Horror Literature
through History

Horror Literature through History

An Encyclopedia of the Stories That Speak to Our Deepest Fears

VOLUME 1

MATT CARDIN, EDITOR

 GREENWOOD™

An Imprint of ABC-CLIO, LLC
Santa Barbara, California • Denver, Colorado

Library of Congress Cataloging-in-Publication Data

Names: Cardin, Matt, editor.
Title: Horror literature through history : an encyclopedia of the stories that speak
    to our deepest fears / Matt Cardin, editor.
Description: Santa Barbara, California : Greenwood, 2017. |
    Includes bibliographical references and index.
Identifiers: LCCN 2017000044 (print) | LCCN 2017000211 (ebook) |
    ISBN 9781440842016 (set : acid-free paper) | ISBN 9781440847561
    (volume 1 : acid-free paper) | ISBN 9781440847578 (volume 2 : acid-free
    paper) | ISBN 9781440842023 (ebook)
Subjects: LCSH: Horror tales—History and criticism—Encyclopedias.
Classification: LCC PN3435 .H665 2017 (print) | LCC PN3435 (ebook) |
    DDC 809.3/8738—dc23
LC record available at https://lccn.loc.gov/2017000044

ISBN: 978-1-4408-4201-6 (set)
      978-1-4408-4756-1 (vol. 1)
      978-1-4408-4757-8 (vol. 2)
      978-1-4408-4202-3 (ebook)

21 20 19 18 17   1 2 3 4 5

This book is also available as an eBook.

Greenwood
An Imprint of ABC-CLIO, LLC

ABC-CLIO, LLC
130 Cremona Drive, P.O. Box 1911
Santa Barbara, California 93116-1911
www.abc-clio.com

This book is printed on acid-free paper ∞

Manufactured in the United States of America

Contents

Guide to Related Topics

Interviews

Laird Barron
Ramsey Campbell
Ellen Datlow
Caitlín R. Kiernan
Joe R. Lansdale
Thomas Ligotti
Chelsea Quinn Yarbro

Horror Literature through History

Horror in the Ancient World
Horror in the Early Modern Era
Horror in the Middle Ages
Horror in the Eighteenth Century
Horror in the Nineteenth Century
Horror from 1900 to 1950
Horror from 1950 to 2000
Horror in the Twenty-First Century

Horror Types and Subgenres

Apocalyptic Horror
Dark Fantasy
Eco-horror
Ghost Stories
The Gothic Literary Tradition
Gothic Poetry
Horror Comics
Horror Literature and Science
   Fiction
Lovecraftian Horror
New Weird
Occult Fiction
Psychological Horror

Vampire Fiction from Dracula to Lestat
   and Beyond
Weird and Cosmic Horror Fiction
Young Adult Horror Fiction

Monsters, Creatures, Threats, and Villains

Devils and Demons
Doubles, Doppelgängers, and Split
   Selves
Gothic Hero/Villain
Incubi and Succubi
Mad Scientist
Monsters
Mummies
Vampires
Werewolves
Witches and Witchcraft
Zombies

Topical Studies

Body Horror
Cthulhu Mythos
Gender, Sexuality, and the Monsters of
   Literary Horror
Horror Anthologies
Horror Criticism
Horror Literature in the Internet Age
Horror Literature as Social Criticism
   and Commentary
Horror Publishing, 1975–1995: The
   Boom Years
Horror Video Games

Preface

Horror is not only one of the most popular types of literature but one of the oldest. People have always been mesmerized by stories that speak to their deepest fears. *Horror Literature through History*, in both the scope of its coverage and the currency of its contents, is uniquely suited to speak to this primal and perennial fascination.

It is also a pointedly timely work, as it arrives at a cultural moment when horror is experiencing a fierce resurgence after having gone through a relative cultural downswing during the previous decade. It was not that horror had ever actually died, for it is, as many have enjoyed noting, an undying—or perhaps undead—form of art and entertainment. But it had become somewhat sluggish in the mid- and late 1990s, aided by the flaming out of the great horror publishing boom of the previous decade-plus, whose high-water mark on the mass market end was represented by the soaring popularity of novels by the likes of Stephen King, Peter Straub, Anne Rice, Ramsey Campbell, and Dean Koontz. And so the revival of the early 2000s constitutes a distinct and discernable phenomenon.

Significantly, this revitalization of horror has not been just a literary matter; in this new era, horror's chief audience and consumer base, consisting largely of high school–aged and college-aged young people, has begun eagerly absorbing horror, especially of the supernatural variety, from a variety of sources. Along with novels and short fiction collections, there are television programs, movies, comic books, and video (and other types of) games. Weird horror fiction—a form to be defined and discussed in the pages to follow—has entered what some began to call a new golden age, not just in literary form but in film and television, as in HBO's *True Detective*, whose first season in 2014 displayed the distinct influence of such authors as Robert W. Chambers, Thomas Ligotti, and Laird Barron. Horror gaming—like other gaming—has rapidly attained new heights of technological and narrative sophistication. Horror movie subgenres both old (such as exorcism) and new (such as "torture porn" and the found-footage world of movies like *Paranormal Activity*) have become enormously popular and profitable. Armies of zombies have begun to infest the pages of comic books and the proliferating sea of screens both large and small.

And throughout it all, the various nonliterary forms continue to draw deeply on their literary cousins for their basic plots, themes, and ideas. This was always true of horror films, but it is critically important to recognize that it remains equally true during the present era of exploding new forms and media, when it might be possible for a partaker of these new forms—the horror video games, the creepypastas, and so on—to ignore or forget the literary foundations of the whole phenomenon.

Literary horror predates all of the other types. It has a vastly longer, and therefore richer and deeper, history. And this is where and why a reference work like the present one comes in: because it serves to illuminate the roots of modern horror, both literary and otherwise, by laying out the field's deep history and evolutionary development.

To this end, *Horror Literature through History* is presented in a three-part structure that is designed for maximum usefulness in assisting all kinds of readers, including those who seek a comprehensive overview of horror's rich literary heritage and those who want to conduct a focused study of specific authors, works, and/or topics. It is also well suited to piecemeal browsing.

Part One, titled "Horror through History," consists of eight essays presenting a comprehensive chronological overview of horror literature during different historical periods. These essays take the form of narrative and critical surveys that situate literary works within the social, cultural, historical, and intellectual currents of their respective eras, creating a seamless narrative of the genre's evolution from ancient times to the present

Part Two, "Themes, Topics, and Genres," contains twenty-three essays that show how otherwise unrelated works of horror have influenced each other, how horror subgenres have evolved, and how a broad range of topics within horror—such as ghosts, vampires, religion, and gender roles, as well as the academic study of these things—have been handled across time.

Part Three, "Reference Entries," presents nearly 400 alphabetically arranged reference entries on authors, works, and specialized topics. It serves as both a source of stand-alone reference reading in its own right and, importantly, a supplement to the encyclopedia's preceding sections. In effect, many of the reference entries serve as "close-ups" on information and concepts presented in the preceding two sections, allowing readers to understand specific authors, works, and topics within the wider context of horror literature's evolutionary history and thematic universe.

Supplementing the main entries are seven original interviews with important contemporary horror authors and editors plus nearly 150 sidebars featuring mini-analyses of literary works, excerpts from primary and secondary works, excerpts from reviews, timelines, trivia, information about media adaptations, and more.

With this unique structure, *Horror Literature through History* offers a variety of uses both to students and to general readers:

- The excerpts from horror novels and stories exemplify topics discussed in the entries, such as theme, language, and characterization. Students are thus able to read these excerpts critically in light of the entries. This supports Common Core State Standards for English language arts.
- The excerpts from background texts work in tandem with the entries by providing contextual material to help students read the literary works critically and understand how authors have engaged the major scientific, social, artistic, psychological, religious, and other issues of their respective eras.

- The historical overview essays in Part One and the topical essays in Part Two distinguish *Horror Literature through History* from works consisting of relatively short A–Z entries. These essays prompt readers to consider the nature of horror as a genre and the ways in which horror literature intersects with mainstream concerns such as religion, politics, education, and more.
- The information on such topics as film adaptations, television shows, video games, and other nonliterary matters helps readers connect horror literature to popular culture at large.
- The interviews provide insights from horror authors about what they have written and why, as well as their thoughts on other writers, works, themes, trends, and issues in the field. Students can apply these views and opinions to analyzing and evaluating the work of the interviewees, as well as many additional works, authors, and topics.

In sum, the encyclopedia enables readers to discover the roots of modern horror literature, trace the evolution of horror literature across time, recognize the influence of literary horror on popular culture, examine how works of horror have related to key issues at different periods in history, and conduct focused research on specific authors, literary works, genres, themes, and topics related to horror. Written by seventy scholars and authors from half a dozen countries, *Horror Literature through History: An Encyclopedia of the Stories That Speak to Our Deepest Fears* offers the reader an in-depth education, in two volumes, about the literary background of popular modern horror entertainments and the rich intrinsic value of this enduring art form in its own right.

Introduction: Spookhouses, Catharsis, and Dark Consolations

Why Horror?

From the outset, a reference work like this one begs an important question, and one that strikes right to the heart of the stated project: *Why horror?* Why do people seek stories, novels, movies, plays, and games that horrify? It is an old question, and one that has become virtually clichéd from overuse, as many horror novelists and movie directors can testify after years of having been asked some version of it by multiple interviewers, often with an affected attitude of mild amazement or disbelief: "Why horror? Why do you (or how can you) write, direct, imagine, envision, such unpleasant things? Why do you think your readers/viewers flock to them? Why are we insatiably addicted to tales of horror and dread?"

What Is Horror?

In answering this question, one could immediately jump into offering various theories and speculations, but to do this would be to beg yet another question, one that is usually missed or ignored by those attempting to deal with the "Why?" question, but that is properly prior to it: namely, the question of horror's *definition*. The very word and concept of "horror" is a noun, and also an adjective (as in "horror novel" and "horror movie"), that is too often left uninterrogated. Not by everyone, to be sure, but by a great many of the people who read the books, watch the movies, and play the games labeled as "horror" year in and year out. Many such people, if pressed, would likely say something to the effect that horror has something to do with being scared, and leave it at that. They would assert that "horror" is simply another word for "fear."

But a moment's reflection is enough to disabuse one of that notion. Certainly, horror does involve fear, but simple introspection shows that the word refers to something more than this, to fear *plus* something, fear with an admixture or addition of *something else*. A person may fear losing a job, or facing a tiger, or being mugged or beaten up; this does not mean someone in those positions is experiencing horror. Conversely, one may witness, say, the emotional abuse of a child, or the despoiling of an ecosystem, or the ravaging of a loved one by cancer—things that do not involve the supernatural trappings or operatic violence and gore associated with many books and movies bearing the "horror" label—and yet say in all honesty that one feels *horrified*. What exactly is it, then, about the emotional response to such situations that warrants the use of the "h" word to describe it?

These, along with a multitude of additional possible examples, may allow us to triangulate the inner element that makes horror horrifying, and to identify this element as some quality of *wrongness* or *repulsiveness*—physical, metaphysical, moral, or otherwise—that leads one to shrink from someone, something, some event, some idea, a monster, the sight of blood, a situation of gross immorality or injustice, or any number of other things. Horror, it seems, involves an irreducible element of revulsion or abhorrence, centered on a primal gut feeling, often implicit, that something *should not be*, that something is somehow fundamentally *wrong* about a given person, creature, act, event, phenomenon, environment, or situation. (Additionally, and significantly, there is a distinction to be made between horror and *terror*—another word that is of critical importance to the type of art generally labeled "horror" today—and this is addressed in the pages of this encyclopedia.)

In his 1990 study of the aesthetics of horror titled *The Philosophy of Horror, or Paradoxes of the Heart* (1990), the philosopher and film scholar Noël Carroll famously noted the interesting and revealing fact that horror as a genre is named for the chief emotional reaction with which it is concerned, the emotional reaction that we have here called into question. Horror *horrifies*: it sets out to inspire a sense of fear and dread mingled with revulsion. Or, if one follows the lead of Leo Tolstoy (1828–1910), R. G. Collingwood (1889–1943), and other significant representatives of the expressive theory of art, one might argue that the works of horror that actually achieve the true status of art as such (defined as imaginative works possessing and displaying an intrinsically higher level of quality than "mere" genre or formula fiction, whose purpose is to entertain) do not so much seek to inspire horror in the reader or viewer as to communicate a sense of horror that has been experienced by the author. The horror critic and scholar S. T. Joshi, in such books as *The Weird Tale* (1990) and *The Modern Weird Tale* (2001), has advanced the idea that what distinguishes the most important and enduring authors of weird and supernatural horror fiction is their tendency to imbue their work with a consistent vision or worldview. In keeping with this, and regardless of the overall merit of Joshi's specific assertion (which some have disputed), it may well be that one of the distinguishing qualities of the greatest authors in this area is an uncommonly and acutely deep personal sensitivity to the more fearsome, dark, and distressing aspects of life, so that these aspects become a true source of fear, suffering, and, yes, *horror*. Following Tolstoy and Collingwood, one would say that when this quality is present in an individual who possesses (or is possessed by) the inbuilt drive and skill that motivates some people to become writers and artists, it will naturally lead such an individual to tell the rest of us the truth about these dark insights and experiences. And it will empower such a person to use the vehicles of prose fiction, and/or poetry, stage drama, film, television, comic books, or video games, to communicate to others an actual experience of horror by recreating it, to some extent, in the reader, viewer, or player.

Interestingly, and as demonstrated repeatedly over the long history of horror literature, this does not necessarily mean that such writers and artists convey their horror in just a single, easily identifiable type of work that can automatically be given a category or genre label. Horror, as has been persuasively argued—perhaps most famously by Douglas E. Winter in his 1998 speech, and later essay, "The Pathos of Genre"—is not really a genre, defined as a type of narrative that has developed recognizable characteristics through repeated use, which can then be used as a kind of formula for producing other, similar works. Rather, it is "a progressive form of fiction, one that evolves to meet the fears and anxieties of its times. . . . [S]ometimes it wears other names, other faces, marking the fragmentation and meltdown of a sudden and ill-conceived thing that many publishers and writers foolishly believed could be called a genre" (Winter 2000, 182). In other words, horror in art is not a genre but a *mode* that can be employed in any form or genre. Horror has thus had a long and fruitful relationship with, for example, science fiction, from such Ur-texts as Mary Shelley's *Frankenstein* (1818) and H. P. Lovecraft's *At the Mountains of Madness* (1936), to the advent of the "New Weird" at the turn of the twenty-first century in such works as China Miéville's *Perdido Street Station* (2000), to the fifty-year reign of zombies over the realm of apocalyptic and postapocalyptic horror that began in 1968 with writer/director George Romero's *Night of the Living Dead*, which was itself partly inspired by Richard Matheson's classic 1954 horror/science fiction novel *I Am Legend*. And there are also horror Westerns, horror romance novels, religious horror stories, horror thrillers, horror mysteries, and so-called "literary" horror (with "literary" denoting nongenre writing).

Being so portable, as it were, horror can spread out into all types of storytelling, and indeed, this is what has been happening with increasing visibility and pervasiveness in the horror renaissance of the early twenty-first century, to the point where the creeping spread of horror throughout the literary and entertainment landscape is one of the defining characteristics of this new era. Horror has become unbound, and its fortunes have become those of literature at large. In this new state of things, horror's reputation has begun to transcend its former questionable status, as some darlings of the literary establishment have produced works that could be considered pure horror even though they do not bear the category label. In fact, if these had been published during the great horror boom of the 1980s, when not just Stephen King and Anne Rice but a host of lesser authors virtually owned drugstore bookshelves and bookstore window displays, they would have been every bit as horrifying as (if not more so than) any 1980s paperback novel with garish Gothic typography and a leering monster on the cover.

Again: Why Horror?

So these, then, are some of the issues involved in identifying and defining horror in life and art. But the question with which we opened still remains: *Why* horror? Even having answered—perhaps provisionally, arguably, necessarily incompletely—the question of why some writers write it (because they are themselves subject to a deeper-than-average experience of the horrors of life and consciousness), the question remains as to why readers read it. Fear and loathing are conventionally unpleasant emotions. Why do people seek to be subjected to them?

There are a number of customary answers to this question, many of which have been resorted to repeatedly by the interviewees mentioned above, and all of which carry some merit. For instance, what has sometimes been termed the roller coaster or funhouse theory of horror is surely true to an extent. There is something pleasant, even delightful—so this answer has it—about absorbing fictional stories of darkness, danger, and dread while remaining safely in one's easy chair. There is something purely entertaining and enjoyable about entering an imaginative world of horror, rather like a carnival funhouse ride, in order to enjoy the thrills to be found in such a place. From this point of view, seeking horror in fictional, cinematic, or any other form is no different in principle from seeking an adrenaline rush by reading a thriller or seeking a laugh by watching a comedy. And some people do approach all of these things on this very level. Some horror fiction, including most (but not all) of what appeared in *Weird Tales* and the other classic horror, fantasy, and science fiction pulps of the 1920s through the 1940s, as well as most of what was published during the late twentieth-century horror boom, seems precisely aimed at fulfilling this function.

There is also surely something to the more profound theory of horror as catharsis, a position first advanced by Aristotle in his *Poetics* and still invoked more than two thousand years later to explain all kinds of artistic engagements, but especially those of a powerfully stark and unpleasant nature. Aristotle was talking specifically about Greek tragic plays, which brim with grief, betrayal, dark secrets, and unhappy endings, not to mention supernatural horrors and gruesome violence (as in, for example, Euripides's *Medea* and Aeschylus's *Oresteia* trilogy, both from the fifth century BCE). Such productions, the great philosopher argued, serve to purge viewers of their pent-up emotions of fear and pity in a safely walled-off fictional world, thus preparing them better to deal with the anxieties of real life. One would be foolish and naïve to deny that today's horror fiction (and other forms) may serve this kind of function for some, and perhaps many, people.

But even granting the validity of these views, there is another and deeper answer to be given, and this is where the possible sensitivity of the reader meets the sensitivity of the writer who uses imaginative literature to convey his or her own sense of profound horror at the vicissitudes and strangenesses of life, the world, consciousness, and everything. Perhaps, for some people, the great works of horror provide a deep, visceral, darkly electrifying confirmation of their own most personal and profound experiences and intuitions. After the spookhouse ride has let out, and after the catharsis has come and gone, horror in art, as Thomas Ligotti put it in his essay "The Consolations of Horror," may actually, weirdly, provide some readers with a kind of *comfort* by showing that "someone shares some of your own feelings and has made of these a work of art which you have the insight, sensitivity, and—like it or not—peculiar set of experiences to appreciate" (Ligotti 1996, xxi). What is more, horror accomplishes this artistic-alchemical feat not by denying or diminishing the dark, dismal, dreadful, terrifying, and horrifying elements of life, but by *amplifying* them. Never mind the possible therapeutic or other conventionally beneficial results that might be imputed to such a thing; the point, for both writer and reader, is simply to confront, recognize, experience, name, and know horror as such, because it is in fact real. It is part of the human experience. We are, from time to time (and some of us more often than others), haunted by horror. The type of art named as such is an expression of this truth, a personal and cultural acknowledgment of and dialogue with it, a means by which we know it, and affirm it, and "stay with" it, instead of denying it and looking away, as is otherwise our wont.

Like all art, horror literature and its associated other forms play out in ways that link up with a host of additional issues: historical, cultural, sociological, ideological, scientific, artistic, philosophical, religious, spiritual, and existential. It is the story of how exactly this has played out over the long span of human history, especially, but not exclusively, since the birth of literary Gothicism in the eighteenth century with the publication of Horace Walpole's *The Castle of Otranto* (1764), that is the central focus of this encyclopedia. Whatever the reader's purpose in picking up this work, and whichever the level at which he or she tends to engage personally with horror—as funhouse ride, cathartic tool, or personal consolation—it is hoped that the contents herein will help to clarify and illuminate the history, present, and possible futures of horror in both literary and other forms, while also fostering an enhanced appreciation of the central mystery and core of darkness that lies at the heart of the whole thing. It is in fact this darkness that serves as horror's source of enduring power, and that makes it an undying and undead form of human literary and artistic endeavor.

Matt Cardin

Further Reading

Carroll, Noël. 1990. *The Philosophy of Horror, or Paradoxes of the Heart*. New York: Routledge.

Joshi, S. T. 1990. *The Weird Tale*. Austin: University of Texas Press.

Joshi, S. T. 2001. *The Modern Weird Tale*. Jefferson, NC: McFarland.

Ligotti, Thomas. 1996. *The Nightmare Factory*. New York: Carroll & Graf.

Winter, Douglas E. 2000. "The Pathos of Genre." In *The Year's Best Fantasy and Horror*, edited by Ellen Datlow and Terri Windling, 176–183. New York: St. Martin's Press. Also available at http://omnimagazine.com/eh/commentary/winter/pages/0799.html.

Timeline of Horror Literature Through History

ca. 2100 BCE	The *Epic of Gilgamesh*
ca. 750–700 BCE	Homer's *Iliad* and *Odyssey*, featuring tales of gods, monsters, magic, a trip to the underworld; Hesiod's *Theogony*, with additional descriptions of monstrous and supernatural entities
5th century BCE	Heyday of Greek tragedy in works of Aeschylus, Sophocles, and Euripides, featuring supernaturalism and grisly scenes of physical horror
3rd century BCE	Apollonius Rodius, *Argonautica*, showing Jason and the Argonauts encountering multiple monsters and supernatural threats
ca. 200 BCE	Plautus, *Mostellaria* ("The Haunted House")
1st century CE	Petronius, *Satyricon*, featuring the first extant account of a werewolf in ancient literature; Ovid, *Metamorphoses*, with tales of human beings transforming into plants and animals
2nd century CE	Apuleius, *Metamorphosis*, a.k.a. *The Golden Ass*, with transformation, witchcraft, and more
ca. 750–1000	*Beowulf*
12th century	Romance narratives rise to prominence in Europe, featuring many fantastical elements, including ghosts, fairies, werewolves, supernatural transformations, and mysterious castles
14th century	Middle English romances flourish, including tales of women seduced by demons (e.g., *Sir Gowther*), werewolves (*William of Palerne*, translated from Old French), and *Sir Gawain and the Green Knight*, which teems with supernaturalism and horror
1308–1320	Composition of Dante Alighieri's *Divine Comedy*, whose second section, *Inferno*, profoundly shapes Western Christian conceptions of demons, devils, Satan, and hell
1487	Heinrich Kramer and Jacob Sprenger, *Malleus Maleficarum* (*The Hammer of the Witches*)—the most famous (notorious) of the witch-hunting manuals

1572	English translation of Swiss theologian Ludwig Lavatar's *Of ghostes and spirites walking by nyght*
1584	Reginald Scot, *Discoverie of Witchcraft*
1587	Thomas Kyd, *The Spanish Tragedy*
1594	Christopher Marlowe, *Doctor Faustus*; Thomas Nashe, *The Terrors of the Night*; William Shakespeare, *Titus Andronicus*
1597	King James I, *Daemonologie*
1599	John Marsten, *Antonio's Revenge*
1600	William Shakespeare, *Hamlet*
1605	English translation of French scholar Pierre le Loyer's *A treatise of spectres or straunge sights, visions and apparitions appearing sensibly unto men*
1607	Thomas Middleton, *The Revenger's Tragedy*; William Shakespeare, *Macbeth*
1612	Thomas Middleton, *The Witch*
1621	Thomas Dekker, John Ford, and William Rowley, *The Witch of Edmonton*
1623	John Webster, *The Duchess of Malfi*
1634	Thomas Heywood and Richard Brome, *The Late Lancashire Witches*
1667	Publication of John Milton's *Paradise Lost*, with a profoundly influential depiction of Christian angels, demons, and Lucifer
1681	Joseph Glanvill, *Saducismus Triumphatus*, an apparition narrative arguing for the reality of both biblical/Christian supernaturalism and witches, revenants, and other horrific supernatural beings
1692	Beginning of the Salem witch trials
1693	Publication of Cotton Mather's *Wonders of the Invisible World*, focusing on the dangers of witchcraft, and published in the immediate wake of the Salem witch trials
1704	Publication of John Dennis, *Grounds of Criticism in Poetry*, an essay promoting the terror of the sublime as the most powerful driver of great poetry
ca. 1722–1751	Rise of the so-called Graveyard Poets, who wrote melancholy poetry set in graveyards and reflecting on death and mortality, e.g., Robert Blair's "The Grave," Edward Young's *The Complaint:*

	Or Night-Thoughts on Life, Death and Immortality, and Thomas Gray's "Elegy Written in a Country Churchyard"
1727	Daniel Defoe, *An Essay on the History and Reality of Apparitions*
1746	Publication of Antoine Augustin Calmet's "Dissertations on the Apparitions of Spirits and on the Vampires or Revenants of Hungary, Moravia, and Silesia"—an exhaustive study of angels, demons, witchcraft, lycanthropy, and related beings and occult phenomena (and a book of major importance in driving popular fascination with vampires for the next century)
1757	Publication of Edmund Burke's *A Philosophical Enquiry into the Origins of Our Ideas of the Sublime and Beautiful*, an essay articulating an aesthetics of death, pain, power, and cosmic immensity that proved hugely influential for subsequent Gothic and horror literature
1764	Horace Walpole, *The Castle of Otranto*
1774	August Bürger, *Lenore*
1778	Clara Reeve, *The Old English Baron*
1781	Henry Fuseli, *The Nightmare* (painting)
1786	William Beckford, *Vathek*
1787–1789	Friedrich von Schiller, *Der Geisterseher* (*The Ghost-Seer*)
1793	Christian Heinrich Spiess, *Petermännchen* (*The Dwarf of Westerbourg*)
1794	Ann Radcliffe, *The Mysteries of Udolpho*
1796	Matthew Lewis, *The Monk*
1797	Samuel Taylor Coleridge, *Christabel*; Matthew Lewis, *The Castle Spectre*; Ann Radcliffe, *The Italian*
1798	Charles Brockden Brown, *Wieland, or The Transformation*; Samuel Taylor Coleridge, *Rime of the Ancient Mariner*
1799	Charles Brockden Brown, *Edgar Huntly*
1801	Robert Southey, *Thalaba the Destroyer*
1816	Lord Byron, John Polidori, Percy Shelley, and Mary Shelley hold a ghost story contest while staying together for the summer at the Villa Diodati on the shores of Lake Geneva, giving rise to the literary vampire (via Polidori's "The Vampyre") and Mary's *Frankenstein*
1817	E. T. A. Hoffmann, "The Sand-man"; Lord Byron, *Manfred*

1818	Jane Austen, *Northanger Abbey*; Mary Shelley, *Frankenstein, or The Modern Prometheus*
1819	John Polidori, "The Vampyre"
1820	Washington Irving, "The Legend of Sleepy Hollow"; Charles Maturin, *Melmoth the Wanderer*
1824	James Hogg, *The Private Memoirs and Confessions of a Justified Sinner*
1826	Posthumous publication of Ann Radcliffe's essay "On the Supernatural in Poetry"
1831	Nikolai Gogol, *Evenings on a Farm Near Dikanka*; Victor Hugo, *Notre Dame de Paris* (*The Hunchback of Notre Dame*); Mary Shelley, *Frankenstein* (revised version)
1835	Nikolai Gogol, *Mirgorod* and *Arabesques*; Nathaniel Hawthorne, "Young Goodman Brown"
1837	Nathaniel Hawthorne, *Twice-Told Tales*
1838	Edgar Allan Poe, "Ligeia" and *The Narrative of Arthur Gordon Pym*
1839	J. Sheridan Le Fanu, "Schalken the Painter"; Edgar Allan Poe, "The Fall of the House of Usher"
1840	Edgar Allan Poe, *Tales of the Grotesque and Arabesque*
1842	Edward Bulwer-Lytton, *Zanoni*; Edgar Allan Poe, "The Mask of the Red Death" (revised in 1845 as "The Masque of the Red Death")
1843	Edgar Allan Poe, "The Black Cat," "The Pit and the Pendulum," "The Tell-Tale Heart," "The Conqueror Worm"
1844	Nathaniel Hawthorne, "Rappaccini's Daughter"; Karl Adolf von Wachsmann, "The Mysterious Stranger"
1845	Edgar Allan Poe, "The Raven"
1845–1847	James Malcolm Rymer and Thomas Peckett Prest, *Varney the Vampire* (published in installments)
1846	Edgar Allan Poe, "The Cask of Amontillado"
1847	Charlotte Brontë, *Jane Eyre*; Emily Brontë, *Wuthering Heights*; Thomas Peckett Prest, *Sweeney Todd, The Demon Barber* (first published as *The String of Pearls*); Count Jan Potocki, *The Manuscript Found in Saragossa*
1848	The young Fox sisters of Hydesville, New York, report hearing "spirit raps," leading to the explosive birth of Spiritualism,

	which will play a significant role in much supernatural horror fiction
1851	Nathaniel Hawthorne, *The House of the Seven Gables*
1855	Elizabeth Gaskell, "The Old Nurse's Story"
1857	Charles Baudelaire, *Les Fleurs du Mal* (*The Flowers of Evil*)
1859	Edward Bulwer-Lytton, "The Haunted and the Haunters"; Wilkie Collins, *The Woman in White*; Fitz-James O'Brien, "What Was It?"
1866	Charles Dickens, "The Signal-man" (first published as "No. 1 Branch Line: The Signal-man")
1869	Comte de Lautréamont, *The Songs of Maldoror*; J. Sheridan Le Fanu, "Green Tea"
1872	J. Sheridan Le Fanu, *In a Glass Darkly* (includes *Carmilla*)
1881	Robert Louis Stevenson, "Thrawn Janet"
1882	The Society for Psychical Research is founded in London.
1884	J. K. Huysmans, *A rebours* (*Against the Grain*); Robert Louis Stevenson, "The Body Snatcher"
1885	Rudyard Kipling, "The Phantom 'Rickshaw"; Robert Louis Stevenson, "Olalla"
1886	F. Marion Crawford, "The Upper Berth"; H. Rider Haggard, *She: A History of Adventure*; Robert Louis Stevenson, *The Strange Case of Dr. Jekyll and Mr. Hyde*
1887	Guy de Maupassant, "The Horla"
1888	Rudyard Kipling, *The Phantom 'Rickshaw, and Other Tales*
1889	W. C. Morrow, "His Unconquerable Enemy"
1890	Arthur Conan Doyle, "The Ring of Thoth"; Rudyard Kipling, "The Mark of the Beast"; Vernon Lee, *Hauntings*; Oscar Wilde, *The Picture of Dorian Gray*
1891	Ambrose Bierce, "An Occurrence at Owl Creek Bridge" and "The Death of Halpin Frayser"; Thomas Hardy, *Tess of the d'Urbervilles*; J. K. Huysmans, *Là-Bas* (published in English as *Down There* or *The Damned*); Henry James, "Sir Edmund Orme"; Rudyard Kipling, "The Recrudescence of Imray"
1892	Charlotte Perkins Gilman, "The Yellow Wall-Paper" Arthur Conan Doyle, "Lot No. 249"
1893	Ambrose Bierce, "The Damned Thing" and *Can Such Things Be?*

1894	George du Maurier, *Trilby*; Arthur Machen, *The Great God Pan and the Inmost Light*
1895	Robert W. Chambers, *The King in Yellow*; Arthur Machen, *The Three Impostors* (with "The Novel of the Black Seal")
1896	H. G. Wells, *The Island of Dr. Moreau*
1897	Arthur Machen, *The Hill of Dreams*; Richard Marsh, *The Beetle*; Bram Stoker, *Dracula*; H. G. Wells, *The Invisible Man*
1898	Henry James, *The Turn of the Screw*
1899	Vernon Lee, "The Doll"
1900	Lafcadio Hearn, "Nightmare-Touch"; Robert Hichens, "How Love Came to Professor Guildea"
1901	Arthur Conan Doyle, *The Hound of the Baskervilles*; M. P. Shiel, *The Purple Cloud*
1902	W. W. Jacobs, "The Monkey's Paw"
1903	Bram Stoker, *The Jewel of Seven Stars*
1904	Lafcadio Hearn, *Kwaidan: Stories and Studies of Strange Things*; M. R. James, *Ghost Stories of an Antiquary* (with "Oh, Whistle, and I'll Come to You, My Lad"); Arthur Machen, "The White People"
1905	F. Marion Crawford, "For the Blood Is the Life"
1906	Leonid Andreyev, "Lazarus"; Algernon Blackwood, *The Empty House*
1907	Algernon Blackwood, *The Listener and Other Stories* (with "The Willows")
1908	Algernon Blackwood, *John Silence: Physician Extraordinary*; F. Marion Crawford, "The Screaming Skull"; Hanns Heinz Ewers, "The Spider"; William Hope Hodgson, *The House on the Borderland*
1910	Algernon Blackwood, "The Wendigo"; Walter de la Mare, *The Return*; Gaston Leroux, *The Phantom of the Opera*; Edith Wharton, "Afterward"
1911	Hanns Heinz Ewers, *Alraune*; M. R. James, *More Ghost Stories of an Antiquary* (with "Casting the Runes"); Oliver Onions, *Widdershins* (with "The Beckoning Fair One"); Saki, "Sredni Vashtar"; Bram Stoker, *The Lair of the White Worm*
1912	E. F. Benson, *The Room in the Tower*; Walter de la Mare, "The Listeners"; William Hope Hodgson, *The Night Land*

1913	William Hope Hodgson, *Carnacki, the Ghost Finder*
1913–1914	Gustav Meyrink, *The Golem*
1914	Saki, "The Open Window"
1915	Franz Kafka, "The Metamorphosis"
1918	Sax Rohmer, *Brood of the Witch Queen*
1919	Sigmund Freud, "The Uncanny"; Stefan Grabiński, *The Motion Demon*; W. F. Harvey, "The Beast with Five Fingers"
1920	Maurice Renard, *The Hands of Orlac*
1921	A. E. Coppard, "Adam & Eve & Pinch Me"
1922	Walter de la Mare, "Seaton's Aunt"; H. P. Lovecraft, "The Music of Erich Zann"
1923	Walter de la Mare, *The Riddle and Other Stories* (with "Seaton's Aunt" and "Out of the Deep"); launch of *Weird Tales*
1924	H. P. Lovecraft, "The Rats in the Walls"
1925	Franz Kafka, *The Trial*; Edward Lucas White, "Lukundoo"; *Not at Night*, edited by Christine Campbell Thomson
1926	Cynthia Asquith, *The Ghost Book*; D. H. Lawrence, "The Rocking-Horse Winner"; H. P. Lovecraft, "The Outsider"
1927	F. Scott Fitzgerald, "A Short Trip Home"; H. P. Lovecraft, *The Case of Charles Dexter Ward*, "Pickman's Model," "The Colour out of Space," and *Supernatural Horror in Literature*
1928	Frank Belknap Long, "The Space Eaters"; H. P. Lovecraft, "The Call of Cthulhu"; Montague Summers, *The Vampire, His Kith and Kin*; H. R. Wakefield, *They Return at Evening* (with "He Cometh and He Passeth By"); *Great Short Stories of Detection, Mystery, and Horror*, edited by Dorothy Sayers
1929	Frank Belknap Long, "The Hounds of Tindalos"; H. P. Lovecraft, "The Dunwich Horror"; Montague Summers, *The Vampire in Europe*
1930	William Faulkner, "A Rose for Emily"; H. P. Lovecraft, "The Whisperer in Darkness"
1931	Conrad Aiken, "Mr. Arcularis"; Clark Ashton Smith, "The Return of the Sorcerer"
1932	Conrad Aiken, "Silent Snow, Secret Snow"; Jean Ray, "The Shadowy Street"; launch of Charles Birkin's *Creeps* anthology series

1933	Guy Endore, *The Werewolf of Paris*; H. P. Lovecraft, "The Dreams in the Witch House"; Clark Ashton Smith, "Ubbo-Sathla"
1934	Dennis Wheatley, *The Devil Rides Out*
1936	H. P. Lovecraft, *At the Mountains of Madness*, "The Shadow over Innsmouth" "The Shadow Out of Time," and "The Haunter of the Dark"
1937	H. P. Lovecraft, "The Thing on the Doorstep"; Edith Wharton, *Ghosts* (published posthumously)
1938	John W. Campbell, "Who Goes There?"; Robert E. Howard, "Pigeons from Hell"; Daphne du Maurier, *Rebecca*
1939	H. P. Lovecraft, *The Outsider and Others*—the first published collection of Lovecraft's fiction, from the newly founded Arkham House; founding of *Unknown* magazine
1940	John Collier, "Evening Primrose"; L. Ron Hubbard, *Fear*; Theodore Sturgeon, "It"; Jack Williamson, *Darker Than You Think*
1941	Fritz Leiber, "Smoke Ghost"; H. P. Lovecraft, *The Case of Charles Dexter Ward* (published posthumously)
1942	Clark Ashton Smith, *Out of Space and Time*
1943	Robert Bloch, "Yours Truly, Jack the Ripper"; Fritz Leiber, *Conjure Wife*; Jean Ray, *Malpertuis*
1944	Theodore Sturgeon, "Killdozer"; Jack Williamson, *Darker Than You Think: Great Tales of Terror and the Supernatural*, edited by Herbert Wise and Phyllis Fraser; *Sleep No More*, edited by August Derleth
1945	Robert Bloch, *The Opener of the Way*; Elizabeth Bowen, *The Demon Lover*; August Derleth (and H. P. Lovecraft), *The Lurker at the Threshold*
1946	Ray Bradbury, "The Homecoming"
1947	Ray Bradbury, *Dark Carnival*; rebranding of Educational Comics as Entertaining Comics by William Gaines, soon to publish *Tales from the Crypt*, *Haunt of Fear*, and *Vault of Horror*
1948	Shirley Jackson, "The Lottery"; Theodore Sturgeon, "The Perfect Host"
1949	Fritz Leiber, "The Girl with the Hungry Eyes"
1950	Richard Matheson, "Born of Man and Woman"
1951	Robert Aickman, *We Are for the Dark*; Ray Bradbury, *The Illustrated Man*; John Wyndham, *The Day of the Triffids*

1952	Daphne du Maurier, "The Birds"
1953	Sarban, *The Doll Maker and Other Tales of the Uncanny*
1954	Richard Matheson, *I Am Legend*
1955	Jack Finney, *The Body Snatchers*; Flannery O'Connor, "Good Country People"
1955	Ray Bradbury, *The October Country* (revised version of 1947's *Dark Carnival*)
1957	John Wyndham, *The Midwich Cuckoos*
1959	Robert Bloch, *Psycho*; Shirley Jackson, *The Haunting of Hill House*; the first *Pan Book of Horror Stories*, edited by Herbert van Thal; *The Macabre Reader*, edited by Donald A. Wollheim
1961	Richard Matheson, "Nightmare at 20,000 Feet"; Ray Russell, "Sardonicus"
1962	Ray Bradbury, *Something Wicked This Way Comes*; Shirley Jackson, *We Have Always Lived in the Castle*; Ray Russell, *The Case Against Satan*
1963	Manly Wade Wellman, *Who Fears the Devil?*
1964	Robert Aickman, *Dark Entries* (with "Ringing the Changes"); Ramsey Campbell, *The Inhabitant of the Lake and Less Welcome Tenants*; *Creepy* #1, from Warren Publishing
1966	*Eerie* #1, from Warren Publishing
1967	Ira Levin, *Rosemary's Baby*; Colin Wilson, *The Mind Parasites*; *Dangerous Visions*, edited by Harlan Ellison
1968	Robert Aickman, *Sub Rosa* (with "The Cicerones"); Fred Chappell, *Dagon;* launch of the magazine *Weirdbook*; creation of modern zombie archetype in George Romero's *Night of the Living Dead*
1971	William Peter Blatty, *The Exorcist*; T. E. D. Klein, "The Events at Poroth Farm"; Richard Matheson, *Hell House*; Thomas Tryon, *The Other*; *The Seventh Fontana Book of Great Ghost Stories*, edited by Robert Aickman
1973	J. G. Ballard, *Crash*; Ramsey Campbell, *Demons by Daylight*; Harlan Ellison, "The Whimper of Whipped Dogs"; Robert Marasco, *Burnt Offerings*; Thomas Tryon, *Harvest Home*
1974	James Herbert, *The Rats*; Stephen King, *Carrie*; Brian Lumley, *Beneath the Moors* and *The Burrowers Beneath*; Karl Edward Wagner, "Sticks"

1975   J. G. Ballard, *High-Rise*; Harlan Ellison, *Deathbird Stories*; James Herbert, *The Fog*; Stephen King, *'Salem's Lot*; establishment of the World Fantasy Award at the first World Fantasy Convention

1976   Ramsey Campbell, *The Doll Who Ate His Mother*; John Farris, *The Fury*; Russell Kirk, "There's a Long, Long Trail A-Winding"; Ray Russell, *Incubus*; *Frights*, edited by Kirby McCauley

1977   Gary Brandner, *The Howling*; Stephen King, *The Shining*; Fritz Leiber, *Our Lady of Darkness*; Joyce Carol Oates, *Night-Side*; *Whispers*, edited by Stuart David Schiff

1978   Stephen King, *The Stand* and *Night Shift*; Whitley Strieber, *The Wolfen*; Chelsea Quinn Yarbro, *Hotel Transylvania*; launch of the *Shadows* horror anthology series, edited by Charles L. Grant

1979   Ramsey Campbell, *The Face That Must Die* and "Mackintosh Willie"; Angela Carter, *The Bloody Chamber*; Charles L. Grant, *The Hour of the Oxrun Dead*; George R. R. Martin, *Sandkings*; David Morrell, *The Totem*; Peter Straub, *Ghost Story*; Thomas Tessier, *The Nightwalker*

1980   Jonathan Carroll, *The Land of Laughs*; Suzy McKee Charnas, *The Vampire Tapestry*; Jack Ketchum, *Off Season*; Russell Kirk, "The Watchers at the Strait Gate"; Michael Shea, "The Autopsy"; *Dark Forces*, edited by Kirby McCauley

1981   Dennis Etchison, *The Dark Country*; Thomas Harris, *Red Dragon* (the novel that introduced Hannibal Lecter); Stephen King, *Cujo* and *Danse Macabre*; Robert R. McCammon, *They Thirst*; Sandy Peterson, *The Call of Cthulhu* (role-playing game); Whitley Strieber, *The Hunger*; F. Paul Wilson, *The Keep*; launch of *Rod Serling's Twilight Zone Magazine*, edited by T. E. D. Klein, Michael Blaine, and Tappan King

1982   Thomas Tessier, *Shockwaves*

1983   William Peter Blatty, *Legion* (sequel to *The Exorcist*); Robert Bloch, *Psycho 2*; Susan Hill, *The Woman in Black*; *Black Water*, edited by Alberto Manguel; *Fantastic Tales*, edited by Italo Calvino; *The Guide to Supernatural Fiction*, edited by E. F. Bleiler

1984   Clive Barker, *The Books of Blood*; Octavia E. Butler, "Bloodchild"; Stephen King and Peter Straub, *The Talisman*; T. E. D. Klein, *The Ceremonies*; Alan Moore takes over DC's *Swamp Thing*; John Skipp and Craig Spector, *The Light at the End*; S. P. Somtow, *Vampire Junction*

1985	Clive Barker, *The Damnation Game*; Stephen King, *Skeleton Crew*; T. E. D. Klein, *Dark Gods*; Thomas Ligotti, *Songs of a Dead Dreamer*; Anne Rice, *The Vampire Lestat*; Ray Russell, *Haunted Castle: The Complete Gothic Tales of Ray Russell*; Dan Simmons, *Song of Kali*
1986	Clive Barker, *The Hellbound Heart*; Stephen King, *It*; Brian Lumley, *Necroscope*; Lisa Tuttle, *A Nest of Nightmares*; "splatterpunk" coined by David J. Schow
1987	Clive Barker, *Weaveworld*; Stephen King, *Misery*; Robert R. McCammon, *Swan Song*; Toni Morrison, *Beloved*; Michael Shea, *Polyphemus* and *Fat Face*; Whitley Strieber, *Communion*; founding of the Horror Writers Association (as Horror Writers of America) and establishment of the Bram Stoker Award Dean Koontz, *Watchers*
1988	Clive Barker, *Cabal*; Neil Gaiman, *Sandman* (launch of comic book series); Thomas Harris, *The Silence of the Lambs*; Anne Rice, *The Queen of the Damned*; John Skipp and Craig Spector, *The Scream*; *Prime Evil*, edited by Douglas A. Winter; revival of *Weird Tales* by George H. Scithers, John Gregory Betancourt, and Darrell Schweitzer
1989	Neil Gaiman, *Sandman* #1; Jack Ketchum, *The Girl Next Door*; Joe R. Lansdale, *On the Far Side of the Cadillac Desert with Dead Folks*; Patrick McGrath, *The Grotesque*; Anne Rice, *The Mummy, or Ramses the Damned*; Dan Simmons, *Carrion Comfort*
1990	Robert Bloch, *Psycho House*; Noël Carroll, *The Philosophy of Horror: Or, Paradoxes of the Heart*; Thomas Ligotti, "The Last Feast of Harlequin"; Robert R. McCammon, *Mine*; Anne Rice, *The Witching Hour*; *Lovecraft's Legacy*, edited by Robert Weinberg and Martin H. Greenberg; *Splatterpunks: Extreme Horror*, edited by Paul Sammon
1991	Clive Barker, *Imajica*; Bret Easton Ellis, *American Psycho*; Thomas Ligotti, *Grimscribe: His Lives and Works*; Alan Moore, *From Hell* (issue 1); launch of the Dell Abyss line of horror paperbacks; founding of the International Gothic Association
1992	Poppy Z. Brite, *Lost Souls*; Tanith Lee, *Dark Dance* and *Heart Beast*; Kim Newman, *Anno Dracula*
1993	Poppy Z. Brite, *Drawing Blood*; Ramsey Campbell, *Alone with the Horrors*; Stefan Grabiński, *The Dark Domain*; Laurell K. Hamilton, *Guilty Pleasures*
1994	Elizabeth Hand, *Waking the Moon*; Jack Ketchum, "The Box"; Joe R. Lansdale, *Bubba Ho-Tep*; Thomas Ligotti, *Noctuary* and

	The Agonizing Resurrection of Victor Frankenstein and Other Gothic Tales; Joyce Carol Oates, *Haunted: Tales of the Grotesque*
1995	Joyce Carol Oates, *Zombie*; establishment of the International Horror Guild Award (which will run to 2008)
1996	Poppy Z. Brite, *Exquisite Corpse*; Ramsey Campbell, *The House on Nazareth Hill*; Thomas Ligotti, *The Nightmare Factory*
1997	Thomas Tessier, *Fogheart*
1998	Tom Holland, *The Sleeper in the Sands*; Caitlín R. Kiernan, *Silk*
1999	Michael Cisco, *The Divinity Student*; Thomas Harris, *Hannibal*; H. P. Lovecraft, *The Call of Cthulhu and Other Weird Stories* (first of three Penguin Classics volumes that help to canonize Lovecraft as a major American author); Peter Straub, *Mr. X*; launch of the journal *Gothic Studies*
2000	Mark Z. Danielewski, *House of Leaves*; Stephen King, *The Bullet* (published online as a freely downloadable eBook for the first week); Sarah Langan, *The Keeper*; Patrick McGrath, *Martha Peake*; China Miéville, *Perdido Street Station*; Jeffrey Thomas, *Punktown*
2001	Tananarive Due, *The Living Blood*; Neil Gaiman, *American Gods*; Charlaine Harris, *Dead Until Dark* (first novel in *The Southern Vampire Mysteries*, later adapted for television as *True Blood*); Stephen King and Peter Straub, *Black House*; Kelly Link, *Stranger Things Happen*; Chuck Palahniuk, *Lullaby*; Jeff VanderMeer, *City of Saints and Madmen*
2002	Matt Cardin, *Divinations of the Deep*; Neil Gaiman, *Coraline*; Thomas Ligotti, *My Work Is Not Yet Done*; China Miéville, *The Scar*; David Morrell, *Long Lost*
2003	Brian Keene, *The Rising*; Reggie Oliver, *The Dreams of Cardinal Vittorini*; Mark Samuels, *The White Hands and Other Weird Tales*; Jeff VanderMeer, *Veniss Underground*; awarding of the National Book Foundation's Medal for Distinguished Contribution to American Letters to Stephen King; debut of Robert Kirkman's comic series *The Walking Dead*
2004	China Miéville, *Iron Council*; Adam Nevill, *The Banquet of the Damned*
2005	Elizabeth Kostova, *The Historian*; Octavia E. Butler, *Fledgling*; John Ajvide Lindqvist, *Handling the Undead*; Joe Hill, *20th Century Ghosts*; *H. P. Lovecraft: Tales*, edited by Peter Straub and published by Library of America; Stephenie Meyer, *Twilight*; Chuck Palahniuk, *Haunted*

2006	Max Brooks, *World War Z: An Oral History of the Zombie War*; Thomas Ligotti, *Teatro Grottesco*; launch of *The Irish Journal of Gothic and Horror Studies*
2007	Laird Barron, *The Imago Sequence and Other Stories*; Joe Hill, *Heart-Shaped Box*; Sarah Langan, *The Missing*; John Ajvide Lindqvist, *Let the Right One In*; Cormac McCarthy, *The Road*; Reggie Oliver, *Masques of Satan*; Dan Simmons, *The Terror*; establishment of the Shirley Jackson Awards
2008	John Langan, *Mr. Gaunt and Other Uneasy Encounters*; Mark Samuels, *Glyphotech and Other Macabre Processes*; *Poe's Children*, edited by Peter Straub; launch of Creepypasta.com
2009	Jane Austen and Seth Grahame-Smith, *Pride and Prejudice and Zombies*; Caitlín R. Kiernan, *The Red Tree*; John Langan, *House of Windows*; Joe McKinney, *Dead City*
2010	Laird Barron, *Occultation and Other Stories*; Matt Cardin, *Dark Awakenings*; Justin Cronin, *The Passage*; Joe Hill, *Horns*; Thomas Ligotti, *The Conspiracy against the Human Race*; Isaac Marion, *Warm Bodies*; Adam Nevill, *Apartment 16*; Helen Oyeyemi, *White Is for Witching*; debut of *The Walking Dead* television series on AMC; launch of the academic journal *Horror Studies*
2011	Laird Barron, *The Light Is the Darkness*; Livia Llewellyn, *Engines of Desire: Tales of Love and Other Horrors*; Adam Nevill, *The Ritual*; Mark Samuels, *The Man Who Collected Machen*; *The Weird*, edited by Ann and Jeff VanderMeer
2012	Laird Barron, *The Croning*; Richard Gavin, *At Fear's Altar*; Jack Ketchum, *I'm Not Sam*; Caitlín R. Kiernan, *The Drowning Girl: A Memoir*; Adam Nevill, *Last Days*
2013	Laird Barron, *The Beautiful Thing That Awaits Us All*; Joe Hill, *NOS4A2*; John Langan, *The Wide Carnivorous Sky and Other Monstrous Geographies*
2014	Kelly Link, *Magic for Beginners*; Adam Nevill, *No One Gets Out Alive*; Simon Strantzas, *Burnt Black Suns*; Jeff VanderMeer, the *Southern Reach Trilogy*
2015	Clive Barker, *The Scarlet Gospels*; Elizabeth Hand, *Wylding Hall*; Thomas Ligotti, *Songs of a Dead Dreamer and Grimscribe* (Penguin Classics edition with revised texts); Paul Tremblay, *A Head Full of Ghosts*; National Medal of the Arts awarded to Stephen King

Part One: Horror through History

HORROR IN THE ANCIENT WORLD

Horror and the supernatural enter literature with one of the earliest extant literary documents, the *Epic of Gilgamesh* (ca. 1700 BCE), which was a product of ancient Mesopotamian culture. This fragmentary text already features such elements as the superhero, prophetic dreams, a descent into the underworld, and the quest for eternal life. But it was the writers of classical antiquity, especially the Greeks, who, with their prodigal creation of gods and monsters, definitively infused terror and strangeness into literature. The term "classical antiquity" itself refers to the fusion of ancient Greek and Roman culture, lasting from about the eighth century BCE to the fifth century CE, a period whose literature, art, and philosophy have exercised and continue to exercise an immense influence on Western civilization.

It is problematical to speak of "ancient Greece" as a unified entity, because the region was for centuries a series of largely autonomous and often warring city-states, chief of which were Athens, Sparta, and Corinth. The commencement of Greek civilization can be dated to around 1200 BCE (the approximate date of the Trojan War), although extant Greek literature does not emerge in abundance until the fifth century BCE. Alexander the Great did unify Greece politically and militarily in the later fourth century, but the Romans subjugated Greece two centuries later.

The Romans dated the founding of their city to 753 BCE, but did not emerge as a world power until the third century BCE. With the establishment and expansion of the Roman Empire in the course of the first and second centuries CE, the entire Mediterranean came under the sway of a single military power. The result was that both Greek and Latin literature flourished throughout the region, with leading writers emerging from Spain, North Africa, and elsewhere. The end of classical antiquity is canonically dated to 476 CE, when the Goths sacked Rome and over-threw the last Roman emperor.

The Greeks and the Romans initiated—and in many ways perfected—some of the major genres of literature, ranging from epic poetry (Homer, Virgil) to the drama, both tragic (Aeschylus, Sophocles, Euripides, Seneca the Younger) and comic (Aristophanes, Plautus), to lyric poetry (Pindar, Horace), to history (Herodotus, Thucydides, Polybius, Livy, Tacitus), and even the novel (Lucian, Apuleius). Within these diverse genres there was abundant room for the expression of horrific themes, and both the Greeks and the Romans took occasional advantage of it.

In Homer's *Odyssey* (codified around 700 BCE, but based on oral sources extending as far back as the twelfth century), Odysseus provides a first-person account of his travels throughout the known and unknown world that spans three books

A Timeline of Horror in the Ancient World

ca. 750–700 BCE	Homer's *Iliad* and *Odyssey* feature tales of gods, monsters, and magic. The *Odyssey* features Odysseus's trip to the underworld. Hesiod's *Theogony* presents additional descriptions of monstrous and supernatural entities.
5th century BCE	Greek tragedy has its heyday in the works of Aeschylus, Sophocles, and Euripides, featuring supernaturalism and grisly scenes of physical horror.
3rd century BCE	Apollonius Rhodius's *Argonautica* narrates Jason and the Argonauts' encounters with multiple monsters and supernatural threats.
1st century BCE	The supernatural plays a significant part in the works of Horace and Virgil.
1st century CE	Petronius's *Satyricon* presents the first extant account of a werewolf in ancient literature. Ovid's *Metamorphosis* relates tales of human beings transforming into animals and plants. The plays of Seneca the Younger retell Greek stories full of blood and thunder.
2nd century CE	Apuleius's *Metamorphoses*, a.k.a. *The Golden Ass*, includes transformation, witchcraft, and more.

(books 9–12) and includes encounters with such curious entities as the Laestrygonians (a giant cannibal race who eat some of Odysseus's men), the sorceress Circe (who can turn human beings into animals), the Sirens (hybrid creatures, half bird and half woman, whose songs are fatally alluring), and Scylla and Charybdis (the one a whirlpool, the other a sea creature with six heads and twelve feet). Perhaps most memorable is Odysseus's battle with Polyphemus, a creature belonging to a race called the Cyclops (literally "round-eyed," with the implication that the creature has only one eye in the center of his forehead). Some of these entities are only alluded to in the *Odyssey*, but they are described more exhaustively in Hesiod's *Theogony* (ca. 700 BCE), an account of the origin of the gods that is as close as the Greeks ever came to having a sacred text.

Odysseus's venture into the realm of the dead (book 11) has a number of curious features. First, this realm is not actually under the earth, as in the standard Greek view, but instead in a remote region far to the west. Homer does not name the region aside from calling it "the house of Hades," referring to the god who rules the realm; but later sources sometimes use Hades to refer to the place itself. When he encounters the shades of the dead, Odysseus tries to embrace them, but they "fluttered out of my hands like a shadow / or a dream" (11.207–208). The suggestion is that the shades resemble the forms they had in life but are virtually immaterial.

Greek tragedy—flowering especially during the fifth century BCE in Athens, where annual contests were held among dramatists—contributed to the elaboration of Greek myth while at the same time probing human nature and social conflict with unprecedented subtlety and emotive power. Medea (whose name means "the cunning one") was the focus of Euripides's great play *Medea* (431 BCE). When her husband Jason, who brought her from Colchis (a remote city in Asia Minor) to be his wife, takes up with a younger woman, Medea appeals to Hecate (the goddess of magic and witchcraft) and prepares a dress and a golden diadem laced with poison. A Messenger's speech telling of the grisly deaths of both Creon (Jason's father-in-law) and Creon's daughter (*Medea*, lines 1121–1230) is one of the most vivid passages of physical horror in classical antiquity. Somewhat similar, albeit nonsupernatural, is Euripides's *Bacchae* (The Bacchantes; 405 BCE), in which women inflamed by the god Dionysus dismember King Pentheus of Thebes. (This event is also described by a Messenger rather than presented on stage.)

In Euripides's *Trachiniae* (The Women of Trachis; ca. 425 BCE), Deianira gives Herakles a robe that has been poisoned by the blood of Nessus, a centaur who had attacked her. Herakles suffers horrible agony when he puts the robe on. The Herakles (Hercules in Latin) cycle, embodied in the twelve "labors" that he was forced to undertake, is largely separate from the Homeric cycle, but features such distinctive creatures as the snake-headed Hydra and the three-headed dog Cerberus, who guards the entrance to Hades.

Ghosts also make striking appearances in Greek literature. In Homer's *Iliad* (ca. 750 BCE), the ghost of the slain soldier Patrocles berates his friend Achilles for not burying his corpse, thereby preventing him from crossing "the river" (i.e., the Styx, in Hades) and mingling with other shades in the underworld. Ghosts also appear in Greek tragedy, chiefly as baleful prognosticators of future woe. In Aeschylus's *Persae* (The Persians; 472 BCE), a distinctive melding of contemporary history and supernaturalism, the Persian queen Atossa summons the ghost of King Darius, who is unaware that his forces have been decisively defeated by the Greeks in the battle of Salamis (480 BCE). In Aeschylus's *Eumenides* (458 BCE—the middle play in the trilogy *Oresteia*), the ghost of Clytemnestra upbraids Orestes for murdering her and urges the Furies to plague him. The prologue to Euripides's *Hecuba* (ca. 425 BCE) is spoken by Polydorus, the son of Hecuba and Priam of Troy, who now "hovers as a wraith over my mother's head" (line 29).

With Athens's defeat by Sparta at the end of the Peloponnesian War (404 BCE), Greek literature entered a phase referred to as Hellenistic, when highly sophisticated writers used mythic figures to display their own erudition and exhibit a bland cynicism about life and society. Many of the leading writers of the period flourished in the Egyptian city of Alexandria, although at this point it was thoroughly Greek in culture. Apollonius Rhodius's epic *Argonautica* (third century BCE) recounts the quest for the Golden Fleece, as Jason gathers an illustrious band of cohorts for his voyage on the *Argo*. Along the way he encounters the bronze giant Talos; meets the prophet Phineus, who, having offended Zeus, is plagued by the

Harpies (birdlike creatures; their name means "the snatchers") who pluck his food away just as he is about to eat it; and braves the Clashing Rocks, immense cliffs that, at the Bosporus, clash together, crushing any ships that attempt to make their way through them. But a substantial portion of the *Argonautica* deals with Medea, who helps Jason obtain the Golden Fleece. At the very outset Medea is described as "something of a witch" (3.89); one of her most distinctive potions is a magic ointment made from the ichor of Prometheus, the demigod whom Zeus punished for giving the secret of fire to human beings.

The defeat of the Greeks at the battle of Corinth in 146 BCE spelled the definitive subordination of the Greek city-states to the increasing power of Rome. The sturdy, practical Romans developed a reputation in antiquity of scorning the fine arts, including literature, for the more "manly" arts of warfare and governance; and while it is true that many Latin authors—including the greatest of them, Horace and Virgil—were heavily reliant upon Greek models, Latin literature does include many imperishable works of poetry, drama, and history; and the supernatural plays a significant part in this array of writing.

Latin drama began in earnest with the comic playwright Plautus (T. Maccius Plautus). One play in particular is of interest in tracing the course of horror literature in the ancient world: *Mostellaria* (The Haunted House; ca. 200 BCE). Here no ghost actually appears; instead, the play deals with a clever slave, Tranio, who fabricates a ghost as a way of distracting Theopropides, father of the wastrel Philolaches. Tranio tries to maintain that the house in question has become haunted because its former owner had killed his guest (an appalling crime in Greco-Roman civilization), but the ruse collapses very quickly. The play is really a send-up of the superstitiousness and credulity that may have afflicted even wealthy and educated Romans.

In his memorable fifth *Epode* (ca. 38 BCE), Horace (Q. Horatius Flaccus) speaks of the witch Canidia, who has "locks and disheveled head entwined with short vipers" and who utters a mad incantation intended to prevent a hapless youth from falling in love with any other woman but her. Then there is the utterly bizarre Poem 63 (ca. 55 BCE) of Catullus (C. Valerius Catullus), written in a highly unusual meter and telling of the hideous self-castration of Attis (spelled Atys by later writers), the son and lover of Cybele, the Great Mother of the gods. While nothing strictly supernatural occurs here, the vivid first-person depiction of religious frenzy and madness makes it virtually unique in ancient literature.

Also unique, but in a very different way, is the *Satyricon* (ca. 65 CE) of Petronius (T. Petronius Arbiter). What survives of this sprawling novel—if it can be called that—is probably less than one-fifth, and perhaps less than one-tenth, of the complete work. Its centerpiece is the *Cena Trimalchionis* (Trimalchio's Dinner), where different speakers tell amusing or fantastic tales for the enjoyment of the guests. It is here that we find the first extant account of a werewolf in ancient literature. This blandly told story depicts a soldier who takes his clothes off, urinates on them, and turns into a wolf. He proceeds to howl and run off into the woods; the clothes, meanwhile, have turned to stone. Later the teller of the tale learns that a wolf has killed many of the sheep on a nearby farm.

Of the *Metamorphoses* (ca. 10 CE) of Ovid (P. Ovidius Naso) it is difficult to speak in small compass, for its very premise is supernatural: the transformation of human beings into all manner of animals, and even into plants. Along the way we have many gripping set-pieces, among them Perseus's slaying of a sea monster and his rescue of Andromeda (4.663–764), a lengthy account of the witcheries of Medea (7.1–424), a rendering of the transformation of the maiden Scylla into a birdlike monster (8.1–151), and perhaps the most poignant surviving account (although many others must once have existed) of the failed attempt of Orpheus to rescue his dead wife Eurydice from the underworld (10.1–85). Ovid's purpose is rarely to induce terror; instead, he seeks to evoke wonder at the very process of shape-shifting.

The most celebrated Roman account of the underworld is, of course, the *Aeneid* (ca. 20 BCE) of Virgil (P. Vergilius Maro), but here we are even farther from terror. The moving passage (book 6) describing Aeneas's descent into the underworld to seek the shade of his father Anchises, and also that of his dead lover Dido of Carthage, whom he abandoned, is notable for Anchises's magnificent prophecy of future Roman greatness. A later epic, the *Bellum Civile* or *Pharsalia* (ca. 65 CE) of Lucan (M. Annaeus Lucanus), treating of the civil war between Julius Caesar and Pompey, is notable for the entire absence of the standard pantheon of gods, but features a striking passage (6.419–830) in which Pompey's son seeks the counsel of the witch Erictho, who uses a "lunar poison" to reanimate a corpse and make him utter a prophecy.

The plays of Seneca the Younger (L. Annaeus Seneca, ca. 4 BCE–65 CE) are full of blood and thunder, among them *Hercules Oetaeus*, about the Hercules/Deianira story, and *Medea*. The *Metamorphoses* (ca. 180 CE) of Lucius Apuleius, usually translated as *The Golden Ass*, is a deliberate echo of Ovid, but focuses on a single metamorphosis: that of a man named Lucius into an ass. Lucius had seen a reputed witch named Pamphile turn herself into an owl and wished to become one himself; but the slave girl Fotis gives him the wrong potion, and he becomes an ass. The rest of the novel is an adventure story in which Lucius seeks to eat roses that will (for some unexplained reason) turn him back into a human being.

Terror and the supernatural are not absent from the work of otherwise sober historians. The Greek biographer Plutarch (46–120 CE) mentions ghosts with some frequency, as in *Brutus* (where Brutus confronts his "evil spirit"), *Cimon* (where the ghost of a murderer is seen haunting the public bath where he was killed), and elsewhere. Pliny the Younger's famous letter to Licinius Sura (7.27; ca. 100 CE) speaks with apparent belief of a haunted house in Athens. The curious *Peri thaumasion* (On Wonderful Events; second century CE) by the Greek writer Phlegon of Tralles recounts the tale of Philinnion, a young woman who returned from the dead six months after her funeral because of her love for Machates, spending several nights with him before dying again.

Ancient Greek and Roman civilization established a number of the major motifs that would be used in subsequent horror literature, including the ghost, the haunted house, the werewolf, the sorcerer/sorceress/witch, and monsters emerging from the depths of hell. While classical literature was largely the preserve of a small segment of the population during the Middle Ages, when literacy was restricted to a tiny intellectual elite, the horrific motifs in that literature were ripe for use whenever the heavy hand of Christian orthodoxy would be loosened to allow the appreciation of this "pagan" writing. While individual writers of the Middle Ages did find inspiration in classical writing, it took the radical scientific, philosophical, and aesthetic revolution of the Renaissance to restore this literature to a position of centrality in Western culture.

S. T. Joshi

See also: Horror in the Middle Ages; *Part Two, Themes, Topics, and Genres*: Ghost Stories; Religion, Horror, and the Supernatural; *Part Three, Reference Entries*: The Haunted House or Castle; Monsters; Transformation and Metamorphosis; Werewolves.

Further Reading

Colavito, Jason. 2008. "Introduction: From Prometheus to Faust." In *Knowing Fear: Science, Knowledge, and the Development of the Horror Genre*, 5–24. Jefferson, NC: McFarland.

Felton, D. 1999. *Haunted Greece and Rome: Ghost Stories from Classical Antiquity*. Austin: University of Texas Press.

Joshi, S. T. 2014. *Unutterable Horror: A History of Supernatural Fiction, Volume 1: From Gilgamesh to the End of the Nineteenth Century*. New York: Hippocampus Press.

Lovecraft, H. P. [1927] 2012. *The Annotated Supernatural Horror in Literature*. Edited by S. T. Joshi. New York: Hippocampus Press.

Mark, Joshua J. 2014. "Ghosts in the Ancient World." *Ancient History Encyclopedia*, October 30. http://www.ancient.eu/ghost.

Ogden, Daniel. 2009. *Magic, Witchcraft, and Ghosts in the Greek and Roman World: A Sourcebook*. 2nd ed. New York: Oxford University Press.

HORROR IN THE MIDDLE AGES

The Middle Ages (or medieval period) is the term used to designate the period of European history between the end of antiquity and the beginning of the early modern era. As neither of these transitions occurred on a fixed date, there are no definitive dates for the beginning and end of the medieval period. Broadly speaking, the Middle Ages begins with the fall of the Roman Empire, usually classed as occurring with the deposition of the last Western emperor in 476 CE. The end of the Middle Ages is harder to place, as there are substantial regional differences in political, religious, and social development. Some historians suggest that the Middle Ages ended with Christopher Columbus's first voyage to the Americas (1492); others suggest that the endpoint comes with Johannes Gutenberg's invention of the printing press (ca. 1440), or with the Protestant Reformation (beginning in 1517).

When attempting to characterize the entirety of the European medieval period, it is most common to use 1500 as an approximate endpoint—thus delineating a Middle Ages that lasted roughly 1,000 years.

In order to give more focus to the study of a millennium-long era, medievalists now frequently divide the Middle Ages into two or three subperiods. Some historians use the terms "high" and "low" to distinguish between the earlier and later parts of the era. English-speaking historians use "early," "high," and "late" to differentiate the periods of the Middle Ages, and this is the result of linguistic shifts across the era. Thus, the early Middle Ages refers to the period before 1066, when Old English (the Anglo-Saxon language) was the dominant spoken and written language in England. The High Middle Ages are the years following the Norman Conquest, when Anglo-Norman was the dominant language. An early form of Middle English began to develop toward the end of the High Middle Ages, leading to a decline in Anglo-Norman and the dominance of Middle English in the late Middle Ages (toward the end of the twelfth century and the beginning of the thirteenth).

It used to be common to find the term "Dark Ages" used to describe the medieval period. In fact, this term is still sometimes used to refer to the early Middle Ages. The phrase emerged as a way to differentiate the period from the Renaissance and the Age of Enlightenment that followed, and it was intended to conjure an image of a superstitious, ignorant, and barbaric period of European history. Developments in our understanding of the time have changed this perception, and more sensitive understandings of religious, intellectual, and social history have questioned this characterization. Although contemporary popular culture still often depicts the "darkness" of the period, scholarship has focused some attention on the cultural and intellectual achievements of the so-called Dark Ages. It is common nowadays to find medievalists challenging persistent misconceptions about the era, which include the myth of the "flat earth" belief, the idea that the Catholic Church suppressed scientific development, and the belief that diseases were universally misunderstood and mistreated.

The extent of time and space encompassed by a conception of the Middle Ages makes it difficult to summarize the significant shifts in religious, political, scientific, and literary culture during this time. However, there are some important developments that are worth noting for their impact on fiction writing. In 800 CE, Pope Leo III crowned the Frankish king Charlemagne emperor, the first time the title had been used in Western Europe since 476. Charlemagne's coronation marked the beginning of the Holy Roman Empire (though it was not explicitly called this until the thirteenth century). The Holy Roman Empire claimed ascendancy through its descent from the Roman Empire, and Charlemagne used his title to expand the lands of the Carolingian kings and to further develop a close allegiance with the papacy. The Holy Roman Empire was a powerful—though not undisputed—complex of territories in the Middle Ages, which came to include the kingdoms of Germany, Italy, and Burgundy. Charlemagne himself is a key figure in both history and literature, as his legendary exploits were recounted in numerous narratives.

Along with the formation of the Holy Roman Empire and the coronation of Charlemagne, the Crusades would also play an important part in shaping European literature. The Crusades were a series of religious wars that were fought in the eleventh to fifteenth centuries. While contemporary popular culture imagines these wars as a conflict between Christians and Muslims, taking place entirely in what is now the Middle East, there were, in fact, multiple conflicts involving Western (Catholic) and Eastern (Orthodox) Christians, Muslims, Jews, and Mongols—among others—and taking place in Asia, Africa, and Europe. While ostensibly a battle for the Holy Land, initiated in 1096, the Crusades had a huge impact on the political landscape of Europe. Not only did these wars lead to anti-Semitic violence across Europe, inflame tensions between Western and Eastern Christians, and enable the sacking of cities such as Antioch and Constantinople, the financial and military burden on Crusading territories was not insubstantial. Crusades in Northern Europe saw regions such as Livonia annexed and converted to Christianity, and the papacy was able to expand its control (and taxation) of the West through its success during the wars. Crusading nations were able to use seized and stolen property to fund local developments, and trading principalities (such as Genoa and Venice) were able to capitalize and prosper. In addition to this, the Crusades elevated the role of "knight" from that of a military horseman to a figure of elite aristocratic power. The Crusades added a religious dimension to the burgeoning code of chivalry first introduced by Charlemagne and his descendants.

This background is necessary for understanding some of the important changes in literature that occurred during the Middle Ages, which would have a big impact on the fiction that followed in later centuries. Some of the changes in literary trends as a result of events such as the Crusades are still clearly visible in contemporary literature.

There was no concept of "horror" as a genre in medieval writing. However, there are a number of tropes in contemporary horror fiction that have their ancestors or predecessors in medieval writing. Distinctions between "fiction" and "nonfiction" are also a more modern concept, so it is necessary to look at a broader range of types of writing in order to discern elements of horror in medieval narratives.

Literary storytelling in the Middle Ages took a number of different forms, including histories, chronicles, epics, and (later) romances. Medieval historiography worked differently than its modern counterpart, and so there is some crossover between these forms. A narrative that was designated as a "history" might, to modern audiences, seem like a work of fiction; the idea was that it revealed some "truth" about the world, even if it was not grounded in precise adherence to actual circumstances and events. In this way, some of the earliest stories of King Arthur were entitled histories, though the character later appeared in epic and romance narratives as well.

One of the best-known pieces of Old English literature is the epic poem *Beowulf*. Composed between 750 and 1000 CE (the exact date is unknown), this narrative describes the adventures of the eponymous Geatish king as he destroys the monsters besieging the Danish kingdom, ascends to the throne of Geatland, rules peacefully for fifty years, and then dies in a final battle with a dragon. The narrative makes a number of allusions to historical individuals, but also creates a fictional hero for whom there is no "real life" counterpart. The poem survives in only one manuscript, and there is little evidence of its being known in the later Middle Ages; however, it was rediscovered in the early modern era and successfully translated in the nineteenth century. At first, the poem was studied for its linguistic and

A Timeline of Horror in the Middle Ages

ca. 441–451	Beginning of Anglo-Saxon incursions and migration to Britain.
476	Deposition of Romulus Augustulus, last emperor of the Western Roman Empire.
ca. 750–1000	Composition of *Beowulf*, an Anglo-Saxon epic poem about kings and monsters.
800	Charlemagne crowned emperor by Pope Leo III in Rome.
1066	Norman conquest of England.
1096–1099	First Crusade: Pope Urban II sends military assistance to Byzantine emperor Alexios I Komnenos to fight the Turks.
1147–1149	Second Crusade: Pope Eugene III, Louis VII of France, and Conrad III of Germany are defeated by Seljuk Turks.
ca. 1170	*Erec and Enide*, the first of Chrétien de Troyes's romance poems, is completed.
1189–1192	Third Crusade: King Henry II of England, King Philip II of France, and Holy Roman Emperor Frederick Barbarossa attempt to conquer the Holy Land. Henry dies and is succeeded by King Richard I (known as Richard the Lionheart). Frederick Barbarossa also dies en route to the Holy Land.
ca. 1190–1200	The *lais* of Marie de France, short romance tales of chivalry and the supernatural, are completed.
1202–1204	Fourth Crusade: Crusaders sack the city of Constantinople, the capital of the Christian-controlled Byzantine Empire, destroying relations between Western and Eastern Christians for centuries to come.
ca. 1340	The Auchinleck Manuscript is produced, including the Middle English romances of *Sir Degaré*, *Floris and Blancheflour*, *Sir Orfeo*, and *Amis and Amiloun*.
1347–1350	The Black Death ravages Europe, killing about a third of the population.
ca. 1380	Composition of *Sir Gawain and the Green Knight*, a Middle English Arthurian romance.
ca. 1440	Johannes Gutenberg invents the printing press.
1476	William Caxton introduces the printing press to England.

historical implications, but in 1936 J. R. R. Tolkien gave a groundbreaking lecture in which he argued that the poem is, at its heart, about monsters. The monsters of *Beowulf*—Grendel, his mother, and the dragon—have been of abiding interest to scholars and creative writers ever since.

Despite its modern popularity, *Beowulf* is somewhat unusual as a piece of medieval epic poetry, though it does share some key concerns with later Norse poetry and Icelandic sagas, and there is little evidence of its influence on later narratives. The more influential forms of epic that circulated in Europe were tales of the military exploits of historical (and legendary) kings, and of the men who served them. In the late eleventh century, a form of Old French narrative poetry called *chansons de geste* (literally "songs of deeds") began to emerge, telling stories about the exploits of Charlemagne (the "Matter of France"), King Arthur (the "Matter of England"), and the heroes of the Trojan War (the "Matter of Rome"). As the genre developed, the knights who served the legendary kings began to be the central focus of the *chanson de geste* (reflecting the growing power of the aristocratic knight in the wake of the Crusades). Fantastic and supernatural elements also began to be added, including monstrous enemies—particularly giants—and the use of magic. These elements were introduced as part of the hero's development: monster-slaying was an important attribute of heroism, and the world of adventures began to incorporate exotic and preternatural realms.

However, the *chansons de geste* cannot really be characterized as "horror" fiction, as they lack a fully developed psychological component. There are numerous descriptions of fear in these texts, but this is most commonly presented as a straightforward and easily overcome response to a life-threatening situation. It was only with the development of a new type of fiction that emotions of dread and terror would start to be explored.

In the twelfth century, the first romance narratives started to circulate in Europe. The earliest examples of romance include the Arthurian stories of Chrétien de Troyes and the *lais* of Marie de France (short narrative poems that combined chivalric and supernatural themes). The rise of the knightly class in twelfth-century France, partly as a result of the Crusades and partly as a result of political power shifts, meant that this fiction, while often written by clerical and monastic writers, was commissioned and owned by royalty and the aristocracy. The figure of the knight (rather than the king) was central to this new fiction, and the stories abounded with fantastical elements, including monsters, ghosts, fairies, werewolves, magical weapons, supernatural transformations, and mysterious castles.

The increasing power of the aristocracy led to the development of "courtly" culture, including romanticized "codes of conduct" for knights, elaborate entertainments, and an increased desire for fiction that reflected this idealized self-image. Hand-in-hand with this, however, were shifts in theological thinking, particularly in terms of the conceptualization of the figure of Christ. Early medieval representations of Christ had focused on his divine strength and his role as the "King of Heaven" (and it is possible that Beowulf was intended to reflect this all-powerful masculine Messiah). By contrast, the twelfth century began to see a focus on Christ's suffering as the "Man of Sorrows," with iconography drawing attention to his wounds and his pain. As a figure of idealized masculinity, the romance knight also suffered—both physically and mentally. Later medieval narratives are often concerned with the interior life of the knight, and with the toll his adventures might take on his mind, body, and soul.

The first Middle English romances appeared in the late thirteenth century, but the genre really flourished in the fourteenth century. In the 1330s, a number of narratives appeared that told of fairy knights and kings who threatened and attacked the human realm, including *Sir Orfeo* and *Sir Degaré*, and of women seduced by demons, including *Sir Gowther*. Old French romances were adapted for English-speaking audiences, including *William of Palerne*, a werewolf story translated in the mid-fourteenth century. For modern audiences, one of the best-known Middle English romances is *Sir Gawain and the Green Knight* (late fourteenth century), which tells the story of a monstrous intruder at Arthur's court at Camelot. The hero's battle with the monster, the desolate and terrifying landscape through which he must travel, the constant indications of the man's fear, and the final supernatural denouement are all features that connect this poem to contemporary horror fiction. Less well known—at least to modern audiences—is the later, shorter version of the same story, known as *The Greene Knight*, in which the inner thoughts and motivations of the supernatural intruder are presented, paving the way for many of horror fiction's monstrous antiheroes.

When looking at medieval fiction, it is important to view it in relation to broader cultural concerns. These narratives did not occur in isolation, and various elements—for example, ideas about monsters, the physical body, and death—are reflected in all sorts of contemporaneous cultural productions, from religious sermons to medical writing, and from architectural decoration to maps of the world. It is possible to discern cultural patterns and trends, and to situate romance fiction, with its terrifying monsters, sadistic fairies, and traumatized werewolves, within this broader picture. Like a lot of horror fiction, these narratives reveal a profound concern with understanding the human condition, and with determining the limits to which a person can be pushed.

Hannah Priest

See also: Horror in the Ancient World; Horror in the Early Modern Era; *Part Two, Themes, Topics, and Genres*: Religion, Horror, and the Supernatural; *Part Three, Reference Entries*: Devils and Demons; Incubi and Succubi; Monsters; Transformation and Metamorphosis; Werewolves; Witches and Witchcraft.

Further Reading

Bildhauer, Bettina, and Robert Mills, eds. 2003. *The Monstrous Middle Ages*. Toronto and Buffalo: University of Toronto Press.

Database of Middle English Romance. 2012. University of York. http://www.middleenglishro
    mance.org.uk.

Heng, Geraldine. 2004. *Empire of Magic: Medieval Romance and the Politics of Cultural Fan-
    tasy*. New York and Chichester: Columbia University Press.

Pernoud, Régine. 2000. *Those Terrible Middle Ages: Debunking the Myths*. Translated by Anne
    Englund Nash. San Francisco: Ignatius Press.

Priest, Hannah. 2014. "Christ's Wounds and the Birth of Romance." In *Wounds in the Middle
    Ages*, edited by Anne Kirkham and Cordelia Warr, 131–150. Farnham: Ashgate.

Steinberg, Theodore L. 2003. *Reading the Middle Ages: An Introduction to Medieval Literature*.
    Jefferson, NC: McFarland.

Tolkien, J. R. R. 2006. *The Monsters and the Critics and Other Essays*. Edited by Christopher
    Tolkien. London: HarperCollins.

HORROR IN THE EARLY MODERN ERA

The early modern era is generally defined as between 1500 and 1800, although many disciplines consider the eighteenth century the period of the Enlightenment. As a literary period, the early modern era is renowned for the output of what used to be called the Renaissance (a term that has fallen out of fashion because what is understood by "Renaissance" took place at different times in different parts of Europe) and is dominated by major canonical figures such as Christopher Marlowe, William Shakespeare, John Donne, and John Milton. Traditionally horror is considered to begin after this time, with many studies citing Edgar Allan Poe as the first writer of true horror. More recently, however, critics have begun to highlight the rich veins of horror texts to be found in the sixteenth and seventeenth centuries. The period as a whole is characterized by upheaval—both social and religious. Although encompassing the artistic achievements of the Renaissance, the early modern era also contained persecution, torture, and colonization on a massive scale. The uncertainties created by radical shifts in religion, science, and exploration created a space in which writers of various literary modes could utilize the embryonic motifs and tropes of horror to comment on and interrogate the issues of their time.

The main forms of literature in the early modern era all utilize early notions of horror. Drama and poetry have been the focus of most critical attention over the centuries, but prose writing and ballads are becoming more important in understanding the concerns and ideas of the time. The increased visibility of these popular forms enables the recognition of the more sensationalist aspects of early modern horror. As can be seen in later periods, horror literature took a range of forms and approaches, each of which can be linked to particular anxieties in the wider culture of the time.

One of the key sources of horror in the early modern era was the religious domain. Conflicts between the worldviews of traditional Catholicism and the newer reformed Protestant theologies led to fault lines that were explored in literary works (and that have continued to be explored even today). Religion was a fundamental part of early modern society and identity, and therefore the ruptures of the Reformation were powerful and long lasting. This can be seen in the popularity of supernatural and demonic figures such as ghosts, demons, and witches throughout the period.

A series of important prose works set out the parameters of early modern supernatural belief and therefore its implementation in horror. The demand for such writing can be seen by the translation into English of several prominent European examples, although surprisingly not the most infamous, *Malleus Maleficarum* (1487). Perhaps the two most influential of these translated works are *Of ghostes and spirites walking by nyght, and of strange noyses, crackes, and sundry forewarnynges, which commonly happen before the death of menne, great slaughters & alterations of kyngdomes* (1572) by the Swiss theologian Ludwig Lavatar, and French scholar Pierre le Loyer's *A treatise of spectres or straunge sights, visions and apparitions appearing sensibly unto men* (1605). Important vernacular works include Reginald Scot's *Discoverie of Witchcraft* (1584), in which the skeptical author reveals the misconceptions and artifices that lie behind many superstitious ideas, and King James I's *Daemonologie, In Forme of a Dialogue, Divided into three Books* (1597). Although these texts are not traditionally considered to be horror, the lurid details and fascination with the darker aspects of human behavior contained within speak to a similar desire on the part of the reader. In fact, these "nonfiction" texts work in the same way as modern-day true-crime narratives in which information and sensationalism sit side-by-side. The potential for such texts to be intended as entertainment can be seen by the popularity of Thomas Nashe's satirical *Terrors of the Night* (1594), a convincing parody of the kind of beliefs described in the other works.

Accounts of hauntings and suspected witchcraft were not restricted to large published tracts, however. Scores of cheap, popular ballads and chapbooks (small, cheap, paper-covered books of mass popular appeal) recounted supernatural happenings of every imaginable kind, clearly illustrating the demand for horror as entertainment. This demand can also be seen by the popularity of supernatural horror in the dramatic works of the time. Shakespeare's *Macbeth* is probably the most famous example, but there were also hugely popular plays by other playwrights, such as Christopher Marlowe's *Doctor Faustus* (1594), featuring a cast of demons that infamously caused contemporary audiences to believe they were real, and Thomas Middleton's *The Witch* (1612), a play largely overshadowed by its textual links to *Macbeth*. Thomas Dekker, John Ford, and William Rowley's *The Witch of Edmonton* (1621) and Thomas Heywood and Richard Brome's *The Late Lancashire Witches* (1634) were both dramatic versions of "real" accounts of witchcraft. This "true-horror" subgenre shows the closeness between literature and other cultural uses of horror in the period. Alongside these plays centered on aspects of haunting or demonology, the tropes and devices of supernatural horror became widely used on stage, with ghosts in particular being a defining characteristic of the hugely successful genre of revenge tragedy.

Revenge tragedies are perhaps the clearest horror texts of the time, featuring as they do lurid representations of blood, death, and mutilation. Even William

A Timeline of Early Modern Horror

1440　Johannes Gutenberg invents the printing press, signaling the beginning of the literary early modern period.

1487　*Malleus Maleficarum* is published in Germany.

1517　Martin Luther posts his Ninety-five Theses on the door of Wittenburg Cathedral, generally seen to be the formal beginning of the Reformation.

1576　The Theatre is built in Shoreditch, London.

1587　*The Spanish Tragedy* is first performed.

1594　Thomas Nashe's *The Terrors of the Night* is published, showing a demand for literary treatment of demonological ideas.

1607　Shakespeare's *Macbeth* stages horror and witchcraft.

1623　Webster's *Duchess of Malfi* cements his role as playwright of horror.

1649　The English king, Charles I, is executed. The civil wars that follow bring a new kind of horror to the population.

1701　The Age of Enlightenment commences, in which science and skepticism replace the superstition of what came before. Such a view, despite its reductive aspects, does provide an end point to the early modern period.

Shakespeare was not immune to the savage delights of the form, as can be seen in his blood-drenched *Titus Andronicus*. The origins of the revenge tragedy can be traced to a particularly English combination of the ghosts and described atrocities of classical drama and the highly visual and physical staging of the medieval mystery plays. The result was a style of drama that pushed the limits of taste and decency much as horror continues to do today. Although all revenge tragedies contain some element of supernatural or physical horror, particular exemplars illustrate the extremes to which playwrights took the horror. Thomas Kyd's *The Spanish Tragedy* (ca. 1587) is the most famous early revenge tragedy and is often considered alongside *Titus*. Detailing the mental disintegration and torment of the Knight Marshal of Spain, Hieronimo, the play contains a litany of mutilations and murders, including an onstage glossectomy (removal of a tongue) and the *Saw*-like (2004) display of Hieronimo's murdered son's corpse. The play also popularized the metatheatrical ideas of plays-within-plays and a supernatural observer on stage—here both in the personification of Revenge and a Ghost. The inevitable bloodbath at the conclusion of the play brings to mind the tagline to the classic horror movie *The Texas Chainsaw Massacre* (1974): "Who will survive, and what will be left of them?" Indeed, this question can be applied to the entire genre of revenge tragedy.

The development of revenge tragedy can be compared to that of horror cinema, as writers competed to include ever more bloodthirsty and horrific content. *Antonio's Revenge* (1599) by John Marston repeats the cannibalistic banquet utilized earlier by Shakespeare in *Titus* (and taken from the classical tragedian Seneca's *Thyestes*, ca. 62) but furthers the horror by the meal being made from a young child—a choice made even more horrific by the fact that the play was written for one of the boy's companies. Thomas Middleton's *The Revenger's Tragedy* (ca. 1607), a play often considered to be a commentary on the entire genre, features a poisoned and disguised skull used to murder a corrupt duke, and the line that perhaps best sums up the particular blend of sensationalism and moralizing that defined the revenge tragedy: "When the bad bleeds, then is the tragedy good" (Middleton 1988, Act 3, Scene 5, line 200).

Despite their surprisingly modern approach to violent representation, early modern revenge tragedies are clearly steeped in the conventions of the period. Revengers generally receive fatal punishment for taking matters into their own hands rather than leaving justice to the state or God (an approach often rendered impossible due to the villain being in a position of power), and the final words are invariably spoken by the highest ranked character left alive. The fate of almost all female characters in revenge tragedies also predicts their treatment in horror cinema as figures of desire but with little chance of survival.

Following from these hugely successful plays, the mantle of horror passes to John Webster, a writer so infamous for his macabre approach that he features as a child cameo in the Oscar-winning *Shakespeare in Love* (1998), declaring: "Plenty of blood. That's the only writing." Alongside the obligatory mutilations, stabbings, and poisonings of revenge tragedy, Webster further adds to the horror in his masterpiece, *The Duchess of Malfi* (1623), through use of contemporary ideas of lycanthropy as an extreme form of mental disorder. The villainous Ferdinand, brother to the titular Duchess, conspires to have her killed out of a mixture of jealousy and family pride when she takes a lover he does not approve of. Following her death, he rapidly descends into madness, a madness that finally manifests itself in wolf-like behavior: "Said he was a wolf, only the difference / Was, a wolf's skin was hairy on the outside" (Webster 1996, Act 5, Scene 2, lines 16–17). Such use of creature horror was in part influenced by the popularity of Ovid's *Metamorphoses* (ca. 8 CE) as a school text and also in part by anxieties and uncertainties about the barriers between human and animal brought about through accounts of strange beasts in travel narratives.

Horror's existence on the boundaries can also be seen in early modern literature's treatment of the closeness of horror and laughter. Modern expectations of comedy as funny and tragedy as sad do not apply to early drama, in which moments of extreme bloodshed and atrocities were punctuated with dark humor and a plethora of puns. This clear literary awareness of the proximity of horror and laughter is a defining characteristic of many forms of horror literature from revenge tragedies onward. The laughter, whether genuine or the result of discomfort at what is being witnessed, becomes a key part of audience response, and the high moral purposes of tragedy described by early modern theorists such as Sir Philip Sidney are subsumed into sensationalism and spectacle.

The influence of early modern horror literature can be seen across many aspects of later writing, as the period continues to be a popular setting for films and books that set out to exploit the superstitious pretechnological world. In fact, the rural European settings of later classics of Gothic horror such as *Frankenstein* and *Dracula* enable an atmosphere that has far more in common with the sixteenth century than the increasingly urbanized and industrialized England. Modern films such as *Bram Stoker's Dracula* (1992) and *Van Helsing* (2004) emphasize this difference through costume and setting. M. Night Shyamalan's *The Village* (2004) plays on these cinematic conventions, depicting a primitive community that shares beliefs and traditions that set them aside from the modern setting of the film. More specifically, horror texts set in the early modern era continue to be popular, particularly within the subgenre of folk horror. Notable examples include the novels *Deliver Us from Evil* (1997) by Tom Holland and *The Tale of Raw Head and Bloody Bones* (2013) by Jack Wolf, and films ranging from the early classics *Hexen* (1922) and *Day of Wrath* (1943) to later standouts such as *Witchfinder General* (1968) and *Blood on Satan's Claw* (1971), and, more recently, *A Field in England* (2013). The success, critically and commercially, of writer/director Robert Eggers's *The Witch* (2015) demonstrates that the popularity and influence of horror in the early modern era is still strong.

Stephen Curtis

See also: Horror in the Ancient World; Horror in the Middle Ages; Horror in the Eighteenth Century; *Part Two, Themes, Topics, and Genres*: Religion, Horror, and the Supernatural; Shakespearean Horrors; *Part Three, Reference Entries*: Devils and Demons; Witches and Witchcraft.

Further Reading

Clark, Stuart. 1999. *Thinking with Demons: The Idea of Witchcraft in Early Modern Europe*. Oxford: Oxford University Press.

Joshi, S. T. 2014. *Unutterable Horror: A History of Supernatural Fiction, Volume 1: From Gilgamesh to the End of the Nineteenth Century*. New York: Hippocampus Press.

Middleton, Thomas. [ca. 1606] 1988. *The Revenger's Tragedy*. In *Five Plays*, edited by Bryan Loughrey and Neil Taylor, 71–160. Houndsworth: Penguin.

Sage, Victor. 1988. *Horror Fiction in the Protestant Tradition*. London: Macmillan.

Shakespeare in Love. 1998. Directed by John Madden. Universal Studios.

Simkin, Stevie. 2006. *Early Modern Tragedy and the Cinema of Violence*. Houndmills, Basingstoke: Palgrave Macmillan.

Thomas, Keith. 1971. *Religion and the Decline of Magic: Studies in Popular Beliefs in Sixteenth and Seventeenth Century England*. Oxford: Oxford University Press.

Walter, Brenda S. Gardenour. 2015. *Our Old Monsters: Witches, Werewolves and Vampires from Medieval Theology to Horror Cinema*. Jefferson, NC: McFarland.

Webster, John. [ca. 1614] 1996. *The Duchess of Malfi*. In *The Duchess of Malfi and Other Plays*, edited by René Weis, 103–200. Oxford: Oxford University Press.

HORROR IN THE EIGHTEENTH CENTURY

The roots of horror literature run back through the Middle Ages, the classical age of the ancient world, and beyond, to the fireside stories and cave paintings of our Paleolithic ancestors. And while "horror fiction" would not be used as a generic label until the mid-twentieth century, there is nevertheless ample justification for stating that it was in the eighteenth century that horror as a popular fictional genre emerged. During the last decade of this century—roughly contemporaneously with the French Revolution—that crucial precursor to modern horror, the Gothic novel, became among the most widely consumed literary forms.

A wide variety of literary developments earlier in the century fed into the Gothic and the development of horror as a genre. Indeed, most early eighteenth-century writings that focused on the supernatural as a source of fear and excitement were not conceived as fiction at all. In reaction to the loss of religious faith occasioned by the rise of skeptical philosophy, empirical science, and materialism, the closing decades of the seventeenth century saw the publication of a variety of books and pamphlets dedicated to persuading their readers of the reality of supernatural beings, including ghosts, revenants, and demons. Later termed "apparition narratives," such texts sought to combat growing skepticism toward religious, and specifically Christian, teachings, using supposedly empirical accounts of supernatural beings and occurrences to defend the reality revealed by scripture against the encroachments of Enlightenment science and philosophy.

Probably the most influential of these was *Saducismus Triumphatus* (1681). Written by English cleric Joseph Glanvill (1636–1680) and published shortly after his death, the book is a compendium of witchcraft and related subjects that is ultimately a defense of the truth of Christian scripture. As suggested by the title, which can be translated as "The Triumph over Sadducism"—with the latter term coming from the ancient Jewish sect of the Sadducees, which held a skeptical viewpoint about supernatural matters such as angels and the afterlife—Glanvill aligns skepticism toward supernatural menaces including witches and revenants with skepticism toward the Bible. Heavily influenced by Glanvill, American Puritan theologian and prolific writer Cotton Mather (1663–1728) published his *Wonders of the Invisible World* (1693) shortly after the conclusion of the Salem witch trials. A work of natural theology that catalogues a wide variety of supernatural phenomena in the New World, *Wonders* focuses particularly on the dangers of witchcraft and the need to punish and prevent its practice, drawing on the cases presented during the Salem trials and serving as a justification for the trials themselves. Tremendously influential at the time of their publication, in the succeeding two centuries both Glanvill's and Mather's works would continue to exert an influence quite unlike anything their authors had intended, as they would be drawn upon by many eighteenth- and nineteenth-century writers who would reweave these accounts into fictional fabrics.

Many eighteenth-century writers speculated about the attraction such supernatural terrors held, often tying them both to the important role folklore and superstition played in the development of national and cultural identities, and to the supposedly more universal concept of the sublime. An affective state combining awe and terror, the sublime became a major aesthetic category in Britain and throughout Western Europe following the rediscovery of the ancient Greek rhetorician Longinus's *Peri Hypsous* and its translation into modern languages. (Nicholas Boileau's 1674 French translation was probably the most influential, but the most widely read in the English-speaking world of the eighteenth century was William Smith's 1739 translation, titled *On the Sublime*.) Longinus saw the elicitation of great passion, *ekstasis*, as both the hallmark of genius in a writer and as a way of elevating the reader, and this concept of the sublime became widely discussed by critics and philosophers, and even more widely aspired to by writers and artists. English dramatist and critic John Dennis (1658–1734) explained the importance of sublime terror in poetry and theater in his 1704 essay "Grounds of Criticism in Poetry," claiming that no passion is more "capable of giving a great spirit to poetry" than the "enthusiastic terror" of the sublime (Dennis 2000, 101). Dennis went on to iterate some sources of such terror in what amounts to an ingredients list for later Gothic writers: "gods, demons, hell, spirits and souls of men, miracles, prodigies, enchantments, witchcraft, thunder, tempests, raging seas, inundations, torrents, earthquakes, volcanoes, monsters, serpents, lions, tigers, fire, war, pestilence, famine, etc." (102). Dennis concluded that such terrors are important both morally and theologically, as "of these ideas none are so terrible as those which show the wrath and vengeance of an angry god" (102). Building on Dennis's ideas, Joseph Addison (1672–1719) provided a more psychological account of sublime terror in his journal *The Spectator* in 1712, claiming "it does not arise so properly from the description of what is terrible, as from the reflection we make on our selves at the time of reading it," situating those things that terrify us at the center of our attempts to understand our own identity (Addison 2000, 105).

Following such critical statements, more writers would come to see the creation of a feeling of terror in readers as a worthy aspiration. One crucial example was prolific English writer Daniel Defoe (1660–1731). Best remembered for his protorealist novels *Robinson Crusoe* (1719) and *Moll Flanders* (1722), Defoe also wrote numerous tracts, pamphlets, and books about the reality of supernatural phenomena, and this work occupies a prominent position between the apparition narratives of the late seventeenth century and the Gothic fictions of the latter half of the eighteenth. His longer and more influential works in this vein include *The Political History of the Devil, As Well Ancient as Modern* (1726), *A System of Magic, or the History of the Black Art* (1726), and *An Essay on the History and Reality of Apparitions* (1727). Presenting itself initially as a compendium of apparition narratives in the tradition of Glanvill, the latter essay is particularly ingenious in its blending of encyclopedic and narrative elements, tied together by a narrating theologian who serves as a modest witness while creating an uncanny atmosphere through an eye for eerie details. Defoe brings to bear his verisimilar skills here just as he did with *Robinson Crusoe*, making the *Essay* important as much for its literary techniques as for its apparition accounts.

French Benedictine monk and researcher Antoine Augustin Calmet (1672–1757) took an approach similar to Defoe's in producing what is probably the most influential collection of eighteenth-century apparition narratives. Calmet undertook an exhaustive study of the apparitions of angels, demons, various other spirits, and related occult phenomena, including witchcraft and lycanthropy. The fruits of his labor, *Dissertations sur les apparitions des anges, des démons et des esprits, et sur les revenants et vampires de Hongrie, de Bohême, de Moravie et de Silésie* (*Dissertations on the Apparitions of Spirits and on the Vampires or Revenants of Hungary, Moravia, and Silesia*) was published in 1746 and in an expanded revised edition in 1751, and was quickly translated into English and numerous other languages, reaching a wide audience. Calmet's work, though it ultimately attempts to discount the reality of many of these phenomena on Catholic theological as well as on empirical grounds, was often read for the vivid and chilling details of its accounts. In particular, his description of the supposed vampires and revenants of Eastern Europe continued to fuel the popular fascination with such creatures for well over a century, serving as a major source for vampire narratives from Robert Southey's *Thalaba the Destroyer* (1801) through John Polidori's "The Vampyre" (1819), and Bram Stoker's *Dracula* (1897).

The middle decades of the eighteenth century also saw a number of British poets produce religious ruminations on mortality that relied heavily on images of death and decay, ostensibly to serve as memento mori (reminders of mortality) and aids to pious meditation. The earliest and most influential example was Anglo-Irish poet Thomas Parnell's (1679–1718) "Night-Thoughts on Death" (posthumously published by his friend Alexander Pope in a 1722 collection of Parnell's poetic works). The popular success and critical attention paid to Parnell's work would inspire many later poets to work in a similar mode. Other important examples include Scottish poet Robert Blair's (1699–1746) blank verse poem "The Grave" (1743), English poet Edward Young's (1683–1765) *The Complaint: Or Night-Thoughts on Life, Death and Immortality* (serially published between 1743 and 1745), and English poet Thomas Gray's (1716–1771) "Elegy Written in a Country Churchyard" (1751). Critics of some of the later and more formulaic examples of what would come to be known as the "Graveyard" or "Boneyard" school of poetry, however, saw the gruesome images of such poems as ultimately exploitative, and their supposed moral and theological purpose as an excuse to revel in morbidity, an accusation that would also be frequently leveled against later Gothic and Dark Romantic writers who learned vital aesthetic lessons from the poets of the "Graveyard school."

In 1757, the literary aesthetics of death, pain, power, and cosmic immensity that continue to play a vital role in modern horror were influentially articulated when Irish philosopher and statesman Edmund Burke (1729–1797) published his treatise, *A Philosophical Enquiry into the Origins of Our Ideas of the Sublime and the Beautiful*. Building extensively on the work of earlier writers including Addison as well as philosophers Lord Shaftesbury and Francis Hutcheson, and exemplifying his ideas through the work of great writers including William Shakespeare and John Milton,

Burke drew on empirical psychological principles to argue that terror was the most powerful emotion a human being was capable of experiencing, and thereby provided an aesthetic justification that would be seized upon by writers devoted to inspiring awe and terror in readers. Burke could not have anticipated the tremendous influence his *Enquiry* would have in shaping literary tastes for centuries to come. It would be read, referenced, and reacted to not only by early Gothic writers including Horace Walpole and Ann Radcliffe, but also by later writers including Edgar Allan Poe and H. P. Lovecraft, the latter of whom would paraphrase Burke in declaring fear to be "the oldest and strongest emotion of mankind" (Lovecraft 2012, 25).

A Timeline of Horror in the Eighteenth Century

1681	Joseph Glanvill publishes *Saducismus Triumphatus*.
1692	The Salem witch trials commence.
1693	The Salem witch trials continue. Cotton Mather publishes *Wonders of the Invisible World*.
1711–1712	Addison and Steele publish their journal *The Spectator*, including essays on the role of the sublime and fantastic in literature as well as short Orientalist narratives such as "Santor Barsisa" that will later inspire Gothic writers.
1727	Daniel Defoe publishes *An Essay on the History and Reality of Apparitions*.
1746	Augustin Calmet publishes his "Dissertations on the Apparitions of Spirits and on the Vampires or Revenants of Hungary, Moravia, and Silesia."
1757	Edmund Burke publishes his *Philosophical Enquiry*.
1762	The Cock Lane Ghost becomes the subject of popular fascination and is investigated by notable intellectuals including Samuel Johnson and Oliver Goldsmith.
1764	Horace Walpole publishes *The Castle of Otranto*.
1787–1789	Friedrich von Schiller's unfinished novel *Der Geisterseher* (*The Ghost-Seer*) is serially published in the journal *Thalia*.
1789	The storming of the Bastille occurs ten days after the Marquis de Sade is transferred to the insane asylum at Charenton. The French Revolution continues until 1799, contemporaneous with the peak popularity of the Gothic novel.
1793	Louis XVI and Marie Antoinette killed by the Revolutionaries. William Godwin publishes his rationalist Gothic novel *Caleb Williams*.
1794	Ann Radcliffe publishes her wildly popular Gothic novel *The Mysteries of Udolpho*.
1796	Matthew Lewis publishes his Gothic romance *The Monk*, retrospectively recognized as the first novel of supernatural horror in English.

It was Horace Walpole (1717–1797) who invented the Gothic as a literary form. Inspired by the medieval revivalism of poets including James Macpherson and Thomas Chatterton, Walpole combined his antiquarian enthusiasms with an interest in folkloric superstitions and a desire to explore his own dreams and nightmares, and the result was his pseudo-medieval romance *The Castle of Otranto* (1764). He presented the first edition of the book as a translation from a thirteenth-century Italian manuscript, and even as historians and philologists decried it as an obvious hoax, the book became a popular success. Walpole appended an apology to the book's second edition (1765), coining the term "Gothic story" for this new literary form that combined history with fantasy in a manner meant to evoke both wonder and terror, one that would become a vital precursor to modern horror literature.

By the 1780s in Germany, another precursor emerged in the form of *Schauer-romane* (shudder-novels). An extension of the *Sturm und Drang* ("storm and stress") aesthetic of early romanticism, these novels combined tragedy with mystery and supernaturalism, often focusing on conspiracies, secret societies, and black magic. Despite never being completed, one of the most influential was Friedrich von Schiller's (1759–1805) *Der Geisterseher* (*The Ghost-Seer*, serially published between 1787 and 1789). Also seminal was Christian Heinrich Spiess's *Das Petermännchen* (1793; translated as *The Dwarf of Westerbourg*). Like Walpole's *Otranto*, this was a ghost story set in the thirteenth century. These and other *Schauer-romane* anticipated the British Gothic novels of the 1790s in both subject matter and style, and in some cases would be directly imitated by British writers including Matthew Lewis.

Lewis was a young English aristocrat whose first and only Gothic novel, *The Monk* (1796), has a strong claim to be considered the first novel of supernatural horror in English. Partly inspired by the Gothic romances of Ann Radcliffe (1764–1823), whose popular *Mysteries of Udolpho* (1794) Lewis had devoured and sought to imitate, *The Monk* draws heavily on the *Sturm und Drang* writers Lewis avidly consumed as a student of German literature. With its frenetic style, florid descriptions of sexuality and violence, and its unapologetic portrayal of a world in which satanic supernatural powers conspire against humanity, *The Monk* rejected both Radcliffe's decorum and the Enlightenment values that led her to explain the seemingly supernatural occurrences in her fictions according to rational, materialist principles. These excesses led a scandalized Radcliffe to distinguish between her own moralistic "terror" Gothic romances and Lewis's "horror" Gothic in an essay titled "On the Supernatural in Poetry" (1826) that in many ways serves as the first critical attempt to distinguish "horror" as its own literary genre. Radcliffe's distinction between terror and horror corresponds closely with how horror as a literary genre evolved in the two centuries to come, and would be echoed by later studies including Lovecraft's *Supernatural Horror in Literature* (1927) and by Stephen King's *Danse Macabre* (1981).

Lewis's novel became an international sensation, its scandalous success carrying it not only throughout Britain, but to France, Germany, and the New World. In

Britain, it would inspire more transgressive and horror-focused Gothic fictions including Charlotte Dacre's *Zofloya* (1806), Mary Shelley's *Frankenstein* (1816), and Charles Maturin's *Melmoth the Wanderer* (1820). In France, it spurred the popular appetite for the *roman noir*, inspiring writers including François Guillaume Ducray-Duminil and the Marquis de Sade, and later nineteenth-century writers of horrific fiction including Victor Hugo, Honoré de Balzac, and Guy de Maupassant. In America, though Charles Brockden Brown's early Gothic novels *Wieland* (1798) and *Edgar Huntly* (1799) took a psychological approach informed by William Godwin's *Caleb Williams* (1793), they would nevertheless echo *The Monk's* use of a vicious and religiously deluded antihero, whereas Poe's later forays into the Gothic would share Lewis's emphasis on overt supernaturalism and the grotesque.

Sean Moreland

See also: Horror in the Middle Ages; Horror in the Nineteenth Century; *Part Two, Themes, Topics, and Genres*: The Gothic Literary Tradition; Gothic Poetry; *Part Three, Reference Entries*: Brown, Charles Brockden; *The Castle of Otranto*; Lewis, Matthew Gregory; *The Monk*; *The Mysteries of Udolpho*; Psychological Horror; Radcliffe, Ann; Romanticism and Dark Romanticism; The Sublime; Terror versus Horror; Vampires; Walpole, Horace.

Further Reading

Addison, Joseph. [1712] 2000. "Joseph Addison (1672–1719), *The Spectator*, No. 419 (1712)." In *Gothic Documents: A Sourcebook 1700–1820*, edited by E. J. Clery and Robert Miles, 104–107. Manchester and New York: Manchester University Press.

Bloom, Clive. 2007. *Gothic Horror: A Guide for Students and Readers*. 2nd ed. Basingstoke: Palgrave Macmillan.

Crawford, Joseph. 2013. *Gothic Fiction and the Invention of Terrorism: The Politics and Aesthetics of Fear in the Age of the Reign of Terror*. London and New York: Bloomsbury.

Dennis, John. [1704] 2000. "John Dennis (1657–1734), *The Grounds of Criticism in Poetry* (1704)." In *Gothic Documents: A Sourcebook 1700–1820*, edited by E. J. Clery and Robert Miles, 100–104. Manchester and New York: Manchester University Press.

Hogle, Jerrold E. 2002. *The Cambridge Companion to Gothic Fiction*. Cambridge Companions to Literature. Cambridge: Cambridge University Press.

Joshi, S. T. 2014. *Unutterable Horror: A History of Supernatural Fiction, Volume 1: From Gilgamesh to the End of the Nineteenth Century*. New York: Hippocampus Press.

Lovecraft, H. P. [1927] 2012. *The Annotated Supernatural Horror in Literature*. Edited by S. T. Joshi. New York: Hippocampus Press.

HORROR IN THE NINETEENTH CENTURY

As the nineteenth century began, it seemed, at least in Europe, to mark a new beginning following the upheaval of the French Revolution and Napoleon's empire, which occupied Europe until 1815. America was relatively unconcerned with such developments, which seemed distant in spite of their repercussions in Latin

America and the Caribbean. The United States seemed relatively well settled after its own revolution, in spite of seething disputes between the North and South that would remain in uneasy balance for the first sixty years of the century, the continuing conquest and taming of the West providing a safety-valve of sorts.

France was not done with revolutions yet—it was to have two more in 1830 and 1848, and another, albeit brief and localized, in 1871—and other European nations, even when they kept the lid on ever-seething domestic social upheavals, were by no means done with international wars, the Crimean War providing a particularly bloody midcentury interlude, and the traumatic reverberations of the Franco-Prussian War of 1870 extending beyond France, especially in their apparent implications as to the probable shape of wars to come. The imaginative significance of those two European wars and the American Civil War of 1861–1865 went far beyond the political questions they appeared to settle temporarily, by virtue of the innovative newspaper reportage that brought the horrors of war to the domestic hearth in an unprecedented fashion and complemented their dire reality with a new urgency that sowed fear for the future as well as horror.

The news in question revealed, all too clearly, that war was something that affected civilians as well as soldiers in devastating fashion, and that as weaponry became more powerful, civilians were being moved ever closer to the battle lines as increasingly easy cannon fodder. Writing about the horrors of war became much more intimate and immediate in the nineteenth century, not merely because the images of death and devastation became sharper but because they became much closer in time and space. For the first time, people began to produce fictional images of wars that were historically very recent, or even still in progress, sometimes even yet to come. Such fiction is not generally categorized as "horror fiction" because that genre tends to be defined primarily in terms of supernatural horror and the horror of psychological aberration, but no shift in the spectrum of horror, considered in its broadest sense, can occur without reverberations in other parts of the spectrum.

Supernatural horror fiction did not slide toward oblivion as the spectrum of real horrors began to take a much greater place in the popular imagination—after war, the most newsworthy topic by far was murder, the more gruesome the better, and murder involving passion and rape the best of all—but it did mutate, as it had to do, to adapt to the new imaginative ambience. To some extent it did so by absorption; as the news suffered from the effects of melodramatic inflation, having to pile on increasing amounts of agony to procure the same level of shock and awe, so horror fiction reached for new extremes of gruesomeness, passion, and violation, but it was hampered and shackled in so doing by standards of literary decency. Even the news was censored of actualities too nasty to be reported, but fiction, devoid of the justification of accurate reportage, was more severely constrained by prudishness.

Inevitably, therefore, the most prominent strategy of adaptation was not a matter of taking real horrors aboard, but a matter of seeking and discovering oblique approaches to stimulation that could achieve telling effects without too much cru-dity. Even in France, which did not suffer from English Victorianism or American prudishness, the Marquis de Sade's reckless indulgence in the horrors of rape and cruelty remained banned throughout the century, and it required special circum-stances for a catalogue of physical atrocities like the one featured in Louise Michel's *Les Microbes humains* (1886; translated as *The Human Microbes*) to slip through the net. The supernatural was, in that regard, something of a literary refuge, offering abundant scope for the creation of horror by implication, but it did not take long for writers to begin to exploit the inevitable hesitation of any character confronted with apparently supernatural manifestations, as to whether they were to be con-strued as objective facts or as symptoms of madness—or, in the most sophisticated works of all, the hesitation over whether that supposed difference ultimately really matters.

Against the background of this overall pattern of evolution, the Gothic novel was already doomed by the time the nineteenth century began. One of the first reflections of the developments of the philosophical and literary movement of romanticism, it had already reached its peak in the 1790s and was entering a phase of decline by 1801. The precedents laid down by Ann Radcliffe and Matthew Gregory Lewis were still influential, but anyone intending to achieve something new in the genre was required at least to broaden it out somewhat, and in so doing begin its transformation.

Most of the nineteenth-century novels subsequently to be labeled Gothic and established retrospectively as landmark works, most notably Mary Shelley's *Frank-enstein* (1818), Charles Robert Maturin's *Melmoth the Wanderer* (1820), and James Hogg's *Private Memoirs and Confessions of a Justified Sinner* (1824), are considerably more sophisticated, psychologically and conceptually, than the eighteenth-century Gothic classics and helped mark a transition toward narrative that aspired both to more profundity and delicacy. Radcliffe, Lewis, and their imitators had given the imaginative lexicon of Gothic horror a new location on the literary map, from which the writers of the nineteenth century were to take selected items of that lexi-con in several new directions, often refining its horrific element, both in the detail of its imagery and the imagined subtlety of its psychological effect.

By 1825 the Gothic vogue in Britain was well and truly past, although it lingered in the lowest strata of the marketplace, continuing to fuel "penny dreadfuls" like *Varney the Vampire* (1845–1847) for some time thereafter. When imported into America in the work of Charles Brockden Brown, it had already undergone a psychological adaptation that fitted it for the kinds of endeavors that Nathaniel Hawthorne and Edgar Allan Poe were to carry forward with such artistry, and a similar sophistication occurred, even more flamboyantly, in Germany, largely due to the endeavors of E. T. A. Hoffmann. It was Hoffmann who produced the most crucial exemplars of supernatural horror fiction in the first two decades of the century, not merely in his own country but in France, where his works were enormously popular. Hoffmann was the writer who first blurred the boundaries

A Timeline of Horror in the Nineteenth Century

1815	The Battle of Waterloo ends Napoleon's imperial ambitions for good.
1818	Mary Shelley's *Frankenstein* establishes one of the key archetypes of modern horror fiction.
1820	Charles Robert Maturin's *Melmoth the Wanderer* brings down the curtain on Gothic horror.
1824	James Hogg's *Private Memoirs and Confessions of a Justified Sinner* begins the new era of psychological horror in English-language fiction.
1839	Edgar Allan Poe's "The Fall of the House of Usher" reaches new depths of psychological symbolism.
1842	Edward Bulwer-Lytton's *Zanoni* helps to lay the foundations of the occult revival.
1853–1856	The Crimean War is the first to be extensively reported in newspapers as it happens.
1857	Charles Baudelaire's *Les Fleurs du mal* establishes the key exemplar of the Decadent style of consciousness.
1861–1865	The American Civil War brings the horrors of war to the United States.
1870–1871	The Franco-Prussian War ends with the bombardment of Paris and the brief establishment of the Paris Commune.
1886	Robert Louis Stevenson's *The Strange Case of Dr. Jekyll and Mr. Hyde* establishes another key archetype of horror fiction, and Louise Michel's *Les Microbes humains* illustrates the extent to which no one else was allowed to go in the depiction of fictitious horrors.
1890–1891	Oscar Wilde's *The Picture of Dorian Gray* adds a further petal to the flower of Decadent aesthetics.
1895	Robert W. Chambers's *The King in Yellow* imports the Decadent style to American horror fiction, following precedents set by Ambrose Bierce.
1897	Bram Stoker's *Dracula* supplies the last of the great nineteenth-century archetypes.

between manifestation and hallucination so completely that it became impossible to discern, and thus set the direction and the tempo for the development of modern horror fiction.

If there is one dominant theme in the post-Gothic weird fiction of the nineteenth century, it is the theme of the dead returning to pester the living, not necessarily literally, but insistently. Some authors stuck to the traditional motives of waiting to reveal the truth of hidden crime and to harry the guilty, but ghostly visitations were often more enigmatic than that, and the fright they caused more heavily impregnated with puzzlement and mystery.

Death had changed its social status in the nineteenth century; funerals, funereal monuments, and mourning became more ostentatious, to the extent that their extravagance could not help but be seen by many as gross hypocrisy. Thus, efforts made to soothe consciences by making more fuss of the dead often inflamed anxiety, and the angry psychological sores that resulted can be seen in the supernatural fiction of the period, as well as the remarkable growth of Spiritualism.

In America, the Fox sisters, who began to open new channels of communication between the forgiving dead and the reassurance-seeking living in 1848, were put on public display by P. T. Barnum. Their career as mediums served as the origin point for the Spiritualist movement, and as the century progressed it became increasingly difficult for people to let the dead rest in peace, especially as they seemed to be clamoring for attention with insistent rappings, levitating tables, and clouds of ectoplasm, while they waited their turn to use the overstrained vocal cords of entranced mediums, who responded as best they could to audiences' demands to have their guilty anxieties soothed away. Their clients wanted to be told that their loved ones were safe in heaven, and that they—the living—had been forgiven for all their petty trespasses and sins of neglect. Horror fiction, which told a very different story, was the other side of the coin of conscience.

Skeptics fought to demonstrate that the apparitions of Spiritualism were merely products of fevered imagination. If they hoped by that means to drive out anxiety, however, they had mistaken their enemy; sufferers who were convinced that the cause was internal rather than external simply became haunted by demons within rather than demons without. In the nineteenth century the phenomena of madness were brought decisively into the context of medical research and medical explanation, and the idea of "mental illness" achieved its final victory, in order that the fear of the diseased psyche could take on its modern aspect. In stories of derangement written after 1825, therefore, an advancing clinicality was inevitable. The transformation that clinicality wrought sharpened rather than blunted the horrific aspect of tales of disturbing encounters with enigmatic apparitions. The medical association of madness with tertiary syphilis, under the euphemistic label of "general paralysis of the insane," remained largely submerged in fiction by prudishness, but it lurks beneath the surface of nineteenth-century horror fiction, detectable to the psychoanalytic eye.

Because of its preoccupations with extraordinary extrapolations of guilt and medically defined madness, the history of the horror story throughout the nineteenth century is largely an account of growing introversion, as the moaning specters and deformed monsters of the Gothic were gradually relocated within the psyche, graphically depicted in such archetypes as Robert Louis Stevenson's monstrous Mr. Hyde, lurking within the personality of the respectable Dr. Jekyll. Where ghosts and monsters retained independent existence, their connection with the people they haunted grew gradually more intimate and at least covertly sexual—a pattern particularly obvious in classic vampire stories from John Polidori, Théophile Gautier, and J. Sheridan Le Fanu to the full flowering of *Dracula* (1897).

There is nothing surprising in that growing intimacy, given the social dramatization of death and the clinicalization of madness. However the horrid specters of nineteenth-century supernatural fiction manifest themselves, there is something in the mind of their victim that summons them; the eye of the beholder is already prepared to catch sight of them. The Gothic villain, especially in his Byronic mode, was already an ambivalent figure, seductive as well as cruel; after 1825 his literary descendants evolved in two opposed directions, sometimes becoming more human and sometimes surreal, but they retained the power of the predisposition of their victims to be perversely fascinated by their symbolic status and force. There is a third line of development, in which the Gothic villain moves toward heroic status, foreshadowed in Edward Bulwer-Lytton's Rosicrucian romances, which served as an inspiration to many of the lifestyle fantasies of the occult revival that played such a prominent role in British and European (particularly French) culture during the Victorian period.

Brian Stableford

See also: Part Two, Themes, Topics, and Genres: The Legacy of *Frankenstein*: From Gothic Novel to Cultural Myth; *Part Three, Reference Entries*: Baudelaire, Charles; Bierce, Ambrose; Brown, Charles Brockden; Bulwer-Lytton, Edward; Chambers, Robert W.; *Dracula*; "The Fall of the House of Usher"; Gautier, Théophile; Gothic Hero/Villain; Hawthorne, Nathaniel; Hoffmann, E. T. A.; *The King in Yellow*; Le Fanu, J. Sheridan; Lewis, Matthew Gregory; Maturin, Charles Robert; *Melmoth the Wanderer*; Penny Dreadful; *The Picture of Dorian Gray*; Poe, Edgar Allan; *The Private Memoirs and Confessions of a Justified Sinner*; Psychological Horror; Radcliffe, Ann; Shelley, Mary; Spiritualism; Stevenson, Robert Louis; *The Strange Case of Dr. Jekyll and Mr. Hyde*; "The Vampyre"; *Varney the Vampire; or, The Feast of Blood*.

Further Reading

Frayling, Christopher. 1996. *Nightmare: The Birth of Horror*. London: BBC Books.

Hennessy, Brendan. 1979. "The Gothic Novel." In *British Writers*, vol. 3, edited by Ian Scott-Kilvert, 324–346. New York: Charles Scribner's Sons.

Joshi, S. T. 2014. *Unutterable Horror: A History of Supernatural Fiction, Volume 1: From Gilgamesh to the End of the Nineteenth Century*. New York: Hippocampus Press.

Sage, Victor. 1988. *Horror Fiction in the Protestant Tradition*. London: Macmillan.

Scarborough, Dorothy. 1917. *The Supernatural in Modern English Fiction*. New York: Putnam.

Wisker, Gina. 2005. *Horror Fiction: An Introduction*. New York: Continuum.

HORROR FROM 1900 TO 1950

Culturally, socially, and artistically, the first decade or so of the twentieth century in America and Britain actually belonged to the nineteenth. It was effectively an extension of the Victorian Age, and this holds equally true for the significant horror literature of the period. In 1900, Bram Stoker's (1847–1912) *Dracula* was three years old. Robert W. Chambers's (1865–1933) groundbreaking *The King in Yellow* was five years old. As the new century was beginning, Arthur Conan Doyle (1859–1930), best known for his Sherlock Holmes stories of the late 1800s, wrote a variety of weird and ghostly stories. Indeed, his Holmes novel *The Hound of the Baskervilles*, published in 1901, is rich with a Gothic atmosphere and seems to promise the supernatural before its rationalized resolution.

The turn of the century saw the emergence of a number of significant new horror authors in Britain. One of the most important new writers of the age was M. R. James (1862–1936), who had been reading his ghost stories aloud to friends and groups of schoolboys (he was a British scholar and academic, later Provost of Eton) since about 1893. His first collection, *Ghost Stories of an Antiquary*, appeared in 1904, and others followed, with all of them ultimately assembled as the still-standard *Collected Ghost Stories* (1931). James's hallmark was a refined subtlety of technique, in which a series of clues and hints usually led to an explicit (and often distressingly physical) encounter with some menace from the past better left buried. His work represented the highest development of the classical English ghost story, and it has been enormously influential on a whole school of followers and on such moderns as Ramsey Campbell and Robert Aickman. A contemporary and similar figure was E. F. Benson (1867–1940), who is best known today for social comedies comparable to those of P. G. Wodehouse, but whose ghost stories, beginning with the collection *The Room in the Tower* (1912), form a significant and surprising appendage to his main career.

Another Englishman, Algernon Blackwood (1869–1951), also did much of his best work about this time, producing the psychic-detective sequence *John Silence: Physician Extraordinary* (1908) and such collections as *The Empty House* (1906) and *The Lost Valley* (1910). Blackwood is notable for his nature mysticism and his use of outdoor settings, as is seen in his most famous stories, "The Willows" and "The Wendigo." H. P. Lovecraft rated the former as the finest weird story in the English language. The great Lord Dunsany (Edward John Moreton Drax Plunkett, eighteenth Baron Dunsany, 1878–1957) published his first book, *The Gods of Pegana,* in 1905. While most of his work would be classified as fantasy or even as comic, he could be eerie or horrifying when he chose, and his influence on subsequent writers, particularly Lovecraft and his school, is tremendously significant. Walter de la Mare (1873–1956) published a supernatural novel, *The Return*, in 1910 and became notable for such short stories as "Seaton's Aunt" and "All Hallows," which blended the ghostly and the psychological powerfully and subtly.

The literary impact of the First World War (1914–1918) extended well beyond killing off such talented writers as William Hope Hodgson (1877–1918), who excelled at both cosmic and nautical horror stories (such as *The House on the Borderland*, 1908), and Saki (the pen name of H. H. Munro, 1870–1916), whose short, ironic horror stories are found scattered through his larger collections. Effectively, the twentieth century begins in 1919, in the wake of the war. One of the most important social changes of this transitional period was a blurring of class distinctions, and this is reflected in literature, both in Britain and in the United States. Thus the polite, elegant ghost story for upper-class audiences—and featuring upper-class characters—began to merge with something a bit earthier and less sophisticated. In Britain this meant the appearance of such lowbrow anthologies as Charles Birkin's *Creeps* series (1932–1936), as well as novels of occult horror such as Dennis Wheatley's (1897–1977) *The Devil Rides Out* (1934). In America, it meant pulp magazines.

"Pulp" is a technical term that refers to the quality of paper used, in which flecks of wood pulp are visible, but it became synonymous with cheaply printed and often luridly illustrated popular magazines. Pulps soon began to specialize in particular genres, with magazines featuring detective stories, Westerns, sea stories, and the like. The first weird fiction magazine was actually German, *Der Orchideengarten* (1919–1921), but the first in English, and the most important, is *Weird Tales* (1923–1954 plus several revivals, with the most recent issue published in 2014).

The earliest issues of *Weird Tales* may have seemed none too promising to readers at the time, since much of the contents were crude, material horror that was badly written by any standard. However, the magazine persisted and began to develop important writers, so that much of the story of English-language horror, particularly in the second quarter of the twentieth century, is the story of *Weird Tales*.

By far the most important *Weird Tales* writer was H. P. Lovecraft (1890–1937), whose popularity and influence made him the central figure in horror fiction for much of the twentieth century and well into the twenty-first. Lovecraft's first appearance in *Weird Tales* was with the short story "Dagon" in 1923. His "The Rats in the Walls" (1924) must have had a tremendous impact on the readership at the time, as it was so obviously superior to most of what appeared around it. The first editor of *Weird Tales*, Edwin Baird, accepted anything Lovecraft sent him, but Lovecraft's relations with Baird's successor, Farnsworth Wright, who edited the magazine from late 1924 to early 1940, were sometimes difficult. Wright was a brilliant editor who not only raised the magazine to greatness, but kept it going through the Great Depression, even when at one point the magazine's assets were wiped out in a bank failure. However, Wright could be overcautious. For example, he first rejected Lovecraft's "The Call of Cthulhu" because he was afraid his readers would not understand it, but then asked to see it again, and published it in 1928. He also published the majority of Lovecraft's work, including such classics as "The Dunwich Horror" (1929), "Pickman's Model" (1927), and "The Whisperer in Darkness" (1930), and singled out "The Outsider" (1926) for editorial praise in the highest possible terms. Wright rejected some of Lovecraft's longer narratives, including *At the Mountains of Madness* and "The Shadow over Innsmouth," which severely damaged Lovecraft's self-confidence and slowed down his creativity in his last years. (*At the Mountains of Madness* was eventually published in another magazine in 1936, the same year that "The Shadow over Innsmouth" was published as a stand-alone book with a miniscule print run.) When Wright published Lovecraft's "The Haunter of the Dark" and "The Thing on the Doorstep" in two successive issues (December 1936, January 1937), it must have seemed that all was suddenly well again, but by March of 1937, Lovecraft was dead.

In the meantime, Lovecraft had managed to gather a whole circle of colleagues around him, including such established contemporaries as Henry S. Whitehead

A Timeline of Horror from 1900 to 1950

1904 *Ghost Stories of an Antiquary* by M. R. James. First collection.

1906 *The Empty House* by Algernon Blackwood. First collection.

1907 "The Willows" by Algernon Blackwood, published in *The Listener and Other Stories*.

1908 *The House on the Borderland* by William Hope Hodgson.

1912 *The Room in the Tower* by E. F. Benson. First collection.

1923 *Weird Tales* founded (March). First Lovecraft story published in *Weird Tales*, "Dagon" (October). *The Riddle and Other Stories* by Walter de la Mare published (includes "Seaton's Aunt").

1924 *Weird Tales* publishes Lovecraft's "The Rats in the Walls" (March). Farnsworth Wright takes over as *Weird Tales'* editor (November).

1926 "The Abominations of Yondo," first weird story by Clark Ashton Smith, published in *The Overland Monthly* (April).

1927 Early version of Lovecraft's "Supernatural Horror in Literature" published in *The Recluse.*

1928 Lovecraft's "The Call of Cthulhu" published in *Weird Tales* (February).

1929 Lovecraft's "The Dunwich Horror" published in *Weird Tales* (April).

1933 *The Werewolf of Paris* by Guy Endore.

1936 Lovecraft's *The Shadow over Innsmouth* published as a limited edition book. M. R. James dies.

1937 Lovecraft dies. *To Walk the Night* by William Sloane published.

1939 *Unknown* magazine founded (March).

1940 Dorothy McIlwraith succeeds Farnsworth Wright as editor of *Weird Tales*. Jack Williamson's "Darker than You Think" (short version) published in *Unknown* (December).

1943 "The Wind" by Ray Bradbury in *Weird Tales* (March). Fritz Leiber's *Conjure Wife* published in *Unknown* (April). *Unknown* folds (October). "Yours Truly, Jack the Ripper" by Robert Bloch published in *Weird Tales* (July).

1947 *Dark Carnival* by Bradbury published. First collection.

1948 "The Lottery" by Shirley Jackson published in *The New Yorker* (June 26).

1950 "Born of Man and Woman" by Richard Matheson published in *The Magazine of Fantasy and Science Fiction* (Summer).

(1882–1932), Clark Ashton Smith (1893–1961) and Robert E. Howard (1906–1936), as well as a host of newcomers such as Robert Bloch (1917–1994) and Fritz Leiber (1910–1992), whom he encouraged and mentored with great generosity. His influence extended further through his revision clients. Stories in *Weird Tales* by Hazel Heald, Zealia Bishop, and others read a lot like Lovecraft and even mentioned his forbidden books and elder gods—because Lovecraft had, in fact, ghost-written those stories. Two of Lovecraft's younger colleagues, August Derleth (1909–1971) and Donald Wandrei (1908–1987), not only wrote stories in the Lovecraftian tradition, with Derleth more or less taking over the "Cthulhu Mythos" in the 1940s and 1950s and putting his own quite un-Lovecraftian spin on it, but they changed the history of horror fiction profoundly by creating the publishing firm of Arkham House, first to preserve Lovecraft's work in book form, and then to reprint other *Weird Tales* writers.

Of Lovecraft's contemporaries and colleagues, Robert E. Howard is certainly the most popular and widely reprinted, though he is primarily an action-adventure writer, best known for his stories of Conan the Barbarian (who also made his debut in *Weird Tales* in 1932). Howard could evoke the supernatural and horrific powerfully in his fiction, but it was often tangential to his main interests. Clark Ashton Smith, on the other hand, was a strikingly original writer, obsessed with the grotesque and the cosmic. He often expressed a desire to reach "beyond the human aquarium" in his fiction and to depict alien worlds and beings on their own terms. This led him, as it did Lovecraft, to something approximating science fiction, but he also wrote of vampires, ghouls, and dire sorcery in such realms as Averoigne (medieval France), prehistoric Hyperborea, or Zothique, Earth's last continent, which will arise sometime in the remote future.

By the early 1940s, Wright had died and his successor Dorothy McIlwraith did her best to keep the magazine going. It slowly declined, but continued to publish fine work, including many notable early stories by Ray Bradbury, Fritz Leiber, Robert Bloch, and numerous others. Bradbury (1920–2012) became one of the dominant figures in twentieth-century science fiction, but he also made significant contributions to horror in his *Weird Tales* stories, some of which were later collected in the Arkham House book *Dark Carnival* (1947) and its later transformation into *The October Country* (1955). Where many of the *Weird Tales* writers tended to be a bit old-fashioned, even Victorian in their approaches, Bradbury was thoroughly modern and addressed emotions directly through a style derived more from Ernest Hemingway and Thomas Wolfe than from pulp fiction. He and other such writers helped give horror fiction a broader appeal, which made the tremendous horror boom of the 1980s and 1990s possible. Many of Bloch's 1940s *Weird Tales* stories, including the famous "Yours Truly, Jack the Ripper" (1943), were widely reprinted and adapted for television in later decades.

In the 1940s *Weird Tales* began to suffer serious competition from the magazine *Unknown* (later called *Unknown Worlds*), which ran thirty-nine issues between 1939 and 1943 and was edited by John W. Campbell Jr. (1910–1971), who is better remembered as one of the great science fiction editors for his work on *Astounding* and *Analog*. Campbell's approach was radically different from *Weird Tales*: he wanted stories that were thoroughly modern in style and content. Except for a few with historical or imaginary settings, most *Unknown* fiction was firmly set in the contemporary world. Much was humorous, but *Unknown* did publish two particularly notable horror novels. Jack Williamson's (1908–2006) *Darker Than You Think* (1940; expanded 1948) tells of werewolves, a distinct, shape-changing species that has always coexisted with humankind, but that has gained a terrible advantage now that people no longer believe in them. Similarly, in Fritz Leiber's *Conjure Wife* (1943), set in a college, the faculty wives are all secretly witches who use their spells to advance their husbands' careers and curse their rivals. Again, skepticism puts the hero in grave danger. Both of these novels, and a good deal of *Unknown's* short fiction, are the immediate predecessors of what today is marketed as "urban fantasy."

Outside of the pulp magazines, horror sank to a low ebb by the middle of the twentieth century, but some continued to appear. William Sloane (1906–1974) published two outstanding novels on the borderline of science fiction and horror. *To Walk the Night* (1937) concerns an alluring woman who seems to be an alien entity possessing the body of a human idiot, and *The Edge of Running Water* (1939) is about a scientific attempt to contact the dead. Robert Bloch and Fritz Leiber cited *To Walk the Night* as a particular favorite. Both novels are superbly atmospheric and written in a fully literate style, without any of the crudities typical of much pulp fiction. However, Sloane wrote no more, instead becoming a publisher. The mid-twentieth century also saw the birth of horror comics, most notably those published by EC comics (*Tales from the Crypt*, *The Haunt of Fear*, and *The Vault of Horror*), which went on to form their own important substream within the larger tradition of purely literary horror fiction.

Horror could still slip into the mainstream on occasion. Shirley Jackson's (1919–1965) famous story "The Lottery," about a rural town where one person is ritually stoned every year, caused a sensation in 1948 when it was published in *The New Yorker*. In 1950, Richard Matheson (1926–2013) published "Born of Man and Woman," his first story, told from the point of view of a monster child kept chained under the basement stairs. Both of these stories are completely modern in style and approach, remaining subtle and understated, with great psychological depth, but told in deceptively plain prose.

The development of horror in the first half of the twentieth century can be defined as the evolution that went from M. R. James to Shirley Jackson and Richard Matheson. Jackson went on to write *The Haunting of Hill House* (1959), one of the greatest ghost novels ever published. Matheson, for his part, defined horror for the generation of Stephen King and his contemporaries, and has been second only to Lovecraft in subsequent influence.

Darrell Schweitzer

See also: Horror in the Nineteenth Century; Horror from 1950 to 2000; *Part Two, Themes, Topics, and Genres*: Horror Anthologies; Horror Comics; Horror Literature and Science Fiction; Weird and Cosmic Horror Fiction; *Part Three, Reference Entries*: Arkham House; Benson, E. F.; Blackwood, Algernon; Bloch, Robert; Bradbury, Ray; Chambers, Robert W.; Cthulhu Mythos; de la Mare, Walter; Derleth, August; Hodgson, William Hope; Howard, Robert E.; Jackson, Shirley; James, M. R.; Leiber, Fritz; Lovecraft, H. P.; Lovecraftian Horror; Matheson, Richard; Pulp Horror; Saki; Smith, Clark Ashton; Wandrei, Donald; *Weird Tales*; Wheatley, Dennis; Whitehead, Henry S.

Further Reading

Colavito, Jason. 2008. *Knowing Fear: Science, Knowledge, and the Development of the Horror Genre*. Jefferson, NC: McFarland.

Everett, Justin, and Jeffrey H. Shanks. 2015. *The Unique Legacy of Weird Tales: The Evolution of Modern Fantasy and Horror*. Lanham, MD: Rowman & Littlefield.

Joshi, S. T. 2014. *Unutterable Horror: A History of Supernatural Fiction, Volume 2: The Twentieth and Twenty-first Centuries*. New York: Hippocampus Press.

Lovecraft, H. P. [1927] 2012. *The Annotated Supernatural Horror in Literature*. Edited by S. T. Joshi. New York: Hippocampus Press.

Weinberg, Robert. 1999. *The Weird Tales Story*. Berkeley Heights, NJ: Wildside Press.

HORROR FROM 1950 TO 2000

Between 1950 and 2000 horror literature underwent a major shift in focus and direction that contrasted with approaches to the tale of horror in the first half of the twentieth century. In the immediate postwar years horror fiction shed many of the crudities of style and content that had distinguished pulp horror in favor of more sophisticated storytelling. The second half of the twentieth century also saw the emergence of Stephen King, whose best-selling fiction had an incalculable impact on horror fiction written in the wake of his phenomenal success, including the popularization of the novel over the short story as the most important vehicle for horror fiction.

In the 1940s, wartime paper shortages killed off most pulp magazines that published short horror fiction. *Weird Tales*, the longest-lived of all pulp magazines that catered to tastes for weird fiction, struggled on into the 1950s and published its last issue in September 1954. By that time not only *Weird Tales* but the type of horror fare that it offered had fallen out of vogue. As Les Daniels observed in *Living in Fear: A History of Horror in the Mass Media*, "The Second World War, climaxing with the explosion of nuclear weapons and capped by the hideous revelations unearthed in a beaten Germany, had temporarily exhausted the public's appetite for horrors of any kind" (Daniels 1975, 156).

Horror fiction written by Robert Bloch, August Derleth, Joseph Payne Brennan, Manly Wade Wellman, Fritz Leiber, and other *Weird Tales* alumni continued to be published in science fiction magazines (then enjoying a postwar boost in popularity) and in mystery magazines, where it frequently absorbed influences from those very different genres. At the same time, horror stories from Richard Matheson, Charles Beaumont, Ray Russell, and other writers whose careers were launched in the 1950s began appearing in the burgeoning men's magazine market, whose publications demanded a higher level of literary sophistication and maturity than the pulps. Their work bore out the perception that, in the aftermath of World War II, the traditional monsters of horror fiction were now irrelevant to contemporary readers. "Sad, but true," Beaumont wrote flippantly in his introduction to the anthology *The Fiend in You*, "after centuries of outstanding service to the human imagination, the classic terrors—the ghosts, the vampires, the werewolves, the witches, the goblins, all the things that go bump in the night—have suddenly found themselves unable to get work, except as comedians" (Beaumont 1962, vi). A world contending with the very real anxieties over the dawning nuclear age demanded horror stories that were more believable than fantastic.

Horror fiction had already been moving in that direction via the stories of Ray Bradbury and Shirley Jackson. Throughout the 1940s Bradbury published horror stories in *Weird Tales* set in familiar small-town America, whose ordinary characters leading their mundane lives share more of a kinship with the everyday people of Edgar Lee Masters's Spoon River or Sherwood Anderson's Winesburg, Ohio, than they do with the creepy residents of H. P. Lovecraft's legend-haunted Arkham, Massachusetts. More often than not the horrors in these stories grow out of ordinary human experience rather than some horrific incursion of the supernatural. In his novel *Something Wicked This Way Comes* (1962), a distillation of themes and ideas that he had addressed in his *Weird Tales* stories, Bradbury describes the people of Green Town, Illinois as "tired men and women whose faces were dirty with guilt, unwashed of sin, and smashed like windows by life that hit without warning, ran, hid, came back and hit again" (Bradbury 1998, 24). The unrelieved frustration and disillusionment with life expressed in this passage proves a magical incantation that summons Cooger & Dark's Pandemonium Shadow Show, a dark carnival that magically appears in town one October, on the cusp of Halloween, to mock the residents and their unfulfilled dreams with Faustian temptations.

The fiction of Shirley Jackson can be read as a complement to Bradbury's weird tales. Jackson's work appeared mostly in mainstream publications such as the *New Yorker, Charm,* and *Good Housekeeping,* and a very thin line separates her stories of amusing characters' mishaps from those in which similar mishaps prove more ominous. At the core of much of Jackson's writing is a vision of the individual perilously out of step with his or her society and the status quo, most evident in such stories as "The Lottery" (1948), about a small New England town where long-established traditions have deteriorated into menacing rituals, and "The Summer People" (1951), in which a vacationing family discovers the terrible fate that awaits any out-of-towners who overstay the summer season. Her best-known novels— *The Sundial* (1958), *The Haunting of Hill House* (1959), and *We Have Always Lived in the Castle* (1962)—are modern Gothics in which characters who are usually more sensitive and self-conscious than others around them retreat to insular environments that bring their feelings of personal dislocation sharply into focus and concentrate what critic S. T. Joshi refers to as the "pervasive atmosphere of the odd" that pervades all of her work (Joshi 2001, 13).

The "banalization" of the macabre seen in the writing of Bradbury and Jackson became commonplace in much of the better horror fiction written in the 1950s and 1960s, notably in the work of Richard Matheson and Charles Beaumont. The leitmotif in all of Matheson's stories, as he described it in his introduction to *The Collected Stories of Richard Matheson,* is "the individual isolated in a threatening world, attempting to survive" (Matheson 2005, 252–253). In the paranoid world of Matheson's fiction, even the most common situations and settings have the potential to threaten: household appliances turn murderous toward their owner in "Mad House" (1953), and every slight or unwanted encounter in the everyday world is proof of a sinister conspiracy again the individual in "Legion of Plotters" (1953). In his novel *The Shrinking Man* (1956), a character shrinking in size daily as the result of a toxic exposure suddenly finds the house he has lived in comfortably for years to be full of dangerous snares and pitfalls—among them the household cat and a spider in his basement—as his diminishing size renders him more vulnerable. In Charles Beaumont's fiction, horror often grows out of the stultifying effects of social conformity. In his story "The New People" (1958), a couple newly moved into an upper-crust community are horrified to discover that all of their neighbors participate in a black magic coven to alleviate the boredom of their successful lives. "The Dark Music" (1956), "The Hunger" (1955), and "Miss Gentibelle" (1957) all are concerned with sexual repression and the strange forms that its expression can assume. Matheson and Beaumont became two of the most prolific screenwriters for Rod Serling's *The Twilight Zone* (1959–1964), a television program that frequently focused on the dark side of ordinary human experience. The interplay between horror stories and representations of horror in extraliterary media such as television and film was another influence that shaped horror fiction in the postwar years in a way that it never had before.

The familiarizing of horror also extended to its most iconic tropes as writers sought to adapt and reconceive classic horrors to fit a postwar sensibility. Fritz Leiber, for instance, had begun doing this in the 1940s through short stories such as "Smoke Ghost" (1941), which conjured spectral presences out of the smoke and grime of industrial cities, and "The Girl with the Hungry Eyes" (1949), in which an advertising model feeds vampirically off the sexual passions that she arouses in men. In his novel *The Sinful Ones* (1980), a man and woman awaken one day from their routine lives to discover that the world and all of its people are zombie-like automatons who go mechanically about their routines, oblivious to anything that deviates from the prescribed program. Another American writer, Jack Finney, reimagined the tale of supernatural possession in terms of extraterrestrial invasion in *The Body Snatchers* (1955), in which aliens from outer space appropriate the bodies

A Timeline of Horror from 1950 to 2000

1954	*Weird Tales* publishes its final issue in September. Richard Matheson publishes *I Am Legend*.
1955	Jack Finney, *The Body Snatchers*.
1959	Shirley Jackson, *The Haunting of Hill House*.
1959–1964	Robert Bloch publishes *Psycho*. Rod Serling's *The Twilight Zone* brings high-quality horror, SF, and fantasy to a prime-time American television audience, featuring scripts written by the likes of Charles Beaumont and Richard Matheson.
1960	Alfred Hitchcock directs his iconic film adaptation of Robert Bloch's *Psycho*.
1962	Ray Bradbury, *Something Wicked This Way Comes*.
1963	Ray Russell, *The Case Against Satan*; director Robert Wise's *The Haunting*; a cinematic adaptation of Shirley Jackson's *The Haunting of Hill House*.
1967	Ira Levin, *Rosemary's Baby*.
1968	Writer/director George Romero's *Night of the Living Dead*, partly inspired by Matheson's *I Am Legend*, creates the modern zombie archetype. Roman Polanski directs a film adaptation of Ira Levin's *Rosemary Baby*.
1971	William Peter Blatty, *The Exorcist*; Thomas Tryon, *The Other*.
1973	Nine months after the United States' withdrawal from Vietnam in March, director William Friedkin's film adaptation of William Peter Blatty's *The Exorcist*—with a screenplay written by Blatty himself—becomes a cultural sensation and launches the era of the modern movie "blockbuster." Ramsey Campbell publishes *Demons by Daylight*.
1974	Stephen King publishes his first novel, *Carrie*.
1976	Anne Rice publishes her first novel, *Interview with the Vampire*.
1977	Stephen King, *The Shining*.
1979	Stephen King, *The Dead Zone*; Peter Straub, *Ghost Story*.
1983	Stephen King, *Pet Sematary* and *Christine*.
1984–1985	Clive Barker, *Books of Blood*.
1987	David G. Hartwell edits *The Dark Descent*.
1991	Kathe Koja's *The Cipher* launches the Dell Abyss line of contemporary horror novels.
1992	Poppy Z. Brite, *Lost Souls*.
1998	Caitlín R. Kiernan, *Silk*.
2000	The publication of China Miéville's *Perdido Street Station* marks the advent of the "New Weird."

of residents of a small California town, depriving them of their emotions and free will and forging a community through rigid social conformity. In his controversial novel *Some of Your Blood* (1961), Theodore Sturgeon expanded on the vampire theme, dispensing with traditional representations of the vampire as a creature of supernatural evil and presenting, instead, a case study of aberrant psychology in which a young man's craving for menstrual blood provides him with the emotional fulfillment denied him by the norms of society. Norman Bates, the psychologically disturbed young man in *Psycho* (1959), who periodically assumes the persona of his overprotective dead mother to kill women who arouse his passions, was arguably Robert Bloch's refurbishing of horror's shape-shifter or werewolf theme for the tale of the modern serial killer. In *Rosemary's Baby* (1967), Ira Levin reimagined the witch's coven of gothic horror fiction as a clique of tenants in a modern Manhattan apartment building who worship Satan in order to reap advantages crucial to their social advancement.

Levin's novel, Thomas Tryon's *The Other*, and William Peter Blatty's *The Exorcist* were all marketed as mainstream novels that gradually revealed undertones of horror in varying degrees. They epitomize the degree to which the horror tale embraced mainstream conventions through the familiarization of its themes, settings, and characters. These novels, all popular best-sellers, laid the foundations for the modern horror boom and set the stage for the meteoric ascent of Stephen King, whose phenomenal popularity is understandable in part in terms of the achievements of these novels. Like Levin, Tryon, and Blatty, King uses horror fiction effectively as a vehicle for exploring fundamental human dramas. Perhaps more than any other writer of contemporary horror fiction, King is the preeminent creator of fables that use fantasy to transform ordinary individuals into archetypes, and the personal, social, and political conflicts that shape their lives into struggles with mythic resonance. As a member of the baby boom generation, he became a mouthpiece through his tales of horror for the anxieties of his peers as they matured from rambunctious childhood to doubt-ridden adulthood. His novels *Carrie* (1974) and *Christine* (1983) are both powered by their insights into the cruelty of teenage peer groups. *The Dead Zone* (1979) presents its protagonist with a difficult moral choice that sums up the political dilemmas facing the counterculture of the 1960s. *The Shining* (1977) is concerned partly with the devastating effects that one individual's personal demons can have on a family, and *Pet Sematary* (1983) with the devastating grief that comes with the death of a loved one. At the same time, King's very contemporary tales of horror often nod to or reprise ideas and themes from classic horror fiction in a way that shows his keen understanding of the mechanics of the horror story and his appreciation of horror's ideas and formulas as an endlessly interpretable set of myths that can be resurrected and reshaped to fit the anxieties of each new age.

Although King's success was one of the main drivers of the horror boom of the 1980s, the movement was also catalyzed to some degree by the era's social and political realities. King emerged as a popular writer in the years immediately following

America's withdrawal from the Vietnam War (1955–1975) and the political turmoil of the Watergate scandal, when distrust of authority and paranoia about once-sacred institutions were at their highest in the United States. Horror fiction spoke to the anxieties of the generation that had come of age in the 1960s and that was now wrestling with apprehensions about the state of the world that they were inheriting. Abetted by publishers who, rightly or not, interpreted King's success as a sign of the reading public's appetite for horror fiction, rather than for King's inimitable style of storytelling, a new generation of writers began turning out works of horror, some of which specifically addressed the fears and concerns that readers felt as both individuals and members of their society, but much of which simply reworked the themes of classic horror, albeit with a contemporary spin. Several writers, including Peter Straub, Anne Rice, Dean R. Koontz, Clive Barker, and Robert R. McCammon, achieved best-seller status, a reality all but unthinkable before the phenomenon of Stephen King. The proliferation of horror fiction and the profusion of writers devising new approaches to horror themes helped to transform several of the fiction's classic monsters in these years. Anne Rice, with her novel *Interview with the Vampire* (1976), aided by the scores of vampire novels by other writers that it inspired, helped to transform the vampire into a sympathetic individual marginalized by his society. And the zombie, once a relatively innocuous entity resurrected by voodoo, was reinterpreted by writers nurtured on George Romero's *Night of the Living Dead* films as a relentless, mindless, undead, flesh-eating predator.

The rise of the zombie in late twentieth-century horror fiction coincides with the emergence of "splatterpunk," a horror literature distinguished by graphic and occasionally gratuitous revels in gore and violence. Splatterpunk found its impetus in the fiction of Clive Barker, whose six *Books of Blood* collections published in 1984 and 1985 were notable for their artful but explicit depictions of sex and violence. Splatterpunk was also a response to the dark fantasy movement—promulgated at the start of the horror boom and popularized by Charles L. Grant through his *Shadows* anthologies—which encouraged the crafting of subtle horror stories with mainstream literary appeal. Splatterpunk's most talented contributors—David J. Schow, John Skipp, and Craig Spector—produced work of indisputable merit, but the vast amount of splatterpunk fiction's violation of taboos, for no better reason than to shock or revolt, constituted a new decadence, not unlike that seen at the twilight of the Gothic novel era two centuries before. The controversies the fiction raised among readers and writers foreshadowed the implosion of horror markets in the 1990s, as publishers retrenched from a genre label and a glut of fiction most of which never achieved the same success as the work of horror's standard bearers.

Two trends that developed in horror publishing in the final decades of the twentieth century have persisted into the new century. A vibrant and dedicated small press, which helps to nurture new writers and assist developing writers in honing their craft, has become an indispensable fixture in horror publishing, one with fewer aesthetic constraints or reservations than commercial publishing. And the horror periodical has been largely replaced by the original anthology, whose varying thematic and nonthematic orientation has resulted in a renaissance for the short horror story. The legacy of horror fiction in the second half of the twentieth century is best measured by the profusion of works published and the pervasive presence of horror fiction in Western popular culture (and also world popular culture) at large. Once a subliterature that catered to the tastes of a small audience of devoted readers, horror emerged during the postwar years as a vital fiction that reflected the anxieties of its age and became a part of that age's culture. Any literature of the next century that would present an accurate portrait of its time would have to contend with horror fiction as a ubiquitous presence in the modern literary landscape and a regular part of the general cultural vocabulary.

Stefan R. Dziemianowicz

See also: Horror from 1900 to 1950; Horror in the Twenty-First Century; *Part Two, Themes, Topics, and Genres*: Horror Anthologies; Horror Publishing, 1975–1995: The Boom Years; Page to Screen: The Influence of Literary Horror on Film and Television; Small Press, Specialty, and Online Horror; *Part Three, Reference Entries*: Barker, Clive; Beaumont, Charles; Bloch, Robert; *Books of Blood*; Bradbury, Ray; Brennan, Joseph Payne; Campbell, Ramsey; Dark Fantasy; Derleth, August; *The Exorcist*; "The Girl with the Hungry Eyes"; Grant, Charles L; Harris, Thomas; Herbert, James; *Interview with the Vampire*; Jackson, Shirley; Ketchum, Jack; King, Stephen; Klein, T. E. D.; Koontz, Dean; Lansdale, Joe R.; Leiber, Fritz; Matheson, Richard; McCammon, Robert R.; Novels versus Short Fiction; *The Other*; Rice, Anne; Russell, Ray; *The Shining*; *Something Wicked This Way Comes*; Splatterpunk; Straub, Peter; Sturgeon, Theodore; Vampires; *Weird Tales*; Wellman, Manly Wade; Zombies.

Further Reading

Beaumont, Charles. 1962. *The Fiend in You*. New York: Ballantine.

Bradbury, Ray. [1962] 1998. *Something Wicked This Way Comes*. New York: Avon.

Daniels, Les. 1975. *Living in Fear: A History of Horror in the Mass Media*. New York: Scribners.

Dziemianowicz, Stefan. 1999. "Contemporary Horror Fiction, 1950–1998." In *Fantasy and Horror,* edited by Neil Barron, 199–343. Lanham, MD: Scarecrow Press.

Joshi, S. T. 2001. "Shirley Jackson: Domestic Horror." In *The Modern Weird Tale: A Critique of Horror Fiction*, 13–49. Jefferson, NC: McFarland.

King, Stephen. 1981. *Danse Macabre*. New York: Everest House.

Matheson, Richard. 2005. *Collected Stories, Vol. 2*. Colorado Springs: Edge Books.

Skal, David J. 1993. *The Monster Show: A History of Horror.* New York: Norton.

HORROR IN THE TWENTY-FIRST CENTURY

The twenty-first century has seen an accentuation and continuation of events, trends, and inventions begun or created in the twentieth century that came to fruition in the 2000s. The widespread use and development of communication and digital technologies, the completion of the Human Genome Project, terrorist panic after the attacks of 9/11, and the culmination of neoliberal agendas and globalization have led to a consolidation of mistrust in governments and corporations. Horror has been affected by these events and shows a clear tendency toward apocalyptic scenarios, best captured by the zombie pandemic narrative, a form of dystopian fiction that focuses on the lives of survivors in a world of little hope and much suffering. But horror has also been positively affected, on a practical side, by the development of digital books. A significant number of out-of-print horror novels, especially from the 1980s' "boom" period, have gradually become available as eBooks at low prices that make them easily accessible and affordable. At the same time, the possibility of self-publishing, via platforms like Amazon, means that horror novels have multiplied. In fact, it is safe to say that, although not as mainstream as it was in the 1980s, horror is undergoing a species of second golden age, with hundreds of horror novels having been published in the new millennium.

If horror literature is, indeed, experiencing a revival, this is partly because horror writers such as Stephen King, Clive Barker, Ramsey Campbell, Anne Rice, Peter Straub, Tanith Lee, and Dean Koontz, all of whom began writing in the 1970s or 1980s, have acted as role models for a new generation. Their establishment as auteurs, regardless of their (in some cases) dwindling or niche readerships, have made horror writing an appealing venture. Stephen King, in particular, with his tireless championing and promotion of the genre, whether through book tours, encouraging reviews, or talks at universities, has become a spearhead figure for the indefatigable horror writer and has even received recognition from outside horror circles; he was awarded the 2003 National Book Foundation Medal for Distinguished Contribution to American Letters and, in 2015, the National Medal of Arts. King has also managed to produce a string of successful novels, novellas, and short stories, including *Under the Dome* (2009) and *A Good Marriage* (in *Full Dark, No Stars,* 2010), that have been or are being swiftly adapted to television or film.

Although some of these writers, such as Barker, have switched gears and now work in genres such as YA (young adult) fiction—or else, like Caitlín Kiernan, have never considered themselves to be horror writers—they have still managed to produce significant works of literary horror, such as Kiernan's haunting novel *The Red Tree* (2009) and Barker's *The Scarlet Gospels* (2015), which chronicles the return of the iconic Pinhead (best known from the Hellraiser movies). This exodus or evolution of some writers of genre horror has also helped "clear" horror's image, so that more literary or mainstream writers, such as Bret Easton Ellis (*Lunar Park*, 2005), Chuck Palahniuk (*Haunted*, 2005), Mark Z. Danielewski, who actually began his career with the labyrinthine postmodernist horror novel *House of Leaves* (2000), and David Mitchell (*Slade House*, 2015), have successfully turned to horror at occasional points. The perennial return of the Gothic, in novels by the likes of Sarah Waters (*The Little Stranger*, 2009), Susan Hill (*Dolly*, 2011), Jeanette Winterson (*The Daylight Gate*, 2012), Lauren Owen (*The Quick*, 2014), and Kate Mosse (*The

Taxidermist's Daughter, 2014), has also been important in keeping the flame of subtle horror burning bright.

While the twenty-first century has seen the death or retirement of more than one key figure—such as Richard Matheson, James Herbert, and Poppy Z. Brite, to name a few—these have been swiftly replaced with young blood. A remarkable example of this new generation is Joe Hill, who, despite beginning his career by hiding the fact that he is Stephen King's son, has quickly built up a significant bibliography that tackles ghosts (*Heart-Shaped Box*, 2007), devils (*Horns*, 2010), vampires (*NOS4A2*, 2013), and world-changing plagues (*The Fireman*, 2016). Importantly, Hill has also worked in another medium that has seen a rise in horror-themed volumes: comics. His *Locke and Key* series (2008–2013) deserves particular praise for its innovative magical "keys" premise, which rethinks the haunted house narrative.

Adam Nevill is another writer on the rise who has consistently produced solid works and is developing an ever-growing readership. His brand of supernatural horror, high on suggestion and cinematic in style, features horrific creatures that range from evil presences such as the Brown Man (*The Banquet of the Damned*, 2004), to a pagan beast looking for sacrificial prey (*The Ritual*, 2011), to heretic ghosts awaiting remanifestation (*Last Days*, 2012), to an ancient fertility rite spirit (*No One Gets Out Alive*, 2014), to deadly portals (*Apartment 16*, 2010). The occult cult, a recurring trope in Nevill, is also present in *House of Small Shadows* (2013).

A few other noteworthy contemporary horror writers are Sarah Pinborough, Gillian Flynn, John Shirley, Alison Littlewood, Jonathan Maberry, David Moody, Glen Duncan, Conrad Williams, Joseph D'Lacey, Nicole Cushing, Graham Joyce, Joel Lane, Guillermo del Toro and Chuck Hogan, Sarah Langan, Brian Keene, Tom Fletcher, and Tim Lebbon.

Monsters continue to play a significant role in horror fiction, and none have been a more steady focus of attention than the vampire and the zombie. The vampire, despite largely having been co-opted by the romance genre and YA fiction, especially after Stephenie Meyer's record-breaking *Twilight* series (2005–2008) established sparkling Edward Cullen as the vampire *du jour*, has also been at the heart of several notable twenty-first-century horror novels. John Ajvide Lindqvist's *Let the Right One In* (2007), a work that aligns its child vampire, Eli, with another social outsider, twelve-year-old incontinent and bullied Oskar, develops pity for the monster, who in turn becomes a savior and, as we find out in Ajvide Lindqvist's short story "Let the Old Dreams Die" (2009), even a lover.

But apart from exploring "human" bonds and the modern sympathetic monster, Ajvide Lindqvist's novel is representative of the gradual change that monsters experienced in the late twentieth and twenty-first centuries, when their monstrosity became linked to the idea of disease and infection, an idea first explored at length in Richard Matheson's *I Am Legend* (1954). Vampires, for instance, became the result of viral infections and partially shed their religious connections to a Manichean notion of evil (that is, the idea that vampires are simply and purely evil, as absolutely opposed to good). Justin Cronin's *The Passage* (2010) takes this trope to the extreme and merges it with the postapocalyptic narrative, itself particularly popular after Cormac McCarthy won the Pulitzer Prize for Fiction in 2007 for *The Road*. Market forces aside, it could be argued that vampires are becoming viral as a result of an increased awareness of pandemics and their spread, following recent international disease crises such as the various outbreaks of AIDS, mad cow disease, avian flu, and Ebola.

The contemporary fascination with infection has also traveled underground, deep into the graves of the restless undead. If late 1960s cinema saw the birth of the nuclear, meat-eating zombie in George Romero's *Night of the Living Dead*, then the twenty-first century has fathered the viral zombie, the rabid subject that is human but shows all the signs of being a traditional flesh- and/or brain-craving zombie. Apart from the obvious filmic, comic, and television influences—the films *Resident Evil* (2002) and *28 Days Later* (2002), and Robert Kirkman's comic series *The Walking Dead* (debuted in 2003) and its corresponding AMC television series (debuted in 2010) have all been seminal—two novels have been key in the establishment of zombie fiction, which was never predominant in the twentieth century, as the postmillennial subgenre *par excellence*: Max Brooks's *World War Z: An Oral History of the Zombie War* (2006) and Jane Austen and Seth Grahame-Smith's *Pride and Prejudice and Zombies* (2009). The former followed scrupulously the template of the global pandemic and showed that horror could still be well written and politically committed, while the latter kick-started the mash-up parody subgenre, which splices together literary classics with pulp horror fiction. The zombie has, like the vampire, proved very versatile. Novels such as Isaac Marion's *Warm Bodies* (2010) have given prominence to the zombie romance, and others, such as M. R. Carey's *The Girl with All the Gifts* (2014), have explored the possibilities of fungus-based plagues and of zombies retaining mental powers. Most likely, zombie fiction is popular not just because of the simple laws of supply and demand; the zombie resonates with the hyperconnected masses of the twenty-first century. Its alienation, horde-like qualities, and, ultimately, helplessness constitute a strong metaphor for the feelings of disenchantment brought about by late capitalism and the invigoration of multinational corporations.

The other main horror subgenre to develop strongly in the twenty-first century is the weird, particularly following the rehabilitation of its flagship writer, H. P. Lovecraft. Three volumes of his stories were published by Penguin Classics between 1999 and 2004. Then, in 2005, a selection of his tales appeared in a prestigious edition by the Library of America, effectively canonizing him as a major American author. The weird, "a rather breathless and generically slippery macabre fiction, a dark fantastic ('horror' plus 'fantasy') often featuring non-traditional alien monsters (thus plus 'science fiction')" (Miéville 2009, 510), may be seen to be thriving in the work of writers such as Simon Strantzas, Quentin S. Crisp, John Langan, Richard Gavin, Paul Tremblay, Livia Llewellyn, Mark Samuels, Matt Cardin, and Laird Barron. The latter's fictional universe, largely constructed through

A Timeline of Horror in the Twenty-First Century

2001	Terrorists attack the World Trade Center in New York City and the Pentagon in Washington, D.C., and a fourth hijacked airliner crashes in Pennsylvania. A coalition of U.S.-led forces invades Afghanistan.
2003	Mapping of the human genome is completed. The first issue of *The Walking Dead*, by Robert Kirkman, Tony Moore, and Charlie Adlard, is published.
2004	Exploration rovers land on Mars.
2005	H. P. Lovecraft's *Tales* are published in a Library of America volume.
2006	Max Brooks publishes *World War Z: An Oral History of the Zombie War*.
2007	John Ajvide Lindqvist publishes *Let the Right One In*.
2007–2008	The world is rocked by a cascading series of global financial crises.
2008	The first season of HBO's *True Blood* airs, indicating a growing interest in high-budget horror television.
2010	The first season of *The Walking Dead* premiers on AMC.
2011	Thomas Ligotti publishes *The Conspiracy against the Human Race*.
2013	Stephen King publishes the long-awaited sequel to *The Shining*, *Doctor Sleep*.
2014	Anne Rice returns to her vampire chronicles with *Prince Lestat*.
2015	Clive Barker kills off his most famous character, Pinhead, in *The Scarlet Gospels*. Stephen King is awarded a National Medal of the Arts. Mark Z. Danielewski publishes the first book in his ambitious 27-volume *The Familiar* series.

intricately crafted short stories and in the novel *The Croning* (2013), has been gathering such attention that an homage anthology of stories by various writers, *The Children of Old Leech: A Tribute to the Carnivorous Cosmos of Laird Barron*, was published in 2014. Samuels received a similar treatment in 2016 with a tribute anthology titled *Marked to Die: A Tribute to Mark Samuels*.

Another writer of weird horror who rose to prominence in the early years of the century and who exerted a profound influence on the new crop of writers is Thomas Ligotti. Having established a cult reputation during the 1980s and 1990s with his extremely literary and philosophically pessimistic style of horror fiction, Ligotti was a key progenitor of the weird renaissance at the turn of the millennium, even as he continued to produce work of his own, including *The Conspiracy against the Human Race* (2010), a nonfiction book of horror-centered philosophical and literary commentary. Ligotti's significance was then amplified in 2014 when his name suddenly came to mainstream awareness as the first season of HBO's *True Detective* drew on the tradition of weird supernatural horror fiction, and in particular the work of Ligotti (along with Robert W. Chambers's *The King in Yellow*, 1895), as a chief inspiration.

The weird has also played a major role in the speculative turn in horror philosophy, especially in the work of media scholar Eugene Thacker, author of three books comprising a trilogy on the "horror of philosophy": *In the Dust of This Planet* (2011), *Starry Speculative Corpse* (2015), and *Tentacles Longer Than Night* (2015). Another significant writer in this vein is philosopher Graham Harman, author of, among others, *Weird Realism: Lovecraft and Philosophy* (2012).

The extent to which the "new weird," understood as a hybrid of the science fiction new wave of the 1960s and the new horror of the likes of Clive Barker—and practiced by, for example, China Miéville and Jeff VanderMeer—is "new" (innovative) or simply a periodic marker (of the modern or contemporary) is still very much up for debate. In any case, the new weird shows how horror has, in some cases, hybridized to the point where its generic allegiance becomes less interesting than a specific writer's own style and influences.

All in all, horror fiction in the twenty-first century is in good health, a situation that is surprising considering that written fiction now has to compete with other, similarly immersive horror products, such as comics and video games. Although the rise of the zombie and the interest in an impending apocalypse demonstrate a marked pessimism and skepticism about global capitalism and the neoliberal triumph of free trade—Žižek has astutely referred to the current period as "living in the end times" (in a 2010 book of that very title)—it would be unfair to say that all horror fiction shows signs of a social and political engagement with the zeitgeist. The continuations and further mutations of well-known myths, alongside the nurturing of subgenres such as the weird, as well as the arrival of a new generation of writers who are influenced by the horror "boom" of the 1980s—all of this makes twenty-first-century horror, still in its infancy, a fascinating and multiple-headed beast.

Xavier Aldana Reyes

See also: Horror from 1950 to 2000; *Part Two, Themes, Topics, and Genres*: Apocalyptic Horror; Horror Comics; Horror Literature as Social Criticism and Commentary; Horror Literature in the Internet Age; Small Press, Specialty, and Online Horror; Weird and Cosmic Horror Fiction; *Part Three, Reference Entries*: Ajvide Lindqvist, John; Barker, Clive; Barron, Laird; Campbell, Ramsey; Hill, Joe; *House of Leaves*; Keene, Brian; Kiernan, Caitlín R.; King, Stephen; Koontz, Dean; Lee, Tanith; Ligotti, Thomas; Lovecraft, H. P.; Miéville, China; New Weird; Palahniuk, Chuck; Rice, Anne; Samuels, Mark; Straub, Peter; Vampires; VanderMeer, Jeff; Zombies.

Further Reading

Aldana Reyes, Xavier. 2016. "Post-Millennial Horror, 2000–16." In *Horror: A Literary History*, edited by Xavier Aldana Reyes, 189–214. London: British Library.

Joshi, S. T. 2014. *Unutterable Horror: A History of Supernatural Fiction. Volume 2: The Twentieth and Twenty-First Centuries*. New York: Hippocampus Press.

Luckhurst, Roger. 2015. *Zombies: A Cultural History*. London: Reaktion.

Miéville, China. 2009. "Weird Fiction." In *The Routledge Companion to Science Fiction*, edited by Mark Bould, Andrew M. Butler, Adam Roberts, and Sherryl Vint, 510–515. London and New York: Routledge.

Nelson, Victoria. 2013. *Gothicka: Vampire Heroes, Human Gods, and the New Supernatural.* London and Cambridge, MA: Harvard University Press.

Sederholm, Carl H., and Jeffrey Andrew Weinstock, eds. 2016. *The Age of Lovecraft.* Minneapolis, MN: University of Minnesota Press.

VanderMeer, Ann, and Jeff VanderMeer, eds. 2008. *The New Weird.* San Francisco, CA: Tachyon Publications.

VanderMeer, Jeff. 2008. "The New Weird: 'It's Alive?'" In *The New Weird*, edited by Ann and Jeff VanderMeer, ix–xviii. San Francisco, CA: Tachyon Publications.

Žižek, Slavoj. 2010. *Living in the End Times.* London: Verso.

Part Two: Themes, Topics, and Genres

APOCALYPTIC HORROR

Apocalyptic horror is concerned with the end of the world or the end of humanity. It has been a popular subgenre of horror fiction since the nineteenth century, though its antecedents are much older. The word "apocalypse" comes from Ancient Greek and means "revelation" or "uncovering." It is the name (in Greek) of the final book of the New Testament, known as the Book of Revelation in English, in which the ultimate destiny of the world is revealed by Jesus Christ to John of Patmos. As a result, "apocalypse" has come to be used as a catch-all term to describe various end-of-world scenarios, with the earlier sense of "revelation" being obscured. Given the cataclysmic and terrifying nature of the apocalypse(s), almost all apocalyptic fiction is, in one way or another, horror fiction.

Theological conceptualizations of the final events of history, "end times" or "end of days," are called eschatology. Many religions include eschatological writings within their scriptures, including Judaism, Islam, Hinduism, Zoroastrianism, Buddhism, and Jainism. In a number of cases, this eschatology is concerned with the completion of the world's preordained life cycle or the attainment of some ultimate state of existence, thus rendering any further human endeavor unnecessary. In many eschatological scriptures, this end point is signaled by a period of degeneration, the coming (or return) of a messianic figure, the resurrection of the dead, the collection or redemption of the pious, and the violent destruction of the remains of humanity and (in most cases) the world itself. In some literature, including Christian and Hindu writings, this destruction includes a final battle (at Armageddon and Keekatpur respectively) in which the unrighteous are massacred. This last battle signals the end of history, leading either to the obliteration of the earth or the transition to another phase of existence. The "final battle" motif is also found in other apocalyptic myths, including the Viking myth of Ragnarök, which has led to the theorization of a common Proto-Indo-European source for these myths.

Eschatological writing treats the degeneration and destruction of the Earth as the means to an end, as the true significance of the event lies in the spiritual transcendence or elevation that comes in the aftermath. However, artistic representations and responses to the apocalypse commonly focus on the events leading to transcendence, rather than on the endpoint itself. In medieval representations of the Book of Revelations, for example, it is common to find detailed (and often lavish) depictions of the beast (Rev. 13:1–10), the dragon (Rev. 12:9, 20:2), "Babylon the Great" (also known as the "Whore of Babylon," Rev. 17:4–20), and the lake of fire (Rev. 19:20). One of the more famous examples of this type of representation is Cambridge, Trinity College MS R.16.2 (ca. 1250), known as the Trinity Apoca-lypse, in which the various stages of the destruction of sinners are represented in colorful illuminations alongside biblical text and commentary. Significantly, me-dieval illuminated manuscripts often incorporate contemporary concerns into visual representations of biblical figures, including depicting "Babylon the Great" in Muslim dress, despite the fact that most Christian interpretation claims the figure is intended to represent Rome.

Illuminated medieval apocalypse manuscripts, and the wealth of other visual and textual material that was produced at the same time, reveal some of the founda-tions on which the subgenre of apocalyptic horror is built. These manuscripts reveal an enthusiasm for vivid scenes of pain, suffering, and terror, but representa-tions can vary dramatically. This, along with the inclusion of contemporary political and social issues, reveals a tradition of artists interpreting and redefining religious texts in individual ways. Moreover, the artistic focus on degeneration and destruc-tion (rather than on spiritual transcendence) points to the didactic purpose of the eschatological texts. If illustrations and elaborations were to depict only the suc-cessful survival of the righteous, the warning message would be lost. Medieval apocalypses were not intended to present reassurances about the aftermath of Armageddon; they were intended to present a stark (if often entertaining) message about what would happen to the majority of humanity at the end of days.

As well as illuminated manuscripts, the medieval (Christian) apocalypse was also known to wider audiences through the performance of mystery plays. These public performances told stories from the Bible, from the Creation to the Last Judg-ment, with musical accompaniment. These plays were often performed in "cycles," which included the full spread of "pageants," and performances would sometimes take place over several days. In some areas of England, the cycle would be per-formed during the Feast of Corpus Christi (the festival following Trinity Sunday, usually falling in late May or early June), and each pageant would be performed on a decorated wagon by a local trade or craft guild. One of the best-known cycles of English plays comes from York, and this is the only cycle that has completely survived. In the York cycle, the "Doomsday" play was performed by the guild of mercers (merchants of luxury cloth and textiles) and represented the spectacular climax of a long day of popular street entertainment. The mercers were wealthy and powerful citizens of York, and records show that their pageant was particularly lavish. As well as hiring professional actors and laborers to stage the play, the mer-cers decorated their pageant wagon with specially constructed artificial angels and banners decorated with gold and silver leaf. The players performed in costumes and masks as devils, sinners, and redeemed souls, and Christ's costume included a diadem and gilded mask. Surviving records also show that later performances of the play included two additional carts that represented the mouth of Hell and a coffin from which the resurrected dead would emerge. The mercers' Doomsday play depicts the glorious terror of the apocalypse, and, like all the mystery plays, its official purpose was a didactic one: the pageant cycle was intended to bring the (mostly) nonliterate audiences into close proximity to biblical teachings and to encourage personal reflection on the meaning of these teachings, particularly during a Eucharistic holiday. However, surviving civic records and criticisms of the Corpus Christi cycles reveal that concerns were raised over incidents of drunkenness, revelry, and "wantonness" during the performances, suggesting that the message of the Doomsday play (and others) may have been obscured at times by its entertainment.

Performance of mystery plays was banned during the Reformation of the sixteenth century, but apocalyptic art did not go away. Early modern theater, literature, and visual art continued to develop the fascination with the end of days. While this was still conceived in terms of religious eschatological writings, there was an increasing focus on situating historical and contemporary events into the timeline of the apocalypse. For example, millenarianism, or the belief in an impending cataclysmic event that will effect a transformation of the world, flourished during the English Civil War (1642–1651) and its aftermath, which is reflected in literature such as John Milton's *Paradise Lost* (1667). Additionally, in various parts of Protestant Europe, popular entertainment (particularly carnivals) raised the specter of the "Antichrist" of Christian eschatology, or the false prophet who will face Christ at Armageddon. Religious thinkers and writers of the time, such as Martin Luther and John Knox, identified this figure as the Roman Catholic papacy, and more popular responses followed in the form of vulgar broadsheets, effigy burning, and public celebrations such as Elizabeth Day and Guy Fawkes Day in England. As with the earlier Doomsday plays, it is clear (from the secular continuation of Guy Fawkes Night, for example) that the eschatological message was often concealed by the apocalyptic entertainment.

Early modern European apocalyptic art and entertainment continued to draw directly on Christian eschatology. However, the advent of the Industrial Age saw the birth of a new vision of the end of days: the secular apocalypse. This new type of apocalypse would come to be represented in artistic works, but it would also become a focus of science and ethics. The secular apocalypse is the basis of much contemporary apocalyptic horror, though it can take many forms.

One of the earliest examples of secular apocalypse fiction is Mary Shelley's *The Last Man* (1826), in which humanity is destroyed by a plague. Shelley's introduction to the book suggests it is a prophetic story, but notably the author claims she found the tale among writings of the Cumaean Sibyl, a legendary priestess of the Apollonian oracle whose messianic prophecies were of interest to both pre-Christian and Christian writers. By linking her fiction to this mythic figure, Shelley is able to both connect and disconnect from the traditions of presenting the apocalypse. Elements of Christian eschatology remain embedded in the apocalypse, but these are overwritten by broader (and older) concerns about how humanity will be destroyed. The mention of the Cumaean Sibyl is a literary conceit on Shelley's part (*The Last Man* is her own work of fiction); however, it sets the stage for a new type of horror fiction, which foregrounds its prophetic nature over its biblical allusions

Types of Apocalypse in Horror Fiction

- **Alien Invasion and Animal Uprising**. Human beings are annihilated or enslaved by extraterrestrials or the accelerated evolution of a terrestrial species.

  EXAMPLES: *The Midwich Cuckoos* by John Wyndham (1958), *Zoo* by James Patterson and Michael Ledwidge (2012)

- **Anthropogenic Environmental Disaster**. Human activity disrupts the earth's climate or ecosystem, destroying life as we know it.

  EXAMPLE: *The Burning World* by J. G. Ballard (1964)

- **Astronomical or Natural Disaster**. The destruction of earth and/or humanity by a large-scale natural event, such as asteroid impact or volcanic eruption.

  EXAMPLES: *Lucifer's Hammer* by Larry Niven and Jerry Pournelle (1978), *Ashfall* by Mike Mullin (2011)

- **Global Warfare and Genocide**. Annihilation of the human race through military aggression, often involving nuclear or chemical weapons. Global warfare often acts as the catalyst for other apocalyptic horrors, such as postnuclear contagion, environmental disaster, and the rise of tyrannical regimes.

  EXAMPLE: *Z for Zachariah* by Robert C. O'Brien (1974)

- **Pandemic**. An outbreak of a disease afflicts the world's population, including engineered viruses, zombie contagion, and extraterrestrial contagion.

  EXAMPLES: *The Stand* by Stephen King (1978), *World War Z* by Max Brooks (2006)

- **Revelations and Rapture**. The apocalypse as imagined in religious writings, usually Christian, reimagined from a contemporary perspective.

  EXAMPLE: *Left Behind* by Tim LaHaye and Jerry B. Jenkins (1995)

- **Rise of the Machines**. Artificial intelligence reaches the point of sentience and overthrows humanity.

  EXAMPLE: *R.U.R.* by Karel Čapek (1921)

- **Tyranny and Dystopia**. Often facilitated by a previous apocalyptic event, a totalitarian regime dictates the limits of human existence and experience.

  EXAMPLE: *The Handmaid's Tale* by Margaret Atwood (1985)

(though these are still present). *The Last Man* also presents a number of narrative tropes that will recur throughout apocalyptic horror fiction. A specific date is given (the end of the twenty-first century); characters initially ignore warning signs, believing that the plague will not affect them; growing panic and chaos threaten to cause almost as much damage as the pandemic itself; society divides into violent factions; a group of survivors die as a result of the selfish actions of their leader.

Shelley's protagonist, Lionel Verney, is the only survivor of the plague and ends the novel as the last man on Earth. In this respect, the novel is both apocalyptic and postapocalyptic. This is also a feature that resonates with later apocalyptic horror. While the ultimate endpoint of eschatology is the transcendence or redundancy of human endeavor, the secular apocalypse has revealed an increasing interest in the possibility of survival and continuation. Other nineteenth-century forerunners of this type of fiction include Edgar Allan Poe's short story "The Conversation of Eiros and Charmion" (1839), in which two spiritual beings discuss the annihilation of the Earth by a comet after the event; Richard Jefferies's novel *After London* (1885), in which the apocalypse itself is never described and the narrative focuses on the postapocalyptic lifestyle of a small group of survivors; and H. G. Wells's *The War of the Worlds* (1898), which features a successful alien invasion of Earth followed by humanity's last-minute diversion of the apocalypse. Like medieval and early modern apocalypses, these nineteenth-century fictions draw on religious, historical, and political ideas to inform their vision of the end of days; however, these secular apocalypses also clearly and directly address contemporary scientific developments, including vaccinology, astronomy, Darwinism, and early environmentalism. These fictions also indicate an increasing interest in the anthropogenic apocalypse, in which the end of the world is brought about, not by the supernatural forces of evil, but by the hubristic endeavors of human development. Nevertheless, they also reveal a new strategy of decentering humanity, suggesting that the world—and, in some cases, the universe—will go on even after human life is destroyed.

In the twentieth and twenty-first centuries, apocalyptic horror proliferated with potential ends of the human race. Alien invasion remains a popular trope, as does environmental disaster, including both anthropogenic climate change and astronomical catastrophe. The pandemic is also a common cause of apocalyptic horror, and since the mid-twentieth century this has also included the "zombie apocalypse" (a mixture of contagion narrative and supernatural terror). Advances in robotics and artificial intelligence are reflected in technological apocalypses, in which computerized or (bio-)robotic machines enslave, destroy, or mutate the human race. Christian eschatology is not absent entirely from these narratives—and some fictions continue to draw directly on (or retell) the biblical apocalypse—but, overwhelmingly, religious elements are reimagined and incorporated into a more secular end-of-world view. Thus, "Armageddon" can be used to refer to a number of violent scenarios, including global and extraterrestrial warfare, genocide, and cosmological collision. The Four Horsemen of the Apocalypse (Rev. 6:1–8), the biblical harbingers of Christ's Last Judgment, are reimagined as avatars of human self-destruction, with "War," "Pestilence," "Famine," and "Death" all being key themes in apocalyptic horror.

Apocalyptic horror in the twenty-first century remains an important vehicle for exploring the nature of human existence and the nature of our relationship to other species, the planet, and the universe. Whether a narrative focuses on the period of degeneration and destruction or the postapocalyptic aftermath, whether the characters are overwhelmed by the cataclysm or survive to wander a depopulated wasteland, apocalyptic horror consistently addresses and exploits humanity's existential fears. Nevertheless, the sheer number of popular and creative responses to these fears reveals humanity's persistent ability to revel in the specter of its own demise.

Hannah Priest

See also: Horror Literature and Science Fiction; Religion, Horror, and the Supernatural; Weird and Cosmic Horror Fiction; *Part One, Horror through History*: Horror in the Twenty-First Century; *Part Three, Reference Entries*: Cthulhu Mythos; *I Am Legend*; *The Night Land*; Shelley, Mary; Zombies.

Further Reading

Cambridge, Trinity College MS R.16.2 (Trinity Apocalypse, digitized). ca. 1250. Accessed March 19, 2016. http://trin-sites-pub.trin.cam.ac.uk/james/viewpage.php?index=1199.

Carey, Frances, ed. 1999. *The Apocalypse and the Shape of Things to Come*. Toronto and Buffalo: University of Toronto Press.

Himmelfarb, Martha. 2010. *The Apocalypse: A Brief History*. Chichester: Wiley-Blackwell.

Johnston, Alexandra F., and Margaret Dorrell. 1972. "The York Mercers and Their Pageant of Doomsday." *Leeds Studies in English* 6: 11–35. http://digital.library.leeds.ac.uk/122/1/LSE1972_pp11-35_JohnstonDorrell_article.pdf.

Rosen, Elizabeth K. 2008. *Apocalyptic Transformation: Apocalypse and the Postmodern Imagination*. Lanham, MD, and Plymouth, UK: Lexington Books.

Wagar, W. Warren. 1982. *Terminal Visions: The Literature of Last Things*. Bloomington: Indiana University Press.

Williamson, Arthur H. 2008. *Apocalypse Then: Prophecy and the Making of the Modern World*. Westport, CT: Praeger.

ECO-HORROR

The idea that nature can be frightening is certainly not new. Yet "eco-horror," the subgenre of horror that deals most explicitly with these fears, is comparatively modern. Eco-horror—also known as "natural horror," "environmental horror," or "green horror"—is now a widely known term. But despite this, there is still some uncertainty and inconsistency in its usage. Broadly understood, an eco-horror text is any text in which the natural environment is in some way horrific: it may exploit "obvious" fears of violent and repulsive nature, or it could more subtly address the gloomy and pervasive sense that now, in the age of modern sciences and technologies, humans have somehow severed themselves from the natural world. More specifically, there are two main elements that define eco-horror narratives. First, there is a central theme of nature's *revenge* exacted on humankind. This "golden rule" of eco-horror is always as follows: humans harm nature, and nature, in turn, delivers its own bloody retribution. Second, the eco-horror text is always intended to encourage its audience toward a more ecocentric (naturecentric), rather than anthropocentric (humancentric), viewpoint. In other words, it is designed explicitly to increase environmental awareness.

Though eco-horror has quite wide delineations—and so should, in theory, encompass a multitude of literary and cinematic texts—the term is used almost exclusively in relation to horror *films*, and usually in relation to a specific cluster of horror films from the 1970s. This subgenre, for whatever reason, has blossomed onscreen, and is, ordinarily, never discussed within the context of horror literature. This is surprising considering the fact that eco-horror finds its origins in horror literature and has continued its existence, alongside its filmic counterparts, in this literary form. Though seldom discussed, the subgenre of eco-horror holds a significant place and history inside the canon of horror literature. In order to examine this, however, it is first necessary to become aware of how exactly "eco-horror" has come to be understood in the history of horror cinema.

The general consensus holds that the eco-horror film was not truly born until the 1970s. This is due to the fact that the eco-horror genre has been intimately tied to the environmental movement, which only fully surfaced in the 1960s. There was a widespread popularization of environmental issues in this decade. For example, 1962 saw the publication of Rachel Carson's *Silent Spring*, a work on conservation that focused on the indiscriminate and dangerous use of pesticides. Most importantly, the book brought environmental concerns to the American public and has been lauded as the very first example of ecocriticism. The 1960s also saw such seminal measures as the passing, in the United States, of the Wilderness Act in 1964 and the formation of the Environmental Protection Agency (EPA), which became operative in 1970. It makes sense, then, that while there were such seminal eco-horror texts as Alfred Hitchcock's *The Birds* (1963) in this decade, the true deluge of eco-horror titles came subsequently, in the 1970s, in reaction to this suddenly widespread eco-awareness.

Indeed, *natural horror*—along with body horror and satanic horror—was one of the three main cinematic horror genres in this period. There were countless nature nasties, such as *Willard* (1972), *Frogs* (1972), *Night of the Lepus* (1972), *The Bug* (1975), *Killer Bees* (1974), *Jaws* (1975), *Grizzly* (1976), *Squirm* (1976), *Orca* (1977), *Day of the Animals* (1977), *Piranha* (1978), and *Nightwing* (1979), to name just a few. In these stories, viewers were warned again and again that if they disturb, depredate, and destroy the natural world, this will have devastating results, and Mother Nature will turn darkly against them. For example, in *Frogs* (1972), various amphibians and reptiles (and even the occasional butterfly) turn violently on the humans who are releasing pesticides into the natural environment. In *Orca* (1977), the titular whales only become violent after they have been harpooned and harmed by human fishermen. Though the sheer volume of eco-horror films made in the 1970s has never been rivaled, there has been a steady production of such texts in subsequent years. Titles such as *Cujo* (1983), *Little Shop of Horrors* (1986), *Arachnophobia* (1990), *Lake Placid* (1999), and *The Happening* (2008) collectively confirm the tenacity of this onscreen subgenre.

A Timeline of Eco-horror

1800s

Texts: *The Castle of Otranto*, *The Monk*, *Frankenstein*, "Young Goodman Brown," *Walden*, "The Great God Pan," *Dracula*

Events:

- 1816: Mount Tambora global disaster
- 1854: *Walden* by Henry David Thoreau
- 1892: John Muir forms the Sierra Club

Early 1900s

Texts: "The White People," "The Willows," "The Wendigo," "The Man Whom the Trees Loved," "The Shunned House," "The Colour out of Space"

Events:

- 1905: Formation of the Bureau of Forestry

1950s/1960s

Texts: *The Birds* (short story and film), *Silent Spring*, *The Night of the Grizzly*

Events:

- 1964: Wilderness Act
- 1968: Publication of *The Population Bomb* by Paul Ehrlich
- 1969: Santa Barbara oil spill

1970s

Texts: *Jaws* (novel and film) *Willard*, *Night of the Lepus*, *Grizzly*, *Tarantulas*, *Tentacles*, *Piranha*, *The Swarm*, etc.

Events:

- 1970: Formation of EPA
- 1970: Clean Air Act
- 1971: Formation of Greenpeace
- 1972: Clean Water Act
- 1973: Endangered Species Act
- 1979: Nuclear meltdown of Three Mile Island

1980s

Texts: *Cujo*, *The Rats*, *The Ceremonies*, *Croaked*, *Little Shop of Horrors*

Events:

- 1980: World population hits 4.5 billion.
- 1982: Nuclear Waste Policy Act
- 1985: Evidence confirms hole in the ozone layer over Antarctica.
- 1988: NASA warns Congress about global warming.
- 1989: *Exxon Valdez* oil spill

1990s	Texts: *Outbreak, Aberration, Sphere, Bats, Lake Placid*

Events:

- 1990: Oil Pollution Act
- 1990: Pollution Prevention Act
- 1996: Federal Insecticide, Fungicide, and Rodenticide Act
- 1997: Kyoto Protocol is signed by 38 industrialized nations

2000s	Texts: *Seeders, Uprooted, The Last Winter, The Happening, Birdemic, Cloverfield, The Thaw, The Bay*

Events:

- 2001: President George W. Bush refuses to sign the Kyoto Protocol.
- 2006: The documentary *An Inconvenient Truth* is released.
- 2007: Energy Independence and Security Act
- 2010: *Deepwater Horizon* BP oil spill
- 2014: IPCC release a devastating report promising dire environmental consequences if leading economies do not reduce greenhouse gas emissions immediately.
- 2016: The Paris Agreement, within the United Nations Framework Convention on Climate Change, is signed by 193 UNFCCC member nations.

It is this cinematic background that illuminates the intriguing and less well-known subject of eco-horror literature. When examining eco-horror themes in a literary context, the parameters are much broader than those in the discussion of film. The horror of nature has been depicted since the very beginning of literature with *Gilgamesh* (ca. 2100 BCE) and has continued as a dominant theme throughout the human traditions of myths, fairy tales, and countless other literary narratives. Most relevantly, it has held a consistently prominent place in Gothic and horror literature, right from the outset. The emphasis on truly sublime landscapes is central to many of the classic Gothic novels: vast terrains of ice, mountains, and forest create the awesome and eerie ambience in such classic texts as *The Castle of Otranto* (1764), *The Monk* (1796), *Frankenstein* (1818), and *Dracula* (1897). This extends beyond the European Gothic and into the American Gothic, where the darkness of the natural world is equally prevalent, while the image of the fearsome forest, inspired by inherited fears of the New World wilderness, is even more dominant. This is seen, for example, in the works of writers such as Charles Brockden Brown and Nathaniel Hawthorne. Indeed, critics such as Lisa Kröger have convincingly argued that the trope of the "Deep Dark Forest" is so recurrent that it is as much a central tenet of the Gothic text as the castle, crypt, or convent.

The two main elements of the eco-horror text as outlined above—the revenge of nature and the focus on an ecocentric perspective—have been utilized, both subtly and explicitly, by many of the most esteemed authors of the horror genre. Recently, there has been some discussion of the environmental themes to be found in the works of H. P. Lovecraft. In particular, stories of his such as "The Colour out of Space" (1927) and "The Shunned House" (1924) have been retrospectively read in light of fears of widespread pollution. *The Day of the Triffids* (1951) has been read as the epitome of "plant horror" (a subset of eco-horror). A key figure, due to his somewhat unique position as both nature and horror writer, is Algernon Blackwood. In his infamous tale "The Willows" (1907), two men fatally underestimate the majesty of nature and are consequently terrorized by the trees that surround them; in "The Temptation of the Clay" (1912), a man is horribly punished for viewing the natural world in material terms; in "The Transfer" (1912), human greed is rewarded by an all too literal demonstration of nature's voracious appetite; and in "The Man Whom the Trees Loved" (1912), the imagined "union" between humans and nature is made truly monstrous. T. E. D. Klein has strong elements of eco-horror in his fiction, too, as for example in *The Ceremonies* (1984). Here, the main antagonist is aligned firmly with nature, and the protagonist, Jeremy, seems to be truly endangered only when he disrespects the natural environment. He poisons small creatures and bugs with insecticide and later—in a pure moment of eco-horror revenge—is slowly poisoned himself by the same insecticide, which is used in his food. Many "obvious" examples of eco-horror literature can also be found in literary examples of animal horror, including such classic texts as James Herbert's *The Rats* (1982) and Stephen King's *Cujo* (1981). (In fact, many examples can be found throughout King's work, such as the haunted hedge in 1977's *The Shining*). It is also important to note that two of the most infamous eco-horror films of all time, *The Birds* and *Jaws*, each originated as horror literature: Daphne du Maurier wrote the short story "The Birds" in 1952, and Peter Benchley wrote *Jaws* in 1974. There is more symbiosis between eco-horror film and eco-horror literature than many might first imagine.

Currently, the genre of eco-horror is still dominated primarily by filmic texts such as *The Bay* (2006), *The Happening* (2008), and *The Last Winter* (2012). These recent films carry a very different tone from what might be considered the "classic" eco-horror films of the 1970s. Instead of giant insects, mutant rats, and killer sharks, the threat of nature is shown to be much more insidious and pervasive; it is now often *nature itself* that is depicted as the collective and malevolent force, turning unanimously on a transgressive and now unwelcome humankind. This is representative of an increasing sense that humans have severed themselves from the natural world, which they are consciously—and continually—destroying. In this battle of humans vs. nature, it is clear that *people*, collectively, are the monsters.

When it comes to the place of contemporary eco-horror *literature*, the emphasis is not so much on the production of new books (although there are interesting examples to be pointed to, such as Jeff VanderMeer's Southern Reach trilogy) but on the attention that horror literature is now receiving within the *context* of eco-horror themes. Indeed, there has been a general increase in academic interest in visions of nature and environment in fiction. This has, significantly, resulted in the birth of the "ecoGothic," which is firmly related to (and at times imbricated with) eco-horror. However, this term refers not to a genre of text but to the means of its deconstruction: in other words, the ecoGothic is the heading under which ecocritical and environmental themes may be interrogated within horror fictions. Eco-horror texts have always provided an important social and political commentary on environmental issues, but now—in a time when humans have affected everything in nature, from the ozone layer down—they are more relevant and essential than ever before. This is only emphasized by the fact that humans are, as Anil Narine credibly attests, collectively experiencing "eco-trauma": a state in which people are so terrified by the overwhelming seriousness of environmental issues that they paradoxically deal with these fears not only by ignoring them, but by actively *repressing* them (Narine 2015). It is more important than ever, therefore, to examine in detail the texts in which these fears may still find expression.

Elizabeth Parker

See also: The Gothic Literary Tradition; Horror Literature and Science Fiction; *Part Three, Reference Entries*: Blackwood, Algernon; *The Ceremonies*; "The Colour out of Space"; Forbidden Knowledge or Power; Lovecraft, H. P.; Mad Scientist; *The Rats*; The Sublime; "The Willows."

Further Reading

Gambin, Lee. 2012. *Massacred by Mother Nature: Exploring the Natural Horror Film.* Baltimore, MD: Midnight Marquee Press.

Hillard, Tom J. 2009. "'Deep into the Darkness Peering': An Essay on Gothic Nature." *Interdisciplinary Studies in Literature and the Environment (ISLE)* 16, no. 4 (Autumn): 685–695.

Muir, John Kenneth. 2007. *Horror Films of the 1970s.* London: McFarland.

Narine, Anil. 2015. *Eco-trauma Cinema.* London: Routledge.

Smith, Andrew, and William Hughes, eds. 2013. *EcoGothic.* Manchester and New York: Manchester University Press.

Tabas, Brad. 2015. "Dark Places: Ecology, Place, and the Metaphysics of Horror." *Miranda* 11. https://miranda.revues.org/7012.

GENDER, SEXUALITY, AND THE MONSTERS OF LITERARY HORROR

From its inception, horror has offered an ambivalent space for the construction and exploration of gender and sexuality. On the one hand, anxieties about gender roles and sexuality are cast off onto the monsters of horror fiction and social norms are constructed through the "othering" of "deviations" and "perversity." On the other hand, horror also provides a space for the expression of transgressions of sexual and social norms. Hence, for example, the vampire's long history as a figure of both repulsion and fascination, of fear and desire. In terms of its critical reception and history, horror is a literary form split along gender lines, often conceived of by critics as comprising two distinct traditions. At the "feminine" pole lies "Gothic Romance," which includes the novels of Ann Radcliffe in the eighteenth century as well as the "paranormal romance" of the twenty-first. This "feminine" form is characterized by stories of monstrous (yet desirable) male antagonists, of the incarceration and flight of the heroine, and the struggle over the control and possession of her body and property. At the "masculine" end of the pole lies the horror tradition inaugurated by Mary Shelley's *Frankenstein* (1818), which includes works that blend adventure, science fiction, and body horror, such as Robert Louis Stevenson's *The Strange Case of Dr. Jekyll and Mr. Hyde* (1886). Fred Botting suggests that this tradition contrasts with its feminine counterpart because it "subordinat[es] love adventure" and "licens[es] more 'masculine' tendencies towards power and violence" (Botting 2008, 11). Botting's delineation of these two gendered traditions also reveals the way in which the "masculine" form (characterized by its transgression and violence) has been critically valued to the detriment of the "feminine." The latter is often seen as conservative and clichéd, and Botting dismisses it accordingly as an "embourgeoisif[ied]" form traceable "through the Brontës, Collins, Corelli, du Maurier and the host of popular romantic fictions packaged as 'Harlequins', 'Gothics', 'Mills and Boon' . . . and on" (Botting 2008, 11). However, it is not so easy to delineate a "feminine" tradition from a "masculine" tradition in horror, nor should either be valued over the other as a space in which ideas of gender and sexuality are constructed and critiqued.

Horror provides an interface for the traversing and crossing of such gender boundaries as those drawn in critical accounts of the form. As Judith Halberstam's study of monstrosity shows, horror narratives never "turn so neatly around gender identifications" (Halberstam 1995, 18). In its exploration of sexuality, perversity, and monstrosity, horror provides a space for the negotiation of the extremes of ideas about gender, often revealing the constructed and fluid nature of gender in the process. Feminist scholars have noted the way that horror can express frustration with the lot of women and is able to critique the polarization of women through binary sexual categories such as virgin and whore, victim and monster. Yet, horror can also reinforce gender stereotypes and express misogyny, pathologizing women who fail to conform. For example, Barbara Creed's study of horror film argues that the "monstrous feminine" expresses "male fears" about female sexuality (Creed 1993, 7). Thus, horror is always ambivalent; it is not simply a patriarchal and oppressive space, but nor is it easily recuperable by feminist politics. The afterlives of horror literature's most enduring monsters reveal this ambivalence. Frankenstein's monster, the vampire, and the werewolf are all sites of monstrosity that continue to negotiate between the extreme poles of masculinity and femininity and offer a fantasy space for the expression of anxieties and desires surrounding sexuality.

The monsters of horror literature have often been read as ciphers for "perverse" sexuality and non-normative gender identities, the expulsion of their monstrous otherness serving to reinforce social norms. However, the long literary afterlives of Frankenstein's monster, Bram Stoker's Dracula, and the werewolves of Victorian horror fiction in numerous rewritings and adaptations show how the monster has served as a way of negotiating and celebrating aspects of gender and sexual identity not often given expression in mainstream culture and society.

Shelley's *Frankenstein* (1818) is cited by critics as the inception of a masculine horror tradition (as above in Botting's 2008 *Gothic Romanced*) and the beginning of a female tradition (as in Ellen Moers's 1978 essay in which she coins the term "Female Gothic"). The novel explores both a repressive feminine sphere of domesticity and a masculine sphere of scientific discovery. Yet, as Moers insists, the relationship between its male antiheroes is an exploration of the trauma (and failure) of motherhood as much as it is of Promethean rebellion. The birth of Frankenstein's monster reimagines the birth myth through the images of body horror, and the death of Frankenstein's own mother looms large both in his decision to create his creature and to destroy its female mate. In this latter episode in particular, the novel registers anxieties about the power of generation. Frankenstein refuses to make the monster a mate for fear that together they will produce a "race of devils" (Shelley 1992, 170). It is the sexual reproductive power of the female monster that Victor fears most, suggesting that any female monster may be "ten thousand times more malignant than her mate" (Shelley 1992, 170). Marie Mulvey-Roberts argues that through Victor's brutal destruction of the monster, *Frankenstein* exposes the violent misogyny of fears about female sexuality (Mulvey-Roberts 2016, 111). The idea that *Frankenstein* explores the cultural construction of "monstrous" female sexuality has a long afterlife in twentieth-century horror film, notably in works such as *Alien* (1979).

Drawing on this influence, feminist writers have found *Frankenstein* a rich text for adaptation and rewriting. Shelley Jackson's hypertext revision of the novel, *Patchwork Girl* (1995), reassembles the fragmented female monster and imagines a narrative for each body part, giving voice to the female monster so brutally silenced in the original. In a more recent rewriting of the novel, Chris Priestley considers the construction of masculinity and links the destruction of the monster's mate thematically to another act of misogynist violence in nineteenth-century literature, the murder of Nancy in Dickens's *Oliver Twist* (1839). Priestley's *Mister Creecher* (2011) pairs the monster with a young Bill Sykes in an exploration of how masculine violence is culturally and socially produced. *Frankenstein* has also been read as a queer text into which might be read the repression of homosexual desire. Eve Kosofsky Sedgwick describes the novel as "a tableau of two men chasing each other across the landscape," their relationship ambiguously amorous and/or murderous (Sedgwick 1986, ix–x). The queer subtext of the novel is developed in Kate Horsley's recent novelistic adaptation, *The Monster's Wife* (2014), which focuses on the friendship and desire between two young women, one of whom is taken by Frankenstein for his experiments. It is the bond between two female protagonists that is foregrounded here, and the antagonism between Shelley's male antiheroes plays out in the background of Horsley's novel.

Whereas the sexual appetites of Frankenstein's monster are denied, those of the vampire run rampant in Bram Stoker's 1897 novel, *Dracula*. Stoker's predatory Count Dracula represents a perverse sexual desire that disturbs middle-class systems of marriage and offspring and passes as a contagion to his victims. Though most famous of the vampires of horror literature, Dracula was not the first and is predated by J. Sheridan Le Fanu's Carmilla by twenty-five years. In *Carmilla* (1872) Le Fanu depicts a more sympathetic vampire whose lesbian desire for her friend Laura comprises the text, rather than the subtext, of the story. Stoker's tale acts as a corrective to Le Fanu's, recasting the vampire as male (and so placing sexual agency in the realm of masculine virility) and violently punishing the count's female progeny for their perverse manifestations of sexual appetite. The most obvious recipient of Stoker's punitive violence is Lucy Westenra, who is staked, decapitated, and has her mouth stuffed with garlic by the three men who had previously competed for her affections. As a vampire, Lucy is able to express sexual appetites and refuse the confining structures of bourgeois femininity. When the "Crew of Light," as Christopher Craft has characterized them (Craft 1984, 130) encounter her in Kingstead cemetery, she callously throws aside a child she has fed from and makes overt advances to the waiting men. This scene reveals what Gina Wisker notes is typical of female vampires: they are able to critique and problematize received notions of femininity, but negotiate a constant tension between punishment and celebration of their transgressions (Wisker 2016, 150).

Yet Dracula has also proved a more ambivalent and open symbol than he was perhaps intended by his creator. Though a masculine sexual predator, against whom the Crew of Light must safeguard their women, he is also feminized as a degenerate, racial other. Patrick Bratlinger notes that through the count's advances on Lucy and Mina, *Dracula* constructs the myth of a "demonic invasion" from the colonies of the British Empire (Bratlinger 1988, 234). Halberstam also notes that Dracula's perverse sexuality is racialized as Jewish, showing that Stoker's description of the count reflects the anti-Semitism of the period. Feminist and queer rewritings of *Dracula* often seek to make plain the punitive misogyny and racism of the source material, or else to draw out its ambiguities. Angela Carter's story "The Loves of Lady Purple" (1974) shows the female vampire a victim of abjection and othering before she turns on her creator and revives herself by drinking his blood. Lady Purple offers a model for a host of powerful lady vampires in horror fiction ever since, from Anne Rice's *Queen of the Damned* to the fiction of Poppy Z. Brite. Helen Oyeyemi's novel *White Is for Witching* (2010) also concerns itself with female vampirism and tackles racist fears still extant in British culture. Set in a British border town at the forefront of contemporary discussions of immigration, *White Is for Witching* casts white Miranda as a vampiric figure who cannot help but drain her black girlfriend, Ore. As well as suggesting the continuing damage racist discourses do to nonwhite subjects, *White Is for Witching* also resurrects the figure of Carmilla in Miranda's desire for Ore. The two girls experience their vampiric coupling as pleasurable, and Miranda's desire to consume Ore works to transgress both racist boundaries between self and other, as well as norms of femininity and heterosexuality.

In contrast to the feminized figure of the vampire, the werewolves of horror fiction often serve as an image of unambiguous hypermasculinity. However, the hypermasculine werewolves of contemporary horror fiction such as Charlaine Harris's *The Southern Vampire Mysteries* (2001–2014) (popularized in HBO's television adaptation, *True Blood* [2008–2014]) or *Underworld* (2003) belie the complex history of the werewolf in horror literature. In Victorian fiction, female werewolves were as common as their male counterparts. In Clemence Housman's "The Werewolf" (1890), a wandering stranger called White Fell uses her feminine sexuality to seduce a Scandinavian warrior before revealing herself as a fierce and deadly wolf, luring him to his doom. Frederick Marryat's "The White Wolf of the Hartz Mountains" (1839) portrays a similarly transgressive female, who seduces a widowed trapper in order to consume his children. Though they kill the wolf, the father and remaining son are punished for their transgressions against nature and women (it is revealed that the widower killed his first wife) with madness and death. Chantal Bourgault du Coudray notes that female werewolves in these early stories are characterized by "unrepentant hedonism and physicality," whereas their male counterparts are "psychologized . . . reflecting the widespread association of masculinity with the mind." This mind/body division in werewolf fiction guarantees the male's salvation, "whereas the demonic female werewolf was always destroyed" (Bourgault du Coudray 2006, 55–56). Similar to the stories of female vampires, these tales of the werewolf construct and condemn "aberrant" female behavior and sexuality, but at the same time reveal transgression as an empowering possibility.

The 2001 B-movie horror film *Ginger Snaps* offers an interesting reworking of the complex gender politics of the werewolf in its reimagining of the werewolf as an adolescent girl. The film knowingly offers multiple readings of its monster: a metaphor for incipient teenage female sexuality, a response to the double standards in what feminists have called Western rape culture (that is, the normalization of sexual coercion and violence against women), and a morality tale about the dangers of unprotected sex, among others. The film opens with a montage of images of fetishized young female victimhood common in horror film as the protagonists reenact sexualized and horrific death scenes for a school art project. As the film progresses, however, its teenage protagonist, Ginger, morphs from a fetishized victim of horror into a violent, hedonistic, and sexually voracious monster, a transformation that is both psychological and physical. The film flirts with images of the monstrous feminine, but also critiques these images as well as bitterly commenting on the limited social roles into which girls and young women are asked to place themselves. Ginger's death at the climax of the film means that the figure of the werewolf retains its essential ambivalence. For Ginger, becoming a werewolf is neither definitely empowering, nor wholly punitive.

Halberstam argues that the monsters of Gothic and horror fiction are radically open to interpretation. Monsters are "overdetermined" because they incorporate fragments of otherness from a multitude of sources into one body (Halberstam 1995, 92). Because its monsters cause such "interpretive mayhem" (2), horror, in both its classic and contemporary incarnations, offers a space to interrogate and challenge normative constructions of gender and sexuality. As a form it is available to any number of readings of gender and sexuality, even where individual texts may initially seek to reinforce gender norms or punish transgressions. Through the continued reinventions of its monsters, horror fiction offers a space in which to negotiate, challenge, and reimagine ideas about sexuality and gender into the contemporary moment.

Chloé Germaine Buckley

See also: Horror Criticism; Horror Literature as Social Criticism and Commentary; The Legacy of *Frankenstein*: From Gothic Novel to Cultural Myth; Vampire Fiction from Dracula to Lestat and Beyond; *Part Three, Reference Entries*: Brite, Poppy Z.; *Carmilla*; Carter, Angela; *Dracula*; du Maurier, Daphne; *Interview with the Vampire*; Le Fanu, J. Sheridan; Rice, Anne; Shelley, Mary; Stoker, Bram; *The Strange Case of Dr. Jekyll and Mr. Hyde*; Vampires; Werewolves; Witches and Witchcraft.

Further Reading

Botting, Fred. 2008. *Gothic Romanced: Consumption, Gender and Technology in Contemporary Fictions*. London: Routledge.

Bourgault du Coudray, Chantal. 2006. *The Curse of the Werewolf: Fantasy, Horror and the Beast Within*. London: I. B. Tauris.

Bratlinger, Patrick. 1988. *Rule of Darkness: British Literature and Imperialism 1830–1914*. Ithaca and London: Cornell University Press.

Craft, Christopher. 1984. "Kiss Me with Those Red Lips: Gender and Inversion in Bram Stoker's *Dracula*." *Representations* 8: 107–133.

Creed, Barbara. 1993. *Monstrous Feminine: Film, Feminism, Psychoanalysis*. London: Routledge.

Easley, Alexis, and Shannon Scott, eds. 2013. *Terrifying Transformations: An Anthology of Victorian Werewolf Fiction*. Kansas City, MO: Valancourt.

Halberstam, Judith. 1995. *Skin Shows: Gothic Horror and the Technology of Monsters*. Durham and London: Duke University Press.

Horner, Avril, and Sue Zlosnik. 2006. "Introduction" to *Women and the Gothic*, edited by Avril Horner and Sue Zlosnik, 1–14. Edinburgh: Edinburgh University Press.

Moers, Ellen. 1985. *Literary Women: The Great Writers*. Oxford: Oxford University Press.

Mulvey-Roberts, Marie. 2016. "The Female Gothic Body." In *Women and the Gothic*, edited by Avril Horner and Sue Zlosnik, 106–119. Edinburgh: Edinburgh University Press.
Priestley, Chris. 2011. *Mister Creecher*. London: Bloomsbury.
Sedgwick, Eve Kosofsky. 1986. *The Coherence of Gothic Conventions*. New York: Methuen.
Shelley, Mary. [1818] 1992. *Frankenstein*. London: Penguin.
Wisker, Gina. 2016. "Female Vampirism." In *Women and the Gothic*, edited by Avril Horner and Sue Zlosnik, 150–165. Edinburgh: Edinburgh University Press.

GHOST STORIES

In its strict sense, the ghost story genre includes tales of haunting that rely upon supernatural or unexplained presences to invoke fear, create suspense, and challenge rationality. Intuitively, the ghost story may be considered a literature of terror rather than horror. Full of occluded spaces and unspoken secrets, the mode often relies upon suspense or creeping fear, which are perhaps followed by revelations, to invoke and maintain its macabre effects. Yet, in a number of examples from the long history of ghost stories that have come to constitute the "classic" tradition, horrific figures are rendered at the corner of the reader's vision, so to speak. Even the most formalistic of ghost story writers, the influential Cambridge don M. R. James, invokes the horrific, for instance, in the white, obscure apparition that pursues the antiquarian Parkins in "Oh, Whistle, and I'll Come to You, My Lad" (1904), or in the dark figure that creeps and steals along the living painting of "The Mezzotint" (1904). Forming a particularly important strand to Victorian, modern, and contemporary Gothic, the short ghost story very rarely explains away the supernatural in its pages, and the malignity that propels the narrative often resonates with readers long after they have finished the tale's last line. Yet, ghost stories are not merely contained in the short story form, and many of the texts mentioned below are novellas or have film, television, or radio adaptations that are just as powerful as their literary originals.

The first modern ghost stories may be credited as being published in the German tradition. Perhaps the most famous is E. T. A. Hoffmann's "The Sand-man" (1816). Hoffmann's story is a horrific tale of doubling that Sigmund Freud would come to draw from in his formulation of the "uncanny" in 1919 when he was particularly intrigued by two of Hoffmann's central, strange figures: Coppelius and Olympia. A discomforting return of the repressed for Freud, the feeling of the uncanny arises when a sense of the homely is invaded by the unhomely. Purists may not regard "The Sand-man" as the same type of story that we associate with the British ghost story tradition, but the ghost as an unhomely guest within a narrative is a well-established trope, and many of the early ghostly British tales themselves appear within longer host narratives; for instance, Sir Walter Scott's embedded narrative "Wandering Willie's Tale" within his *Redgauntlet* (1824). The ghost story as it came to be recognized as a distinct literary genre in the British tradition dates back to Scott's short story "The Tapestried Chamber" (1828), which was penned for the Christmas annual *The Keepsake for 1829*.

Of course, ghosts are folkloric in origin, and the oral tradition of telling such stories was the genesis of two key texts in the development of horror: those monstrous tales that arose from the retreat of Lord Byron, Percy Shelley, Mary Shelley, Claire Clairmont, and John Polidori to the Villa Diodati on Lake Geneva in 1816. After evenings of German ghost story telling, followed by discussions of galvanism between Byron's guests, Mary Shelley was visited by the monstrous visions of the waking dream that inspired *Frankenstein* (1818/1831), while the physician John Polidori drew inspiration from Bryon's own writing to pen "The Vampyre," the first modern vampire tale. The opening decades of the nineteenth century were just as important to the American tradition of horror. Washington Irving published his "The Legend of Sleepy Hollow" in 1820. In the years that followed, the ghost story as a genre developed fully alongside the literary magazine cultures of the Victorian, Edwardian, and Georgian periods, as well as resonating with practices of spiritualism investigated by, for instance, the Society for Psychical Research, which was founded in London in 1882.

The exact temporal framing of the ghost story genre's heyday or high point is disputable—reasonable estimates tend to lie within the period 1840–1930—but, certainly, from the late Victorian period into the mid-twentieth century there was a conscious theorizing of the form in Anglo-American letters, one that engaged with many of the cultural anxieties of the age. In an essay arguing that the ghost story should employ an unexplained supernatural or malign force, Henry James, one of the greatest writers of the ghostly tale, suggests the skill and care—indeed, the literariness—with which the best of these stories have been fashioned. In the "Author's Preface" to his *The Turn of the Screw* (1898), James professes his aesthetic preference for rendering what he termed the "withheld glimpse," a technique that allows readers' minds to create the horror in a story for themselves: "Make him *think* the evil, make him think it for himself, and you are released from weak specifications" (James 2001, 8). For James, readers may be most disturbed by a tale when they furnish it with horrors made complete in their own imaginations.

Published half a century after Henry James's "Preface," a particularly cogent theorization of the ghostly tale is found in the Anglo-Irish writer Elizabeth Bowen's preface to a 1952 collection of ghost stories edited by Cynthia Asquith. Bowen, whose most well-read collections of stories include her debut *Encounters* (1923) and the post–World War II collection *The Demon Lover and Other Stories* (1945), contends that the ghost story addresses the unspeakable: that which cannot be uttered without trepidation and fear. As with Henry James, it seems that Bowen takes a typically modernist approach to understanding the ghost story: understatement and aesthetic refinement are privileged over horror in her formulation that "modern" ghost stories should "abjure the over-fantastic and grotesque, operating, instead, through series of happenings whose horror lies in their being just, just out of the true" (cited in Foley 2011). Yet there are modernist writers, such as D. H. Lawrence, May Sinclair, and Edith Wharton, who generate a sense of dread and disease that are close to horror.

A Timeline of Important Ghost Stories, 1816–1945

Summer 1816   Recognized as the genesis of Mary Shelley's *Frankenstein* (1818/1831) and John Polidori's "The Vampyre" (1819), the famous ghost story competition occurs at the Villa Diodati, Lake Geneva.

1817   E. T. A. Hoffmann's story collection *Die Nachtstücke* (*The Night Pieces*) is published in Berlin. It opens with his influential "The Sand-man."

1820   Washington Irving's "The Legend of Sleepy Hollow" appears in his collection *The Sketch Book of Geoffrey Crayon, Gent.*

1829   Sir Walter Scott's "The Tapestried Chamber" is published in the Christmas annual *The Keepsake for 1829.*

1842   Edgar Allan Poe's "The Mask of the Red Death" (later revised in 1845 as "The Masque of the Red Death") appears in the May volume of *Graham's Lady's and Gentleman's Magazine.*

1843   Charles Dickens's *A Christmas Carol* is published by Chapman & Hall on December 19 in London.

1855   Elizabeth Gaskell's "The Old Nurse's Story" is commissioned by Dickens for the Christmas issue of *Household Words.*

1866   Charles Dickens's "The Signal-Man" is published in the Christmas number of *All the Year Round.*

1872   J. Sheridan Le Fanu's collection *In a Glass Darkly* is published; it includes M. R. James's favorite Le Fanu ghost story, "The Familiar."

1898   Henry James's *The Turn of the Screw* is published in his *The Two Magics* by the Macmillan Company in New York.

1904   M. R. James's first collection, *Ghost Stories of an Antiquary,* is published, which includes "Oh, Whistle, and I'll Come to You, My Lad."

1910   Edith Wharton's "Afterward" is first published in *The Century Magazine* in January.

1914   Arthur Machen's ghostly war story "The Bowmen" is published on September 29.

1926   Cynthia Asquith's *The Ghost Book* is published. It includes contributions by May Sinclair, D. H. Lawrence, Arthur Machen, and Algernon Blackwood.

1945   Elizabeth Bowen's collection of wartime ghost stories, *The Demon Lover,* is published.

Somewhat misguidedly, James once wrote of his distaste for what he termed the "primitive" mindset of those who indulged in the writings of the American master of the Gothic horror short story: Edgar Allan Poe (Gargano 1990). Poe's "The Masque of the Red Death" (1842), with its bodiless specter, can be considered a ghost story in the strictest of terms. Yet, more generally, when the repressed returns in Poe its nature is intentionally ambiguous. In "The Black Cat" (1843), his gruesome tale of haunting that stages the return of the seemingly vanquished, the protagonist of the story is overcome by a dark, psychological force—what he terms in the opening meditation of the story as "the spirit of PERVERSENESS"; in turn, he becomes compelled to mutilate his cat Pluto by gouging out one of its eyes and then hanging the feline from a tree. The narrator soon encounters an uncanny double of Pluto in a tavern: this cat, missing an eye, has a patch of mutable white hair on its chest that soon takes on the shape of a noose. As the narrator tries to murder Pluto's double with an axe, his wife intervenes, only to be murdered herself. The story's super-natural element, its claim to being a ghost story, is validated when the vengeful apparition of Pluto's double reveals the whereabouts of the narrator's wife to police. By the end of the narrative the law restores order but there is an ambiguous, Gothic remainder left over: just what gave Pluto's uncanny double its powers of malignity?

Affirming its intimate relationship with the evolution of the Gothic from the Victorian period onward, the ghost story has also been said to continue the Female Gothic mode: a genre that critics identify as beginning during the Romantic period in novel form. The critic Diana Wallace argues that the ghost story "allowed women writers special kinds of freedom" with which "to offer critiques of male power and sexuality" (Wallace 2004, 57). The more nuanced appropriations of this standard involve "a rewriting of the Gothic elements of the Bluebeard story, especially the figure of the husband" (Wallace 2004, 58). Such an example is found in May Sin-clair's "The Villa Désirée," which, collected by Cynthia Asquith for her *The Ghost Book* (1926), includes a paradoxical figure of ghostly monstrosity. Alone in the bedroom of the Villa Désirée, the space in which a murderous calamity had once befallen her husband Louis's first betrothed, Mildred is visited by a composite and monstrous apparition, "its body . . . unfinished, rudimentary, not quite born" (Sin-clair 2006, 438), with a face that gives the impression of absolute horror. In this otherwise restrained ghost story, horror comes to signal the danger posed to inde-pendent, feminine identity by patriarchal tyranny.

The ghost story need not only be cautionary in theme; it relies, too, upon nu-anced psychological and temporal techniques to unnerve its reader. Many of the most popular ghost stories are associated with the festive period: a time at which the ghosts of the past visit to intervene in the present. A prominent example in this regard, Charles Dickens's *A Christmas Carol* (1843), now predominantly remem-bered for the redemption of its central miserly character Ebenezer Scrooge, con-tains, too, a series of disturbing passages that culminate in death's apparition as a ghost from the future (to cite Shakespeare's Prince Hamlet, "the time is out of joint" in Dickens's famous tale). Perhaps the most unnerving of Dickens's short ghost stories is "The Signal-Man" (1866). In this uncanny tale, a horrific apparition ap-pears to an isolated signalman only to lure him to his death. The BBC's adaptation of this story, with a screenplay provided by Andrew Davies and direction by Law-rence Gordon Clark, is one of the highlights of the corporation's *A Ghost Story for*

Christmas series. Other adaptations in this series include tales originally penned by M. R. James and his important nineteenth-century precursor, writing in the Irish tradition, Sheridan Le Fanu. The continued adaptation of these classics of the genre suggests that their themes still resonate with contemporary anxieties surrounding the return of the repressed.

Indeed, since the 1950s, many modern, enduring ghost stories have been added to the literary canon, and these often invite film and television adaptations. Shirley Jackson's *The Haunting of Hill House* (1959) continues and updates the Female Gothic; Susan Hill's *The Woman in Black* (1983) returns to the Gothic tradition of M. R. James; and Sarah Waters's *The Little Stranger* (2009) draws from a range of nineteenth-century American, Victorian, and Edwardian ghostly standards in its charting of the fall of the aristocratic Ayres family in Clement Attlee's post–World War II England. American modern and contemporary horror is replete, too, with powerful stories in which ghostliness, or the return of the dead, is intertwined with the psychological dissolution of characters, including Stephen King's *The Shining* (1977), Peter Straub's *Ghost Story* (1979), Mark Z. Danielewski's *House of Leaves* (2000), and Bret Easton Ellis's *Lunar Park* (2005). Thus, even if we may regard the ghost story as a genre that was most welcomed by readerships of the mid-nineteenth through the mid-twentieth centuries, its endurance and influence upon modern Gothic and horror literature remains significant and its possibilities barely exhausted.

Matt Foley

See also: The Gothic Literary Tradition; Religion, Horror, and the Supernatural; *Part One, Horror through History*: Horror in the Ancient World; *Part Three, Reference Entries*: "The Demon Lover"; *Ghost Story*; Hartley, L. P.; The Haunted House or Castle; *The Haunting of Hill House*; *House of Leaves*; *In a Glass Darkly*; James, M. R.; Poe, Edgar Allan; "The Sand-man"; *The Shining*; Spiritualism; The Uncanny; Wharton, Edith; *The Woman in Black*; "The Yellow Wall-Paper."

Further Reading

Briggs, Julia. 1977. *Night Visitors: The Rise and Fall of the English Ghost Story*. London: Faber and Faber.

Foley, Matt. 2011. "Bowen's Thoughts on the Ghost Story." *The Gothic Imagination* at University of Stirling, January 5. http://www.gothic.stir.ac.uk/blog/bowens-thoughts-on-the-ghost-story.

Gargano, James. 1990. "Henry James and the Question of Poe's Maturity." In *Poe and His Times: The Artist and His Milieu*, edited by Benjamin Franklin Fisher IV, 247–255. Baltimore: The Edgar Allan Poe Society. http://www.eapoe.org/papers/psbbooks/pb1990 1x.htm.

Hay, Simon. 2011. *A History of the Modern British Ghost Story*. New York: Palgrave Macmillan.

James, Henry. 2001. "Author's Preface to *The Turn of the Screw*." In *Ghost Stories of Henry James*, edited by Martin Scofield, 3–10. Hertfordshire: Wordsworth Editions.

"Shelley's Frankenstein: The Ghost Story Challenge." 2014. British Library, May 15. http://www.bl.uk/teaching-resources/shelley-frankenstein-the-ghost-story-challenge.

Sinclair, May. [1926] 2006. "The Villa Désirée." In *H. P. Lovecraft's Book of the Supernatural*, edited by Stephen Jones, 427–442. New York: Pegasus Books.

Smith, Andrew. 2010. *The Ghost Story, 1840–1920: A Cultural History*. Manchester: Manchester University Press.

Wallace, Diana. 2004. "Uncanny Stories: The Ghost Story as Female Gothic." *Gothic Studies* 6.1: 57–68.

THE GOTHIC LITERARY TRADITION

Horror fiction, as we understand it today, would be unthinkable without the genesis of a Gothic literary tradition in the eighteenth century and its development throughout the nineteenth and twentieth. In fact, after the cinematic successes of Universal's horror films in the 1930s and Hammer Horror in the 1950s and 1960s, the most relevant of which were adaptations of the Gothic novels *Dracula* (1897) and *Frankenstein* (1818), the term "Gothic" is often used to designate work that would be more easily defined as "horror." Even then, a distinction is often traced between the Gothic, perceived as a subtle and suggestive literary form connected to the uncanny and the sublime, and horror, understood as its more graphic, visceral, explicit, and shocking cousin. This also means that horror is often devalued as a descriptive term in favor of the more sober and literary Gothic. It is possible, however, to distinguish between the two and to see the Gothic as an artistic mode that conjures up a series of recognizable tropes, characters, settings, images, and stock situations, and horror as constituting a solid genre, that is, a type of artistic manifestation marked much less clearly by its constituents than by the overall emotion it attempts to convey, namely, fear in its various manifestations (shock, dread, suspense, and disgust, among others). This terminological difficulty is, however, proof of the extent to which the Gothic literary tradition and horror fiction overlap.

The Gothic is roughly agreed to begin with Horace Walpole's *The Castle of Otranto* (1764), although certain aspects of William Shakespeare's plays, revenge tragedies, and graveyard poetry have been identified as clear precursors by critics. A purely historicist view would insist that the Gothic ends in 1820 with the rather late *Melmoth the Wanderer* (1820) by Charles Robert Maturin, but the more popular view is that the Gothic is best understood as an artistic mode that has been present in literature throughout the last 250 years and which has adapted to various societal changes to maintain its relevance, and has further hybridized with genres like science fiction or noir. Walpole's novel initially pretended to pass for an English translation by the fictional William Marshall of a 1529 manuscript by one Onuphrio Muralto, canon of the Church of St. Nicholas at Otranto, printed in Naples but found in the north of England. It was only after the success the novel experienced that Walpole felt daring enough to include his name on the second edition and explain his intention of "blend[ing] the two types of romance, the ancient and the modern" (Walpole 2014, 9), that is, the fantasy of the chivalric romance with the social accuracy of the novel of sensibility. This second edition of 1765, more importantly, bore a significant subtitle: *A Gothic Story*. Many of the trappings of the Gothic, literal and figurative, are already present in this early novel, from the underground passages and the lugubrious medieval castle to the presence of the ghost of the past and the persecution of the damsel in distress. The reception of the novel would sour, however, after the fake manuscript ploy was revealed, for there was no follow-up Gothic novel for more than a decade until *The Champion of Virtue* (1777) was published anonymously, first by Clara Reeve and subsequently under the new title of *The Old English Baron*.

It would be in the hands of several female writers—Reeve, but also Sophia and Harriet Lee, Regina Maria Roche, Eliza Parsons, and Charlotte Turner Smith—that the Gothic would develop throughout the late eighteenth century, sometimes incorporating heavy didacticism and moralistic messages. No writer contributed more to the development of the Gothic than Ann Radcliffe, who, with the publication of her fourth novel, *The Mysteries of Udolpho* (1794), became the best paid novelist of her time. She is seen as the writer who popularized the use of "the explained supernatural" in her own brand of Gothic fiction, where seemingly supernatural phenomena eventually would be revealed to have been tricks, hoaxes, or coincidences. It was precisely this preference for a technique that would dispel horrors, rather than hone in on them, that has, retrospectively, been understood to differentiate her writing (taken to be a token of Female Gothic) from that of more visceral and shocking authors like Matthew Lewis, whose *The Monk* (1796) was a convoluted tale of the demonic seduction of a priest interspersed with gory episodes that include a bleeding apparition, a decomposing child, and a trampled nun. Lewis's novel, which caused a massive uproar upon publication and had to be purged of its most sacrilegious passages, infused new blood into the Gothic and is a key book in the so-called German School of Terror, influenced by German romances. Its notorious shock ethic means we could rethink *The Monk* as a first example of the horror novel, but always in retrospect, for, as Dale Townshend has noted, horror "was yet to be generically formulated as such, and was unthinkable outside of the broader 'Gothic' mode in literature in which it first took shape" (Townshend 2016, 20).

This is not to say that there were no contemporary debates around horror and terror. In fact, the late eighteenth and early nineteenth centuries are precisely when these debates began to germinate, if not coalesce. Works by Anna Laetitia Aikin, James Beattie, and Nathan Drake began to sound the possible pleasures of horror, as well as its workings, especially after the publication of Edmund Burke's *A Philosophical Enquiry into the Origins of Our Ideas of the Sublime and Beautiful* (1757). This treatise included a lengthy discussion of the sources of terror (and thus, of the sublime, the highest expression of which is astonishment), and included sections dedicated to "obscurity," "vastness," or "pain." Its ideas would hold sway, and the sublime has become both a tool through which to understand eighteenth-century

Major Gothic Novels: A Timeline

1764 *The Castle of Otranto* by Horace Walpole

1778 *The Old English Baron* by Clara Reeve (first published anonymously as *The Champion of Virtue* in 1777)

1786 *Vathek* by William Thomas Beckford

1794 *The Mysteries of Udolpho* by Ann Radcliffe

1796 *The Monk* by Matthew Lewis

1798 *Wieland, or The Transformation* by Charles Brockden Brown

1818 *Frankenstein* by Mary Shelley

1820 *Melmoth the Wanderer* by Charles Robert Maturin

1845 *The Mysteries of London* by George W. M. Reynolds

1847 *Varney the Vampire* by James Malcolm Rymer and Thomas Peckett Prest; *Jane Eyre* by Charlotte Brontë; *Wuthering Heights* by Emily Brontë

1859 *The Woman in White* by Wilkie Collins

1886 *The Strange Case of Dr. Jekyll and Mr. Hyde* by Robert Louis Stevenson

1897 *Dracula* by Bram Stoker; *The Beetle* by Richard Marsh

1910 *The Phantom of the Opera* by Gaston Leroux

1938 *Rebecca* by Daphne du Maurier

1954 *I Am Legend* by Richard Matheson

1976 *Interview with the Vampire* by Anne Rice

1979 *The Bloody Chamber* by Angela Carter

1983 *The Woman in Black* by Susan Hill

1987 *Beloved* by Toni Morrison

1995 *Patchwork Girl* by Shelley Jackson

2000 *House of Leaves* by Mark Z. Danielewski

2001 *The Shadow of the Wind* by Carlos Ruiz Zafón

2004 *The Historian* by Elizabeth Kostova

2005 *Twilight* by Stephenie Meyer

2009 *The Little Stranger* by Sarah Waters

Matt Cardin and Xavier Aldana Reyes

Gothic and a theoretical concept worth studying in its own right. Radcliffe herself, in an excerpt from her posthumous novel *Gaston de Blondeville* (1826) that was published in *New Monthly Magazine* that same year, attempted a first distinction between terror and horror, a distinction premised on affect (the emotional effects of the literary piece) that, it would seem, has partly evolved into the twenty-first-century misconception that the Gothic should be connected to the eerie and the uncanny, and horror with the shocking and explicit.

After the famous ghost story challenge at the Villa Diodati yielded two of the most significant and long-living of horror monsters, Frankenstein's creature in Mary Shelley's *Frankenstein* (1818) and the aristocratic vampire in John William

Polidori's "The Vampyre" (1819), the Gothic would travel in two directions in the mid-to-late nineteenth century: inward, in order to explore the dark recesses of the mind—especially in Edgar Allan Poe's paranoid fictions and in Robert Louis Stevenson's *Strange Case of Dr. Jekyll and Mr. Hyde* (1886)—and toward urban centers, especially in penny dreadfuls like George W. M. Reynolds's *The Mysteries of London* (1845) and James Malcolm Rymer and Thomas Peckett Prest's *Varney the Vampire* (1847), cheap serial publications that included lurid topics and sometimes supernatural phenomena. The Gothic would hybridize with the suspense story in the sensation novel, the best examples of which are Wilkie Collins's *The Woman in White* (1859) and Mary Elizabeth Braddon's *Lady Audley's Secret* (1862), and would be further shaped by the Decadent movement (especially Oscar Wilde and Joris-Karl Huysmans) and by fears directly connected to degeneration (H. G. Wells, Rudyard Kipling's "The Mark of the Beast," 1890) and the fall of the British Empire (Richard Marsh, H. Rider Haggard). By the end of the nineteenth century, Gothic fiction had largely shed its medieval trappings and adopted modern ones, to the point where we might want to question why novels like *The Beetle* (1897) are referred to as Gothic and not as straightforward horror. However, horror had yet to coalesce into a distinct genre. H. P. Lovecraft's study *Supernatural Horror in Literature* (1927), where recent "weird" (another interstitial, slippery term) writers like William Hope Hodgson, Algernon Blackwood, or Arthur Machen are presented as part of a longer literary tradition reaching back to Walpole, would be the first to connect the various strands of the Gothic–horror continuum, albeit with the main purpose of claiming the value of the weird, and not of theorizing horror as a category.

A precedent was set in 1937 with the development of the "H for Horrific" certificate, used to identify the films that followed Universal's *Dracula* and *Frankenstein*, and which was intended to inform audiences about the dangerous nature of that material. It is safe to say that horror developed much more readily as a cinematic category and was subsequently applied to certain types of fiction, even when some of these, as was the case with a number of the short stories collected in *The Pan Book of Horror Stories* (1959–1989), would have been referred to previously as Gothic or weird. The banning of horror comics in the 1950s, again on the grounds that these texts could have deleterious effects on the young, brought the debates more readily onto the publishing industry, and by the 1980s, it is possible to speak of a burgeoning and "booming" horror market, with designated genre spaces in bookshops and publishers like Tor developing horror lines. The success throughout the late 1970s and 1980s of horror auteurs like Stephen King, Clive Barker, and Ramsey Campbell, as well as extreme fiction ("splatterpunk"), served to entrench the dividing line between the Gothic (Anne Rice, Angela Carter) and horror, even when a number of "splatterpunk" (extreme horror) novels would seemingly return to well-known Gothic monsters like the vampire.

Where exactly the Gothic and horror may lie within the modern and contemporary period has been the subject of much debate. Gothic studies has been steadily institutionalized in academia through a dedicated stream of publications since the early 1980s, but especially in the 1990s, which saw the founding of the International Gothic Association and the publication, in 1999, of the first issue of the specialist journal *Gothic Studies*. This interest in the Gothic has permeated education, to the point where the Gothic is an option in British A-levels (high school examinations), it is present in most degrees in Britain and the United States, and it can be further studied through specialist master's degrees. The Gothic has also experienced a public resurgence, with the British Film Institute and the British Library running Gothic-themed seasons and exhibitions (2013–2014 and 2014–2015, respectively). All this investment in the legitimization of the Gothic has naturally led to a concomitant reevaluation of horror fiction (and film), and to studies on its history, such as Darryl Jones's *Horror: A Thematic History in Film and Fiction* (2002), *Horror Fiction: An Introduction* (2005), and the edited collection *Horror: A Literary History* (2016), as well as S. T. Joshi's *Unutterable Horror: A History of Supernatural Fiction* (2014), which includes a number of horror texts.

For all that, the difference between the Gothic and horror is still less than clear. It would seem that we must either extricate the Gothic (as an aesthetic and thematic marker) from horror (as an emotive and affective one), or else celebrate their overlaps.

Xavier Aldana Reyes

See also: The Legacy of *Frankenstein*: From Gothic Novel to Cultural Myth; Page to Screen: The Influence of Literary Horror on Film and Television; *Part One, Horror through History*: Horror in the Eighteenth Century; Horror in the Nineteenth Century; *Part Three, Reference Entries*: Carter, Angela; *The Castle of Otranto*; Lewis, Matthew Gregory; *Melmoth the Wanderer*; *The Monk*; *The Mysteries of Udolpho*; The Numinous; Penny Dreadful; Poe, Edgar Allan; Radcliffe, Ann; Rice, Anne; *The Strange Case of Dr. Jekyll and Mr. Hyde*; The Sublime; Terror versus Horror; "The Vampyre"; *Varney the Vampire; or, The Feast of Blood*; Walpole, Horace.

Further Reading

Bloom, Clive, ed. 2007. *Gothic Horror: A Guide for Students and Readers*. 2nd ed. Basingstoke: Palgrave Macmillan.

Botting, Fred. 2013. *Gothic*. 2nd ed. London and New York: Routledge.

Chaplin, Sue. 2011. *Gothic Literature: Texts, Contexts, Connections*. York: Longman.

Hogle, Jerrold E., ed. 2002. *The Cambridge Companion to Gothic Fiction*. Cambridge: Cambridge University Press.

Punter, David. 1996. *The Literature of Terror, Volume 1: A History of Gothic Fiction from 1765 to the Edwardian Age* and *The Literature of Terror, Volume 2: The Modern Gothic*. 2nd ed. London and New York: Routledge.

Punter, David, ed. 2015. *A New Companion to the Gothic*. Malden, MA: Wiley-Blackwell.

Spooner, Catherine. 2007. "Gothic in the Twentieth Century." In *The Routledge Companion to Gothic*, edited by Catherine Spooner and Emma McEvoy, 38–47. London and New York: Routledge.

Townshend, Dale. 2016. "Gothic and the Cultural Sources of Horror, 1740–1820." In *Horror: A Literary History*, edited by Xavier Aldana Reyes, 19–51. London: British Library.

Walpole, Horace. 2014. *The Castle of Otranto*. Oxford: Oxford University Press.

GOTHIC POETRY

Gothic poetry began in the eighteenth century and accompanied the rise of Gothic architecture. The poetry was partly the product of the rediscovery of medieval history, exemplified in the building of Strawberry Hill House by Horace Walpole, and partly an interest in what Walpole called "gloomth," that mysterious half-understood world of shadows and bizarrerie that could be experienced from visits to ruins, and that was attached to the personal universe that the eighteenth century called sentiment. Sentiment was an irrational and highly subjective emotional response to the sublime, which itself inspired both terror and horror and could only be felt in extreme situations.

Gothic poetry emphasized this interior world and especially dealt with the feelings accompanying the attractions of fear and disorientation when faced with a universe devoid of the rationality preached by Enlightenment thinkers. The best way to experience such feelings was to revisit the ruined world of the past in one's mind, or to inhabit a supernatural world where God was no longer present.

Gothic literature was originally inspired by the world of Shakespeare, but Gothic poetry had a slightly different trajectory. Memorial poetry of the time produced by England's metaphysical poets in the seventeenth century, stripped of its word play and religious intention, soon became the memorial elegy as produced by Thomas Gray. This in turn led others to take a more sanguinary view of decay, and the new vogue for tourism sent crowds to ruins such as Netley Abbey, where they mused and wrote sonnets on the picturesque charms of death and decay.

Poets as different as Lord Byron and Susan Evance produced poetry on decay and ruination, while novelists such as Ann Radcliffe (*The Mysteries of Udolpho*, 1794) incorporated poetry of meditations on the picturesque. Her own blandly soothing poems on nature ("The Glow-Worm") and scenery were accompanied by poems of dead brides ("The Mariner"), murdered pilgrims ("The Pilgrim;" originally "The Traveller"), and the mountain abyss ("Storied Sonnet"), in which there is a decided hint of Samuel Taylor Coleridge's "Kublai Khan."

Nevertheless, Byron was the most famous poet of Gothic thrills for his generation, supplying vampires in "The Giaor" (1813) and metamorphosing into the first vampire character in "The Vampyre" (1819) by his doctor John Polidori. Yet it was Coleridge whose influence was eventually the strongest. The French Revolution deeply influenced both William Wordsworth and Coleridge, and through its prism they discovered the sublimity of nature and nature's resonance with human emotion in a world in which nature is supreme. Coleridge's interest in the border ballad form, then current, led to *The Rime of the Ancient Mariner* (1798), in which the death of an albatross has to be atoned for by the sailor who has murdered the bird.

The moment the mariner fixes his unknowing listener with his tale of woe, and thereby curses him to repeat the story to the reader, became the spine of Mary Shelley's tale of *Frankenstein* (1818).

Nevertheless, it was the German writer August Bürger's poem of doomed love that was to become the most influential of all Gothic poems. Bürger was the son of strict Lutheran parents, and he was set to join the church. But he rebelled, and his interest in law gained him a magistrate's position while his interest in British border ballads led him to become a poet. His most famous poem, "Lenore," was translated into English by William Taylor for the March 1796 edition of *The Monthly Magazine* as "Lenora."

The story follows Lenore as she waits for her William to return from the Crusades. Her despair leads her to renounce God despite her mother's entreaties. Suddenly, in the night, William, although clearly a specter, appears on a steed and carries off Lenore in her night shirt to be his bride. At cock crow they plunge to earth, William returning to his tomb and Lenore left dying amid the graves.

Walter Scott translated Bürger's "Der Wilde Jager" as "The Wild Huntsman" and published it to great acclaim in Matthew Lewis's *Tales of Wonder* in 1796, while Lewis himself produced his own version of the ballad in his scandalous Gothic novel *The Monk* (1796). "Lenore" introduced the "corpse bride," the girl who dies when she is about to marry, a character trait reproduced in the characters of Victor Frankenstein's bride Elizabeth in *Frankenstein* and Miss Haversham in Charles Dickens's *Great Expectations* (1860) and reproduced in such films as Tim Burton' s *The Corpse Bride* (2005). The poem's most famous line, "stil Denn die Todten reiten schnell" ("for the dead travel fast"; Bürger 1900, 27), was used by Bram Stoker in *Dracula* (1897) when Jonathan Harker first encounters the count.

Charles Maturin's *Melmoth the Wanderer* (1820) was the last great Gothic novel of the Romantic period (ca. 1760–1830, with romanticism as such surviving several decades longer). It also set the tone for a different sort of Gothic sensation. Instead of the horrors attendant on the supernatural world, there was a greater attention to material fears made manifest by the cruelty of authority and the perversity of human nature. It was to human nature that the writers of the late Romantic Gothic would turn their attention. Theirs would be a world where horror was not a consequence of violating nature, but instead would be a consequence of mental disturbance. Such mental disturbance was first analyzed by James Prichard in *A Treatise on Insanity and Other Disorders Affecting the Mind* (1835). He called the condition "moral insanity," a term for those whose outward signs are perfectly normal, but who are insane within.

Coleridge had led the way in the exploration of the imagination in *Biographia Literaria* (1817), in which he proposed a new way of understanding the world. This was through pure imagination, which to Coleridge had the power to transform base reality and transcend material being. This "new" world was opposed to the merely combinational aspects of our perception, which he called "fancy." To get to the imagination one might use drugs or other hallucinogens, the point being to reconnect with the spiritual aspect of human existence. This was Coleridge's poetic solution to the loss of God, which had taken place with the secularization of French life amid the upheavals of the French Revolution (1789–1799). Nevertheless, if a person were to reconnect with the supernatural and what amounted to a natural religiosity, there was nothing to stop him or her from simply imagining a reality that was at odds with experience. In simple terms, this might lead a person to impose his or her will through perverse and hallucinatory desire brought on by mania or drug addiction or both.

The first English writer to understand this contradiction and to become fascinated by it was Thomas De Quincey, who published a satiric article in *Blackwood's Magazine* in 1827 titled "On Murder considered as one of the Fine Arts." In it he proposed a "Society of Connoisseurs in Murder" whose aim was to analyze the "design, gentlemen, grouping, light and shade" (De Quincey 2006, 10) and "poetry" essential to study the "great artists" (4) of murder whose lives were eaten up by the secret passions of "jealousy, ambition, vengeance and hatred" (4).

De Quincey's proposal, absurd though it seemed, suggested a new heightened interest in criminal psychology, the murders themselves creating a world only a fraction apart from normality, determined by secret passions harbored by all people. It was simply too "vulgar" and unimaginative to knock someone on the head for his money bag. From now on there had to be "sympathy" for the murderer rather than the victim.

De Quincey had been drawn to the subject by his fascination with the notorious Ratcliffe Highway murders, which occurred in 1812 between December 7 and 19. An unknown assailant had butchered two families, including their young children, beating them senseless and cutting their throats. John Williams was apprehended and charged, but hanged himself in prison before any proof could be brought. His body was buried with a stake in its heart at a crossroads near the scene of the crime. This interest in the psychological aspects of Gothic mentality greatly influenced two of the most important Gothic poets of the years 1830 to 1850, Robert Browning and Edgar Allan Poe.

Browning's great gift was for psychological monologues, a term applied later to the series of poetic narratives he created between the middle 1830s to 1842, when he published the collection *Dramatic Lyrics* (1842). Such monologues are interior conversations with the reader, who is drawn into the mad world of the speaker to the point where it is impossible to escape the knowledge that is imparted, a technique invented years earlier by Coleridge in *The Rime of the Ancient Mariner*.

Porphyria's Lover, which Browning wrote in 1836 and published in the January edition of the *Monthly Depository* (but without its present title), was an early attempt to understand the mind of a killer who yet believes he is a lover. It was reprinted in *Dramatic Lyrics* under the title "Madhouse Cells." The tale is told as Porphyria returns to her lover at night through a rainstorm. Although wet, she sits next to the narrator and puts her arm around his waist as she gently lays his cheek on her bare shoulder. The eroticism is heightened by the disheveled nature of her clothes and by her "yellow hair" and "white shoulder bare" (Browning 1836, 43). The narrator meditates on her absolute love for him and that at the moment of their silent clinch "she was mine" (44). The reader might expect a kiss or vow of love from the narrator, yet what he does next is both shocking and inexplicable:

> . . . I found
> A thing to do, and all her hair
> In one long yellow string I wound
> Three times her little throat around,
> And strangled her. (44)

The infantilized tone, "I found a thing to do," and the use of diminutives such as "little" suggest an innocence about the narrator's actions that speak directly of moral insanity. Indeed, he even rationalizes the assumption that

> No pain felt she;
> I am quite sure she felt no pain. (44)

However, murder now has no moral consequence as the poem pointedly finishes with the cynical "God has not said a word!" (44). It is no coincidence that Porphyria is a disease of the blood and skin that may lead to manic depression in sufferers. This hint at medical complications nevertheless leaves a world where perverse desire (in this case, possibly fetishistic sexual desire: Porphyria's hair) and the personal will of the narrator override spiritual elements and confuse moral certainties, replacing material reality with the inner disorientation consequent upon absolute loss of faith.

The same effect is to be found in Browning's more famous "My Last Duchess," which was anthologized in 1842. It takes place in the corridors of the Duke of Ferrara's palace during 1564. The duke is showing an ambassador around his picture collection while discussing his next potential bride. Everything is told in an urbane and disinterested tone created by the technique of enjambment (the continuation of a sentence or clause across a poetic line break, without a pause), which gives the poem a conversational tone, the better to disarm its reader before the denouement.

The duke begins the conversation by stopping at a portrait behind a curtain that he has drawn back and pointing out his "last duchess." Sinisterly, he notices that she is presented "looking as if she were alive" (Browning 1842, 25), and that, even more disturbingly, the ambassador is privileged to see what is shown. The duke points out the way the painter has caught the "half flush that dies along her throat," but this aesthetic detail sends the duke off into a reminiscence regarding the duchess's perceived overfamiliarity with those around her and her apparent disregard of his gift to her of "a nine-hundred-years-old name" (26). The duke turns to his interlocutor and admits that something in the duchess "disgusts him." It appears he has had her murdered, something of so little consequence to him that he continues his tour oblivious of his revelation. The implication, however, is clear: the next duchess will meet the same fate, and the duke will continue with the same casual disregard.

Browning was the master of insidious intent. His exploration of perverse states of mind rationalized beyond sense was a symptom of mid-century concerns regarding the nature of human consciousness in a world beset with existential doubts, social upheaval, rapid industrialization, and class conflict. These concerns found their greatest expression in Alfred Tennyson's "Locksley Hall" (1842).

All of these conflicting problems seemed unwittingly to focus on women. Edgar Allan Poe, although an American, was influenced by the currents of British thought regarding mental hygiene and psychological well-being. In a series of short tales— "Berenice" (1835), "Eleonora" (1842), and "Ligeia" (1838)—Poe explored the nature of that male monomania that he named "the imp of the perverse." It was Poe who first integrated previously written poems into his tales to give greater psychological insight into the characters and the way they experienced the world. It was also Poe who integrated assonance (the repetition of vowel sounds) and sibilance (the repetition of *s*, *sh*, *z*, and related sounds) into his prose to give it a dreamlike feeling, which Poe remarked had the effect of language and imagery recalled from reverie or the moment between waking and sleeping.

Ligeia occupies this dreamlike and hallucinatory world, in which an unnamed narrator sits with his dying wife (a wife who may be a hallucination brought about by opium consumption), who intones the poem "The Conqueror Worm." The poem concerns a "theatre" of human woes where "puppets" act out "mimes" "at [the] bidding of vast formless things" (Poe 2008, 88). The action of the poem is that of humanity (or, at least, sentient beings) manipulated by the mindless entities of a meaningless universe in an endless cycle of anarchy and chaos. Into this terrifying world crawls "the Conqueror Worm," a fanged and gory entity to whom all must submit. Against this disaster Ligeia poses the overriding importance of the human will, all that is left of the spiritual possibilities of Coleridge's imagination. When Ligeia returns at the end of the tale, it is not merely the triumph of her will, but that of the narrator's, who literally wills her into life out of the corpse of his second wife. As with Browning, it is the fetish of her raven hair that is the symbol of her resurrection.

Poe again made use of the incorporated poem in "The Fall of the House of Usher," where "The Haunted Palace" is a metaphoric description of Roderick Usher's mental decline, the Gothic imagery of the castle serving as a perfect foil for the disintegration of Roderick's mind, where red eyes and a humorless laugh betray mental disorder.

The poem most associated with Gothic goings-on is Poe's "The Raven" (1845), whose central character, the raven itself, may have been suggested by Grip, the talking raven in Dickens's *Barnaby Rudge* (1841). The poem's complicated rhyme scheme may have been further suggested after Poe reviewed the trochaic octameter poem "Lady Geraldine's Courtship" by Elizabeth Barrett, published in 1845. Regardless of its sources, the poem follows the incident of a raven landing on a bust

Edgar Allan Poe's "The Conqueror Worm": Horror the Soul of the Plot

While Poe's "The Raven" may be the first thing that comes to mind for most people when they try to think of a Gothic poem, his "The Conqueror Worm," which allegorically portrays conscious life as a hideous play presided over by incomprehensible powers and performed for an angelic audience, delivers a dose of Gothic gloom that at least equals that of its dark-feathered cousin.

Lo! 't is a gala night
   Within the lonesome latter years—
A mystic throng, bewinged, bedight
   In veils, and drowned in tears,
Sit in a theatre, to see
   A play of hopes and fears,
While the orchestra breathes fitfully
   The music of the spheres.

Mimes, in the form of God on high,
   Mutter and mumble low,
And hither and thither fly—
   Mere puppets they, who come and go
At bidding of vast shadowy things
   That shift the scenery to and fro,
Flapping from out their Condor wings
   Invisible Wo!

That motley drama—oh, be sure
   It shall not be forgot!
With its Phantom chased forevermore,
   By a crowd that seize it not,
Through a circle that ever returneth in
   To the self-same spot,
And much of Madness and more of Sin,
   And Horror the soul of the plot.

But see, amid the mimic rout,
   A crawling shape intrude!
A blood-red thing that writhes from out
   The scenic solitude!
It writhes!—it writhes!—with mortal pangs
   The mimes become its food,
And the angels sob at vermin fangs
   In human gore imbued!

Out—out are the lights—out all!
    And, over each dying form,
The curtain, a funeral pall,
    Comes down with the rush of a storm,
While the angels, all pallid and wan,
    Uprising, unveiling, affirm
That the play is the tragedy, "Man,"
    And its hero, the Conqueror Worm.

Source: Poe, Edgar Allan. *The Works of Edgar Allan Poe*. 1914. Vol. 10. New York: Charles Scribner's Sons. 34–35.

of Pallas inside the door of a young scholar who is reading books of occult knowledge while mourning his lost love, who is called Lenore (a clear reference to Bürger's poem). It begins,

Once upon a midnight dreary, while I pondered, weak and weary,
Over many a quaint and curious volume of forgotten lore—
    While I nodded, nearly napping, suddenly there came a tapping,
As of some one gently rapping, rapping at my chamber door.
"'Tis some visitor," I muttered, "tapping at my chamber door—
    Only this and nothing more." (Poe 1845, 143)

The poem became an instant success, as its theatricality made it a parlor performance favorite. It brought Poe fame, but little money, and created a host of parodies, remaining still the most famous Gothic poem ever written. With its raven intoning the meaningless "Nevermore," the public loved the mysterious nature of the work, so much so that Poe attempted to cash in on his success with an explanation of the poem's creation. Nevertheless, his essay "The Philosophy of Composition" (1846) did little to explain away the mysteries of what was intended. The main theme seems to be the perverse desire to both forget and remember a traumatic event, but beyond that, the narrator's need to make sense of the raven's meaningless repetitions suggests the loss of an irretrievable past. Beyond all this remains the attraction of the poem's mesmeric alliteration and its verbal dexterity, which is both formulaic and yet surprising.

Poe's work represents the end for Gothic taste in poetry, although the taste for medievalized Gothic poetry continued up to the end of the nineteenth century, with the work of Browning and Poe evolving into the work of Decadents such as Charles Baudelaire and Symbolists such as Algernon Swinburne, with poetry that catered to urban and perverse tastes unaccompanied by any interest in Gothic trappings. Gothic poetry was finally sublimated into the imaginative world of the silent movie and European cabaret.

Clive Bloom

See also: The Gothic Literary Tradition; *Part One, Horror through History*: Horror in the Eighteenth Century; Horror in the Nineteenth Century; *Part Three, Reference Entries*: Baudelaire, Charles; Byron, Lord; Lewis, Matthew Gregory; "Ligeia"; *Melmoth the Wanderer*; *The Monk*; *The Mysteries of Udolpho*; Poe, Edgar Allan; Radcliffe, Ann; The Sublime; Terror versus Horror; "The Vampyre"; Walpole, Horace.

Further Reading

Bloom, Clive, ed. 2007. *Gothic Horror: A Guide for Students and Readers*. 2nd ed. New York: Palgrave Macmillan.

Browning, Robert. 1836. "The rain set early in to-night." Sixty lines signed "Z," in *Monthly Repository*, vol. x., N.S., 1836, pp. 43–44.

Browning, Robert. (1842). *Bells and Pomegranates. No. III. – Dramatic Lyrics*. London: Edward Moxon.

Bürger, August Gottfried. [1774] 1900. *Lenore*. Translated by Dante Gabriel Rossetti. London: Ellis and Elvey.

De Quincey, Thomas. 2006. *On Murder*. Oxford: Oxford University Press.

Duggett, Tom. 2010. *Gothic Romanticism: Architecture, Politics, and Literary Form*. New York: Palgrave Macmillan.

Kendrick, Walter M. 1991. *The Thrill of Fear: 250 Years of Scary Entertainment*. New York: Grove Weidenfeld.

Poe, Edgar Allan. 1845. "The Raven." *American Review*, February, 1:143–145.

Poe, Edgar Allan. 2008. *The Complete Poetry of Edgar Allan Poe*. New York: Signet Classics.

Punter, David. 2014. "Gothic Poetry, 1700–1900." In *The Gothic World*, edited by Glennis Byron and Dale Townshend, 210–220. New York: Routledge.

Smith, Andrew. 2013. *Gothic Literature*. Edinburgh: Edinburgh University Press.

Wagner, Corinna, ed. 2014. *Gothic Evolutions: Poetry, Tales, Context, Theory*. Ontario: Broadview Press.

HORROR ANTHOLOGIES

An anthology is a collection of thematically linked works by different authors. (In the modern publishing industry, the term "collection" itself is used for books consisting of works by a single author.) The thematic linkages can be weak, and, importantly, the works do not have to be prose fiction but can include material from other forms of literature—verse, drama, essays, correspondence—as well as such other genres as music and theology. Anthologies have played a significant role in the history of horror literature and the establishment of a canon, helping to shape the field by shaping assumptions about which works are important to reprint, read, and remember.

Those wanting to establish horror as a many-rooted genre would do well to look at the depictions of horrific punishments and general bloodlust in the collections of Christian sermons and homiletics that were at one time popular. If one concentrates on fiction anthologies, it helps to remember that although short fiction predates the invention of movable type, the printing press, and even the Christian era, it was Christians' development of the codex—the progenitor of the modern form of the book, created from separate pages bound together along one edge—that permitted different works by different authors to be cumulated into one binding. The earliest known anthologies would thus be manuscript collections, and arguably the earliest horror anthology is MS. Cotton Vitellius A XV, which dates from prior to 1631 and collects not only *Beowulf*, the earliest monster story in English, but Christian apocrypha such as the Gospel of Nicodemus, as well as containing numerous illustrations of monsters and the monstrous.

Despite such an auspicious beginning, and despite the appearance of horrific elements in the works of such widely read medieval authors as Geoffrey Chaucer, Giovanni Boccaccio, and Dante Alighieri, it was not until the Renaissance and the Age of Enlightenment that formal collections of thematically linked works began to be systematically published, although it must be emphasized that such literary genres as horror and fantasy did not then exist and are relatively recent in invention. One of the earliest print collections was the English writer Thomas Bromhall's marvelously titled *A Treatise of Specters, or, An History of Apparitions, Oracles, Prophecies, and Predictions with Dreams, Visions and Revelations and the Cunning Delusions of the Devil to Strengthen the Idolatry of the Gentiles and the Worshiping of Saints Departed, with the Doctrine of Purgatory: a Work very Seasonable for Discovering the Impostures and Religious Cheats of These Times, Collected out of Sundry Authors of Great Credit and Delivered into English from Their Several Originals by T.B.* (1658). While hardly free from religious argumentation, Bromhall's book nevertheless would have provided its susceptible readers with horrific chills. The eighteenth century likewise had such works as *The History of Apparitions, Ghosts, Spirits or Spectres; Consisting of Variety of Remarkable Stories of Apparitions, Attested by People of Undoubted Veracity* (1762), whose author is listed simply as "Clergyman." However, perhaps the most significant work to emerge from this period was Daniel Defoe's often anthologized and still occasionally read ghost story, *A True Relation of the Apparition of One Mrs. Veal, the Next Day After Her Death, to One Mrs. Bargrave at Canterbury, the 8th of September, 1705* (1706)—a book that, despite its title, is fiction.

It was during the nineteenth century that anthologies of horrific literature—which is to say, literature deliberately written to a specific sensationalistic aesthetic—began to be consciously compiled. There was a contemporary awareness that this material was different in content and approach from other works, and editors recognized that such material could be cumulated and collected. Such a collection was the five volumes of the *Gespensterbuch*, edited by Johann August Apel and Friedrich August Schulze (as F. Laun) and published between 1811 and 1815. The title means *Ghost Book*, and it included not only works of Germanic folklore but also works of supernatural horror. This is an especially significant book in the history of horror anthologies, for in 1812 a selection of the tales was translated into French and published as *Fantasmagoriana; ou Recueil d'Histoires d'Apparitions, de Spectres, Revenans, Fantômes, &c.*, after which a selection of these along with the introduction to the French volume were translated into English as *Tales of the Dead* (1813) by one Sarah Utterson. Her introduction is well informed, revealing a historical awareness of the literature of the horrific, and the French introduction recognizes the existence of horrific literature and provides an argument for its existence: "the wonderful ever excites a degree of interest, and gains an attentive ear; consequently, all recitals relative to supernatural appearances please us" (iv). Moreover, the French introduction provides bibliographic discussions of and references to those eighteenth-century works that discuss aspects of the supernatural. As if this were not significant enough for one small volume, *Tales of the Dead* was one of those books read by Lord Byron, John Polidori, and Percy and Mary Shelley during their legendary 1816 sojourn at Lake Geneva, and thus almost certainly helped inspire Mary Shelley's writing of *Frankenstein* (1818) and Polidori's "The Vampyre" (1819).

The lack of an international copyright meant that, for most of the nineteenth century, works could be published in England and Europe and almost immediately reprinted in America, and vice versa. This led to the first multivolume fantastic fiction anthology in English, the *Popular Tales and Romances of the Northern Nations* (1823; 3 volumes). Also having a thoroughly cosmopolitan set of contents were John Y. Akerman's *Tales of Other Days* (1830) and Henry St. Clair's *Tales of Terror* (1835). In addition to a number of anonymously translated European tales, the latter also included American writer William Austin, whose widely anthologized "Peter Rugg, the Missing Man" (1824) is an American utilization of the idea of the Flying Dutchman, a man cursed to travel forever, unable to recognize when he arrives at his destination, and horrifying by implication.

The nineteenth century saw numerous anthologies of horrific work, and there was no social stigma against authors, whether men and women, writing works that were fantastic and horrific. Reprints of anthologies, often with expanded contents, became more common. This was the case with Akerman, mentioned above, and it included such later works as *A Stable for Nightmares*, whose 1867 English edition contained twelve stories, only some of which were reprinted in an 1896 edition, which added new material. American writers began to vie for space with the English and Europeans; in *Strange Happenings* (1901), the American regionalist (a writer focusing on conveying the "local color" of a specific region of the United States) Hamlin Garland could rub shoulders with such male English writers as Grant Allen and W. Clark Russell and such women as Beatrice O'Connor, Mrs. Fleming, and Clara Savile-Clarke. The Victorian love of the supernatural led to such collections as *Stories with a Vengeance* (1883), which was also sold as the *Bow Bells Annual* for 1883. Similarly, individual magazines began to be mined for their fantastic contents: *Strange Doings in Strange Places* (1890) reprinted eighteen stories that had appeared in *Cassell's Sunday Journal* during 1888.

The subject matter of the stories remained essentially static, however, and although there were significant stylistic differences, and individual authors such as Fitz-James O'Brien and J. S. Le Fanu could and did offer unique approaches, the material published in the early nineteenth century was essentially the same as the material published at its conclusion: stories of hauntings, punishments natural and supernatural, covenants with demons and devils, premature burials, and the ever-popular stories of adventures with vampires and werewolves. It was only in the 1920s and 1930s, with the advent of such magazines as *Weird Tales* in the United States, coupled with the prescience of English editors and the rivalries of various English newspaper chains, that the subject content of horrific anthologies began to be consciously expanded. English editor Christine Campbell Thomson began the trend with *Not at Night* (1925), which reprinted a number of stories that included several first published in *Weird Tales*. The series lasted for eleven volumes, concluding with *Nightmare by Daylight* (1936). The next year, 1937, saw the publication of *The Not at Night Omnibus* (1937), collecting thirty-five selected stories from the previous volumes. Starting in 1928, with *Great Short Stories of Detection, Mystery, and Horror* (1928), Dorothy Sayers began editing a series of massive collections, whose title indicates its mix of genres. The horrific and fantastic writers included many of the finest writers then alive, and Sayers continued to edit similar anthologies until the early 1940s. H. R. Wakefield and Charles Birkin, editors at the publisher Philip Allan, began what is now popularly known as the *Creeps* series in 1932 with the publication of *Creeps* (1932), *Shivers* (1932), and *Shudders* (1932). Ultimately, some fourteen titles were published, with the contents either horrific or dark fantasy, and *The Creeps Omnibus* (1935) cumulated the contents of the first three volumes. (The latter contained seven stories by Wakefield.)

While the above were being published, the rival English newspaper chains began offering subscribers inexpensive sets of historically important writers and also massive subject-based anthologies that collected material old and new. Readers interested in the horrific could thus acquire, among many others, *A Century of Creepy Stories* (1934), *A Century of Thrillers from Poe to Arlen* (1934), *The Mystery Book* (1934), *A Century of Thrillers: Second Series* (1935), *The Great Book of Thrillers* (1935; revised, 1937), *Century of Ghost Stories* (1936), and *A Century of Thrillers* (1937, 3 vols.).

Although some of the above had American editions, anthologies of horror and the fantastic published originally in America were much less common during this period, though one of the more significant works was *The Moon Terror* (1927). Anonymously edited by Farnsworth Wright, who was then editing *Weird Tales*, *The Moon Terror* reprinted four stories published in the original *Weird Tales* and was offered as a subscription premium for new subscribers. It apparently did not attract many, but it is the first American fantastic anthology whose contents were derived completely from a genre magazine. During the 1940s, however, several events occurred roughly simultaneously. More anthologies began to be published, their contents derived from the genre magazines, and because most major publishers did not wish to commit themselves to publishing what they undoubtedly did not consider literature, these anthologies were published by the fans and the smaller publishers, who were more inclined to take risks. Perhaps the most notable of these was *The Garden of Fear* (1945), edited by William L. Crawford, consisting of five stories originally published in *Marvel Tales*, which was also owned and edited by Crawford. Forty-eight thousand copies were printed, and had this book received the newsstand distribution Crawford had been promised, horror anthologies might have been accorded more respect.

A Selective Timeline of Horror Anthologies

1813 *Tales of the Dead*, translated from the French by Sarah Utterson
1835 *Tales of Terror*, edited by Henry St. Clair
1867 *A Stable for Nightmares*, edited by John Y. Akerman
1883 *Stories with a Vengeance*
1925 *Not at Night*, edited by Christine Campbell Thomson (first of eleven volumes)
1927 *The Moon Terror*, edited (anonymously) by Farnsworth Wright
1928 *Great Short Stories of Detection, Mystery, and Horror*, edited by Dorothy Sayers (first of a series)
1932 *Creeps, Shivers,* and *Shudders* (three separate volumes), edited by Charles Birkin
1944 *Sleep No More*, edited by August Derleth; *Great Tales of Terror and the Supernatural*, edited by Herbert Wise and Phyllis Fraser
1945 *The Garden of Fear*, edited by William L. Crawford
1947 *Dark of the Moon: Poems of Fantasy and the Macabre* (first anthology from Arkham House); *The Avon Fantasy Reader*, edited by Donald Wollheim
1967 *Dangerous Visions*, edited by Harlan Ellison
1973 *Demon Kind*, edited by Roger Elwood
1980 *Dark Forces*, edited by Kirby McCauley
1983 *Fantastic Tales*, edited by Italo Calvino; *Black Water*, edited by Alberto Manguel
1987 *The Dark Descent*, edited by David G. Hartwell
1988 *Prime Evil*, edited by Douglas A. Winter
2011 *The Weird*, edited by Ann and Jeff VanderMeer

One of the few anthologies to be published by a major press was *Sleep No More* (1944), edited by August Derleth, a well-respected Wisconsin regionalist writer. Derleth, however, was also co-founder in 1939, with Donald Wandrei, of the publishing firm Arkham House. Originally intended to put into print the works of the recently deceased and much missed H. P. Lovecraft, Arkham House rapidly began to publish dark fantasies and weird science by such living writers as Clark Ashton Smith, Ray Bradbury, Fritz Leiber, Frank Belknap Long, and Derleth himself. Its first anthology was *Dark of the Moon: Poems of Fantasy and the Macabre* (1947). Another anthology from a major press was *Great Tales of Terror and the Supernatural* (1944), edited by Herbert Wise and Phyllis Fraser, which collected fifty-two stories by such writers as Edgar Allan Poe, H. P. Lovecraft, Henry James, Algernon Blackwood, and Guy de Maupassant, as well as such contemporary mainstream writers as Ernest Hemingway and Dorothy Sayers. Its publication as part of Random House's Modern Library helped it to achieve, like Sayers's anthologies mentioned above, the status of a genre- and canon-defining book.

Unbound and softcover books—if not exactly paperbacks—had existed almost since the existence of movable type, and during the nineteenth and early twentieth centuries the German Tauchnitz imprint was well known for providing English-language editions of books for European readers. Furthermore, the American readers of the late nineteenth and early twentieth centuries were familiar with such paperbound works as dime novels and the book-sized imprints of Street & Smith. Nevertheless, no standardizations existed for size or pagination, and it was not until 1939—coincidentally, the year in which Arkham House's first book was published—that publisher Robert de Graaf partnered with American publisher Simon & Schuster to issue the Pocket Books imprint, thus creating what has become known as the "mass market paperback." Pocket Books proved sufficiently successful that other publishers rapidly followed suit, including, during the Second World War, the Council on Books in War Time, which issued paperbacks for the U.S. military and thus prepared an entire generation of readers for small and portable paperback books. Many of the Armed Services Editions were genre literature, but so far as is known, only one was horrific: H. P. Lovecraft's *The Dunwich Horror and Other Weird Tales* (1945?). Perhaps not coincidentally, a paperback collection of Lovecraft's writings was already in existence from another publisher, *The Weird Shadow over Innsmouth and Other Stories of the Supernatural* (1944).

Accompanying the development of the paperback was the realization that fiction could be anthologized and reprinted only so many times, and that purchasing audiences existed for paperbacks that printed original material. It would seem that American publisher and writer Donald Wollheim was the first to extend this recognition to fantasy and horror, with the series that became *The Avon Fantasy Reader* (1947). Other publishers followed suit.

From the late 1940s forward, then, horror anthologies existed in hardcover and paperback, their contents as likely to be original as reprint, and editors tended not to be too restrictive on definitions. Indeed, although representing ostensibly edgy science fiction, many of the stories in Harlan Ellison's *Dangerous Visions* (1967) were fantastic, and some, such as Fritz Leiber's "Gonna Roll the Bones" and Norman Spinrad's "Carcinoma Angels," were overtly horrific. Starting in the late 1960s, American editor Roger Elwood edited a number of anthologies, beginning with reprints in *The Little Monsters* (1969) and *Horror Hunters* (1971), and rapidly progressing to original contents in such works as *Demon Kind* (1973) and *The Berserkers* (1974). Furthermore, although children had often been protagonists in fairy tales and horror fiction, genre anthologies intended for a younger readership interested in horror literature had not previously been published. But these, too, began to appear at this time.

English-language horror anthologies were thus relatively widely available from the 1970s, in paperback as well as hardcover, and published by small presses as well as major publishers. Two events occurred to change the concept of anthologies. First, although numerous editors had compiled numerous horror anthologies, and a number of series had existed since Donald Wollheim's *Avon Fantasy Reader*, nobody had attempted to combine a widespread systematization of the selection of the contents with the systematic marketing of genre-specific anthologies. In 1974, Martin Harry Greenberg, a recent PhD in political science, compiled (with Patricia Warrick) *Political Science Fiction: An Introductory Reader* (1974) to assist with a class they were co-teaching. Recognizing that a market existed, he soon compiled other anthologies dealing with science fiction, and then he began branching into other subjects. He assembled a group of scholars and enthusiasts who were willing to assist him in compiling the contents, and found numerous writers willing to write genre-specific stories. The former included such people as Stefan Dziemianowicz and Robert E. Weinberg, and the books they co-edited included such titles as *Weird Tales: 32 Unearthed Terrors* (1988), *100 Ghastly Little Ghost Stories* (1993), *100 Creepy Little Creature Stories* (1994), and *Miskatonic University* (1996, only by Greenberg and Weinberg). At the time of his death in 2011, Greenberg had edited nearly 1,300 books, the majority of them fantastic, with a sizable percentage of these being fantasy and horror.

Changes in printing technology—the birth of so-called "desktop publishing"—and the near simultaneous digital revolution of the 1990s and beyond likewise changed the concept of anthologies. The former meant that costs of printing and binding could be minimized, there would be no costs for storage, and material could be distributed directly to purchasers rather than through intermediaries (bookstores). The latter initially meant that horror anthologies could be made available on CD-ROM at a fraction of the cost of a printed volume, and the new technology meant that not only could anthologies offer more stories, but their contents could include audio and video files to supplement the reading experience. Although CD-ROMs remain available, active horror anthologists who wish to avoid traditional print technologies now distribute their fiction via the World Wide Web and may use text, images, and sound in combination. Horror anthology websites exist for apparently all tastes. The traditional-minded will find fictive homages to such writers as Bram Stoker, William Hope Hodgson, and H. P. Lovecraft; the technologically inclined will find science fiction horror anthologies; and there is a great deal of erotic horror.

Finally, the digital revolution has allowed self-publishing to become reinvented and achieve a semi-respectability. While for some the term "self-publishing" implies an obsession with a photocopy machine—and before this, either a mimeograph or a hectograph—self-publishing is an enormous business, with such multinationals as Amazon competing with such companies as Lulu and Xlibris and iUniverse to deliver fiction to the reader, either in traditional book form or to such ereaders as Kindles and Nooks. That readers may likewise determine the contents of their anthologies, downloading and swapping out stories at will, not only guarantees the future of the anthology but permits the creation of communities of like-minded enthusiasts. The horrific anthology is, like so many monstrous and horrific beings, effectively immortal.

Richard Bleiler

See also: Horror Literature in the Internet Age; The Legacy of *Frankenstein*: From Gothic Novel to Cultural Myth; *Part One, Horror through History*: Horror in the Middle Ages; Horror in the Early Modern Era; Horror in the Nineteenth Century; Horror from 1900 to 1950; Horror from 1950 to 2000; Horror in the Twenty-First Century; *Part Three, Reference Entries*: Arkham House; Derleth, August; Ellison, Harlan; Le Fanu, J. Sheridan; Leiber, Fritz; Lovecraft, H. P.; O'Brien, Fitz-James; Wakefield, H. R.; Wandrei, Donald; *Weird Tales*.

Further Reading

Ashley, Mike, and William G. Contento. 1995. *The Supernatural Index: A Listing of Fantasy, Supernatural, Occult, Weird, and Horror Anthologies*. Westport, CT: Greenwood Press.

Chalker, Jack L., and Mark Owings. 1998. *The Science-Fantasy Publishers: A Bibliographic History, 1923–1998*. Westminster, MD, and Baltimore: Mirage Press.

Fraser, Phyllis, and Herbert Wise. [1944] 1994. *Great Tales of Terror and the Supernatural*. New York: Random House.

Hartwell, David G., ed. 1987. *The Dark Descent*. New York: Tor.

Hartwell, David G., ed. 1992. *Foundations of Fear*. New York: Tor.

Joshi, S. T. 2009. *Classics and Contemporaries: Some Notes on Horror Fiction*. New York: Hippocampus Press.

Utterson, Sarah. 1813. *Tales of the Dead*. London: White, Cochrane. http://knarf.english.upenn.edu/EtAlia/tdtp.html.

HORROR COMICS

Horror comics have long been a staple in the comic book industry, and they also have a curious history. Born in the 1940s as an offshoot of mainstream comic books, horror comics went on to color the imaginations of generations of readers, with an impact extending beyond comic books as such to influence the wider world of horror entertainment at large. They were also implicated in the mainstreaming of formerly "outsider" viewpoints in American society beginning in the 1970s.

In 1933 publisher Max Gaines (ca. 1895–1947) created the pamphlet-style "comic book" form. A decade later, in 1944, he founded Educational Comics (EC), which published such fare as *Picture Stories from the Bible* and other titles meant to ground children in morality. But this was not what his audiences wanted to read. Instead, they desired mainly tales of action and adventure. Gaines was also instrumental in the history of another early comics company, All-American Publications, which was later consolidated—along with National Comics and Detective Comics—into DC. He was also centrally involved in bringing both *Wonder Woman* and *Superman* to market. On his own, he tried new methods and continually worked to refine his approach, despite the lackluster performance of his overtly moralistic efforts.

Gaines died in a boating accident in 1947 while on vacation, and his son, William M. Gaines (1922–1992), known as Bill to his friends, became the president of the failing EC brand that same year, at the age of 25. One of the first things Bill Gaines decided to do was to change the company's name from "Educational Comics" to "Entertaining Comics," which signaled an internal shift of focus while retaining the recognizable EC logo. Ironically, the new EC would become—in a sense—even more instructive than its former incarnation, presenting readers with stories far more educational than any verbatim reading of Bible tales or classic literary fare.

After changing the company's name, the younger Gaines's next initiative was to carve away the titles that underperformed while adding others that appeared to have greater potential. The staff was not exempt from this reform: some of the existing artists and writers did not appeal to Gaines's personal aesthetic (he was an atheist, and also an ardent reader of science fiction and horror), and so he put out a call for interested novices to send their portfolios to his attention at EC's New York City headquarters. The resulting shakeup in the creative lineup at EC led to groundbreaking results, with a wholesale shift to publishing horror, science fiction, war, and satirical comics.

Of course, EC, although today it is the most recognizable brand name associated with the original golden age of such comics, was not the first comic book company to tackle these types of stories. Others had laid the groundwork by taking the elder Gaines's notion of the comic book and attempting to create sales through an assortment of approaches, including supernatural offerings and other popular trends, such as detective and crime stories. With a large debt to the pulps that had preceded them, these adventure-oriented comics were tinged with spectacular and often horrific elements. The first dedicated horror comic was likely Gilberton Publications' *Classic Comics* #13 (1943), which adapted Robert Louis Stevenson's 1886 novella *The Strange Case of Dr. Jekyll and Mr. Hyde*. Later, Avon Publications produced *Eerie* #1 (1947, the same year of Max Gaines's untimely death), which was comprised of all original horror content (and which is not to be confused with Warren Publishing's identically named title of the 1960s through the 1980s).

In light of these developments in the market, and freed from his father's overly moralistic influence, the third thing Bill Gaines did was to permanently move away from Max Gaines's vision and concentrate instead on the types of stories that interested him personally: tales of a speculative nature. Before he came to understand the real desires of his readership, Bill Gaines had played it cautious and tried to straddle the line between his ideas and those of his father. But this new and complete shift of focus was a stroke of genius all his own. Though it took some time to transition the old vision to the new, by about the end of 1951, the trajectory had been set and Gaines had assembled an amazing collection of new artists, writers, and editors for the EC stable: Al Feldstein, Johnny Craig, Jack Kamen, Ray Bradbury, Joe Orlando, Bernard Krigstein, Wally Wood, Jack Davis, Frank Frazetta, Graham Ingels, Al Williamson, Harvey Kurtzman, Will Eder, siblings John and Marie Severin, and more.

During this productive time for Gaines and EC, other companies played catch-up with Gaines's successful formula, though several of them had been dabbling in these areas prior to the conversion of EC from "Educational" to "Entertaining." EC, though now the most popular of these companies, was being eroded in the market due to competition from its rivals, who upped the ante with respect to the salacious and graphic images they were willing to offer. EC and Gaines, along with his support staff, such as Craig and Feldstein, were less interested in outdoing their competitors with gore and smut, and more interested in ensuring the quality of their stories and final product. They even began an exclusive partnership with the very popular author Ray Bradbury to adapt his works in comic book format with his approval and input.

Adding to these pressures of success were the condemnations of Dr. Fredric Wertham, an eminent American psychiatrist who turned his attention to the study of the comic book industry. As a senior psychiatrist with the New York Department of Hospitals, he focused on the very successful EC (which was also based in New York City) and its more lurid imitators, drawing bogus conclusions that boredom and entertainment, and comic books in particular, were the root causes of the rise in juvenile delinquency in the United States during this time. For good or ill, the foundations of his arguments—laid out in his shocking book *Seduction of the Innocent* (1954)—still resonate today, though the stress has now shifted away from comic books to sexuality and violence in video games, television, music, film, and other artistic and entertainment forms; and the criticism has expanded to encompass not just juvenile delinquency but an erosion or coarsening of the culture as a whole. Ironically, Wertham later renounced some of his beliefs; unfortunately, the die was cast.

Later in 1954, the U.S. Senate Subcommittee on Juvenile Delinquency convened hearings to address these concerns. Bill Gaines admirably defended the practices of the industry in general and EC particularly, but in spite of his strong performance in this battle, he and the rest of the trade would ultimately lose the war. As a result of the intense political pressure, the industry capitulated to self-regulation rather than risking further government intervention, and in the same year established the so-called Comics Code Authority (CCA), which oversaw a strict new "Code of Conduct" modeled on the motion picture Hays Code. These restrictions were solely for comic books; magazines—defined as an oversized format not aimed at children (though many of EC's most ardent readers were adult males)—were exempt. This would actually prove to be a boon for DC and Marvel Comics, two companies that had already mined the superhero concept to great effect, since the loss of, and refocus away from, horror and science fiction titles was less onerous for them than for some other publishers, especially Gaines's EC empire. As a result of these developments, EC was forced, after a brief and failed attempt at rebranding, to cancel all of its titles due to the burdensome restrictions. Only their popular *MAD* magazine survived, as it was already published in magazine format.

Later in the 1960s, one publisher decided to tackle the underrepresented horror comics market by staying in the larger magazine format, thus avoiding the quicksand of the CCA seal. Warren Publishing, owned by James Warren, was already

Significant Events in the History of Horror Comics

1933	Creation of the familiar pamphlet "comic book" by publisher Max Gaines (ca. 1895–1947).
1943	Gilberton Publications' *Classic Comics* #13 adapts Robert Louis Stevenson's 1886 novella *The Strange Case of Dr. Jekyll and Mr. Hyde*.
1944	Max Gaines founds Educational Comics (*Picture Stories from the Bible*, etc.).
1947	Avon Publications produces *Eerie* #1, comprised of all original horror content. Max Gaines dies in a boating accident, and his son, William M. Gaines, inherits Educational Comics.
1949–1950	William Gaines changes the direction of the company toward more genre-related works (horror, sci-fi, fantasy, war, Western, etc.); the name is changed to Entertaining Comics (commonly known as EC).
1954	Dr. Fredric Wertham publishes his bombshell book *Seduction of the Innocent*. U.S. Senate Subcommittee on Juvenile Delinquency convenes. The comic book industry agrees to self-regulate rather than risk further government intervention, establishing the Comics Code Authority (CCA) seal and a "Code of Conduct" modeled on the motion picture Hays Code.
1955	Due to CCA restrictions, EC cancels all titles except *MAD*, which is exempt from the CCA restrictions since it is in magazine format. Other companies comply with the CCA seal.
1957	James Warren founds Warren Publishing.
1958	Warren Publishing releases the first issue of *Famous Monsters of Filmland*.
1964	Warren Publishing: *Creepy* #1.
1966	Warren Publishing: *Eerie* #1.
1960s–late 1980s	Marvel and DC publish "light" horror titles (CCA approved): *House of Secrets* (DC), *House of Mystery* (DC), *Werewolf by Night* (Marvel), *Tomb of Dracula* (Marvel). Smaller independent houses such as Charlton and Gold Key publish dark or sci-fi fare (CCA approved): *The Twilight Zone*, *Star Trek*, *The Many Ghosts of Doctor Graves*, *Ghost Manor*, etc. Non-CCA fare flourishes as Underground Comix (counterculture in nature).
2011	The CCA is effectively abandoned.

successful in the magazine business as the publisher of *Famous Monsters of Film-land*, edited by the now-legendary Forrest J. Ackerman. Warren would eventually go on to publish several magazines—including the horror titles *Creepy*, *Eerie*, and *Vampirella* (a female vampire character created by Ackerman)—and to employ a number of EC alumni, including Jack Davis, Frank Frazetta (by then a well-respected fine artist), Al Williamson, John Severin, Joe Orlando, Johnny Craig, and others.

Beginning during this same era and peaking in the mid-to-late 1970s (as well as extending into the 1980s), Marvel and DC published lighter horror titles, including *House of Secrets* (DC), *House of Mystery* (DC), *Werewolf by Night* (Marvel), and *Tomb of Dracula* (Marvel). Some of these even boasted a "horror host" in the vein of the Crypt-Keeper, Vault-Keeper, and Old Witch characters that had provided introductions and closing commentary for EC's classic horror titles. Other independent houses such as Charlton and Gold Key continued offering dark or sci-fi fare (*The Twilight Zone*, *Ghost Manor*, *Star Trek*, *The Many Ghosts of Doctor Graves*, and more). Some of the proper superhero titles even got into the supernatural on occasion as the market and taste for "real" horror returned. Interestingly, comic book treatments (as opposed to magazines) burgeoned for the first time in years, causing their new creators to chafe at the restrictive CCA. The Code continued to exert a stranglehold on the mainstream comics industry, even as a few iconoclasts tried to push the envelope, most notably the Code-less "Underground Comix" in the late 1960s and 1970s, which, in keeping with the era's counterculture vibe, tried to stun the establishment awake by dealing overtly with themes, characters, situations, and images of sex, drug use, and violence, as opposed to using mere sociopolitical implication. Most of these eventually folded or morphed into something more "respectable," though a number of fine writers and artists—Greg Irons, William Stout, Robert Williams, Dan O'Bannon, Moebius, and others—were involved throughout this period of civil and artistic upheaval, arriving on the far side to enjoy larger rewards as their prescient outsider viewpoints were finally ingested and assimilated by society as a whole, and by popular culture specifically.

By the dawn of the 1980s, several new independent companies had sprung up, pushing the boundaries of eroticism/sexuality, violence, and conceptualism to fill the horror/sci-fi/mature comics void, among them Vortex (*Black Kiss*), First (*American Flagg!*), Eclipse (*The Rocketeer*), and Pacific (*Twisted Tales*, *Alien Worlds*). Eschewing the CCA, they would use artists and writers from EC and Warren on occasion, but would also highlight individuals greatly influenced by EC's long shadow, as well as the Underground Comix movement, including Dave Stevens, Bruce Jones, Richard Corben, Bernie Wrightson, Howard Chaykin, and Jeff Jones.

Ironically, the final blow for the end of self-censorship and the resurgence of horror comics into the world of "acceptable" fodder for mass entertainment would not come from indie publishers, most of whom would collapse under their own ambitions, though Dark Horse, Fantagraphics, and DC's more mature-oriented Vertigo still exist and are still publishing at the time of this writing. The real progress was foreshadowed by one venerable DC title that had originally been created by Len Wein and Bernie Wrightson in the early 1970s: *Swamp Thing*. In 1982 this was revamped and relaunched under the title *The Saga of the Swamp Thing*. In the hands of the writer Alan Moore (who would go on to work further revolutionary changes on the comic book form with the likes of *From Hell* and *Watchmen*), *Saga* lived up to its full potential, though Moore, a Brit, found it difficult to work under the strictures imposed by the CCA. *Saga* soon stopped carrying the seal, becoming the first comic to do so since the industry's adoption of the code in 1954. DC followed suit four years later with Frank Miller's groundbreaking Batman limited-series *The Dark Knight Returns* (1986). The CCA self-regulating code and seal have since been abandoned entirely.

The impact of horror comics on extraliterary forms of horror entertainment has been significant. In the 1970s the British film company Amicus released two anthology films (part of a wider series of horror-themed anthology films) based on EC comics, *Tales from the Crypt* (1972) and *Vault of Horror* (1973), starring major name actors such as Joan Collins, Peter Cushing, Christopher Lee, and Ralph Richardson. *Tales from the Crypt* was also adapted as a popular HBO television series (1989–1996) and two accompanying feature films, *Demon Knight* (1995) and *Bordello of Blood* (1996). EC comics have also been adapted for radio and children's television cartoons. Novelist Stephen King and film director George Romero collaborated on a well-received anthology movie consisting of EC-style stories, 1982's *Creepshow*, which was followed five years later by a (distinctly lesser) sequel. The production company behind *Creepshow*, Laurel Entertainment, went on to produce two popular American horror television series in the same vein, *Tales from the Darkside* (1983–1988) and *Monsters* (1988–1991). Swamp Thing has been the subject of two feature films (1982 and 1989) and a cable television series on USA Network (1990–1993). Alan Moore's graphic novel about Jack the Ripper, *From Hell*, was adapted as a major Hollywood movie starring Johnny Depp in 2001. Both artistically and socially, horror comics have a long, large, and important legacy.

Jason V Brock

See also: Horror Literature as Social Criticism and Commentary; Small Press, Specialty, and Online Horror; *Part One, Horror through History*: Horror from 1900 to 1950; Horror from 1950 to 2000; *Part Three, Reference Entries*: Bradbury, Ray; Moore, Alan; Pulp Horror.

Further Reading

Arndt, Richard J. 2013. *Horror Comics in Black and White: A History and Catalog, 1964–2004*. Jefferson, NC, and London: McFarland.

Benton, Mike. 1991. *Horror Comics: The Illustrated History*. Dallas: Taylor.

Gifford, Denis. 1984. *The International Book of Comics*. New York: Crescent Books.

Goulart, Ron. 1986. *Great History of Comic Books*. Chicago: Contemporary Books.

Hajdu, David. 2008. *The Ten-Cent Plague*. New York: Picador.

Round, Julia. 2014. *Gothic in Comics and Graphic Novels*. Jefferson, NC: McFarland.
Wright, Bradford W. 2001. *Comic Book Nation: The Transformation of Youth Culture in America*. Baltimore: Johns Hopkins University Press.

HORROR CRITICISM

Although horror studies is generally seen as a component of or a tool for evaluating cultural history, its significance alongside other, more "established" disciplines is seen by certain disciplines as somehow outside the study of intellectual ideas and patterns. However, modern developments over the last four decades have featured a broadening of the range—and acceptability—of inclusion in intellectual history, revealing in the process a rich sense of communication between "high" and "low" culture. The study of horror both in literature and in film was, in many ways, seen as outside the study of intellectual ideas and patterns perhaps because scholars failed to see the ways in which more established disciplines and horror criticism have mutually appropriated ideas and subject areas from one another. However, history has shown that horror's critical relegation would not stay that way for long.

Horror films are narratively constructed under an elaborate, self-cognizant, yet continuously evolving sociopolitical system of ideas and beliefs, a system that was not, to use the words of Peter E. Gordon, "developed chiefly by intellectuals," but that was developed collectively through empowered groups and individuals before diffusing into culture (Gordon 2014, 10). It is interesting to note that, in addition to culture, intellectual history, according to Gordon, is also concerned with politics, yet both culture and politics are inextricably tied to horror and vampire films. It may be speculated that, in part, intellectual history discounts horror and vampire studies because their particular objects of intelligent study are first mass culturally circulated and consumed, that is, dirtied or sullied, in "the realm of public discourse" before they are taken up for examination by scholars (Gordon 2014, 10). This may or may not be the case, but what can be said, with relative certainty, is that horror and vampires, when treated by intellectuals, reveal an elaborate design that has existed since their inception.

Horror studies, to cite the "Editorial" of the inaugural issue of the academic journal *Horror Studies*, examines "all cultural manifestations of horror, from the more familiar forms it assumes in literature and film, through to such lesser-known modes of expression as fashion, dance, fine art, music and technology" (*Horror Studies* 2010, 3). In the discipline's early years, however, it focused almost exclusively on the study of horror cinema, a subject area that, until the 1970s and 1980s, made only sporadic appearances in film studies journals and other discourses. This changed with the work of film critic Robin Wood, whose influential essay "An Introduction to the American Horror Film" (1979) is commonly credited with jumpstarting the discipline. Until that point, the horror genre itself had been treated like a second-class citizen, despite its apparent success among theater houses. In fact, little has changed today: the horror genre is still deemed "lowbrow," yet it has not lost its ability to draw in audiences. Wood's real scholarly achievement, notes contemporary horror studies scholar Adam Lowenstein, was in organizing (with Richard Lippe) "The American Nightmare," a special retrospective at the Toronto International Film Festival in 1979 that screened films by, and included discussions with, directors such as Wes Craven, Brian De Palma, George A. Romero, Stephanie Rothman, and David Cronenberg. Wood introduced horror cinema to Marxism and psychoanalytic theory (his essay "The American Nightmare: Horror in the '70's" [1986] continues this tradition), arguing that the horror genre's true subject is the recognition of all that is repressed or oppressed by civilization. He located at the center of American culture the contemporary American horror film and its conventions. Lowenstein adds:

> The American Nightmare bravely sought to move beyond the conventional associations attached to the horror genre: heartless exploitation, slipshod filmmaking, gratuitous violence, unrelieved misogyny, and an inherent silliness that precludes any substantial aesthetic or political ambitions. Against all odds, Wood wanted to take the horror film seriously. In fact, he titled his wide-ranging essay that opens the program notes "An Introduction to the American Horror Film," with its unmistakable connotations of wiping the slate clean, of showing us anew something we thought we understood perfectly well (or never deigned to understand at all). (Lowenstein 2016, 260)

Australian film studies professor Barbara Creed debuted her influential essay "Horror and the Monstrous-Feminine" in 1986 (expanding it to a book-length project in 1993), and it, like Wood's work, relied heavily upon psychoanalysis (as well as psychosexualism), locating horror within childhood. By 1987, film studies professor Carol J. Clover published "Her Body, Himself: Gender in the Slasher Film" (expanding it to a book-length project in 1992), which introduced the relatively new discipline of gender studies to the study of horror cinema. Finally, philosophy professor Noël Carroll rounded out what has become the canon of horror criticism with his *The Philosophy of Horror: Or, Paradoxes of the Heart* (1990), which examined philosophically, as well as cognitively, the aesthetics of horror fictions from film and radio to novels and short stories. In doing this, Carroll began to push the boundaries of horror studies beyond mere film.

Through the 1990s and mid-2000s, several scholars took up the proverbial torch by following Carroll's lead and moving beyond film, all the while relying upon the initial, seminal studies. Not least among these scholars are (in no particular order): Tony Williams, Adam Lowenstein, David J. Skal, Cynthia Freeland, Ken Gelder, Harry Benshoff, Richard J. Hand, Gregory A. Waller, Steffen Hantke, Rick Worland, Peter Hutchings, James Kendrick, Isabel C. Pinedo, I. Q. Hunter, Jeffrey Jerome Cohen, Mark Jancovich, Steven Jay Schneider, Ian Conrich, Kendall R. Phillips, Stephen Prince, Caroline Picart, Linda Badley, Jeffrew Andrew Weinstock, and many others. Yet, curiously, a closer look at the work of many of these same scholars shows a preoccupation with the much older discipline of literary studies and the Gothic. Fundamentally, Gothic studies are horror studies' older brother, though it is not unusual nowadays to see these two disciplines grouped together in trade publications and anthologies. Gothic studies are primarily concerned with both literature and the Gothic conventions established during the Romantic and Victorian periods. The two primary schools are the English and American Gothic, though in the last ten years these schools subdivided into more specialized units, such as the Southern Gothic, Asian Gothic, Irish Gothic, Australian Gothic, Spanish Gothic, and the more holistic Global Gothic. Yet it is not unusual to see the Gothic conventions and discourses of these schools appropriated by scholarship in horror studies, simply or especially because horror's cinematic roots are chiefly Gothic until the period of the 1940s. Scholarship on Gothic fiction ("horror" to modern eyes) is almost as old as the genre itself; consider, for example, Ann Radcliffe's 1826 essay "On the Supernatural in Poetry" in *The New Monthly Magazine*. However, the first modern studies of the Gothic, both critical and laudatory alike, appear in the 1920s in such distinguished literary journals as the *PMLA (Publications of the Modern Language Association)*, and again in the 1930s at the hands of André Breton and Montague Summers. Today, Gothic studies boasts of a critical and scholarly empire grander even than horror studies, with works from such scholars as Fred Botting, David Punter, Benjamin F. Fisher, Charles Crow, S. T. Joshi, Glennis Byron, Jerrold E. Hogle, William Hughes, Andrew Smith, Glennis Byron, Dale Townsend, Angela Wright, and Carol Margaret Davison, as well as several newer, equally accomplished scholars, not least among them Johan Höglund, Brigid Cherry, Andrew Hock Soon Ng, Catherine Spooner, and Xavier Aldana Reyes, who are bridging the divide between horror and the Gothic.

Monstrous Pedagogies: Seven Texts about Teaching Horror

Burger, Alissa. 2016. *Teaching Stephen King: Horror, the Supernatural, and New Approaches to Literature*. Basingstoke, UK: Palgrave Macmillan.

Golub, Adam, and Heather Richard Hayton, eds. 2017. *Monsters in the Classroom: Essays on Teaching What Scares Us*. Jefferson, NC: McFarland.

Hoeveler, Diane Long, and Tamar Heller, eds. 2003. *Approaches to Teaching Gothic Fiction: The British and American Traditions (Approaches to Teaching World Literature)*. New York: Modern Language Association of America.

Moreland, Sean, and Aalya Ahmad, eds. 2013. *Fear and Learning: Essays on the Pedagogy of Horror*. Jefferson, NC: McFarland.

Nevárez, Lisa A., ed. 2013. *The Vampire Goes to College: Essays on Teaching with the Undead*. Jefferson, NC: McFarland.

Powell, Anna, and Andrew Smith, eds. 2006. *Teaching the Gothic (Teaching the New English)*. Basingstoke, UK: Palgrave Macmillan.

Weinstock, Jeffrey Andrew, and Tony Magistrale, eds. 2008. *Approaches to Teaching Poe's Prose and Poetry (Approaches to Teaching World Literature)*. New York: Modern Language Association of America.

Queer studies has also seen several key players, from Linda Williams, Jack Halberstam, and Harry Benshoff, to Patricia MacCormack, Steven Bruhm, and George Haggerty, who have focused on theories of deviant representation and difference both in horror cinema and in literature of the Gothic(s). Queer writings share a long and curious history with horror and the Gothic. Richard Dyer (1998) notes in "Children of the Night: Vampirism as Homosexuality, Homosexuality as Vampirism" that one of the first gay stories to be published was indeed a vampire story. Early (as well as relatively later) Gothic fiction, when it was not the product of women, Dyer points out, was predominantly written by gay men. Benshoff's work on twenty-first-century queer horror cinema in *Monsters in the Closet: Homosexuality and the Horror Film* (1997) argues that monsters in American cinema were, and continue to be, framed in accordance with the socialized conception of homosexuality—"or more broadly queerness"—of the particular era in which they appear (Benshoff 1997, 131). In a 2012 update to his book, Benshoff examines how queer monsters continue to come out of the closet, and these days in much greater numbers. Studies like Benshoff's are important, for without the use of a queer studies lens, these developments might have remained hidden from horror studies. Moreover, without acknowledging their queer status, or the queer status of certain other past and future monstrous figures, queer studies will remain decidedly limited.

Just as the late 2000s through early 2010s saw a "vampire renaissance" (then, subsequently, a "zombie renaissance") in fiction and film, horror criticism also saw a golden age, which is currently still unfolding with no end in sight as yet. Today, horror criticism has branched out into more disciplines than ever, and the last decade alone has seen an almost daunting number of books and articles going to print in the field. Publishers are finding horror studies more lucrative now than ever, especially university presses, which are finding themselves in need of titles that will keep them afloat. These days, scholarly self-justification for studies in horror is starting to become more and more *passé* given the mass of critical materials on the subject that have appeared since the late 1970s. However, if one publishes in a media studies journal or queer theory journal an analysis of, say, the sexual representations in *Jeepers Creepers* (2001), then the analysis is "media studies" or "queer theory." But if it is published in the journals *Horror Studies* or the *Irish Journal of Gothic and Horror Studies*, or in the University of Wales Press's new "Horror Studies" book series, then the analysis is labeled "horror studies." Publishing in horror studies journals can thus still carry with it a certain taboo, perhaps because horror cinema's grim nature and populist appeal has a tendency to blind some critics to horror studies' intellectual capacity. However, the kinds of contributions horror and Gothic criticism are able to offer to both film and literary studies, as well as queer studies, more than evidence their legitimacy as a division of intellectual history.

Indeed, horror criticism not only broadens film and literary studies, it can help to change minds as well. Educators who use horror studies and criticism in their curricula do not have to limit themselves to giving a historiography of horror fiction, poetry, and film, but can instead help their students to observe and understand horror's functionality within a much broader cultural framework. Jeffrey Jerome Cohen aptly notes in his seminal work *Monster Theory: Reading Culture* (1996) that monsters do cultural work. Helping students to understand monsters through this particular critical lens can incite in them the desire to begin the process of divorcing their minds and actions from oppressive ideologies and promote inclusivity. Few other disciplines have the ability, let alone the capacity, for stimulating such a rich sense of communication between "high" and "low" culture. In the end, perhaps therein lies the real dilemma: that such a restrictive hierarchization is not preserving intellectual history but rather impeding it.

John Edgar Browning

See also: Gender, Sexuality, and the Monsters of Literary Horror; The Gothic Literary Tradition; Horror Literature as Social Criticism and Commentary; *Part Three, Reference Entries*: Monsters; Vampires.

Further Reading

Benshoff, Harry M. 1997. *Monsters in the Closet: Homosexuality and the Horror Film*. Manchester: Manchester University Press.

Browning, John Edgar. 2012. "Towards a Monster Pedagogy: (Re)claiming the Classroom for the Other." In *Fear and Learning: Essays on the Pedagogy of Horror*, edited by Sean Moreland and Aalya Ahmad, 40–55. Jefferson, NC: McFarland.

Carroll, Noël. 1990. *The Philosophy of Horror: Or, Paradoxes of the Heart*. New York: Routledge.

Cohen, Jeffrey Jerome, ed. 1996. *Monster Theory: Reading Culture*. Minneapolis: University of Minnesota Press.

Dyer, Richard. 1998. "Children of the Night: Vampirism as Homosexuality, Homosexuality as Vampirism." In *Sweet Dreams: Sexuality, Gender, and Popular Fiction*, edited by Susannah Radstone, 47–72. London: Lawrence & Wishart.

"Editorial." 2010. *Horror Studies* 1, no. 1: 3.

Gelder, Ken, ed. 2000. *The Horror Reader*. New York: Routledge.

Gordon, Peter E. 2014. "What Is Intellectual History? A Frankly Partisan Introduction to a Frequently Misunderstood Field." Paper presented at the Future of the History of Ideas Workshop, University of Sydney, Australia August 12.

Lowenstein, Adam. 2016. "A Reintroduction to the American Horror Film." In *American Film History: Selected Readings, Vol. II: 1960 to the Present*, edited by Cynthia Lucia, Roy Grundmann, and Art Simon, 259–274. Malden, MA Wiley-Blackwell.

Nelson, Victoria. 2013 *Gothicka: Vampire Heroes, Human Gods, and the New Supernatural*. Cambridge, MA: Harvard University Press.

Skal, David. J. 1993. *The Monster Show: A Cultural History of Horror*. New York: Penguin Books.

HORROR LITERATURE AND SCIENCE FICTION

Horror and science fiction have far more in common than purists of either genre may initially realize. It has been argued that science fiction works from the premise that the universe is inherently knowable. If that is so, then horror is one of the many possible responses to what that knowledge reveals, and the most powerful.

Conversely, horror and its associated emotion, dread, blossom when the rationalist perspective often prioritized in science fiction is found wanting, or when that rationalism leads to a place where it undoes itself. In this sense, horror and science fiction are complementary, if differing, means of knowing the world.

Horror and science fiction are distinguished first and foremost by the marketing strategies of publishers. This was not always the case. Throughout the nineteenth century and into the early twentieth, nonrealist literature appeared in numerous magazines and serials, often with no established generic distinctions. It was not until 1926, when Hugo Gernsback published *Amazing Stories*, that a specific market space was created for science fiction. Gernsback established in the pages of his pulp magazine a back history for his preferred story type (then referred to as "scientifiction") that excluded supernatural-flavored fiction in favor of the scientific romances of H. G. Wells and the engineering speculations of Jules Verne. This historical moment of divergence is a result of a business model based on marketing factors and editorial concerns, including pedagogical concerns, since Gernsback wanted to prepare young men for a technologically rich future that included space travel.

Amazing Stories, however, was not so much a point of genre demarcation as it was a moment of thematic sublimation. Put another way, horror moved forward as a literature preoccupied with the supernatural and otherworldly in publications not devoted exclusively to science fiction even as it continued to play a fundamental role in what was otherwise marketed as science fiction. An example of this sublimation is Edmond Hamilton's "The Man Who Evolved" (1931), first published in another of Gernsback's pulps, *Wonder Stories*. The story follows a scientist who propels himself through various stages of human evolution, with each development ever more horrifying to the two colleagues who watch his progression. The end result of this forced evolution is a return to the primordial protoplasm from which life on Earth sprang. This knowledge drives one of the observers mad while the other is just barely able to escape with his life and sanity. "The Man Who Evolved" is an early example of how the trappings of scientific rhetoric and reasoning work in science fiction, yet its narrative devices are firmly grounded in the supernatural or ghost story of the preceding century. Similarly, C. L. Moore's "Shambleau," first published in *Weird Tales* in 1933, is grounded in the tone and imagery of the horror tale and can be read as a precursor to the body horror that emerged in literature and film in the second half of the twentieth century. The titular Shambleau, a vampiric Medusa-like alien creature that devours the soul of any man unlucky enough to fall in love with it, is a throwback to the supernatural creatures of older literary traditions even as it reconfigures them in a science fictional landscape, in this case Mars.

The stories by Hamilton and Moore are foundational texts in science fiction and demonstrate how horror elements were deeply ingrained in science fiction's generic origin point. This should perhaps come as no surprise given that science fiction, it has been argued, first by Brian Aldiss and subsequently by many others, has its thematic origin in the Gothic, specifically Mary Shelley's *Frankenstein* (1818; revised 1831). Scholars will undoubtedly continue to deliberate the beginning point of science fiction—either 1818, 1926, or hundreds, if not thousands, of years earlier—but what is important to note is that horror is at once the genre's precursor and its simultaneous offshoot. This position is not contradictory, but rather indicative of how the genres inform and influence each other.

Situated between *Frankenstein* and *Amazing Stories* is Algernon Blackwood's "The Willows" (1907). It is hard to overestimate the influence and importance of this story of two men who are terrorized by an unseen force. The language and tone is that of supernatural horror, but the underlying science fictional conceit is that of an agency, which is antithetical to the well-being of the human species, that originates from an unknown yet material dimension. It is Blackwood who introduces the idea of these Other spaces as organic properties of the knowable universe and not as visitations from its opposite, the nonmaterial or spiritual realm. This notion of a hostile universe is not new, but it is science fictionalized by Blackwood and later amplified to great degree and effect by H. P. Lovecraft in stories published from 1921 to 1937, which later came to be associated with the Cthulhu Mythos cycle and which in turn created the cosmic dread subcategory of horror and science fiction that remains popular to this day. That Lovecraft is so often thought of as a writer of horror gives some insight into the power of tone, language, and style. Lovecraft is a horror writer, but he is every bit a science fiction writer, too, with his rich treasury of extraterrestrial and pan-dimensional beings and his mutated, hybrid country folk.

A Selective Timeline of Horror and Science Fiction

1818	*Frankenstein, or The Modern Prometheus* by Mary Shelley
1886	*The Strange Case of Dr. Jekyll and Mr. Hyde* by Robert Louis Stevenson
1896	*The Island of Dr. Moreau* by H. G. Wells
1897	*The Invisible Man* by H. G. Wells
1901	*The Purple Cloud* by M. P. Shiel
1907	"The Willows" by Algernon Blackwood
1912	*The Night Land* by William Hope Hodgson
1927	"The Colour out of Space" by H. P. Lovecraft
1928	"The Call of Cthulhu" by H. P. Lovecraft
1929	"The Hounds of Tindalos" by Frank Belknap Long
1931	"The Man Who Evolved" by Edmond Hamilton
1933	"Shambleau" by C. L. Moore
1936	*At the Mountains of Madness* and "The Shadow out of Time" by H. P. Lovecraft
1944	"Killdozer" by Theodore Sturgeon
1951	*The Day of the Triffids* by John Wyndham
1954	*I Am Legend* by Richard Matheson

1957   *The Midwich Cuckoos* by John Wyndham
1967   "I Have No Mouth and I Must Scream" by Harlan Ellison; *The Mind Parasites* by Colin Wilson
1972   *The Stepford Wives* by Ira Levin
1979   *Sandkings* by George R. R. Martin
1980   "The Autopsy" by Michael Shea
1981   *The Vampire Tapestry* by Suzy McKee Charnas
1984   "Bloodchild" by Octavia E. Butler
1987   *The Tommyknockers* by Stephen King
2000   *Perdido Street Station* by China Miéville; *Punktown* by Jeffrey Thomas
2001   *City of Saints and Madmen* by Jeff VanderMeer
2002   *The Scar* by China Miéville
2003   *Veniss Underground* by Jeff VanderMeer
2004   *Iron Council* by China Miéville
2005   *Fledgling* by Octavia E. Butler
2007   *Deadstock* by Jeffrey Thomas
2008   *Blue Wars* by Jeffrey Thomas
2009   *Under the Dome* by Stephen King
2011   *11/22/63* by Stephen King
2014   The Southern Reach Trilogy by Jeff VanderMeer

A rich cadre of genre writers emerged in the mid-twentieth century who proved themselves adept at writing horror, science fiction, fantasy, or some hybrid of all three. Charles Beaumont, Ray Bradbury, Fredrick Brown, John W. Campbell, Fritz Leiber, Henry Kuttner, Richard Matheson, Frank M. Robinson, Theodore Sturgeon, Manly Wade Wellman, and John Wyndham all moved rather effortlessly between at least two if not all three modes. Writers who have since followed include Clive Barker, Laird Barron, Harlan Ellison, Dennis Etchison, Kelly Link, George R. R. Martin, and Lucius Shepard. But this small sampling of mid- and late-century writers is hardly indicative of the degree to which horror and science fiction overlap. Any attempt to produce an exhaustive list would be impossible and fruitless, and would indicate how on some level the distinction between horror and science fiction is largely one of rhetorical stratagems, narrative devices, and marketing. The work of Ira Levin, author of *Rosemary's Baby* (1967), serves as a good example. His *The Stepford Wives* (1972) develops its science fictional theme, robots, into a novel of escalating horror, while *The Boys from Brazil* (1976) works its science fictional premise, cloning, into a mainstream thriller narrative with political overtones. More central to the horror tradition is Stephen King, whose *Carrie* (1974) is grounded in its titular protagonist's (pseudo) scientific telekinetic ability, a theme revisited in *Firestarter* (1980). Of his many novels, *The Stand* (1978, revised 1990), which depicts human civilization decimated by an engineered plague; *The Tommyknockers* (1987), which depicts how an alien spaceship creates a hive mind out of a local population; *Under the Dome* (2009), which shows alien children trapping a small town within a dome; and *11/22/63* (2011), a time travel story that revolves around the Kennedy assassination, are his most overtly science fictional in their premise, but there are other examples in both his long and short fiction.

Another way of thinking about horror and science fiction is to consider how writers such as Levin and King use genre in the service of ideas, stylistic decisions, or social trends. Such an approach uses the science fictional premise as a springboard toward some other form of narrative play. Other writers, however, seem more invested in core horror and science fiction aesthetics for their own sakes. Contemporary examples include China Miéville, Jeff VanderMeer, and Jeffrey Thomas. Miéville is certainly the most political of the three, as expressed in his New Crobuzon sequence of novels *Perdido Street Station* (2000), *The Scar* (2002), and *Iron Council* (2004). VanderMeer is the most stylistically conscious, as exhibited by *City of Saints and Madmen* (2001), *Veniss Underground* (2003), and the Southern Reach Trilogy (2014). And Thomas is the most—in a good way—pulpish, as conveyed in the thematic collection *Punktown* (2000, expanded 2003) and the novels *Deadstock* (2007) and *Blue War* (2008). These three writers, radically different and singular, nevertheless share one encompassing trait: a disdain for generic divisions that is exceeded only by their commitment to and embrace of the generic treasury of images, themes, styles, and tropes that together define what is thought of most broadly as nonrealist literature. Whatever anxiety may arise from violating generic distinction is totally absent from this group of writers and others like them, and is instead replaced by a sense of freedom and play. Ironically, it may be this complete obliteration of generic distinction that ultimately characterizes horror and science fiction in its purest mode.

Javier A. Martinez

See also: Apocalyptic Horror; The Gothic Literary Tradition; The Legacy of *Frankenstein*: From Gothic Novel to Cultural Myth; Weird and Cosmic Horror Fiction; *Part Three, Reference Entries*: *At the Mountains of Madness*; Ballard, J. G.; Barker, Clive; Barron, Laird; Beaumont, Charles; Blackwood, Algernon; Bradbury, Ray; Butler, Octavia E.; "The Call of Cthulhu"; "The Colour out of Space"; *Communion*; Cthulhu Mythos; Datlow, Ellen; Derleth, August; Dick, Philip K.; Ellison, Harlan; Etchison, Dennis; Forbidden Knowledge or Power; Hand, Elizabeth; *I Am Legend*; "I Have No Mouth and I Must Scream"; *The Invisible Man*; *The Island of Dr. Moreau*; King, Stephen; Kneale, Nigel; Kuttner, Henry; Leiber, Fritz; Link, Kelly; Long, Frank Belknap; Lovecraft, H. P.; Lumley, Brian; Mad Scientist; Matheson, Richard; Miéville, China; *The Mind Parasites*; Morrow, W. C.; New Weird; Newman, Kim; *The Night Land*; Pulp Horror; *Sandkings*; Shea, Michael; Shiel, M. P.; Simmons, Dan; *The Strange Case of Dr. Jekyll and Mr. Hyde*; Sturgeon, Theodore; VanderMeer, Jeff; *Weird Tales*; Wellman, Manly Wade; Wells, H. G.; "The Willows"; Wyndham, John; Zombies.

Further Reading

Aldiss, Brian, and David Wingrove. 1986. *Trillion Year Spree: The History of Science Fiction*. London: Gollancz.

Colavito, Jason. 2008. *Knowing Fear: Science, Knowledge, and the Development of the Horror Genre*. Jefferson, NC: McFarland.

Freedman, Carl. 2002. "Hail Mary: On the Author of *Frankenstein* and the Origins of Science Fiction." *Science Fiction Studies* 29: 253–264.

Lawler, Donald. 1988. "Reframing *Jekyll and Hyde*: Robert Louis Stevenson and the Strange Case of Gothic Science Fiction." In *Dr. Jekyll and Mr. Hyde after One Hundred Years*, edited by William Veeder and Gordon Hirsch, 247–261. Chicago: University of Chicago Press.

Nelson, Victoria. 2012. *Gothicka: Vampire Heroes, Human Gods, and the New Supernatural*. Cambridge, MA: Harvard University Press.

Oakes, David A. 2000. *Science and Destabilization in the Modern American Gothic: Lovecraft, Matheson, and King*. Westport, CT: Greenwood Press.

Rauch, Alan. 1995. "The Monstrous Body of Knowledge in Mary Shelley's *Frankenstein*." *Studies in Romanticism* 34: 227–253.

Skal, David J. 1998. *Screams of Reason: Mad Science and Modern Culture*. New York: W. W. Norton.

Stableford, Brian. 2009. "Horror in Science Fiction." In *Gothic Grotesques: Essays on Fantastic Literature*, 11–23. Rockville, MD: Wildside Press.

Tibbetts, John C. 2012. *The Gothic Imagination: Conversations on Fantasy, Horror, and Science Fiction in the Media*. New York: Palgrave Macmillan.

Wolfe, Gary K. 2011. "Evaporating Genres." In *Evaporating Genres: Essays on Fantastic Literature*, 18–53. Middletown, CT: Wesleyan University Press. http://www.strangehorizons.com/2013/20130722/2wolfe-a.shtml.

HORROR LITERATURE AS SOCIAL CRITICISM AND COMMENTARY

From primordial cosmogonic myths (myths about the origin of the cosmos) to early modern fairy tales, from the Christian theological purpose of seventeenth-century apparition narratives to the liberal working-class ethos of Stephen King's fictions, narratives that use fear and horror to instill moral lessons and provide social commentary have an ancient provenance and a tremendous variety. A brief, partial survey of the history, prospects, and potential problems of such narratives, focusing particularly on those that have had a large role in shaping modern English language horror fiction, can provide valuable insight into the workings of horror fiction as a whole.

Among the oldest extant literary works, the Mesopotamian *Epic of Gilgamesh* (approximately 2100 BCE) presents a mythic protagonist whose initial cruelty to his subjects leads the gods to seek his punishment, and whose later despair at the prospect of his own inevitable death serves both to make him more sympathetically human and to call into question the association between worldly power and divine immortality. The epic thereby both inscribes and interrogates cultural values and social norms, and its focus on the fear of death invests it with a resonance that is practically universal. Recognizing the potency of pathos, many ancient Greek poets and playwrights used horror to both stir audiences and interrogate their beliefs. Tragedies including Aeschylus's *The Oresteia* (approximately 458 BCE), Euripides's *Hecuba* (approximately 424 BCE) and *The Bacchae* (approximately 405 BCE), and Sophocles's *Oedipus the King* (429 BCE) present powerful syntheses of physical violence, emotional extremity, and supernatural control over human affairs, using them to frame questions about Greek religion, culture, and social values in ways that make them key precursors to works of modern horror literature.

Even more pointedly, the final book of Roman poet Lucretius's *De rerum natura* (55 BCE), whose vision of universal atomic transformation and decay had a profound effect on the development of modern cosmic horror, provides a harrowing account of the effects of the plague at Athens derived from the historian Thucydides. Its horrors, however, are wielded as didactic weapons by Lucretius, who uses the inevitable terror and sufferings of death as the capstone for his attempt to persuade the reader of the value, even the necessity, of rejecting religious superstitions and accepting Epicurean epistemology and ethics. Lucretius emphasizes that it is the lack of comprehension of the nature and necessity of death that leads the plague's victims to their violent and irrational behaviors.

However, Lucretius's modern reception also suggests the degree to which horror's visceral manifest content can entirely overshadow its ability to function as social criticism, as it is the poem's visions of suffering and disintegration that made the greatest impression on most of its readers throughout the intervening millennia, to the extent that its vision of panicked putrescence is echoed by two of the most important early examples of literary body horror, Edgar Allan Poe's (1809–1849) "Facts in the Case of M. Valdemar" (1845) and H. P. Lovecraft's (1890–1937) "Cool Air" (1928). In both these tales, the attempt to prolong human life through (pseudo) scientific means leads to putrid conclusions.

Some literary works use horror to effect social criticism more overtly and explicitly than others, often through an emphasis on the allegorical or symbolic dimensions of supernatural threats. In works of literary horror from Matthew Lewis's *The Monk* (1796), which satirizes Roman Catholic beliefs, to Richard Matheson's *I Am Legend* (1954), which crystallizes and interrogates Cold War and civil rights–era anxieties, to Joe Hill's *The Fireman* (2016), which connects a deadly infection to the escalating role of outrage in contemporary cultural politics, elements of supernaturalism are often used to frame social issues.

When handled this way, horror as a form of social criticism can potentially be pointed and specific, and tends to function much like satire; where the latter targets certain beliefs, behaviors, or types of people by ridiculing them, the former transfigures anxieties about certain beliefs, behaviors, or people into objects of terror. The use of supernatural threats as allegories of social crisis goes back at least to the early modern era; one striking example occurs in the early eighteenth century, during the apparent epidemic of bloodthirsty revenants in Eastern Europe that helped spark the popular rise of the literary vampire. In response to various accounts of corpses rising from their graves and attacking their family and neighbors, one anonymous commentator wrote to the British journal *The Craftsman*: "These Vampyres are said to torment and kill the Living by sucking out all their Blood; and a ravenous Minister, in this part of the World, is compared to a Leech or a Blood-sucker, and carries his Oppressions beyond the Grave, by anticipating the publick Revenues, and entailing a perpetuity of Taxes, which must gradually drain the Body Politick of its Blood and Spirits" (Butler 2010, 53).

Of course, the history of horror fiction, like the history of literary satire, offers many examples of social criticism that are more likely to be understood as reactionary rather than radical. For example, *The Monk* notably propagated a wide variety of specious Anglican stereotypes about Roman Catholic belief; Bram Stoker's *Dracula* (1897) is inseparable from its author's patriarchal, Victorian anxieties about the social dangers of female sexuality and the "dangers" of foreign immigration into England; Lovecraft's obsession with the "corrupting" dangers of multiculturalism and his desire to police the boundaries of white, Anglo-American culture are writ large even in many of his least polemical fictions; and Dean Koontz's (1945–) conservative family values are obvious in many of his horror novels. This prevailing tendency led King, in his influential autobiographical study of horror, *Danse Macabre* (1981), to compare horror writers to Republican bankers in three-piece suits, exploiting social anxieties for their own gain.

On the other hand, there are many examples of classic horror fictions producing positive social change through pointed criticism. While her best-known tale, "The Yellow Wall-Paper" (1892), is a chilling psychological variation on the ghost story often reprinted in Gothic anthologies, Charlotte Perkins Gilman (1860–1935) expressly wrote it as a critique of the Victorian medical profession's damaging, infantilizing treatment of women diagnosed with hysteria. Though the story became widely read and vitally influential, Gilman was aware that many readers, appreciating it primarily as a work of fictional horror, remained unaware of the story's autobiographical and social-critical context, and wrote the brief essay "Why I Wrote the Yellow Wallpaper" (1911) nearly two decades later in an attempt to counter this. The tendency of Gilman's readers to understand "ghost story/horror story" and "literary social criticism" as mutually exclusive categories anticipates a prevailing critical tendency through much of the twentieth century to see horror fiction, as well as related speculative genres, as purely pop-cultural entertainment, and therefore divorced from the probing social and moral scrutiny associated with and expected from "high" literature. This misperception of horror, as well as the other speculative genres, is both as widespread and as mistaken today as it was in Gilman's time. As influential American writer Joyce Carol Oates (1938–) states, "The essential horror springs from life—fiction is a mirror of life, sometimes distorted in the interests of meaning, sometimes raw and unmediated. There is no fiction so horrifying as the horror of actual life—not just life in wartime, or life amid violence, but the incursions of our ordinary lives upon us: aging, illness, gradual loss of family and friends.

Sometimes to tell a realistic story, you must choose a non-realistic form to emphasize a point—this is the power of genre" (Morton 2014).

Despite this recognition, the perceived association between horror and, on the one hand, purely sensationalistic entertainment and, on the other, a departure from realism and an embrace of fantastic and supernatural elements, has led many modern and contemporary writers to query or outright reject the label "horror" as applied to their work. American writer Flannery O'Connor (1925–1964), for example, known for her use of Gothic and grotesque elements, viewed classification of her stories as "horror" as misguided, writing, "The stories are hard but they are hard because there is nothing harder or less sentimental than Christian realism. I believe that there are many rough beasts slouching toward Bethlehem to be born and I have reported the progress of a few of them, and when I see these stories described as horror stories I am always amused because the reviewer always has hold of the wrong horror" (O'Connor 1988, 90). Contemporary weird fictionist Caitlín R. Kiernan has similarly rejected the term "horror" for her fiction, precisely because she sees it as antithetical to her desire to pose ethical questions and challenge the reader's ability to empathize and identify with the Other.

If "horror" is defined primarily as the intention to elicit a strong emotional response from readers that combines fear and disgust with other affective, ethical, or

The Heresy of the Didactic

In his posthumously published essay "The Poetic Principle" (1850), Edgar Allan Poe articulated what he called the "heresy of the didactic," rejecting the idea that literature should provide moral instruction; instead, the province of art, he said, was the creation of beauty, of effect, of atmosphere. Thus Poe anticipated much of the art for art's sake sensibility of the later Symbolist and Decadent movements, as well as twentieth-century movements including Dada and surrealism, which influenced twentieth-century horror and weird fiction.

However, the rejection of overt didacticism and the possibility of literature as social criticism are not mutually exclusive. Poe's attack on the nineteenth century's idol of didacticism was itself a social criticism. As many readers have noted, Poe's tales are not without moral undercurrents or social engagements. Indeed, the question of moral culpability is one Poe turns to time and again in tales like "The Black Cat" (1843) and "The Tell-Tale Heart" (1843). The social relevance of such tales is amplified as they were written at a moment when British and American jurisprudence wrestled with the complex issue of legal culpability in cases where mental illness was a factor, an issue that would lead to the M'Naghten rules in British law in 1843, and one that continues to haunt, and be haunted by, contemporary horror fictions including Patrick McGrath's *Spider* (1990) and Joyce Carol Oates's *Zombie* (1995).

Source: Poe, Edgar Allan. 1902. *The Complete Works of Edgar Allan Poe: Literary Criticism IV*. Edited by James A. Harrison. New York: Society of English and French Literature.

aesthetic concerns viewed as only secondary effects, then surely O'Connor and Kiernan are right to reject the label. Understood this way, horror is necessarily an exploitative genre, predisposed to demonize and denigrate difference and change, converting it into a transient "buzz" of subjective intensity. While this description surely seems suited to some works of horror fiction, it is ultimately reductive. If, however, influential film theorist Robin Wood's view that what constitutes "radical," and therefore valuable, horror is that it cultivates the audience's (or reader's) sympathy for the monster, and uses this sympathy to challenge normative and hegemonic assumptions, then the possibilities for horror's functioning as a form of radical social commentary are greatly expanded.

While they are arguably examples of science fiction as much as of horror, vampirism-focused fictions including Suzy McKee Charnas's *The Vampire Tapestry* (1980), Jewelle Gomez's *The Gilda Stories* (1991), and Octavia E. Butler's *Fledgling* (2005) demonstrate this possibility by using many recognizable tropes of horror fiction to produce salient and nuanced examinations of the way racial and sexual difference is constructed in contemporary American society. Both of these novels suggest and problematize parallels between their "supernatural" protagonists and marginalized social groups, refusing easy allegorical interpretations while still vividly reframing widespread cultural concepts.

The critical role played by horror literature also need not be limited to its overt framing of particular topics. Indeed, if Poe's rejection of the "heresy of the didactic" and his criticisms of allegory are taken seriously, horror, like any literary form in which affect, tone, and atmosphere are crucial, will tend to be more effective when its social-critical or symbolic aspects are an undercurrent, however forceful. More broadly, critics and theorists of horror including Barbara Creed and Noël Carroll have argued that horror can itself best be understood through the work of abjection (confrontation with the fear and loathing of the rejected "other") and the transgression of cultural categories, in which case horror only exists as a literary mode when it offers unsettling challenges to accepted cultural norms.

As Gina Wisker writes, "the objects and subjects of horror are not always what they appear to be and are very often socially, politically, and culturally transgressive and challenging. Restoring order, which is itself dubious and questionable, destructive, and illegitimate (oppressive gender roles, slavery, imperialism, capitalism, etc.) is not always the aim of the radical horror writer" (Wisker 2005, 10). This view is shared by influential British horror writer Ramsey Campbell, who states: "Horror fiction is in the business of going too far, of showing the audience things they've avoided seeing or thinking. Very much like humour, it's in the business of breaking taboos, and it follows that once those taboos are broken the fiction tends to lose power, to become 'safe'" (quoted in Joshi 2001, 20).

Sean Moreland

See also: Gender, Sexuality, and the Monsters of Literary Horror; Horror Criticism; *Part One, Horror through History*: Horror in the Ancient World; Horror in the Early

Modern Era; *Part Three, Reference Entries*: Butler, Octavia E.; Campbell, Ramsey; Charnas, Suzy McKee; Hill, Joe; *I Am Legend*; Kiernan, Caitlín R.; Koontz, Dean; Lovecraft, H. P.; *The Monk*; Oates, Joyce Carol; O'Connor, Flannery; "The Yellow Wall-Paper."

Further Reading

Butler, Erik. 2010. *Metamorphoses of the Vampire in Literature and Film: Cultural Transformations in Europe, 1732–1933*. Studies in German Literature, Linguistics, and Culture (Unnumbered). Rochester, NY: Camden House.

Joshi, S. T. 2001. *Ramsey Campbell and Modern Horror Fiction*. Liverpool: Liverpool University Press.

Morton, Lisa. 2014. "Interview with Joyce Carol Oates." *Nightmare Magazine* 25. http://www.nightmare-magazine.com/nonfiction/interview-joyce-carol-oates.

O'Connor, Flannery. 1988. *The Habit of Being: Letters of Flannery O'Connor*. Edited by Sally Fitzgerald. New York: Farrar, Straus and Giroux.

Poe, Edgar Allan. 1902. *Collected Works XI*. Edited by James A. Harrison. New York: Crowell. 71. See also *X*, 60–71; *XI*, 67–85; and *XIII*, 148–155.

Wisker, Gina. 2005. *Horror Fiction: An introduction*. New York: Continuum.

HORROR LITERATURE IN THE INTERNET AGE

The Internet age is the current period of contemporary history. Alternatively referred to as the computer age, the digital age, or the new media age, this period is marked by the computerization of information and the growth of online connectivity via social, financial, and informational networks. In addition, it also corresponds to the growth of digital technology. Though much of the relevant technology has its origins in the latter decades of the twentieth century, the Internet age is largely considered an umbrella term for the twenty-first century so far. The advent of Web 2.0 is of particular significance, since this saw the Internet change from a largely static information source to a fluid, user-generated, networked community. It was crucial in the movement toward an interactive online "life."

As with all technological and cultural developments, the Internet age and its attendant technologies has had a profound impact on the landscape of horror. The increasing power of digital technology has afforded filmmakers, game designers, and artists the means to create horror with unprecedented visual sophistication. Equally, online networks provide both a marketplace for global sales of horror media and the opportunity for fans of the genre to meet, discuss, and create. The Internet is full of websites devoted to horror in all its guises.

In addition to advancing both the production and promotion of horror, the Internet has also become the focus of horror in its own right. Horror has always exploited anxieties about new technologies, and in recent years the Internet has become a recurrent trope, particularly in cinema. Recent horror films such as *Fear.com* (dir. William Malone, 2002), *Pulse* (dir. Jim Sonzero, 2006), *Unfriended* (dir. Leo Gabriadze, 2014), and *Friend Request* (dir. Simon Verhoeven, 2016) emphasize the terrifying potential of the Internet's indistinct relationship with reality. The more recent films dwell much more heavily on the inherent menace posed by social media, imposing a supernatural horror aesthetic over real-world concerns about privacy, anonymity, and the misuse of information.

In comparison with cinema, horror fiction's engagement with the Internet initially appears relatively slight. At first glance the Web seems to have gained less of a foothold in horror fiction than it has in science fiction or the mainstream techno-thriller. However, closer scrutiny reveals a significant link between online culture and the horror writing of recent years. Though the Internet has yet to become as common a trope within horror fiction as it has within the horror movie, there are a number of important contemporary novels that either feature the Internet as a major concern or that are influenced by its formal properties.

One of the first horror novels to interact with the Internet was Mark Z. Danielewski's *House of Leaves* (2000). The novel is now widely considered a key text in twenty-first-century horror, due largely to its reorientation of what a "book" can do. Much of the attention is focused on the novel's experimentation with text and its interest in modern media. Though *House of Leaves* makes little direct reference to the Internet, it is worth noting that much of the early interest in the novel was raised by its online presence. Before the book was bought for mainstream publication, Danielewski uploaded a fifty-page excerpt to his own website in 1997. The file was copied and appeared in various places around the Web in an early (and unplanned) example of viral proliferation. Encountering *House of Leaves* in this way effectively furthered the blurring of realities that is so crucial to the novel's plot and form. Danielewski's novel maintains the pretense that it is a "found" document, in which competing narratives consistently query each other's authenticity. Indeed, it directly addresses a parallel concern of the digital age: the waning of trust in the photographic or video image. *House of Leaves'* central narrative behaves like an urban legend, in which not only is verification impossible, but that impossibility is the point. Danielewski's novel is not about the Internet per se, but it does construct a terrifying narrative around the very anxieties that mark the Internet era: worries about accuracy, authenticity, and basic truth.

These same issues recur in Mira Grant's *Newsflesh* Trilogy. Comprising *Feed* (2010), *Deadline* (2011), and *Blackout* (2012), the trilogy depicts the aftermath of a zombie uprising in which online blogging has usurped conventional journalism. The story follows a team of young bloggers who are invited to cover a presidential campaign, during which they stumble across a major political conspiracy. While the postzombie backdrop is well developed and fairly original (insofar as the world has come to terms with the outbreak and civilization endures), Grant's major innovation is in using the outbreak to reveal the inadequacy of mainstream journalism as an information source. In this way the *Newsflesh* trilogy can be read as a commentary on real-world media responses to global issues, especially relating to politics and disaster scenarios. In *Feed* in particular, the importance of firsthand accounts via professional bloggers corresponds to the media's increasing reliance on amateur footage and the way that traditional news channels fail to keep pace with user-generated sources such as YouTube and Twitter.

This same phenomenon is addressed in "found-footage" horror movies, such as *Cloverfield* (2008), in which horror is viewed through the firsthand lens of a personal video camera. The exploding popularity of found footage horror seems to reflect the fact that amateur recordings are now the standard way of encountering real-world horror. Cinema broke ground first in this regard, but horror fiction has begun to explore the same concerns. Novels such as those by Danielewski and Grant drive this home, as does the more recent *A Head Full of Ghosts* (2015). This Bram Stoker

A Timeline of Horror in the Internet Age

1972   Ray Tomlinson, a computer scientist in Cambridge, Massachusetts, sends the first email.

1974   Computer scientist Larry Tesler first programs the copy and paste function into computer text-editing software.

1989   Tim Berners-Lee, a scientist at CERN, develops the World Wide Web as a new way of sharing information across computer networks.

1997   Mark Danielewski uploads a fifty-page excerpt of *House of Leaves* to his own website for friends to read. This is copied and reappears across the Web, garnering interest.

1999   *The Blair Witch Project* is released in cinemas. It is one of the first films to use online "viral" marketing. This includes a website that presents the cast members as authentically missing, complicating the audience's understanding of whether the film is real or fictional.

2000   *House of Leaves* is published in book form.

2004   The emergence of "Web 2.0" (the transformation of the World Wide Web into a user-generated online community of social networking, blogs, wikis, and so on) is widely hailed in the mass media.

2005   YouTube is founded. This later proves essential to the development of Web-based multimedia fiction.

2006   The term "copypasta" is used for the first time on the online forum 4chan.

2008   Creepypasta.com is launched.

2009   Victor Surge uploads two doctored photos to the somethingawful.com competition. This marks the first mention of the online figure known as Slender Man.

2010   Creepypasta experiences peak popularity when it is the focus of an editorial piece in the *New York Times*.

2014   Creepypasta achieves notoriety following the attempted murder of a twelve-year-old Wisconsin girl by two twelve-year-old school friends who allegedly committed the attack as a sacrifice to Slender Man.

2015   *A Head Full of Ghosts* by Paul Tremblay wins the Bram Stoker Award for best novel.

Award–winning novel by Paul Tremblay has been compared to *House of Leaves* and features a self-conscious commentary on the negative impact of mass media, particularly that driven by the Internet and reality television. It follows the trials of an American family whose daughter, Merry, is the purported victim of demonic possession. Merry becomes the subject of an exploitative TV show, which only worsens the supernatural episodes. Added to this mix of competing realities is a series of online blog posts that further critique and complicate any sense of objective experience. Tremblay's novel may not be as elaborate or as profound as Danielewski's, but it has the benefit of hindsight where the Internet is concerned. As such it is perhaps the most focused treatment of new media in horror fiction so far.

This is only one half of the Internet's impact on horror fiction, however. Perhaps more important still is the way that the Internet has provided the space for a new (or at least resurgent) form of horror writing, one that relies on the Internet's tendency toward ambiguity and elusive origins. These online horror stories are known collectively as "creepypasta."

The term is a horror-inflected variation on "copypasta," which originally referred to any material that was copied and shared around the Web. One of the earliest examples is smiledog, which consisted only of an image of a husky dog and the accompanying warning of a curse that threatened anyone who saw the photograph with madness and/or imminent death. This type of "cursed artifact" is a common trope in early creepypastas and constitutes little more than a macabre version of chain emails and spam that infested communication channels in the early years of the Web. Soon, however, creepypastas became more substantial and sophisticated. They are now a recognized online phenomenon, and entire websites and online forums are devoted to creating and analyzing the stories. Major websites include creepypasta.com and the No Sleep section of Reddit.com. Some breakout stories have since been published in traditional book form. One notable example is *Penpal* by Dathan Auerbach, which originated on the No Sleep forum but was subsequently self-published by the author to acclaim within the horror community.

The stories themselves tend to cluster around themes, with nostalgia for 1980s and 1990s media being a major trend. Many creepypastas center on video footage, usually a television program or old video game that they present as having either sinister content or dangerous consequences. Two famous examples are "Ben Drowned" and "Candle Cove." The former tells of a teenager who buys a second-hand copy of a video game at a yard sale. The game turns out to be haunted by the spirit of a drowned boy, whose presence manifests in technical glitches in the game. Some recent versions of the story include video footage of the supposed glitches. "Candle Cove" is written in the form of an online forum thread, in which numerous parties discuss episodes of a fictional children's television show from the 1970s. The "conversation" turns increasingly to disturbing aspects of the show, involving a monster known as the Skin Taker. At the close of the thread a final contributor reveals that once he asked his mother about the show, only to be told that no such show ever existed and that he merely used to sit in front of the television and watch static for thirty minutes.

Both stories are representative of creepypasta's interest in the uncanny or spectral nature of digital content. They exploit ignorance about how such content is actually created and stored, as well as gesturing to the issues of nostalgia and faulty memory. At the heart of creepypasta's effectiveness is the inability of readers to verify the extent of truth involved. Was *Candle Cove* a real TV program? The writer describes it as "half-remembered," and it is reminiscent enough of actual children's shows of the time that it could well be conflated in readers' memory with another "real" show. Similarly, "Ben Drowned" features an existing Zelda game. Creepypastas blur the lines between reality and fiction, and their folklorish proliferation, copied and told across online communities, further complicates their dismissal as fiction.

One creepypasta stands above all others in its reach and impact, however. This is the modern phenomenon known as Slender Man: a figure who has been termed "the first great myth of the Web," and who has, in disturbing fashion, effectively breached the Web's fourth wall to influence acts of real-world violence: in 2014 two twelve-year-old girls in Wisconsin lured a classmate into the woods and stabbed her multiple times, later explaining their actions by saying they had been trying to become Slender Man's "proxies" or followers, and that in order to do this, they had to murder someone. Ironically, unlike most creepypastas, the origins of the Slender Man myth are known and documented. In 2009 Victor Surge, a forum user on somethingawful.com, entered a competition to make a Photoshop monster. Surge (real name: Eric Knudson) doctored a pair of photographs of children to include an elongated, tentacular figure. Both photographs were accompanied by fragmented prose suggesting that something evil befell the children. From this obscure beginning the Slender Man has grown in stature to become a recognizable cultural icon, the subject of fiction, movies, video games, and merchandise. His story is now told across multiple platforms, including an interlocking network of digital narratives that use both video and text to build the mythology. The main narratives are Marble Hornets, EverymanHybrid, and Tribe Twelve, each of which uses a mixture of text websites and YouTube videos in the construction of narrative.

Slender Man is the strongest example of the Internet's impact on horror fiction. Freed from the constraints of traditional storytelling, creepypastas are able to expand beyond the confines of a single authorial vision. As such, creepypastas, and Slender Man in particular, are representative of a newly democratic, collaborative form of storytelling that evolves over time and across cultures. Thomas Pettitt suggests that creepypasta signals the closing of the "Gutenberg Parenthesis." By this he means that it ends the period of literary history in which conventional printing (beginning with the Gutenberg printing press) cemented stories in specific forms. The Internet, in contrast, has created the opportunity to return to the campfire tale in a globalized oral tradition. Horror stories have always flourished in the oral tradition, and they have been given a major boost by the technology of the Internet age.

Neil McRobert

See also: Horror Literature as Social Criticism and Commentary; Horror Video Games; Page to Screen: The Influence of Literary Horror on Film and Television; Small Press, Specialty, and Online Horror; *Part One, Horror through History*: Horror in the Twenty-First Century; *Part Three, Reference Entries*: Bram Stoker Award; *House of Leaves*; New Weird; Unreliable Narrator.

Further Reading

Auerbach, Dathan. 2012. *Penpal.* N.p: 1000Vultures Press.

Blake, Linnie, and Xavier Aldana Reyes, eds. 2015. *Digital Horror: Haunted Technologies, Network Panic and the Found Footage Phenomenon.* New York and London: I. B. Tauris.

Blank, Trevor, ed. 2009. *Folklore and the Internet: Vernacular Expression in a Digital World.* Logan: Utah State University Press.

Boyer, Tina Marie. 2013. "Anatomy of a Monster: The Case of Slender Man." *Preternature: Critical and Historical Studies on the Preternatural* 2/2: 240–261.

Chess, Shira, and Eric Newsome. 2015. *Folklore, Horror Stories, and the Slender Man: The Development of an Internet Mythology.* New York: Palgrave Macmillan.

Edwards, Justin D., ed. 2015. *Technologies of the Gothic in Literature and Culture: Technogothics.* New York: Routledge.

"The Gutenberg Parenthesis: Oral Tradition and Digital Technologies." 2010. MIT Communications Forum. http://cmsw.mit.edu/thomas-pettitt-gutenberg-parenthesis.

Jones, Abigail. 2014. "The Girls Who Tried to Kill for Slender Man." *Newsweek*, August 13. http://www.newsweek.com/2014/08/22/girls-who-tried-kill-slender-man-264218.html.

Krotoski, Alex. 2012. "Tales." *Digital Human*, Series 2, Episode 5, October 29. http://www.bbc.co.uk/programmes/b01nl671.

Pettitt, Thomas. 2013. "Bracketing the Gutenberg Parenthesis." *Explorations in Media Ecology* 11: 95–114.

Wiles, Will. 2013. "Creepypasta." *Aeon*, December 20. https://aeon.co/essays/creepypasta-is-how-the-internet-learns-our-fears/.

HORROR PUBLISHING, 1975–1995: THE BOOM YEARS

The great "Horror Boom" of the late twentieth century began slowly. Before it, there was no such thing as a "horror category" in publishing. Publishers had no "horror editor" the way they might have a science fiction editor or a mystery editor. There was no horror section in a bookstore.

Change began in the early 1960s. While there had always been ghost story anthologies and books now recognized as classics of horror published in the mainstream, such as Shirley Jackson's *The Haunting of Hill House* (1959), there was a significant difference in Donald A. Wollheim's paperback *The Macabre Reader*

(Ace, 1959) and *More Macabre* (1961). These began to define what a horror paperback looked like. Soon Ballantine Books followed with the first discernable line of horror paperbacks, all of them with Richard Powers covers of semi-abstract, swirling menace. Some books in this line included a paperback of H. R. Wakefield's Arkham House collection, *The Clock Strikes Twelve* (1961), Fritz Leiber's *Shadows with Eyes* (1962), and some others. Such packaging is very important in commercial publishing. Books aimed at a specific readership must be made to resemble other books aimed at that readership. What these were doing, cautiously, was determining that a horror audience actually existed, and that books made to look like "horror books" could be pitched to it. Meanwhile, during this period, the only press specializing in horror or weird fiction continued to be Arkham House, which issued the occasional new volume and began repackaging all of the works of H. P. Lovecraft in hardcover, opening up a new readership through library sales.

Things remained in this state for about a decade. Meanwhile, as horror scholar S. T. Joshi has suggested, the public's taste for and familiarity with supernatural or horror motifs was being built up through the films of Alfred Hitchcock and such TV shows as *Thriller, Way Out*, and especially Rod Serling's *The Twilight Zone*.

The horror explosion was the result of three blockbuster novels and their associated film adaptations: *Rosemary's Baby* by Ira Levin (1967), *The Exorcist* by William Peter Blatty (1971), and *The Other* by Thomas Tryon (1971). These, followed by the enormous success of Stephen King's *Carrie* (1974) and *'Salem's Lot* (1975), changed the publishing scene completely. With King the publishing industry had a writer who could produce not just one fluke bestseller, but a whole series of bestsellers in a repeatable fashion, often more than one a year. The industry, as it inevitably does in such instances, suddenly began looking for more books of the same type, or more books to be pitched to the same audience. Suddenly lucrative careers could be made by writing only horror, and writers as varied in temperament and ambition as Ramsey Campbell, Peter Straub, Robert R. McCammon, F. Paul Wilson, Charles L. Grant, John Farris, J. N. Williamson, Rick Hautala, Bentley Little, Richard Laymon, and John Saul were cranking out enormous quantities of material. (McCammon is a rare example of a writer who began as an obvious King imitator, but broke free and discovered a significant and powerful voice of his own.) Dean Koontz, formerly a midlist science fiction writer, reinvented himself as a horror/suspense writer, and his best-seller status continues to this day.

Packaging had changed with the times. Now a horror paperback was thick. It usually featured a dark or black cover, often see-through, with something brighter (a drop of blood or the grinning face of a demonic child) on the inner cover. There was a growing section of such volumes in the bookstore, as distinct as the sections for other genres. While there were some who predicted a flood of formulaic drivel followed by a bust, for a time such voices were not heard, and horror seemed to have conquered the commercial marketplace.

This caused expansions in other areas beyond mass-market paperbacks. While there had been some attempts at horror magazines in the past, the most significant since the demise of *Weird Tales* in 1954 had been Robert A. W. Lowndes's low-paying and mostly reprint *The Magazine of Horror* (1963–1971) and its companion, *Startling Mystery Stories* (1966–1971), which published Stephen King's first fiction. But by 1981 there was a high-budget, and initially high-circulation, publication, *Rod Serling's The Twilight Zone Magazine*, edited by T. E. D. Klein, Michael Blaine, and Tappan King, which lasted until 1989. It had a digest-sized companion, *Night Cry*, edited by the writer Alan Rodgers, which was even more explicitly a horror magazine. Most of the leading writers of the period appeared in these magazines, and *Twilight Zone* also featured many interviews and a great deal of media coverage.

There were also many small-press horror magazines, ranging from the Lovecraft-oriented fanzines edited by Robert M. Price, *Crypt of Cthulhu* and its companions, to Stuart Schiff's elegant *Whispers* and W. Paul Ganley's less flamboyant but excellent *Weirdbook*, and many others, such as *Cemetery Dance* (still being published), *Grue, Eldritch Tales, The Horror Show, Fantasy Tales,* and more, all of which encouraged a new generation of writers, including such eccentrics as Thomas Ligotti and W. M. Pugmire, whose work did not fit easily into commercial molds. On a somewhat larger scale, *Weird Tales* was revived on a solid basis by George Scithers, John Betancourt, and Darrell Schweitzer. This was the most sustained of all revivals of *Weird Tales,* which only began to become seriously erratic in its schedule in 2014.

Anthologies proliferated. Two of the most important were edited by the anthologist/agent Kirby McCauley, *Frights* (1976) and *Dark Forces* (1980). This last was something of a *Dangerous Visions* of horror (*Dangerous Visions* having been a groundbreaking and genre-defining science fiction anthology edited by Harlan Ellison in 1967), showcasing the finest talents, new and old, and containing everything from one of the last stories of Theodore Sturgeon to an original short novel ("The Mist") by Stephen King. Poppy Z. Brite (now known as Billy Martin) was inspired by this book to become a horror writer, because it showed so many possibilities of the form. Charles L. Grant's eleven-volume *Shadows* series was a showcase for "quiet" as opposed to loud and splashy horror, and published numerous excellent stories by a wide variety of writers.

In contrast to Grant's "quiet horror," the "splatterpunk" movement arose about 1989–1990. It was very short-lived, and some of the writers associated with its hype notably distanced themselves from it (particularly David J. Schow), but for a time there was a distinct school of self-proclaimed rude, crude, gross-out horror fiction that might be described as the horror fiction equivalent of death metal rock music. There were two anthologies edited by Paul Sammon, *Splatterpunks: Extreme Horror* (1990) and *Splatterpunks II* (1995). The leading novelists of the splatterpunk movement were undoubtedly John Skipp and Craig Spector, whose vampire novel *The Light at the End* (1984) was the first of several such books. Skipp and Spector (and later Skipp by himself) also edited the 1989 anthology *Book of the Dead* and sequels, which mark the beginnings of modern zombie fiction, itself almost a subfield of its own. Such stories and novels featured zombies of the apocalyptic, brain-eating variety, as popularized by George Romero's *The Night of the Living Dead* and similar films, not the shuffling, undead slaves of Haitian folklore.

Horror had a huge impact on the small press book market. Driven by hysterically high prices paid by collectors for first editions of, in particular, Stephen King, specialty publishers turned out more and more for the collector. Donald M. Grant, who had previously specialized mostly in the works of Robert E. Howard, published a deluxe "limited" edition of King's *The Gunslinger* (1984), which, in addition to the genuinely limited signed version, had at least two printings of the trade edition, making it the commonest "rare" book of its generation. But this sort of thing proliferated. Dennis Etchison's first book, a collection of stories called *The Dark Country* published by Scream Press in 1982, reportedly sold out 16,000 copies in four hardcover printings, very quickly. The conventional publishing wisdom was that a book of stories by a writer who did not have any novels would not be commercially viable at all, but a one-man small publisher had just done vastly better than a regular New York publisher would have with that book. Scream Press was one of many such horror-only imprints of the boom years. It also got into the Stephen King business with a deluxe, limited edition of King's short fiction collection *Skeleton Crew* illustrated by J. K. Potter. For a time, fortunes were being made in the horror field at all levels, and there seemed to be no end to the public's appetite for such product.

Phenomenon followed phenomenon. The works of Anne Rice, beginning with *Interview with the Vampire* (1976), opened up vast new areas of erotic horror fiction, and virtually turned vampires into a genre all to themselves. (Indeed, Warren Lapine, the publisher of *Weird Tales* in the 1990s, had an all-vampire magazine titled *Dreams of Decadence* going for a while.) All manner of other vampiric fiction proliferated, among the most notable being Chelsea Quinn Yarbro's long series about the immortal Comte St. Germain, beginning with *Hotel Transylvania* in 1978; Les Daniels's series about Don Sebastian de Villanueva, beginning with *The Black Castle* (1978); and Whitley Strieber's *The Hunger* (1981). Vampire fiction became historical, romantic, and even occasionally funny. A notable funny example is *I, Vampire* by Jody Scott (1984). Suzy McKee Charnas's *The Vampire Tapestry* (1980) brilliantly analyzed the character of its vampire, but with a quasi-science fictional rationale. Michael Talbot's *The Delicate Dependency* (1982) was one of the outstanding vampire novels of the period, with a claustrophobic atmosphere, surprisingly little explicit violence, and a gay subtext. His vampires are secret masters, Illuminati, wiser than mankind and always feared. S. P. Somtow's *Vampire Junction* (1984) tells of a vampire who is perpetually a child with an ethereally beautiful voice. In the twentieth century, he is a rock star.

Explicitly erotic horror fiction also became a recognizable category. Jeff Gelb's *Hot Blood* series of anthologies proved successful and long-running, and Cecelia Tan's Circlet Press became an entire imprint devoted to erotica, much of it horror.

The early career of Clive Barker was almost unprecedented in the history, not only of horror fiction, but of all literature. An unknown writer suddenly came out

Even an extremely brief and selective list of significant authors and titles from the great horror boom of the late twentieth century demonstrates the extent to which this striking publishing and literary phenomenon affected popular perceptions of horror literature, for many of these titles have become iconic, even legendary, in the collective mind of two and three generations of readers:

1975	Stephen King, *'Salem's Lot*
1976	Anne Rice, *Interview with the Vampire*
1977	Stephen King, *The Shining*
1979	Peter Straub, *Ghost Story*
1984–1985	Clive Barker, *The Books of Blood*
1986	Stephen King, *It*
1988	Thomas Harris, *The Silence of the Lambs*

Matt Cardin

(in England) with six volumes of stories, the *Books of Blood* (1984–1985), most of them previously unpublished. They were soon an international sensation, and, as the originals had been paperbacks, specialty presses raced to publish deluxe hardcover editions for the collectors. Barker certainly had the field's attention. Stephen King proclaimed him "the future of horror." When his first novel, *The Damnation Game*, came out in 1985, his continued success was assured, but, as with Etchison, it was established that a writer could make a successful career with short fiction before he had a novel published.

Anything seemed possible. Horror was prospering in many categories. It was on the best-seller lists. It was in the collector's market. Small press horror magazines came and went at a bewildering rate. There was loud horror, quiet horror, erotic horror, erotic romantic horror, historical horror, contemporary horror, whole subgenres about zombies and vampires, with the occasional werewolf thrown in. Laurell K. Hamilton began a long series of vampire, erotic, noir, detective fiction with *Guilty Pleasures* (1993), the first novel in her series titled *Anita Blake: Vampire Hunter*.

The stage was at this point set for the institution of a high-budget, high-prestige horror publishing project, and it came in the form of the Dell Abyss line of horror paperbacks, edited by Jeanne Cavelos and launched in 1991 with very high expectations. The first books seem to have done well, but before long it was clear that the majority of them did not. To make matters worse, the publisher took the one really successful discovery, Poppy Z. Brite, out of the line, to be published as mainstream instead of horror, so that thereafter, on paper at least, the entire enterprise looked even less profitable than it was. For a brief time Brite (Martin) was a genuine cultural phenomenon, with two vampire novels, *Lost Souls* (1992) and *Drawing Blood* (1993), which appealed strongly to a young, alienated, Goth audience, but this did Dell Abyss little good. In any case, two books, no matter how successful, could not sustain a failing imprint or genre for long. The last Abyss books were published in 1995 with much smaller print runs and far less publicity than the earlier ones.

The obvious conclusion was that the horror bubble had burst. The horror sections in bookstores shrank or disappeared altogether. There would, of course, be survivors, revivals, and new trends. In the late 1990s there was a flurry of nonsupernatural serial-killer novels, inspired by the success of Thomas Harris's *The Silence of the Lambs* (1988), and many horror writers tried to save their careers with a leap into the lifeboat of "dark suspense." Others ended up writing media fiction, or fell silent. The really major figures, King, Straub, Campbell, Koontz, Rice, and a few others, rode out the collapse. The revival of interest in all things Lovecraftian, which was marked by the centennial anthology *Lovecraft's Legacy*, edited by Robert Weinberg and Martin H. Greenberg in 1990, was just getting started. But horror bestsellers were rare. Much of it retreated to the small presses. The boom had definitely gone bust.

Darrell Schweitzer

See also: Horror Anthologies; Vampire Fiction from Dracula to Lestat and Beyond; *Part One, Horror through History*: Horror from 1900 to 1950; Horror from 1950 to 2000; *Part Three, Reference Entries*: Arkham House; Barker, Clive; *Books of Blood*; Brite, Poppy Z.; Campbell, Ramsey; Charnas, Suzy McKee; *The Damnation Game*; Etchison, Dennis; *The Exorcist*; Farris, John; Grant, Charles L.; Harris, Thomas; *Interview with the Vampire*; Joshi, S. T.; King, Stephen; Klein, T. E. D.; Koontz, Dean; Ligotti, Thomas; McCammon, Robert R.; *The Other*; Rice, Anne; *Rosemary's Baby*; Schweitzer, Darrell; Splatterpunk; Straub, Peter; Wilson, F. Paul; Yarbro, Chelsea Quinn; Zombies.

Further Reading

Dziemianowicz, Stefan. 1999. "Contemporary Horror Fiction, 1950–1998." In *Fantasy and Horror: A Critical and Historical Guide to Literature, Illustration, Film, TV, Radio, and the Internet*, edited by Neil Barron, 199–344. Lanham, MD: Scarecrow Press.

Glover, John. 2016. "The Life and Afterlife of Horror Fiction." *Postscripts to Darkness*, June 12. https://pstdarkness.com/2016/06/12/1707.

Hantke, Steffen. 2008. "The Decline of the Literary Horror Market in the 1990s and Dell's Abyss Series." *Journal of Popular Culture* 41, no. 1: 56–70.

Joshi, S. T. 2012. *Unutterable Horror, a History of Supernatural Fiction, Vol. 2: The Twentieth and Twenty-First Centuries*. Hornsea, UK: PS Publishing.

HORROR VIDEO GAMES

From the outset, horror video games have been indebted to horror cinema. Indeed, famous game designers such as Frédérick Raynal (*Alone in the Dark*, Infogrames, 1992) and Shinji Mikami (*Resident Evil*, Capcom, 1996) have overtly acknowledged that they take their inspiration from film and wish to give gamers the feeling of being the main character in a horror movie. As both *Alone in the Dark* and *Resident Evil* depict a mansion where the action takes place through predetermined camera angles, the connection could not be clearer. However, such a link should not obscure the bearing of literature on horror games. Fully as much as cinema, the horror video game—especially the third-person action-adventure games labeled as survival horror—borrows many of its themes and narratives, and much of its iconography, from the Gothic and from fantastic short stories and novels recast in an interactive media. As the Gothic is known to actively involve the reader in the construction of a story to provoke strong emotions of horror, fear, and terror, video game scholars have underlined how natural was its adaptation into games, what Tanya Krzywinska calls the "gamification of Gothic" (2015). The dominant tropes of the Gothic have found a renewed breath in games.

The old mansion, the crypt, the sewer, the graveyard, or the abandoned public building, the deserted laboratory, the subway tunnel—all of these locales have to be explored by the horror gamer. The gloomy and oppressive mood described in detail in Gothic novels is transposed in a forthright manner to the videoludic realm (that is, the realm combining the visual [video] with gaming and play [the ludic]). Horror video games privilege atmosphere over action, providing a dreadful experience that needs to be lived, rendering the surroundings unsafe or likely to become dangerous without warning. This relationship to spatial exploration is intimately linked to the history of video games. As early as the 1970s, *Colossal Cave Adventure* (Crowther, 1976) and *Zork* (Infocom, 1979) offered adventures in mysterious caves, dungeons, and houses to gamers who typed commands in textually depicted environments. Far from being disadvantaged compared to graphical representation, the use of words allowed the creation of vivid and deep fictional worlds. At a time when technology was a great obstacle to the pioneering attempts at the horror genre, text adventures offered great opportunities for ambiance and plot development. British video game publishing company CRL Group released games mostly based on landmark Gothic tales, such as *Dracula* (Pike & Ellery, 1986), *Frankenstein* (Pike & Derrett, 1987), and *Wolfman* (Pike & Derrett, 1988). Previously, *The Rats* (GXT, 1985), based on the eponymous novel by James Herbert, not only relied on the text adventure's tools but also integrated simulation elements, allowing the gamer to organize the governmental response to the rat outbreak. Rodents would swarm the text as well, clouding the perception of the action and conveying the panic afflicting the characters. Such ludic experimentations became more and more frequent as the downfall of text adventures brought by technological advancement permitted the development of other types of games.

The actional dimension of video games asks for an embodiment of the threat. Unlike the student filmmakers in *The Blair Witch Project* (dir. Daniel Myrick and Eduardo Sánchez, 1999), the player-character encounters actual evil foes during the videoludic adaptation *Blair Witch Volume 1: Rustin Parr* (Terminal Reality, 2000). In side-scrolling platform games such as *Ghost House* (Sega, 1986), *Castlevania*

(Konami, 1986), or *Vampire: Master of Darkness* (SIMS, 1992), the gamer faces the whole Gothic bestiary: ghosts, vampires, mummies, demons, skeletons, zombies, demons, and so on. While those monsters do not breed fear, as they are more obstacles to be destroyed in order to move on instead of monstrous evil threats, 3-D action games do stage frightening confrontations. This change is salient in the first-person shooters *Clive Barker's Undying* (DreamWorks Interactive, 2001) and *Clive Barker's Jericho* (Mercury Steam Entertainment, 2007). Additionally, with *Clive Barker's Nightbreed: The Action Game* and *Clive Barker's Nightbreed: The Interactive Movie*, developed by Impact Software Development in 1990, the author of *Cabal* (1988) and writer-director of *Hellraiser* (1987) is one of the very few writers to have his name upfront regarding his involvement in the video game industry. *Harlan Ellison: I Have No Mouth, and I Must Scream* (Dreamers Guild, 1995) is another notable example.

That said, one of the most influential authors on horror video games is, undoubtedly, H. P. Lovecraft. Since the famous text adventure *The Lurking Horror* (Infocom, 1987), dozens of adaptations of the Cthulhu Mythos have been made, demonstrating an important compatibility between Lovecraft's horrific fictional universe and adventure video games: Lovecraft's cosmic fear works well with, and makes up for, the slow pacing and lack of sensory-motor challenges in adventure games. Plus, their basic dynamic—putting together clues in order to unlock new areas with more mysteries—is at the heart of the Lovecraftian plot, and these mechanics remain an essential part of horror video games. Here, the literary influence is expressed in a manner specific to the videoludic medium. Lovecraft's emphasis on the loss of cosmic landmarks and sanity allows for much experimentation: sanity meters, inherited from a first ludification of his universe through the role-playing game *The Call of Cthulhu* (Chaosium, 1981), appear in both *Eternal Darkness: Sanity's Requiem* (Silicon Knights, 2002) and *Call of Cthulhu: Dark Corners of the Earth* (Headfirst Production, 2005), and may lead the gamer to see the image on the screen distorted by hallucinations when his or her character loses his mind. More psychological than gore-oriented, the vision may be interpreted as obscured or unreliable, and the clear-mindedness of the protagonist questioned (like the loss of consciousness leading to the Otherworld in *Silent Hill* [Konami, 1999]). The unreliable narrator from fantastic literature, such as those found in so many stories by Edgar Allan Poe— whose short stories were adapted in *The Dark Eye* (Inscape, 1995)—has become an unreliable playable character. The testimony form cherished by this genre has also proved to be quite amenable to horror video games, which are filled with written texts and hidden secrets scattered everywhere, explaining what took place or giving access to a lost history (as with the many files and documents found in *Resident Evil's* Spencer Mansion). In *Fatal Frame* (Tecmo, 2001), the camera obscura allows the gamer to fight off or liberate ghosts by taking pictures of them, while in *Outlast* (Red Barrels, 2013) the gamer can use a video camera to record dreadful events.

The subversion of aesthetics that is used to immerse the reader in literary horror has become characteristic of survival horror games, which merge the adventure

A Timeline of Significant Horror Video (and Computer) Games

1985   *The Rats* (GXT), based on James Herbert's 1974 novel

1986   *Castlevania* (Konami); *Dracula* (CRL Group); *Ghost House* (Sega)

1987   *Frankenstein* (CRL Group); *The Lurking Horror* (Infocom), based on H. P. Lovecraft's 1923 short story

1988   *Wolfman* (CRL Group)

1990   *Clive Barker's Nightbreed: The Action Game* and *Clive Barker's Nightbreed: The Interactive Movie* (Impact Software Development)

1992   *Alone in the Dark* (Infogames); *Dark Seed* (Cyberdream); *Vampire: Master of Darkness* (SIMS)

1993   *Gabriel Knight: Sins of the Father* (Sierra On-line, 1993)

1995   *The Dark Eye* (Inscape), based on the short fiction of Edgar Allan Poe; Harlan Ellison, *I Have No Mouth, and I Must Scream* (Dreamers Guild)

1996   *Resident Evil* (Capcom)

1999   *Silent Hill* (Konami)

2000   *Blair Witch Volume 1: Rustin Parr* (Terminal Reality)

2001   *Clive Barker's Undying* (DreamWorks Interactive); *Fatal Frame* (Tecmo)

2002   *Eternal Darkness: Sanity's Requiem* (Silicon Knights)

2005   *Call of Cthulhu: Dark Corners of the Earth* (Headfirst Productions); *Resident Evil 4* (Capcom)

2007   *Clive Barker's Jericho* (Mercury Steam Entertainment)

2010   *Alan Wake* (Remedy Entertainment); *Amnesia: The Dark Descent* (Frictional Games)

2013   *Outlast* (Red Barrels)

2014   *P.T.* (Kojima Productions)

Matt Cardin

and action genres. While adventure games rely mainly on finding objects and solving puzzles, horror games use these moments to trigger the appearance of the aforementioned embodied threats. Such is the case in *Silent Hill*, where the discovery of the first key item (a radio) leads to a creature bursting through the window. While action games emphasize confrontation and empowerment, games like *Alone in the Dark* make controls so clumsy, combat so difficult, and ammunition so scarce that players are better off avoiding fighting. They are forced to forsake their habits and circle around monsters rather than overcome them. *Resident Evil 4* (Capcom, 2005) created a new trend of horror games in which reflex and precision are required to defeat numerous enemies. *Amnesia: The Dark Descent* (Frictional Games, 2010)—whose engine is called "HPL," after Lovecraft—transformed the genre once again by setting its action in the first-person perspective with enemies that cannot be looked at without draining sanity. Hence, the agonistic progression in first-person shooters in which the gamer always points a weapon at what he or she looks at eventually led to disarmament and a Lovecraftian perilous gaze. Going one step further, the "playable teaser" *P.T.* (Kojima Productions, 2014), developed for the canceled game *Silent Hills*, offered an experience voided of any confrontation: the gamer explores a never-ending corridor, filled with strange events and apparitions, and must solve its mysteries in order to escape. Fear and enigmas are the main obstacles within this impossible architecture of looping rooms, with doors leading to different places each time, and with inverted floors, ceilings, and walls. Such experiences renew horror video games with the literary heritage of horror as they throw the gamer into dark and strange worlds that she or he tries to understand in order to reconstitute the story.

Perhaps because of its relationship with imagination and investigation, the writer figure abounds in horror video games, from the author of *Gabriel Knight: Sins of the Father* (Sierra On-line, 1993) or of *Silent Hill* to the would-be novelist in *Dark Seed* (Cyberdream, 1992) or the best-selling thriller author à la Stephen King in *Alan Wake* (Remedy Entertainment, 2010). The gamer is not only put in the shoes of such a character, but is somehow always writing her or his own story of the game itself. Perhaps in the end this makes the player of such games assume the role of the famous "wreader" (the intermingling of writer and reader) that interactive fiction authors have been talking about since the 1990s.

Bernard Perron and Jean-Charles Ray

See also: The Gothic Literary Tradition; Horror Literature in the Internet Age; Page to Screen: The Influence of Literary Horror on Film and Television; *Part One, Horror through History*: Horror in the Twenty-First Century; *Part Three, Reference Entries*: Barker, Clive; Cthulhu Mythos; Ellison, Harlan; Herbert, James; "I Have No Mouth and I Must Scream"; Lovecraft, H. P.; Lovecraftian Horror; Monsters; Psychological Horror; *The Rats*; Unreliable Narrator.

Further Reading

Kirkland, Ewan. 2012. "Gothic Videogames, Survival Horror and the *Silent Hill* Series." *Gothic Studies* 14, no. 2 (November): 106–122. http://dx.doi.org/10.7227/GS.14.2.8.
Krzywinska, Tanya. 2015. "Gamification of Gothic." In *Diversity of Play*, edited by Mathias Fuchs, 21–38. Lüneburg: Meson Press.
Perron, Bernard, ed. 2009. *Horror Video Games: Essays on the Fusion of Fear and Play*. Jefferson, NC: McFarland.

THE LEGACY OF *FRANKENSTEIN*: FROM GOTHIC NOVEL TO CULTURAL MYTH

Frankenstein is a Gothic novel by Mary Wollstonecraft Shelley. The novel was published in 1818 when Mary was just twenty years old. Though it received little immediate recognition, theatrical adaptation raised the profile of *Frankenstein*, and it was issued again in 1831 in a revised form. It has never been out of print since and has become horror's most enduring myth. The novel itself has been reimagined, reinvented, parodied, and recontextualized in countless ways, and numberless texts have been derived from its central themes. The figure of the Creature, the theme of science gone awry, and the Faustian power struggle between Creature and creator underpin a whole spectrum of modern narratives, both within the horror genre and more widely.

Brian Aldiss has described *Frankenstein* as the "first great myth of the industrial age" (Aldiss 1973, 23), but it could be argued that Mary Shelley's novel is in fact the most fundamental of all modern myths. Itself a modernization of Faustian and Promethean myths—the former about a learned magician who sells his soul to the devil, the latter about an ancient Greek deity who incurs drastic punishment by stealing fire from the gods to give to humans—*Frankenstein* is in turn the model for all subsequent attempts to present the dangers of hubris (that is, foolish pride or arrogance) and the threat of unfettered scientific ambition.

The story of *Frankenstein* is among the most famous in Western literature and is well known to any student with even a passing interest in horror. In brief, it tells of Victor Frankenstein's scientific ambitions and his ruin at the hands of the Creature he has constructed from the fragments of corpses. Victor is driven to understand the principles of life, but once he has given life to his Creature he abandons it in disgust. The Creature is cast out in solitude to face the cruelty of the world. Lonely, he asks Victor to make him a mate, and when Victor changes his mind—horrified at the prospect that "a race of devils would be propagated upon the earth" (Shelley 1994, 121)—the Creature vows to destroy the man he sees as the architect of his misery. The remainder of the novel is filled with violence and death as the Creature embarks on his revenge.

The story has been adapted and altered innumerable times. Its first adaptation was in Richard Brinsley Peake's play *Presumption; or, the Fate of Frankenstein* (1823). Peake's play was largely responsible for the growing success of Mary Shelley's novel after it had an initial lukewarm reception. *Presumption* is perhaps most significant for establishing the emphasis on the Creature's nameless status. The playbill famously represented the Creature merely as a series of dashes, foreshadowing the postmodern interest in the Creature as a representation of the unrepresentable.

There were other theatrical adaptations, but it was cinema that established *Frankenstein*'s place in the fabric of popular culture. The first cinematic treatment of the novel is Edison Studios' silent film (1910), but by far the most famous early cinematic version of *Frankenstein* is James Whale's 1931 adaptation for Universal Studios. Whale's film is considered a classic of the early era of horror cinema, and almost all subsequent representations of the Creature are derived from Boris Karloff's appearance as a rectangular-headed giant with bolts through his neck. Whale's film, which was not based on Shelley's novel but on a 1927 stage adaptation by the British playwright Peggy Webling, deviates significantly from the original source, and in doing so it introduces numerous motifs that have since become enshrined as part of a parallel, cinematic mythology. These include the hunchbacked hench-man, Igor, the use of electricity to give life to the Creature, and the pitchfork-wielding villagers who destroy the monster.

Whale's sequel, *The Bride of Frankenstein* (1935), is considered by many critics to be superior to the first film, though it now has only tangential links with the source material. Elsa Lanchester's portrayal of the titular Bride, with her iconic, lightning-patterned beehive hair, has entered the modern horror pantheon in its own right. *The Bride of Frankenstein* is also noteworthy for its inclusion of a pro-logue depicting Mary, Percy Shelley, and Lord Byron discussing Mary's novel. The film is thus introduced by Mary's claim that there is more story to tell. The scene highlights the way in which the biographical background of *Frankenstein* is often indivisible from the novel itself.

There are literally hundreds of other cinematic adaptations. Most of them ad-here loosely (if at all) to the source material and frequently represent the Creature as a brutish monster, stripped of the subtlety and sympathy that was so integral to the original story. Some of the more outlandish examples include *I Was a Teenage Frankenstein* (1957), *Frankenstein Versus Dracula* (1971), and *Blackenstein* (1973). These, like most modern treatments, apply the name Frankenstein to the monster rather than his creator.

Frankenstein has proved ripe for parody as well. Famous examples include *Ab-bott and Costello Meet Frankenstein* (1948), Mel Brooks's *Young Frankenstein* (1974), and the stage show and subsequent film *The Rocky Horror Picture Show* (1975).

As well as direct revisions of Shelley's novel, the legacy of *Frankenstein* can be identified in any narrative in which scientific ambition has dangerous, uncontain-able consequences. Thus, *Frankenstein* can be seen as the fundamental science fiction narrative, and it is widely regarded as the first example of the genre. Its in-fluence can be seen in such prominent science fiction films as *2001: A Space Odys-sey* (1968) and *Blade Runner* (1982), both of which question the nature of life and intelligence, as well as the dangers of technology. *Frankenstein* has reemerged in the contemporary era as a referent for the potential pitfalls of scientific progress. In particular, anxieties about the ethics and consequences of advances in genetics have found fertile ground in the *Frankenstein* myth. Horror films such as *The Fly* (1986), *Species* (1995), and *Splice* (2009) each center on the horrific results of meddling with the natural order of life. In real-world terms, the prefix *Franken*—as in "Frankenfoods," referring to foods that have been genetically modified or other-wise changed by human intervention; and "Frankenstorm," a term coined for the possible "monstrous" merging of Hurricane Sandy with other violent weather in 2012—is now synonymous with the threat of unrestricted human interference. As science progresses toward artificial intelligence and human-technological inter-faces, and further exerts an ostensible control over the natural world, the legacy of *Frankenstein* continues to be useful as an expression of anxiety.

However, alongside this particular perpetuation of the *Frankenstein* narrative, the novel's genesis has itself accrued mythical overtones. There is no other novel whose composition is so famous. Mary Shelley wrote *Frankenstein* in 1816 while holidaying on the banks of Lake Geneva. That year was famously the "year without a summer," when meteorological anomalies meant poor weather and confinement indoors. Mary was spending the summer in Geneva with a literary gathering that included her soon-to-be husband, the poet Percy Bysshe Shelley; the iconic Lord Byron, another of the era's most famous poets; and his physician John Polidori. Trapped in the gloomy Villa Diodati by the weather, it was suggested that they each attempt to write a ghost story. *Frankenstein* was Mary Shelley's contribution.

There are many suggestions as to what inspired Mary to write *Frankenstein*. Critics point to the revolutionary attitude of the time, which Mary's parents—the political philosopher William Godwin and the novelist and feminist philosopher Mary Wollstonecraft—had helped shape. The theme of rebellion against authority is laced throughout the novel, most spectacularly in the Creature's violence against his master. Equally, some see the death of Mary's infant daughter in 1815 as the wishful inspiration for a story focused on overcoming the restrictions of mortality. *Frankenstein*

Frankenstein's Monster: Adam or Satan?

The monster as originally portrayed in Mary Shelley's novel differs dramatically from the mute, shambling version of it that was burned into public consciousness by Universal Studios' 1931 film adaptation. Mary's monster learns to speak and read, and it ponders the nature of its own existence with intense emotional agony. Here are its reflections as it reads John Milton's *Paradise Lost* and relates that epic cosmic story of Satan, God, Adam, and Eve to its own circumstance:

> But *Paradise Lost* excited different and far deeper emotions [than the other books I had read]. I read it, as I had read the other volumes which had fallen into my hands, as a true history. It moved every feeling of wonder and awe, that the picture of an omnipotent God warring with his creatures was capable of exciting. I often referred the several situations, as their similarity struck me, to my own. Like Adam, I was apparently united by no link to any other being in existence; but his state was far different from mine in every other respect. He had come forth from the hands of God a perfect creature, happy and prosperous, guarded by the especial care of his Creator; he was allowed to converse with, and acquire knowledge from beings of a superior nature: but I was wretched, helpless, and alone. Many times I considered Satan as the fitter emblem of my condition; for often, like him, when I viewed the bliss of my protectors [a poor family whom the monster spied on to learn about human behavior], the bitter gall of envy rose within me. (Shelley 1823, 36–37)

Matt Cardin

Source: Shelley, Mary. [1818] 1823. *Frankenstein*. A New Edition. London: Printed for G. and W. B. Whittaker, Ave Maria Lane.

is filled with symbolic resonance and is open to seemingly limitless interpretation. It is perhaps this very adaptability that has perpetuated its importance in contemporary culture, whereas other monstrous myths have been exhausted.

What is clear is that Mary was interested in the scientific principle of galvanism, the application of electrical current to organic tissue. It was at the time being practiced in London by Erasmus Darwin (grandfather of Charles). In the foreword to the 1831 edition of her novel, Mary recounts a conversation between Byron and Percy Shelley that touched upon the subject of Darwin's experiment, in which a piece of vermicelli was galvanized into "voluntary motion." Mary goes on to wonder: "perhaps a corpse would be reanimated; galvanism had given token of such things: perhaps the component parts of a Creature might be manufactured, brought together, and endured with vital warmth" (Shelley 1994, xv). Famously, Mary would then go on to dream of "the pale student of unhallowed arts kneeling beside the thing he had put together . . . the hideous phantasm of a man stretched out, and then, on the working of some powerful engine, show signs of life, and stir with an uneasy, half-vital motion" (Shelley 1994, viii). Mary had her story, and two years later it was published.

Significantly, *Frankenstein* was not the only horror legacy to be birthed in that friendly competition. Both Byron and Polidori wrote stories based upon the folklore of the vampire that they had heard while touring the Balkans. Byron abandoned his attempt, but Polidori went on to complete a draft of "The Vampyre" (1819) a full eighty years before Bram Stoker would create his own horror icon in *Dracula* (1897). And though Dracula is credited with introducing the notion of the vampire as an urbane and seductive monster, Polidori's vampire is all this and more, being based largely on Byron himself.

As with *Frankenstein* itself, the most famous depictions of these events at the Villa Diodati are cinematic. As mentioned, Whale's *The Bride of Frankenstein* features a conversation between Shelley and her circle as an introduction to the film. The most famous fictionalization of the events at Villa Diodati is director Ken Russell's *Gothic* (1986). Like the later *Haunted Summer* (1988), Russell's film presents the gathering as a hedonistic, psycho-sexual degeneration. The film won several awards and has since garnered a cult following.

Both *Frankenstein* and the story of its creation live on in popular culture. Increasingly, postmodern meta-inclinations have led to a blurring of the lines demarcating these two distinct stories. For example, Brian Aldiss's *Frankenstein Unbound* (1973) features a time-traveler who visits 1816, where he encounters both the monster and a young woman named Mary Shelley. Peter Ackroyd's *The Casebook of Victor Frankenstein* (2008) similarly conflates the world of the story and the figures involved in its creation. In Ackroyd's novel, Victor Frankenstein meets the Shelley circle and is inspired to create his monster by their revolutionary zeal. Laurie Sheck's *A Monster's Notes* (2009) is presented as the diary of the monster who, having lived through the ages since the publication of Shelley's novel, looks back at his own role in its inspiration.

Interestingly, all of this blurring of boundaries has been present since the publication of the 1831 edition of the novel. In her foreword Shelley clearly outlines the association between her book and the sutured Creature it contains, both of which could be referred to by her famous phrase "my hideous progeny" (ix). *Frankenstein* is a novel about creativity, and it is therefore unsurprising that the novel has been employed in contemporary fiction's tendency toward self-consciousness. Shelley's novel has endured so long and remained so central to popular culture because of its adaptability. In the current cultural moment, it is a useful metaphor for tortured literary creation and frightening scientific advancement.

Neil McRobert

See also: Eco-horror; The Gothic Literary Tradition; Horror Literature and Science Fiction; Page to Screen: The Influence of Literary Horror on Film and Television; *Part One, Horror through History*: Horror Literature in the Nineteenth Century; *Part Three, Reference Entries*: Body Snatching; Byron, Lord; Frame Story; Gothic Hero/Villain; Koontz, Dean; Mad Scientist; Monsters; Romanticism and Dark Romanticism; Shelley, Mary; "The Vampyre."

Further Reading

Aldiss, Brian. 1973. *Billion Year Spree: The True History of Science Fiction*. New York: Doubleday.

Baldick, Chris. 1987 *In Frankenstein's Shadow: Myth, Monstrosity and Nineteenth Century Writing*. Oxford: Clarendon Press.

Friedman, Lester, and Allison B. Kavey. 2016. *Monstrous Progeny: A History of the Frankenstein Narratives*. New Brunswick, NJ and London: Rutgers University Press.

Glut, Donald F. 2002. *The Frankenstein Archive: Essays on the Monster, the Myth, the Movies, and More*. London: McFarland.

Graham, Elaine L. 2002. *Representations of the Post/Human: Monsters, Aliens and Others in Popular Culture*. New Brunswick, NJ and London: Rutgers University Press.

Hitchcock, Susan Tyler. 2007. *Frankenstein: A Cultural History*. New York and London: W. W. Norton.

Hoobler, Dorothy, and Thomas Hoobler. 2006. *The Monsters: Mary Shelley and the Curse of Frankenstein*. New York: Little, Brown.

Levine, George, and U. C. Knoepflmacher, eds. 1979. *The Endurance of* Frankenstein: *Essays on Mary Shelley's Novel*. Berkeley: University of California Press.

Mellor, Anne K. 1988. *Mary Shelley: Her Life, Her Fiction, Her Monsters*. London: Routledge.

Shelley, Mary. [1831] 1994. *Frankenstein*. Mineola, NY: Dover.

Tyler Hitchcock, Susan. 2007. *Frankenstein: The Cultural Legacy*. New York: Norton.

OCCULT FICTION

The field of occult fiction is immensely wide and reflects the ongoing concern, spread across all ages and all cultures, with magic. A very short definition of magic would focus on the possibility of change: change of shape, change of the future, change of perception. All science has to do with change, but magic proposes to effect change through means that do not conform to rational standards, typically in the West through alchemical process and through ritual. Figures such as Simon Magus (from the first century CE), Albertus Magnus (ca. 1200–1280), Cornelius Agrippa (1486–1535), Paracelsus (1493–1541), Giordano Bruno (1548–1600), and Eliphas Levi (1810–1875), among many others, are frequently cited as the precursors and progenitors of occult fiction, along with the apocryphal "Hermes Trismegistus." All of these are thought to have been involved in "practical magic," attempts to influence the world's affairs through unorthodox means, which are often said to be secret except to the initiate.

The more modern attempts to speak of the history of the world as having been influenced by magicians and occult forces beyond our control have a rich history, involving the "Illuminati," Rosicrucianism, and freemasonry; a recent flowering of this attitude is seen in the popularity of works by Dan Brown and his many imitators. But in the nineteenth century, there was a particularly strong crossover between notions of the occult and the practice of Gothic and horror fiction in the hands of such writers as Edward Bulwer-Lytton (1803–1873), Helena Blavatsky (1831–1891), Annie Besant (1847–1933), and Marie Corelli (1855–1924).

Probably the best-known "occult association" is still the Order of the Golden Dawn, which counted among its members Aleister Crowley and W. B. Yeats, and which still flourishes today across many continents, as does its darker brother, Ordo Draconis. Six crucial works that display the development of occult fiction as

Occult Fiction since the Nineteenth Century: A Selective Chronology

1842	Edward Bulwer-Lytton, *Zanoni*
1889	Marie Corelli, *Ardath: The Story of a Dead Self*
1892	Helena Blavatsky, *Nightmare Tales*
1894	Arthur Machen, *The Great God Pan*
1903	Bram Stoker, *The Jewel of Seven Stars*
1917	Aleister Crowley, *Moonchild*
1926	Dion Fortune, *The Secrets of Dr Taverner*
1934	Dennis Wheatley, *The Devil Rides Out*
1941	H. P. Lovecraft, *The Case of Charles Dexter Ward*
1992	M. John Harrison, *The Course of the Heart*
1993	Peter Ackroyd, *The House of Doctor Dee*
1993	Arturo Pérez-Reverte, *The Club Dumas*
1995	Alice Hoffman, *Practical Magic*
2003	Dan Brown, *The Da Vinci Code*
2007	F. G. Cottam, *The House of Lost Souls*
2013	Jeanette Winterson, *The Daylight Gate*

a genre are Arthur Machen's *The Great God Pan* (1894); Crowley's *Moonchild* (1917); Dennis Wheatley's *The Devil Rides Out* (1934); M. John Harrison's *The Course of the Heart* (1992); Peter Ackroyd's *The House of Doctor Dee* (1993); and F. G. Cottam's *The House of Lost Souls* (2007).

"The Great God Pan" was described by the *Westminster Gazette* on its first publication as "an incoherent nightmare of sex" (Spender 2016, 101) but it is actually a work of the occult, in which one Dr. Raymond proposes to use magical means to open up human perception in order to see the spiritual world. His "patient," Mary, is exposed to this operation and becomes reduced to idiocy. Later, various characters encounter a woman known as Helen, and terrible results ensue. It is then revealed that Helen is in fact the daughter of Mary and the Great God Pan, who has been allowed into the human world through Dr. Raymond's occult practices. Helen is eventually cornered and confronted, and dies an extraordinary death, in which she appears to return to various states between beast and human before finally dying.

The concern with the occult here is, as so often, with transgression: Raymond has breached the gap between ordinary human operation and a different, amoral, and finally destructive world which reveals humanity as a thin skin stretched between different realms. In the search for knowledge, he has gone beyond that which is permitted, and what is then revealed is a state where we find our place in a wider swathe of being, but one in which humanity as such can no longer continue.

Aleister Crowley is probably the most famous magician in the Western tradition, a man who was proud to boast of himself as the Great Beast and as the "wickedest man in Europe." It may be that a certain irony is needed when dealing with Crowley; he was widely regarded as a charlatan, but in the world of the occult it is difficult to know what this means, since such a judgment in fact reflects unwittingly the possibility that there may indeed be such a thing as "true magic" even if it is not that which is ritualistically practiced by the Order of the Golden Dawn. With Crowley, magic becomes inextricably confused with drugs and addiction, as he says in his *Diary of a Drug Fiend* (1970).

Moonchild centers on a battle between white (benevolent and selfless) and black (malevolent and self-serving) magicians. Various magicians of the day figure in the novel, including MacGregor Mathers, A. E. Waite, the theosophist Annie Besant, Mary D'Este, the companion of Isadora Duncan, and others; and intriguingly, the conclusion of the book bends occult practice back toward the dread actualities of history, with the white magicians appearing to support the Allies in the First World War, while the black magicians are on the side of the enemy, thus asserting that the occult is not without practical effects. The heart of the book is also quite similar to that of "The Great God Pan," since the essence of magical practice is claimed to be the ritual birth of a "savior," thus justifying "sexual magic" as being the essential ingredient in the search for superhuman powers.

In Wheatley's *The Devil Rides Out*, the Duc de Richleau and Rex van Ryn find that their friend Simon Aaron has become involved with a group of devil-worshippers, whose leader is the highly ambiguous Mr. Mocata. Aaron is rescued from a Sabbath ritual held in one of the most magical of sites, Stonehenge, but although until this point the reader may well believe that the scenario is one of fake magic, what happens next as unearthly forces begin to appear and gain strength suggests that occult powers are not so easily disposed of.

This suggests one of the principal aspects of occult fiction, which is that of belief. Is the reader encouraged to believe that, as with so much late nineteenth-century spiritualism and fortune-telling, magic is mere illusion, a set of conjuring tricks designed to impose on minds weakened by drugs and promises of eternal life? Or is the reader instead encouraged to believe that, on the contrary, magical practices can genuinely cleanse the doors of perception and lead into a wider, fuller view of life where the human is merely one aspect of a set of universal truths, wider than history, deeper than reason? The best of occult fiction remains ambiguous about this: obviously the reader might say that there is no such thing as "genuine" magic at all, but the occultist will riposte that there are, indeed, more things in heaven and earth—and in hell—than we customarily imagine, and it is clear that there is a cultural appetite for belief, even if this involves the thought that to discover new worlds might involve the death of the soul as we usually know it.

M. John Harrison's *The Course of the Heart* follows the lives of three Cambridge students who meet a man named Yaxley, who may—or may not—be a magician. In any case, under his direction they perform a series of magical experiments, and although the processes and results of these experiments are entirely unclear, it appears that this subsequently puts an occult curse on their lives. In order to help his friends—who have married, but whose relationships are bedeviled by depression, recurring hallucination, and worse—the third of the students, who is the narrator, invents a mythical country, the "Coeur," and much of the novel is spent in a fruitless search for this unreal land. Across twenty years, it is supposed that failed magic—if indeed it has failed—is directing the friends' lives and condemning them to various kinds of misery; meanwhile Yaxley himself continues with his attempts to enter forbidden realms, which results in his extremely ugly death.

It is suggested at several points in the book that what is happening is only doing so in a realm of dream; but the question thrown up is whether magic can in fact operate to counter a recurring sense of drudgery and tedium, or whether it is merely that our more depressive encounters with the repetitions of quotidian life are what feeds our constant desire to believe in and engage with the paranormal, even in its seediest aspects.

The Course of Heart is resolutely set in an inescapable present; Ackroyd's *The House of Doctor Dee* takes us back to one of the heartlands of the occult tradition, the sixteenth century, and to perhaps the most celebrated of all Renaissance magicians, John Dee. Dee himself was an impressive intellectual, an astronomer and mathematician, an adviser to Queen Elizabeth, as well as being an astrologer and occultist; he spent a great deal of time trying to converse with angels. He became a feared figure as well as a respected one, and in his novel Ackroyd develops this view of Dee by counterpointing his life and intellectual struggles with those of a contemporary character, Matthew Palmer, who has inherited his house.

The brilliance of the book consists in the way Ackroyd uses magic to illustrate the complexities of history and time. Although Dee and Palmer are separated by four centuries, it appears that something in the house—or in the spells that Dee wrought, which may by now be unshakeable—prevents history from moving forward and ties the characters into an entirely different chronology in which everything is repeated and they are bound into an interminable, and perhaps impossible, search for a realm beyond the human. The power of magic here is frightening, although whether there is any objective basis for this power remains a hovering thought, unsusceptible of final proof; perhaps, again, it is simply a desire for escape and transcendence that motivates our fascination with the occult, although clearly Dee, at his peculiar juncture of history, saw magic as an essential extension, or deepening, of the developing sciences.

F. G. Cottam's *The House of Lost Souls* is a fair representation of contemporary engagements with magic and the occult. Four students visit a derelict house, known as the Fischer House, which has been the scene of a number of magical experiments involving well-known figures from the occult tradition including Wheatley, but also tying this in with a different account of "secret history" involving ghosts, Nazis, and the history of the Second World War. Klaus Fischer has hosted a Crowley-esque gathering devoted to magic, and its reverberations continue to roll down through the decades. The mystery remains whether a real disruption of conventionally imagined historical processes has taken place, or if the protagonists are the victims of a series of hallucinations.

None of this becomes entirely clear, but the themes are evident: the conflict between a malevolent use of magic and the possibility that a version of "enlightenment" might dispel the haunting effects of a previously laid and entrenched magical plot; the relations between dark magic and the recurrence of "evil" throughout history; the question of whether impressionable minds can ever serve as reliable witnesses to events that never fully emerge into clarity; and other questions as to whether the effects of magic are simply produced by drink, drugs, and fear.

Reading on through the history of occult fiction could take us to the other secret histories embodied in the work of authors such as Dan Brown and Donna Tartt, although here the emphasis is not so much on magic as on conspiracy, two themes that are perhaps not so far apart since magic involves the idea that history can be, and perhaps always has been, manipulated by powers operating in the shadows, outside the rational consensus. At its best, as in Jeanette Winterson's *The Daylight Gate* (2012), magic (here in what is perhaps its alternative guise as witchcraft) may be regarded as a kind of empowerment; at its worst, as in historical assumptions and prejudices about the Rosicrucians and the Illuminati, it may be seen as an occult means by which those already in positions of authority preserve, spread, and strengthen their influence over society. Either way, the occult is intrinsically connected with the exercise of power. It is for the writer to persuade the reader that these beliefs are tenable or that they are the very substance of delusion, and here occult fiction has, through the ages, patrolled or hovered over the boundary between the real and the imagined, desire and the defeat of desire, the will toward the superhuman and the draw back toward the bestial.

David Punter

See also: Part Three, Reference Entries: Blackwood, Algernon; Bulwer-Lytton, Edward; *The Case of Charles Dexter Ward;* "Casting the Runes"; *The Devil Rides Out;* Devils and Demons; "The Dunwich Horror"; Ewers, Hanns Heinz; *The Golem;* "The Great God Pan"; "Green Tea"; Haggard, H. Rider; *John Silence: Physician Extraordinary;* Machen, Arthur; Meyrink, Gustav; *The Monk;* Occult Detectives; *Vathek;* Wheatley, Dennis; Witches and Witchcraft.

Further Reading

Bloom, Clive. 2007. "Introduction: Death's Own Backyard." In *Gothic Horror: A Guide for Students and Readers*, edited by Clive Bloom, 1–24. New York: Palgrave Macmillan.

Cowan, Douglas E. 2015. "The Occult and Modern Horror Fiction." In *The Occult World*, edited by Christopher Partridge, 469–477. New York: Routledge.

Geary, Robert F. 1992. *The Supernatural in Gothic Fiction: Horror, Belief, and Literary Change.* Lewiston, NY: Edwin Mellen Press.

Killeen, Jarlath. 2009. "Ghosting the Gothic and the New Occult." In *Gothic Literature 1824–1914*, 124–159. Cardiff: University of Wales Press.

Messent, Peter B., ed. 1981. *Literature of the Occult.* Englewood Cliffs, NJ: Prentice-Hall.

Spender, J. A. [1895] 2016. *The New Fiction: (A Protest against Sex-Mania) and Other Papers.* Routledge Revivals. New York: Routledge.

Willard, Thomas. 1998. "Occultism." In *The Handbook to Gothic Literature*, edited by Marie Mulvey-Roberts, 165–167. New York: New York University Press.

PAGE TO SCREEN: THE INFLUENCE OF LITERARY HORROR ON FILM AND TELEVISION

Modern horror grew out of Gothic literature but was transformed by film and television, which added sights and sounds to the guilty pleasures of dark stories. In the early twentieth century, as film grew from a curiosity that recorded spectacle to a narrative art form, filmmakers turned to written fiction to provide plots and characters for their movies, and horror writers provided moviemakers with dramatic narratives that quickly became a staple of the new industry. Although early screenwriters of horror drew on folklore and mythology for some films, popular horror fiction provided the filmmakers with their richest source of ideas.

Horror Fiction and Horror Films

Prior to the development of the cinema, novelists often secured the dramatic rights to their work because in the nineteenth and early twentieth centuries many popular novels were turned into plays. Bram Stoker's *Dracula* (1897) was one of the earliest works of horror adapted to the screen, remains one of the most popular and often adapted, and provides a textbook example of the problems and possibilities of adaptation. Stoker secured the dramatic rights to *Dracula* with a public reading on the day the novel was published. Two early film adaptations, the Russian *Drakula* and the Hungarian *Drakula halala* (*Dracula's Death*), are now lost. F. W. Murnau's classic German Expressionist film *Nosferatu: eine Simphonie des Grauens* (1922), starring Max Schreck, was both successful and influential. Murnau did not secure permission to use the novel, and Stoker's widow sued to have the film destroyed. Fortunately, some copies remained, and the film was successfully restored in 2005. Despite Murnau's changes in character and location, many critics today consider *Nosferatu* the most successful adaptation of *Dracula*, with Schreck's portrayal of the vampire as a disease-like predator being especially horrific. The first authorized adaptation of Stoker's novel was Tod Browning's 1931 *Dracula* for Universal Pictures, starring Bela Lugosi as a caped, romantic, seductive Dracula. The film was Universal's most successful picture of 1931 and spawned a host of other Universal monster movies, including *Frankenstein* (1931), *The Mummy* (1932), *The Wolfman* (1941), and *The Invisible Man* (1933), all based at least in part on earlier works of fiction. In addition, Universal released numerous sequels based on the original adaptations.

In the 1950s Britain's Hammer Films remade many of the Universal features, including *Dracula* (1958), starring Christopher Lee as a powerful and attractive Dracula and Peter Cushing as an intelligent and aggressive Abraham Van Helsing. Over the next decade and a half, Hammer Films released eight sequels of the popular film, with Christopher Lee starring in six of them. *Dracula* continued to be adapted throughout the twentieth century. Many of these are forgettable, but some are of continued interest, such as Philip Saville's 1978 *Dracula*, made for BBC television and starring Louis Jourdan as a tragically romantic vampire; and John Badham's 1979 *Dracula*, based on the Deane/Balderston play commissioned by Stoker's widow, which served as the screenplay for Universal's 1931 adaptation. In 1992 Francis Ford Coppola released *Bram Stoker's Dracula*, starring Anthony Hopkins as Van Helsing, Wynona Ryder as Mina Harker, and Gary Oldman as Dracula. As much a love story as a horror narrative, *Bram Stoker's Dracula* remains the most expensive and financially successful *Dracula* adaptation to date. A telling indicator of the significance of Stoker's *Dracula* among horror adaptations is that *Dracula* has been adapted more times than any other character; Sherlock Holmes is second (Guiley 2005, 108; Melton 2011, 210).

Mary Shelley's *Frankenstein* (1818) was first adapted to film by Edison Studios in 1910, and later as *Life Without Soul* in 1915. The most famous and influential adaptation was James Whale's for Universal Studios in 1931. Starring Boris Karloff as the monster, Whale's *Frankenstein* shifts the focus from Dr. Frankenstein's ethical dilemma to the pathos of the creature he created, and in the process foregrounds the sympathetic monster. Karloff's performance here, and in the Universal sequel

Some Notable Cinematic Horror Adaptations

Bram Stoker's *Dracula* (1897):

- *Nosferatu* (1922), dir. F. W. Murnau
- *Dracula* (1931), dir. Tod Browning, starring Bela Lugosi
- *Dracula*, a.k.a. *Horror of Dracula* (1958), dir. Terence Fisher, starring Christopher Lee and Peter Cushing
- *Dracula* (1978), dir. Philip Saville, starring Louis Jordan
- *Dracula* (1979), dir. John Badham, starring Frank Langella
- *Bram Stoker's Dracula* (1992), dir. Francis Ford Coppola, starring Gary Oldman

Mary Shelley's *Frankenstein* (1818):

- *Frankenstein* (1910), Edison Studios
- *Frankenstein* (1931), dir. James Whale, starring Boris Karloff
- *Bride of Frankenstein* (1935), dir. James Whale, starring Boris Karloff
- *The Curse of Frankenstein* (1957), dir. Terence Fisher, starring Peter Cushing and Christopher Lee
- *Mary Shelley's Frankenstein* (1994), dir. Kenneth Branagh, starring Robert De Niro

Robert Louis Stevenson's *The Strange Case of Dr. Jekyll and Mr. Hyde* (1886):

- *Dr. Jekyll and Mr. Hyde* (1920), starring Lionel Barrymore
- *Dr. Jekyll and Mr. Hyde* (1931), dir. Rouben Mamoulian, starring Fredric March
- *Dr. Jekyll and Mr. Hyde* (1941), dir. Victor Fleming, starring Spencer Tracy and Ingrid Bergman

Richard Matheson's *I Am Legend* (1954):

- *The Last Man on Earth* (1964), starring Vincent Price
- *The Omega Man* (1971), starring Charlton Heston
- *I Am Legend* (2007), starring Will Smith

Other notable horror adaptations:

- *The Haunting of Hill House* by Shirley Jackson (1959) → *The Haunting* (1963), dir. Robert Wise and *The Haunting* (1999), dir. Jan de Bont
- *Rosemary's Baby* by Ira Levin (1967) → *Rosemary's Baby* (1968), dir. Roman Polanski
- *The Exorcist* by William Peter Blatty (1971) → *The Exorcist* (1973), dir. William Friedkin
- *Carrie* by Stephen King (1974) → *Carrie* (1976), dir. Brian De Palma
- *The Shining* by Stephen King (1977) → *The Shining* (1980), dir. Stanley Kubrick
- *Misery* by Stephen King (1987) → *Misery* (1990), dir. Rob Reiner
- *Interview with the Vampire* by Anne Rice (1976) → *Interview with the Vampire* (1994), dir. Neil Jordan

Matt Cardin

Bride of Frankenstein (1935), created the iconic image of the monster that remains embedded in popular culture. *Frankenstein* has been adapted more than seventy times, including seven adaptations by Hammer Films, the best of which is *The Curse of Frankenstein* (1957), directed by Terence Fisher and starring Peter Cushing as Victor Frankenstein and Christopher Lee as the monster. Other notable adaptations include Kenneth Branagh's *Mary Shelley's Frankenstein* (1994), starring Robert De Niro as the monster, and Mel Brooks's comic masterpiece *Young Frankenstein* (1974), starring Gene Wilder as Victor Frankenstein's grandson and Peter Boyle as the monster.

Robert Louis Stevenson's *The Strange Case of Dr. Jekyll and Mr. Hyde* (1886), with its dramatic transformation of the morally upright Dr. Jekyll into the depraved Mr. Hyde, attracted numerous film adapters. As early as 1912 James Cruze directed and starred in a twelve-minute version of the story. John Barrymore starred in a 1920 silent adaptation, and in 1931 Paramount Pictures released a sound version directed by Rouben Mamoulian and starring Fredric March, who won an Academy Award for his performance. The film was so successful that in 1941, when MGM bought the rights to the story, the studio attempted to buy and withdraw all copies of the 1931 film before releasing their adaptation, starring Spencer Tracy and Ingrid Bergman, which was not as critically or popularly successful. There have been more than thirty film adaptations of Stevenson's novel, and aside from the 1931 Fredric March film, the most acclaimed is *Mary Reilly* (1996), starring Julia Roberts and John Malkovich.

Several other notable adaptations of horror fiction were released in the 1930s. In 1933 Universal Pictures released *The Invisible Man*, loosely based on H. G. Wells's popular novel. Directed by James Whale and starring Claude Raines, *The Invisible Man*, like its source novel, explored the boundaries between horror and science fiction. Universal Studios' two other classic monster movies, *The Mummy* (1932), starring Boris Karloff, and *The Wolf Man* (1941), starring Lon Chaney Jr., were not directly adapted from novels but were influenced by them. *The Mummy* was made in response to the discovery of the tomb of Tutankhamun ("King Tut"), but the film has strong similarities to Arthur Conan Doyle's short story "Lot No. 249" (1892) and Bram Stoker's novel *Jewel of the Seven Stars* (1903). *The Wolf Man*, for its part, was inspired by European folklore, but two early novels, Alexandre Dumas's *The Wolf-Leader* (1857) and Erckmann-Chatrian's *Hugues-le-Loup* (1869), translated into English as *The Man-Wolf*, may have influenced the filmmakers.

Two studios, Universal Pictures and Hammer Films, dominated the horror market during the studio era (ca. 1930–1948), but with the breakup of the studios after the Second World War (1939–1945), outstanding horror films were produced by many companies, although American International Pictures cornered the market on grade B horror thrillers such as *I Was a Teenage Werewolf* and *I Was a Teenage Frankenstein*, both in 1957. AIP also released better films, including four adaptations of Edgar Allan Poe's fiction: *The Fall of the House of Usher* (1960), *The Pit and the Pendulum* (1961), *The Haunted Palace* (1963), and *The Masque of the Red*

Death (1964), all starring Vincent Price. In the postwar period and the years following, both horror fiction and horror films moved from the margins of the popular to the mainstream, no longer being a genre defined by grade B films and cheap paperback novels. The popularity and quality of the horror adaptations that have appeared since the 1960s reflects the renewed interest of writers, filmmakers, and audiences.

Two horror novels published in 1954 became film horror classics when adapted. Jack Finney's horror science fiction novel *The Invasion of the Body Snatchers* captured the paranoid mood of Cold War America when released by Allied Artists as a film in 1956, and Richard Matheson's classic *I Am Legend*, about the lone human survivor of a worldwide plague of vampires, was adapted three times: as *The Last Man on Earth* (1964), starring Vincent Price; *The Omega Man* (1971), starring Charlton Heston; and *I Am Legend* (2007), starring Will Smith. Robert Bloch published *Psycho* in 1959, and in 1960 Paramount released Alfred Hitchcock's memorable adaptation starring Janet Leigh as the unwitting victim of Anthony Perkins's homicidal mania. Hitchcock's masterful control of mystery and horror elevated the film to the status of a cultural icon. Also published in 1959 was Shirley Jackson's *The Haunting of Hill House,* a chilling story of a group of psychic explorers who visit a house that may or may not be haunted. Robert Wise's 1963 adaptation, *The Haunting*, starring Julie Harris and Claire Bloom, effectively combines elements of horror and psychological thriller. In 1999 MGM released a second, and decidedly inferior, adaptation starring Liam Neeson.

In 1968 Paramount released *Rosemary's Baby*, based on Ira Levin's best-selling 1967 novel. Directed by Roman Polanski and starring Mia Farrow, the film successfully combines psychological realism with supernatural horror as a young woman slowly discovers the child she is carrying may be Satan's. Another successful adaptation that combined elements of the occult with psychological realism was William Friedkin's 1973 *The Exorcist,* based on William Peter Blatty's 1971 novel of demonic possession in modern Washington, D.C. Both films were financially and critically successful, establishing the genre of cinematic occult horror. In 1974 Peter Benchley released *Jaws*, his wildly successful novel of a vengeful great white shark terrorizing a Long Island beach community. For the film adaptation Universal Pictures hired director Steven Spielberg, who worked quickly through production; the film was released the next year to popular success. In 1976 Anne Rice reinvented the vampire novel with *Interview with the Vampire*. Set in New Orleans, Rice's novel revolves around the relationships among three vampires—Louis, Lestat, and Claudia—and begins to develop a cultural history of vampires that Rice continues to expand through her *Vampire Chronicles*. In 1994 Warner Brothers released the film adaptation, starring Brad Pitt and Tom Cruise, to positive reviews. Another film adaptation from the series, *The Queen of the Damned* (2002), was not as successful.

If earlier periods of horror film were dominated by studios such as Universal Pictures, Hammer Films, and American International, the latter part of the twentieth century was dominated by the novels and adaptations of the work of one man, Stephen King, who in addition to writing more than seventy books has had over one hundred films and television programs adapted from or based on his work. Several works, such as *The Shining* and *Carrie*, have been adapted more than once. Adjusted for inflation, King's films have grossed nearly eight hundred million dollars. Five of his highest grossing films are horror adaptations: *The Shining* (1980), *Carrie* (1976), *Misery* (1990), *Pet Sematary* (1989), and *Secret Window* (2004). Three of these films have become cultural icons, defining film horror in the late twentieth century. In adapting King's 1974 supernatural horror novel *Carrie*, Brian De Palma emphasized the terror of a young abused girl who discovers her telekinetic ability when she has her first period, and the horrific results of bullying by her high school classmates. Sissy Spacek received an Academy Award nomination for her performance in the title role. Director Rob Reiner directed the adaptation of King's 1987 psychological horror novel *Misery*. James Caan plays Paul Sheldon, writer of romance novels, who writes a manuscript killing off the series heroine. Kathy Bates plays Annie Wilkes, a nurse who rescues Sheldon after an automobile accident, and while helping him recover discovers his intentions to kill her favorite character. She imprisons him, eventually hobbling him by breaking his ankles with a sledgehammer. Sheldon eventually kills his tormentor. Bates received an Academy Award for her performance. Stanley Kubrick's adaptation of King's 1977 novel *The Shining* starred Jack Nicholson, Shelley Duval, Danny Lloyd, and Scatman Crothers. Kubrick's depiction of the descent of Jack Torrance, played by Nicholson, into madness and murder in an isolated and haunted resort hotel stands as one of the most terrifying films ever made, and Nicholson's performance has become legendary.

Early filmmakers found stories to adapt in other literary forms, drama and history being the most obvious examples, but they also drew upon comic strips and comic books. Later, graphic novels joined these other forms in serving as source material. Science fiction and fantasy filmmakers have adapted these sources early and often, as the long relationship between the Superman, Batman, and now Marvel Universe characters in print and on the large and small screens clearly demonstrates. Directors of horror films have recently explored this genre. Stephen Norrington in *Blade* (1998) and its sequels, and Guillermo del Toro in *Hellboy* (2004) and its sequel, both provide successful horror/fantasy crossovers. Another recent trend has been the adaptation of young adult fiction, especially popular mixed-genre fiction combining horror with either fantasy or romance, such as the film adaptations of J. K. Rowling's seven *Harry Potter* novels and Stephenie Meyer's *Twilight* saga.

Horror Fiction and Horror Television

Television began and survived with adoption and adaptation, borrowing formats and content from radio, drama, film, and literature. Commercial television modeled news, musicals, comedy, and dramatic programming on that of radio, which permitted frequent advertising breaks, and when, in the mid-1950s, film studios began to make their pre-1948 content available to television networks and stations, many of the Universal horror films, such as *Dracula* and *Frankenstein* and their sequels, began to appear on television, often as late-night or weekend content.

Television adopted another format, the anthology, from literature. Drawing on the growing popularity of science fiction and horror films in the late 1950s and early 1960s, American networks presented genre material, some original and some adapted from fiction, in such anthology series as *Alfred Hitchcock Presents* (CBS/NBC, 1955–1962), *One Step Beyond* (ABC, 1959–1961), *The Twilight Zone* (CBS, 1959–1964), *Thriller* (NBC, 1960–1962), and *The Outer Limits* (ABC, 1963–1965). All of these series presented science fiction, supernatural, and horror stories, but *Thriller*, hosted by Boris Karloff, was more focused on Gothic horror stories, including several by Robert Bloch. The anthology series has remained a significant form in providing viewers with original and adapted horror narratives, as shown in the popularity of such series as *Tales from the Crypt* (HBO, 1989–1996), with a title and format adapted from the classic 1950s pulp horror comic book of the same name, and *Tales from the Dark Side* (1983–1988). Networks continued to develop new sources and formats for horror material. ABC adapted Charles Addams's *New Yorker* cartoons for its comic Gothic *Addams Family* (1964–1966), a satire on American life featuring a macabre family living in a decaying Victorian mansion. More comic and less satiric was CBS's *The Munsters* (1964–1966), which adapted characters based on *Dracula* and *Frankenstein*, as well as their Universal Studios incarnations. Dracula and Frankenstein's monster have become cultural icons thanks to television as well as film and fiction, appearing everywhere from Public Television to breakfast cereal boxes (Count Chocula and Frankenberry).

Because of the need for broadcast content, television producers, in addition to acquiring the rights to earlier-released films, introduced made-for-television movies, which were usually less costly and time consuming to bring to the small screen than traditional films. As over-the-air stations and cable networks proliferated, the demand for new content increased, and made-for-television horror movies, adapted both from classics of Gothic horror and from popular horror fiction, became popular to both broadcasters and audiences.

The popularity of Mary Shelley's *Frankenstein* and Bram Stoker's *Dracula* made them both attractive to television producers. In 1972 NBC released *Frankenstein: The True Story*, starring Leonard Whiting, Jane Seymour, and James Mason. The film was originally aired in two ninety-minute segments, and it presented the monster as handsome upon creation, only to grow uglier as the film progressed. In 2004 the Hallmark Channel released a miniseries adaption of *Frankenstein* starring Alec Newman, Luke Goss, and Donald Sutherland, which follows Shelley's novel more closely than most adaptations.

In 1974, CBS broadcast released a made-for-television adaptation of *Dracula*, directed by Dan Curtis and starring Jack Palance. Outside the United States it was given a theatrical release. The film is noted for Palance's performance and for suggesting a connection between the fictitious Dracula and the historical Vlad Tepes, or Vlad the Impaler, the fifteenth-century Wallachian warlord. The television adaptations of the works of Stephen King—thirty-four made-for-television movies, television series, and episodes in other series—can provide an overview of adapted-for-television works by a popular contemporary writer. Television is a medium that can be adapted for narratives of varying lengths, and many of Stephen King's longer works have been adapted for television miniseries rather than for the cinema, although some of his works have appeared on both the large and small screens. Four of King's most popular works have been adapted twice. 'Salem's Lot, King's vampire novel published in 1975, first appeared as a successful miniseries produced by Warner Brothers in 1979, starring David Soul and James Mason. It was recreated by TNT starring Rob Lowe in 2004. Similarly, The Shining, published in 1977, was readapted (after Kubrick's 1980 version) for television by ABC as a miniseries starring Rebecca de Mornay and Steven Weber in 1997. It, King's epic novel of a cosmic horror terrorizing a small town in Maine across multiple generations, was adapted as a successful miniseries in 1992, with Tim Curry starring as the terrifying Pennywise the Clown, who preys on children. In 2017 a new theatrical adaptation was released with Pennywise played by Bill Skarsgård. In addition, King's The Dead Zone, published in 1979, was adapted twice, first for the large screen by David Cronenberg in 1983 and later as a series for television that ran on USA Network from 2002 until 2006.

Stephen King is not the only successful horror author whose work has been adapted as successful television miniseries. The Vampire Diaries is a successful young adult series of novels published between 1991 and 2012 by L. J. Smith about a beautiful young high school student who falls in love with two attractive vampires. Three additional novels based on the series were written by ghostwriter Aubrey Clark and published in 2012 and 2013. In 2006 the CW network began airing a television adaptation, and it ran for many seasons. The Walking Dead is another popular adapted horror television series. Based on the comic book series of the same name written by Robert Kirkman and drawn by Tony Moore, the series revolves around the adventures of Rick Grimes, a sheriff's deputy who awakens from a coma in the middle of a quarantine Georgia faced with a zombie apocalypse. The series began airing on AMC in 2010, and in 2015 a spin-off series, Fear the Walking Dead, was produced by the same network.

The attraction of many of the classic Gothic horror monsters is that they are able to overcome natural law and defy death. Mummies, Frankenstein's monster, Dracula, and zombies all come back from the dead. The economics of film and television, with ever increasing audiences and formats, demands a constant supply of characters and stories. It would seem inevitable that undying creatures that appeared first in print would be kept alive through adaptations, sequels, spin-offs, and parodies that have come back to life on the large and small screens.

Jim Holte

See also: The Gothic Literary Tradition; Horror Comics; The Legacy of *Frankenstein*: From Gothic Novel to Cultural Myth; *Part One, Horror through History*: Horror from 1900 to 1950; Horror from 1950 to 2000; Horror in the Twenty-First Century; *Part Three, Reference Entries*: Bloch, Robert; *Dracula*; *The Exorcist*; *I Am Legend*; *Interview with the Vampire*; King, Stephen; Mummies; Poe, Edgar Allan; *Rosemary's Baby*; *The Strange Case of Dr. Jekyll and Mr. Hyde*; Vampires; Werewolves; Zombies.

Further Reading

Backer, Ron. 2015. *Classic Horror Films and the Literature That Inspired Them*. Jefferson, NC: McFarland.

Broderick, James F. 2012. *Now a Terrifying Motion Picture!: Twenty-Five Classic Works of Horror Adapted from Book to Film*. Jefferson, NC: McFarland.

Guiley, Rosemary. 2005. *The Encyclopedia of Vampires, Werewolves, and Other Monsters*. New York: Facts on File.

Hanke, Ken. 2013. *A Critical Guide to the Horror Film Series*. London: Routledge.

Holte, James. 1997. *Dracula in the Dark: A Study of the Dracula Film Adaptations*. Westport, CT: Greenwood Press.

Jowett, Laura, and Stacey Abbott. 2013. *TV Horror: Investigating the Dark Side of the Small Screen*. London and New York: I. B. Tauris.

Melton, J. Gordon. 2011. *The Vampire Book: The Encyclopedia of the Undead*. Canton, MI: Visible Ink Press.

RELIGION, HORROR, AND THE SUPERNATURAL

The critical commonplace, largely uncontested, is that horror is marked by a prevalent concern with the material and psychological. However, horror is also concerned with invoking a sense of spiritual and religious anxiety. In fact, authors from Arthur Machen to Clive Barker agree that the roots of horror literature are embedded in religious traditions or theological conflicts. While scholarship on the area of religious horror is relatively new, there are several exemplary books and essays on its literary origins in supernatural Gothic literature. British Gothic literature is marked by certain prevalent religious prejudices both anti-Catholic and anti-Semitic. These strains of theological conflict can be read as the attempt to assert a hegemonic Protestantism against the threat of foreign and, in the case of Catholicism, former religious traditions. Although the religious and supernatural codes and conventions set out by the Gothic in the eighteenth and nineteenth centuries are crucial to any consideration of religion's connection with horror and supernatural literature, it is important to understand that horror goes beyond the traditions and inheritances of Christian Britain and is created within the contexts of different faiths and nationalities. Consequently, the representation of religion and the supernatural in horror fiction does not flow in one direction or from one nation or religion, but is created out of a cultural exchange of religious symbols, narratives, and themes.

It was the religious imagination of such early Christian theologians as Augustine of Hippo that first introduced the Western world to the horror of the human condition, and it was visionaries such as the Italian Dante Alighieri who first journeyed in the imagination to the depths and limits of hell. Their Protestant and Catholic illustrations of divine punishment and human perversity and sin greatly inform European horror to this day. This is not to suggest that horror fiction, as a whole, is orthodox or faithful. The ideology and form of horror fiction tends to focus on the corrupt and perverse; therefore, it is inclined toward showing the reader what is dreadful about church and God. Since the establishment of Anglicanism during the Protestant Reformation in 1534, supernatural and religious horror has become associated with an increasingly secularized form of literature preoccupied with questioning rather than preaching religious lessons and dogmas. As early as the Renaissance period, authors such as Edmund Spenser (1552–1599) and William Shakespeare (1564–1616) used modes of horror, supernaturalism, and the religious to undermine church and state. In the seventeenth century, the English poet John Milton's epic, *Paradise Lost* (1667), caused religious controversy by suggesting a remarkably seductive and sympathetic devil. It was, however, the emancipatory project of the Enlightenment from the mid-eighteenth century onward that influenced two generations of darkly supernatural writing. This writing was tethered to certain religious and sociohistorical events that would breed religious horror. Events such as the tensions surrounding the Catholic Emancipation campaign through the 1770s, the French Revolution in 1789, and the eventual passing of the Catholic Emancipation Act in 1829 all had an effect on the supernatural and religious themes of Gothic novels like Horace Walpole's *The Castle of Otranto* (1764), Ann Radcliffe's *The Mysteries of Udolpho* (1794), and Matthew Lewis's *The Monk* (1796). These early Gothic writers made common the tropes of medieval and foreign European settings, entrapments in a monastery or convent, evil clergy and the Inquisition, wandering Jews, satanic or occult ritual, and supernatural occurrences. The holy terrors of the Catholic Church continued to be a favorite theme well into the twentieth century. J. M. Barrie's Scottish Gothic story, *Farewell Miss Logan* (1932), for example, tells the story of a Protestant minister working in a lonely highland glen beset by ambiguous vampires, ghosts, and Roman Catholic Jacobites.

However, "foreign" Catholicism was not the only aspect of the religious to make Gothic and horror writers uncomfortable. A second wave of Gothic novels in the second and third decades of the nineteenth century established new religious and supernatural conventions. Taking inspiration from both science and religion, Mary Shelley gave scientific and theological form to the supernatural in *Frankenstein* (1818). Charles Maturin's *Melmoth the Wanderer* (1820) features a scholar who sells his soul for longer life only to become doomed to wander the world seeking death and redemption. Subsequent scholarship identifies the accursed wanderer—a literary inheritor of the anti-Semitic religious identity of Jews—as another horrifying figure popular among Gothic and Romantic writers. The first American Gothic novel is also a religious horror story. Charles Brockden Brown's *Wieland* (1798) introduced the subject of America's oppressive Puritan mindset by featuring a minister driven over the edge of sanity by his supernatural suspicions and sense of spiritual failure. Fanatical Protestant sects and Puritan paranoia are also the principal targets in Nathaniel Hawthorne's *The Scarlet Letter* (1850) and *The House of Seven Gables* (1851). Gothic Scotland is the setting for James Hogg's *The Private Memoirs and Confessions of a Justified Sinner* (1824) and Robert Louis Stevenson's *Dr. Jekyll and Mr. Hyde* (1886). These stories work through Calvinism's oppressive guilt, self-scrutiny, and God by describing men pursued by their own demonic doubles.

An interesting thing to note in early Gothic novels is the differences between the authors' perspectives on the representation of the religious and supernatural. Lewis's parade of ghosts, demons, and, ultimately the devil himself is at once outrageous and irreverent. Radcliffe, on the other hand, showed timidity when it came to religious and otherworldly matters, offering natural but complicated explanations of the supernatural. Furthermore, the fact that all early Gothic writers show timidity about representing God has been read as underlying Christian values by some scholars and evidence of God's increasing obsoleteness by others.

This nervousness around the representation of the supernatural was to change with mainstreaming of Gothic in Victorian literary culture and its branching off into subgenres such as the ghost story and weird or cosmic fiction. By the mid- to late nineteenth century, the clergy had been replaced with other fears also tethered to certain religious and social transformations, namely, the increased intrusion of science and materialism into people's lives. This was sharpened by the discoveries of Charles Darwin on the evolution of the human in *The Origin of the Species* (1859) and the antimodernist scholarly work *Degeneration* (1895) by Max Nordau, both of which ignited diverse fears about what it means to be human. In response to the perceived threat of scientific materialism, a variety of spiritual and religious movements—such as, to name one notable example, Spiritualism—sprang up throughout the middle and latter part of the nineteenth century, each in its own way attempting to bridge the divide between the rational and the spiritual.

The Victorian occult horror story and supernatural tale features séances, mesmerism, paganism, alchemy, medieval occult religions, and a more exuberant and varied supernaturalism. This indicates that the supernatural was becoming less tethered to fundamental religions or conventional concepts of God. It also suggests that the evocation of strange worlds, peculiar rituals, and exotic supernatural entities enabled readers to entertain spiritual notions that were otherwise fading in their everyday lives. Arthur Machen's stories are filled to the brim with pagan gods and occult demons and an ambivalent attraction to medieval rituals and religions. Another writer who commonly exploited the occult was Oscar Wilde. In *The Picture of Dorian Gray* (1890), Wilde used the standard aesthetics of Catholicism and an occult narrative to tell the story of the separation of one man's soul from his body, but turned this into an exploration of his own Catholic tendencies. The fascination with paganism and occult religions remained well into the twentieth century where it was used to develop the idea of a person being caught between the oppressive horrors of the past and the soulless materialism of the present.

Horror, which is loosely deemed a subgenre of Gothic literature, shares many of that genre's fears and anxieties as well as its religious ambiguities. But along with being traceable in this way to a late eighteenth-century English literature, there is, in fact, a wealth of horror from a diverse range of spiritual traditions from Judaism to Islam and Asia, each of which use the supernatural to explore the horrors of religious experience.

The zombie, for example, has its roots in the African-derived religious systems of Haitian Vodou—more commonly known in horror literature and film as Voodoo—Jamaican Obeah, and Cuban Santéria. As perhaps the most ubiquitous icon of the horror genre in the early twenty-first century, the zombie lends itself to both shifts and transformations in the religious and cultural experiences of Caribbean and Latin American people. This includes their racist displacement and oppression by white colonialism. The zombie, along with other Vodou spirits such as the Jumbie, was first brought to the attention of colonial readers in horrific tales of slave religion, barbaric ritual, and black magic. Vodou and its ceremonies also played an integral role in the uprising of Haitian and Jamaican slaves during two separate rebellions. However, despite repeated attempts to suppress and delegitimize its practice, Vodou survived by becoming intermixed with the European colonists' native Catholicism. The interest in Vodou traditions was rekindled in the early twentieth century by both white and African authors playing to colonial mythology and romanticism, and by Caribbean authors looking to understand their religious traditions and the horrors of their past.

The reinvigoration of the zombie in the twentieth century also fit with the turn to the body in the mid-twentieth-century horror aesthetic. As well as making literature more recognizably categorized as horror, the body was the focus of multiple religious and theological fears. In a great many of these books, possession and dispossession symbolize a persistent supernatural dimension. By portraying the evil invasion of the female body, for example, Ira Levin's *Rosemary's Baby* (1967) and William Blatty's *The Exorcist* (1971) suggest a threat from forces not only above and beyond but also within. Unnatural violations also occur in Noel Scanlon's *Black Ashes* (1986), a book on the insidious horrors of reincarnation and a Hindu god-demon named Ravana who incarnates as a creepy and charismatic leader of an Indian cult. Other authors return to more typical psycho-religious Gothic ground, albeit in more gruesome manifestations. While echoes of America's dark English heritage and sinister pagan rites appear in Thomas Tryon's *Harvest Home* (1973), Haitian Vodou is to blame for a series of child sacrifices in Nicholas Condé's *The Religion* (1987).

Other authors reflexively explored these literary themes alongside historical events and interpretations of scripture. For example, racism and anti-Semitism are the essence of evil in Dan Simmons's novel *Carrion Comfort* (1989). Similarly, in his earlier book, *Song of Kali* (1985), the setting of Calcutta, the grotesque Hindu goddess Kali, and the hideous ceremony of human sacrifice are used to address such diverse fears as the fear of women, the fear of losing children, and humanity's

Religious Horror around the World

Although **Asian horror** occasionally borrows the aesthetics of Western Christianity and the Gothic, its supernatural concepts are derived not from Christian notions of sin, evil, or anti-Catholicism, but from various forms of Hindu, Taoist, and Buddhist philosophy. In Japanese religious folk tradition, for instance, the *Onryō* are female ghosts that have died in tragic or unlawful circumstances and are revered as minor deities. Unless pacified by homage and ritual (*onyrōgami*), these spirits can become restless and nasty, inflicting terrible justice and vengeance upon the guilty.

Islamic horror stories are populated by Jinns, unseen spirits that are derived from the Qur'an and that can manifest as human or animal. Jinns can be good or bad, playful or vengeful. However, as is often the case in these largely conservative stories, an evil Jinn can also be neutralized by prayer and leading a good Muslim life.

American Jewish Gothic stories convey complex fears about the mutability and instability of memory, time, place, and "authentic" Jewish identity. The Dybbuk is a Jewish poltergeist whose name is derived from Hebrew meaning "attachment" or "cling to." Other undead spirits seeking homes in human bodies appear in early Kabbalistic texts.

unholy passion for violence. In all of these twentieth-century examples, the body—its sexuality, transgression, and ruin—continues to pose as our most absorbing theological conundrum. This culminates most perversely in the "splatterpunk" movement that marked the closing of the century. The supernatural vocabulary and Christian values that underpin the prolific writings of Stephen King, James Herbert, Dean Koontz, Clive Barker, and Peter Straub are made strange and ambivalent by their alternation between apocalyptic and emancipatory transgressions of the body.

Religion and the supernatural continue to be a characteristic of contemporary horror. Religious horror is shaped by many issues, including nationality, race, sexuality, history, politics, and, of course, theology. It is also the case that the genre's use of supernaturalism challenges and complicates such issues as the boundary between flesh and spirit, the material and immaterial world, and transcendence and transgression. There is not just one religious horror, but religious horrors with many different forms and levels of dread and fear. These change as writers transform and renew the form in order to explore shifting cultural and religious concerns.

Eleanor Beal

See also: Apocalyptic Horror; Occult Fiction; *Part One, Horror through History*: Horror in the Ancient World; Horror in the Middle Ages; Horror in the Early Modern

Era; *Part Three, Reference Entries*: Barker, Clive; Devils and Demons; *The Exorcist*; *Harvest Home*; Herbert, James; King, Stephen; Koontz, Dean; Machen, Arthur; *The Monk*; The Numinous; *Rosemary's Baby*; *Song of Kali*; Spiritualism; Straub, Peter.

Further Reading

Beal, Timothy. 2002. *Religion and Its Monsters*. New York: Routledge.

Geary, Robert F. 1993. *The Supernatural in Gothic Fiction: Horror, Belief and Literary Change*. New York: Edwin Mellen Press.

Ingebretson, Edward J. 1996. *Maps of Heaven, Maps of Hell: Religious Terror as Memory from the Puritans to Stephen King*. New York and London: M. E. Sharpe.

Nelson, Victoria. 2001. *The Secret Life of Puppets*. Cambridge, MA: Harvard University Press.

O'Malley, Robert. 2006. *Catholicism, Sexual Deviance and Victorian Gothic Culture*. Cambridge, UK: Cambridge University Press.

Porte, Joel. 1974. "In the Hands of an Angry God." In *The Gothic Imagination: Essays in Dark Romanticism*, edited by G. R. Thompson, 42–64. Pullman: Washington State University Press.

SHAKESPEAREAN HORRORS

William Shakespeare (1564–1616) has been an important influence on almost all genres and modes of literature; he casts a significant shadow over literary endeavors to this day. Known principally as a playwright, he also wrote poetical works, acted, and was a partner in the business of the Globe Theatre. He has rarely been considered specifically in regard to horror writing, however, despite the wealth of horror tropes and horrific images contained within his work. This is perhaps mainly due to the perceived gulf between Shakespeare as exemplar of high literary culture and the traditionally low esteem paid to horror as trashy sensationalism. Such a tradition ignores the ways in which the bodily effect of horror fits perfectly with the ideas of humors and passions that prevailed in Shakespeare's time. Theater was believed to have a physical effect on its audiences, with their emotional response being a result of actual changes to their humoral makeup (changes that still have a metaphorical afterlife even after the decline of humoral theories).

Shakespearean horrors are largely in keeping with the early modern contexts of their authorship. Consequently, supernatural and spectral horror predominates. The ghosts and witches of contemporary cultural belief find their place on Shakespeare's stage, alongside the flair for horrific spectacle that characterized the new professional theater. Competing with—often sharing the same performance spaces as—popular public entertainments such as bearbaiting meant that playwrights were keen to appeal to the more bloodthirsty interests of their paying customers. The hugely popular genre of revenge tragedy in particular fits well with horror, as it used increasingly lurid and sensational ways to torture its participants and thrill its audience.

The one play that has attracted most attention for its horror elements is *Titus Andronicus* (ca. 1594), although this attention has traditionally been far from positive.

Generally dismissed as immature juvenilia and, indeed, often argued against being by Shakespeare at all, this dark tragedy bursts onto the stage with mutilations, decapitations, sacrifices, and forced cannibalism. In exploring the results of a corrupt emperor's rule, the play revels in a view of the human body that is surprisingly close to the modern "torture-porn" of the likes of *Saw* (2004) and *Hostel* (2005). It is perhaps no surprise that productions of *Titus* invariably result in audience members fainting—a fact that publicity material delights in mentioning. In the figure of Titus's daughter, Lavinia—savagely raped and then mutilated (her hands cut off and tongue removed)—we can see an early example of the displayed victim that haunts horror throughout the ages. Because she is unable to express the identity of her attackers, her family is forced to attempt to interpret what has happened through their engagement with her horrific wounds, a clear metaphorical comparison with the role of horror literature in culture more generally. Although clearly an early work, *Titus* is far more sophisticated than traditional critics' dismissals might indicate. The play highlights the traumatic and horrific results of war, and its layering of staged atrocities leads to a bloody climax that wipes the stage clean of the majority of the combatants. The audience is left simultaneously appalled and thrilled by the excesses that they have witnessed—a conflation of feelings that is quintessentially related to the literature of horror.

Shakespearean Horrors in the Modern World

Such is Shakespeare's influence and importance, there have been many attempts to adapt his plays into every imaginable media form. Notable examples within horror literature and film include:

- *Theatre of Blood* (1973): Possibly the greatest work of Shakespearean-influenced horror, this delightful movie stars Vincent Price as Edward Lionheart, an actor who takes vengeance on his scornful critics through elaborate devices taken straight from Shakespeare's plays.
- *Titus* (1999): Julie Taymor's film version of Shakespeare's bloodiest play combines arthouse and horror techniques to provide a stunning and spectacular adaptation. Extra horror associations are achieved by the casting of Anthony Hopkins as Titus following his performance as Hannibal Lecter in *Silence of the Lambs* and its sequels, particularly given the cannibalistic ending.
- *Romeo and Juliet vs. the Living Dead* (2009): Low-budget and enthusiastic movie mash-up of Shakespeare's classic tale of doomed love and the ubiquitous zombie.
- *Shakespeare Undead* (2010): Along the lines of many horror mash-ups such as *Pride and Prejudice and Zombies*, this novel recasts William Shakespeare as an immortal vampire with powers of necromancy, handily explaining the breadth of his knowledge and experience. While the first novel is equal parts *Twilight* and *Shakespeare in Love*, the sequel, *Zombie Island*, retells the story of *The Tempest* through a period version of the Romero-esque zombie movie.

While *Titus Andronicus* may be the clearest and most visceral of Shakespearean horrors, it is certainly not his only dalliance with darkness. The social and religious upheaval of the early modern era in which he was writing meant that there was a wealth of Gothic horror tropes on which he could draw. Not surprisingly, these moments of horror found expression predominantly, although not exclusively, in Shakespeare's tragedies. Ghosts populate his history plays, and the fairies of *Midsummer Night's Dream* are not necessarily the innocent Victorian sprites of contemporary understanding. The transformation of Bottom in the same play also has potential for a much more horrific portrayal of the closeness between human and animal than its usual slapstick performance. However, it is the tragedies that represent the most developed and engaged examples of Shakespearean horrors.

Julius Caesar (1600) can be seen as a precursor of the more surreal moments of Giallo movies, with its horrific portents, highly choreographed stabbing, and musically driven ghost scene. Although far less overtly horror-based than Shakespeare's earlier Roman play, the supernatural and gory elements drive the play's narrative and drama, with the focus on Caesar's bloodied robe in particular bringing the audience face-to-face with the violent result of ambition. Such a use of horror elements is continued in *Hamlet, Prince of Denmark* (1600–1601). Shakespeare's most celebrated play is dramatically dominated by the Freudian/supernatural presence of the former king's ghost. The repeated calls for Hamlet to "Remember" his father set the tone for centuries of hauntings, and productions on stage and screen have continually been heavily influenced by contemporary horror techniques in their representations of this spectral figure.

The claustrophobic tragedy of *Othello* (1604) contains a vein of problematic racist representations of the titular Moor. The play itself is more nuanced but does depict an early modern idea of the black soldier as monstrous and inhuman. This representation is a development from that of the villainous Aaron in *Titus*—a character who takes great relish in his role as villain. Instead, the horror of *Othello* is in the readiness of civilized society to dehumanize an individual labeled as "other." This effect is achieved in part through reference to contemporary ideas of truly monstrous races that were popular in travel literature of the time: "And of the Cannibals that each other eat, / The Anthropophagi, and men whose heads / Do grow beneath their shoulders" (Shakespeare 1997, Act 1, Scene 3, Lines 142–144). The introduction of such creatures leads to a spectrum of humanity that Iago exploits in horrific terms of proto–white supremacy. The eventual death of Desdemona is a prototypical foreshadowing of the enraged and murderous madman that would become a staple of sensationalist horror literature.

If *Othello* is claustrophobic and enclosed geographically, then *King Lear* (1606) takes the horror inside and relocates it into the mental degeneration of the eponymous ruler. While most famously providing a chilling examination of the effects of alienation and senility, the play also makes use of early modern traditions of demons and fairies throughout Lear's isolation on the heath. The liberal use of Samuel Harsnett's *Declaration of Egregious Popish Impostures* (1603) relocates the satirical listing of demons into a pagan, primitive version of folk horror in which individu-als feel threatened by forces lurking just outside of their understanding. Of course, *Lear* also infamously features perhaps Shakespeare's most vivid use of "splatter" as the Duke of Gloucester's eyes are savagely removed onstage and then stamped on.

Macbeth (1607) can be seen as the culmination of Shakespeare's various uses of horror imagery and motifs, containing as it does a veritable "best of" with gore, ghosts, witches, and supernatural omens. Often considered to be capitalizing on contempo-rary concerns with witchcraft (James VI and I having written a book on the subject), its repeated use of motifs such as the omens and hauntings from *Julius Caesar* suggest that Shakespeare was providing his paying audience with what they were demand-ing. This popular aspect of Shakespeare as a writer further undermines the traditional split between him as high culture and horror; in many ways he was working within a tradition similar to that of the sensationalist writers of later periods.

In *Macbeth* the horror elements are crucial in developing and furthering the plot, resulting in the play being more clearly identifiable as a horror text than any other of Shakespeare's works, apart perhaps from the body horror of *Titus An-dronicus*. The dark setting, full of supernatural and folkloric aspects, creates an oppressive world that serves as a combination of the claustrophobia of *Othello* and the pagan outdoors of *Lear*. Aside from this atmosphere of dread, *Macbeth* contains a number of key iconic moments of stage horror. The uncanny appearance of the bearded witches, Banquo's bloody ghost, and gory visions emanating from the witches' cauldron are all powerful moments of horror that have been memorably depicted on both stage and screen. The associations with horror are perhaps most clearly shown by the borrowings form horror cinema in movie versions of *Macbeth*, ranging from Roman Polanski's 1971 version to the most recent one directed by Justin Kurzel (2015). The latter's use of ideas of post-traumatic stress disorder is a particularly effective marriage of old and new to update the horrific elements of Shakespeare's text.

Macbeth and horror are connected outside of the realms of the text, however, as can be seen in long-standing theatrical superstition. Actors traditionally refuse to utter the name of the "Scottish play" outside of performance for fear that it will lead to a horrific accident. It is surely no coincidence that this superstitious belief applies to the most developed horror text of Shakespeare's canon. The dark and malevolent atmosphere of *Macbeth* leaks from the world of the play and into its wider cultural reception. While *Macbeth* is the culmination of Shakespeare's use of tragic horror, it is not his last exploration of horror in drama.

Shakespeare's late plays have often proved difficult to categorize, representing a departure from the traditional genres of comedy and tragedy, and variously labeled as romances, tragicomedies, or simply "late plays." Some of this generic confusion can be attributed to their use of horror—moments that often seem particularly out of place with the general mood of these plays. *Cymbeline* features a decapitated corpse during one particularly horrific scene when the play's heroine, Imogen (or Innogen depending on the edition), marks her face with its blood under the false belief that it is her fiancé, Posthumous. This visceral set piece shows the tragicomic turn in these plays, as it simultaneously provides a moment of stage horror and the potential for a comic ending as the audience knows the body is in fact that of the villainous Cloten. *The Winter's Tale* takes place in an atmosphere of pagan belief and suspected witchcraft, seemingly concluding with the magical transformation of a statue into a living person. The play also includes the most famous stage direction in theater—*Exit, pursued by a bear*—a nod to the shared performance space and a precursor of the creature feature genre that would rise to prominence in twentieth-century horror.

Shakespeare's *The Tempest* is often considered one of his most modern plays, being understood as an exploration of colonialism and Western exploitation. The incursion onto the island by the shipwrecked Italians plays out like a prototype for *King Kong* with the monstrous ape represented by the problematic figure of Caliban, variously described as a fish and a monster. The drunkard Trinculo's first reaction is to consider the potential rewards for exhibiting the islander at shows in England. Of course, more modern approaches to the play reposition Caliban as the colonized victim and Prospero as the oppressive monster.

Shakespearean horrors, therefore, cover a wide range of the areas that subsequent horror writers would go on to use, cementing his role as an important influence on—and participant in—the literature of fear. The centrality of his works in culture and education mean that Shakespeare's use of horror creates and works within a shared cultural space in which his poetry and horror sit side by side.

Stephen Curtis

See also: Ghost Stories; *Part One, Horror through History*: Horror in the Early Modern Era; *Part Three, Reference Entries*: Witches and Witchcraft.

Further Reading

Aebischer, Pascale. 2004. *Shakespeare's Violated Bodies*. Cambridge: Cambridge University Press.

Desmet, Christy, and Anne Williams, eds. 2009. *Shakespearean Gothic*. Cardiff: University of Wales Press.

Drakakis, John, and Dale Townsend, eds. 2008. *Gothic Shakespeares*. Abingdon, UK: Routledge.

Pridham, Matthew. 2012. "Razors to the Heart: William Shakespeare and Horror Fiction." *Weird Fiction Review*, April 10. http://weirdfictionreview.com/2012/04/razors-to-the -heart-william-shakespeare-and-horror-fiction.

Shakespeare, William. [1604] 1997. *Othello*. In *The Norton Shakespeare*, edited by Stephen Greenblatt, Walter Cohen, Jean E. Howard, and Katharine Eisaman Maus, 2091–2174. New York and London: Norton.

Theatre of Blood. [1973] 2002. DVD. Directed by Douglas Hickox. Twentieth-Century Fox.

Yeo, Colin. "'Supp'd full with horrors': 400 years of Shakespearean Supernaturalism." *The Conversation*, April 20, 2016. http://theconversation.com/suppd-full-with-horrors-400 -years-of-shakespearean-supernaturalism-57129.

SMALL PRESS, SPECIALTY, AND ONLINE HORROR

Since the beginning of the twentieth century, horror fiction has found a comfortable home within small presses, specialty presses, and "alternative" outlets. These venues have functioned as markets for less commercial works and as proving grounds for authors developing their skills. The small press market has been traditionally dependent on both the technologies that support cheap production and the trends popularized by mainstream publishers. Yet small presses have often flourished in those periods of history when mainstream horror publishing has been declining, as popular and midlist writers have sought out new or niche venues for their works.

The early history of these venues centered upon the works of H. P. Lovecraft, an amateur press enthusiast whose work was first published in pulp magazines such as *Weird Tales*. He and his circle—Frank Belknap Long, August Derleth, Clark Ashton Smith, Robert E. Howard, and a few others—frequently shared materials. After Lovecraft's death in 1937, a prominent member of this circle, August Derleth, joined with Donald Wandrei to establish Arkham House in Sauk City, Wisconsin, to release a memorial collection of Lovecraft's short stories, *The Outsider and Others* (1939). After the end of World War II a number of other small presses such as Prime Press (established by Oswald Train in 1947) similarly made it their mission to rescue material that had once been published in the pulp magazines.

The 1950s and 1960s saw the rise of paperback and trade publishing of horror books. Consequently, the small presses that had flourished in the postwar period began to decline, although Arkham House continued to publish a small but steady list under pressure from trade publishers and science fiction small presses. During this period, it was in comics, such as EC Comics' *The Haunt of Fear, The Vault of Horror,* and *The Crypt of Terror*, where horror remained most popular until the U.S. Senate Subcommittee on Juvenile Delinquency in 1953 caused many horror comics to fold. A few high-quality magazines such as Paul Ganley's *Weirdbook* (1968) and Stuart Schiff's *Whispers* (1970) began to pick up the slack in the tail end of the decade.

In the 1970s the public interest in horror surged, driven by the mainstream successes of works such as William Peter Blatty's *The Exorcist* (1971) and the early novels of Stephen King, including *Carrie* (1974), *'Salem's Lot* (1975) and *The Shining* (1977), many of which were popularized by film adaptations. The small press market fed off these successes, spawning magazines such as *The Horror Show, Grue, Pulphouse,* and *Cemetery Dance* and presses such as Necronomicon Press, which continued alongside the stalwart Arkham House. Throughout the late seventies, a number of important writers got their start in the small presses, including Thomas Ligotti, Kathe Koja, and Poppy Z. Brite. Other commercially successful writers such as Joe R. Lansdale, Lucius Shepard, Ramsey Campbell, Dennis Etchison, and Stephen King published in both large and small venues, depending on the nature of their work.

The importance of small presses was consolidated in the 1980s as Cemetery Dance Publications, Dark Harvest, Borderlands Press, and Dark Regions, among

A Selective Timeline of Small Press, Specialty, and Online Horror

1923 H. P. Lovecraft publishes "The Horror at Martin's Beach" in the second issue of *Weird Tales*.

1939 Arkham House is founded by August Derleth and Donald Wandrei to produce a memorial volume of Lovecraft's fiction.

1954 Estes Kefauver leads the U.S. Senate Subcommittee on Juvenile Delinquency, causing many horror comic publishers to censor or cancel their series.

1974 The hardcover edition of Stephen King's *Carrie* is released by Doubleday, marking the beginning of the horror boom.

1986 Tor begins the first dedicated horror line from a major press.

1988 *Weird Tales* is revived by George H. Scithers, John Gregory Betancourt, and Darrell Schweitzer.

1996 Zebra Press, the flagship imprint of Kensington Publishing and one of the last remaining major publishers of horror, is discontinued.

1997 Sponsored by Leisure Books, ChiZine.com is founded as an online magazine.

1998 Darren McKeeman conceives of connecting a worldwide community of horror lovers through www.Gothic.net.

2009 The global recession initiates a substantial decline in the traditional publishing industry.

2010 Leisure Books announces that Dan D'Auria will no longer edit its horror line, and all print publications are slated to continue as eBooks.

2012 John Joseph Adams successfully crowdfunds the launch of *Nightmare Magazine*.

others, began their operations. These presses produced a range of titles from high-quality hardcover releases to limited editions for collectors to trade paperbacks. In 1988, John Gregory Betancourt, Darrell Schweitzer, and George H. Scithers revived *Weird Tales*, the magazine famous for publishing many of Lovecraft's original works, which had ceased operations in 1954. It saw success initially with authors such as Ligotti, Tanith Lee, and Brian Lumley.

But by the second half of the decade the genre had begun to stagnate as the market became saturated. In 1990, Tor, the first company to begin a dedicated horror line, shifted from genre to mainstream, and by 1996 Zebra was discontinued, sounding the death knell for the last of the major American horror lines. Leisure Books, an imprint of the mid-sized company Dorchester Publishing, continued to publish horror alongside Westerns and thrillers, but it was one of the few remaining publishers with industry heft. While the main market was faltering, small presses picked up some of the slack. By 1993, they were responsible for publishing almost 25 percent of all new horror novels, anthologies, and collections. Three influential editors of anthologies came to prominence within this period: Ellen Datlow, Stephen Jones, and Paula Guran.

A number of important new presses entered the field as the end of the 1990s approached. Of these, two of the most important were, arguably, the San Francisco–based Night Shade Books and Peter Crowther's PS Publishing in Hornsea, established in 1997 and 1999, respectively. PS Publishing continues to be one of the most successful small presses in Britain. Other presses of this period included Sarob Press, which produced collectors' editions of new and old fiction; Subterranean Press, which produced a quarterly magazine alongside novels collections and chapbooks; Ash-Tree Press in Canada, which rescued forgotten works in the ghost story tradition by writers such as M. R. James; Necronomicon Press, devoted to the Lovecraft tradition and responsible for a range of scholarly magazines; and Tartarus Press, which specialized in literary fiction with a supernatural bent and supported authors such as Robert Aickman. Magazine publishing continued with *The 3rd Alternative*, primarily focused on science fiction, fantasy, and slipstream stories.

By end of the century, the Internet was beginning to offer new possibilities. In March, 2000, Stephen King published his novella *Riding the Bullet* as an eBook freely downloadable for the first week. The publicity stunt was so successful that the hosting servers crashed. Digital publishing offered small presses and magazines a way to reduce their printing and distribution costs while still making fiction available to the reading public. A popular electronic market during this phase was Darren McKeeman's www.Gothic.net, but others arose with varying levels of success, including *Imaginary Worlds, Sinister Element,* and *Terror Tales. Chiaroscuro: Treatments of Light and Shade in Words* (known as ChiZine.com), founded by Brett Alexander Savory in 1997, was one of the few eZines that worked its way up to paying professional rates. In 2009 it was expanded to include a successful print arm, ChiZine Publications.

As the global recession devastated the published industry in 2009, the small press market offered alternatives to the midlist writers who were increasingly under pressure within larger houses. New technologies such as print-on-demand continued to make publishing an attractive, if perilous, pursuit for those with an entrepreneurial spirit. A number of imprints took advantage of these circumstances, including Hippocampus Press, Grey Friar Press, Mythos Books, and Shroud Publishing. Cemetery Dance, Subterranean Press, and Tartarus Press continued to produce high-quality works of fiction, and editor Sean Wallace acquired Prime from Wildside Press, which by this point was publishing the long-running *Weird Tales* magazine. But the economic climate and the changes to the publishing environment caused a number of small presses to fold, including Andrew Hook's Elastic Press and Chris Teague's Pendragon Press.

In 2009, online giant Amazon also released its second generation of the Kindle, a specialized e-reader. This would shape the industry for many years as publishers decided how best to integrate eBooks alongside printed books. While this technology benefited small presses to some extent, several experiments in eBook-only publishing were unsuccessful. In 2010, mass market publisher Leisure Books announced that Dan D'Auria, who had been responsible for its horror line, would be let go and that they would no longer produce print publications. In 2011, a group of writers called for the company to be boycotted for publishing eBooks for which they had not acquired digital rights.

During this period, electronic magazines came into their own. *Strange Horizons* was launched in 2000 by Mary Anne Mohanraj and continues to operate today. *Apex Magazine* also continues to publish a range of fiction and reviews, and former editor Lynne M. Thomas recently launched *Uncanny Magazine*. Print-on-demand also made print anthologies more attractive than magazine publication for many editors. One of the few surviving print-only publications is *Black Static*, which was previously published as *The Third Alternative* and was acquired in 2005 by Andy Cox and TTA Press. These venues tended to divide themselves along internal genre lines, with some favoring a more literary strand while others such as Sinister Grin and Raw Dog Screaming Press have explored bizarro fiction, a visceral brand inspired by the late 1980s turn to schlock and gore. Authors who have found their foothold in the small presses of the late 1990s and early 2000s include Brian Evenson, Laird Barron, Kelly Link, and Reggie Oliver, among others.

As the publishing industry has begun to stabilize, the last decade has seen some presses falter while others have reached maturity. In 2010 Night Shade Books, a prominent publisher, was placed on probation by the Science Fiction and Fantasy Writers of America for irregularities in payment. Two years later the company, facing bankruptcy, was sold to Skyhorse Publishing and Start Publishing. And yet PS Publications and Tartarus Press continue to produce high-quality specialty editions in the United Kingdom, while Small Beer, Dark Regions, Hippocampus Press, Samhain Publishing, and Permuted Press publish a range of new fiction in America. Canada has distinguished itself largely through the efforts of ChiZine Publications and Undertow Press launched by Michael Kelly, while Australian publishers such as Ticonderoga, Severed Press, and Twelfth Planet Press have also taken advantage of the new paradigm of digital production. *Nightmare Magazine,* edited by John Joseph Adams, released its first issue in 2012 after a successful crowdfunding campaign. Likewise, a greater number of writers who first published with small presses have moved into mainstream success, including Joe Hill, Paul Tremblay, Jeff VanderMeer, and, most recently, Michael Andrew Hurley, whose novel *The Loney* was first published by Tartarus Press in 2014, only to win Costa's prestigious First Novel Award after a successful reissue by John Murray in 2015.

Small press and specialty publishing from the beginning of the twentieth century onward has been driven in part by a desire to innovate and in part a desire to conserve the materials of the past. The small presses have traditionally been home to materials that were not expected to find a widespread audience, either because the writing was too experimental or extreme or because the traditional market for those works was declining. But as technology has made small-scale production cheaper, there has been a concomitant rise in publishing of exactly this kind. The chapbooks and hand-stapled ephemera of the past decades have largely migrated to digital formats or else been collected into cheap print-on-demand anthologies. Likewise, the specialty presses that traditionally made their money from expensive limited editions have also begun to branch out into the mass eBook and print-on-demand trade market. Whereas in the horror boom of the 1980s small press publishing was influenced by the large publishers such as Tor, in fact, the trend seems to be reversing, with independent publishing providing the impetus for innovation. The result is that readers and writers are likely to encounter more choice in the materials they read and the formats available to them in the future.

Helen Marshall

See also: Horror Anthologies; Horror Comics; Horror Literature in the Internet Age; Horror Publishing, 1975–1995: The Boom Years; *Part One, Horror through History*: Horror from 1900 to 1950; Horror from 1950 to 2000; Horror in the Twenty-First Century; *Part Three, Reference Entries*: Aickman, Robert; Arkham House; Barron, Laird; Campbell, Ramsey; Datlow, Ellen; Derleth, August; Etchison, Dennis; King, Stephen; Lee, Tanith; Ligotti, Thomas; Link, Kelly; Lovecraft, H. P.; Lovecraftian Horror; Oliver, Reggie; *Weird Tales*.

Further Reading

Barron, Neil. 1999. *Fantasy and Horror: A Critical and Historical Guide to Literature, Illustration, Film, TV, Radio, and the Internet.* Lanham, MD: Scarecrow Press.

Hantke, Steffen. 2008. "The Decline of the Literary Horror Market in the 1990s and Dell's Abyss Series." *Journal of Popular Culture* 41.1: 56–70.

Herald, Diana Tixier, and Wayne A. Wiegand, editor. 2006. *Genreflecting: A Guide to Popular Reading Interests.* Westport, CT: Libraries Unlimited.

Jones, Stephen. 2014. *Best New Horror: # 1.* Hornsea, UK: PS Publishing.

Morrison, Michael A. 1996. "After the Danse: Horror at the End of the Century." In *A Dark Night's Dreaming: Contemporary American Horror Fiction*, edited by Tony Magistrale and Michael A. Morrison. Columbia: University of South Carolina Press.

Sutton, David, and Stan Nicholls. 2000. *On the Fringe for Thirty Years: A History of Horror in the British Small Press.* Birmingham: Shadow Publishing.

VAMPIRE FICTION FROM DRACULA TO LESTAT AND BEYOND

Vampire fiction finds its origins in the vampire hysteria that swept across Europe in the early part of the eighteenth century, a period that saw officially sanctioned exhumations of villagers suspected of being vampires. German poets like Johann Wolfgang von Goethe and Gottfried August Bürger, as in his ballad *Lenore* (1774)—which included a verse that gave rise to the line "Denn die Todten reiten schnell" (*For the dead travel fast*) in Bram Stoker's *Dracula* (1897)—soon began integrating into their works the figure of the vampire. But by the early part of the nineteenth century, romantics such as Lord Byron, Samuel Taylor Coleridge, and John Keats began to try their own hands at vampire poetry in works such as *The Giaour* (1813), *Christabel* (1816), and *Lamia* (1820), respectively, which gave rise to the vampire as a distinct fictional trope.

It was not until Dr. John William Polidori's anonymously published "The Vampyre; A Tale" (1819) in *The New Monthly Magazine and Universal Register*, however, that the enduring features of the vampire still seen today came into being. The first story of the undead "successfully to fuse the disparate elements of vampirism into a coherent literary genre," according to Sir Christopher Frayling, "The Vampyre" was falsely attributed upon publication to Lord Byron, for whom Polidori had previously worked as a personal physician (Frayling 1991, 108). Polidori based his work on the fragment of a novel Byron wrote during the now celebrated ghost story competition (at which Polidori was present) between him, Percy Bysshe Shelley, and Mary Shelley at Byron's home, the Villa Diodati, by Lake Geneva in the summer of 1816, the same competition that would produce *Frankenstein* (1818). Polidori's chief vampire, Ruthven, which he stylized after Byron, is an enigmatic lord who enters London society where he encounters a young Englishman named Aubrey. They become fast friends and travel together, but various events during their adventures reveal to Aubrey that Ruthven is in fact a vampire. The novel ends with Aubrey dying insane and Ruthven marrying Aubrey's sister, who turns up dead with her blood drained. Polidori's story found immediate popular success, no doubt partially as a result of being initially attributed to Byron, but mainly due to its appropriation of the Gothic conventions for which the public longed. Despite its success, "The Vampyre," and Byron's public refutation of and disdain for the story, destroyed Polidori's career. However, it transformed the vampire from the hideous walking corpse of folklore into the form recognized today of an aristocrat who feeds upon high society.

Polidori's formula surfaces again in the short story "The Mysterious Stranger," first published in German as "Der Fremde" by Karl Adolf von Wachsmann in *Erzählungen und Novellen* (1844), then in installments in the popular literary magazine *Würzburger Conversationsblatt* (May–June 1847), and then it was translated into English and published anonymously as "The Mysterious Stranger" in *Chambers's Repository of Instructive and Amusing Tracts* (October–December 1853) and later reprinted in *Odds and Ends* (1860). The story begins with a party of Austrian travelers led by the Knight of Fahnenberg, who has just inherited a large estate in the Carpathian Mountains. Among the party are Franziska, the knight's daughter, her cousin and suitor, the Baron Franz von Kronstein, and Bertha, Franziska's female companion who is admired by the courageous Knight of Woislaw, presently off in Turkey fighting in a war. Soon it becomes apparent that a torrential snowstorm is upon them, so they hasten their journey onward only to find that howling "reed-wolves" have encircled the party. The travelers soon approach the abandoned ruins of Castle Klatka, and fearing an attack, they seek refuge there. Before the travelers can reach the ruins, however, the wolves begin their assault. They fear the worst until suddenly a tall man appears out of nowhere between the wolves and the party. Knightly and old-fangled in dress, the stranger raises his hand in a waving gesture, which halts the advance of the wolves and sends them in retreat into the woods. The travelers watch as their rescuer says nothing and simply returns to the path leading up to the castle, where he seems to vanish into the ruins.

The travelers eventually return to explore the castle, finding among its ruins the coffin of "Ezzelin de Klatka, Eques." At sunset, appearing out of nowhere again is the tall stranger, who calls himself Azzo von Klatka. Like Dracula, he is about forty, tall, thin, and pale, with piercing grey eyes, black hair, and black beard. The thankful travelers invite their rescuer to pay them a visit at their neighboring estate, and soon the stranger makes frequent dinner visits after nightfall. In the meantime, Franziska, who has taken a fancy to the stranger, slowly becomes anemic, complains of bad dreams and nightly visitors who enter her bedroom in mist, and starts to bear a small wound on her throat. Then, arriving just in time is the Knight of Woislaw, a proto–Van Helsing character who, given his dealings abroad, suspects almost immediately that a vampire is afoot. Woislaw then takes Franziska back to Castle Klatka, where he instructs her to drive three long spikes through the coffin lid of "Ezzelin de Klatka." Afterward, Franziska quickly recovers from her strange illness, and Azzo, the mysterious stranger, is not seen or heard from again.

"The Mysterious Stranger," like Polidori's *The Vampyre*, obviously had a great effect on Stoker's writing of *Dracula*, but it was not the last to do so. Serialized works like James Malcolm Rymer and Thomas Peckett Prest's "penny dreadful" *Varney the Vampire: Or, The Feast of Blood* (1845–1847) and Sheridan Le Fanu's novella *Carmilla*, first published in *The Dark Blue* (1871–1872), then reprinted in Le Fanu's collection *In a Glass Darkly* (1872), did much to firmly establish the vampire in the popular imagination of the Victorian era, and, in doing so, influenced Stoker. Sir Francis Varney was the first vampire to establish, at least in English, what would become several standard tropes in vampire fiction: vampires bearing fangs and entering through windows at night to attack sleeping maidens, leaving behind two puncture wounds in the neck, and displaying hypnotic powers coupled with incredible strength and agility. Though it is not unreasonable to speculate whether Rymer or Prest had indeed read "Der Fremde" in its original German and mirrored Varney somewhat after Wachsmann's "Azzo," what is certainly their creation is a vampire who drinks and eats as a human, if only to disguise himself, and who acts upon his vampirism only when his energy is running low, an unfortunate condition Varney simultaneously loathes and is powerless to ignore. In this way, Varney is a prototype of the "sympathetic vampire" that would come into its own more than a hundred years later. The erotic elements seen in Le Fanu's lesbian vampire novella *Carmilla* show through in Stoker's *Dracula* as well, particularly in Stoker's characterization of his vampire women. *Carmilla* is also set in Styria, where Stoker originally set *Dracula* before moving the count's home to Transylvania.

Stoker's greatest achievement in *Dracula*, a novel he spent seven years writing (longer than any of his other novels), lies in his combining a number of tropes from previous vampire literature and displaying them to perfection in *Dracula's* pages. Although Stoker did not invent many of the tropes he used, he did build upon them, and *Dracula's* incredible popularity and immensely positive reception by critics only helped to fan the public's association of these tropes with his novel. One example is Count Dracula's transformation into a bat. Étienne Geoffroy Saint-Hilaire, no doubt influenced by the vampire hysteria and poetic verse of the previous century, identified and named the vampire bat (*Phyllostoma rotundum*) in Paraguay in 1810, and it was during the nineteenth century that the vampire bat and the supernatural vampire slowly fused together. American newspapers had appropriated the figure of the vampire as early as the eighteenth century and through the nineteenth century, as a pejorative to describe everything from corporations and banks to bankers and politicians. But when science invoked the vampire to name and describe certain species of bat (and later, squid), and with the publication of Polidori's instantly popular *The Vampyre* in 1819, newspapers and literature worked eagerly at fusing the supernatural vampire and the vampire bat into one mythology. For a while, a new vampire hysteria spread across the globe when folks started seeing (i.e., misidentifying) vampire bats everywhere (despite their being a species native to Central and South America only). Eventually, a conflation of the supernatural vampire with the relatively harmless vampire bat occurred in the figures of the "winged vampire" or vampire "bat-winged" person, who alternately began to play a prominent role in figurative political rhetoric and even as an American literary trope. This conflation is also almost assuredly what fanned the late-Victorian image of the vampire as having fangs (a trait the European vampire of folklore lacked entirely). (Take, for example, the fanged vampire in the form of the beautiful "Vespertilia" in Anne Crawford's "A Mystery of the Campagna" [1887], *vespertilio*, or "evening bat," being a common variety of bat found the world over.) Thus, although the eighteenth-century vampire of folklore and poetic verse was responsible for the vampire bat's subsequent nomenclature and frightening mystique, it was probably the vampire bat that, in turn, fitted the literary vampire with its iconic fangs. After *Dracula*, fangs, crucifixes, traveling boxes (or coffins), mirrors, and garlic were to become standard fare in vampire literature through the next century and into the twenty-first.

Draculas the World Over in Film, Television, and Video Games

1921	*Drakula halála* (Hungary/Austria)
1922	*Nosferatu, eine Symphonie des Grauens* (Germany)
1931	*Dracula* (USA); *Drácula* (USA)
1936	*Dracula's Daughter* (USA)
1943	*Son of Dracula* (USA)

1944	*House of Frankenstein* (USA)
1945	*House of Dracula* (USA)
1948	*Bud Abbott and Lou Costello Meet Frankenstein* (USA)
1953	*Drakula Istanbul'da* (Turkey)
1956	*Matinee Theatre*, "Dracula" (USA)—Television
1958	*Dracula* (UK); *The Return of Dracula* (USA)
1959	*Onna Kyuketsuki* (Japan)
1961	*El Mundo de los vampiros* (Mexico)
1963	*Mga Manugang ni Drakula* (Philippines)
1964	*Tetsuwan Atom*, "Vampire Vale" (Japan)—Television, Animation; *Kulay Dugo ang Gabi* (Philippines/USA)
1966	*Dracula: Prince of Darkness* (UK); *Emotion: densetsu no gogo=itsukamita Dracula* (Japan)
1967	*Zinda Laash* (Pakistan)
1968	*Dracula Has Risen from the Grave* (UK); *Kaibutsu-Kun* (Japan)—Animation
1969	*Dracula and the Boys; aka Does Dracula Really Suck?* (USA)—Adult; *Drakulita* (Philippines); *Santo en El Tesoro de Dracula* (Mexico)
1970	*El Conde Drácula* (Spain/West Germany/Italy/Liechtenstein); *Scars of Dracula* (UK); *Taste the Blood of Dracula* (UK)
1971	*The Electric Company* (USA)—Television
1972	*Blacula* (USA)
	Dracula A.D. 1972 (UK)
1973	*Dracula* (UK)—Television; *Santo y Blue Demon contra Drácula y el Hombre Lobo* (Mexico); *The Satanic Rites of Dracula* (UK); *Scream, Blacula, Scream* (USA)
1974	*Blood for Dracula* (Italy); *The Legend of the 7 Golden Vampires* (Hong Kong/UK)
1975	*Deafula* (USA)
1977	*Count Dracula* (UK)—Television
1979	*Dracula* (USA/UK); *Love at First Bite* (USA); *Nosferatu: Phantom der Nacht* (West Germany)
1981	*The Count* (USA)—Video Game
1983	*Gayracula* (USA)—Adult; *Spider-Man and His Amazing Friends*, "Transylvanian Connection" (USA)—Animation/Television
1985	*Kyûketsuki hantâ D* (Japan)—Animation
1990	*Akumajo Dracula* (Japan)—Video Game
1992	*Bram Stoker's Dracula* (USA); *Khooni Dracula* (India)
2000	*Buffy the Vampire Slayer*, "Buffy vs. Dracula" (USA)—Television; *Dracula 2000* (USA)
2012	*Hotel Transylvania* (USA)—Animation
2013	*Dracula* (UK/USA)—Television
2014	*Dracula Untold* (USA); *Penny Dreadful* (USA/Ireland/UK)—Television

Short fiction featuring vampire characters continued to see print in the early part of the twentieth century, but with *Dracula's* lucrative adaptation on the British and American stage from the mid- through late 1920s, and the subsequent film version by Universal in 1931, Count Dracula would continue to dominate the public's image of the vampire. However, one notable exception came in 1954 with Richard Matheson's *I Am Legend* (1954), a postapocalyptic zombie-vampire novel that is now considered a contemporary classic among horror fiction in general and vampire literature in particular. The story's protagonist is Robert Neville, a resident of Los Angeles who has become the only survivor of a pandemic whose victims have returned from the dead, hide out by day, and venture about by night in search of human blood. Neville is immune to the disease as a result, he thinks, of being bitten by a vampire bat years earlier. While *I Am Legend* is revered for its vampiric storyline, of equal note is the way in which Matheson's vampires break radically from the traditional literary archetype of the Romantic and Victorian periods by reverting back to the older, preliterary vampire that had ruled the "vampire hysteria" of the eighteenth century (though, in Matheson's novel, vampire hunters may now add to their arsenal the use of garlic, stakes, and mirrors, tools deriving from folklore but popularized in Stoker's *Dracula*).

Although the late twentieth century continued to see traditional works of vampire fiction, such as Stephen King's immensely popular *'Salem's Lot* (1975), which reimagined Stoker's *Dracula* story around modern-day small-town America (in Maine, to be precise), something thematically important happened in the late 1960s that was to have a lasting effect on vampire fiction, remaining visible even today. Barnabas Collins, the Dracula-type vampire in Dan Curtis's television series *Dark Shadows* (1966–1971), firmly planted into the American consciousness the prospect of an incredibly sad, flawed, yet redeemable vampire with whom audiences could at last sympathize. This new character trait became immediately fashionable, surfacing again in *Blacula* (1972), Dan Curtis's televised movie *Dracula* (1973), and in *Andy Warhol's Dracula* (1974). However, it was to have an equally profound effect on vampire literature, the mode that would prove to have the most lasting effect on subsequent vampire narratives—on screen and in print. Anne Rice's *The Vampire Chronicles* series, beginning with *Interview with the Vampire* (1976)—and, albeit to a lesser extent, Chelsea Quinn Yarbro's Count Saint-Germain series (1978–), beginning with *Hôtel Transylvania* (1978)—took the vampire mythos by storm.

Today, the current state of vampire literature and film is most immediately the result of the "vampire renaissance" that occurred roughly from the late 2000s through the early 2010s. This period heralded not only an explosion of vampire fictions, from Charlaine Harris's *Sookie Stackhouse* series (2001–2013) and the subsequent televised adaptation *True Blood* (2008–2014) to Stephenie Meyer's *Twilight* series (2005–2008) and the subsequent film adaptations (2008–2012), but the decisive and definitive proliferation of the sympathetic vampire, a theme that began in its earliest form in *Varney the Vampire*, before being reimagined and redeveloped over a century later in *Dark Shadows* and then perfected in *Interview with the Vampire*.

John Edgar Browning

See also: Page to Screen: The Influence of Literary Horror on Film and Television; *Part Three, Reference Entries: Carmilla; Dracula; I Am Legend; Interview with the Vampire*; Penny Dreadful; Rice, Anne; Stoker, Bram; Vampires; "The Vampyre"; *Varney the Vampire: Or, The Feast of Blood*; Yarbro, Chelsea Quinn.

Further Reading

Anderson, Douglas A. 2010. "A Note on M. R. James and Dracula." *Fastitocalon: Studies in Fantasticism Ancient to Modern* 1(2): 189–194.

Barber, Paul. 2010. *Vampires, Burial, and Death: Folklore and Reality*. New Haven, CT: Yale University Press.

Browning, John Edgar. 2010. "The Mysterious Stranger." In *The Encyclopedia of the Vampire: The Living Dead in Myth, Legend, and Popular Culture*, edited by S. T. Joshi. Westport, CT: Greenwood Press.

Browning, John Edgar, ed. 2012. *Bram Stoker's Dracula: The Critical Feast, An Annotated Reference of Early Reviews and Reactions, 1897–1913*. Berkeley, CA: Apocryphile Press.

Carter, Margaret L., ed. 1988. *Dracula: The Vampire and the Critics*. Ann Arbor, MI: UMI Research Press.

Carter, Margaret L. 1989. *The Vampire in Literature: A Critical Bibliography (Studies in Speculative Fiction)*. Ann Arbor, MI: UMI Research Press.

Crawford, Heide. 2016. *The Origins of the Literary Vampire*. Lanham, MD: Rowman & Littlefield.

Eighteen-Bisang, Robert, and Elizabeth Miller, eds. 2008. *Bram Stoker's Notes for Dracula: A Facsimile Edition*. Jefferson, NC: McFarland.

Frayling, Christopher. 1991. *Vampyres: Lord Byron to Count Dracula*. London: Faber and Faber.

Matheson, Richard. 1954. *I Am Legend*. New York: Gold Medal Books/Fawcett Publications.

Miller, Elizabeth, ed. 2005. *Bram Stoker's Dracula: A Documentary Volume (Dictionary of Literary Biography*, vol. 304). Farmington Hills, MI: Thomson Gale.

Polidori, John William. 1819. *The Vampyre: A Tale*. London: Sherwood, Neely, and Jones.

Wachsmann, Karl Adolf von. 1844. *Erzählungen und Novellen* 21. Leipzig: Verlag von Carl Focke.

WEIRD AND COSMIC HORROR FICTION

While they have applications beyond his conceptions, the terms "weird fiction" and "cosmic horror" are both widely associated with the critical and fictional writings of H. P. Lovecraft (1890–1937), whose influential study *Supernatural Horror in Literature* (1927) helped to popularize and to some degree define them. However, Lovecraft's essay does not consistently distinguish between them, nor does it serve as the final authority on their meaning. Later writers have understood both "weird" and "cosmic" horror in different but closely related ways. Cosmic and weird horror are closely intertwined, but at the same time they are potentially distinct literary modes that intersect in multiple ways with horror. Though there are many important writers of the weird and cosmic whose work is not generally understood as horror, it is also true that many of the writers who have had the greatest influence on the history of horror literature have done so largely because of their work in cosmic and weird fiction.

In *Supernatural Horror in Literature*, Lovecraft defined a weird tale as one involving supernatural elements, but which nonetheless did not conform to the conventions of the Gothic novel as established initially by eighteenth-century British writers including Horace Walpole, Ann Radcliffe, and Matthew Lewis and carried on in the nineteenth century by writers from Mary Shelley to Bram Stoker, or to those of the ghost story, which had been formalized particularly by Victorian writers including M. R. James and Rudyard Kipling. Lovecraft claims that the *sine qua non* (the irreducible element) of the weird tale is the creation of a "certain atmosphere of breathless and unexplainable dread" and the suspension, if not violation, of "fixed laws of Nature" (Lovecraft 2012, 28).

Lovecraft presents Edgar Allan Poe as the most important figure in the development of weird fiction, claiming: "Before Poe the bulk of weird writers had worked largely in the dark; without an understanding of the psychological basis of the horror appeal, and hampered by more or less of conformity to certain empty literary conventions" (Lovecraft 2012, 55). Lovecraft provides an alternative definition of weird fiction in a 1926 letter that also emphasizes Poe's centrality: "As to what is meant by 'weird'—and of course weirdness is by no means confined to horror—I should say that the real criterion is a strong impression of the suspension of natural laws or the presence of unseen worlds or forces close at hand," going on to claim that "perhaps the supreme weird tale of all the ages—is to me *The Fall of the House of Usher*" (Lovecraft 1997, 2.69–70).

Here, too, the central idea behind Lovecraft's definition of the weird is "the suspension of natural laws," and this characteristic is one way of formulating a distinction between cosmic horror and weird fiction. In its narrowest and most identifiable sense, cosmic horror is an approach that fuses the affect and tone of horror with science fictional premises while following naturalistic principles, remaining to some degree compatible with contemporaneous scientific thought. In this sense, it is a literary mode closely related to the cosmic irony beloved of American naturalist writers (ca. 1890–1925) including Theodore Dreiser and Stephen Crane (both of whom were admired by Lovecraft), and to Lovecraft's philosophy of cosmic indifferentism, which emphasizes the insignificance of humanity in the unknown vastness of the universe. This breed of cosmic horror uses verisimilar writing techniques (i.e., techniques that make fictional stories appear true) to undermine the human presumption of knowledge, displaying the abyssal contrast between delusions of human exceptionalism and the reality that we are but one species of animal among thousands, struggling for survival on one planet among millions, in a universe whose virtually infinite reaches are beyond our meager ability to grasp or understand. Lovecraft's "The Colour out of Space" (1927) and *At the Mountains of Madness* (1936) are his greatest achievements in this mode, and important later examples include John W. Campbell's "Who Goes There?" (1938), Theodore Sturgeon's "It" (1940), Fritz Leiber's *Our Lady of Darkness* (1977), Michael Faber's *Under the Skin* (2000), Caitlín R. Kiernan's *The Dry Salvages* (2004), Peter Watt's *Blindsight* (2006), and Jeff VanderMeer's *Southern Reach Trilogy* (2014), as well as films including Ridley Scott's *Alien* (1979) and John Carpenter's *The Thing* (1982, itself based loosely on Campbell's 1938 story).

However, as Lovecraft's privileging of Poe's "Usher" (a story whose occult themes and baroque style make it far removed from these examples) suggests, what he calls "weird" and in other instances "cosmic" is often markedly different from this narrow conception. In its broader sense, cosmic horror need not be tied to either realism or science fiction. It can draw on a wide variety of techniques, approaches, and literary modes to suspend or erode presumptions about the nature of reality,

---

The word "weird," originally associated with fate, predestination, prophecies, and related phenomena, has a venerable lineage in the English language. The *Oxford English Dictionary* records its first adjectival uses in Middle English near the turn of the fifteenth century, where it was often used attributively to describe the Fates and the three witches of British and European folklore that are descended from them. This usage appeared in *Holinshed's Chronicles* in 1587, which would become the primary inspiration for the witches of Shakespeare's *Macbeth*.

The term's use in delineating a particular kind of fiction, however, dates to the early twentieth century. While clear links exist between the weird and literary modes of earlier epochs, most commentators agree that it is very much a twentieth- and twenty-first-century phenomenon. Central to the shift in meaning that led to "weird fiction" becoming a distinct literary concept and marketing category in the early twentieth century was the magazine *Weird Tales*, founded in 1923 by J. C. Henneberger and J. M. Lansinger as a companion publication to Henneberger's pulp crime magazine *Detective Tales* that would be devoted exclusively to horror fiction. Over the first two decades of its existence, *Weird Tales* became associated with fiction that moved away from the folkloric supernaturalism associated with earlier Gothic horror. Writers including H. P. Lovecraft, C. L. Moore, and Francis Stevens contributed stories in which science fictional concepts produced the combination of awe and terror that had once been the provenance of the supernatural beings of traditional folklore.

Nevertheless, Lovecraft was critical of *Weird Tales'* tendency to publish more readily classifiable works of Gothic horror and action-oriented pulp science fiction, often to the exclusion of the more interstitial and challenging work that he considered "true" weird and cosmic fiction. His development of a germinal theory of weird fiction, which began in earnest two to three years after the magazine's appearance, is partially informed by this critical reaction.

and this broader sense of the term becomes more nebulous, difficult to classify, and impossible to disentangle from weird fiction generally.

As Ann and Jeff VanderMeer's compendious anthology *The Weird* (2012) demonstrates, the twentieth-century Anglo-American tradition of weird fiction, with its close ties to American naturalism on the one hand and pulp fiction on the other, drew upon and existed parallel to numerous other threads of weird fiction. These threads run through the work of writers from different cultural and linguistic traditions, with the canon that Lovecraft's influential essay helped to establish being but one cluster in a much larger constellation.

Nevertheless, *The Weird*'s conception of weirdness shares the central epistemological emphasis of Lovecraft's: it "strives for a kind of understanding even when something cannot be understood, and acknowledges that failure as sign and symbol of our limitations" (VanderMeer and VanderMeer 2012, xv). In S. T. Joshi's words, "the weird tale is an inherently philosophical mode in that it frequently compels us to address directly such fundamental issues as the nature of the universe and our place in it" (Joshi 1990, 11).

Rather than a fixed literary form or genre, weird fiction is best understood as a series of mutations and hybridizations of other literary forms. According to the VanderMeers, "As a twentieth and twenty-first century art form the story of The Weird is the story of the refinement (and destabilization) of supernatural fiction within an established framework but also of the welcome contamination of that fiction by the influence of other traditions, some only peripherally connected to the fantastic" (VanderMeer and VanderMeer 2012, xv–xvi). Similarly, influential writer and scholar of weird fiction Michael Cisco (1970–), who describes his own work as "de-genred," maintains that its transgeneric state is the most identifiable quality of weird fiction.

This makes weird fiction closely related to other modern and contemporary interstitial fictional modes, including New Wave science fiction, slipstream fiction, and bizarro fiction. Indeed, British writer Anna Kavan's (1901–1968) 1967 novel *Ice*, which Christopher Priest identifies as a quintessential work of slipstream, could, with its menacing strangeness, ghastly beauty, and gradual creation of an atmosphere of anxious dread, be as productively read as an important mid-century example of weird horror.

This interstitial relationship between weird fiction and different precedent or contemporaneous literary movements can best be illustrated with a brief list of selected examples. The weird fictions of British writer Arthur Machen (1863–1947), one of the greatest influences on Lovecraft and his circle, bear many similarities to the Victorian Gothic novels of Bram Stoker or Richard Marsh. Like Stoker's *Dracula* and Marsh's *The Beetle* (both 1897), Machen's novella *The Great God Pan* (1894) and novel *The Three Impostors* (1895, as much short story cycle as novel) are ultimately invasion narratives. Rooted in cultural anxieties linked to a particular moment in British colonial history and industrial globalization, they also share in common modernized approaches to the epistolary novel form.

Contrarily, the weird fictions of early twentieth-century Japanese writer Ryuno-suke Akutagawa (1892–1927) and the Poe-inspired Edogawa Rampo (1894–1965) are closely tied to the Edo-era popular movement Ero-Guro-Nansensu (Erotic-Grotesque Nonsense), which emphasized eroticism, decadence, and aestheticism. Those of Polish fine artist, playwright, and novelist Bruno Schulz (1892–1942), who produced an important body of weird work including the story collection *The Street of Crocodiles* (1934) and the delirious autobiographical novel *Sanatorium Under the Sign of the Hourglass* (1937), like those of Austrian writer Franz Kafka (1883–1924), share more in common with literary modernism, while anticipating in many ways the existentialist and absurdist movements of the mid-twentieth century. Notably, both these writers continue to exert a powerful influence over many contemporary weird fiction writers, including Thomas Ligotti (1953–) and Michael Cisco.

Some of the most important mid- to late twentieth-century English-language works of weird horror, including fictions by J. G. Ballard (1930–2009), Harlan Ellison (1934–), James Tiptree Jr. (1915–1987), Joanna Russ (1937–2011), Philip K. Dick (1928–1982), and Angela Carter (1940–1992), are closely linked to the New Wave movement(s) in speculative fiction. Coalescing first in the United Kingdom and then in North America in the second half of the twentieth century, New Wave writers fused genre tropes with avant-garde literary techniques and an adversarial stance toward received social and literary conventions. Similarly, a number of the most important weird writers of the 1990s, including Clive Barker (1952–), Poppy Z. Brite (1967–), Kathe Koja (1960–), and Caitlín R. Kiernan (1964–), became known for sexually transgressive work that both drew upon and subverted the literary techniques of mainstream horror boom icons including Stephen King and Peter Straub.

Since the 1990s, writers including China Miéville (1972–), M. John Harrison (1945–), and Jeff VanderMeer (1968–) have identified with what they call the "New Weird," in part as a way to forcefully differentiate their genre-resistant approach to weird fiction both from the horror genre and from the pulp-era roots of the Anglo-American tradition centering on Lovecraft and *Weird Tales*. Others, including Laird Barron (1970–), Gemma Files (1968–), and Mark Samuels (1967–), tend to work recognizably with and through both the horror genre and the Lovecraft tradition.

Sean Moreland

See also: Horror Literature and Science Fiction; Religion, Horror, and the Supernatural; *Part Three, Reference Entries*: Ballard, J. G.; Barker, Clive; Barron, Laird; Blackwood, Algernon; Brite, Poppy Z.; Cisco, Michael; Dick, Philip K.; Dreams and Nightmares; Ellison, Harlan; "The Fall of the House of Usher"; Joshi, S. T.; Kafka, Franz; Kiernan, Caitlín R.; Ligotti, Thomas; Lovecraft, H. P.; Lovecraftian Horror; Machen, Arthur; The Numinous; Poe, Edgar Allan; Samuels, Mark; Schulz, Bruno; VanderMeer, Jeff.

Further Reading

Everett, J., and Jeffrey H. Shanks, eds. 2015. *The Unique Legacy of Weird Tales: The Evolution of Modern Fantasy and Horror*. Studies in Supernatural Literature. Lanham, MD: Rowman & Littlefield.

Joshi, S. T. 1990. *The Weird Tale*. Austin: University of Texas Press.

Joshi, S. T. 2012. "Poe, Lovecraft, and the Revolution in Weird Fiction." Paper presented at Ninth Annual Commemoration Program of the Poe Society, October 7. https://www.eapoe.org/papers/psblctrs/pl20121.htm.

Lovecraft, H. P. 1997. *Selected Letters*. Edited by August Derleth and Donald Wandrei. Sauk City, WI: Arkham House.

Lovecraft, H. P. [1927] 2012. *The Annotated Supernatural Horror in Literature*. Edited by S. T. Joshi. New York: Hippocampus Press.

Ralickas, Vivian. 2008. "'Cosmic Horror' and the Question of the Sublime in Lovecraft." *Journal of the Fantastic in the Arts* 18, no. 3: 364.

VanderMeer, Ann, and Jeff VanderMeer. 2012. "The Weird: An Introduction." In *The Weird*, edited by Ann and Jeff VanderMeer, xv–xx. New York: Tor.

YOUNG ADULT HORROR FICTION

Controversies over the consumption of horror fiction by young adults began as early as 1796 with the publication of then twenty-year-old Matthew Lewis's shocking novel, *The Monk*. A story of Satanism, incest, and rape, *The Monk* is characterized by critics today as the product of "adolescent fantasy" and at the time of its publication was subject to venomous attacks by reviewers (Spacks 1990, 149). Samuel Taylor Coleridge argued that "*The Monk* is a romance, which if a parent saw in the hands of a son or daughter he might reasonably turn pale" (Coleridge 1936, 356–357). Seen as the product of a juvenile imagination and assumed to have a deleterious effect on young minds, *The Monk* typifies the way horror fiction written for, or read by, young adults prompts polarized responses. Though many critics of the day echoed Coleridge's consternation, some Romantic writers vociferously argued the benefit of terrifying tales on young minds, or expressed nostalgia for their own juvenile appreciation of horror. In "Witches and Other Night Fears" Charles Lamb laments how "tame and prosaic" his adult dreams have grown in contrast to a younger self "dreadfully alive to nervous terrors" (Lamb 1835, 75). In his discussion of these Romantic responses to frightening fiction, Dale Townshend notes that William Wordsworth praised the gruesome chapbooks of his youth for giving the energy of the young imagination free rein. For Wordsworth, horror in literature (in the form of chapbook romances and gruesome fairy tales) "enabled him to withstand the potentially annihilating effects of horror" encountered in real life (Townshend 2008, 29). As a brief look at the history of the subject will show, debate about the merits (or lack thereof) of horror literature for young adult readers continues through the nineteenth and twentieth centuries, and well into the twenty-first.

Since its inception in the form of the chapbooks so beloved by William Wordsworth, through the Gothic romances derided by critics in the eighteenth century, into the scandalous penny dreadfuls of the late nineteenth century, and on into the pulp horror of the twentieth century, horror literature has consistently been weighed against pedagogical criteria, with critics concerned as to how it will help (or hinder) the education and psychological development of young adults. Accordingly, critical approaches to young adult horror in the twentieth century borrow variously from developmental psychology, psychoanalysis, or some variety of ego-relational therapeutic psychology in an attempt to understand the effects horror might have on young adult readers. J. A. Appleyard argues that adolescent readers exhibit a predilection for horror and the supernatural; they "demand that stories not just embody their wishes and fantasies, but also reflect realistically the darker parts of life" (Appleyard 1991, 109). Appleyard characterizes adolescence as a psychologically "dark" period that horror stories help readers navigate. This view echoes Bruno Bettelheim's famous thesis on fairy tales, *The Uses of Enchantment: The Meaning and Importance of Fairy Tales* (1976), in which he deployed Freudian theories to argue that fairy tales help children negotiate the various phases of psychological development. In her assessment of the appeal of frightening fiction to young adult readers, Kimberley Reynolds is at first wary of such "well-rehearsed psychoanalytic arguments," though she agrees that the monsters of horror offer the "perfect metaphor for this stage in a young person's development . . . 'the beast' many teenagers suspect they harbor within themselves can be externalized, encountered and finally overcome" (Reynolds 2001, 6). Reynolds also suggests that the "abject" aspects of YA horror writing, that is, its use of disgusting imagery, helps young adult readers replay and so finally overcome the oedipal conflict of their early childhood (Reynolds 2001, 7). This narrative about the therapeutic benefits of horror for young adult readers endures today. In a an essay at the Tor.com blog titled "Why Horror Is Good for You (And Even Better for Your Kids)," writer and artist Greg Ruth states that childhood and adolescence are a "terrifying ordeal" that the horror writer can "help children survive" (Ruth 2014). The direction of commentary such as this, even though it acts in praise of horror fiction, is as paternalistic as Coleridge's consternation over *The Monk*. The critics allot a therapeutic role to horror administered by adults to aid young adults on their road to developing maturity.

Since the publication of Matthew Lewis's *The Monk* in 1796, critics have argued about the suitability of horror fiction for young adult readers. From eighteenth-century Gothic romances to fin de siècle penny dreadfuls, from the furor over horror comics in the 1950s to the 1980s' "video nasty" panic, young adult horror fiction has prompted moral panic among its detractors as well as impassioned defenses by others who see the value of frightening fiction for developing young minds. Increasingly, in the twenty-first century, horror is lauded as an important and valuable mode of writing, though many works defy accepted ideas about the ways horror fiction aids in the maturation and psychological development of young adult readers.

This association of frightening fiction with the developing maturity of the young adult reader plays out in a continual back and forth about suitability, and the history of horror literature and young adult readers through the nineteenth and twentieth centuries is also a history of moral panic. In the 1870s, cheap installment fiction aimed at a juvenile, working-class readership, known as "penny dreadfuls," were big business for various entrepreneurial publishers. Popular titles such as *The Wild Boys of London; Or, The Children of the Night* (1846–1866) contained violent imagery and often "borrowed" plots (without acknowledgment) from older Gothic romances. Many contained stories about violent criminals, and John Springhall argues that they became the scapegoat for a host of social problems in the late Victorian period in Britain. In 1877, the Society for the Suppression of Vice instituted summonses against the publishers of *The Wild Boys of London* under the 1857 Obscene Publications Act (Springhall 1994, 326). As Springhall points out, the moral panic over penny dreadfuls was also a class conflict. The 1852 Government Select Committee on Criminal and Destitute Juveniles promoted standard middle-class morality in its attempt to suppress penny dreadfuls, part of working-class culture (Springhall 1994, 328). A similar moral panic occurred a century later in the United States when a public outcry against horror comics on the newsstands coincided with a congressional investigation on juvenile delinquency. The investigation linked delinquency to comic books thanks in part to Fredric Wertham's indictment of the industry in *Seduction of the Innocent* (1954). Comic book titles such as *The Vault of Horror, Tales from the Crypt*, and *The Haunt of Fear* by pulp comic publisher EC Comics were placed under scrutiny and, as a result, publishers agreed to self-censor to prevent further damage to reputation and sales. Among its restrictions, The Comics Code Authority forbade the depiction of excessive violence, gruesome illustrations, and vampires, werewolves, or zombies. These restrictions loosened over time, with publishers abandoning the code one after another in the late twentieth century (Marvel in 2001 and DC in 2011), rendering the code, finally, defunct.

Penny dreadfuls and horror comics are two examples that reveal how the development of horror for young adult readers seems to follow a "masculine" direction. Typically, horror fictions are conceived of as being written for and consumed by male readers. Reynolds argues that the twentieth century saw the development of "a peculiarly male form of horror/frightening fantasy [that] has emerged in tandem with youth culture's male rebels and the rejection of the cozy domestic world fetishized in the books, radio and television programs of the postwar period" (Reynolds 2001, 5). Despite this association of horror fiction with male youth culture, evidence abounds that female readers have also found horror fiction compelling. British writer Celia Rees counts classic "pulp" horror works of the twentieth century like *The Pan Book of Horror Stories* (1959–1989) and Dennis Wheatley's *The Devil Rides Out* (1934) among the works that have influenced her own writing the most. As a teenager, she would "borrow" such illicit titles from under her older brother's bed and consume them "voraciously" (Rees 2012). Rees's juvenile appetite for horror is present in her own writing for young adults, such as the 1996 vampire novel *Blood Sinister*.

In the late twentieth century, the two most popular print horror series, *Point Horror* and *Goosebumps* (category fiction imprints from Scholastic), borrowed overtly from slasher movies and B-movie horror tropes (two genres also associated with male audiences) to address female teens. *Point Horror*, in particular, was aimed at girls and rewrote the early twentieth century domestic genre of the "school story" as a paranoid mode in titles such as *Prom Dress* by A. Bates (1989) and *Teacher's Pet* by Richie Tankersley Cusick (1990). Kevin McCarron notes that the *Point Horror* series employed distinctly masculine and feminine modes, with masculine "thrillers" that offered the appearance of realism (typified by R. L. Stine's work) and feminine "supernatural" works that resisted such realism (typified in the vampire fictions of Caroline B. Cooney) (McCarron 2001, 42). McCarron characterizes *Point Horror* as conservative fiction, which tends to establish and maintain boundaries such as insider vs. outsider, often reinforces social norms (including heterosexuality and marriage), and reestablishes social cohesiveness in the resolution of its plots (Reynolds 2001, 28). Likewise, for Reynolds much of the popular fiction of the late twentieth century marketed as horror for young adults lacks the "all pervasive sense of fear and ghastly transgression which characterizes true horror" (Reynolds 2001, 3). In these evaluations of young adult horror, McCarron and Reynolds implicitly reinforce a masculine/feminine binary that runs throughout discussions of horror literature. Demanding that "true" horror be radical and subversive, they align horror with "masculine" subcultures and reject popular, or mainstream, culture, which is implicitly regarded as "feminine."

Radical or not, these horror fictions of the late twentieth century prompted their own moral panic among adult commentators and educationalists. Reynolds notes that British newspapers branded the *Point Horror* series "vile and truly pernicious," echoing the language used about penny dreadfuls, and lists various campaigns that sought to have the books excluded from school libraries (Reynolds 2001, 2). Reynolds likens the concerns raised over the *Point Horror* books to the moral panic over horror comics, though they are most likely the consequence of the British "video nasty" panic of the 1980s and 1990s, which involved a media outcry about the effects of horror film violence on teenagers able to watch "adult" horror through the unregulated medium of VHS. This panic was intensified by the killing of the toddler James Bulger in 1993 by two teenagers from Merseyside who were supposedly influenced by the film *Child's Play 3*. However, such damning commentary about the effects of horror abated by 2001, a shift that is in part due to the *Harry Potter* phenomenon. Nick Hunter notes that by the time all seven of J. K. Rowling's *Harry Potter* titles had been published in 2008, the series had sold more than 375 million copies in 63 languages. In response, the *New York Times* introduced a children's best-sellers list in 2001 after *Harry Potter* titles had filled the first three spots on their regular best-seller list for more than a year (Hunter 2013, 46). Though *Harry Potter* is not horror fiction, Rowling's use of "dark" fantasy appealed to adult readers and critics, and its popularity with these gatekeepers led to the fantastic mode in general becoming more culturally valuable. At the same time, innovations on the small screen were also changing critical perceptions of horror for young adults. Joss Whedon's genre-defining television series *Buffy the Vampire Slayer* (1997–2003) was playful and self-aware in its use of horror tropes. The show explicitly interrogated the typical gender roles of horror narratives and played with critical assumptions about gendered responses to horror. After *Harry Potter* and *Buffy,* there occurs a distinct shift in discourse on horror fiction for young adults away from the centuries-old back and forth about its merits and pitfalls, and toward a more positive association.

In the twenty-first century, young adult horror fiction not only proliferates in the publishing market, but it is also generally well received by critics both in the academy and in wider culture. No longer ghettoized as category fiction, as Scholastic's *Point Horror* series was, young adult horror can be found across publishers and genres. Notable examples include Chris Priestley's portmanteau horror series *Tales of Terror* (2007–2009) and the now canonical (and critically acclaimed) *Coraline* by Neil Gaiman (2002), which has since been adapted into a successful film by Henry Sellick and Laika (2009). Pulp horror also remains popular, exemplified by the gory zombie serials by Darren Shan (*Zom-B,* published between 2012 and 2016) and Charlie Higson (*The Enemy,* published between 2009 and 2015). These two series in particular attempt to exceed previous limits of acceptability in terms of gross-out aesthetics and violent content, though critics now seem more sanguine about such transgressions. The *Telegraph,* a British newspaper at the forefront of the condemnation of *Point Horror,* favorably reviewed *Zom-B* as "a clever mix of horror, fantasy and realism" (Chilton 2012). Finally, there is also an emergent trend for young adult weird fiction, inspired by the Cthulhu Mythos of H. P. Lovecraft. Titles include Anthony Horowitz's *Power of Five* series (2005–2012) and Celia Rees's novel *The Stone Testament* (2007).

Though much commentary on this recent fiction continues to evoke long-standing ideas about horror as essentially therapeutic or helpful in developing the maturity of young adult readers, the works themselves often resist this pedagogical function. Darren Shan's first *Zom-B* novel, for example, offers an unlikely hero protagonist whose moral, social, and physical maturation is cut short when she is turned into a zombie at the close of the book. In subsequent books, it proves difficult to map a developmental schema or moral lesson onto Shan's foul-mouthed and violent zombie hero protagonist. Likewise, the nihilistic conclusion to Anthony Horowitz's *Power of Five* series, *Oblivion* (2012) refuses the bildungsroman (i.e., coming-of-age) structure of much young adult fiction. As the title suggests, the hero protagonist of this series does not achieve maturation and mastery in the resolution of the plot, but rather complete oblivion. Finally, young adult readers are beginning to make themselves heard in the continuing dialogue about the suitability and function of horror fiction. In 2014, pupils of the Richmond Park Academy, London, self-published an anthology titled *Dare You?* that challenges the

assumption that adult gatekeepers might know what is best for young adult readers. The collection defies many of the accepted notions of what critics and writers
think is appropriate. The stories frequently refuse resolution, and the reader is left
feeling disoriented; there are no safe spaces, and barriers are frequently ruptured;
shocking body horror erupts at unexpected moments. Like Shan's *Zom-B,* there are
thoroughly unlikeable personalities who disrupt notions of empathy and conventional morality. In many ways, *Dare You?* recalls the work of Matthew Lewis in
1796, who, at the age of twenty, produced a shocking, discordant, and fascinating
work that proved as popular with young adult readers as it was shocking to adult
critics.

Chloé Germaine Buckley

See also: Gender, Sexuality, and the Monsters of Literary Horror; Horror Comics;
Part One, Horror through History: Horror in the Nineteenth Century; Horror from
1900 to 1950; Horror from 1950 to 2000; Horror in the Twenty-First Century;
Part Three, Reference Entries: Body Horror; Coleridge, Samuel Taylor; Cthulhu
Mythos; *The Monk*; Penny Dreadful; Pulp Horror; Zombies.

Further Reading

Appleyard, J. A. 1991. *Becoming a Reader: The Experience of Fiction from Childhood to Adulthood.* Cambridge: Cambridge University Press.

Bettelheim, Bruno. 1976. *The Uses of Enchantment: The Meaning and Importance of Fairy
Tales.* London: Thames and Hudson.

Chilton, Martin. 2012. "Zom-B by Darren Shan, Review." *The Telegraph*, September 28, 2012.
http://www.telegraph.co.uk/culture/books/children_sbookreviews/9568888/Zom-B-by
-Darren-Shan-review.html.

Coleridge, Samuel Taylor. 1936. *Coleridge's Miscellaneous Criticism.* Edited by Thomas M.
Raysor. Cambridge: Harvard University Press.

Hunter, Nick. 2013. *Popular Culture: 2000 and Beyond.* London: Raintree.

Lamb, Charles. [1823] 1835. *Essays of Elia [Both Series].* Paris: Baudry's European
Library.

McCarron, Kevin. 2001. "Point Horror and the Point of Horror." In *Frightening Fiction*,
edited by Kimberley Reynolds, Geraldine Brennan, and Kevin McCarron, 19–52. London and New York: Continuum.

Pulliam, June. 2014. *Monstrous Bodies: Feminine Power in Young Adult Horror Fiction.* Jefferson, NC: McFarland.

Rees, Celia. 2012. "Interview about a Vampire and Other Gothic Topics." *The History Girls
Blog*, October 18. http://the-history-girls.blogspot.co.uk/2012/10/interview-about
-vampire-and-other.html.

Reynolds, Kimberley. 2001. "Introduction." In *Frightening Fiction*, edited by Kimberley
Reynolds, Geraldine Brennan, and Kevin McCarron, 1–18. London and New York:
Continuum.

Ruth, Greg. 2014. "Why Horror Is Good for You (and Even Better for Your Kids)." *Tor.com*,
May 29. http://www.tor.com/2014/05/29/why-horror-is-good-for-you-and-even
-better-for-your-kids.

Spacks, Patricia Meyer. 1990. *Desire and Truth: Functions of Plot in Eighteenth-Century English Novels*. Chicago, IL: University of Chicago Press.

Springhall, John. 1994. "'Pernicious Reading'? 'The Penny Dreadful' as Scapegoat for Late-Victorian Juvenile Crime." *Victorian Periodicals Review* 27, no. 4: 326–349.

Townshend, Dale. 2008. "The Haunted Nursery: 1764–1830." In *The Gothic in Children's Literature: Haunting the Borders*, edited by Roderick McGillis, Karen Coats, and Anna Jackson, 15–38. London: Routledge.

Part Three:
Reference Entries
(Authors, Works, and
Specialized Topics)

A

AICKMAN, ROBERT (1914–1981)

Robert Fordyce Aickman was a British writer of fiction and nonfiction, best known for his supernatural "strange" tales. His interests were many and various: he was a noted conservationist, a champion of the restoration of the British canal system; he loved to travel; he was a passionate patron of the arts; and he was a lifelong believer in ghosts and the paranormal, an advocate and theorist of supernatural literature, as well as a writer of it.

"The Cicerones": Numinous Horror

"The Cicerones" is one of Aickman's most memorable tales, and also one of his shortest. It was first collected in *Sub Rosa*. It also appeared in *The Seventh Fontana Book of Great Ghost Stories* (1971), which Aickman edited, and in the posthumous compilation *The Unsettled Dust*. It is apparently based on something that actually happened to Aickman. The title is an old term for a city guide.

John Trant, a bachelor approaching middle age, visits the Cathedral of Saint Bavon in Belgium, entering at almost exactly 11:30 a.m., anticipating the midday closure of the building. He finds the cathedral surprisingly empty. Wandering through the building, he has a series of uncanny encounters with young men and strange children, the cicerones of the title, who show him the cathedral's morbid paintings of monsters and martyrs. At the story's end, Trant is penned in by the cicerones, down in the cathedral's crypt. The clock then strikes twelve, and the cicerones close in on him and begin to sing. The story derives its disconcerting power from linking the gruesome ends of the martyrs in the paintings with Trant's own fate, though all is implicit, and the story ends in ambiguity.

"The Cicerones" brings together a number of key Aickman themes, including travelers who, through ignorance or misfortune, stray across a boundary into some strange place, and ordinary time coming to a standstill in the face of the strange. It is also imbued with a strong sense of the numinous, that strong religious or spiritual quality that indicates or suggests the presence of a divinity. Here, though, as in other Aickman tales, this sense is turned to horror. A 2002 short film directed by Jeremy Dyson and starring Mark Gatiss was based on the story.

Timothy J. Jarvis

Aickman was born just before World War I (1914–1918). He would never quite feel that he "fitted in" in the modern world, feeling instead that he rightly belonged to a lost era of gentility that the war had ended forever. He had a fraught upbringing. His parents were unsuited to each other, and they fought continuously. He survived his early years by taking refuge in books, his imagination, and the supernatural, which provided him with a sense of profound communion. Aickman also had a Gothic family inheritance: Richard Marsh, a popular author who was most famous for the horror novel *The Beetle*, was his grandfather.

After World War II, Aickman met the author Elizabeth Jane Howard through his conservation work, and the two had an affair. Howard encouraged Aickman to write his first ghost stories, and they published a volume together in 1951, *We Are for the Dark*. From that point on, Aickman concentrated more and more on his writing. In 1964, he published a novel, *The Late Breakfasters*, and a collection of ghost stories, *Dark Entries*. He also began editing the Fontana series *Great Ghost Stories*.

Over the next sixteen years, Aickman published a volume of autobiography, *The Attempted Rescue* (1966), and six more volumes of supernatural tales. He also received recognition for his writing, winning a World Fantasy Award for the story "Pages from a Young Girl's Journal" in 1975 and a British Fantasy Award for his short story "The Stains" in 1980.

Very few of Aickman's supernatural tales contain anything like a conventional haunting. In fact, though *We Are for the Dark* was subtitled "Six Ghost Stories," he later adopted, for the subtitle of his 1968 collection *Sub Rosa*, "Strange Stories." And he would use the term "strange" to describe his work throughout the remainder of his life. The term has become synonymous with the Aickmanesque story.

In various critical writings, Aickman outlines a unique philosophy of the supernatural tale and a singular mode of composition. Aickman had a strong interest in Freudian psychoanalysis, which may well have stemmed from therapy undergone to make sense of the damage his childhood did him. He believed in Freud's notion that only one-tenth of the mind is conscious, and that the remaining nine-tenths is unconscious. Because he felt the conscious one-tenth, the intellect, to be responsible for the ills of modernity, he thought it important to get in contact with the other nine-tenths. Of all literature, he considered the ghost story best equipped to do this. But though he believed in the supernatural, he didn't think that the "ghost" in a ghost story had to be an actual revenant, though it did have to be, in Freudian terms, a return of the repressed, something rising up from the unconscious mind.

Aickman had particular ideas about the compositional strategies that might be used to draw out the submerged nine-tenths of the mind. He felt that the best ghost stories are close to poetry in that they are only partly constructions of the conscious mind. He wrote that his most successful tales came to him in a half-trance. Aickman's strange stories, then, arising from the unconscious, are akin to dreams. And they work because they are dream-like; though they have no surface logic, they hang together because they are the emanations of Aickman's psyche and have a clear symbolic skeleton. The reader cannot shake the idea that there might be solutions to their puzzles. Of course, as is often remarked, there is nothing duller than someone relaying a dream, and sometimes Aickman's stories miss their mark. But when they do work they are as strange and off-kilter as the oddest dreams, as chilling as the worst nightmares. And, like dreams, they are often startling in their frankness and grotesquery, comical in their bizarreness, melancholy in their affect, and chilling in their insinuation. Aickman's novel *The Late Breakfasters* and his posthumously published novella *The Model* (1987) take the same themes and techniques, and develop them in different modes—satire in the case of *The Late Breakfasters* and magical realism in the case of *The Model*.

In the autumn of 1980, Aickman became ill with cancer. He refused conventional treatment, choosing instead to consult a homeopathic physician. Following a brief illness, he died in London's Royal Homeopathic Hospital on February 26, 1981.

Since Aickman's death, his reputation as one of the most significant British writers of supernatural short fiction of the late twentieth century has grown. His influence can be seen in the work of writers such as Ramsey Campbell, Neil Gaiman, Stephen King, Peter Straub, Joel Lane, Reggie Oliver, and M. John Harrison. His stories have been adapted for television. He has also influenced comedy: the bizarre and unsettling British troupe called the League of Gentlemen took much from Aickman's tales. His work has been reprinted. And a new generation of writers has been influenced by him: 2015 saw the publication of an anthology, *Aickman's Heirs*, edited by Simon Strantzas, which contains a number of British, U.S., and Canadian authors, including Lisa Tuttle, writing stories of Aickmanesque strangeness.

Timothy J. Jarvis

See also: Dreams and Nightmares; "Ringing the Changes"; Surrealism; World Fantasy Award.

Further Reading

Crawford, Gary William. 2011. *Robert Aickman: An Introduction*. Ashcroft, BC, Canada: Ash Tree Press. Kindle edition.

Crawford, Gary William. 2012. *Insufficient Answers: Essays on Robert Aickman*. Baton Rouge: Gothic Press.

Joshi, S. T. 2001. *The Modern Weird Tale*. Jefferson, NC: McFarland.

Russell, R. B., and Rosalie Parker. 2015. *Robert Aickman: Author of Strange Tales*. Leyburn, North Yorkshire, UK: DVD. Tartarus Press.

Strantzas, Simon, ed. 2015. *Aickman's Heirs*. Pickering, ON, Canada: Undertow Publications.

AINSWORTH, WILLIAM HARRISON (1805–1882)

William Harrison Ainsworth was a popular English novelist who, though trained in law, chose to write creatively, specializing in historical romances. An immensely prolific writer, he published forty novels over a span of five decades, many of which contained elements of horror. In the words of H. P. Lovecraft, Ainsworth's "romantic novels teem with the eerie and gruesome" (Lovecraft 2012, 46).

His early stories often involved crime and criminals, and made use of such Gothic motifs as thwarted heirs, secret passages, ruined edifices, burial vaults, corpses, and ghosts, the latter genuine as well as rationalized. His first success, *Rookwood* (1834), is ramshackle in plotting and construction but utilizes all of these devices, as well as a legend involving the fall of a tree branch leading to a death; it describes a dispute over an inheritance and the legitimacy of an heir. (There are, additionally, false identities, gypsies, and excessive praise of highwaymen, particularly the infamous Dick Turpin, as the story gradually resolves itself in favor of the legitimate claimant.) Though not supernatural, *Jack Sheppard* (1839) is more genuinely horrific, describing the monstrously villainous thieftaker (someone hired to capture criminals) and thief Jonathan Wild (1682?–1725) and his role in the creation, persecution, and ultimate destruction of the titular criminal (1702–1724). Although it proved popular with readers, *Jack Sheppard* reveals problems that were increasingly to affect Ainsworth's prose, specifically weak characterizations and narrative padding. Even allowing for the market, the latter is egregious.

Ainsworth's next significant successes were a trio of overtly historical novels—*The Tower of London* (1840), *Guy Fawkes* (1841), and *Old St. Paul's* (1841)—whose turgid plots combined with historical events proved initially popular with contemporaries. These, too, often contained horrific material, as in the latter's depiction of the spread of the black plague and the Great Fire of 1666; their success permitted Ainsworth to establish his own magazine (*Ainsworth's Magazine*, 1842–1854). He thus serialized *Windsor Castle* (July 1842–June 1843), a historical romance describing the events around Henry VIII's courtship of Anne Boleyn; a strong Gothic element involves the presence of the supernatural Herne the Hunter, who haunts Windsor Forest, who leads ghostly hunts through the forest, and whose origins are variously given. *Windsor Castle* proved very popular, not because of the uninspired retelling of the historical narrative, but because of Herne, who is more vital and convincing than the humans surrounding him.

Following this relatively promising beginning, Ainsworth's fortunes began a long, slow, and sad decline. His once large readership dwindled, as did his income, and where he was once considered almost Charles Dickens's equal, he gradually became no more than another impoverished second-rater, though it would be inaccurate and unfair to refer to him as a hack, as he undoubtedly cared about his writing. Late in his life, the City of Manchester honored him for his writings featuring the history of that city, but the accolades did not include financial security, and he died shortly thereafter. His obituaries tended to be dismissive and sometimes included erroneous material.

Though specialists and scholars still occasionally read Ainsworth and note that his fiction often possesses narrative drive, he is unlikely to be rediscovered by later audiences. The general academic consensus is that he was neither an innovator nor particularly talented as a writer or a creator of character, and that he provided a popular readership with historical novels featuring familiar and generally unin-spired horrific devices. Still, there are some who appreciate his fleeting and faded charms. Rosemary Mitchell, a British scholar of Victorian literature and history, writes that Ainsworth may well have been forgotten because his "attraction was to the gothic historical, to the black and the bloody, to haunted history," which made his writings serve in effect as "the dark side of those progressive Victorians we all know about, with their trains and telegraphs, their technological advances and their scientific discoveries, their liberal politics and their enlightened skepticism." She characterizes Ainsworth as a "precursor of [legendary Hollywood director and producer] Cecil B. DeMille and [best-selling author of *The Da Vinci Code*] Dan Brown, a master of the spectacle and the sinister, king of the colourful and the clichéd" (Mitchell 2011).

Richard Bleiler

See also: Part One, Horror through History: Horror in the Nineteenth Century; *Part Two, Themes, Topics, and Genres*: The Gothic Literary Tradition.

Further Reading

Lovecraft, H. P. [1927] 2012. *The Annotated Supernatural Horror in Literature*. Edited by S. T. Joshi. New York: Hippocampus Press.

Mitchell, Rosemary. 2011. "'What a Brain Must Mine Be!': The Strange Historical Romances of William Harrison Ainsworth." *Open Letters Monthly*, August 1. http://www.open lettersmonthly.com/what-a-brain-must-mine-be-the-strange-historical-romances-of -william-harrison-ainsworth.

Schroeder, Natalie. 1985. "William Harrison Ainsworth." In *Supernatural Fiction Writers: Fantasy and Horror*, vol. 1, edited by Everett Franklin Bleiler, 187–194. New York: Charles Scribner's Sons.

AJVIDE LINDQVIST, JOHN (1968–)

Of Algerian descent, horror writer John Ajvide Lindqvist is popularly referred to as Sweden's answer to Stephen King, an appropriate soubriquet given the author's interest in childhood and the decidedly supernatural bent of his fiction. Ajvide Lindqvist is notable for having produced one of the most original vampire novels of the twenty-first century, but also because he is one of a very few number of hor-ror auteurs to have broken into the international market without writing in Eng-lish. His novels are transnational enough to appeal to a wider public, yet remain decidedly Swedish in references and subject matter.

Ajvide Lindqvist was born in Blackeberg, Sweden. He rose to fame with his first and, to date, most famous novel, *Låt den rätte komma in / Let the Right One In*, pub-lished in his home country in 2004 and translated into English in 2007. The novel was made into a successful Swedish film in 2008 and was remade for the American market in 2010. Thematically, his writings have thus far covered, and updated, traditional horror figures such as the vampire (lonely and sympathetic in *Let the Right One In*), the zombie (an empty, post-traumatic shell of her/his former self in *Hanteringen av odöda / Handling the Undead* [2005; 2009]), and the ghost (capable of physically possessing the living in *Människohamn / Harbour* [2008; 2010]). But Ajvide Lindqvist has also conjured up less familiar scenarios, such as those of *Lilla stjärna / Little Star* (2010; 2011), in which a psychic child is capable of sucking the life out of humans, and of the surreal mood pieces collected in *Let the Old Dreams Die* (2010), a translation of *Pappersväggar* (2006) that included the story "Låt de gamla drömmarna dö" / "Let the Old Dreams Die" (2011). In the latter, Oskar and Eli from *Let the Right One In* make a brief reappearance.

One of the things that separates Ajvide Lindqvist from other contemporary authors is the allegorical quality of his writings, which work narratively as well as more metaphorically. This personal trait is particularly obvious in his last novel to be translated to English, *I Am behind You* (2017; published in Swedish as *Himmelstrand* in 2014), where an apocalyptic scenario serves as an excuse to probe the dark recesses of human despair. Similarly, in *Harbour*, what starts off as a fairly standard haunting turns into a reflection on Sweden's historical connection to the sea.

Xavier Aldana Reyes

See also: Vampires; Zombies.

Further Reading

Aldana Reyes, Xavier. 2016. "Post-Millennial Horror, 2000–16." In *Horror: A Literary History*, edited by Xavier Aldana Reyes, 189–214. London: British Library Publishing.

Bruhn, Jørgen, Anne Gjelsvik, and Henriette Thune. 2011. "Parallel Worlds of Possible Meetings in *Let the Right One In*." *Word and Image*, 27, no. 1: 2–14.

Costorphine, Kevin. 2010. "Panic on the Streets of Stockholm: Sub/urban Alienation in the Novels of John Ajvide Lindqvist." In *The Gothic: Probing the Boundaries*, edited by Eoghain Hamilton, 137–144. Oxford: Inter-Disciplinary Press.

ALCOTT, LOUISA MAY (1832–1888)

Louisa May Alcott was the renowned writer of *The Little Women Trilogy* (1868–1886), and her Gothic and sensation fictions were often pseudonymous, anonymous, or lost. Her children's fiction (Jo March's tabloid fiction in *Little Women*), correspondence, journals, and scholars occasionally referenced her shadow oeuvre of thrillers before their recovery by Madeline Stern in six volumes (1975–1993). As the daughter of Bronson Alcott, she was connected to the Transcendentalist movement and progressive educational initiatives from birth, with her circle of family friends including the likes of Ralph Waldo Emerson and Henry David Thoreau.

Joel Myerson and Daniel Shealy recovered Alcott's unpublished first novel *The Inheritance* (1849, 1997), with Gothic landscapes and a secret family history influenced by Ann Radcliffe and Charlotte Brontë. Alcott published sentimental yet sensational tales in 1850s Boston weeklies, but her 1860s thriller career involved two cheap publishing empires, Frank Leslie's and Elliot, Thomes, & Talbot. Three different Leslie publications ran at least twenty-seven original Alcott tales (1863–1870), beginning with prizewinner "Pauline's Passion and Punishment" (1863, 1975) about a U.S. femme fatale marrying a Cuban planter to aid her revenge against her U.S. ex-fiancé. Another confidence woman tale, "V. V." (1865, 1976), is an early detective fiction and initiated Alcott's run with Elliott, Thomes, & Talbot (1865–1867). That firm published several poems and six novelettes (four as A. M. Barnard and two relatively upbeat Gothics with her own name), including her final two con artist narratives. These con narratives exhibit Alcott's career-long interests in gender struggles, often defined in terms of mastery and slavery, as well as theatricality and masquerade, which threaten family structure in "Pauline's" and "V. V." but prove liberating for characters marginalized by gender and/or class hierarchy in "Behind a Mask" (1866, 1975) and "The Mysterious Key" (1867, 1975).

Alcott's thrillers invoke the supernatural, the Orientalist, and drugged states. "The Abbot's Ghost" (1867, 1975), a late Barnard tale, is a Christmas ghost story with her usual theme of secret family history. "Lost in a Pyramid" (1869, 1998), a late Leslie work rediscovered by Dominic Montserrat, expands upon Théophile Gautier with a sorceress-mummy's cursed flower seeds, and holds the distinction of being one of the earliest stories about defilers of an Egyptian tomb being hounded by a curse. Her anonymous novel *A Modern Mephistopheles* (1877) reprises Faustian bargains, foreign drugs, and moral or physical confinement from Goethe, Nathaniel Hawthorne, and Alcott's "A Whisper in the Dark" (1863, 1976) and *A Long Fatal Love Chase* (1866, 1995), a novel rejected by Elliott and recovered by Kent Bicknell. Before her death, Alcott agreed to reprint (1889) under her own name *Mephistopheles* and "Whisper." Alcott's parallel oeuvre illustrates supernatural and sensational themes and imagery informing nineteenth-century sentimental literature as well as dilemmas of female authorship in a patriarchal literary market.

Alcott suffered from ill health for many years, and she died of a stroke in Boston at the age of fifty-five. She is buried in Sleepy Hollow Cemetery in Concord, Massachusetts, near Emerson, Hawthorne, Thoreau, and many other notable U.S. writers in the section of the cemetery now known as Authors' Ridge.

Bob Hodges

See also: Forbidden Knowledge or Power; Gothic Hero/Villain; The Haunted House or Castle; Hawthorne, Nathaniel; Mummies.

Further Reading

Eiselein, Gregory, and Anne Phillips, eds. 2001. *The Louisa May Alcott Encyclopedia*. Westport, CT: Greenwood.

Porter, Nancy, and Harriet Reisen, eds. 2008–2016. *Alcott Project*. www.alcottfilm.com.

Smith, Gail. 1995. "Who Was That Masked Woman? Gender and Form in Alcott's Confidence Stories." In *American Women Short Story Writers: A Collection of Critical Essays*, edited by Julie Brown, 45–59. New York: Garland.

Stern, Madeline. 1995. Introduction to *Louisa May Alcott Unmasked: Collected Thrillers*. Boston: Northeastern University Press.

ALONE WITH THE HORRORS

Alone with the Horrors: The Great Short Fiction of Ramsey Campbell 1961–1991 was published in 1993 by Arkham House. It is a revision and expansion of *Dark Feasts: The World of Ramsey Campbell* (1987) and was fittingly published by the firm that issued Campbell's first book, *The Inhabitant of the Lake and Less Welcome Tenants* (1964), when he was a teenager. The selection of stories is Campbell's own, and the stories are dated by year. These dates do not indicate date of publication but date of composition. Campbell has kept a scrupulous record of the writing, publication, and translation of his work. Campbell does not include a story for every year of his literary career since 1961; both early in his career and later on, when he turned his attention to writing novels, he wrote few or no short stories; in this volume, there are no stories for the years 1962–1965, 1969–1972, 1981–1982, and 1988–1990.

The volume is a scintillating assemblage of some of the best weird fiction written during the years it covers. "Cold Print" (1966) constitutes Campbell's ultimate refinement of his adaptation of motifs borrowed from the work of H. P. Lovecraft, which was the focus of the juvenile pastiches of his first volume. Campbell reprints several stories from his second—and, arguably, best—story collection, *Demons by Daylight* (1973), which embody his distinctive melding of dream imagery, sexuality, and luminous prose.

A full eight stories are taken from *Dark Companions* (1982), in which Campbell's exposition of urban horror reaches its pinnacle. "Mackintosh Willy" (1977), for example, finds terror in a homeless person who appears to live in a bus shelter and is mercilessly tormented by two adolescent boys—but they pay for their cruelty when Mackintosh Willy revives from the dead to exact vengeance. "The Depths" (1978) features a prototypical mingling of dream and reality, where a writer discovers that if he doesn't write down the horrible nightmares he suffers, the events they depict occur in the real world.

Later stories feature grim and sardonic humor ("Seeing the World" [1983], in which a couple who have returned from an overseas trip are revealed to be zombies); a focus on aberrant psychological states ("Boiled Alive" [1986], where a man cannot distinguish between the real world and the pseudo-reality of film); and a clever use of modern technology to incite terror ("End of the Line" [1991], in which a telemarketer may be receiving calls from his deceased ex-wife and child).

Overall, *Alone with the Horrors* includes the full range of Campbell's short fiction and exhibits the wide-ranging imagination, the relentless focus on aberrant psychological states, and the manipulation of evocative, smooth prose that distinguish

Campbell's work in both the novel and the short story. In 1994 the book was awarded the World Fantasy Award for Best Collection.

S. T. Joshi

See also: Campbell, Ramsey; "Mackintosh Willy"; World Fantasy Award.

Further Reading

Campbell, Ramsey, Stefan Dziemianowicz, and S. T. Joshi. 1995. *The Core of Ramsey Campbell: A Bibliography & Reader's Guide.* West Warwick, RI: Necronomicon Press.
Joshi, S. T. 2001. *Ramsey Campbell and Modern Horror Fiction.* Liverpool: Liverpool University Press.

ALRAUNE

Alraune is the second novel in a loose trilogy that focuses on the character of Frank Braun, a thinly veiled idealization of its author, Hanns Heinz Ewers. *Alraune* was originally published in Ewers's native Germany in 1911, and it went on to become the most successful book of his career. S. Guy Endore's original English translation first appeared in 1929, published by the John Day Company of New York in an illustrated edition with drawings by the acclaimed artist of the grotesque, Mahlon Blaine.

Named after the novel's main character, *Alraune* is a play on the legend of the mandrake root (*Alraune* is German for *mandrake*) that was said to grow from the spilt semen of a hanged man at the foot of the gallows tree. In the novel, Braun, buried under gambling debts, retreats to the secluded home of his uncle Ten Brinken, a wealthy biologist and collector of arcana and oddities. Among this collection is a mandragora root. Braun appeals to his uncle's prideful and curious temperament by suggesting that he could be the first scientist in history to create a living *Alraune*-creature, the first to, as Braun phrases it, "make truth out of the old lie" (Ewers 1929, 58). The requirements for the task were the seed of a condemned criminal and a prostitute who would serve the Mother Earth role in the myth. Braun posits that "earth is also the eternal prostitute. Does she not give herself to all, freely?" (59).

Thus was spawned Alraune. Her diabolical conception resulted in her body being poisonous, her soul evil. Frank Braun returns, after further travel and adventures, to find that the "project" has matured into a woman. In keeping with Ewers's fascination with the Lilith archetype of the demonic or otherworldly female, Alraune is practically irresistible to men, whose blood is enflamed by her presence. This, naturally, is a disastrous attraction, as Alraune leaves a string of corpses in her wake before love itself leads to her ultimate destruction.

The double current of Alraune herself, that of Eros and Thanatos, not only makes for a stimulating novel, but it also resonates with the structure of the classical mandragora myth, which was said to bring boons to one person and disaster to another. Alraune's poisonous flesh and callous soul give the novel something of a Sadean flavor (that is, reminiscent of the notorious eighteenth- and nineteenth-century writer and libertine the Marquis de Sade), while its embrace of blasphemy, individualism, and the Gothic arguably qualifies the book an example of Germany's famous *Sturm und Drang* ("Storm and Stress") literary movement from the latter half of the eighteenth century.

While the creation of life by artificial means links *Alraune* directly to Mary Shelley's *Frankenstein*, it lacks some of the philosophical integrity of its predecessor. Where Victor Frankenstein strove for a Promethean leap in human abilities and comprehensions of life, Ewers's protagonists seem to approach the endeavor with a certain mouth-watering zeal for sin for sin's sake. The theme of parental responsibility, which served as *Frankenstein*'s moral anchor, tends more to float in *Alraune* like textual driftwood. The novel's substance also bears the clear marks of the author's interest in the question of genetics and environment, or alternately, blood and soil.

Alraune was filmed no fewer than five times, beginning with three silent versions. It was also loosely adapted as a German comic book between 1998 and 2004. The novel itself was brought back into print in the twenty-first century in a new translation by Joe E. Bandel, and the original English translation by Endore was also given a new edition.

Richard Gavin

See also: Ewers, Hanns Heinz.

Further Reading

Ashkenazi, Ofer. 2012. "Assimilating the Shrew: *Alraune* and the Discussion of Biological Difference in Weimar Horror Film." In *Weimar Film and Modern Jewish Identity*, 77–110. New York: Palgrave Macmillan.

Ball, Jerry L. 1996. "Alraune." *Magill's Guide to Science Fiction and Fantasy Literature* 1–2.

Ewers, Hanns Heinz. [1929] 2013. *Alraune*. Translated by S. Guy Endore. London: Birchgrove Press.

Koger, Grove. 2007. "Hanns Heinz Ewers." *Guide to Literary Masters and Their Works* 1. Salem, MA: Salem Press.

ANCESTRAL CURSE

Curses are forms of magical thinking that give intercessionary power to gods and spirits. An ancestral or family curse is one that accompanies a family and causes misfortune across multiple generations.

Many ancient cultures have ritual forms of curses on rivals and enemies, or which are used to protect family and property, or preserve memory. Assyrian memorial stones laud the powerful, but condemn those who dishonor their name. Egyptian scribes formalized "execration texts" in which the names of the enemies of the pharaoh were written on clay pots and smashed. These "threat formulas" could also be addressed to personal enemies. In the Greco-Roman tradition, *defixiones,* or curse tablets, appealed to the infernal gods or spirits with messages written on thin lead sheets that were then rolled and buried (sometimes in graves). In Greece, many shadowed legal disputes. Roman curses could be more personal and were composed in an obscure, occult language designed to address the gods in their own language. The Semitic god of the Old Testament issued regular curses that traveled down family lines, "visiting the iniquity of the fathers upon the children unto the third and fourth generation" (Exodus 20:5) for disobeying the jealous god. There is rich evidence of curses in northern tribes, particularly in Gaelic and Icelandic traditions.

Highly formalized, curses promise oblivion to the enemy, usually by ending the family line. "May his name and his seed disappear in the land," reads one Assyrian curse on a memorial stele (Holloway 2014). The content of curses has remained remarkably consistent across millennia and cultures. Curses are often paired with "lucks," talismans that bring good fortune, countermagics that work to block the hexes of enemies. This is the purpose of the evil eye: it neutralizes the threat by cursing those who curse first. Curses are also recursive, in that it has long been feared that to come into contact with one is to become bound to its logic and suffer its consequences.

Curses are associated with premodern thought, the kind of superstitious belief that Enlightenment thinkers believed a rational and scientific worldview would eradicate. To Victorian anthropologists, belief in curses was a sign of "primitive" thought. Yet just as Gothic literature emerged in the eighteenth century, so did a revamped idea of the family or ancestral curse. The Gothic and family curses are linked from the first avowed Gothic romance, Horace Walpole's *The Castle of Otranto* (1764). Walpole's fiction concerns the perversion of the proper patriarchal line, and the usurper Manfred meets his end in accord with an ancestral curse. This plot was repeated across many key early Gothic novels, from Matthew Lewis's *The Monk* (1796) to Charles Maturin's *Melmoth the Wanderer* (1820).

In response to the social and economic transformations of eighteenth-century England, a new interest in genealogy was common. Families sought legitimacy and security by digging for aristocratic or even royal roots (the Walpoles being a prime example). Hence, alongside the Gothic, stories of ancestral lucks and curses became a new kind of folklore, the stories commonly told and widely known.

Family curse stories might be typified by the Cowdray Curse, in which the nobleman Sir Anthony Browne was rewarded for his loyalty to Henry VIII by the gift of lands during the dissolution of the monasteries. Browne's family was cursed by a monk cast out at the dissolution. Over the centuries, several disasters among the descendants culminated in the extinguishing of the line in 1793. The most notorious family curse concerned the Tichbornes. The luck of the ancient family was said to depend on the annual payment of a dole to the local poor. When the family discontinued the Tichborne Dole in 1796, the curse was activated. The heir to the baronetcy was lost at sea in 1854; ten years later a man in Australia declared himself the lost baronet. The "Tichborne Claimant" dragged the family through the courts at vast expense and much public scandal in two trials in the 1870s. The Tichbornes restored the dole, but the family was ruined.

Many fictional family sagas followed patterns of ancestral curses. Walter Scott's *The Bride of Lammermoor* (1818) typified the ubiquity of clan curses in the Scottish imagination and his use of these plots, tinged with the supernatural, were hugely influential. The Gothic or horror version was common to tales published by *Blackwood's Magazine*. The anonymity of *Blackwood* stories such as "The Curse" (1832) left a shivery boundary of uncertainty as to the truth status of these narratives. Soon, family curses bled into mainstream fiction, such as the doom that haunts the Dedlock family in Charles Dickens's *Bleak House* (1853). The sensation fiction boom of the 1860s was dominated by melodramas driven by family secrets and ancestral shame, a device often used by writers like Ellen Wood and Wilkie Collins. By the late nineteenth century, biological determinism colored the imagination of family inheritance. The curse in Arthur Conan Doyle's *The Hound of the Baskervilles* (1902) turns out not to be a spectral dog but the evolutionary taint of criminality in the family blood.

Another key element of curse stories is that they are often a kind of exercise of primitive retributive justice of the weak against the strong. They are populated by monks, shepherds, the itinerant, and the dispossessed who curse feudal power, challenging its absolute rights with the promise of supernatural retribution. This class resentment figured strongly in the case of the fifth Earl of Carnarvon, the wealthy aristocrat who funded years of excavation in Egypt only to die six weeks after the opening of the tomb of Tutankhamun in 1923. The recursive logic of "Tut's Curse" allegedly killed many associated with the opening, although such a curse had no basis in ancient Egyptian belief. The story fitted into the Western tradition of ancestral curses perfectly, however. The pattern of revenge against transgression in Tut's Curse is the model for horror films from *The Mummy* (1932) all the way to *Drag Me to Hell* (2009).

Curses are effective in horror fiction and film because they evoke this premodern underpinning of nasty and vengeful supernatural agencies, but also because they exist in the shadowy space of rumor, hovering between fact and fiction, the perfect fodder for sensational tabloid reportage. A curse can crawl out of a museum relic, or rest with a mummy, or rise up out of the floors of a house imbued with a hidden, traumatic history. The cursed house is central to the American Gothic from Hawthorne's *The House of the Seven Gables* (1851) to Stephen King's *The Shining* (1977) or Jay Anson's *The Amityville Horror* (1977). Magical thinking still assigns misfortune, poverty, illness, and death to purposive malignant forces: horror fiction simply meets us halfway to disavowed belief.

Roger Luckhurst

See also: *The Castle of Otranto*; *The Hound of the Baskervilles*; *The House of the Seven Gables*; *Melmoth the Wanderer*; *The Monk*; Mummies; *The Shining*.

Further Reading

Holloway, April. 2014. "Assyrian Stele Containing Ancient Curse Will Not Be Reunited with Its Other Half." *Ancient Origins*, March 29. http://www.ancient-origins.net/comment/14174.

Lockhart, J. G. 1938. *Curses, Lucks and Talismans*. London: Geoffrey Bles.

Luckhurst, Roger. 2012. *The Mummy's Curse: The True Story of a Dark Fantasy*. Oxford: Oxford University Press.

Mighall, Robert. 1999. *A Geography of Victorian Gothic Fiction: Mapping History's Nightmares*, 78–129. Oxford: Oxford University Press.

Nordh, Katarina. 1996. *Aspects of Ancient Egyptian Curses and Blessings: Conceptual Background and Transmission*. Uppsala: Uppsala University Press.

ARKHAM HOUSE

As soon as he received news in March 1937 of the death of H. P. Lovecraft, writer August Derleth immediately began to make plans for the preservation of Lovecraft's stories. He had never met Lovecraft, but through correspondence he had developed a close relationship with him. Derleth was by this point a successful writer, both in the pulps and in the literary mainstream. He first submitted a volume of Lovecraft's stories to his regular publisher, Scribner's, but when this failed, he collaborated with fellow writer Donald Wandrei to bring the book out under his own imprint. Derleth had to surreptitiously borrow the money from a bank loan on his house, and Wandrei pitched in what he could. The result was *The Outsider and Others* (1939) under the imprint of Arkham House (the name taken from the imaginary Massachusetts town featured in Lovecraft's fiction). Nothing would ever be

---

Arkham House, founded by August Derleth and Donald Wandrei after the death of H. P. Lovecraft to preserve his work, went on to publish some of the most significant works of fantasy, horror, and science fiction in history, including several important horror "firsts."

1939   *The Outsider and Others*. Arkham House's first book, and the first published collection of Lovecraft's fiction, consisting of thirty-five stories, plus Lovecraft's essay "Supernatural Horror in Literature," plus a short essay about Lovecraft by Derleth and Wandrei.

1942   *Out of Space and Time*. First collection of supernatural stories by Clark Ashton Smith.

1945   *The Opener of the Way*. First book by Robert Bloch.

1947   *Dark Carnival*. First book by Ray Bradbury.

1958   *Nine Horrors and a Dream*. First book by Joseph Payne Brennan.

1964   *The Inhabitant of the Lake and Less Welcome Tenants*. First book by Ramsey Campbell.

Matt Cardin

the same again. Not only was the Lovecraft volume of paramount importance, but the publishing precedent Derleth had set would have wide repercussions.

Derleth's sole intention had been to preserve Lovecraft. Further volumes were planned, including at least one volume of Lovecraft's brilliant letters. But at the same time Derleth had submitted a collection of his own weird stories to Scribner's, and the editor there suggested that a specialized firm, like Arkham House, could publish the book more effectively. This proved to be the case. Despite good reviews, *The Outsider and Others* sold slowly, and Derleth's *Someone in the Dark* actually made a profit first. Derleth and Wandrei then began to consider preserving the work of other *Weird Tales* writers, beginning with Clark Ashton Smith's *Out of Space and Time* in 1942. Another Lovecraft volume, *Beyond the Wall of Sleep,* appeared in 1943, followed by Henry S. Whitehead's *Jumbee* (1944) and another Smith collection. Whether he had planned to or not, Derleth had become a publisher. Wandrei joined the army in 1942, after which Arkham House was mostly Derleth's business.

Derleth was in new territory, but he was well prepared. Prior to him, there had only been sporadic efforts to publish Lovecraft's work in book form, such as William Crawford's very amateurish edition of Lovecraft's *The Shadow over Innsmouth* (1936). But Derleth came on the scene as a professional whose books were taken seriously by critics and the book trade. Within a few years, in the period following World War II, there were many such firms publishing fantasy, horror, and science fiction, such as Fantasy Press and Gnome Press, but it was Derleth who had shown the way. Mainstream publishing was not ready, and small presses run by enthusiasts had to demonstrate that there was a market for such material.

Derleth knew there was a market for Lovecraft. He released *Marginalia* in 1944 as a stopgap, intending to bring out at least one volume of Lovecraft's letters shortly thereafter. But, as frequently happened with Arkham House, economic realities put the project on hold. The *Selected Letters* eventually ran to five volumes, but the first one did not appear until 1965.

After World War II, Derleth had to decide in what direction Arkham House should go. He brought out the first collection of Robert E. Howard's fantasy *Skull-face and Others* in 1946. He experimented tentatively with science fiction, and his edition of A. E. van Vogt's popular *Slan* (1946) was the first science fiction book published in hardcover after the war. He sought the newest talent and published the first story collections of Robert Bloch, Ray Bradbury, and Fritz Leiber Jr. He also reprinted the work of older writers, including J. Sheridan Le Fanu and William Hope Hodgson. He signed up as many of the still-living classic ghost story writers as he could: Algernon Blackwood, H. R. Wakefield, Lord Dunsany, L. P. Hartley, and Cynthia Asquith. He also brought out an extremely important anthology of supernatural poetry, *Dark of the Moon* (1947).

Not all of this worked out well. By the early 1950s, Derleth had to be bailed out by a $2,500 loan from author-physician David H. Keller. Arkham House survived the 1950s on a reduced scale, publishing several volumes of poetry (by Robert E. Howard, Leah Bodine Drake, and Clark Ashton Smith), a collection of Keller's stories, and more Lovecraft. The 1960s saw a general reprinting of all of Lovecraft's work, plus his *Collected Poems* (1963), and the last volumes of Clark Ashton Smith's fiction (ultimately six in all), plus his monumental *Selected Poems* (1971). There were major discoveries: the first books by Ramsey Campbell and Brian Lumley. By the time of his death in 1971, it was clear that Derleth had been a major force in twentieth-century fantasy publishing, and he had done his job superbly, producing attractive volumes much prized by collectors.

Derleth probably did not expect Arkham House to outlive him, but his heirs continued. New volumes by Campbell and Lumley appeared, along with other backlog. In 1975 the dynamic James Turner took over as managing editor. He oversaw the reissue of Lovecraft in carefully revised texts (edited by S. T. Joshi), published a Cthulhu Mythos anthology, and brought out horror collections by Charles L. Grant and Tanith Lee, but outraged Arkham House traditionalists by turning heavily to modern science fiction, so that when a rival firm, Fedogan and Bremer, began to appeal to the old Arkham House market (starting with a collection by Donald Wandrei), fans called it "the new Arkham House." There is no doubt that Turner's books—by Michael Bishop, James Tiptree, Michael Swanwick, Bruce Sterling, Lucius Shepard, J. G. Ballard, and others—sold extremely well. His departure in 1996 left Arkham House in a difficult position. Fedogan and Bremer had captured their old readership and Turner had walked off with the new, founding the Golden Gryphon Press, which published the same sort of books that he would have done for Arkham House. The post-Turner Arkham House has seemed to drift. It has brought out some interesting nonfiction, notably E. Hoffmann Price's book of pulp-era memoirs, *Book of the Dead*, plus a biography of Hugh B. Cave and two volumes of stories by pulp writer Nelson Bond. These may not have sold very well. The firm still exists but has not published a new title in several years.

Darrell Schweitzer

See also: Blackwood, Algernon; Bloch, Robert; Bradbury, Ray; Campbell, Ramsey; Derleth, August; Hartley, L. P.; Howard, Robert E.; Leiber, Fritz; Lovecraft, H. P.; Lumley, Brian; Smith, Clark Ashton; Wakefield, H. R.; Wandrei, Donald.

Further Reading

"Arkham House: Home to Horror, Sci-Fi Writers." 2004. *Weekend Edition Sunday*. NPR, October 31. http://www.npr.org/templates/story/story.php?storyId=4133870.

Barrett, Mike. 2013. "Arkham House: Sundry Observations." In *Doors to Elsewhere*, 17–43. Cheadle, Staffordshire, UK: Alchemy Press.

Joshi, S. T. 1999. *Sixty Years of Arkham House: A History and Bibliography*. Sauk City, WI: Arkham House.

AT THE MOUNTAINS OF MADNESS

At the Mountains of Madness is the longest story that H. P. Lovecraft published during his lifetime, although legend has it that he had set it aside in 1931 when it was rejected by his usual market, *Weird Tales*, and was subsequently submitted by Donald Wandrei without Lovecraft's knowledge to *Astounding Stories of Super-Science*, where it was serialized in a heavily edited version in 1936. A version much closer to the original was included in the Arkham House omnibus *The Outsider and Others* in 1939 and reprinted as the title story of an Arkham House collection in 1964; a corrected version of the latter collection was issued in 1985.

The novella follows the standard format of an archeological mystery story, in which investigators of long-buried ruins disturb entities that might have been better left to lie. The narrative takes the similarly standardized form of an account by geologist William Dyer of a scientific expedition to the Antarctic in 1930–1931, supposedly relating facts previously unrevealed, with the motive of warning future prospective explorers of the dangers they might face.

John W. Campbell's "Who Goes There?": Antarctic Horror with Echoes of Lovecraft

John W. Campbell Jr.'s novella "Who Goes There?" is one of the most original—and influential—treatments of a shape-shifting monster, widely acknowledged as a classic of the science fiction genre. The story was originally published, under the pseudonym "Don A. Stuart," in the August 1938 issue of the pulp *Astounding Stories*.

Set at an Antarctic research station, "Who Goes There?" echoes H. P. Lovecraft's *At the Mountains of Madness* (1931) in its depiction of an isolated group of scientists besieged by alien forces. In Campbell's tale, this extraterrestrial invader is capable of assimilating and perfectly mimicking any life form, including human beings, and the story's horrific charge lies in the growing paranoia of the increasingly harried men, who cannot be sure who is friend and who is foe. Above all, the monster must be prevented from reaching civilization, where its ability to simulate humans would be given free rein, spreading like a contagion.

"Who Goes There?" has influenced much subsequent SF-horror hybrids, such as Jack Finney's 1955 novel *The Body Snatchers* and the 1956 film, *Invasion of the Body Snatchers*, based upon it. Campbell's story also has been adapted for the screen, first in 1951 as *The Thing from Another World*, which removed the shape-shifting premise, and then in 1982, by director John Carpenter, as *The Thing*, which reinstated the original plot line.

Rob Latham

Source: Leane, Elizabeth. 2005. "Locating the Thing: The Antarctic as Alien Space in John W. Campbell's 'Who Goes There?'" *Science Fiction Studies* 32 (2): 225–239.

Dyer explains how the expedition discovered traces of a civilization established there fifty million years ago by extraterrestrial colonists, called Elder Things by the expedition's ill-fated biologist Professor Lake, but probably identical to entities previously introduced in other Lovecraft stories and allegedly known in arcane writings as the "Old Ones." The colonists' cities were built with the aid of monstrous biologically engineered slaves called shoggoths, whose eventual revolution brought the civilization to an end. In the course of the story the members of the expedition realize that the city's final inhabitants were only in suspended animation; having been disturbed, they are now returning to life, apparently continuing their ancient conflict. After a climactic encounter with a shoggoth, the narrator reports that his companion, the graduate student Danforth, was driven insane by the sight of even worse horrors that he was fortunate enough not to glimpse.

Along with the other Lovecraft story published in *Astounding*, "The Shadow out of Time," *At the Mountains of Madness* became a pivotal item of the retrospectively constructed "Cthulhu Mythos," ingeniously redefining entities that had been deemed supernatural in previous stories within a science fictional context, as products of alien biology, and thus decisively altering the assumed metaphysical context of that schema. In consequence, its substance offered more scope than its predecessors for future development and elaboration by the many other hands who added later works to the Mythos, and more temptation to exercise the imagination in extrapolation and variation. It is, therefore, one of the most extensively plundered and supplemented narratives in the sequence, and one of the most influential texts in modern weird fiction.

At the Mountains of Madness has been the subject of various extraliterary adaptations, including a graphic novel and audio dramatizations and readings by the H. P. Lovecraft Historical Society and the BBC. Filmmaker Guillermo del Toro spearheaded an effort to make a big-budget movie adaptation, with James Cameron being named as producer and Tom Cruise attached as a lead actor at one point. However, the project ran into roadblocks at Warner Brothers, and del Toro was reportedly dismayed and discouraged by similarities between his vision of the film and director Ridley Scott's 2012 science fiction–horror film *Prometheus*. At the start of 2017, the project was still in limbo.

Brian Stableford

See also: Arkham House; "The Colour out of Space"; Cthulhu Mythos; Lovecraft, H. P.

Further Reading

Collis, Clark. 2012. "'Prometheus' Kills Guillermo del Toro's Dream Project." *Entertainment Weekly*, June 10. http://www.ew.com/article/2012/06/10/prometheus-ridley-scott-guillermo-del-toro-lovecraft.

Harman, Graham. 2012. *Weird Realism: Lovecraft and Philosophy*, 148–172. Winchester, UK: Zero Books.

Long, Christian. 2015. "The Story of Guillermo del Toro's Fight to Bring Lovecraft's 'At the Mountains of Madness' to the Screen." *Uproxx*, August 20. http://uproxx.com/movies /guillermo-del-toro-mountains-madness.

Lovecraft, H. P. [1936] 2005. *At the Mountains of Madness: The Definitive Edition*. New York: Modern Library.

Mosig, Dirk W., and Donald R. Burleson. 1979. "At the Mountains of Madness." In *Survey of Science Fiction Literature*, vol. 1, edited by Frank N. Magill, 97–101. Englewood Cliffs, NJ: Salem Press.

"On *At the Mountains of Madness*: A Panel Discussion." 1996. *Lovecraft Studies* 34 (Spring): 2–10.

B

BALLARD, J. G. (1930–2009)

James Graham Ballard was known primarily as an author of science fiction, although the tones and textures of his best work converged with horror literature. Ballard was interned in a Japanese prison camp during World War II, enduring trials that left him with an abiding alienation from the values of Western modernity, convinced that advanced civilization is merely a screen for violent and irrational impulses. Influenced by Freudian psychological theory and European surrealism, Ballard's early work—gathered in such collections as *The Voices of Time* (1962) and *The Terminal Beach* (1964)—pointed the way toward a sophisticated and cynical new breed of science fiction, skeptical about the scientific mastery of nature and the essential heroism of the human species. His trilogy of disaster novels—*The Drowned World* (1962), *The Drought* (1964), and *The Crystal World* (1966)—challenged every convention of the genre: rather than battling to preserve the remnants of civilization in the face of adversity, his protagonists pursued a psychic accommodation—virtually a mystical fusion—with the forces destroying their worlds. In these works, the pessimistic impulses of horror literature seemed to overcome the essential optimism of science fiction.

This movement toward horror was even more pronounced in Ballard's mid-career trilogy chronicling the crushing boredom and despair of modern urban experience: *Crash* (1973), *Concrete Island* (1973), and *High-Rise* (1975). *Crash* evokes the automobile as a kind of demon lover, with fatal collisions becoming emblems of perverse eroticism, of denatured humanity bleakly coupling with machines, while *High-Rise* centers on an apartment building swiftly descending into chaos, driven by the low-grade tensions and rivalries that mark urban existence itself. Disturbingly surreal examinations of the tenuousness of civilization, these works—both memorably filmed (*Crash* by David Cronenberg in 1996, *High-Rise* by Ben Wheatley in 2015)—depict eruptions of the wanton irrationalism lurking beneath life's surface pleasantries.

These novels' grim tone and inclination to explore the basest of human impulses made Ballard a controversial figure within science fiction, with many fans arguing that he was not a science fiction author at all. Certainly, his later work moved resolutely away from the field, with his culminating tetralogy—*Cocaine Nights* (1996), *Super-Cannes* (2000), *Millennium People* (2003), and *Kingdom Come* (2006)—extrapolating the vein of social horror plumbed in *Crash* and *High-Rise*. All of these works are set in artificial environments, planned communities where their denizens' darkest fantasies can be given free rein, and their tone is consistently somber, though enlivened by flashes of ferocious satire. When Ballard died in London in 2009, he was widely celebrated as one of the most important British authors of the postwar period.

Rob Latham

See also: Psychological Horror; Surrealism.

Further Reading

Baxter, Jeanette, and Rowland Wymer, eds. 2012. *J. G. Ballard: Visions and Revisions*. New York: Palgrave Macmillan.

Luckhurst, Roger. 1997. *The Angle Between Two Walls: The Fiction of J. G. Ballard*. Liverpool: Liverpool University Press.

Oramus, Dominika. 2015. *Grave New World: The Decline of the West in the Fiction of J. G. Ballard*. Toronto: Terminal Press.

Sellars, Simon, and Dan O'Hara, eds. 2012. *Extreme Metaphors: Interviews with J. G. Ballard*. London: Fourth Estate.

BARKER, CLIVE (1952–)

Clive Barker is a celebrated horror author, a member of the *Masters of Horror* elite, a film and theater director, and an artist. He is best known in horror literature and film for his thematic blending of body horror and transcendence, frequently incorporating transgressive sexual symbolism and transformations of the body. His influential original creations are often bound up in twisted transfigurations of the flesh, the most infamous of which is the Hell Priest "Pinhead" from Barker's novella *The Hellbound Heart* (1986), adapted and directed by Barker for the screen as *Hellraiser* (1987). He attained acclaim in the mid-1980s in Britain for his unique short stories and novels that celebrate graphic body horror, as well as his unique S&M-style monsters, all of which combine erotic suggestion with the desire and torment of human transcendence. His novels and short stories are known for their lyrical descriptive prose, recalling H. P. Lovecraft's style of describing the unimaginable. Barker is particularly interested in themes and motifs of gaining access to other worlds and hidden realms, doorways which are often concealed from view and discovered only by those worthy to glimpse their wonders.

Born in Liverpool, England, in 1952, Barker displayed a keen interest in art, drawing, painting, models, and puppets from an early age, and he soon began creating dark creatures and fantastical worlds. He was keen on detailing his own unique creatures and tales, which soon translated to an interest in theater. Alongside both former school friends and upcoming actors and writers, he formed an avant-garde theater group, the Dog Company, which served as his first foray into professional writing and stage work. The group earned some critical praise in London and Edinburgh for their avant-garde original plays and performance style. By the late 1980s, Dog Company members directly featured in or contributed to

A Selective Clive Barker Chronology: Books and Films

Books

1984–1985	*Books of Blood*
1985	*The Damnation Game*
1986	*The Hellbound Heart*
1987	*Weaveworld*
1988	*Cabal*
1989	*The Great and Secret Show*
1991	*Imajica*
1992	*The Thief of Always*
1994	*Everville*
1996	*Sacrament*
1998	*Galilee*
2001	*Coldheart Canyon*
2002	*Abarat*
2004	*Abarat: Days of Magic, Nights of War*
2007	*Mister B. Gone*
2011	*Abarat: Absolute Midnight*
2015	*The Scarlet Gospels*

Films (as writer and/or director)

1973	*Salomé* (short film)—Director
1978	*The Forbidden* (short film)—Director
1985	*Underworld*, a.k.a. *Transmutations*—Writer
1986	*Rawhead Rex* (based on Barker's short story "Rawhead Rex")—Writer
1987	*Hellraiser* (based on Barker's novella *The Hellbound Heart*)—Writer and director
1990	*Nightbreed* (based on Barker's novella *Cabal*)—Writer and director
1992	*Candyman* (based on Barker's short story "The Forbidden")—Writer and producer
1995	*Lord of Illusions* (based on Barker's short story "The Last Illusion")—Writer, producer, and director

Barker's films, both onscreen and off, the most notable of whom is Doug Bradley, who was cast as Pinhead of the *Hellraiser* franchise. Peter Atkins, another Dog Company writer, wrote the screenplays for the first three *Hellraiser* sequels—*Hellbound: Hellraiser II* (1988); *Hellraiser III: Hell on Earth* (1992), and *Hellraiser IV: Bloodline* (1996)—which established his own screenwriting career in horror cinema.

Barker's first success as an author came with the publication of an ambitious collection of horror short stories entitled *Books of Blood* (1984–1985). Published in six volumes over two collections, these imaginative and often visceral horror short stories enjoyed a strong critical reception, garnering Barker enthusiastic endorsements from such horror luminaries as Ramsey Campbell and, most notably, Stephen King, who described Barker in a widely circulated blurb as "the future of horror." This rapid ascent in horror circles was followed by Barker's debut novel, *The Damnation Game* (1985), set in 1980s Britain and celebrating Barker's interest in traditional Gothic and horror tropes. This first novel rapidly established him as a major literary force in British horror literature; by 1986, two years after his publishing debut, he appeared alongside Ramsey Campbell and Lisa Tuttle in the horror anthology *Night Visions 3*, edited by George R. R. Martin. The story featured in the anthology, "The Hellbound Heart," would become a signature piece in Barker's literary and visual storytelling; republished as a separate novella in 1988 due to its successful screen adaptation, *The Hellbound Heart* foregrounded Barker's style as one of fleshy horror and gore combined with body modification, exploring the intermingling of pleasure and pain as a wellspring of fascination and desire. According to Doug Bradley, Barker half-jokingly describes this macabre tale as "Ibsen with monsters" (*Under the Skin,* 2004), in that it is primarily concerned with the disintegration of a marriage by means of infidelity and murder, with monsters hidden in the attic.

Barker's polymathic artistry also flourished with the rare opportunity to adapt and direct his novella into a feature-length film, retitled *Hellraiser.* Barker had previously directed two short films, *Salomé* (1973) and *The Forbidden* (1978), and had previous unsuccessful screen adaptations of his stories with *Underworld* (1985; released as *Transmutations* in the United States) and *Rawhead Rex* (1986), but this new feature-length project was grander in scope and budget, and, crucially, it allowed Barker to completely control its style and tone as director. Its most spectacular element was certainly the S&M-style Cenobites, "demons to some, angels to others" (*Hellraiser* 1987), infernal explorers of pain and pleasure that are striking in their visual design, with each member of the group bearing its own unique body modifications, which include bejeweled pins decorating intersections of precisely carved flesh, exposed abdominal gashes, surgical wounds, and chattering teeth, all made complete by the creatures' bodies being sewn into sculpted leather clothing. The Cenobites, designed directly from Barker's own sketches, also engender a ghostly and gothic contamination of domestic space, an invasion of the psyche made monstrous with forbidden appetites. Barker's monsters peel back open flesh and sinew with bloodied chains and hooks, marking *Hellraiser* as a confrontational visual experience at the time. A striking combination of gory special effects makeup with a plot that evokes the theme of the Faustian bargain, *Hellraiser* is Barker's most successful and widely known film as director to date.

There exists a certain branding tension between Barker's authorial and directorial creations. His name had become synonymous with horror branding as early as 1986, but privately he was undergoing a transition away from his roots in graphic horror fiction. *Hellraiser* was released during this period of generic change in

Barker's writing style, which was characterized by a distinctive moving away from his established exploration of body horror in favor of dark fantasy storytelling. Rejecting rigid genre traditions and expectations, Barker describes his creations as "dark fantastique" (Winter 2001). This notable confluence of fantasy and horror is evidenced in Barker's second novel, *Weaveworld* (1987), a tale of magic and power in a secret realm hidden in the filigree of a magic carpet. *Weaveworld* is better understood as an epic tale of dark adventure rather than one of grisly horror or mutilation. The novel's mantra, "that which can be imagined need never be lost" (Barker 1997, xvii), neatly sums up Barker's thematic transition from his earlier visceral horrors and bleak tone. Released in the same year as *Hellraiser*, Barker's *Weaveworld* began his generic transition in literature over the next decade, while his public (and film) personas were more explicitly wedded to his visceral horror creations. His next three novels, *The Great and Secret Show* (1989), *Imajica* (1991), and *Everville* (1994), crystallized his preoccupation with dark forces and human transcendence, as each tale grapples with themes of Manichean battles (that is, battles between absolute light and darkness) that ripple across time and dominions. For Barker, the fantastic enabled him to create parallel worlds of wonder and horror, glimpsed through a doorway in the everyday world and free from the constraints of any one genre.

Barker has had a mixed relationship with the film industry. His directorial debut with *Hellraiser* was positively received, soon spawning a successful sequel, which he produced. However, in 1990 he directed *Nightbreed*, based on his novella *Cabal* (1988), and the film received a mixed critical response and poor box-office returns. This disappointment left an indelible mark on Barker. *Nightbreed* is a tonally uneven film, but it also suffered from mishandling by Fox Studios that directly affected its box-office returns. Executives were reportedly baffled by the film's insistence that the monsters were its heroes, and the studio rejected the director's cut in favor of a shorter yet narratively confusing theatrical version. Further, Fox's marketing department inaccurately sold the film as a slasher, despite its clear fantasy themes, all of which contributed to unfavorable critical responses and to Barker's personal and professional disillusionment with the film industry. *Nightbreed* has remained a cult favorite with film festival audiences, and it underwent restoration and re-release as a director's cut in 2014.

Barker's final film as director, *Lord of Illusions* (1995), was loosely adapted from his short story "The Last Illusion" in *Books of Blood, Vol. 6*. Starring Scott Bakula as Detective Harry D'Amour, the film combines dark fantasy, stage magic, and horror, generically blending Barker's fascination with trickery, evil, and immortality with strong film noir aesthetics. Garnering positive reviews from critics including Roger Ebert and the *Hollywood Reporter*, the film was more palatable to general audiences outside of Barker's core fan base. However, today Barker avoids further directorial projects while remaining an influential producer through his production company, Seraphim Films, and he continues his contributions to filmmaking through extensive collaboration.

During the mid-to-late 1990s, Barker's novels revealed much about his personal life, including his political and cultural interests beyond the horror genre and filmmaking. Following his relocation to Los Angeles in the early 1990s, he published three "dark fantastique" novels—*Sacrament* (1996), *Galilee* (1998), and *Coldheart Canyon* (2001)—each of which leaves illuminating clues about his personal and emotional life. As an openly gay author, in *Sacrament* Barker articulates his concerns about the horrors of animal extinction and the 1990s AIDS crisis. *Galilee* draws inspiration from Barker's then relationship with photographer David Armstrong in a tale of a mysterious and exotic explorer, the titular Galilee, caught between two warring families. *Coldheart Canyon* is a Gothic haunted house novel critiquing Hollywood's vapid culture and scandalous past. Partially set in Barker's Beverly Hills home, the novel heralded his explicit return to the horror fold, through which he vented his personal frustrations with Hollywood culture, including his place within it.

The inclusion of Barker's original artworks in his novels emerged in the early 1990s and had steadily grown more prominent in his literary career. *The Thief of Always* (1992), his fable-like first published novel for children, included Barker's own sketches, documenting the story's many monsters and ghoulish sights as witnessed by young protagonist Harvey Swick. Abandoning the constraints of filmmaking for the expressive liberation of painting and sketches, Barker was keen to create tales lyrically and visually for young adult (YA) readers at a time when it was unorthodox for horror authors to target different audiences and demographics. The success of *The Thief of Always* prompted him to plan a series specifically addressing a younger readership. *The Books of Abarat*, an intended quintet of novels accompanied by Barker's paintings, chart the tale of heroine Candy Quackenbush, who accidentally discovers a hidden magical realm of monsters and strange creatures scattered across an enchanted archipelago of twenty-five islands. To date, three of the five intended books have been published: *Abarat* (2002), *Abarat: Days of Magic, Nights of War* (2004), and *Abarat: Absolute Midnight* (2011).

A return to more traditional horror fiction was inevitable for Barker. His short novel *Mister B. Gone* (2007) plays with narrative form, as readers encounter the title character and demon Mister B., who wishes to break free from the very pages of the book. The novel is Barker's personal testament to the power of horror literature. In 2015, in the midst of completing his *Books of Abarat* quintet and its accompanying artworks, Barker also published the long-awaited and much anticipated novel *The Scarlet Gospels*, a crossover tale reviving beloved characters from his earlier work. *The Scarlet Gospels* chronicles a battle of wits between Pinhead and Barker's film noir–styled paranormal detective Harry D'Amour, as the Hell Priest journeys into the bowels of hell to claim its throne for himself. Ten years in development, the novel was nominated for the Bram Stoker Award in 2016. More recently, he has hinted on social media that he is preparing a new tale in which Pinhead revisits the character of Kirsty from *The Hellbound Heart* and *Hellraiser* for a final encounter. These developments suggest a desire on Barker's part to return to the type of horror fiction, visceral and gory in theme and style, that originally established his reputation in the 1980s.

Sorcha Ní Fhlainn

See also: "The Beast with Five Fingers"; Body Horror; *Books of Blood*; *The Damnation Game*; Dark Fantasy; Lovecraft, H. P.; Splatterpunk.

Further Reading

Badley, Linda. 1996. "Clive Barker Writing (from) the Body." In *Writing Horror and the Body: The Fiction of Stephen King, Clive Barker and Anne Rice*, 73–104. Westport, CT: Greenwood Press.

Barker, Clive. [1987] 1997. *Weaveworld*. 10th Anniversary Edition. London: HarperCollins.

Brown, Michael, ed. 1991. *Pandemonium: Further Explorations into the Worlds of Clive Barker*. Forestville, CA: Eclipse.

Hellraiser. 1987. Written and directed by Clive Barker. New World Pictures.

Hellraiser. 2004. Special Edition Boxset. Anchor Bay Films.

Hoppenstand, Gary. 1994. *Clive Barker's Short Stories: Imagination as Metaphor in the Books of Blood and Other Works*. Jefferson, NC: McFarland.

Jones, Stephen. 1991. *Clive Barker's Shadows in Eden*. Lancaster: Underwood-Miller.

McRoy, Jay. 2002. "There Are No Limits: Splatterpunk, Clive Barker, and the Body in-Extremis." *Paradoxa* 17: 130–150.

Ní Fhlainn, Sorcha, ed. 2017. *Clive Barker: Dark Imaginer*. Manchester: Manchester University Press.

Under the Skin: Doug Bradley on Hellraiser. 2004. Directed by Jake West. Nucleus Films.

Winter, Douglas. E. 2001. *Clive Barker: The Dark Fantastic*. London: HarperCollins.

BARLOW, R. H. (1918–1951)

Best known for his work as an anthropologist, Robert Hayward Barlow spent his early years as a central figure in the Lovecraft circle, a group of weird fiction writers. Barlow befriended H. P. Lovecraft via correspondence at the young age of thirteen, and Lovecraft collaborated with Barlow on no less than six stories. They became so close that the latter named Barlow his literary executor upon his death. Unfortunately, this appointment drove a wedge between Barlow and the rest of the Lovecraft circle, effectively alienating him from the group and ending his career as a practitioner of the weird tale.

Barlow's fiction more clearly resembles the fantasy tales of Lord Dunsany and Clark Ashton Smith than Lovecraft's speculative realism. The bulk of Barlow's writing is of an amateurish quality, consisting largely of short vignettes and sketches rather than completed stories. However, this work shows the promise of a young writer learning his craft and reveals that Barlow possessed a wry wit and a keen sense of satire. These short pieces recount events occurring in fantasy worlds and are tied loosely together by theme and motif. They often depict the interactions between the gods and the societies that worship them, foregrounding the disastrous consequences of human hubris in confronting larger forces. Barlow also connects his tales through reoccurring characters such as the God Lord Krang, thus demonstrating the early stages of development of a mythos modeled on Lovecraft's Cthulhu mythos.

While the majority of Barlow's work feels unpolished, he produced at least two stories, "The Night Ocean" (1936) and "A Dim-Remembered Story" (1936), that demonstrate professional quality. "The Night Ocean" most resembles Lovecraft's work and is the least fantastic of Barlow's writing. While Lovecraft collaborated with Barlow on this story, his input has been proven minimal. The story, an excellent study in atmospheric horror, centers on an artist on vacation at a small seaside town, building tension through the artist's ruminations on human insignificance next to the terrible vastness of the ocean. "A Dim-Remembered Story," more in line with the rest of Barlow's fantasy work, tells the story of a man who awakens in a seemingly medieval world, only to realize that he is actually eons in the future among the remnants of a fallen civilization. The narrator is then transported further into the future where, as a mere consciousness floating in space, he sees that the universe is completely altered, leaving no trace of humanity's existence. The horror of the story develops from the recognition of human triviality in the gigantic flow of time.

After falling out with the Lovecraft circle, Barlow met Lawrence Hart and began publishing activist poetry. He eventually moved on to a successful career in anthropology at Mexico City College as an expert in Mesoamerican culture and the Náhuatl language. Barlow committed suicide in January 1951.

Travis Rozier

See also: Lovecraft, H. P.; Lovecraftian Horror; Smith, Clark Ashton.

Further Reading

Barlow, R. H. 2002. *Eyes of the God: The Weird Fiction and Poetry of R. H. Barlow*, edited by S. T. Joshi, Douglas A. Anderson, and David E. Schulz. New York: Hippocampus Press.
Berutti, Massimo. 2011. *Dim-Remembered Stories: A Critical Study of R. H. Barlow*. New York: Hippocampus Press.

BARRON, LAIRD (1970–)

Laird Samuel Barron is a writer of weird fiction from the United States. He is one of the most significant early twenty-first-century writers of cosmic horror and has received many plaudits, award nominations, and awards for his work.

Barron was born in Palmer, Alaska, and raised on a wilderness parcel in an isolated area, in general poverty. In Alaska he later worked as a fisherman on the Bering Sea and raced the Iditarod, a punishing long-distance sled-dog race, three times. The wilderness and the harsh conditions of his upbringing have fed his work.

Barron's work falls in the tradition of Lovecraft's cosmicism by portraying humans as living at the mercy of inhuman metaphysical forces and entities whose nature and concerns dwarf the human perspective and emerge as intrinsically horrifying to it. But in contrast to Lovecraft, Barron's outer entities are not utterly Other and indifferent to humankind. They are not expressions of a pessimistic shudder at the insignificance of the planet Earth and its civilizations. Instead, Barron's cosmos is actively malevolent. In his stories, the things from the far corners of the universe are petty and cruel. In this, Barron's fiction bears similarities to Thomas Ligotti's. A black miasma underlies everything, and men and women are little more than puppets of this malicious vital force. But in Barron's work, unlike in Ligotti's, human life is not part of the toxicity. In fact, relationships, drinking, drugs, and sexual encounters offer a kind of reprieve from the torment.

Barron's fiction combines weird horror with other pulp modes, such as the Western (as in "Bulldozer," 2004) and noir (as in "Hand of Glory," 2012). His prose also contains revelatory moments of unnerving lyricism, especially when the weird is encountered. Barron has talked of the influence of Cormac McCarthy and Angela Carter on his work, and the approach of these two writers to language can be seen in his stories.

Much of Barron's work deals with the presence of hostile alien entities in Washington State, which was Barron's home for some years. These works form a cycle known as the Pacific Northwest Mythos that shares characters and incidents. In fact, in all of Barron's stories, players and events recur again and again. This has the uncanny effect of making them feel like recountings rather than fictions. Barron has also, in his most recent work, turned to metatextual, parodic stories, such as "More Dark" (2012), in which he and other prominent horror writers are characters; "More Dark" addresses some of the myth-making surrounding Thomas Ligotti in the community of horror writers and readers.

In the early 2010s Barron moved to the Hudson Valley region of New York State, and in his fiction he has turned away from Pacific Northwest settings to focus on Alaskan themes. His 2016 book *Swift to Chase* (2016) collected some of his Alaskan stories.

Barron's work had a strong influence on early twenty-first-century weird fiction. In 2014, Word Horde published *The Children of Old Leech*, a tribute to Barron's fiction. Barron is a multiple Locus, World Fantasy, and Bram Stoker award nominee and was a 2007 and 2010 Shirley Jackson Award winner for his collections *The Imago Sequence and Other Stories* (2007) and *Occultation and Other Stories* (2010). "Mysterium Tremendum" won a 2010 Shirley Jackson Award for best novella.

Timothy J. Jarvis

See also: Carter, Angela; Ligotti, Thomas; Lovecraft, H. P.; Lovecraftian Horror; Pulp Horror; Shirley Jackson Awards.

Further Reading

Barron, Laird. 2010. "Why I Write." *Publishers Weekly*, July 12. http://www.publishersweekly .com/pw/by-topic/authors/interviews/article/43795-why-i-write-laird-barron.html.

Jarvis, Timothy. 2013. "Stages of Horrific Vision in 'The Forest.'" *Weird Fiction Review*, April 9. http://weirdfictionreview.com/2013/04/101-weird-writers-laird-barron.

Lockhart, Ross E., and Justin Steele. 2014. *The Children of Old Leech: A Tribute to the Carnivorous Cosmos of Laird Barron*. Petaluma, CA: Word Horde.

Tourigny, Yves. *They Who Dwell in the Cracks: A Look at the Works of Author Laird Barron*. Accessed July 11, 2106. http://www.theywhodwellinthecracks.com.

Vanderhooft, JoSelle. 2012. "Laird Barron: I'm a Magnet to Steel—Interview." *Weird Tales* 66, no. 3: 21–25.

An Interview with Laird Barron

October 2016

In this interview, Barron, whose writing is noted for its strong use of voice and setting, discusses the place of these elements in horror fiction. He also talks about the revitalization of weird fiction in the twenty-first century, the significance of H. P. Lovecraft and Thomas Ligotti (and also Cormac McCarthy and T. E. D. Klein) for horror fiction, and the impressive breadth of the new millennium's horror revival.

Matt Cardin: One of the first things an astute reader notices when reading your work is the centrality of voice. Many have noted the use of a noir-type voice, tone, approach, in a significant amount of your work, but it goes beyond that. A distinct voice in general, whether noir-ish or otherwise, is crucial to everything you've written. Can you speak to why this is the case? Because not all horror fiction hinges so heavily on this quality. In fact, a great deal of modern horror fiction has been written in the same "style-less" style and voiceless prose that has characterized much mass-published fiction in the past few decades. Why is it different for you? And what do you see as the role of voice in horror fiction as a whole?

Laird Barron: I'm heavily influenced by noir and pulp from the 1930s through the early 1980s. Most of the authors I admire skew toward narrative traditions that privilege sharp characterization and robust detail in setting and atmosphere.

Music also played a significant role in my development. Country and Western songs from the 1960s and 1970s often defaulted to a ballad format. Singers such as Bobby Bare, Tom T. Hall, and Marty Robbins (and many others) possessed rich and distinctive voices and styles. As a consequence, I'm less interested in modes of contemporary prose that eschew all adornment or tend to neuter voice. Horror works best when synthesized with a strong point of view. Voice: the reason Stephen King reigns as the heavyweight champion of horror forty years into his career.

MC: Setting is also crucial to your stories, as it is to a great deal of horror fiction in general. You've done some striking things with turning Washington State into a kind of haunted land of its own, reminiscent, perhaps, of what Stephen King has done with Maine, or what Lovecraft did with Rhode Island, Massachusetts, and New England in general. You have also given some of the same treatment to Alaska. How do you understand the role of setting in horror literature? What would you say about it to readers of horror fiction—yours or anyone else's—who are looking to increase their understanding, enjoyment, and experience of this particular type of literature?

LB: Setting is integral to the kinds of literature that shaped my youth. For example, Robert E. Howard, Edgar Rice Burroughs, Jack London, and Louis L'Amour dwelled on the physicality of their universes. These writers created pulp heroes who reflected (or stood in marked contrast [to]) the high deserts, frozen wastelands, lush jungles, and alien vistas so ubiquitous in their tales. Setting can provide critical elements to a horror story—perhaps it isolates the protagonist or acts as an obstacle. My own choice has been to occasionally elevate setting, to imbue it with its own agency, and, occasionally, treat it as another character.

Real terror can be derived from a reactive universe. Shirley Jackson's *The Haunting of Hill House* and Cormac McCarthy's *Blood Meridian* demonstrate opposite ends of the spectrum of how a reactionary setting illuminates and amplifies horror. In the context of cosmic horror, the vastness of the natural world, and beyond, reinforce the notion that man is minute, a flea upon the back of a behemoth.

MC: The early twenty-first century has seen a reinvigoration of horror fiction and film, especially, but not exclusively, in the area of weird fiction. You are part of this wave. What do you think has happened? Why now? And what is different, if anything, from the original "horror boom" of circa 1975 to 1995?

LB: These things tend to exist as cycles—perhaps we were simply due for a revival. The current boom separates itself from previous cycles in regard to volume and variety. I'm not sure there's ever been so broad or deep an array of theme, style, or technique. Independent presses and the advent of digital technology are driving the movement.

This latter point can't be stressed enough: the independent press and digital technology have compensated for an ever-shrinking midlist. The Internet and forbearance of small publishers have encouraged authors to experiment and to push the envelope.

MC: Two writers have frequently been mentioned in association with you and your work, and both of them are, like you, quite prominent in the twenty-first century's new wave of horror. Their names may be taken here as questions for you to answer, problems for you to address, and/or enigmas for you to explain, whether in relation to yourself or in relation to the field at large. First: Lovecraft.

LB: My interest in H. P. Lovecraft focuses mainly on the implications of his cosmic obsessions, rather than tilling the same patch of literary earth.

Lovecraft has, with diligent labor by August Derleth and S. T. Joshi, arisen from the dust of obscurity to become a literary monument. He personifies what contemporary authors term cosmic horror. That said, it's important to recognize Lovecraft for what he truly is—an artifact. Much of his personal philosophy is untenable and his visionary approach to fiction is simply a beginning, a jumping-off point for those of us who've followed the trail.

Two major camps have arisen of late, the anti-Lovecraftians and the Lovecraft deifiers. The man made a serious contribution to weird fiction; this can't be lightly dismissed on the basis of his purple prose or his abhorrent personal beliefs. Likewise, he isn't the alpha or omega of the genre. Weird fiction and cosmic horror predate the Bible. Weird fiction and cosmic horror have succeeded Lovecraft and will succeed us as well.

MC: Second: Ligotti.

LB: I've written a substantial number of stories in response to Lovecraft and Lovecraft's successors, especially early in my career. As I said, he's a monument looming over a certain precinct of weird fiction. Conversely, Thomas Ligotti is, at this juncture, a massive subterranean structure, or the submerged bulk of an iceberg that dwarfs its surface presence. The worldview of both men drive their fiction. Lovecraft's gaze turned almost impossibly outward, while Ligotti dwells upon the microcosmic. Somehow they wind up bumping into one another at the end of a long, dark journey.

Ligotti's core strength and main appeal is the sui generis quality of his work. Where Lovecraft (despite xenophobic tendencies) spoke to the interests of a broad spectrum of humanity, Ligotti speaks directly to the disaffected, the despondent, and the depressed in a naturalistic manner that knows no equal among horror writers. The adage goes that one mustn't conflate an artist with his or her creations. Ligotti is an exception to the rule. His philosophy seems largely inseparable from the hellscape of his imagination.

MC: Are there any additional authors and works that you would recommend to those who are looking to explore this wing of the literary universe? Which ones strike you as especially important both for this genre and for literature as a whole?

LB: While Cormac McCarthy isn't widely considered a horror or weird fiction author, I beg to differ. His landmark novel, *Blood Meridian*, numbers among the seminal works of both cosmic horror and North American literature in the main. Few stories so brutally illustrate the minuteness of man in all his depravity, ambition, and hubris when contrasted with the implacability of nature and the larger universe.

T. E. D. Klein's horror collection, *Dark Gods*, is essential reading. To quote something I once wrote about this book: *Dark Gods* is a seminal collection of four dark fantasy novellas epitomizing all that was excellent with 1980s horror. Klein, former editor of *Twilight Zone Magazine,* is a master of creeping dread, of quiet, cerebral horror, requiring nary a drop of blood to nail home his point. One of the smoothest wordsmiths in the business, his knack with observed detail is astounding. His talent is certainly on par with the likes of [Peter] Straub and [John] Updike. Of especial merit: "Petey" and "Black Man with a Horn," this latter an homage to H. P. Lovecraft.

MC: What do you think is most important for contemporary readers to know, remember, bear in mind, about horror literature?

LB: Circling back to comments about Cormac McCarthy (and earlier when I mentioned the role of the small press), I note that horror is where you find it. A welcome aspect to the current horror/weird fiction resurgence is a broad-spectrum approach to the subject. Cosmic horror and its kin aren't confined to explicit genre niches—a new wave of writers continue to unearth and perfect techniques and delivery mechanisms far removed from the pulp trappings of Lovecraft, Clark Ashton Smith, and other forefathers of the tradition. May this trend continue.

BAUDELAIRE, CHARLES (1821–1867)

Charles Pierre Baudelaire was a French poet, critic, and translator whose visionary works signal the shift from romanticism to symbolism in the mid-nineteenth century and represent a definitive example of and inspiration for the Decadent movement of the later nineteenth century (which emphasized degeneration, perversity, and self-conscious artifice), thus paving the way for the crystallization of surrealism in the twentieth century as a philosophical and artistic movement dedicated to giving voice to the unfiltered contents of the unconscious mind. Baudelaire's myriad stylistic and conceptual innovations were designed to create a flux of verse that could extract, from the abyss of urban experience, a vision of reality appropriate to the volatility and uncertainty of modern life. Twentieth-century horror literature, particularly in the weird and cosmic modes, owes a great deal to Baudelaire, whose hallucinatory and erotic meditations on possession, corpses, vampires, nightmares, ghosts, poison, pain, and death conjure overwhelming sensations of fear and wonder while turning inside-out traditional notions of space and time. Indeed, years before H. P. Lovecraft would define the weird in *Supernatural Horror in Literature* (1927), Baudelaire remarked, "The Beautiful is always strange" (Hyslop 1992, 36). Another of the early twentieth century's important authors of cosmic horror, Clark Ashton Smith, explicitly acknowledged Baudelaire as an influence. Commercially successful in his day only for his popular translations of Edgar Allan Poe's works, Baudelaire lived a turbulent life oscillating between idleness and debauchery, culminating in his contraction of syphilis and his death from a paralytic stroke at the young age of forty-six.

Inspired by the Gothic writings of Poe, Baudelaire published, in 1857, *Les Fleurs du mal* (*The Flowers of Evil*), an immeasurably influential volume comprised of 132 breathless poems dedicated to poet Théophile Gautier and later praised by such writers as Émile Deschamps, Gustave Flaubert, and Victor Hugo. These metaphysically pessimistic works deconstruct the Romantic view of a harmonious relationship between inner and outer worlds in favor of an embrace of dizzying multiplicity, of an ironic fall from grace and a satanic rapture in the "spleen" of fear and flight. The ecstatic and funerary poems, included under the headings of "Révolte" and "La Mort," best exemplify the volume's anticipation of and role in shaping the genre of cosmic horror. Six poems from *Les Fleurs du mal*—"Les bijoux" (The Jewels), "Le Léthé" (Lethe—the river of forgetfulness in Hades), "A celle qui est trop gaie" (To She Who Is Too Gay), "Lesbos," "Femmes damnées: Delphine et Hippolyte" (Women Doomed: Delphine and Hippolyta), and "Les métamorphoses du vampire" (The Vampire's Metamorphoses)—were condemned and suppressed on grounds of moral indecency. In 1860, Baudelaire published *Les Paradis artificiels, opium et haschisch* (*Artificial Paradise, Opium and Hashish*), an investigation into the sensorial distortions and changes in perspective that come with the effects of opium and hashish. *Le Spleen de Paris* (*Paris Spleen*), published posthumously in 1869 and dedicated to writer Arsène Houssaye, collects fifty-one prose poems that study the melancholic drone of Parisian life in the nineteenth century through a macabre prism, best evidenced in the languid horror of "Chacun sa chimère" (*To Each His Chimera*) and the creeping dread of "Mademoiselle Bistouri."

Sean Matharoo

See also: Gautier, Théophile; Romanticism and Dark Romanticism; Smith, Clark Ashton; The Sublime; Surrealism.

Further Reading

Balakian, Anna. 1947. *Literary Origins of Surrealism: A New Mysticism in French Poetry.* New York: New York University Press.

Holland, Eugene W. 1993. *Baudelaire and Schizoanalysis: The Sociopoetics of Modernism.* New York: Cambridge University Press.

Hyslop, Lois Boe. 1992. *Charles Baudelaire Revisited.* New York: Twayne.

Sartre, Jean-Paul. 1949. *Baudelaire.* Translated by Martin Turnell. London: Horizon.

"THE BEAST WITH FIVE FINGERS"

W. F. Harvey's now-famous story of a creeping, crawling disembodied hand, "The Beast with Five Fingers," was originally published in the first volume of *The New Decameron* (1919), an anthology series that also saw contributions from Dorothy L. Sayers, Compton Mackenzie, and D. H. Lawrence. In the tradition of the fourteenth-century Italian Renaissance writer Boccaccio, volume one is presented

---

A Suspicious Scuttling Sound . . .

In "The Beast with Five Fingers," Eustace has had a box delivered to him, containing what he thinks is some kind of small animal. It escapes in the library of the "gloomy Georgian mansion" (Harvey 1919, 32) where he lives. He pursues the scuttling sound to the top of the library's iron corkscrew stairs and receives a shock:

> Quickly he stole on tiptoe in the dim moonshine in the direction of the noise, feeling as he went for one of the switches. His fingers touched the metal knob at last. He turned on the electric light.
>
> About ten yards in front of him, crawling along the floor, was a man's hand. Eustace stared at it in utter astonishment. It was moving quickly, in the manner of a geometer caterpillar, the fingers humped up one moment, flattened out the next; the thumb appeared to give a crab-like motion to the whole. While he was looking, too surprised to stir, the hand disappeared round the corner. (42–43)

Matt Cardin

Source: Harvey, W. F. 1919. "The Beast with Five Fingers." In *The New Decameron*, 29–71. New York: Robert M. McBride & Co.

as stories told by holiday-makers of disparate disciplines traveling together. "The Beast with Five Fingers," the first story in the book, is billed as "The Psychic Researcher's Tale."

Although anthologized in the interim, "The Beast with Five Fingers" was not collected until 1928, when it became the title story of Harvey's second collection, *The Beast with Five Fingers and Other Stories*. For this collection, according to Richard Dalby in his introduction to *The Double Eye*, Harvey foundationally changed and rewrote the story's first two pages, while deleting some text from the story's latter half. It is this revised version that tends to be reprinted and that has appeared many times in anthologies of terror and horror. It appears, for example, with one of Harvey's other notable stories, "August Heat," in Alexander Laing's classic anthology *The Haunted Omnibus* (1937), and it was even included by Sayers in her *Great Short Stories of Detection, Mystery and Horror, Second Series* (1931).

The story's prologue concerns the eccentric and wealthy Adrian Borlsover, whose ancestors were "generous patrons of odd sciences, founders of querulous sects, [and] trustworthy guides to the bypath meadows of erudition" (Harvey 2004, 310). Toward the end of his life, Borlsover lost his sight. However, he developed "powers of touch that seemed almost uncanny" (311). For reasons only hinted at, but never made clear, Borlsover's hand develops autonomous sentience, and on its master's death has itself delivered to Borlsover's nephew, Eustace, whom it proceeds to torment. Harvey's storytelling is engaging and the narrative is tightly paced, and both qualities have doubtless contributed to the story's ongoing popularity.

"The Beast with Five Fingers" is perhaps the best-known story in the severed-yet-animated hand subgenre, not to be confused with disembodied hands of a more ghostly and less corporeal taxonomy, such as Arthur Quiller-Couch's "A Pair of Hands" (1898). One of the earlier literary examples of this subgenre is J. Sheridan Le Fanu's "An Authentic Narrative of the Ghost of a Hand" (1861). Another key example is Maurice Renard's influential 1920 horror novel *The Hands of Orlac*. More recently Clive Barker, notable for his grisly explorations of the subgenre known as "body horror," explored similar territory in his story "The Body Politic" (1984). The hands in these stories invariably represent the fragmented self, composed of separate, autonomous, intelligent personalities, often in rebellion, with an ability to scuttle and scheme against the identity of the body as a whole.

There is also no shortage of severed-yet-animated hands in film and television, as seen in *Orlacs Hände* (1924), *The Addams Family* (1964–1966), *The Hand* (1981), and *Evil Dead 2* (1987). The most notable case of Harvey's influence in this subgenre is the loose cinematic adaptation of *The Beast with Five Fingers* released in 1946, directed by Robert Florey and starring Robert Alda and Peter Lorre, with a script by Curt Siodmak, who is best known for his work on Universal Studios' *The Wolf Man* (1941). While Siodmak's adaptation of Harvey's story is highly enjoyable, it substantially departs from Harvey's original narrative, changing the setting to an Italian village, adding a number of characters, and making the character of Adrian

Borlsover, renamed Francis Ingram in the film, a master pianist (a nod, perhaps, to *Orlac*, whose eponymous protagonist was likewise a pianist).

Brian J. Showers

See also: Barker, Clive; Body Horror; Doubles, Doppelgängers, and Split Selves; *The Hands of Orlac*; Le Fanu, J. Sheridan.

Further Reading

Dalby, Richard. 2009. Introduction to *The Double Eye*, by W. F. Harvey, v–xvi. Carlton-in-Coverdale: Tartarus Press.

Forrest, Richard W. 2014. "Body Parts." In *The Ashgate Encyclopedia of Literary and Cinematic Monsters*, edited by Jeffrey Andrew Weinstock, 55–58. London and New York: Routledge.

Harvey, W. F. [1919] 2004. "The Beast with Five Fingers." In *The Wordsworth Book of Horror Stories*, 310–329. Ware, Hertfordshire, UK: Wordsworth Editions.

Rowe, Katherine. 1999. "The Beast with Five Fingers: Gothic Labor Relations in Victorian Ghost Stories." In *Dead Hands: Fictions of Agency, Renaissance to Modern*. Stanford, CA: Stanford University Press.

BEAUMONT, CHARLES (1929–1967)

Charles Beaumont, born Charles Leroy Nutt in Chicago on January 2, 1929, was an American author of horror and science fiction who is probably best known for his classic *Twilight Zone* teleplays from the late 1950s and early 1960s.

His parents, Charles and Letty, were working-class; his father was employed in the railroad industry. Charles was a sickly youngster, and the relationship between mother and son was not always an easy one; he would later write about this period with great detachment and insight, especially his uneasy bond with his mother, in stories such as the acclaimed "Miss Gentilbelle." As a youth, Charles L. Nutt was restricted to a year's bed rest to convalesce from spinal meningitis. He missed a great deal of school, but it was during the recovery from this difficult period that he discovered the world within books. He also took up drawing in earnest, for which he had already displayed a natural aptitude.

As a young man, Nutt, now called Charles Beaumont by his own choosing due to dissatisfaction with his surname (a change that he made legal as an adult), married Helen Broun after leaving the military, and they eventually had four children after striking out on their own for Los Angeles, California.

Once in Southern California, Beaumont was at last able to meet others of similar disposition and was to form deep, lasting friendships with Ray Bradbury, Richard Matheson, William F. Nolan, George Clayton Johnson (*Ocean's 11,* 1959), John Tomerlin (*Challenge the Wind,* 1967), Chad Oliver (*The Winds of Time*, 1957), and several others in a loose alliance that came to be known as the "Southern California Writing School." As their careers progressed, they would each find success as writers of short stories, scripts for television (including *The Twilight Zone* and *Alfred Hitchcock Presents*), film, and novels. Beaumont was the nucleus of this group with his frenetic, sparking energy.

Beaumont's fiction and his television scripts are often marked by exceptional strokes of imaginative whimsy, tinged with a subtextual bent toward social justice, as evinced in works as varied as the 1960 story "The Howling Man" (later adapted by Beaumont into a memorable 1960 *Twilight Zone* episode) and his unfinished novel excerpt, "My Grandmother's Japonicas." His single greatest tale is likely the remarkable "Black Country" from 1954, which explores the societal role of African Americans by describing the posthumous influence of a (fictional) black jazz musician. It was the first work of fiction ever published in *Playboy*.

As a stylist, Beaumont is second only to early Bradbury, his mentor. With regard to themes, he worked a large canvas; from genre works in horror and science fiction to straight literary fiction and even comedy, his talent was immense, seemingly unlimited. He usually painted vivid portraits of conflicted, realistic characters in unusual dilemmas of a moral nature and always did so with sensitivity, insight, and intelligence. As was the norm within his peer group of writers, his stories typically featured only one minor element of supernaturalism, or some aspect of progress gone awry (a frequent supernatural stand-in).

While on the set of his greatest artistic triumph, director Roger Corman's 1962 cinematic adaptation of *The Intruder* from Beaumont's eponymous literary novel, about integrating the Jim Crow South, Beaumont began to exhibit symptoms of neural damage. It was initially believed to be the effects of stress, and he was sent to a variety of experts before finally being diagnosed with an incurable, terminal neurological condition. He succumbed after a four-year struggle, at age 38, on February 21, 1967.

Beaumont was singular in his sphere of influence, in that he could inspire others to do things they would never do on their own. This inspirational aspect of his persona was key to his creative influence and to the way he was able to position himself in the modern mass media. Given that his output was restricted to roughly thirteen short years, he was remarkably prolific and consistent, and he remains one of the key, albeit overlooked, figures in genre literature of the latter half of the twentieth century.

Jason V Brock

See also: Bradbury, Ray; Matheson, Richard; Nolan, William F.

Further Reading

French, Lawrence. 2010. "Richard Matheson Remembers His Good Friend Charles Beaumont." *Cinefantastique Online*, March 24. http://cinefantastiqueonline.com/2010/03/richard-matheson-remembers-his-good-friend-charles-beaumont.

Grams, Martin, Jr. 2008. *The Twilight Zone: Unlocking the Door to a Television Classic*. Churchville, MD: OTR Publishing.

Prosser, Lee. 2010. *Running from the Hunter: The Life and Works of Charles Beaumont*. San Bernardino, CA: Borgo Press.

Zicree, Marc Scott. 1992. *The Twilight Zone Companion*. 2nd ed. Los Angeles, CA: Silman-James Press.

BELOVED

Toni Morrison's novel *Beloved* was published by Knopf in 1987. It won the Pulitzer Prize for Fiction in 1988 and was a finalist for a National Book Award in 1987. In 2006 the *New York Times* named *Beloved* the best work of American fiction of the previous twenty-five years.

While editing *The Black Book* (1974), Morrison read about a slave, Margaret Garner, who, in 1856, escaped from a northern Kentucky plantation with her family into Cincinnati, Ohio. During their recapture, Garner killed one of her children with the intent of killing all four and herself in order to prevent them from returning to the violence of slavery. This horror became the inspiration for *Beloved*, though Morrison has noted that she wished to explore imaginatively the themes that Garner's predicament provokes rather than writing strictly historical fiction. She decided to write a ghost story: "The terrain, slavery, was formidable and pathless. To invite readers (and myself) into the repellant landscape (hidden, but not completely; deliberately buried, but not forgotten) was to pitch a tent in a cemetery of ghosts" (Morrison 2004, xvii).

In *Beloved*, Sethe runs from Sweet Home in Kentucky to her mother-in-law's home near Cincinnati. When slave catchers find the family, Sethe attempts to kill her children and herself, but she only is able to kill her two-year-old girl. *Beloved* has a circular structure as characters try to avoid their pasts. Sethe deliberately works to forget repetitive traumatic memories of her past, or "rememories" as she calls them. Rememories are so vividly horrific that she believes they can hurt her daughter Denver, who is ignorant of her mother's past. Sethe's loss of her mother when she was a child, her sexual and physical torture at Sweet Home, and her infanticide cannot be repressed, and they return in the form of a spectral presence named Beloved.

Beloved is set in a haunted house where the lost child's ghost initially manifests as a poltergeist and then arrives as a lost young woman named Beloved. Most critics agree that Beloved is the ghost of the lost child, the eruption of the past in the present. Through her supernatural knowledge and abilities, Beloved forces Sethe to relive her past and share her pain with others. To represent this violent history, Morrison uses the conventions of supernatural literature to illustrate how the trauma of slavery haunts the present and leaves its mark on later generations. A movie adaptation of *Beloved* directed by Jonathan Demme and starring Oprah Winfrey was released in 1998.

Melanie R. Anderson

See also: The Haunted House or Castle; Morrison, Toni; Psychological Horror.

Further Reading

Anderson, Melanie R. 2013. *Spectrality in the Novels of Toni Morrison*. Knoxville: University of Tennessee Press.

Brogan, Kathleen. 1998. *Cultural Haunting: Ghosts and Ethnicity in Recent American Literature*. Charlottesville: University Press of Virginia.

Denard, Carolyn C., ed. 2008. *Toni Morrison: Conversations*. Jackson: University Press of Mississippi.

Morrison, Toni. [1987] 2004. *Beloved*. New York: Vintage.

BENSON, E. F. (1867–1940)

Edward Frederic Benson was an English writer of novels, short stories, dramas, biographies, and reminiscences. He was the fifth child of Archbishop of Canterbury Edward White Benson (1829–1896), the man who, on January 12, 1895, gave Henry James the idea for *The Turn of the Screw*. His brothers Arthur Christopher and Robert Hugh were also writers.

In 1891, E. F. Benson received a first-class honors degree from King's College, Cambridge, then worked on the staff of the British School of Archaeology in Athens and as a member of the Society for the Promotion of Hellenic Studies. But in 1893, inspired and perhaps assisted by Henry James, Benson published *Dodo*, whose success inspired him to continue writing. From 1895 until his death Benson was a full-time professional writer, and horrific fiction is but a small portion of his output: nine novels and eleven collections of short stories were published during his lifetime.

Among Benson's novels, *The Luck of the Vails* (1901) is supernatural, the ironically named Luck bringing misfortune to generations of the Vail family, but the plot is that of a traditional mystery, complete with unexpected denouement. *The Image in the Sand* (1905) makes use of Benson's Egyptian background to describe an amulet that restrains the evil Set-nekht; when it is broken, Set-nekht possesses young Ida Jervis, who is in turn used by the evil Henderson. *The Angel of Pain* (1905) has as its central theme the idea of communing with nature and discovering the nature god Pan; after some successes, Tom Merivale meets his unhappy fate beneath Pan's crushing hooves. The novel reuses the central ideas from Benson's earlier short story "The Man Who Went Too Far" (1904), but both pieces appear indebted to the works of Algernon Blackwood, whose fiction often used variations of this theme. (The two seem never to have met, but Blackwood was a student in Wellington College, established by Edward White Benson prior to his becoming archbishop.) Benson's *The Inheritor* (1930) reuses Pan on both a literal and a metaphoric level. Steven Gervase inherits the curse that leaves him a spiritual Pan: soulless, unable to love or bond with others; when his child is born a literal Pan, he rather unconvincingly commits suicide. The enormously overlong *Colin* (1923) and *Colin II* (1925) describe the results of an ancestral bargain with the devil; the present Colin Stanier is self-consciously wicked but his son's refusal to embrace

E. F. Benson's "Caterpillars": A Cryptic Nightmare

E. F. Benson's widely anthologized short story "Caterpillars" was first published in *The Room in the Tower and Other Stories*. It is told in flashback, with the nameless narrator describing his stay at the Villa Cascana on the Italian Riviera, where he was once the guest of the Stanleys. He recounts how the villa was beautiful but somehow a place where something was fundamentally wrong. Unable to sleep, he witnessed an unoccupied bedroom swarming with enormous yellowish-grey caterpillars with mouths that opened sideways and pincers rather than legs. It might have been a dream, but the next day fellow guest Arthur Inglis has found such a caterpillar; it survives being thrown into a fountain, and when Inglis and the narrator encounter it again, the caterpillar crawls onto Inglis before it is killed. That night, the narrator glimpses the monstrous caterpillars crawling into Inglis's room. An epilogue occurring six months later, in England, has Mrs. Stanley explaining that Inglis has terminal cancer, that he seems to have developed it at the Villa Cascana, and that there had been a fatal case earlier in the unoccupied bedroom.

The subtext of "Caterpillars" is remarkably muddled. It is unclear if, for example, Benson is implying that certain horrible diseases have malign existences and physical manifestations. Or he may mean to convey that the caterpillars are a metaphor for something else. Though one doubts this was Benson's intention, the story might be seen as an attack on Italy, fair on the outside and corrupt within, and its corruption and destruction of the innocent English. It could likewise be argued that the horrible caterpillars might represent a repressed and emergent sexuality, or the inescapability of destructive fate, or really any number of themes. The story remains a puzzle, presenting situations and images without a resolution.

Richard Bleiler

evil leads at last to Colin's repentance. Benson's last fantastic novel is *Raven's Brood* (1934), an atypical work in that it uses lower- and middle-class characters along with folkloric and paganistic elements reminiscent of those used by Arthur Machen. (Again, the two do not seem to have met.)

Benson's short horror stories are fairly conventional and were collected and published in four books during his lifetime: *The Room in the Tower* (1912), *Visible and Invisible* (1923), *Spook Stories* (1928), and *More Spook Stories* (1934). At the same time, while Benson often used animals as horrific elements—apes and monkeys figure in "The Ape" and "Monkeys," respectively; cats and cat-gods in "The Cat" and "Bagnell Terrace"; giant caterpillars in "Caterpillars"; leeches and slugs in "Negotium Perambulans . . ." and "'And No Bird Sings'"—his most horrible and memorable characters are, interestingly, always women. Lady Sybil Rorke in "Inscrutable

Degrees" and Nellie Mostyn in "Christopher Came Back" are murderers and sadists; Mrs. Stone in "The Room in the Tower" and Mrs. Amworth in "Mrs. Amworth" are vampires and monsters; Mrs. Ray in "The Sanctuary," Mrs. Andrews in "Mrs. Andrews' Control," and Mrs. Cumberbatch in "Mr. Tilly's Séance" are active Satanists and idiotic spiritualists; and the otherwise amiable Mrs. Acres of "The Outcast" is the reincarnation of Judas. In "The Face" horrors are visited on harmless Hester Ward: she is haunted by dreams of ruins and an abandoned grave, then taken by a maligned and misshapen being, never to be seen again.

Benson would certainly have objected to being called misogynistic—and a perhaps unconvincing argument may be made that his tales used and misused women because he recognized that they had been neglected and underutilized as figures of power and terror—but there is no doubt that he would have been delighted that his stories disturbed. Indeed, Benson's brief preface to *The Room in the Tower and Other Stories* states that the stories were written to give "some pleasant qualms to their reader" and concludes by stating that "the author therefore fervently wishes his reader a few uncomfortable moments" (Benson 1912, v). The best of E. F. Benson succeeds admirably in providing these.

Richard Bleiler

See also: Blackwood, Algernon; "The Great God Pan"; Possession and Exorcism.

Further Reading

Ashley, Mike. 1992. "Blood Brothers: The Supernatural Fiction of A. C., R. H., and E. F. Benson." In *Discovering Classic Horror Fiction I*, 100–113. Gillette, NJ: Wildside Press.

Benson, E. F. 1912. *The Room in the Tower and Other Stories.* 1912. London: Mills & Boon.

Joshi, S. T. 2004. "E. F. Benson: Spooks and More Spooks." In *The Evolution of the Weird Tale*, 59–65. New York: Hippocampus Press.

BIERCE, AMBROSE (1842–1914?)

Ambrose Gwinnett Bierce was an American journalist, satirist, and author of short fiction, including horror fiction. In some ways his life reads like one of his stories. The unresolved circumstances of his death, generally listed as having occurred in 1914 with an added question mark, eerily parallel many of his short stories of horror and suspense.

Bierce was born in Horse Cave Creek, Meigs County, Ohio. The Bierces moved to Kosciusko County, Ohio, where the young Ambrose graduated from high school. At fifteen he embarked on his first journalistic experience as an apprentice at a small Ohio newspaper. By all accounts his family circumstances were not happy, but his parents' interest in reading offered an advantage that his peers did not enjoy.

With the outbreak of the Civil War, Bierce joined the 9th Indiana Infantry Regiment in 1861. He saw action, notably at Shiloh in 1862 and the Battle of Kennesaw

"The Damned Thing": Hunting the Invisible Horror

"The Damned Thing" (1893) features a common theme in horror fiction: the invisible evil force that bedevils an unsuspecting soul. It opens with eight men gathered in a cabin at night for an inquest into the death of Hugh Morgan, whose mutilated corpse is in the room with them. A man named Harker, a newspaper columnist who witnessed the death, arrives and reads from some of his notes to recount what happened. He says he and Morgan went hunting and encountered a number of eerie events that Morgan attributed to "the damned thing." Finally, Morgan fired his gun, let out blood-curdling screams, and fell to the ground in convulsive jerks. The assembled jurors claim Harker is insane, and they conclude that Morgan was killed by a mountain lion. The story then becomes a series of extracts from Morgan's diary, revealing that Morgan had been haunted by an invisible being and was determined to hunt it.

Bierce was accused of plagiarizing the "invisible monster" idea from Fitz-James O'Brien's "What Was It?" (1859), and he mounted a vigorous defense of his story's originality, arguing that, instead of an invisible monster, his story posited a wild animal whose *color* was invisible. The idea of an invisible color proved significant because of its apparent influence on H. P. Lovecraft in the conception of one of his major stories, "The Colour out of Space." Bierce's "The Damned Thing" probably also influenced Lovecraft in the writing of "The Dunwich Horror," where a fusion of elements from Bierce's story, O'Brien's story, and de Maupassant's "The Horla" may be discerned.

"The Damned Thing" remains a staple of horror fiction and has been anthologized many times. A few adaptations have also appeared on television, including a 2006 episode of the *Masters of Horror* series directed by Tobe Hooper.

E. Kate Stewart

Mountain, where he sustained a head wound. He returned to active duty later that year and was discharged in 1865. His war experiences accounted for a significant outpouring of his fiction, and some critics suggest that the grisly battle scenes he witnessed inspired many of the horrific aspects of his stories. Although he received some acclaim for his war exploits, they ultimately embittered him, paving the way for his most noted nickname, "Bitter Bierce."

His marriage to Mary Ellen "Mollie" Day on December 25, 1871 did not exactly bring marital bliss. Although the two apparently loved each other, they spent most of their marriage separated and subsequently divorced in 1904. The union produced three children: sons Day and Leigh and daughter Helen. Day and Leigh died in 1889 and 1901, respectively. Day committed suicide and Leigh, an alcoholic, died from pneumonia.

Before Bierce penned his most well-known stories, he enjoyed a successful journalistic career. He spent 1872 to 1875 in London, where he wrote for the magazine

Fun. There he also published his first book, *The Fiend's Delight*, in 1873; it bore the penname Dod Grile and contained a collection of his newspaper pieces. On his return to San Francisco, he worked for a variety of newspapers, most notably, perhaps, *The Wasp*, which he edited from 1881 until 1885. He also wrote frequently for William Randolph Hearst's *San Francisco Examiner*; his association with Hearst continued until 1909.

Between 1888 and 1891, Bierce published the stories that secured his fame as a fictionist. In 1896, Hearst sent him to Washington, D.C., so that he could stop legislation that would allow the Union Pacific and Central Pacific railroad to be excused from repaying loans. Bierce also gained a degree of notoriety because of a poem he had published in the aftermath of the assassination of Kentucky governor William Goebel in 1900. When President William McKinley was assassinated the next year, Bierce and Hearst were accused of inciting the president's death. In 1909, Bierce published a collected volume of his stories and *The Devil's Dictionary*.

In 1913 Bierce traveled to Mexico to join Pancho Villa's army and observe the Mexican Revolution. His last communication with a friend came by letter in December of that year. He disappeared soon after, and the actual date and circumstances of his death remain unknown. The 1985 novel *Old Gringo* by Carlos Fuentes presents a fictionalized imagining of Bierce's experiences in Mexico, including his death. It was adapted as a movie of the same title in 1989, with the part of Bierce being played by Gregory Peck.

Ernest Jerome Hopkins in *The Complete Short Stories of Ambrose Bierce* (1970) divides Bierce's fiction into the following groups: The World of Horror, The World of War, and The World of Tall Tales. Among anthologies of American literature that include Bierce, his war stories are most commonly featured, especially "An Occurrence at Owl Creek Bridge" (1890) and "Chickamauga" (1891). On rare occasions the horror tale "The Boarded Window" (1891) will appear. Because of the notoriety of his war stories, many readers may not realize that both his horror stories and his tall tales have much to recommend them. Common threads run through each of the types of stories that Bierce produced. He was, for example, a master of visual and other sensory detail. In "An Occurrence at Owl Creek Bridge," for instance, he achieves a striking effect by focusing on the haunting sound of protagonist Peyton Farquhar's pocket watch as he descends into a dream world.

Although Bierce harbored an antipathy toward literary realism, arguing instead for the value of romanticism, he distinguished himself as a skilled practitioner of realism's most prominent outgrowth, naturalism, through his talent for creating highly effective descriptions of physical landscapes—a result, perhaps, of his work as a journalist—in which the individual is confronted by mysterious and threatening forces. He also had an interesting habit of creating fictional "authorities" of various kinds for many of his horror tales. For instance, both "An Inhabitant of Carcosa" (1886) and "The Death of Halpin Frayser" (1891) quote Hali, an apparently Bierce-created philosopher who stresses that "there be divers sorts of death—some wherein the body remaineth; and in some others it vanisheth quite away with the spirit" (Bierce 1910, 308). Similarly, in "A Psychological Shipwreck" (1879) Bierce presents an "extract" from the fictional "Denneker's Meditations" containing the haunting passage: "to sundry it is given to be drawn away, and to be apart from the body for a season" (Bierce 1910, 230). It also might not be much of a stretch to view Peyton Farquhar's experiences in "An Occurrence at Owl Creek Bridge" as similarly representing an "out-of-body" episode. A common thread connects each of these musings: the idea of the disembodied soul walking the earth. This walking-dead/zombie theme went on to influence contemporary popular culture, and Bierce can validly be identified as one of the forefathers of the modern zombie fiction subgenre, especially via "The Death of Halpin Frayser."

Bierce's fiction has worn well with the public, and many of his "out-of-body" horror tales enjoy currency through their subtle influence on such prominent B-horror films as *White Zombie* (1932) and such prominent television series as *The Walking Dead*. His most remembered story is unquestionably "An Occurrence at Owl Creek Bridge," which has been studied extensively for its narrative technique, and which has been assigned to generations of high school students. The story has been adapted several times for film and television, including a 1929 silent film and episodes of both *Alfred Hitchcock Presents* in 1959 and *The Twilight Zone* in 1964.

E. Kate Stewart

See also: "The Death of Halpin Frayser"; Zombies.

Further Reading

The Ambrose Bierce Project. Accessed June 29, 2016. http://www.ambrosebierce.org/main .html.

Bierce, Ambrose. 1910. *The Collected Works of Ambrose Bierce, Volume III: Can Such Things Be?* New York and Washington: Neale. http://www.ambrosebierce.org/cansuchthingsbe .htm#frayser.

Cornes, Judy. 2008. "The Nightmare World of Ambrose Bierce." In *Madness and the Loss of Identity in Nineteenth-Century Fiction*, 21–54. Jefferson, NC: McFarland.

Davidson, Cathy, ed. 1982. *Critical Essays on Ambrose Bierce*. Boston: G. K. Hall.

Morris, Roy, Jr. 1995. *Ambrose Bierce: Alone in Bad Company*. New York: Crown.

O'Connor, Richard. 1967. *Ambrose Bierce: A Biography*. Boston: Little, Brown.

BLACKWOOD, ALGERNON (1869–1951)

Algernon Blackwood was a British writer who first achieved popular success in the early twentieth century with his tales featuring psychic investigator John Silence. As well as producing atmospheric ghost stories, children's fiction, plays, and novels that are usually distinguished by a heavy strain of mysticism, many of Blackwood's stories have had an enduring influence on subsequent horror fiction. Notable examples include "The Wendigo" and, particularly, "The Willows."

"The Wendigo": A Frolic in the Fiery Heights

Blackwood's "The Wendigo" (1910), whose title refers to the wendigo of Algonquin folklore, is an example of what Margaret Atwood identifies as a Canadian genre, "Death by Bushing," in which characters are overwhelmed by isolation in the wilderness to the point of insanity.

The narrative is presented as an anecdotal account by a Scottish doctor of a terrifying incident experienced by a hunting party in the Canadian backwoods. One of the party's guides, Défago, succumbs to a maniacal wanderlust, personified in the form of the demonic wendigo. He disappears, before returning (in body only) from what is hinted to be a grotesque frolic in the sky, at heights so vast they burn. Distilling European anxieties in the colonial frontier, the focus of the story's horror is almost entirely on Défago's absorption by the illimitable wilderness, embodied by the wendigo. When Défago eventually returns to camp, his personality seems to be entirely absent; and this, more than his hideously deformed, charred feet, inspires the horror of his companions.

The folkloric myth of the wendigo (or "windigo") has been used in works as diverse as Longfellow's epic poem *The Song of Hiawatha* (1855) and Stephen King's *Pet Sematary* (1983). Thanks in no small part to Blackwood's story, it is now a definite, if minor, horror trope. Two notable iterations in horror cinema are director Larry Fessenden's *The Wendigo* (2001) and Antonia Bird's *Ravenous* (1999). In the latter, the notion of "wendigo psychosis" provides an ambiguously supernatural overtone to an incident of cannibalism in the old West. The 2015 survival horror computer game *Until Dawn* is set in "Blackwood Pines Lodge" at the base of "Blackwood Mountain" in Canada and features the wendigo as the principal antagonist.

James Machin

Born in the southeastern county of Kent, England, Blackwood experienced a childhood marked by stifling religiosity at odds with his own inclinations. He was raised in a household dominated by his father's sternly evangelical Christianity and then educated by similarly severe schoolmasters at the Moravian School in the Black Forest, Germany. He rebelled through clandestine investigations into Buddhism and Theosophy (he would later briefly become a member of a late nineteenth-century occult society, the Hermetic Order of the Golden Dawn) and also through his enthusiasm for the natural world. He would later fictionalize his German education in the story "Secret Worship" (1908), where the protagonist remembers of his school days that he found solace and reprieve from the grimly repressive atmosphere by gazing through "the narrow slit windows with the vistas of enticing field and forest beyond" (Blackwood 1998, 145).

Blackwood led an itinerant early life that included spells living in the United States and Canada, detailed in his lively memoir *Episodes Before Thirty* (1923). By the time of the publication of his first book, *The Empty House*, at the age of thirty-seven, Blackwood had been a farmer, gold prospector, hotel manager, artist's model, and journalist for the *New York Times*. His passion for travel and, especially, for the wilderness led to adventures in the wild expanses of the American north, Egypt, and the Swiss Alps. The tensions between domesticity and the wild, humanity and nature, and between traditional Christianity and pantheism resonate throughout his work, where they are regularly amplified into overt horror.

The most celebrated example of this is "The Willows" (1907), possibly the most widely anthologized of Blackwood's stories, and praised by H. P. Lovecraft as a text in which "art and restraint in narrative reach their very highest development" (Lovecraft 2012, 88). If not representative of Blackwood's variegated output, it is perhaps the story in which Blackwood's powers are most expertly and powerfully deployed, particularly his consummate skill in the inexorable ramping up of weird atmosphere through incremental, barely noticeable turns of the screw. Beginning as a genteel travelogue chronicling the months-long canoe trip of two men along the Danube, Blackwood's story subtly strips away the ordinary and commonplace from the engulfing landscape until, by its climax, the protagonists seem entirely at the mercy of ambiguous supernatural forces threatening their survival.

This ambivalence toward the natural world as a place equally immanent with beauty and dread is also connected with another anxiety regularly evident in Blackwood's horror fiction: the loss of personality or the absorption of the individual into the illimitable wilderness. The colonial frontier was for Blackwood, as it was for the early European settlers, a threatening, predatory entity as much as a liberating, emancipating blank canvas upon which to paint a new life. In "The Wendigo" (1910), the eponymous forest spirit of Algonquian folklore is not simply a physical threat to a small hunting party in the Canadian backwoods. The French-Canadian guide, Défago, is abducted by the monstrous and nebulous entity, and when he reappears it is in body only; his personality has been expunged. Although wildly different in tone, "The Man Whom the Trees Loved" (1912) is a further iteration of this same neurosis. In it, David Bittacy is first obsessed, then ultimately absorbed by the collective consciousness of the forest encircling his home. Bittacy's pantheism is framed in opposition to his wife's Christianity, but, despite Blackwood's Buddhist sympathies, the process of Bittacy's loss of self and ego is cast as terrifying rather than liberating. Despite the gentle, almost ethereal unfolding of the tale, the denouement is shattering.

This ambivalence provides a regular balance to the more visionary flights of mystical yearning of the protagonist O'Malley in the novel *The Centaur* (1911). It is as much an exposition as a narrative, regularly quoting great swathes of Gustav Fechner and William James, and promulgating something approaching a Gaia hypothesis of sentient planethood through the experiences of O'Malley (clearly a proxy for Blackwood himself). O'Malley travels to the Caucasus in the company of an *Urmensch*; a "Cosmic Being," both premodern and more highly developed than the teeming human masses. Again, the risk O'Malley exposes himself to is the loss of personality. The price of enlightenment and connection with the Earth's super-consciousness is engulfment: "Complete surrender would involve somehow a disintegration, a dissociation of his personality that carried with it the loss of personal identity" (Blackwood 1912, 6). Throughout the novel, O'Malley oscillates between feeling an unbearable longing to achieve "genuine cosmic consciousness" and an equally acute dread of the implications of its attainment; for "this, surely, was the inner catastrophe that he dreaded, the radical internal dislocation of his personality" (Blackwood 2012, 149–150). As so often in Blackwood's writing, the threat to O'Malley is one of absorption and amalgamation within a greater, overwhelming whole, rather than physical threat.

Other noteworthy stories include "Ancient Sorceries" (1908), the original inspiration behind Jacques Tourneur's celebrated 1942 horror film *Cat People*. The tale concerns Arthur Vezin's weird encounters in a mysterious little town in northern France. The sleepy populace first baffle, then seduce the lone tourist, before the narrative culminates in a diabolical ritual in service of the "Great Ones," vividly rendered as a dreamlike vision. The increasingly hallucinatory quality of Vezin's experience is intensified when he becomes aware that his will is being sapped from him, rendering him unable to make decisions or initiate the process of departure. He becomes inexorably absorbed into the spell lying over the community as his volition is sapped, and he is transfixed by the seductive and mercurial daughter of the hotelier, who seems to toy with him like a cat batting about a concussed mouse between her paws. Blackwood effectively employs the same trope of the seduction of an older man by a mysterious younger woman in "The Glamour of the Snow" (1911), in which the protagonist (a middle-aged writer in thrall to the mountains—Blackwood himself, in other words) has a strange encounter with a lone skater on a mountain resort ice rink at midnight, a beautiful young woman who is in fact an embodiment of both the pleasures and dangers of snow. The protagonist is gradually isolated from the rest of the tourist party and pursues his obsession with the girl—who, it transpires, is actually some type of elemental spirit—with near fatal consequences.

In 1912's "The Man Who Found Out," ancient Chaldean tablets detailing the ultimate secret of the universe extinguish the spirit of anyone who reads them (typically of Blackwood, marked by the "crumbling away" of personality). The story can be read as a cautionary account of the dangers of scientific overreaching, or—and anticipating Lovecraft's work—a more profoundly pessimistic rumination on complacent belief in the primacy of humanity's place in the universe. Blackwood's occasional cosmic scope is contrasted by low-key pieces like "The Little Beggar" (1919), in which a devastatingly personal blow is dealt to an aging gentleman walking to his club one evening when he experiences a counterfactual encounter with his son-who-never-was, the progeny of a marriage that never happened due to the death of his fiancé twelve years earlier.

As well as his unique and sophisticated contributions to the horror genre, Blackwood also produced more formulaic, though nevertheless engaging writing. For example, 1906's *The Empty House* is an uncomplicated ghost story. "The Nemesis of Fire" (1908), a John Silence story, is a particularly well-executed example of the Edwardian "occult detective" genre, featuring an ancient Egyptian curse causing havoc in an English manor house. Similarly, another Silence adventure, "The Camp of the Dog" (1908), uses the traditional horror trope of the werewolf.

In his later years Blackwood became something of a celebrity due to frequent appearances on British television, mesmerizing the nation with his peerless skill at delivering a chilling tale to the camera. He died at the age of eighty-two, leaving little in the way of personal effects or papers, most of which had been destroyed during the bombing of London during the Second World War. Blackwood's influence on horror fiction was considerable even in his lifetime. Many of the writers associated with *Weird Tales*, including H. P. Lovecraft, Clark Ashton Smith, and Robert E. Howard, cited "The Willows" as among their favorite short stories. Blackwood's impact on Lovecraft can be most keenly felt in Lovecraft's foregrounding of marshlands and backwoods as places replete with immanent evil and supernatural threat in stories such as "The Dunwich Horror" and "The Whisperer in Darkness."

Blackwood's character John Silence is a key link in the development of the "occult detective" genre, representing an early twentieth-century rendering of nineteenth-century forerunners such as Sheridan Le Fanu's Dr. Hesselius and Bram Stoker's Van Helsing. The legacy of Blackwood's John Silence stories—as well as William Hope Hodgson's similar Carnacki tales, which they influenced—can be felt through ensuing genre and popular culture from the pulp magazines to television's *The X Files* and *Supernatural*.

James Machin

See also: John Silence: Physician Extraordinary; Lovecraft, H. P.; The Numinous; Occult Detectives; "The Willows."

Further Reading

Ashley, Mike. 2001. *Starlight Man: The Extraordinary Life of Algernon Blackwood*. London: Constable.

Blackwood, Algernon. 1912. *The Centaur*. London: Macmillan. https://archive.org/details/centaur00blacgoog.

Blackwood, Algernon. 1923. *Episodes Before Thirty*. London: Cassell.

Blackwood, Algernon. 1998. *The Complete John Silence Stories*. Edited by S. T. Joshi. New York: Dover.

Blackwood, Algernon. 2002. *Ancient Sorceries and Other Weird Stories*. Edited by S. T. Joshi. London: Penguin.

Joshi, S. T. 1990. *The Weird Tale*. Holicong, PA: Wildside.

Lovecraft, H. P. [1927] 2012. *The Annotated Supernatural Horror in Literature*. Edited by S. T. Joshi. New York: Hippocampus Press.

BLEILER, E. F. (1920–2010)

Everett Franklin Bleiler was an American editor and scholar. In 1948, a youthful interest in fantastic fiction, combined with his scholarly abilities, led the owners of Shasta Publishers to pay him $500 to compile the book that became *The Checklist of Fantastic Literature*.

From 1949 to 1954, with T. E. Dikty of Shasta, he co-edited the first "best of the year" science fiction anthologies before joining Dover Publications in 1955. While at Dover, he edited a number of collections, including the supernatural works of J. Sheridan Le Fanu, Mrs. Riddell, Ambrose Bierce, Algernon Blackwood, Robert W. Chambers, Arthur Conan Doyle, and M. R. James, as well as anthologies reprinting Gothic novels and Victorian ghost stories, as well as an edition of H. P. Lovecraft's *Supernatural Horror in Literature*. All the books contained serious introductions that provided biographical data and contextualized the works as literary history. Bleiler left Dover in 1977 and joined Charles Scribner's Sons, editing and introducing collections of Victorian genre fiction and two massive bio-critical reference works, *Science Fiction Writers* (1982) and *Supernatural Fiction Writers: Fantasy and Horror* (1985). In 1983 Kent State University Press published his *Guide to Supernatural Fiction*, which attempted to conceptualize a field of literature by providing a summation of, and thematic indexes to, every work of supernatural fiction published prior to 1960. He later published two analogous works dealing with the history of science fiction. In 1978 Bleiler received a Special Award (Professional) from the World Fantasy Awards; in 1988 he was given the World Fantasy Award for Lifetime Achievement. In 1984, he received the Pilgrim Award for his contributions to science fiction scholarship.

Bleiler's editorial work and introductions were solid and scholarly, but he was under no illusions about their durability, for inevitably new scholarship emerged, sometimes obviating his earlier efforts, and over his lifetime the concept of editorship changed. It was no longer sufficient to reprint what were deemed an author's "best" or most representative works; researchers wanted and needed the author's oeuvre, however mediocre or discreditable some of it might be. Bleiler came to see himself as a living fossil and was often dismissive of his earlier work, but he took genuine pleasure in assisting in the bibliographic discoveries and scholarly insights of others. Without his contributions, many premodern writers of the fantastic would not have been readily discovered.

Richard Bleiler

See also: Bierce, Ambrose; Blackwood, Algernon; James, M. R.; Le Fanu, J. Sheridan; World Fantasy Award.

Further Reading

Dirda, Michael. 2012. "Let Us Now Praise Dover Books: The Literary Legacy of E. F. Bleiler." *The American Scholar*, December 28. https://theamericanscholar.org/let-us-now-praise-dover-books.

Showers, Brian J. 2006. "All Hallows Talks with . . . E. F. Bleiler." *All Hallows* 42. http://www.brianjshowers.com/articles_bleiler.html.

BLOCH, ROBERT (1917–1994)

Robert Bloch was an American writer of fantasy, horror, and science fiction who, early in his career, was recognized as a representative of the *Weird Tales* school of pulp horror fiction and one of the most talented contributors to the Cthulhu Mythos, the shared world of stories that colleagues of H. P. Lovecraft wrote in homage to his cosmic horror fiction. In the 1950s and 1960s, Bloch sublimated his talent for writing horror fiction in a succession of crime novels that culminated in the publication of *Psycho* (1959), a landmark novel that established him as a leading exponent of psychological horror fiction.

Psycho: A Landmark of Psychological Horror

Bloch's novel *Psycho* (1959) has been hailed as a landmark of psychological horror, and it was the basis for Alfred Hitchcock's iconic 1960 film adaptation. Bloch explained in his autobiography that the case of real-life serial murderer Ed Gein inspired him to write a novel featuring an apparently ordinary rural character who is actually a psychotic murderer. In *Psycho* this character is Norman Bates, proprietor of the Bates Motel on the outskirts of the Midwestern town of Fairvale. Norman is dominated by his emasculating, verbally abusive mother, who, when Norman shows interest in the newly checked-in Marion Crane, murders her—or so it would appear. When people begin investigating Marion's disappearance, they find discrepancies in Norman's claim that he lives alone with his mother, not the least of which is that local authorities remember attending Mrs. Bates's funeral years earlier. Eventually, it is revealed that the psychologically unhinged Norman, who was morbidly close to his mother, exhumed her corpse, preserved it, and now dresses up like her to sustain the illusion of her continued presence. Any encounter that threatens their relationship causes Norman's "mother" to lash out protectively, as she has done several times before (after which Norman dutifully disposes of the corpses in a swamp behind the motel).

In Bloch's novel, as in the movie, the story is sustained by narrative misdirection. The reader is not aware until the denouement that the conversations between Norman and his mother are taking place entirely inside his head. Bloch wrote two sequels, *Psycho II* (1982) and *Psycho House* (1990), both concerned with how the sickness of the serial killer is mirrored in the society that nurtured him. Hitchcock's film also inspired several sequels and, in 2013, the A&E cable network's series *Bates Motel*. It is sometimes cited as an influence on the slasher film subgenre.

Stefan R. Dziemianowicz

Bloch became a fan of Lovecraft's fiction in 1927, shortly after he started reading *Weird Tales*, and in 1933 he began corresponding with him. At Lovecraft's suggestion Bloch submitted his early ghost story "Lilies" (1934) and his fantasy "Black Lotus" (1935) to William Crawford, publisher of the semiprofessional magazines *Marvel Tales* and *Unusual Stories*. Bloch first appeared in print professionally in the January 1935 issue of *Weird Tales* with "The Feast in the Abbey," a Gothic shocker about a traveler through the forests of medieval France who stumbles upon a monastery of cannibal monks. Written in overwrought purple prose, but perfectly orchestrated for its chilling climax, the story is a prime example of the neo-Gothic horror fare that *Weird Tales*, in its early years, peddled to its audience. It would become one of Bloch's (and the magazine's) most reprinted stories.

Between 1935 and the end of 1939, Bloch placed twenty-six stories in *Weird Tales*, which was virtually his exclusive market for fiction. In "The Secret in the Tomb" (1935), he first made mention of Ludvig Prinn's *The Mysteries of the Worm*, a book of occult lore that was to become one of the canonical grimoires of the Cthulhu Mythos. Most of Bloch's mythos tales are routine horror stories clearly written to please Lovecraft, although several rise above simple pastiche. "The Mannikin" (1937), about a hunchback whose deformity is an undeveloped twin alive to the influence of supernatural evil, ends with a perfectly timed O. Henry–type twist that was to become one of Bloch's trademarks. Bloch's "The Shambler from the Stars" (1935) might have been considered a minor mythos tale but for the decimation of its main character, who was clearly modeled on Lovecraft—an example of how much early Cthulhu Mythos fiction was written as an elaborate in-joke among participating writers. Lovecraft responded in 1936 with one of his masterpieces, "The Haunter of the Dark," in which he killed off one "Robert Blake," and Bloch made the story cycle a triptych when, in the September 1950 issue of *Weird Tales*, he responded with "The Shadow from the Steeple," a story that updated the mythos for the then-nascent nuclear age.

A handful of Bloch's mythos tales—including "The Faceless God" (1936), "The Brood of Bubastis" (1937), "The Secret of Sebek" (1937), and "Fane of the Black Pharoah" (1937)—fuse ancient Egyptian lore with Lovecraftian horrors but are part of a larger cycle of Egyptian tales that include "The Opener of the Way" (1936), "The Eyes of the Mummy" (1938), and "Beetles" (1938), which are Lovecraftian in tone but without mythos content. The majority of these stories feature unsympathetic protagonists—greedy tomb-robbers, self-interested businessmen, and the like—who are served poetically just desserts for their transgressions. These stories show Bloch attempting to distinguish his writing as more than just a slavish imitation of Lovecraft's.

Lovecraft's death in 1937 devastated Bloch, but it also propelled him out of the creative rut he had dug himself working in Lovecraft's shadow. He began attempting stories with diverse horror themes: voodoo in "Mother of Serpents" (1936); Native American curses in "The Totem-Pole" (1939); and deals with the devil in "Fiddler's Fee" (1940). Bloch also began writing for markets other than *Weird Tales*, among them the science fiction magazine *Amazing Stories* and the fantasy pulp *Fantastic Adventures*, both edited by Raymond A. Palmer, whom Bloch had met through his involvement with the Milwaukee Fictioneers, a writing group that he had joined in 1935.

Also in 1939, Bloch began writing for *Unknown* (later *Unknown Worlds*), a magazine of "logical" fantasy fiction launched by editor John W. Campbell as a companion to *Astounding Science-Fiction*, then the leading science fiction magazine. Bloch's "The Cloak" (1939), a comic story about a man turned into a vampire when he dons the cloak of a former vampire owner, lampooned many of the Gothic clichés of horror fiction and broke ground for him as a writer of humorous fantasy. For two more comic fantasies published in *Unknown*, "A Good Knight's Work (1941) and "The Eager Dragon" (1943), Bloch adopted a slangy contemporary storytelling voice inspired by the work of Damon Runyon. He would use the same voice in *Fantastic Adventures* to relate the adventures of Lefty Feep, a born loser with the gift of gab and a penchant for getting caught up in preposterously fantastic escapades. Filled with topical jokes and bad puns, they were not Bloch's best work, although some rose above the others in cleverness, notably "The Weird Doom of Floyd Scrilch" (1942), whose protagonist is such an average person that the products he orders from ads in the back pages of pulp magazines—which are notorious for fulfilling the promises of their manufacturers only for the average person—prove fatally effective for him. Bloch also took a cue from fantasist Thorne Smith and, in stories such as "Nursemaid to Nightmares" (1942) and its sequel "Black Barter" (1943), and later "The Devil with You" (1950) and "The Big Binge" (1955), wrote the equivalent of supernatural screwball comedies in which characters become caught up in a series of bizarre events with amusing outcomes. More than any other writer of weird fiction in the twentieth century, Bloch showed that horror and humor were opposite sides of the same coin in stories such as "House of the Hatchet" (1941) and "The Beasts of Barsac" (1944), which mix irony with serious dramatic incidents, and "Catnip" (1948) and "Hungarian Rhapsody" (1958), which end with darkly amusing puns.

In his autobiography *Once Around the Bloch* (1993), Bloch recalled a primal moment from his childhood when he was frightened by Lon Chaney's unmasking scene in the 1925 film adaptation of *The Phantom of the Opera*. Horror films and the relationship between their illusory horrors and the macabre possibilities in real life became a recurrent theme in a significant number of his stories, including "Return to the Sabbath" (1938), "The Dream Makers" (1953), "Terror over Hollywood" (1957), "Sock Finish" (1957), "Is Betsy Blake Still Alive?" (1958), and "The Movie People" (1969). In the late 1930s and 1940s, Bloch also began to explore the intersection of crime and weird fiction in stories such as "Slave of the Flames" (1938), which provides the pyromaniac responsible for the Great Chicago Fire of 1871 with a supernatural motivation, and "The Skull of the Marquis de Sade" (1945) and "Lizzie Borden Took an Axe" (1946), in which contemporary characters acting under the supernatural influence of legendary murderers are compelled to recapitulate their crimes. Bloch's classic in this vein is "Yours Truly, Jack the Ripper" (1943), in which it is revealed that the titular character is alive in contemporary America and committing another spate of serial murders to appease dark gods in exchange for their gift of personal immortality. The year after its publication, this story, among Bloch's best-known works, was adapted for the radio program *The Kate Smith Hour*. It was part of the program of radio adaptations of thirty-three of Bloch's weird tales aired in his native Milwaukee as *Stay Tuned for Terror*.

In 1945, to fill out his first hardcover collection of short fiction, *The Opener of the Way* (1945), Bloch wrote "One Way to Mars," the story of a hopped-up musician whose slipping grasp on reality—and eventual spiral into psychosis—manifests in the form of a strange-looking man in a brown coat who appears to him repeatedly and offers to sell him a one-way ticket to Mars. It was a foretaste of things to come in his writing, not just tales of psychological horror such as "The Sorcerer's Apprentice" (1949), in which a mentally challenged young man who believes a stage magician's illusions are real attempts to reproduce them with disastrous results, and "Lucy Comes to Stay" (1952), in which a woman projects her psychotic proclivities onto an imaginary friend, but in his work as novelist. In 1947 Bloch published his first novel, *The Scarf,* about a man with a dual personality, one of which is a serial strangler of women. Over the next three decades, Bloch wrote a succession of crime novels, including *Spiderweb* (1954), *The Kidnapper* (1954), *The Will to Kill* (1954), *The Dead Beat* (1960), *Firebug* (1961), *The Couch* (1962), and *Terror* (1962), that are memorable for their explorations of the aberrant psychology of their antagonists. These characters descend directly from the unsympathetic protagonists of Bloch's weird fiction, and the world he presents, as seen through their eyes and shaped by the motivations by which they rationalize their behavior, is as skewed and abnormal as the horror of his supernatural fiction.

In 1959, Bloch wrote *Psycho*, the novel to which his reputation as a writer of horror and suspense fiction is inextricably bound. Inspired in part by the real-life crimes of Wisconsin serial murderer Ed Gein, it tells of Norman Bates, a motel operator whose jealous mother kills any female patron who catches Norman's fancy. At the novel's end, it is revealed that Norman killed his mother and her lover years before, and that, unhinged by guilt, Norman has absorbed her personality and acts out the dark side of their uncomfortably close relationship, sometimes even dressing up in her clothes to commit "her" murders. The novel is a narrative tour de force that doesn't tip its hand, until the denouement, that the conversations Norman is having with his mother throughout are taking place entirely within his tortured psyche. Bloch's novel, and the term "psycho," became important fixtures in popular culture when Alfred Hitchcock adapted the novel as his famous film of the same name in 1960.

The notoriety of Hitchcock's adaptation of *Psycho* helped to further Bloch's career in Hollywood, where he had begun working as a screenwriter in the late 1950s. Bloch contributed scripts to the television programs *Alfred Hitchcock Presents, Boris*

Karloff's Thriller, and *Star Trek.* England's Amicus Studios released three anthology films—*Torture Garden* (1967), *The House That Dripped Blood* (1970), and *Asylum* (1972)—that adapted mostly stories of his that were first published in *Weird Tales,* and also the movies *The Skull* (1965; based on Bloch's story "The Skull of the Marquis de Sade") and *The Deadly Bees* (1966), filmed from Bloch's scripts. Director William Castle also filmed the psychological suspense movies *Strait-Jacket* (1964) and *The Night Walker* (1964) from Bloch's scripts.

Bloch was an active contributor during the horror fiction boom of the 1980s and 1990s. His first novel of the supernatural, *Strange Eons* (1979), was an homage to H. P. Lovecraft and the Cthulhu Mythos. His novels *American Gothic* (1974) and *The Jekyll Legacy* (co-written with Andre Norton in 1990) were historical crime fiction that verged on horror fiction. He also wrote two sequels to *Psycho, Psycho II* (1982) and *Psycho House* (1990), partly to try to reclaim control of *Psycho,* after having sold the rights to the cinematic story line. These stories are memorable for their depictions of a morally sick contemporary society that allows monsters like Norman Bates to flourish unrecognized in its midst. Not surprisingly, Bloch edited two anthologies of psychological horror fiction inspired by *Psycho* under the titles *Psycho-Paths* (1991) and *Monsters in Our Midst* (1993). Among his final books were the novel *Lori* (1989), a tale of ambiguous supernaturalism, and his nostalgic personal memoir *Once Around the Bloch* (1993), subtitled in his trademark pun-laden style *An Unauthorized Autobiography.*

Bloch's six-decade career as a horror writer was one of the longest in the twentieth century. He was one of the last of the generation of horror writers who made their reputations writing short stories rather than novels, and his often darkly funny tales, distinguished by their careful craftsmanship and imaginative flair, continue to be reprinted in collections and anthologies after his death. Bloch's transition from writing supernatural horror stories to works of psychological suspense, and his ability to parlay his skills as a writer of fiction into work as a writer for television and film, are an object lesson in how a writer can maintain his relevance in a culture that changes over time. For his accomplishments he received the World Fantasy Convention's Life Achievement Award in 1975 and the Horror Writer Association's Lifetime Achievement Award (1989). Bloch died of cancer in Los Angeles at the age of 77.

Stefan R. Dziemianowicz

See also: Arkham House; Bram Stoker Award; Cthulhu Mythos; Lovecraft, H. P.; Psychological Horror; Pulp Horror; *Weird Tales;* World Fantasy Award.

Further Reading

Bloch, Robert. 1993. *Once Around the Bloch: An Unauthorized Autobiography.* New York: Tor.

Dziemianowicz, Stefan. 2003. "Robert Bloch." In *Supernatural Fiction Writers: Contemporary Fantasy and Horror,* edited by Richard Bleiler, 99–114. New York: Thomson/Gale.

Joshi, S. T. 2014. "A Literary Tutelage: Robert Bloch and H. P. Lovecraft." In *Lovecraft and a World in Transition: Collected Essays on H. P. Lovecraft*, 548–565. New York: Hippocampus.

Larson, Randall. 1986. *Robert Bloch: Starmont Reader's Guide No. 37*. Mercer Island, WA: Starmont House.

Moskowitz, Sam. 1966. "Robert Bloch." In *Seekers of Tomorrow*, 335–349. New York: World.

Punter, David. 1990. "Robert Bloch's Psycho: Some Pathological Contexts." In *American Horror Fiction: From Brockden Brown to Stephen King*, edited by Brian Docherty, 92–106. New York: St. Martin's.

Shovlin, Paul. 2015. "Psycho-ology 101: Incipient Madness in the Weird Tales of Robert Bloch." In *The Unique Legacy of Weird Tales: The Evolution of Modern Fantasy and Horror*, edited by Justin Everett and Jeffrey H. Shanks, 201–210. New York: Rowman and Littlefield.

Szumskyj, Benjamin, ed. 2009. *The Man Who Collected Psychos: Critical Essays on Robert Bloch*. Jefferson, NC: McFarland.

Winter, Douglas E. 1985. "Robert Bloch." In *Faces of Fear*, 10–22. New York: Berkley.

BODY HORROR

The term "body horror" refers to a type of horror focusing on flesh and its transcendence, challenging the concept of the body as a bounded entity and transgressing the limits of the flesh by pushing toward new, transformed corporeal states. The posthuman configurations of body horror are often depicted as positive alternatives to the banality of the "old" human flesh, as in Katherine Dunn's *Geek Love* (1986): here, the body is a canvas, capable of twisting—with the right chemical and genetic alterations—into something at once frightening and ambiguously beautiful. Flesh is always unfinished, always in motion. Body horror celebrates this capacity for corporeal—and often ontological or metaphysical—transformation, reveling in the materiality of the body and its mutative possibilities.

Though body horror is most often associated with cinema, it is prevalent in literature, video games, and other horror media, and is as old as the genre itself. Mary Shelley's hybrid creature in *Frankenstein* (1818), who occupies a body that is both living and dead, human and nonhuman, provides an early example of the subgenre's preoccupations with transitional or intermediate bodily states and the possibilities inherent in matter. Invasion, contagion, and mutation have been central concerns throughout the body horror canon, where the body's permeability reveals the instability of both flesh and humanness itself. In John W. Campbell's "Who Goes There?" (1938), an extraterrestrial being invades, mutates, and then reassumes the guise of its human hosts, grounding its plot—and its corporeal play—in the flexibility of flesh and the inability to determine humanness by sight. Similarly, H. P. Lovecraft's "The Shadow over Innsmouth" (1936), in which the protagonist is confronted with the inevitability of his transformation into a half-human, half-fish creature, draws on the horror—and the disturbing ecstasy—that arises from surrendering to a body whose humanness is rapidly disappearing. At the story's close, the young man embraces the newness of his flesh and the strange possibilities for being it affords him.

The development of prosthetics-based special effects technologies throughout the 1970s and 1980s contributed much to body horror's prominent place in 1980s horror cinema and is perhaps the reason why the subgenre is most associated with film. David Cronenberg's films—widely considered to be the apotheosis of the subgenre—display special effects technologies to grand effect, celebrating transgressive corporeality and bodily possibility in classic body horror works such as *Videodrome* (1983) and *The Fly* (1986). In *Videodrome*, the protagonist Max Renn's bodily transformation into a human-media corporeal hybrid opens onto new ontological possibilities best encapsulated in the film's memorable line, "Long live the new flesh!"

This idea of "new flesh" is central to body horror: where much of horror has turned on the fear of embodiment and the limits of the flesh, body horror celebrates the transformative capacities and potentialities inherent in embodiment. These bodily transformations are always ambiguous: they are at once violent and liberating, repulsively beautiful.

Brittany Roberts

See also: Books of Blood; The Grotesque; *The Hands of Orlac*; *The Island of Doctor Moreau*; Kafka, Franz; Lovecraft, H. P.; Palahniuk, Chuck; Splatterpunk; Transformation and Metamorphosis.

Further Reading

Aldana Reyes, Xavier. 2014. *Body Gothic: Corporeal Transgression in Contemporary Literature and Horror Film*. Chicago: University of Chicago Press.
Kane, Paul, and Marie O'Regan, eds. 2012. *The Mammoth Book of Body Horror*. Philadelphia: Running Press.

BODY SNATCHING

Body snatching is the act of digging up newly buried bodies for the purpose of selling them to hospitals and anatomists to dissect for research, teaching, or other types of experimentation. Though the term "body snatching" was not adopted until the early nineteenth century, it was active throughout the eighteenth century, when body snatchers were referred to as "resurrection men." Most studies of this still-mysterious subject have focused on Great Britain, particularly on areas of medical innovation in Edinburgh and London, but the practice also occurred in America. In tension with a concurrent fear of live burial, it inspired a series of protective devices and procedures, such as mortsafes, which are iron cages and locks placed around coffins to prevent entry. Body snatching, therefore, found a natural entry into the Gothic imagination, alongside this literary tradition's creative uses of corpses and the abject.

"The Body Snatcher": Guilt and Grave-Robbing

First published in the *Pall Mall Christmas Extra* in December 1884, this story features characters based on criminals employed by Robert Knox, the noted nineteenth-century Edinburgh surgeon who was implicated in the infamous Burke and Hare murders of 1828.

Using a frame story, it narrates the tale of two men named Fettes and Macfarlane, who attended medical school together in Edinburgh under the tutelage of the famous doctor "K" (a disguised reference to Knox). They are responsible for acquiring dissection subjects and paying the suspicious men who arrive with the corpses. When Macfarlane brings in the body of a man named Gray, who recently heckled and insulted him, Fettes is convinced that Macfarlane murdered the man. But he keeps silent, and students dissect the body. Some time later, when the medical school is short on anatomical subjects, Fettes and Macfarlane exhume the body of a recently deceased farmer's wife, but on the nighttime ride back to Edinburgh from the graveyard they accidentally break their lantern and, upon lighting the remaining one, discover to their horror that the body is actually that of the long-dead Gray. They leap, terrified, from the carriage, which continues rolling toward Edinburgh.

Dismissed by some critics as a mere potboiler, "The Body Snatcher" shows Stevenson drawing upon his own family history—one of his uncles had trained under Robert Knox—as well as real-life events in Scottish history. It also shows the author's long-running interest in guilt and moral culpability, which would reach its apex just two years later in his novella *The Strange Case of Dr. Jekyll and Mr. Hyde*.

"The Body Snatcher" was adapted as a well-received 1945 Hollywood film directed by Robert Wise, produced by Val Lewton, and starring Boris Karloff and Bela Lugosi in their final screen appearance together. It has also been adapted for television, radio, and the classic horror comic book *Creepy*.

Jon Greenaway

Source: Richardson, Ruth. 2015. "Robert Louis Stevenson's *The Body Snatcher*." *The Lancet* 385, no. 9966 (January): 412–413. http://dx.doi.org/10.1016/S0140-6736(15)60144-1.

Body snatching arose because it was lucrative. Anatomists paid handsomely for bodies, with no questions asked: the fresher, the better. Dissection of the dead was considered to be a vital element of medical education, a concept that was still relatively new. However, there were few legal opportunities in Great Britain to obtain corpses. William Hunter's successful anatomy school became popular in the mid-eighteenth century for its anatomy lectures, and William's brother, John, facing the task of making sure there were enough bodies to meet the demand, turned to body snatching. He was certainly not alone in this. In the most famous case, William Burke and William Hare murdered sixteen people in Edinburgh in 1828, using a suffocation technique called "burking" and selling the bodies to Dr. Robert Knox. After Burke's execution, his body was, fittingly, dissected before an enthusiastic audience. Two pieces of legislation, separated by nearly a century, addressed concerns over body snatching, although they were not entirely effective. The Murder Act of 1752 gave anatomists the bodies of executed murderers as an additional punishment, while the Anatomy Act of 1832 allowed anatomists to take bodies not claimed from hospitals within forty-eight hours and without specific instructions.

Body snatching in literature appeared as early as the 1797 novel *The Horrors of Oakendale Abbey*, attributed to a "Mrs. Carver," though the best-known body snatcher is of course Victor Frankenstein of Mary Shelley's 1818 novel, who dug up anatomical parts for his creature wherever he could find them. Robert Louis Stevenson's short story "The Body Snatcher" (1884) tells of two students of Knox who are caught up in an increasingly complicated situation involving body snatching for medical education purposes. H. P. Lovecraft also employed the theme of body snatching in his short fiction, although in his *The Case of Charles Dexter Ward* and *Herbert West—Reanimator* the practice is used less for dissection and more for resurrection.

Tales of body snatching still resurface sometimes in the news today, and though such incidents tend to inspire less fear than they did in a former age, they still cause scandal and incur significant legal punishment. Within contemporary Gothic literature and film, body snatching has become a staple associated with mad scientists— who now typically procure the bodies themselves without the use of resurrection men—and with medical horror texts, such as Robin Cook's *Coma* (1977). The ethics of the practice have now expanded beyond dissection and experimentation to include acts that involve both clear benefits, such as organ harvesting, as well as clear injustices.

Laura R. Kremmel

See also: *The Case of Charles Dexter Ward*; *Frankenstein*; Mad Scientist.

Further Reading

MacDonald, Helen. 2005. *Human Remains: Dissection and Its Histories*. New Haven, CT: Yale University Press.

Marshall, Tim. 1994. "*Frankenstein* and the 1832 Anatomy Act." In *Gothick Origins and Innovations*, edited by Allan Lloyd Smith and Victor Sage, 57–64. Amsterdam and Atlanta: Rodopi.

Moore, Wendy. 2005. *The Knife Man: Blood, Body Snatching, and the Birth of Modern Surgery*. New York: Broadway Books.

BOOKS OF BLOOD

The *Books of Blood* are a collection of thirty short horror stories of varying lengths written by Clive Barker. The first three volumes, containing four to five stories each, were published individually by Sphere in Britain in 1984, with three further discrete volumes published in 1985 after the venture proved successful. The different volumes were eventually collected in two omnibus editions.

Thematically, the *Books of Blood* are quite varied and mix modern horror with the Gothic tradition: well-known monsters such as ghosts, werewolves, and doubles appear in some stories, and one in particular—"New Murders in the Rue Morgue"—revisits Poe, but they also include new ones. The stories are marked by effect and are often driven by strong and memorable imagery—the founding fathers of "The Midnight Meat Train," the giants in "In the Hills, the Cities," the sow in "Pig Blood Blues," the severed hands in "The Body Politic"—and by a reclaiming of the monstrous as psychologically complex, a notion Barker has also explored in later novels such as *Cabal* (1988).

The uniting thread of the stories in the *Books of Blood* is the body of the medium Simon McNeal, whose flesh becomes the "book of blood" in the eponymous frame story, which is the first one in the collection and acts as a prologue. The dead, whom he has been mocking, decide to carve their stories (the ones included in the various volumes) on his body and to thus turn him into a living record of their tribulations.

Despite the risk involved in publishing three volumes of short stories by an unknown author, Sphere's investment in Barker paid off. After he was touted by Stephen King as "the future of horror" and the stories were commended by Ramsey Campbell, the *Books of Blood* became an overnight sensation. There are many things that distinguish these stories from previous horror fiction, such as Barker's queer sensibility, but their legacy would be strongly connected to their graphic quality. Although "gore" had already been prominent in James Herbert's *The Rats* (1977), the *Books of Blood* would be credited with generating mainstream interest in horror fiction and with leading to the birth of "splatterpunk," championed by writers such as John Skipp and Craig Spector. The stories' legacy has continued in cinema through a number of adaptations in the twenty-first century.

Xavier Aldana Reyes

See also: Barker, Clive; Body Horror; Dark Fantasy; *The Rats*.

Further Reading

Aldana Reyes, Xavier. 2014. *Body Gothic: Corporeal Transgression in Contemporary Literature and Horror Film*, 42–51. Cardiff: University of Wales Press.

Meyer, Gus, and James van Hise. 1990. "The *Books of Blood*." In *The Illustrated Guide to the Masters of the Macabre*, edited by James van Hise, 103–120. Las Vegas, NV: Pioneer Books.

Morrison, Michael A. 1991. "The Delights of Dread: Clive Barker's First Three *Books of Blood*." In *Clive Barker's Shadows of Eden: The Books, Films and Art of Clive Barker*, edited by Stephen Jones, 157–169. Lancaster, PA: Underword Miller.

BORGES, JORGE LUIS (1899–1986)

Jorge Luis Borges was an Argentinean author of short fiction that has had a massive impact on the fields of fantasy and supernatural horror literature. He began writing during the 1930s but only reached a significant international audience in the 1960s, when many of his most important stories were gathered into two major collections of English translations (with some overlapping content), *Ficciones* (1962) and *Labyrinths* (1962). Elliptical and haunting, Borges's tales explore themes of memory, identity, power, and myth with an imaginative brilliance that, despite their idiosyncrasy, gives them the sweep and cogency of universal statements.

Borges's fictions occupy a space somewhere between the short story and the philosophical essay: searching, meditative, wryly ironic, they delve into the profoundest mysteries of human experience with elegance and panache. Borges's first work to appear in English, "The Garden of Forking Paths" (1941), is characteristic: on the surface a tale of wartime espionage, it imagines history as a proliferating series of potential outcomes, branching off from decisive moments of action, in which protagonists elect their destinies and thus define a collective fate; here, Borges's favored trope of the labyrinth becomes a model for history itself. An even more affecting treatment of this theme is "The Library of Babel" (1941), which evokes an archival universe made up of an infinite expanse of interlocking hexagonal rooms filled with all the books that have been or conceivably could be written, tended by a shadowy cabal of librarians; the possibility that some volumes may contain secret hermetic knowledge provides support for a messianic cult that ceaselessly roams the stacks. The story conveys a powerful otherworldly feel, a sense of dislocation into an alternate universe of occult intensity; Borges, who himself worked for many years as a librarian, manages to capture the bibliomaniacal fantasy of a world made wholly out of books.

Many of Borges's stories inhabit such otherworlds, alternative time-spaces darkly estranged from our own. "The Lottery in Babylon" (1941) depicts a mythical world in which the eponymous game of chance dictates all dimensions of life, offering a kind of parable about the power of random chance to shape human destiny. A similar effect can be found in "Tlön, Uqbar, Orbis Tertius" (1940), which illustrates the implications of epistemological solipsism (the belief that only the contents of one's own mind are really knowable) in its evocation of a world whose inhabitants deny its own objective existence. In such tales, complex ideas take on palpable form; indeed, Borges's stories are invariably conceptually driven, their characters and incidents subordinate to a larger speculative agenda that involves consistently blurring the boundaries between fantasy and reality. These two realms interpenetrate at every level, including the very manner—nonlinear, reflective, recursive—in which the tales are told. Borges's fictions often have dark and paranoiac textures, like a nightmare, and his world is one haunted by numinous presences, thick with ghosts, yet he largely eschews conventional depictions of the supernatural in favor of a hazy sense of lurking immensities, a creative treatment for which the term "Borgesian" has been coined.

Many commentators have observed the deep debts Borges's work owes to Edgar Allan Poe in its oneiric (dreamlike) obsessiveness, its fondness for mercurial or unreliable narrators, and its complex mixture of precise cognition and irrationality. Borges also, in his 1975 story "There Are More Things," highlighted a link with H. P. Lovecraft; though affirming that Lovecraft was, in his view, a lesser artist than Poe, Borges nonetheless produced a characteristically eccentric homage in this tale of a monstrous entity inhabiting a shunned house. While his own style is far from Lovecraftian, much of Borges's work does suggest, as in Lovecraft, the highly precarious nature of human existence in the face of cosmic magnitudes beyond mortal ken, and he also has a fondness for furtive mystical or cabalistic cults hankering after forbidden forms of knowledge.

The influence of Borges can be discerned in authors as diverse as Robert Aickman, whose strange stories show a similar impulse to philosophical reflection, and Iain Banks, whose dark fantasy novels *Walking on Glass* (1985) and *The Bridge* (1986) occupy textual dreamscapes of Borgesian complexity. The most powerful homage to Borges in recent years was Mark Z. Danielewski's novel *House of Leaves* (2000), a metafictional horror story set in the eponymous labyrinth, at whose heart lurks a deeply occulted mystery. The term "slipstream," coined by science fiction author Bruce Sterling in 1989 to describe a form of postmodern fiction that makes the reader feel "very strange," can be seen as a contemporary variant of Borges's playful speculations, wherein fantasy elements coexist with a drive toward rigorous logical thought. In acknowledgment of his importance to the field, Borges was honored with a World Fantasy Award for Lifetime Achievement in 1979.

Rob Latham

See also: Aickman, Robert; Dreams and Nightmares; Forbidden Knowledge or Power; *House of Leaves*; The Numinous; Surrealism; World Fantasy Award.

Further Reading

Bell-Villada, Gene H. 2000. *Borges and His Fiction: A Guide to His Mind and Art*. Austin: University of Texas Press.

Buchanan, C. J. 1996. "J. L. Borges's Lovecraftian Tale: 'There Are More Things' in the Dream Than We Know." *Extrapolation* 37 (4): 357–363.

Burgin, Richard, ed. *Jorge Luis Borges: Conversations*. Jackson: University of Mississippi Press.

Fraser, Howard M. 1977. "Points South: Ambrose Bierce, Jose Luis Borges, and the Fantastic." *Studies in 20th Century Literature* 1 (2): 173–181.

Williamson, Edwin, ed. 2014. *The Cambridge Companion to Jorge Luis Borges*. Cambridge: Cambridge University Press.

BOWEN, MARJORIE (1885–1952)

Gabrielle Margaret Vere Campbell Long was born in Hampshire, England, to an alcoholic father who deserted the family soon thereafter and a cold and ineffectual mother. She wrote her first novel, *The Viper of Milan*, while still in her teens, though it did not see print until 1906, where it has remained under various publishers to the present day. History interpenetrates nearly all of Bowen's work, whether she is writing a travel guide, an essay, a biography, crime fiction, or supernatural fiction; or attempting to recreate a specific historical event entirely from available evidence, or using that evidence as a springboard for her own imagination. As with Vernon Lee, her attention to period detail lends her settings and dialogue a sense of having been "lived in," so that her characters act convincingly as integral players in events with recognizable human motives rather than as cogs in a machine.

All of her books appeared under pseudonyms—nearly one hundred under the name Marjorie Bowen, more than thirty as George Preedy, seventeen as Joseph Shearing, and the remainder by Robert Paye, John Winch, the ghost story anthologist Arthur Neale, and the thinly disguised author of the autobiography. Regardless of the pseudonym used, all twenty of the short story collections Bowen gathered include what she termed "twilight tales." Although these are primarily supernatural, her interest in irony, venality, social injustice, and the annals of criminality also lends a macabre edge to her suspense fiction and much of her historical fiction. Thus, although there are only a handful of supernatural novels—*Black Magic: A Tale of the Rise and Fall of Antichrist* (1909), concerning the legend of Pope Joan; *The Haunted Vintage* (1921), chronicling the nineteenth-century appearance of the goddess Freya in the Rhine Valley; *I Dwelt in High Places* (1923), about the sorcerous adventures of John Dee; *Five Winds* (1927), about the inexorable working out of a family curse; *The Shadow on Mockways* (1932), a grotesque and not entirely successful Gothic melodrama; *The Devil Snar'd* ("by George Preedy," 1932), a novel of diablerie; *Julia Roseingrave* ("by Robert Paye," 1933), dealing with the subtle encroachment of witchcraft in a romantic relationship; and the doppelgänger tale *The Man with the Scales* (1954)—many of Bowen's historical novels and novels based on classic crimes "by Joseph Shearing" focus on the darker side of history. Examples include *The Master of Stair* (1907), dealing with the massacre at Glen Coe, and *The Poisoners* ("by George Preedy," 1936), set in the murderous cabal within the court of Louis XIV. Such novels turn very dark indeed, and even some of her novels on heroic subjects, like the Black Prince in *The English Paragon* (1930), contain episodes of a horrific nature.

This is not meant to imply that her work is unrelievedly grim. There is a tender or lyrical side on display in stories like "The House by the Poppy Field" (1916), "The Sign Painter and the Crystal Fishes" (1917), "Dark Anne" (1923), "The Avenging of Anne Leete" (1923), "Anne Mellor's Lover" (1923), "The Breakdown" (1976), and the vision of the godlings toiling in the vineyard at sunrise in *The Haunted Vintage*, as well as grim humor to leaven the supernatural events in "Decay" (1923), "The Crown Derby Plate" (1931), and "Incubus" (1935). This compensates for the savagery of stories like "Giuditta's Wedding Night" (1916), "The Fair Hair of Ambrosine" (1916), "The Last Bouquet" (1916), "Scoured Silk" (1919), "Kecksies" (1923), "Florence Flannery" (1929), and "The Bishop of Hell" (1929).

At her best, Bowen's work teems with color, drama, pathos, and an often under-appreciated metaphorical richness that belies the haste that leaves perceptible, if forgivable, flaws in many of her novels. These are among the qualities that have appealed to so many writers, including Mark Twain, Arthur Conan Doyle, Walter de la Mare, Horace Walpole, William Roughead, Michael Sadleir, Edward Wagen-knecht, and Jessica Amanda Salmonson. Graham Greene claimed that after reading Bowen's first novel, "From that moment I began to write. All the other possible futures slid away. . . . It was as if I had been supplied once and for all with a sub-ject" (Greene 1951, 15–16).

Jim Rockhill

See also: Ancestral Curse; Doubles, Doppelgängers, and Split Selves; Witches and Witchcraft.

Further Reading

Campbell, Margaret. 1939. *The Debate Continues, Being the Autobiography of Marjorie Bowen*. London: William Heinemann.
Greene, Graham. 1951. *The Lost Childhood and Other Essays*. London: Eyre and Spottiswood.
Salmonson, Jessica Amanda. 1998. "The Supernatural Romances of Marjorie Bowen." In Marjorie Bowen, *Twilight and Other Supernatural Romances*, xix–xl. Ashcroft, BC, Canada: Ash-Tree Press.
Wagenknecht, Edward. 1991. "Marjorie Bowen." In *Seven Masters of Supernatural Fiction*, 152–181. Westport, CT: Greenwood Press.

BRADBURY, RAY (1920–2012)

Raymond Douglas Bradbury was an American short story writer, novelist, poet, essayist, playwright, and screenwriter who produced more than six hundred works of horror, fantasy, mystery, and science fiction. He published in more than fifty books, and provided the creative inspiration for the U.S. Pavilion at the 1964 World's Fair and the Spaceship Earth display at Epcot Center, Disney World. His work continued to be published until a week before his death on June 5, 2012. Although he was most widely known as a science fiction writer, in his early writing life he focused more on horror, and this was a subject to which he returned repeat-edly throughout his career.

Bradbury was born in Waukegan, Illinois, a town he frequently fictionalized as Green Town in works such as *Dandelion Wine* and *Something Wicked This Way Comes*. He included among his ancestors a woman who was tried as a witch in Salem, Massachusetts. He saw magician Harry Blackstone several times when he was young, and when he was twelve a carnival magician who appeared under the name Mr. Electrico tapped him on the nose with an electrified sword and com-manded him to "live forever." Bradbury took the advice to heart and started writing every day for the rest of his life. He later said he imitated Edgar Allan Poe from the time he was twelve until he was eighteen.

Ray Bradbury: Horror Writer

Although he is more widely thought of as a science fiction writer—thanks largely to the branding he received as "the world's greatest living science fiction writer," an epithet printed on the covers of paperback editions of his books in the 1970s and 1980s—Ray Bradbury is actually better described as a writer of fantasy, and it is often quite *dark* fantasy, with much of it shading over into genuine horror. His first book, the short fiction collection *Dark Carnival*, was published in 1947 by Arkham House, which at that point dealt only in supernatural horror. *Dark Carnival* was later transformed into *The October Country* (1955), which went on to become a cherished classic among horror readers. In these and many other works, Bradbury made significant and deliberate contributions to horror. He also spoke and wrote passionately, in stories, essays, and public talks, about the necessity of acknowledging and even celebrating, in art, the fearsome, dark, terrifying, and horrifying aspects of life. In a real sense, it would not have been inaccurate during his lifetime to have branded him as one of the greatest living horror writers.

Matt Cardin

When Bradbury was fourteen, the family moved to Los Angeles, by which time he already considered himself a writer. Unable to afford university, he educated himself after high school by going to the local library several days a week for the following decade. He supported himself by selling newspapers. He self-published some of his early work in magazines and fanzines, using pseudonyms to disguise his numerous contributions, and made his first professional sale in 1941, earning $15 for a story called "Pendulum" published in the November issue of *Super Science Stories*. Two years later, he became a full-time writer, supported by his wife, Marguerite "Maggie" McClure, whom he met in the bookstore where she worked.

He adopted a regimental approach to his chosen profession, drafting a new short story every week—first draft on Monday, revisions over the next several days, submission to a potential publisher on Saturday. His plots were often about the perceptions of children or memories of childhood, and he claimed to have total recall of his earliest years, including the moment of his birth.

Most of his work in the horror genre came during his twenties. He found a willing home for his stories in *Weird Tales*, edited by Dorothy McIlwraith, placing a story in every issue but one between March 1943 and September 1945. In the biographical sketch accompanying his appearances in the magazine, Bradbury said he didn't care much for ghosts, vampires, or werewolves, since they had been killed with repetition. Instead, he said, there were good stories to be found in everyday things, as well as good stuff "buried in the green leaves of childhood and the heaped dead leaves of old age" (quoted in Schweitzer 1988, 31).

He made a significant sale to *Mademoiselle* in 1946 with "The Homecoming," about a normal young boy who feels like an outcast in a family of witches and vampires. It was an unlikely story for the market, but Truman Capote, who was helping out around the editorial offices at the time, pulled it from the slush pile and recommended it to the editors. Charles Addams—of Addams Family fame— was hired to illustrate the story, which became the centerpiece of the magazine's Halloween issue. Over the years Bradbury would return several times to the Elliot family of ghosts, ghouls, and other assorted monsters. The seven Elliot tales, including "Uncle Einar," which was also written during this period, are collected in *From the Dust Returned* (2001).

Many of the stories from *Weird Tales* were collected in Bradbury's first book, *Dark Carnival*, published by specialty press Arkham House in 1947. This edition consisted of slightly over 3,000 copies, and within a couple of years the book was out of print and would remain so until a limited edition reissue by Gauntlet Press in 2001.

Several stories in *Dark Carnival* have two-word titles, in the form "The Noun." These include classics such as "The Jar," about a farmer who buys a jar that has something strange floating in it from a carnival sideshow; "The Lake," where the protagonist returns to his hometown after the body of his childhood friend who drowned a decade earlier is finally discovered; "The Crowd," in which a character discovers the same people appearing in the crowds that gather around accident scenes; "The Scythe," wherein a man learns the burdens and responsibilities of reaping; and "The Emissary," a gruesome tale in which the family dog drags the body of a beloved teacher to a bedridden boy. These stories arose from Bradbury's early habit of writing lists of nouns to generate ideas. After creating these lists, he would do a free association exercise in which he investigated why he chose those particular words and what they meant to him. *Dark Carnival* also contains such notable stories as "Skeleton," where a hypochondriac becomes convinced his skeleton is to blame for his health problems; and "The Small Assassin," in which a woman thinks her newborn baby is conspiring to kill her. Given the opportunity to bring the book back into print in 1955, Bradbury decided instead to extensively revise several of the stories, lightly edit others, add four new tales to the mix, and remove twelve of the original twenty-seven that he deemed weak, primitive, or overly violent.

In the years between *Dark Carnival* and the publication of this revamped edition, titled *The October Country*, Bradbury produced some of his most notable works, including *The Martian Chronicles*, *The Illustrated Man*, *Fahrenheit 451* (expanded from "The Fireman," which was written in the basement of the UCLA library on a typewriter that he rented for ten cents per half hour), and *The Golden Apples of the Sun*, in addition to beginning work, in collaboration with film director John Huston in Ireland, on the script for the Hollywood film adaptation of *Moby Dick*. In addition to his two early collections, his only other foray into overt horror was *Something Wicked This Way Comes* (1962), expanded from the 1948 short story

"Black Ferris," first as a screenplay for Gene Kelly (to whom the book is dedicated) to direct, and then into a novel when Kelly couldn't get funding for the project. He then declared that he had said everything he had to say in the horror field.

Before moving into the realm of science fiction and fantasy, Bradbury tried his hand at writing crime fiction for pulp magazines such as *Dime Mystery Magazine* and *Detective Tales*, although these were more often tales of terror rather than whodunits or mysteries. He then started making regular sales to the higher-class and higher-paying "slick" magazines, including *The New Yorker*, *Esquire*, *The Saturday Evening Post*, and *Harper's*.

Though much of his work was futuristic, he classified his stories and novels—other than *Fahrenheit 451*—as fantasy rather than science fiction, because they were about things that could not happen instead of things that might possibly happen. He likened science fiction to using a mirror to slay Medusa: though the stories seemed to be looking into the future, they were actually a way to explore contemporary issues. Despite his reputation as a visionary, Bradbury was a notorious technophobe, refusing to fly for most of his life and never learning to drive a car.

Even when Bradbury worked in other genres and forms, horror and horrific images continued to play an important part in his stories and novels throughout his career. For example, in the futuristic story "The Veldt," parents fall prey to their children's imagination, and "The Banshee," inspired by his difficult experiences working on *Moby Dick*, pits a John Huston-like character against the traditional Irish title creature. During the early 1950s, more than two dozen of his short stories were adapted for EC Comics magazines, including *Tales from the Crypt* and *The Haunt of Fear*. During the same period, his stories also became installments of radio dramas and television anthology series, including *Alfred Hitchcock Presents* and *The Twilight Zone*, where his story "I Sing the Body Electric" was adapted as the show's 100th episode. Dozens of additional short films, television episodes, and movies have been adapted from his stories. In the 1980s he developed *The Ray Bradbury Theater*, a television series for HBO and, later, the USA Network, for which he adapted sixty-five of his stories. The series ran from 1986 until 1992.

Recognition for his achievements came early in his career. He won the O. Henry Prize for "The Homecoming" in 1947 and was a finalist for "Powerhouse" in 1948. In 1954, on the strength of *Fahrenheit 451*, the National Institute of Arts and Letters honored him for "his contributions to American literature." He received the National Book Foundation Medal for Distinguished Contribution to American Letters in 2000, was awarded a National Medal of Art by President George W. Bush in 2004, was made Grand Master of the Science Fiction Writers of America, and was honored with Lifetime Achievement awards by the Horror Writers Association, the World Fantasy Convention, and the PEN Center USA West. He was nominated for an Academy Award for his animated film *Icarus Montgolfier Wright* and won an Emmy Award for his teleplay adaptation of his short novel *The Halloween Tree*, about the death-like Mr. Moundshroud leading a group of American Midwestern children on a journey through history to discover the meaning of Halloween. In

2007 Bradbury received a special citation by the Pulitzer Prize jury for his "distinguished, prolific, and deeply influential career as an unmatched author of science fiction and fantasy." The same year, the Center for Ray Bradbury Studies was established in the School of Liberal Arts at Indiana University–Purdue University Indianapolis.

After a stroke in 1999 left him unable to type, Bradbury continued to write by dictating his work over the phone to his daughter in Arizona, who recorded and transcribed it before faxing edits back to him. Collections of his earlier works, including some that had not been previously published, continued to appear late in his life, culminating in *The Collected Stories of Ray Bradbury*, a projected eight-volume series that aims to bring together every short story he ever published in chronological order. The week before he died in June 2012, he published an autobiographical essay in *The New Yorker* double issue devoted to science fiction.

Bev Vincent

See also: Arkham House; Dark Fantasy; *The October Country*; *Something Wicked This Way Comes*; *Weird Tales*.

Further Reading

Aggelis, Steven L., ed. 2004. *Conversations with Ray Bradbury*. Jackson: University Press of Mississippi.

Bloom, Harold, ed. 2010. *Ray Bradbury*. New Edition. Bloom's Modern Critical Views. New York: Infobase.

Reid, Robin Anne. 2000. *Ray Bradbury: A Critical Companion*. Westport, CT: Greenwood Press.

Schweitzer, Darrell. 1988. "Tales of Childhood and the Grave: Ray Bradbury's Horror Fiction." In *Discovering Modern Horror Fiction I*, 29–42. Berkeley Heights, NJ: Wildside Press.

Weller, Sam. 2010. "Ray Bradbury, The Art of Fiction No. 203." *Paris Review* 192. http://www.theparisreview.org/interviews/6012/the-art-of-fiction-no-203-ray-bradbury.

Weller, Sam. 2014. *Ray Bradbury: The Last Interview and Other Conversations*. New York: Melville House.

BRAM STOKER AWARD

The Bram Stoker Award came into being with the inception of the Horror Writers Association (HWA) in 1987. It has since become a major literary award for the genres of horror and dark fantasy.

Under the leadership of Dean Koontz, the newly formed Horror Writers Association (then named the Horror Writers of America) agreed to give out an award of accomplishment for "superior achievement" in the horror field. It was decided that the award would be named after an icon of horror, and the short list of recommendations included Mary Shelley, Edgar Allan Poe, H. P. Lovecraft, and Bram Stoker.

The award process involves both recommendations from the HWA's membership at large and a juried selection of published works from a given year, with two rounds of voting (on the preliminary ballot and then the resulting final ballot) determining the winners. At the time of this writing, the award is divided into eleven categories: novel, first novel, graphic novel, young adult novel, long fiction, short fiction, fiction collection, screenplay, poetry collection, anthology, and nonfiction. There is also a Bram Stoker Award for Lifetime Achievement in the horror field. Past winners of this latter award include Ray Bradbury, Robert Bloch, Joyce Carol Oates, Ramsey Campbell, Richard Matheson, Stephen King, Peter Straub, Ellen Datlow, Clive Barker, Chelsea Quinn Yarbro, and Anne Rice.

Notable past winners of a Bram Stoker Award have included Stephen King, Neil Gaiman, Richard Matheson, and Clive Barker. The trophy itself is a whimsical eight-inch replica of a haunted house designed by Steven Kirk.

The Stoker Awards were originally given out in small weekend gatherings, and later at the World Horror Convention. More recently, in 2016, the awards ceremony was moved to the literary horror conference StokerCon in order to accommodate a growing audience.

Chun H. Lee

See also: Shirley Jackson Awards; Stoker, Bram; World Fantasy Award.

Further Reading

"The Bram Stoker Awards." 2009. Horror Writers Association. http://www.horror.org /awards/stokers.htm#about.

Wiater, Stanley. 1996. "A Shockingly Brief and Informal History of the Horror Writers Association." Horror Writers Association. http://www.horror.org/aboutus.htm.

BRENNAN, JOSEPH PAYNE (1918–1990)

Joseph Payne Brennan was an American writer, poet, and editor, and publisher of *Macabre* magazine, which appeared in twenty-three issues between 1959 and 1976. Brennan spent the majority of his life working as a librarian in Yale University in New Haven, Connecticut, but although his stories often made use of New England history, culture, and traditions, and a number were set in New Haven, he apparently eschewed using his place of employment as a setting.

Brennan's literary career began as a writer for Connecticut newspapers, but he rapidly became a contributor to pulp magazines, writing numerous crime, mystery, and Western stories in addition to the weird and horrific fiction for which he is remembered. A capable poet whose verse utilized traditional forms, Brennan's fantastic fiction was equally traditional in its subject matter and plainly written, but traditional and plain do not mean inferior, and he was generally capable of providing the requisite thrills required by editors and readers alike. Among his better known stories are "The Calamander Chest" (1954) and "Slime" (1953), which display the range of Brennan's talents: the former is small-scale and personal, with a haunted chest beckoning Ernest Maax, its new owner, to death, while the latter is large-scale, describing a being of slime, monstrously emergent from the ocean, which causes death and destruction until repelled. (Stephen King has praised the latter for the efficient delivery of its horrors.)

At times Brennan's darker fiction had a moral side, too: "Levitation" (1958) depicts a carnival performer with a genuine skill, with which he briefly silences hecklers, but when the performer collapses, the levitated heckler continues to rise. New England history is repurposed in "Canavan's Backyard": the titular bookseller becomes fascinated by his backyard, which seems unnervingly larger when one is in it than it does from the outside. As the narrator recounts, Canavan's researches have disclosed a disquieting historical injustice and an accompanying curse, but knowledge of these is not sufficient to save Canavan. New England itself is presented in "The House on Hazel Street" (1961) and "Episode on Cain Street" (1967): these take place in New Haven and mourn the destruction of historic New England and its accompanying traditions.

While the above stories are thematically connected, Brennan also had a series of stories featuring a psychic investigator, Lucius Leffing, a resident of suburban Connecticut. Nevertheless, as one would anticipate from stories first published in *Alfred Hitchcock's Mystery Magazine,* Leffing's investigations lead not to the supernatural but to the human beings behind the seeming manifestations.

Brennan was a fairly consistently second-tier writer of fiction, rarely disappointing while rarely achieving greatness, and his fiction thus appeared in books published by the genre's small and private presses, collections that remained available despite the slow sales that would have led to their pulping by more commercial publishers. He seems to have been content with this, regarding himself as a poet who wrote occasional fiction. The World Fantasy Convention honored him in 1982 by giving him its award for life achievement, but presently he is completely out of print.

Richard Bleiler

See also: Arkham House; Occult Detectives; *Weird Tales.*

Further Reading

Dziemianowicz, Stefan. 1991. "Darkness Come to Life: The Weird Fiction of Joseph Payne Brennan." *Studies in Weird Fiction* 9 (Spring): 18–26.

Murray, Will. 2009. "Joseph Payne Brennan Interviewed." In *Conversations with the Weird Tales Circle*, edited by John Pelan and Jerard Walters, 330–333. Lake Wood, CO: Centipede Press.

Warren, Allen. 1999. "American Gothic: Joseph Payne Brennan." In *Discovering Modern Horror Fiction II*, edited by Darrell Schweitzer, 108–114. Berkeley Heights, NJ: Wildside Press.

BRITE, POPPY Z. (1967–)

Billy Martin, whose works have appeared under the name Poppy Z. Brite, is a New Orleans–born writer of horror, Southern Gothic, and dark comedy. Featuring queer characters and explicit descriptions of gay sex narrated in a lush and sensual style, Brite's fiction is among the first American horror to place queer sexuality at its center. Brite's frank acknowledgment of his and his characters' non-normative genders and sexualities, in addition to his evident fondness for subculture, have made him a controversial figure in the genre. Though his earliest novels and short stories—published when Brite was in his mid-twenties—were sometimes dismissed as "naïve," Brite quickly achieved cult status and then mainstream success, earning a devoted readership and much praise for his poetic, languorous style and unapologetic eroticism.

Brite began his career when he was eighteen, publishing his first story, "Missing," in *The Horror Show* in 1986, followed by the publication of a number of short stories that would later be gathered in the collection *Swamp Foetus* (1993; later renamed *Wormwood*, 1996). However, Brite's real breakthrough success came with the publication of his first novel, *Lost Souls* (1992), which firmly established his reputation as a writer of innovative genre fiction. Featuring an imaginative recasting of the vampire as an ambiguously gendered, separate species from humans, *Lost Souls* introduced many elements that would become mainstays in Brite's work: bisexual and gay characters, the alienation and sometimes nihilism of subcultural American youth, and the non-normative family and friend group—often made up of both literal and figurative orphans—as an alternative to the broken nuclear family.

Though much of *Lost Souls* takes place in New Orleans, the novel also introduces readers to Brite's fictional city of Missing Mile, North Carolina, a small, swampy Southern town that exerts a strong atmospheric presence in Brite's second novel, *Drawing Blood* (1993), which doubles as a love story and haunted house tale. Exploring the complexities of love, violence, sexuality, and addiction, *Drawing Blood* anticipated many of the themes that would ground Brite's third horror novel, *Exquisite Corpse* (1996). Though Brite's writing in *Exquisite Corpse* was highly praised, its plot—a brutal romance between two serial killers, modeled after real-life murderers Dennis Nilsen and Jeffrey Dahmer, and set against an HIV-saturated New Orleans—proved to be too extreme for many horror readers and critics, solidifying Brite's reputation as a controversial writer. *Exquisite Corpse* is Brite's last horror novel to be set in his own fictional universe. It was followed, in 1998, by *The Lazarus Heart*, a dark revenge fantasy set in the fictional universe of James O'Barr's *The Crow* series.

Brite's horror work also includes the short story collections *Are You Loathsome Tonight?* (1998), *Wrong Things* (with Caitlín R. Kiernan, 2001), *The Devil You Know* (2003), and *Triads* (with Christa Faust, 2004), as well as the edited vampiric erotica collections *Love in Vein* (1994) and *Love in Vein II* (1997). Brite moved into dark comedy in 2002 with his acclaimed *Liquor* series, and in 2010, announced his retirement from writing.

Brittany Roberts

See also: The Haunted House or Castle; Splatterpunk; Vampires.

Further Reading

Brite, Poppy Z. 2001. *Guilty but Insane*. Burton, MI: Subterranean Press.
Stableford, Brian. 2003. "Poppy Z. Brite." In *Supernatural Fiction Writers: Contemporary Fantasy and Horror*, edited by Richard Bleiler, 147–152. New York: Thomson/Gale.

THE BRONTË SISTERS

Charlotte, Emily, and Anne Brontë were English novelists and poets of the early nineteenth century. Charlotte, the eldest, was born in 1816 and outlived the rest of her siblings, dying in 1855. Emily was born in 1818 and died of tuberculosis in 1848. Anne, the youngest, was born in 1820 and died in 1849, also of tuberculosis. Although their lives were brief, each made an important difference in the development of English literature, and their novels continue to be regarded as classics today. In the history of horror literature, their novels are important for the way they combined aspects of the Gothic with the psychological and social concerns of nineteenth-century English fiction.

Their father, Patrick Brontë, was born in Ireland and moved to England when he became an Anglican clergyman. He was assigned to the parish at Haworth, a village in West Yorkshire, where he continued to work all his life. He and his wife Maria Branwell Brontë had six children, the first two dying young. Maria herself died in 1821, and so her children had to grow up, for the most part, without her. Patrick Brontë did not remarry, but raised the children with the assistance of relatives. In addition to the three surviving daughters, who would come to be known to posterity as the Brontë sisters, he had one son, Branwell, who died of tuberculosis at the age of thirty-one. As children, the Brontës amused themselves by creating interlocking stories in shared imaginary worlds; Charlotte and Branwell invented a kingdom they called "Angria," while Emily and Anne created a Pacific island domain they named "Gondal." In a way, these juvenile first efforts anticipated the development of fantasy fiction as a genre of imaginary worlds.

As adults, the three sisters all arranged to have their first novels published in the same year, 1847. The Brontë family was never especially affluent, and publishing fiction was one of the few available ways that women could make money in Victorian England. The Brontë sisters had not failed to try as many of these ways as they could, having worked as teachers and governesses, both in England and abroad. Charlotte Brontë, using the name "Currer Bell," published *Jane Eyre*, while Emily Brontë, writing as "Ellis Bell," published *Wuthering Heights*, and Anne Brontë,

The nexus of literary creativity and family tragedy that was the Brontës stands as one of the most striking stories in the history of literature—Gothic, horror, or otherwise.

1812   Patrick Brontë and Maria Branwell wed.

1814   Maria Brontë is born.

1815   Elizabeth Brontë is born.

1816   Charlotte Brontë is born.

1817   Patrick Branwell Brontë is born.

1818   Emily Brontë is born.

1820   Anne Brontë is born.

1821   Maria Branwell Brontë dies of uterine cancer at age thirty-eight.

1825   Maria dies of tuberculosis at age eleven. Six weeks later, Elizabeth dies of tuberculosis at age ten.

1847   Charlotte, Emily, and Anne all have their first novels published: Charlotte's *Jane Eyre* (published under the pen name "Currer Bell"), Emily's *Wuthering Heights* (as "Ellis Bell"), and Anne's *Agnes Grey* (as "Acton Bell").

1848   Anne publishes *The Tenant of Wildfell Hall* in June. Three months later, Branwell dies, possibly of tuberculosis or chronic bronchitis, aggravated by drink and/or drugs. Three months later, Emily dies of tuberculosis and complications from a cold she caught at Patrick's funeral.

1849   Anne dies of tuberculosis in May. Five months later, Charlotte publishes *Shirley*.

1853   Charlotte publishes *Villette*.

1855   Charlotte dies of tuberculosis and/or extreme morning sickness.

1861   Patrick Brontë dies at the age of 84, having never remarried, and having outlived all of his children.

Matt Cardin

writing as "Acton Bell," published *Agnes Grey*. They chose to present themselves to the public disguised as the "Bell Brothers" to avoid controversy, since women writers were not as respected as men and were not generally free to write about darker or more intimate topics. Taking a male name was a strategy that women writers in that era often utilized in order to get their work published; novelist "George Eliot," for example, was in reality a woman named Mary Ann Evans.

Of the three "Bell Brothers" novels, *Jane Eyre* and *Wuthering Heights* were immediately successful, selling very well and receiving so much attention that the Brontës found it impossible to avoid revealing their true identities. These two novels, though quite different from each other, both represent very significant developments for Gothic literature. *Agnes Grey* was less well received, and it was Anne Brontë's second novel, *The Tenant of Wildfell Hall* (1848), that proved to be the more successful of her works.

Jane Eyre tells the story of an orphan girl, the title character, who becomes relatively independent and takes a position as a governess at Thornfield Hall. There is a strong attraction between Jane and her employer, Mr. Edward Rochester, but she refuses to become involved with him on an unequal footing. Rochester is a darkly charismatic Gothic character who conceals a terrible secret: his own interracial marriage and the fact that his wife, now insane, is confined to the attic of his estate. What Jane initially takes for signs of a possible haunting are in fact the sounds and actions of this mad wife. Much of the supernatural is invoked, only to be explained away, in the course of *Jane Eyre*, but at one point Jane does appear to receive a psychic message, a cry for help, from the far-off Rochester. Jane Eyre's independence and strength of character, her refusal to abandon herself either for pleasure, by running away with Rochester and becoming his mistress, or for the sake of duty, by marrying her austere missionary cousin, St. John, establishes her as a significant feminist character in English literature.

Charlotte Brontë's next novel, *Shirley* (1849), is centered on two female characters, Shirley, who is strong willed and financially independent, and Caroline, who is self-effacing and meekly submissive. Later in her life, Charlotte Brontë published an autobiographical novel, *Villette* (1853). During the early 1840s, she had worked at a school in Belgium, and there she fell in love with the director of the school, who was already married. *Villette* tells a modified version of this story. This novel is less strongly Gothic in flavor, although it does include a scene in which the protagonist, Lucy Snowe, sees what she believes to be the ghost of a nun.

Of the three sisters, Charlotte was the one who came closest to fulfilling the public role of the contemporary novelist, attending literary events in London and meeting other prominent authors, notably William Makepeace Thackeray. Emily, on the other hand, shunned publicity, avoided people, and remained for the most part close to home. Anne was not much in demand until her second novel was published, by which time her health had already begun to fail.

Wuthering Heights (1847), published a few months after *Jane Eyre*, recounts the story of two Yorkshire families over several generations, centered on the doomed love of Catherine Earnshaw and Heathcliff, an orphan discovered and adopted by Catherine's father. Heathcliff develops into a brooding and occasionally sinister character, largely as a result of Catherine's decision to marry the elegant Edgar Linton instead of him. In a sense, aspects of character that Charlotte imbued into Rochester are divided into two characters by Emily. Edgar acquires the aristocratic finish and status, while Heathcliff is given the passion and the pride. Supernatural elements are slightly stronger in *Wuthering Heights*. Heathcliff seems to be haunted by visions of Catherine after her death, and the ghostly couple may appear on the moors. The narrator of the overall narrative encounters the ghost of Catherine before any of the story has been revealed to him, which is arguably the most unequivocal example of a supernatural event in the novel. *Wuthering Heights* also makes use of nonsupernatural Gothic elements, such as the struggle for the inheritance of property, the association of weather and landscape with human emotions, and the extensive use of stories within stories. Where *Jane Eyre* is retold by Jane herself, *Wuthering Heights* is a story told by a stranger, relayed by him from a trusted old family retainer.

Anne's *Agnes Grey* is the most directly autobiographical of the first "Bell" novels, telling the tale of a young woman who goes to work as a governess for a wealthy family in order to prove herself capable of supporting her own family. In both *Agnes Grey* and *The Tenant of Wildfell Hall*, Gothic attributes are much less obvious than in *Jane Eyre* or *Wuthering Heights*; in both of Anne Brontë's novels, the most recognizably Gothic feature is the morally bankrupt wealthy or aristocratic family, and the image of the country estate as fertile ground for the cultivation of selfishness and secret vice.

Taken together, the Brontës are unusual in that they focus their attention on country life with barely a glance toward London, which looms so large in other works of nineteenth-century English fiction. As outsiders from the English countryside, who did not feel or respect the need to adopt a common or conventional perspective uncritically, they were Romantic in that they insisted on their own point of view. While William Wordsworth and the poets of the English Lake District were also emphatic about the validity of their rural point of view as a commentary on an increasingly alienated and urbanized English society, the Brontës still seemed to regard themselves as outsiders, and the horror theme of "outsideness" is strong with them. Their female characters are as morally centered as any Gothic heroines, but Agnes Grey, Catherine Earnshaw, and Jane Eyre are neither naïve nor weak. The intrepid hero of the Gothic novel is entirely absent from these novels, and, while the villains are still present, they are developed with a new degree of understanding and psychological care. The Gothic villain may be sympathetic, within limits, but with the Brontës there is a stronger sense that the darker attributes of the male characters may not be entirely unknown to the female characters as well. In particular a fierce pride and defiance of convention emerge in the Brontës' novels, a clear sign of the influence of romanticism.

The poet Lord Byron (1788–1824) was one of the most important Romantic figures for the Brontës, as indeed he was for the literary world at large, and many critics regard him as the model for both Rochester and Heathcliff. Byron was notorious for flouting social and moral conventions; a handsome and athletic man, he was in many ways like a modern pop star in his own time. His poetic works, which included *Don Juan, Manfred*, and *Childe Harold's Pilgrimage*, and which made ample use of Gothic imagery, were extremely popular. Nor was his use as a model for literary characters confined to the Brontës alone; he was a close friend of the gifted poet Percy Shelley and his wife Mary, the author of *Frankenstein* (published in 1818), and the character of Victor Frankenstein seems to have blended attributes of both Percy Shelley and Byron. Another friend of Byron's, Dr. John Polidori, wrote one of the earlier examples of vampire literature, simply titled "The Vampyre," and the character of the vampire, Lord Ruthven, was clearly modeled on Byron.

Byron may be taken to exemplify what romanticism meant, in good measure, for the Brontës: an exhilarating, but dangerous, liberation from conventional ideas of morality, coupled with a more psychologically sophisticated understanding of character. The mysterious, largely unexplained "evil" of the older Gothic tale disappears, and instead the Brontës present us with characters who may do good for less than virtuous motives, and who may do evil through being overzealous in the pursuit of virtue. Their skepticism about moral absolutes, at least among human beings, does not cause them to dismiss the Gothic as Jane Austen did, but to look to the Gothic for ways to express a stormy and often obscure idea of human passions and motivations, the mysterious problem of the will, which cannot be perfectly controlled by reason. While their female protagonists are clearly valorized, these novels have no purely exemplary characters or morally pure role models; instead, characters are morally complex, formed in a mixture of moral and psychological thinking. It may be that the Byronic model was the key for all three of the Brontës, enabling them to address grim themes and more violent passions.

While the novels of the Brontës all build toward conventional endings involving marriage, all of their works are marked by pessimism about the possibility of lasting happiness and doubts about the value of mere contentment. Jane Eyre is able to marry Rochester only after he is maimed and nearly killed in a fire, while the marriages of the main characters in Anne's novels only come after they have resigned all hope of achieving happiness. The marriages in *Wuthering Heights* come with dire repercussions, and only the final marriage of Hareton and the young Cathy seems to promise anything like a peaceful reconciliation.

The influence of the Brontë sisters is remarkable. Not all popular works of the late 1840s went on to enduring fame, but theirs did. *Wuthering Heights* has been adapted for film and television numerous times and has appeared on the stage both in play and in operatic form. *Jane Eyre* has been adapted for film even more often and has also been presented on television and the stage. Anne Brontë's works have also been dramatized, albeit less frequently. The fictional stories of the Brontës have been retold from the perspectives of other characters, sequels to their novels have been written, and both the Brontës themselves and their characters have entered popular culture. Their most important contribution to English literature might have been their forthright boldness in setting down and publicizing their stories, their franker treatment of the inequities and hypocrisies of English society, their use of sexual themes, their criticism of the institution of marriage, their unconventional piety, and their opinion of the domination of English society by men. Their contribution to horror literature was nothing less than an elevation of the psychological sophistication of the Gothic character, the introduction of a new kind of heroine, one who is virtuous, but conflicted, more active and passionate than her eighteenth-century predecessors. In the strong women of later horror fiction, characters like Agnes Grey, Jane Eyre, and Catherine Earnshaw continue to be reflected.

Michael Cisco

See also: Byron, Lord; Byronic Hero; Gothic Hero/Villain.

Further Reading

Gaskell, Elizabeth. [1857] 1997. *The Life of Charlotte Brontë*. New York: Penguin.

Losano, Antonia. 2002. "The Brontë Sisters: Charlotte, Emily, and Anne." In *British Writers: Retrospective Supplement 1*, edited by Jay Parini, 49–62. Detroit, MI: Charles Scribner's Sons.

Reef, Catherine. 2012. *The Brontë Sisters: The Brief Lives of Charlotte, Emily, and Anne*. New York: Clarion Books.

Shulevitz, Judith. 2016. "The Brontës' Secret." *The Atlantic* (June): http://www.theatlantic.com/magazine/archive/2016/06/the-brontes-secret/480726.

BROWN, CHARLES BROCKDEN (1771–1810)

Charles Brockden Brown was an American novelist and historian whose accomplishments made him one of America's most important literary figures. As a novelist he wrote mainly in the Gothic tradition, and his work influenced other major writers in the same genre, such as Nathaniel Hawthorne and Edgar Allan Poe.

Late in Brown's Gothic novel *Wieland*, the narrator, Clara, reflects on the uncanny occurrences that have unfolded, especially the hearing of disembodied voices, which have led her brother, Wieland, to murder his family in the belief that it is God's will. Clara, who is intensely intellectual, finds her thoughts leading her in dark directions:

> Ideas thronged into my mind which I was unable to disjoin or to regulate. I reflected that this madness, if madness it were, had affected Pleyel and myself as well as Wieland. Pleyel had heard a mysterious voice. I had seen and heard. A form had showed itself to me as well as to Wieland. . . . What was my security against influences equally terrific and equally irresistable?
>
> It would be vain to attempt to describe the state of mind which this idea produced. I wondered at the change which a moment had affected in my brother's condition. Now was I stupified with ten-fold wonder in contemplating myself. Was I not likewise transformed from rational and human into a creature of nameless and fearful attributes? Was I not transported to the brink of the same abyss? Ere a new day should come, my hands might be embrued in blood, and my remaining life be consigned to a dungeon and chains.
>
> . . . Some times I conceived the apparition to be more than human. I had no grounds on which to build a disbelief. I could not deny faith to the evidence of my religion; the testimony of men was loud and unanimous: both these concurred to persuade me that evil spirits existed, and that their energy was frequently exerted in the system of the world. (218–220)

Matt Cardin

Source: Brown, Charles Brockden. 1798. *Wieland; or, The Transformation: An American Tale*. New York: Printed by T. & J. Swords, for H. Caritat.

Brown was born into a Quaker family on January 17, 1771. His family intended their son to become a lawyer, and to accomplish this they sent him to a Quaker school from 1781 to 1787. After six years of reading law, though, he turned to other interests and published his first collection of essays, entitled *The Rhapsodist,* in a local magazine in 1789. Subsequently, he moved to New York to pursue other interests. There he became associated with the Friendly Club, a "study club," which included such luminaries as Elihu Hubbard Smith and William Dunlap and a number of literary ladies. These intellectuals steered him into the world of imaginative literature. Brief sketches and introductory notes on Brown mention that he was the first professional writer in the colonies and the first American writer to garner an international reputation. At various times, some have designated him as either the "Father of American Romance" or the "Father of the American Gothic." Between 1798 and 1801, Brown published his best-known novels: *Wieland* (1798), *Arthur Mervyn* (1799), *Ormond* (1799), *Edgar Huntly* (1799), *Clara Howard* (1801), and *Jane Talbot* (1801). Shortly thereafter, he entered into a partnership with his brothers in an export business, which failed in 1806. The demands of business notwithstanding, Brown continued his literary endeavors by editing *The Monthly Magazine and American Review* and *The Literary Magazine and American Register.* He died in 1810, apparently of tuberculosis.

The general consensus is that Brown's best novels are those allied with the Gothic. Although most scholars hold that the author was a slovenly stylist, they also assert that he was a "flawed genius," and that *Wieland, Arthur Mervyn,* and *Edgar Huntly* are worthy contributions to the Gothic genre. Undeniably, *Wieland, or The Transformation* stands as his best novel, horror or otherwise. Employing a female narrator, Brown relates the history of the Wieland family as it is plagued by religious freneticism and mental aberration. The family patriarch dies as a result of spontaneous combustion; his unbridled zeal may well have led to his fiery end. The younger Wieland manifests both of these tendencies, and they lead him to murder his wife and children. *Arthur Mervyn* explores the terrors of physical illness in the form of yellow fever, which scourged the environs of Philadelphia in 1793. Brown's treatment of this epidemic looks ahead to Edgar Allan Poe's "The Masque of the Red Death." In *Edgar Huntly*, Brown explores the mysterious world of somnambulism and the dangers of living on the fringes of the wilderness.

In all of his horror fiction, Brown excels in his work with landscapes. On the one hand, he is fairly conventional in his Gothic settings. Brown, though, Americanizes it. In both *Wieland* and *Edgar Huntly*, he describes carefully and thoroughly the Pennsylvania region. The former novel employs the urban "wilderness" in Philadelphia, while the latter uses the Lehigh Valley.

The Godwin Circle (the group of radical thinkers gathered around the English political philosopher and novelist William Godwin, father of Mary Shelley) and other international luminaries praised Charles Brockden Brown's Gothic fiction. In addition to Poe and Hawthorne, Brown also influenced Washington Irving and

Margaret Fuller. In the later nineteenth century, interest in Brown's work waned. In the latter half of the twentieth century, however, scholars revived the almost forgotten novelist, and Brown has carved his niche in the world of the literature anthology and the academic conference.

E. Kate Stewart

See also: Hawthorne, Nathaniel; Irving, Washington; Poe, Edgar Allan.

Further Reading

Axelrod, Alan. 1983. *Charles Brockden Brown: An American Tale*. Austin: University of Texas Press.

Brown, Charles Brockden. 1926. *Wieland, or the Transformation*, ed. Fred Lewis Pattee. New York: Harcourt Brace.

Grabo, Norman S. 1981. *The Coincidental Art of Charles Brockden Brown*. Chapel Hill: University of North Carolina Press.

Kafer, Peter. 2004. *Charles Brockden Brown's Revolution and the Birth of American Gothic*. Philadelphia: University of Pennsylvania Press.

Weinstock, Jeffrey Andrew. 2011. *Charles Brockden Brown*. Cardiff: University of Wales Press.

BULWER-LYTTON, EDWARD (1803–1873)

Edward George Earle Lytton Bulwer, author of several influential works of occult fiction, was born May 25, 1803, in London. He added a hyphenated Lytton to his name after inheriting his mother's estates in 1838 and became Lord Lytton in 1866. Although he is chiefly remembered today for his horror story "The Haunted and the Haunters," his popularity as a novelist in his own day rivaled that of Charles Dickens, influencing everything from clothing styles to the development of Theosophy. He is remembered outside the genre for his historical novel *The Last Days of Pompeii* (1834); for the phrases "the pen is mightier than the sword" and "the great unwashed," and for the perhaps unjustifiably maligned opening line "It was a dark and stormy night," which inspired a whimsical annual contest of bad opening lines. He died in 1873.

Heavily influenced by Lord Byron and Romantic literature as well as Rosicrucianism and the Kabbalah, he took the Gothic novel in a metaphysical direction and explored the use of psychology and archetypal characters. His work represents a transition from Gothic to modern supernatural fiction. His actual beliefs are unclear, but he is known to have done extensive research into such areas as spiritualism, animal magnetism, and ritual magic.

Bulwer's early occult short stories include "The Tale of Kosem Kesamim" (1832), "Monos and Daimonos" (1830), and "Manuscript Found in a Madhouse"(1835). His main contributions to the genre, however, are his two occult novels *Zanoni* (1842) and *A Strange Story* (1862), and the novella *The Haunted and the Haunters*

"The Haunted and the Haunters": A Prototypical Haunted House Story

First published in *Blackwood's Magazine* in 1859, Bulwer-Lytton's "The Haunted and the Haunters; or The House and the Brain" represents a transition from the Gothic novel to the modern ghost story. It is one of the earliest haunted house stories, and despite the Gothic elements of secret rooms and mysterious phenomena, it is set in a contemporary urban environment, and the haunting has physical effects. It is the prototypical story of people spending a night in a haunted house, and it exemplifies Bulwer's philosophy that there are no truly supernatural forces, but only natural ones yet to be explained by science. Unlike those in later stories, the phenomena here have a pseudoscientific explanation. Many of the phenomena described were inspired by séances conducted in the author's home by the noted spirit medium Daniel Dunglas Home.

The protagonist hears of a purportedly haunted house for rent in London and decides to spend several nights there. He brings a servant and a dog, and experiences a variety of frightening manifestations. The normally fearless servant flees, and the dog dies of a broken neck, but the protagonist makes it through by sheer willpower. The story exists in a shorter form, in which the protagonist discovers and destroys an apparatus used to create the phenomena. In a second, unabridged version, he later meets the immortal magician responsible for the haunting.

This story's direct influence can be seen in such later works of supernatural horror as "No. 242 Rue Le Prince" (1895) by Ralph Adams Cram, *The Haunting of Hill House* (1962) by Shirley Jackson, and *Hell House* (1971) by Richard Matheson. "The Haunted and the Haunters" is directly or indirectly responsible for the establishment of an entire horror subgenre.

Lee Weinstein

(1859). The titular character of *Zanoni* is an immortal magician belonging to an ancient secret society, who sacrifices himself for love. The novel also introduces the demonic entity called the Dweller of the Threshold, a guardian that haunts failed initiates to the society. "The Haunted and the Haunters" concerns a house haunted by the willpower of an immortal magician.

A Strange Story has many elements in common with the previous stories and involves a magician, the elixir of life, alchemy, and possible reincarnation. It has been cited as an influence on *Dr. Jekyll and Mr. Hyde*, *Dracula*, *The Picture of Dorian Gray*, and William Hope Hodgson's Carnacki stories. Bulwer regarded the magical forces depicted in his work as natural forces that were as yet unexplained by science, as opposed to actual supernatural forces. This is also true of his later science fictional utopia, *The Coming Race* (1871). "The Haunted and the Haunters" remains his most popular and influential work.

His occult fiction in general was influential on the work of Sheridan Le Fanu, Nathaniel Hawthorne, Marie Corelli, and Edgar Allan Poe, all of whom influenced succeeding generations of horror writers. He died in Torquay, UK, on January 18, 1873.

Lee Weinstein

See also: Forbidden Knowledge or Power; Spiritualism.

Further Reading

Christensen, Allan Conrad. 1976. *Edward Bulwer-Lytton. The Fiction of New Regions.* Athens: University of Georgia Press.

Christensen, Allan C. 1983. "Edward Bulwer-Lytton (25 May 1803–18 January 1873)." In *Victorian Novelists Before 1885*, edited by Ira Bruce Nadel and William E. Fredeman, 73–87. *Dictionary of Literary Biography*, vol. 21. Detroit: Gale.

Mitchell, Leslie. 2003. *Bulwer Lytton: The Rise and Fall of a Victorian Man of Letters.* New York and London: Hambledon and London.

Woolf, Robert Lee. 1971. "Strange Stories: The Occult Fiction of Sir Edward Bulwer-Lytton." In *Strange Stories and Other Explorations in Victorian Fiction*, 143–366. Boston: Gambit.

BURNT OFFERINGS

Robert Marasco's 1973 novel *Burnt Offerings* began as an idea for a screenplay sometime around 1970, when Marasco was working as a high school teacher in Manhattan and had just attained some success with a Broadway production of his play *Child's Play*. *Burnt Offerings*, which was originally conceived as a black comedy, charts the disintegration of the Rolfe family during a summer vacation in a crumbling country mansion that effectively acts as the book's murderous villain.

The narrative focuses primarily on Marian Rolfe, her son Davey, husband Ben, and his Aunt Elizabeth. Marian's love of cleanliness, order, and beautiful furniture prompts her to pester Ben into renting a sprawling and suspiciously affordable house to get away from a suffocating city apartment. Marian throws herself into

Robert Marasco's *Burnt Offerings*, although it has receded from public memory in the decades since its publication, remains an influential haunted house novel, and it still provides a powerful jolt of supernatural horror for those readers who choose to seek it out. It has often been compared to Stephen King's *The Shining*, which it preceded by four years, because both novels tell the story of middle-class families living as caretakers in an isolated mansion that proves to harbor an evil force, which infiltrates their psyches as it tries to destroy them.

Matt Cardin

cleaning and caring for the house and cooking for the reclusive old Mrs Allardyce, who is never actually seen. Meanwhile, her family falls prey to a series of terrible accidents, as the house mysteriously repairs itself around them. What is most horrifying about the novel is how little Marian struggles against the house's manipulation of her desire for domestic perfection, as she abandons her dying loved ones and is ultimately absorbed into the house, taking Mrs Allardyce's place in a locked room at its heart, as a kind of supernatural housekeeper. A series of eerie photographs suggest that the house periodically restores itself to splendor in precisely this way, demanding blood sacrifices every few years.

Burnt Offerings cannot be separated from the American haunted house tradition, epitomized by writers from Charles Brockden Brown to Mark Z. Danielewski. Specifically, it emerged during a wave of late twentieth-century novels and films about supernatural domestic disturbances, such as Shirley Jackson's *The Haunting of Hill House* (1959) and Steven Spielberg's *Poltergeist* (1980), and is often compared to Stephen King's *The Shining* (1977); indeed, King has written about the book on several occasions. When it was first published, reviewers found it effective and chilling, and for today's readers, it offers a neat, convincing, often unnerving account of a woman driven by societal pressures to subordinate her personal affections to housework and a love of material objects.

In this regard, it bears comparison to Ira Levin's *Rosemary's Baby* (1967) and *The Stepford Wives* (1972), and King's *Carrie* (1974), horror novels by American male writers focusing on issues affecting middle-class women and girls. While both the book and Dan Curtis's star-studded 1976 film adaptation are relatively obscure today, *Burnt Offerings* remains an important contribution to horror's explorations of the troubled and troubling relationship between women and the houses that dominate their lives.

Dara Downey

See also: Brown, Charles Brockden; The Haunted House or Castle; *The Haunting of Hill House*; *House of Leaves*; *Rosemary's Baby*; *The Shining*.

Further Reading

Bailey, Dale. 1999. *American Nightmares: The Haunted House Formula in American Popular Fiction*. 1999. Bowling Green, OH: Bowling Green State University Popular Press.

King, Stephen. 1998. "Robert Marasco, *Burnt Offerings*." 1998. In *Horror: 100 Best Books*, edited by Stephen Jones and Kim Newman, 217–218. New York: Carroll and Graf.

BUTLER, OCTAVIA E. (1947–2006)

Octavia Estelle Butler was primarily a science fiction writer whose well-crafted, intelligent, and emotionally resonating—and at times devastating—novels brought her much critical success during her lifetime. It can be argued nonetheless that her themes, which she revisited in all of her writing, are also central to horror fiction.

Her sustained focus on alienation and marginalization, her examination of the crushing effects of power as it is wielded by alien forces, her investigation of bodies that have been colonized and refashioned into something Other yet which remain recognizably and in some instances tragically human, are common threads found in the best horror fiction.

The five novels that together make up Butler's Patternist Series—*Patternmaster* (1976), *Mind of My Mind* (1977), *Survivor* (1978), *Wild Seed* (1980), and *Clay's Ark* (1984)—tell a complex story, beginning in the seventeenth century and continuing into the distant future, of an ancient creature and his son who breed with a female shape-changer to create a new breed of human. Her Xenogenesis trilogy—*Dawn* (1987), *Adulthood Rites* (1988), and *Imago* (1989)—tells the story of a visiting alien race that, through programmatic miscegenation (the interbreeding of different races), offers a dying humanity a chance to continue the species, albeit with changes. The Parable series was left unfinished at the time of her death. *Parable of the Sower* (1993) and *Parable of the Talents* (1998) take place in an early twenty-first century America that has collapsed into political, economic and ecological crisis. The latter of these was awarded the Nebula Award for best novel by the Science Fiction Writers of America.

These novels incorporate horror imagery and themes to varying and perhaps progressively lesser degrees, but her final work, *Fledgling* (2005), more fully embraces the horror treasury in its presentation of the vampire as a different species. The Ina are a shadow species that survive by feeding on human blood, and their saliva, in turn, extends the lifetimes of the humans they bring into their inner circle. Butler's dominant theme—of unequal but beneficial symbiotic relationships that require sacrifice from both parties—plays out against a backdrop of familial infighting and power struggle. Shori, the novel's main character, is an adult Ina who, because of a genetic experiment, resembles a ten-year-old black girl. A powerful family of Inas, all of which are white, see her as an aberration and set out to destroy her. The novel is especially bloody even for Butler, whose stories are often vicious in their telling, but *Fledgling* is nonetheless a powerful and insightful exploration of the intersection of identity and violence.

Butler's shorter fiction numbers barely more than half a dozen short stories, but of these, "Bloodchild" (1984) stands out as an extraordinary exercise in body horror and corporeal violation willingly given between alien and human. It was awarded the Locus, Nebula, and Hugo awards. Also significant is "The Evening and the Morning and the Night" (1987), which details the horrific aftereffects of a cure for cancer. The children of those who took the cure are crippled by extreme psychosis and violent behavior. While the subsequent generation learns how to delay the onset of the aftereffects, the social alienation they experience as a result is no better than the afflictions they will eventually face.

As a female African American science fiction writer, Butler's was for years a lone but necessary voice. Indeed, no one but she could have written a novel like *Kindred* (1979), which illuminates the all-too-real horrors of slave culture. The novel follows an educated black woman in 1976 whose white slave-owning ancestor is able to call her back through time whenever his life is imperiled. She and her white husband are forced to confront, experience, and be complicit in the exploitation of black bodies and the violence wrought upon them. Butler's influence on a current generation of writers, white and of color, is profound and cannot be overstated. Her sudden death from a head injury sustained in an accidental fall in her backyard robbed the field of one of its most distinctive and important voices.

Javier A. Martinez

See also: Body Horror; Vampires.

Further Reading

Francis, Consuela, ed. 2010. *Conversations with Octavia Butler*. Jackson: University Press of Mississippi.

Octavia E. Butler. Accessed July 28, 2016. http://octaviabutler.org.

Pfeiffer, John R. 1999. "Butler, Octavia Estelle (b. 1947)." In *Science Fiction Writers: Critical Studies of the Major Authors from the Early Nineteenth Century to the Present Day*, 2nd ed., edited by Richard Bleiler, 147–158. New York: Charles Scribner's Sons.

Samatar, Sofia. 2013. "Strange Symbiosis in 'Bloodchild.'" *Weird Fiction Review*, June 24. http://weirdfictionreview.com/2013/06/101-weird-writers-26-octavia-butler.

BUZZATI, DINO (1906–1972)

Dino Buzzati was, along with Italo Calvino, one of the most important modern Italian writers of fantastic and surrealistic fiction. A prolific author of novels, stories, plays, and journalism, Buzzati has had, via a handful of English translations, a modest impact on the more literary strains of horror and dark fantasy writing. His most celebrated and widely circulated novel, *The Tartar Steppe* (1945), potently echoes Franz Kafka's *The Castle* (1926) in its depiction of a labyrinthine military fort of inscrutable purpose, infested with self-important bureaucrats, to which the main character, Giovanni Drogo, is assigned in a kind of nightmarish exile; the atmosphere, brilliantly sustained, is one of ironic claustrophobia, with Fort Bastiani offering a potent allegory of psychological entrapment. In this novel, Buzzati, like Kafka, makes the absurd seem genuinely foreboding.

Buzzati's key theme is the way in which fantasy and desire—often incarnated in alluring dreams or visionary quests with vaguely supernatural overtones—manage to survive in a barren secular world. His short stories, many taking the form of crystalline parables that draw on fairy tales and myth, have been distilled into two excellent collections of English translations by Lawrence Venuti: *Restless Nights* (1983) and *The Siren* (1984). Buzzati deploys his considerable skills as a journalist to describe, in matter-of-fact prose, marvelous violations of everyday reality: hallucinations take on palpable form, leading to the death of "The Bewitched Bourgeois" (1948); an uncharted city persistently foils an avid traveler in "The Walls of

Anagoor" (1955); time accelerates or freezes into stasis in "The Time Machine" (1954), a work that verges on science fiction (as does Buzzati's 1960 novel *Larger Than Life* [trans. 1962], in which a scientist's dead wife is seemingly reincarnated in a computer).

Buzzati died in 1972, leaving behind a complex corpus of work, much of it still inaccessible to those unversed in Italian. His influence on modern horror literature has been less obvious than that of Kafka or Jorge Luis Borges, but it has nonetheless exerted a strange fascination for readers unafraid to grapple with its playful mysteries, and it has been cited by the contemporary American horror writer Thomas Ligotti as a significant influence.

Rob Latham

See also: Borges, Jorge Luis; Dreams and Nightmares; Kafka, Franz; Surrealism; The Uncanny.

Further Reading

Atchity, Kenneth. 1978. "Time in Two Novels of Dino Buzzati." *Italica* 55 (1): 3–19.

Cancalon, E. D. 1977. "Spatial Structures in the Narrative of Dino Buzzati." *Forum Italicum: A Journal of Italian Studies* 11 (1): 36–46.

Venuti, Lawrence. 1982. "Dino Buzzati's Fantastic Journalism." *Modern Fiction Studies* 28 (1): 79–91.

BYRON, LORD (1788–1824)

George Gordon Byron, the sixth Baron Byron, became the most famous poet of his era and the central figure of the English Romantic movement. His work was dominated by his image and seen primarily as an aspect of that image; his attire and attitude became enormously influential on the poses struck by young men ambitious to be seen as rebels against conformity, the former defining the dress code of English and French "dandies" for a generation—assisted by the influence of his disciple George "Beau" Brummell—and the latter shaping their lifestyle fantasies. Prompted to flee England in 1816 after the breakdown of his marriage to Anne Millbanke, amid scandal generated by multiple affairs (most famously with Caroline Lamb) and rumors of incest (with his half-sister Augusta Leigh) and sodomy, he apparently poured his feelings of guilt into the classic Faustian fantasy *Manfred* and justified his promiscuity by representing "Don Juan" as a victim unable to resist female seduction rather than a predator.

Byron was the orchestrator of the occasion that gave rise to the most famous legend in the history of horror fiction when his guests at the Villa Diodati at Lake Geneva in 1816 embarked on a competition in which each would write a horror story. He and Percy Shelley never finished theirs, but Mary Shelley developed hers into *Frankenstein*, and Byron's physician, John William Polidori, eventually produced "The Vampyre," whose anonymous publication led to it being widely

Byron's *Manfred*: A Gothic Metaphysical Drama

Byron's *Manfred* is a dramatic poem in the form of a closet drama (a play intended to be read, not performed). First published in 1817, it was written after Byron fled Britain following the breakdown of his marriage, amid scandalous rumor, mostly while he was traveling through the Alps after the famous evening spent at the Villa Diodati when he and his various companions discussed writing horror stories.

Like Byron himself, the poem's eponymous protagonist leaves home to wander the Alps, after summoning seven spirits in a Faustian fashion. They cannot provide him any immediate solution to his predicament, which stems from the death of his beloved Astarte, in regard to which he feels a mysterious but intense guilt. In the course of his quest, Manfred also confronts the Witch of the Alps; Arimanes; an abbot; and various allegorical figures, but the various kinds of bargain that they can offer him—including the abbot's offer of forgiveness and redemption from his sin—are not acceptable to him as exits from his predicament, and he insists on dying on his own defiant terms.

Manfred proved the most fascinating of the various *alter egos* Byron adopted in his long philosophical poems. Although haunted by guilt, Manfred refuses any of the conventional solutions to his plight that are offered to him, manifesting an assertive individualism that seemed to many of Byron's admirers to be a perfect encapsulation of the Romantic spirit and the very essence of the imitative Byronism that became a popular lifestyle fantasy.

Manfred was musically adapted for the stage by Robert Schumann as *Manfred: Dramatic Poem with Music in Three Parts*, first performed in 1852. It was also adapted as a symphony, simply titled *Manfred*, by Tchaikovsky in 1885.

Brian Stableford

misattributed to Byron. The inspiration provided by that occasion thus produced two of the most important archetypes of English horror fiction, and the latter story, which recasts a character clearly based on Byron—given the same name as the villain of Caroline Lamb's vengeful novel *Glenarvon* (1816)—brought out the "satanic" aspects of the Byronic pose in a lurid fashion, with the result that countless future vampires would be modeled, directly or indirectly, with various degrees of stigmatization, on the unwitting baron.

Apart from the phantasmagorical *Manfred*, there is little of the horrific in Byron's own work, save for a few elements in the Oriental fantasy "The Giaour" (1813) and the enigmatic poem "Darkness" (1816). The latter is sometimes interpreted as a vision of the end of the world, but probably adapts a description of the aftereffects of the eruption of the volcano Mount Tambora the previous year—whose ash blotted out the sun temporarily in many parts of the world—to the same feelings of guilt occasioned by the failure of his marriage that produced *Manfred*.

Byron's death in April 1824 added further to the romanticism of his legend. Having taken an active role in the Greek War of Independence, perhaps in a spirit of expiation, he died of an infection probably caused by his physician, employing an unsterilized lancet in his worse-than-futile bloodletting.

Brian Stableford

See also: Byronic Hero; Gothic Hero/Villain; Romanticism and Dark Romanticism; Shelley, Mary; "The Vampyre."

Further Reading

Bloom, Harold. 2004. *Lord Byron*. Philadelphia: Chelsea House.
Cochran, Peter, ed. 2009. *The Gothic Byron*. Newcastle upon Tyne, UK: Cambridge Scholars Publishing.
MacCarthy, Fiona. 2002. *Byron: Life and Legend*. London: John Murray.

BYRONIC HERO

The term "Byronic hero" describes a recurring character type often found in horror literature that is identified by his role as a social rebel. Not virtuous in the traditional sense, the Byronic hero is a larger than life figure that is characterized by arrogance, charisma, confidence, moodiness, and mysteriousness. Flawed and at war with society, the Byronic hero is often a handsome character who has dark overtones that are overwhelming to those around him. Named after the early nineteenth-century British poet Lord Byron, whose lover Lady Caroline Lamb once supposedly described as "mad, bad, and dangerous to know," the Byronic hero has featured in many notable works from the horror genre and continues to appear in modern fiction and film.

The Byronic hero has its literary origins in pre-nineteenth-century literature, such as the plays of William Shakespeare and the early works of Johann Wolfgang von Goethe. The advent of Gothic fiction in 1764 with Horace Walpole's *The Castle of Otranto*, itself a work inspired by Shakespearean drama, established the Gothic hero-villain, in the form of the usurper Manfred, as the central character of this new literary genre. Manfred dominates Walpole's narrative with his villainy and commands the reader's unwavering attention in every scene in which he is present. This character type would be combined with the emotional excesses of the "man of feeling," another literary archetype popular in sentimental fiction, by Byron in his own works with strong traces of his own imposing personality to create the Byronic hero, first appearing in his *Childe Harold's Pilgrimage* (1812). Byron would revisit the Byronic hero in numerous later works, most notably *Manfred* (1817), a supernatural play about a sorcerer whose name is an homage to Walpole's Manfred but remade in Byron's image.

Partly because of the engrossing nature of the character type, and partly because of the then celebrity-like infamy surrounding Byron personally, the Byronic hero became an instant success with nineteenth-century horror writers. Byron's personal physician, Dr. John Polidori, used the Byronic hero to criticize his employer in an unflattering short story entitled "The Vampyre" (1819), which is considered the progenitor of vampiric fiction. Byron's lover, the aforementioned Lady Caroline Lamb, wrote *Glenarvon* (1816), a novel that also features this character trope. Years later, after Byron's death, Charlotte and Emily Brontë wrote their Gothic novels, respectively *Jane Eyre* (1847) and *Wuthering Heights* (1847), with male figures that are clear expressions of the Byronic hero. Continuing to the present day, the Byronic hero is very much alive in horror fiction and film, with examples such as Anne Rice's Lestat de Lioncourt from the *Vampire Chronicles* and Sir Thomas Sharpe in Guillermo del Toro's *Crimson Peak* (2015) demonstrating the continued relevance of this fascinating archetype.

Joel T. Terranova

See also: The Brontë Sisters; Byron, Lord; *The Castle of Otranto*; Gothic Hero/Villain; Rice, Anne; "The Vampyre."

Further Reading

Stein, Atara. 2009. *The Byronic Hero in Film, Fiction, and Television.* Carbondale: Southern Illinois University Press.

Thorslev, Peter. 1962. *The Byronic Hero: Types and Prototypes.* Minneapolis: University of Minnesota Press.

Wootton, Sarah. 2016. *Byronic Heroes in Nineteenth-Century Women's Writing and Screen Adaptation.* London: Palgrave Macmillan.

C

"THE CALL OF CTHULHU"

"The Call of Cthulhu" (1928) is a short story by H. P. Lovecraft. It marks the advent of his most effective and characteristic work, and is a bellwether of cosmic horror. In this tale, worn-out supernatural themes (e. g., the vampire) are boldly replaced by philosophical concerns (e.g., humanity's place in the cosmos and the mind's tenuous grip on reality) as the sources of horror.

Francis Thurston pieces together information from disparate sources around the world, and realizes an alien called Cthulhu came to Earth eons ago in the company of beings called the Great Old Ones. The latter used magic to suspend Cthulhu in the sunken city of R'lyeh, from which he will reemerge when the "stars are ready" to rule the planet.

Lovecraft was inspired in part by Arthur Machen's *The Three Impostors* (1895), which also employs the collation of unrelated documents and subnarratives. Another key source is Guy de Maupassant's "The Horla" (1887), about an invisible being that sways men's minds. Other influences include A. Merritt's *The Moon*

The opening paragraph of "The Call of Cthulhu" has justly become one of the most famous passages in all of Lovecraft's fiction, and in weird and cosmic horror fiction as a whole, for it brilliantly encapsulates not only the guiding philosophical ethos of this particular story, but that of the entire cosmic-horrific substream of weird fiction that Lovecraft pioneered. The basic thrust is that an accurate "big picture" understanding of humankind's cosmic circumstance would reveal horrors so vast and profound that they would annihilate the race:

> The most merciful thing in the world, I think, is the inability of the human mind to correlate all its contents. We live on a placid island of ignorance in the midst of black seas of infinity, and it was not meant that we should voyage far. The sciences, each straining in its own direction, have hitherto harmed us little; but some day, the piecing together of dissociated knowledge will open up such terrifying vistas of reality, and of our frightful position therein, that we shall either go mad from the revelation or flee from the deadly light into the peace and safety of a new dark age. (Lovecraft 2016, 139)

Matt Cardin

Source: Lovecraft, H. P. 2016. *The Call of Cthulhu and Other Weird Stories.* New York: Penguin.

Pool (1918–1919) and W. Scott-Elliot's theosophist treatise *Atlantis and the Lost Lemuria* (1925).

The story is characterized by Lovecraft's unique blend of scientific realism and weird atmosphere. Humans and the world, in contrast to traditional religion, have no special place in the cosmos but are merely "recent and transient." Cthulhu is master of time, space, and even mind (he communicates with human beings in dreams); the geometry of his city is non-Euclidean; and even the phonetics of his name are absolutely nonhuman. The narrator realizes that an alien intrusion undermines human science, belief, art, morals, law, and custom—"the liberated Old Ones would teach [men] new ways to shout and kill and revel and enjoy themselves, and all the earth would flame with a holocaust of ecstasy and freedom" (Lovecraft 2002, 155)—and portends complete oblivion for the race.

The work shows a high degree of artistic finish. Its structure, with narrative time folding back on itself, reflects its themes. The prose is carefully modulated, and deft touches of surrealism and dada (the early twentieth-century artistic and literary movement driven by disillusionment with conventional values) appear in the apparently random juxtaposition of events, the use of dreams, and the encounter with Cthulhu. The latter, with its octopus-like head, scaly body, clawed feet, and wings, is the most vivid creation in modern weird fiction. "The Call of Cthulhu" consolidates elements of what would later be called the "Cthulhu Mythos." It has inspired a vast number of imitations and sequels in various media, as well as a 2005 independent film adaptation that was created as a silent black-and-white production, thus mimicking the look and feel of a movie that would have been produced in 1926 when the story was first published.

Steven J. Mariconda

See also: Cthulhu Mythos; Frame Story; Lovecraft, H. P.; Lovecraftian Horror; Machen, Arthur; Maupassant, Guy de.

Further Reading

Cannon, Peter. 2016. *H. P. Lovecraft.* New York: Hippocampus Press. Kindle edition.

Joshi, S. T. 1996. *A Subtler Magick: The Writings and Philosophy of H. P. Lovecraft.* 1996. Gillette, NJ: Wildside Press.

Joshi, S. T., and David E. Schultz. 2004. *An H. P. Lovecraft Encyclopedia*, 27–30. New York: Hippocampus Press.

Lovecraft, H. P. 2002. *The Call of Cthulhu and Other Weird Stories.* S. T. Joshi, ed. London: Penguin.

CAMPBELL, RAMSEY (1946–)

Born in Liverpool, England, Ramsey Campbell has been described as "Britain's most respected living writer" of horror fiction by the *Oxford Companion to English Literature* (Birch 2009, 499). A highly prolific and versatile author, editor, anthologist, and critic, Campbell's literary output to date includes more than three dozen novels and around three hundred short stories. His early work was lauded by Stephen King and T. E. D. Klein as making a significant and original contribution to the genre. During his long career, Campbell has won recognition from the British Fantasy Society, the Horror Writers' Association, and the International Horror Guild, among many others. In 2015 he was given the World Fantasy Award for Lifetime Achievement.

Campbell's fiction has dealt with both supernatural and nonsupernatural themes, especially psychological horror, in a contemporary setting. However, his knowledge of the history of horror literature and the Anglo-American tradition are comprehensive, and his work is, as a consequence, highly allusive. Robert Aickman, Algernon Blackwood, M. R. James, Fritz Leiber, and Arthur Machen have all been cited as influences by Campbell. The primal role of H. P. Lovecraft, in particular, in the writer's development has been acknowledged, then disavowed in the late 1960s and 1970s, before being reembraced in the following decade in the short story collection *Cold Print* (1985).

Campbell is still perhaps best known for his short stories, and he has continued to use this form. He began writing horror at eleven years of age. What was to become his first published story, "The Church in High Street," was accepted by August Derleth at Arkham House in 1962, appearing in the anthology *Dark Mind, Dark Heart*. Arkham House also published Campbell's first collection, *The Inhabitant of the Lake and Less Welcome Tenants* (1964), when the author was eighteen. An anthology of rewritten Lovecraftian tales, it is notable for Campbell's creation, under the advice of Derleth, of a distinctively British setting for his narratives. The fictional "Brichester" of many of Campbell's stories is a thinly disguised stand-in for his native Liverpool. Campbell was to return consistently to a Merseyside and Severn Valley locale throughout his career, for example in *Creatures of the Pool* (2009), thematically in part a novel-length expansion of Lovecraft's fable of miscegenation, "The Shadow over Innsmouth."

However, it was the appearance of his second collection of short stories, *Demons by Daylight* (1973), which really heralded the arrival of Campbell as an original voice within the genre. Stories like "Concussion" and "The Guy" mark a departure from the influence of Lovecraft, marrying modern urban settings and social critique with a subtle and precise prose style. Technique was, and has remained, a central concern for Campbell. Although defining horror as "the branch of literature most often concerned with going too far," Campbell has consistently rejected what he sees as the "disgustingness" of much modern writing in the genre (Campbell 2002, 49; Joshi 2001, 4). As with M. R. James, the horror in Campbell's work evokes shudders but is glimpsed briefly rather than explicitly dwelt upon. For example, the story "Chucky Comes to Liverpool" in the late collection *Holes for Faces* (2013) combines wry social comment with oblique horror. With the media's attribution of horror videos as a cause behind the real-life 1993 murder of a British toddler by two older boys serving as a backdrop, "Chucky" portrays the ironic transformation of an antiviolence campaigner's teenage son into a murderous arsonist. A cinema projectionist becomes a vividly dehumanized "figure covered with flames and partly composed of them" (Campbell 2010, 167). Like the unfortunate projectionist, Campbell's prose is crisp and pared down. These characteristics have led to Campbell being described as "the poet of urban squalor and decay" (Joshi 2001, 97).

A third collection of short stories, *The Height of the Scream*, followed *Demons by Daylight* in 1976. Campbell's important anthology of pieces written during the first thirty years of his career, *Alone with the Horrors*, appeared in 1993. But although his short stories have attracted great acclaim, his output of longer fictions has been prodigious. These novels, and the occasional novella, have become Campbell's most frequently used form of publication and are gaining increasing attention.

Campbell's first novel, *The Doll Who Ate His Mother* (1976), and in particular its successor, *The Face That Must Die* (1979, revised 1983), established him as a specialist in depicting social alienation and madness. The author was drawing from personal experience. His vivid autobiographical preface to *The Face That Must Die* recounts a Catholic childhood and adolescence marked by parental estrangement, in which Campbell's father continued to share the family house as an unseen but frequently heard presence, and his mother descended into paranoid schizophrenia. Perhaps informed by this Gothic-sounding upbringing, Campbell's fiction prominently features abnormal psychology. Diseased minds and mental illness are rendered horrific through probing with "uncomfortable intensity" (Joshi 2001, 12), often from the antagonist's point of view. Characters fantasize about killing their elderly relatives (*Obsession*, 1985), or, as with the malignant great-aunt Queenie in *The Influence* (1988), are possessed or displaced by them. The plot of *Incarnate* (1983), a long novel written during the last year of Campbell's mother's illness, draws on a schizophrenia-like collapse between dream and reality.

Beginning with Horridge in *The Face That Must Die*, the deranged serial murderer as main character is a recurrent theme of Campbell's. Significantly, Campbell began this focus prior to the popularization of the serial killer by thriller writers like Thomas Harris. Campbell's writing has a consistent strain of black humor, though. He even produces a further innovative riff, the comic serial killer, in *The Count of Eleven* (1991) with its sympathetic antihero, Jack Orchard, and his pathetic refrain: "Got to laugh, haven't you?" (Campbell 1991, 29). Like *The Count of Eleven*, many of Campbell's novels, particularly his crime fictions of the 1990s and 2000s, have no supernatural content. However the violent subject matter of murder, child abuse, and the vulnerability of children and women are still, in Campbell's broad imaginative definition, viable sources of horror. Even the suspense thriller, *The One Safe Place* (1995), "becomes" a horror story through its grim conclusions regarding the contagion of violence (Campbell 2002, 43). Throughout Campbell's fiction, those who struggle against the experience of evil tend to do so unaided. Professional support services such as the church, senior educational figures, police, and social workers are depicted negatively, as variously insensitive, buffoonish, or sinister.

Concern with the vulnerability of the nuclear family unites Campbell's nonsupernatural and his supernatural work, particularly the novels. Villains like Peter Grace (*The Parasite*, also known as *To Wake the Dead*, 1980) or Kasper Ganz (*The Nameless*, 1981), who seek to exploit children, exemplify a threat to the family unit, with the satanic cult acting as a metaphor for invasive evil. Yet often with Campbell the threat is much closer to home: "in coming face to face with the monsters we may find ourselves looking not at a mask but a mirror" (Campbell 2002, 53). Even in the Lovecraftian novel *The Darkest Part of the Woods* (2002), inspired by Lovecraft's *The Case of Charles Dexter Ward*, the evil represented by the villainous Nathaniel Selcouth thrives by exploiting family dysfunction. Repeatedly with Campbell's fictions, the central figure is a father. For example, *Midnight Sun* (1990), a novel in the cosmic horror tradition of Lovecraft, Blackwood, and Machen, features a protagonist who, in becoming possessed by an alien intelligence, gradually becomes an emotionally detached and unfeeling monster. In a dramatic climax, Ben Sterling undergoes a last-minute recovery and finally sacrifices himself out of love for, and to save, his own family. *The House on Nazareth Hill* (1996), Campbell's novel-length contribution to the haunted house subgenre, narrows its cast of characters to become a claustrophobic two-hander between an increasingly psychotic, possessed father and his abused teenage daughter.

Campbell became a parent himself for the first time in 1978, and some critics, notably S. T. Joshi, have regretted the increasing focus on middle-class family life in the plots of his novels, preferring instead what they see as the undiluted purity of his short stories. Nevertheless, domesticity continues to be a significant theme for the author, as attested by the late novella *The Pretence* (2013), about a central character trying to protect his family in the last few hours before some unspecified apocalyptic event.

Campbell's horror writing also reflects an ongoing interest in and engagement with other media. He was a film and later DVD critic for BBC Merseyside radio for many years (1969–2007), and early in his career he produced novelizations for several classic Universal Horror movies such as *The Bride of Frankenstein* under the pseudonym Carl Dreadstone (1977). Film itself has a central role in two of Campbell's original novels. *Ancient Images* (1988) features a lost, but entirely fictional, Boris Karloff and Bela Lugosi horror movie of the 1930s in a story about cursed land. *The Grin of the Dark* (2007) draws upon silent film comedy and transpires to be a narrative about a satanic medieval historian seeking to allow an evil intelligence a portal into the world. Although the subject is, again, a traditional one for the genre, the latter novel also employs electronic mail as a new source of horror. Websites, photography, and the sculptures of Antony Gormley feature in *The Seven Days of Cain* (2010), while *Think Yourself Lucky* (2014), with its murder blog, uses the latest trending in social media to uncanny effect.

Such blurring of the boundaries between the real world and a virtual or artificially created one is central to Campbell's horror fiction. For example, the plot of *The Seven Days of Cain* concerns Internet characters, including a sadistic, shape-shifting villain, who keep "writing themselves" after their creation, and culminates in a fictional character's consciousness of her own fictionality and desire for independent existence through being "ashamed of not being real" (Campbell 2010, 143, 306). That this is the photographer hero's girlfriend lends poignancy: "losing Claire felt like abandoning the best part of himself" (Campbell 2010, 314). However, it also reflects Campbell's own consistent authorial self-consciousness. Repeatedly, his work centers on writers or booksellers, their relationship with readers, and the processes and consequences of literary creativity. The novella *Needing Ghosts* (1990), told in the first person and urgent present tense, is perhaps his most confessional if not autobiographical work. The protagonist John Mottershead, a horror writer who, it is revealed, has murdered his own family, is caught in a narrative of entrapment in which he has become the central character of his own story. Writing, the narrator complains, "won't leave you alone, ever," and the mind is likened to a predator, "a spider which is trying to catch reality and spin it into patterns" (Campbell 1990, 34). Unable to distinguish between dream and memory, Mottershead appears doomed to repeat the events of a single day, including sinister encounters with public transport officials, bookstores and a writers' group, and a suicide attempt: "Hadn't he tried this before," he wonders, "more than once, many times?" (Campbell 1990, 80). The theme of recurrent nightmare without closure follows a long tradition, exemplified by Melmoth in Charles Maturin's *Melmoth the Wanderer* (1820), while the self-haunted, unreliable narrator reflects the influence of Aickman.

Despite the appearance of vampires in his recent novel *Thirteen Days at Sunset Beach* (2015), Campbell's vision of horror has largely avoided such familiar generic figures in favor of monstrosity of a more human kind. Although shifting between supernatural and nonsupernatural story lines and often returning to old themes, there has been a development from early use of Anglo-American horror motifs to familial concerns and an increasingly sophisticated preoccupation with psychological processes and existential questions. Campbell's subtle, intensely referential and literary style, his self-description as a horror writer, and his reluctance to allow the parameters of his horror to be easily defined or pigeonholed possibly account for a relative lack of commercial success to date compared to other authors, with Harris, or the even more prolific King, being obvious examples of this. As an editor, Campbell has also championed the work of others. The anthology *Uncanny Banquet* (1992) revives less familiar texts, including the first reprint of Adrian Ross's 1914 novel, *The Hole of the Pit*. Still, Campbell was presented by Liverpool John Moores University with an Honorary Fellowship for outstanding contribution to literature in 2015. His own website, ramseycampbell.com, continues as a forum for discussion of views on horror fiction.

Keith M. C. O'Sullivan

See also: Aickman, Robert; *Alone with the Horrors;* Blackwood, Algernon; James, M. R.; Leiber, Fritz; Lovecraft, H. P.; Lovecraftian Horror; Psychological Horror.

Further Reading

Birch, Dinah, ed. 2009. *The Oxford Companion to English Literature*. 7th ed. New York: Oxford University Press.

Campbell, Ramsey. 1990. *Needing Ghosts*. Bergvlei, South Africa: Century.

Campbell, Ramsey. 1991. *The Count of Eleven*. London: Macdonald.

Campbell, Ramsey. 2002. *Ramsey Campbell, Probably*. Edited by S. T. Joshi. Hornsea: P. S. Publishing.

Campbell, Ramsey. 2010. *The Seven Days of Cain*. Cincinnati, OH: Samhain Publishing.

Campbell, Ramsey. 2013. *Holes for Faces*. Ashland, OR: Dark Regions Press.

Crawford, Gary William, ed. 2014. *Ramsey Campbell: Critical Essays on the Modern Master of Horror*. Lanham, MD: Scarecrow Press.

Joshi, S. T., ed. 1993. *The Count of Thirty: A Tribute to Ramsey Campbell*. West Warwick, RI: Necronomicon Press.

Joshi, S. T. 2001. *Ramsey Campbell and Modern Horror Fiction*. Liverpool: Liverpool University Press.

An Interview with Ramsey Campbell

October 2016

Campbell shares his thoughts and observations about the long-term arc of horror literature from the 1950s to the early 2000s. In addition, he discusses horror as an intensely personal type of writing, the role of nightmares and nightmarish intrusions and irruptions in horror fiction, and the importance of several notable authors in the field, including, especially, H. P. Lovecraft. He concludes by offering some insights about the central characteristics of horror literature that distinguish it from other types.

Matt Cardin: In 2015 you received the World Fantasy Award for Lifetime Achievement. Your career as a published author spans six decades. From this seasoned vantage point, what are some of the most significant developments in horror fiction that you've seen? What do you regard as some really noteworthy aspects of the field's literary evolution from the mid-twentieth century up to now?

Ramsey Campbell: The 1950s saw some crucial developments. On the one hand, there was the rise of [the] California school of contemporary horror, a group of writers—Ray Bradbury, Richard Matheson, William F. Nolan, Charles Beaumont—who founded their sense of the fantastic in everyday reality and in the experience of characters who might live next door if not in the reader's own house (although urban supernatural horror had come to crucial life some years earlier in Fritz Leiber's "Smoke Ghost," where the mundane environment is no longer invaded by the supernatural but is its source, producing an entity manifested in the kind of suggestive glimpse Leiber learned from M. R. James). Shirley Jackson raised the tale of terror to a new peak of delicate reticence, and not just in *The Haunting of Hill House*. Without these developments I doubt we would have the teeming tapestries of contemporary life that Stephen King creates, drawing also, I think on the traditions of [Edgar Allan] Poe and Mark Twain to convey his highly personal vision. Peter

Straub has shaped his own elegant form, a marriage of mystery fiction and horror. T. E. D. Klein demonstrates how cumulatively powerful allusiveness can be in long narratives, while Dennis Etchison pares his accounts of contemporary darkness down to a starkness reminiscent of [Ernest] Hemingway—whose conciseness influenced Bradbury, of course. Thomas Ligotti's vision is as dark as that of any writer in the field, and perhaps outside it, too, but its sense of the cosmic gives it largeness.

In Britain, the 1950s saw the rise of Robert Aickman, the greatest master of the enigmatic strange tale since Walter de la Mare. In the sixties Thomas Hinde (*The Day the Call Came*, *The Investigator*) developed comedy of paranoia, in which dark humor is inextricably bound up with menace. In the seventies James Herbert based *The Rats* on his own youthful experience and brought a working-class view to the field. In the eighties Clive Barker celebrated the monstrous with his gorgeously gruesome horrors, depicted with a painter's eye. Later British writers—Joel Lane, Gary McMahon, Simon Bestwick, and others—have used horror fiction to scrutinize contemporary experience, often in political terms. And there's a strong female sensibility in the field these days, represented by such varied talents as Nina Allan, Sarah Pinborough, Allison Littlewood, Thana Niveau, Lynda Rucker. . . .

MC: Some of your stories and novels have drawn quite directly on your own personal, painful experiences, "Chimney" being a notable example. All writers draw on personal experience, of course, but your practice of it has been particularly intense at times. Do you think there's something about horror fiction as such that makes it a particularly potent literary vehicle for this?

RC: I wouldn't separate horror from other fiction that digs deep. The first three novels of John Franklin Bardin may be nominally crime fiction, but they have a powerful sense of paranoia, based on the author's years with his schizophrenic mother. For that matter, has any horror novel surpassed Samuel Beckett's *L'Innomable* for unrelenting dread? In my case it isn't so much that I choose horror fiction to convey my experience as that aspects of my life find their way into the fiction, often generating it. That's to say, my love of the genre preceded the themes that have become central to many of my tales—psychological disturbance, the vulnerability of children, the willingness to espouse belief systems that deny the right to question, and so on. I'm sure I would write horror, but my preoccupations shape the kind I write.

MC: Much of your work is characterized by a blurring of boundaries between reality and unreality, wakefulness and dream (or nightmare), and sanity and insanity, with frequent irruptions of the strange, the supernatural, and the uncanny. These are all long-lived tropes in Gothic and horror fiction, as is the basic idea of boundaries being violated or broken. Why should this be? What makes this such a central concern in horror stories?

RC: In my case I must invoke autobiography once more. By the time I was three years old I had to distinguish objective reality from my mother's way of seeing it, and so it's hardly surprising if I often write about misperception and about first sights that prove to be something other. More generally, I'd say that disturbing intrusions—whether from without, in the form of the uncanny or the physical or a combination of both, or from the depths of the mind (repressed terrors, the child who we never really cease to be, both of which may lie dormant)—aren't merely the underlying themes of our field but its core. Surely they're so widespread because they're among the basic human dreads, and in many cases the writers are conveying, however metaphorically, some experience of their own.

MC: From the beginning of your career, you had a literary relationship with H. P. Lovecraft. With his legacy growing ever more prominent even as it grows ever more problematic, how do you regard his place in literature and culture, and in relation to your own work? Can you offer any advice or guidance to those who are perhaps wondering what to make of him and how, or whether, to start reading him?

RC: I take Lovecraft to be the most important single writer of the weird, insofar as he unites the traditions that preceded him on both sides of the Atlantic and builds on their strengths. His *Supernatural Horror in Literature* is not only an appreciation of all that he found best in the genre and a critique of the flaws he saw, but also a statement of his own artistic ambitions. His fiction gives them life. To an extent his reputation is the victim of his most famous creation, the Lovecraft Mythos. It was conceived as an antidote to conventional Victorian occultism—as an attempt to reclaim the imaginative appeal of the unknown—and is only one of many ways his tales suggest worse, or greater, than they show. It is also just one of his means of reaching for a sense of wonder, the aim that produces the visionary horror of his finest work (by no means all of it belonging to the Mythos). His stories represent a search for the perfect form for the weird tale, a process in which he tried out all the forms and all the styles of prose he could. For modulation and orchestration of prose, for the accretion of suggestive detail that builds to awe and terror—in fact, for his exemplary sense of structure—his best work is worthy of the closest study. In my first book I tended to imitate the aspects of his work that seem easiest to replicate, but I've found his example inspiring enough to attempt to scale his heights once more in some recent work. Among the Lovecraft tales I'd recommend to new readers: "The Colour out of Space," "The Call of Cthulhu," "The Rats in the Walls," *The Case of Charles Dexter Ward*, "The Shadow out of Time." All of them convey a sense of powers and presences larger than the prose can quite contain.

MC: What other authors and works would you recommend in general to those who are looking to explore this wing of the literary universe? Which ones strike you as especially important and profound both for this genre and for literature as a whole?

RC: Apart from all those I've already cited, Poe and J. Sheridan Le Fanu both compressed the Gothic mode and intensified its sense of the supernatural and psychological. Algernon Blackwood at his finest ("The Wendigo," "The Willows") conveys real uncanny ecstasy, as Arthur Machen does more insidiously in his masterpiece, "The White People." M. R. James can convey intense spectral terror in a sentence or even a phrase that shows just enough to suggest far worse. William Hope Hodgson is the great master of oceanic terror, while his novels *The House on the Borderland* and *The Night Land* are milestones of cosmic horror.

MC: In the end, what really distinguishes horror from other types of literature? What is its singular, *sui generis*, darkly beating heart?

RC: Horror is the branch of literature most often concerned with going too far. It is the least escapist form of fantasy. It shows us sights we would ordinarily look away from or reminds us of insights we might prefer not to admit we have. It makes us intimate with people we would cross the street to avoid. It shows us the monstrous and perhaps reveals that we are looking in a mirror. It tells us we are right to be afraid, or that we aren't afraid enough. It also frequently embraces, or at least is conterminous with, the ghost story. It flourishes here and there in the fields of science fiction and crime fiction, and not infrequently it bobs up in the mainstream, whatever that is. Despite its name, it is often most concerned to produce awe and terror in its audience, but it is not unusual for a horror story to encompass a wider emotional range. This said, I'd suggest that our field is related to real-life horror both directly, in sometimes (I think increasingly often) seeking to examine it, and metaphorically. But let's not underrate the aesthetic experience of terror: some of the finest work in the field is lyrical. Horror and beauty can be a potent combination.

CARMILLA

Carmilla is a vampire novella written by J. Sheridan Le Fanu (1814–1873). It was originally published serially in the journal *Dark Blue* during 1871–1872 in a version that included illustrations by D. H. Friston (1820–1906). It was then published in its entirety with an additional prologue in Sheridan Le Fanu's *In a Glass Darkly* (1872), which brought together five of Le Fanu's short stories. Le Fanu created the character of Doctor Hesselius, an occult detective, to present *In a Glass Darkly* as a case book of supernatural occurrences. Doctor Hesselius has been

---

The scene in *Carmilla* when the narrator suffers a kind of waking nightmare of being attacked by a large cat demonstrates Le Fanu's skill in delivering an authentic chill to the reader. The narrator, Laura, has a sense of awakening in the dead of night. She sees something moving at the foot of her bed:

> . . . it was a sooty-black animal that resembled a monstrous cat. . . . I felt it spring lightly on the bed. The two broad eyes approached my face, and suddenly I felt a stinging pain as if two large needles darted, an inch or two apart, deep into my breast. I waked with a scream. The room was lighted by the candle that burnt there all through the night, and I saw a female figure standing at the foot of the bed, a little at the right side. It was in a dark loose dress, and its hair was down and covered its shoulders. A block of stone could not have been more still. There was not the slightest stir of respiration. As I stared at it, the figure appeared to have changed its place, and was now nearer the door; then, close to it, the door opened, and it passed out.
>
> I was now relieved, and able to breathe and move. My first thought was that Carmilla had been playing me a trick, and that I had forgotten to secure my door. I hastened to it, and found it locked as usual on the inside. I was afraid to open it—I was horrified. I sprang into my bed and covered my head up in the bed-clothes, and lay there more dead than alive till morning. (Le Fanu 1872, 147–149)

Matt Cardin

Source: Le Fanu, Joseph Sheridan. 1872. *In a Glass Darkly, Volume III*. London: R. Bentley & Son.

identified as the first occult detective in literature. His influence can be seen in pulp horror with characters such as Seabury Quinn's Jules de Grandin.

Carmilla follows Laura and her English father, who live in Styria. Following a carriage accident, they take in a young woman, Carmilla. Laura is entranced by her new friend, recognizing her from a dream she had as a child. After Carmilla's arrival, young women in the village start dying. Laura herself becomes ill and dreams of being attacked by a large cat. Her father takes her to meet an old family friend, General Spielsdorf, whose young daughter has recently died. The general recognizes Carmilla as Millarca the vampire, a descendant of the ancient Karnstein family, who preyed on his daughter. Together with Baron Vordenburg, a vampire expert, the general and Laura's father stake Carmilla/Millarca in her tomb before cutting off her head. Laura recovers.

The relationship between Laura and Carmilla has been categorized by many readers and scholars as a lesbian relationship. During the Victorian period, especially approaching the fin-de-siècle—the late nineteenth-century period in Europe and Britain characterized by a growing sense of cultural exhaustion, pessimism, and fears of societal degeneration and civilizational collapse—there was a growing concern over what was perceived to be sexual abnormality, including homosexuality. Carmilla's choice of prey, young women, suggests that she is a predatory deviant, and the trope of vampirism is used to explore these fears. Carmilla's vampirism is horrifying because it represents an attack on societal codes. Le Fanu's novella may have been influenced by Samuel Taylor Coleridge's lyrical poem "Christabel" (1797), which also features a close friendship between a young woman and a female supernatural creature.

Carmilla falls into the genre of Gothic horror. Like earlier Gothic stories it features an absent mother (Laura's mother is dead), which makes Laura vulnerable to attack. The Styrian landscape is replete with forests, abandoned villages, and a gloomy graveyard in which stands a tomb to the ancient Karnstein family. A foreign setting in mainland Europe is regularly used in early Gothic narratives. The horror elements are seen in Carmilla's attack on innocent young women and her vampiric identity. Laura notices a similarity between Carmilla and a portrait of one of her ancestors, a typical Gothic conceit and a cause for uncanny unease. At the end of the novel Carmilla is discovered lying in a coffin full of blood, adding to the sense of horror.

Although less popular than Bram Stoker's *Dracula* (1897), *Carmilla* influenced Stoker, whose notes show that his novel was originally to have opened in Styria where Jonathan Harker, the protagonist, would meet with a beautiful female vampire. Though Stoker ended up changing the opening setting of his novel to Transylvania, there is a parallel between the character of Baron Vordenburg in Le Fanu's novella and the character of Doctor Van Helsing—another vampire expert—in Stoker's novel. Likewise, Carmilla's ability to transform into a cat to attack Laura is echoed in Dracula's ability to shape-shift. Both Le Fanu and Stoker were Irish, and their vampire stories have been analyzed as engaging with Irish politics and as part of the Irish Gothic tradition.

Carmilla has been adapted for film a number of times. Notable adaptations include Carl Dreyer's *Vampyr* (1932), though the lesbian sexuality was excised, and Roger Vadim's *Blood and Roses* (1960). Le Fanu's vampire heavily influenced the British Hammer Horror film productions of the 1960s and 1970s, including *The Vampire Lovers* (1970), which starred Ingrid Pitt and was the first installment of the Karnstein Trilogy. Most recently the novella has been adapted as a Web series on YouTube also titled *Carmilla* (2014–2015).

Kaja Franck

See also: Le Fanu, J. Sheridan; Vampires.

Further Reading

Auerbach, Nina. 1995. *Our Vampires, Ourselves.* Chicago: University of Chicago Press.
Crawford, Gary William, Jim Rockhill, and Brian J. Showers, eds. 2011. *Reflections in a Glass Darkly: Essays on J. Sheridan Le Fanu.* New York: Hippocampus Press.
Nethercott, Arthur H. 1949. "Coleridge's 'Christabel' and Le Fanu's *Carmilla.*" *Modern Philology* 47: 32–38.
Signorotti, Elizabeth. 1996. "Repossessing the Body: Transgressive Desire in 'Carmilla' and *Dracula.*" *Criticism* 38: 607–632.
Ulin, Julieann. 2013. "Sheridan Le Fanu's Vampires and Ireland's Invited Invasion." In *Open Graves, Open Minds: Representations of Vampires and the Undead from the Enlightenment to the Present Day*, edited by Sam George and Bill Hughes, 39–55. Manchester: Manchester University Press.

CARRION COMFORT

Carrion Comfort is Dan Simmons's second novel, published by Dark Harvest in 1989. In it, Simmons reinvents the concept of vampires by applying the word to characters who gain strength and forestall aging by forcing others, through mind control, to perpetrate acts of violence. The book's title is taken from a Gerard Manley Hopkins sonnet that chronicles the protagonist's struggle with the temptation to yield to despair. In a blurb on the book's cover, Stephen King called Simmons's novel "one of the three greatest horror novels of the 20th century."

The plot centers on three "mind vampires," Nina Drayton, Melanie Fuller, and Willi Borden, who have been playing a game for half a century. They gather annually to award each other points based on the difficulty of individual feats of mind control and on the amount of notoriety each violent incident gains. Rivalries and decades-old animosities spark a power struggle within their group. America becomes the playing field for their conflict, and they turn innocent bystanders into the weapons in their attacks against each other. Only Willi wants to join with and control other mind vampires—powerful gifted individuals who have infiltrated almost every level of American society.

The book's Van Helsing is holocaust survivor Saul Laski, who has been hunting Willi for decades. He enlists the help of Sheriff Bobby Joe Gentry and photographer

Natalie Preston, both of whom have been exposed to the violence arising from the vampires' battles. Gentry is killed halfway through the book, and the remaining human combatants stage an attack on a private island where the elite group meets to play chess with human pieces. They kill all of the vampires except for Melanie, whose thoughts turn to the possibility of controlling a nuclear submarine in the closing pages.

The supernatural creatures in *Carrion Comfort* are considered vampires because the author says they are. They rarely come into direct contact with their victims, and they do not extract anything material from them. Their main driving force is a lust for power rather than hunger, although they do benefit physically from feeding. Simmons uses his unconventional concept of vampires to explore the corrupting influence of nearly limitless power and the effect such power has on those who refuse to be victims of it.

At roughly half a million words, *Carrion Comfort* is an ambitious epic, part horror novel, part thriller, with an enormous cast, multiple viewpoint characters (including Melanie's first-person narrative), and numerous settings.

The opening section of *Carrion Comfort* was published as a novella of the same name in *OMNI* (1983) and collected in *Prayers to Broken Stones*. Mainstream American publishers deemed the book too long, though, so its hardcover release came from a small press. It won August Derleth, Bram Stoker, and British Fantasy awards for Best Novel and found a wider audience in paperback the following year.

Bev Vincent

See also: Bram Stoker Award; Dark Fantasy; Simmons, Dan; Vampires.

Further Reading

Gelder, Ken. 1994. *Reading the Vampire*, 130–133. New York: Routledge.
Simmons, Dan. 2009. "Introduction to the Twentieth Anniversary Edition of *Carrion Comfort*." In *Carrion Comfort*, ix–xxxi. New York: Thomas Dunn Books.

CARROLL, JONATHAN (1949–)

Jonathan Carroll is an American writer (long resident in Vienna, Austria) whose work can be characterized as surrealism or American "magic realism." He tends to write about sophisticated, artistic people, reflecting his background as the son of noted screenwriter Sidney Carroll and Broadway actress and lyricist June Carroll (Sillman). Carroll's stories often establish a realistic, contemporary setting and a convincing narrative voice. Somewhere along the way, the story will get very strange, merely because life *is* strange, without any rational explanation. Carroll has said in an interview that he is not consciously writing in a fantasy or horror tradition (Schweitzer 2013, 38).

His approach is typified by his masterful first novel, *The Land of Laughs* (1980), which is about two people who are great fans of a famous children's book author,

Marshall France. The narrator, Thomas Abbey, hopes to write France's biography. He is invited by the author's daughter to come to France's hometown, live in his house, and do research. But gradually he is bringing France's works and then France himself to life. For about 60 percent of the way through, this is a realistic novel that lovingly conveys a sense of literary worship. But then, startlingly, the fantastic begins to intrude. The book ends as the townspeople go to the train station to greet Marshall France, who is coming back from the dead. The fate of Thomas Abbey and his companion is uncertain, now that he has fulfilled his usefulness to the townspeople, who may well be France's creations as well.

Carroll can achieve similarly sinister effects in his short fiction. In the World Fantasy Award–winning "Friend's Best Man" (1987), a man loses a leg saving his dog from a train. While in the hospital, he befriends a terminally ill young girl. The girl seems to be able to talk to the dog. This seems a charming fancy until, just before her death, the girl warns the man that soon animals will revolt and wipe out humans. There are increasing signs that other things the girl learned from the dog are true, so this may be true as well.

Carroll has written (as of 2016) fifteen novels and two novellas published as separate books. *Bones of the Moon* (1987) takes place within the serial dreams of a woman who is led through them by the spirit of the aborted child she never had. (Dreams are a very important motif in Carroll's work and often a major plot element.) *Sleeping in Flame* (1988) is loosely based on the Rumpelstiltskin story. It is about a writer/actor who begins to develop magical talents. Most of Carroll's novels are about people from the normal, everyday world slipping into strangeness. *The Ghost in Love* (2008) reverses this by starting in the afterlife. There is a certain sameness to some of Carroll's later novels, but this is not a major defect because of their uniformly high quality.

Darrell Schweitzer

See also: Dark Fantasy; Dreams and Nightmares; Surrealism.

Further Reading

Rottensteiner, Franz. 1986. "Jonathan Carroll: The Wonder and the Threat of Existence." *Fantasy Review* 9, no. 11 (December): 10–13.
Schweitzer, Darrell. 2013. "Jonathan Carroll" (an interview). In *Speaking of the Fantastic*, 38–58. Rockville, MD: Wildside Press.
Stableford, Brian. 2003. "Carroll, Jonathan 1949–." In *Supernatural Fiction Writers: Contemporary Fantasy and Horror*, 2nd ed., vol. 1, edited by Richard Bleiler, 201–207. New York: Charles Scribner's Sons.

CARTER, ANGELA (1940-1992)
Angela Carter was an English novelist whose revival of Gothic horror in the early days of second wave feminism exposed complacencies of romance and domestic

relationships, emphasizing the essential performativity, and imposed and internalized imprisonment, of gender roles. Her work won several awards, including the John Llewellyn Rhys prize for *The Magic Toyshop* (1967), the Somerset Maugham award for *Several Perceptions* (1968), and the James Tait Black Memorial Prize for *Nights at the Circus* (1987). Influenced by William Shakespeare, William Butler Yeats, and Charles Dickens, always irreverent, and mixing disturbingly dark, glittering, and bawdy carnivalesque themes with horror, her work grows from and rewrites myths, fairy tales, popular fictions, the Marquis de Sade, and Hollywood movies. It undercuts and exposes their sexually constraining, damaging narratives.

Influenced by Edgar Allan Poe, E. T. A. Hoffmann, and H. P. Lovecraft, Carter was more down to earth than any of these three, using fantasy and humor, finding the terrible and vicious in the everyday, such as in domestic tyranny and incarceration in *The Magic Toyshop,* where a severed hand in a kitchen drawer suggests bondage, and orphaned Melanie is turned into a living puppet playing Leda to puppeteer Uncle Philip's gross, homemade swan, Zeus (as in the Greek myth of Leda and the Swan). This latter event indicts classical art and mythology as patriarchal sadism, while satirizing the vanity and violence of attempts to control women's sexuality and agency, here through the figure of the lumpy, comedic, homemade swan. Carter uncovers the horror latent in the familiar, in domestic servitude (as with Aunt Margaret in *The Magic Toyshop*, silenced by her necklace choker), and in pornographic reification and fetishization of women (as in *Nights at the Circus* with its protagonist Fevvers, a Cockney winged circus aerialist, and her friends in alcoves at Madame Schreck's all-female freak show).

Carter's living dolls fight back, even destroying their puppet masters, so in "The Loves of Lady Purple" (1974), a marionette, "petrification of a universal whore" (Carter 1995, 44), refuses her nightly titillating and punished performance, coming to vengeful life, draining the puppeteer's blood, and stalking off to the village brothel. Carter rewrites romantic fictions of eternal undying love and horror scenarios (which they often resemble). In the reversed vampire myth of "The Lady of the House of Love" (1979), Dracula's descendant mourns her vampire nature, falls in love, and is ultimately betrayed/released by a kiss from a traveling bicyclist on his way to die in the First World War.

Carter's version of the romantic lies and tortuous entrapment of the popular "Bluebeard" tale in "The Bloody Chamber" (1979) links de Sade with feminism, revealing a penniless young wife's sexual desires, a duke's commodification of her as so much meat on a slab, and a warrior mother's rescue of her daughter. In Carter's werewolf tale, "The Company of Wolves" (1979), she empowers Rosaleen, a feisty Little Red Riding Hood, to recognize, come to terms with, and celebrate the beast in herself and the lover in the beast, embracing the werewolf. Technically and linguistically, her work operates at the level of paradox, irony, and the oxymoron, refusing binary gender and power divisions, and the Otherizing of difference. Both in its theme and in its form, Carter's writing blends the everyday with the monstrous. She confronts the gender imbalances in traditional fairy tales, showing conventional horror as patriarchal fabrication based on conservative values to control woman as hag, victim, and whore, her virginity a talisman, her innocence a jewel to own and preserve. Lorna Sage, recognizing Angela Carter for her gendered, politicized Gothic horror as "a witch or wise woman" (1994, 1), says her "fictions prowl around the fringes of the proper English novel like dream monsters—nasty, exotic, brilliant creatures that feed off cultural crisis" (Sage 1977, 51).

A number of Carter's works have been adapted for radio, television, and film. Probably the most prominent among these are *The Magic Toyshop*, adapted to film in 1987 with a screenplay by Carter, and *The Company of Wolves*, directed by Neil Jordan and with a screenplay by Jordan and Carter.

Gina Wisker

See also: Dracula; Hoffmann, E. T. A.; Lovecraft, H. P.; Poe, Edgar Allan; Vampires; Werewolves.

Further Reading

Carter, Angela. 1995. *Burning Your Boats: The Collected Short Stories*. New York: Penguin.

Cavallaro, Dani. 2011. *The World of Angela Carter: A Critical Investigation*. Jefferson, NC, and London: McFarland.

Munford, Rebecca. 2013. *Decadent Daughters and Monstrous Mothers: Angela Carter and European Gothic*. New York: Palgrave Macmillan.

Sage, Lorna, ed. 1994. *Flesh and the Mirror: Essays on the Art of Angela Carter*. London: Virago.

Sage, Lorna. 1977. "The Savage Sideshow: A Profile of Angela Carter." *New Review* 39/40: 51–57.

Wisker, Gina. 1993. "At Home All Was Blood and Feathers: The Werewolf in the Kitchen—Angela Carter and Horror." In *Creepers: British Horror and Fantasy in the Twentieth Century*, edited by Clive Bloom, 161–175. London: Pluto Press.

THE CASE OF CHARLES DEXTER WARD

At 51,000 words, this is H. P. Lovecraft's one true novel, if a short one. It is the most Gothic of his major works, a final exercise in that mode before he turned to more science fictional tales such as *At the Mountains of Madness*. Joseph Curwen, of Salem, moves to Providence, Rhode Island in the late seventeenth century. He establishes himself as a merchant, but attracts undue attention by his failure to age. Even when he marries into a respectable family, he cannot dispel sinister rumors of secret experiments and mysterious cemetery delvings. In 1771, a posse raids Curwen's farm in nearby Pawtuxet, when Curwen, still young and vigorous, should be nearly a century old. What they find is only hinted at. Curwen is killed. As much as possible, all trace of him is erased from the historical record.

In 1918, a teenager, Charles Dexter Ward, discovers that he is Curwen's descendant. Already obsessed with the past, he devotes all his energy (indulged by

Charles Dexter Ward by Any Other Name

The Case of Charles Dexter Ward has been the subject of two well-regarded cinematic adaptations, but neither of them used its title. In the first, director Roger Corman's *The Haunted Palace* (1963), the Lovecraft connection is buried beneath a veneer of Poe; "The Haunted Palace" is the title of an 1839 poem by Poe, and the movie was marketed as "Edgar Allan Poe's *The Haunted Palace*" in order to promote it as another entry in Corman's popular series of Poe adaptations for American International Pictures. But the plot was directly drawn from Lovecraft's short novel (with the screenplay penned by Charles Beaumont), right down to the fact that the film's protagonist is named Charles Dexter Ward. *The Haunted Palace* is widely considered a high point in Lovecraftian cinema.

The second *Charles Dexter Ward* adaptation arrived twenty-eight years later under the title *The Resurrected* (1991), although *The Ancestor* and *Shatterbrain* were alternative titles before its release. Directed by Dan O'Bannon, who was already a known quantity in the horror world for writing *Alien* (1979) and directing *Return of the Living Dead* (1985), the film is dark, frightening, and smart, and is regarded as another high point in Lovecraftian cinema. Despite this, it received only a tiny theatrical release (although a wider one had been planned) and was shunted to video in 1992.

Matt Cardin

wealthy parents) to learning about his ancestor. He finds Curwen's grave, and by replicating certain of Curwen's own techniques, resurrects him from his "essential saltes."

Soon Ward confides to the family physician, Marinus Willett, that his "triumph" has turned into unimaginable horror. Disturbing events ensue, both in Charles's laboratory at home and then at the old Pawtuxet farm. His parents fear for his sanity, but Dr. Willett discovers far worse: that Curwen, who so resembles Ward that one can pass for the other, has murdered Charles and is impersonating him. Willett visits the farm and discovers pits inhabited by malformed horrors, left over from Curwen's original resurrection experiments in the 1700s. He manages to have "Ward" committed to a madhouse, and there confronts him, as Curwen, with what he knows. Curwen attempts magic. Willett counters it and Curwen crumbles into dust. Curwen's original scheme went well beyond cheating death. He and two colleagues, who are still alive in the present, were resurrecting learned men and compelling them to surrender their secrets, working toward some goal that threatened all of humanity, even the universe, if a panicked Charles Ward is to be believed.

This is the one Lovecraft story that rises to the dignity of genuine tragedy, as the noble Dr. Willett strives unsuccessfully to save the innocent Charles from the consequences of his actions. Despite this, Lovecraft apparently thought the work a failure and never made any attempt to have it published even when, in the 1930s, publishers began to ask him for a novel-length work. It was only published posthumously, first abridged in *Weird Tales* in 1941 and then complete in *Beyond the Wall of Sleep* in 1943. It is in a slightly unpolished state, with some loose ends and inconsistencies, but it still contains some of his best writing and is, for Lovecraft, a rare triumph of characterization. It can be read as a story of the "Cthulhu Mythos." Yog-Sothoth is mentioned and invoked for the first time in this tale, but the precise nature of the entities Curwen is trafficking with is never made clear.

Darrell Schweitzer

See also: Ancestral Curse; *At the Mountains of Madness*; Lovecraft, H. P; *The Return*.

Further Reading

Joshi, S. T. 2010. *I Am Providence, The Life and Times of H. P. Lovecraft*, 664–670. New York: Hippocampus Press.

Joshi, S. T. 2014. "*The Case of Charles Dexter Ward.*" In *Lovecraft and a World in Transition: Collected Essays on H. P. Lovecraft*, 393–409. Tampa, FL: University of Tampa Press.

Ward, Richard. 1997. "In Search of the Dread Ancestor: M. R. James' 'Count Magnus' and Lovecraft's *The Case of Charles Dexter Ward*." *Lovecraft Studies* 36: 14–17.

"CASTING THE RUNES"

This short story is one of the best-known works of Montague Rhodes (M. R.) James. It appeared in *More Ghost Stories*, published in 1911, as a follow-up to his first collection, *Ghost Stories of an Antiquary*. With its subtle onset of "quiet horror" that creeps into the everyday and slowly builds in the imagination of the reader, it is a classic Jamesian tale.

"Casting the Runes" tells of a malevolent scholar, Victor Karswell, who takes horrible revenge upon his critics by employing his occult expertise to conjure up an "awful demon creature" that pursues, terrifies, torments, and finally kills its target (James 1992, 142). Another scholar, named Edward Dunning, gives one of Karswell's articles a poor review, setting in motion Karswell's vengeance. Dunning receives a slip of paper from him with runes hidden within its contents. Upon learning that he has been cursed, Dunning, with the help of Henry Harrington, the brother of one of Karswell's previous victims, eventually manages to turn the tables on Karswell by tricking him into taking back the paper, thereby consigning him to the same fate that he has meted out to others—a frightful and mysterious death.

Like other Jamesian monsters, such as Count Magnus's tentacled and hooded accomplice in "Count Magnus" (1904), or the billowing sheet-thing of "Oh, Whistle, and I'll Come to You, My Lad" (1904), the demon that haunts first Harrington and then Dunning, the protagonist of "Runes," is most effective for appearing only partially glimpsed in monstrous fragments, such as the "unnaturally rough and hot" (135) hand that thrusts a pamphlet with the name of Karswell's victim Harrington at Dunning, who cannot afterwards recall the exact appearance of the

---

Night of the Demon: The Too-Explained Supernatural

RKO, the Hollywood studio known for its elegant, sophisticated, and restrained suspense and horror films in the 1940s (which stood in marked contrast to the more garish horror films put out by Universal Studios), would have seemed the perfect studio for adapting James's elegant, sophisticated, and restrained occult horror tale "Casting the Runes." And indeed, more than 95 percent of director Jacques Tourneur and screenwriter Charles Bennett's 1957 adaptation *Night of the Demon* (released in the United States as *Curse of the Demon*) lived up to that expectation (although the film ended up being made and released not by RKO, as that studio had originally hoped, but by Columbia). But the producer balked at Tourneur's and Bennett's plan to retain the ambiguity of James's story by leaving the question of a natural or a supernatural explanation unanswered, and opted instead to show a giant demon clearly and unmistakably existing at the beginning and killing the villainous Karswell at the end, in scenes shot without Tourneur's participation. Notwithstanding the fact that the creature's design drew on demonic imagery from medieval woodcuts and delivered a fairly impressive moment of cinematic-demonological iconography, the final result betrayed the director's, the screenwriter's, and James's visions. *Night/Curse of the Demon* remains one of the most notorious instances of a studio's tampering with a filmmaker's artistic intention.

Matt Cardin

---

pamphleteer. In one of the story's most memorable scenes, Dunning puts his hand under his pillow, only to encounter "a mouth, with teeth, and with hair around it" (137). The demon is also alluded to in the excerpt from the Coleridge poem *Rime of the Ancient Mariner* that appears in the text. Finally, it appears as something stalking the doomed Karswell that is mistaken for a dog by a startled porter. At the story's conclusion, its final appearance is in the unspeakable nightmares that Harrington apparently suffered before dying, which Dunning cannot bear to hear recounted.

"Casting the Runes" has frequently been adapted for television and radio, and was retold most famously in director Jacques Tourneur's classic, atmospheric horror film *Night of the Demon* (1957). An amusing pastiche of this story, which yet retains somewhat of the horrific bite of the original, can be found in James Hynes's *Publish and Perish: Three Tales of Tenure and Terror* (1997), where a young assistant professor, Victoria Dunning, takes on the culture wars in the person of the senior professor Karswell, who plagiarizes her work and curses her for refusing to allow him to do so. Currently director Joe Dante is planning to re-adapt James's story for a new film.

Aalya Ahmad

See also: Devils and Demons; James, M. R.

Further Reading

Cox, Michael. 1987. "Introduction." In *Casting the Runes, and Other Ghost Stories* by M. R. James, xi–xxx. Oxford: Oxford University Press.

Hynes, James. 1997. *Publish and Perish: Three Tales of Tenure and Terror.*

James, M. R. 1992. *Collected Ghost Stories*. Hertfordshire: Wordsworth Editions.

Joshi, S. T. 1990. *The Weird Tale*. Austin: University of Texas Press.

Michalski, Robert. 1996. "The Malice of Inanimate Objects: Exchange in M. R. James's Ghost Stories." *Extrapolation* 37, no. 1: 46–62.

THE CASTLE OF OTRANTO

Written and published by Horace Walpole in 1764, *The Castle of Otranto: A Gothic Story* was an immediate success with the British reading public and established the genre of Gothic fiction as numerous writers in subsequent years were directly influenced to follow its haunted footsteps. Originally presented to the reading public as an actual sixteenth-century Italian manuscript in translation regarding events that occurred during the Crusades, *The Castle of Otranto* later received a second edition where Walpole added the subtitle "A Gothic Story" and claimed ownership of the text, explaining that he had been influenced by Shakespeare to create a new genre of romance by blending both the new and the old.

Focusing on Manfred, the prince of Otranto, *The Castle of Otranto* opens on the wedding day of Conrad, Manfred's son, and Isabella. Conrad, however, is killed by

---

Walpole's novel is striking for the way it almost single-handedly invented an entire genre. Common characteristics of Gothic novels—not to mention the multitude of stories, poems, and movies that have descended from the same source—include:

- A setting in a gloomy castle or mansion
- A plethora of fantastic, strange, and often supernatural-seeming events
- Inflated melodrama accompanied by breathless emotions heightened to a fever pitch
- Lovely, virginal women threatened, menaced, manipulated, and pursued by a dark, powerful, tyrannical king, lord, or other authority figure
- A chase through murky catacombs or hidden passageways in or beneath the castle or mansion
- Disturbing dreams and/or other ominous portents of an ancient curse's or prophecy's imminent fulfillment

These all abound in *The Castle of Otranto*, which synthesized them into a singular form for the very first time, and which, although it is not the greatest of novels in terms of pure literary quality, must therefore be acknowledged as one of the single most influential works of literature ever written.

Matt Cardin

a massive helmet that falls on him from the sky, stunning everyone. In shock over his son's death and fearing the collapse of his bloodline, Manfred decides to divorce his wife Hippolita so that he can marry Isabella instead. Manfred jails a young man named Theodore and pursues Isabella against her will until a priest named Father Jerome appears who tells Manfred that the young maiden is under his protection. Jerome discovers that Theodore is his long-lost son and petitions Manfred not to execute him. Manfred demands that he will release Theodore only if Isabella is turned over to him. Meanwhile, Isabella's father, Frederic, arrives to challenge Manfred's rulership of Otranto. Eventually, after a series of supernatural occurrences that culminate with Manfred's accidental murder of his daughter Matilda, it is revealed that Manfred's line is illegitimate and Theodore is actually the true heir to Otranto. The young man marries Isabella, with Manfred retiring to a convent to atone for his sins.

At the center of *The Castle of Otranto*'s narrative is its concern with legitimacy. The text explains that Manfred's line has ruled for three generations, starting with his grandfather and continuing to the present day. The ruler previous to Manfred's grandfather was Alfonso, a man who is spoken of as having been kind and just. As the novel opens and introduces the reader to Manfred's family, the narrator notes a cryptic prophecy that will result in the end of Manfred's line when the ruler becomes too large to inhabit his castle. As the narrative progresses, strange supernatural events take place that involve giant pieces of armor, the first being the helmet that crushes Conrad. When Theodore is shown as Alfonso's heir, and thus the true lord of Otranto, it is also revealed that Manfred's grandfather had committed murder and forgery to take control of Otranto. The supernatural powers at play in the text, while horrific at times, are divine in nature and act to restore the legitimate order, casting aside the usurping force of Manfred's family in favor of Theodore's authentic bloodline.

Almost the entirety of Walpole's text can be looked at in terms of legitimacy. It was composed in a mock-castle that appeared ancient but was actually quite modern (Walpole's famous Strawberry Hill House). When first published, its author declared it to be a medieval work from the Crusades in translation. Neither Walpole's castle at Strawberry Hill nor the text's origins as a medieval work are authentic. Likewise, the plot's focus on one group of aristocrats who are illegitimate compared to another group who are legitimate raises questions as to Walpole's intent. Prior to the elevation of Walpole's father as prime minister in 1721, the family had been well-off country gentry. By the time of *The Castle of Otranto*'s publication in 1764, the family's wealth had put it on the level of some of the most lucrative dukedoms in the nation. The circumstance of being aristocratic in terms of power and influence but not in blood is something Walpole would certainly have been aware of, and this concern seems to have psychologically manifested in his Gothic novel.

In the two and a half centuries since its first publication, *The Castle of Otranto* has continued to have an impact on the horror genre. Not only was it the first

Gothic novel, but numerous tropes, such as the uncanny portrait, weeping statues, and haunted castle, originated with Walpole's novel and are now considered commonplace. Indeed, the use of the haunted castle, which over time has been expanded on to include locations such as houses, forests, ships, schools, and even dreamscapes, is probably the most important contribution *The Castle of Otranto* has made to the modern horror genre that would be instantly recognizable by anyone who has ever seen a scary movie or read a work of Gothic fiction.

The Castle of Otranto directly inspired other writers, such as Clara Reeve, who wrote the second Gothic novel, *The Old English Baron* (1777/1778), to try their hand at this new species of romance, which continues to thrive in the present day. Other writers such as Ann Radcliffe, Edgar Allan Poe, H. P. Lovecraft, and Stephen King have all acknowledged *The Castle of Otranto's* significance in their own discussions of the horror genre. While it is true that several scenes in *The Castle of Otranto* could be considered laughable by today's horror standards, such as the gargantuan-sized helmet that falls from the sky and crushes a man to death, this is nonetheless a work that has rightfully earned its place as historically important and should be read at least once by anyone who studies the horror genre.

Joel T. Terranova

See also: Ancestral Curse; Byronic Hero; Gothic Hero/Villain; The Haunted House or Castle; Radcliffe, Ann; Walpole, Horace.

Further Reading

Clemens, Valdine. 1999. *The Return of the Repressed: Gothic Horror from Castle of Otranto to Alien*. New York: State University of New York Press.

Clery, E. J. 1995. *The Rise of Supernatural Fiction 1762–1800*. Cambridge: Cambridge University Press.

Ellis, Markman. 2000. *The History of Gothic Fiction*. Edinburgh: Edinburgh University Press.

Mack, Ruth. 2008. "Horace Walpole and the Objects of Literary History." *ELH* 75 (2): 367–387.

Rumore, Michael Angelo. 2016. "The Terror of Translation: Ruins of the *Translatio* in *The Castle of Otranto* and *Vathek*." *Studies in the Fantastic* 3: 3–22.

THE CEREMONIES

T. E. D. Klein has been described as "one of the twentieth-century masters of the horror genre" (Mariconda 1986, 28) despite the fact that he has written very little in this field. His fame stems primarily from his singular novel, *The Ceremonies* (1984), and his collection of short stories in *Dark Gods* (1985)—both of which have been widely regarded as modern classics.

The Ceremonies is based on a 1971 short story by Klein entitled "The Events at Poroth Farm." Over several years, Klein developed this much more simplistic tale into a 600-page novel, which is now the classic that we have today. *The Ceremonies*

A Stealth Course in Literary Horror History

The Ceremonies not only stands as an effective (and momentous) horror novel in its own right, but it also offers the reader what amounts to a mini-course in the history of weird, Gothic, and supernatural horror literature. In making Jeremy, the protagonist, a graduate student and college instructor who is preparing to write his dissertation on Gothic and weird literature, Klein creates a narrative vehicle for conveying reflections on many classic texts, presented as entries in Jeremy's journal. These encompass the likes of Walpole's *The Castle of Otranto*, Radcliffe's *The Mysteries of Udolpho*, Lewis's *The Monk*, Maturin's *Melmoth the Wanderer*, Stoker's *Dracula*, Le Fanu's *Carmilla* and "Green Tea," Blackwood's "Ancient Sorceries," Jane Austen's *Northanger Abbey*, Robert W. Chambers's *The King in Yellow*, H. P. Lovecraft's *Supernatural Horror in Literature*, and Arthur Machen's "The White People." These same works—especially the last—also form a thematic background to the cosmic horror at the center of Klein's novel.

Matt Cardin

---

is a thoroughly layered and richly textured work, but its essential narrative elements are as follows. The story centers on a young academic named Jeremy Friers, who visits an isolated community on the edge of the forests outside of New York, in order to pursue an extensive reading list in Gothic studies. Here, in the fictional and devoutly religious setting of Gilead, New Jersey, he stays with a married couple named Deborah and Sarr Poroth, who are part of a vaguely Amish-like religious sect called the Brethren of the Redeemer. He stays in a small cabin at the edge of their garden, immediately beside the woods, in a situation that is, interestingly, very similar to Henry David Thoreau's when writing *Walden* (1854). Jeremy is later visited there by his girlfriend Carol, who is meanwhile employed back in New York City by a man named Rosie (or Rosebottom), who has her researching the darkest origins of people's everyday games and rituals. It transpires that Rosie is in league with mysterious forces in the woods and requires both Jeremy and Carol for an elaborate series of ceremonies. His ultimate aim is to sacrifice this couple in the woods, as this will result in the awakening of a primordial monster that resides, hidden, inside Earth itself. The Poroths become possessed and ultimately killed by the evil forces at hand, but Jeremy and Carol survive their tribulations. The final sacrifice is interrupted just in time, and so the monster slumbers on, temporarily undisturbed. Its presence, however, undercuts this happy end; with the novel's final imagery, there is a tangible sense of the chaos and horror that dwells just beneath human existence.

The novel has been described as a "monumental tribute" (Joshi 1990, 235) to the works of Arthur Machen, and especially to his short story "The White People" (1904), which tells the tale of a young girl's mysterious interactions with her surrounding countryside. Machen's story is famed for its portentous vagueness—a style that is very much emulated throughout the majority of *The Ceremonies*. Klein directly lifts and uses elements of Machen's tale: for example, the narrator of the Green Book (the diary featured in "The White People") refers mysteriously to "the ceremonies" and to something called the "dôl" (Machen 2006, 119)—inspirations, surely, not only for the novel's title, but for its monstrous entity, "the Dhol." In another of his infamous and highly mysterious works, "The Great God Pan" (1890), Machen talks ominously of what he terms "that awful secret of the wood" (106). Though he never reveals what exactly this "awful secret" is, in *The Ceremonies* it seems to have been taken as Klein's central subject, as the vast mysteries of the woodland haunt the novel throughout and are only somewhat revealed at its very end. Klein explicitly draws on the horrors of Machen when he has Jeremy eventually wonder, in horror, "what if Machen told the truth?" (484).

Klein's love and knowledge of Gothic literature extend well beyond the works of Machen and are vividly represented throughout *The Ceremonies*. The protagonist, Jeremy, is not only a scholar of literature, but of Gothic literature specifically. Throughout his time in Gilead, he is slowly working his way through an extensive collection of horror classics, and his reactions to each of these are recorded in detail. There are several instances in which Jeremy's own experiences mirror the texts he reads—for example, when journeying into the wilderness of Gilead, he is reading about Jonathan Harker's entering the woods of Transylvania (*Dracula*, 1897), and later, when one of the animals on the farm is possessed, he is reading about the demonic monkey in Le Fanu's short story "Green Tea" (1872). There is thus a rich intertextuality throughout *The Ceremonies*, which firmly underlines Klein's assertion that horror literature is—or should be—"a tradition-conscious genre" (Tibbetts 2011, 51).

There are many reasons why *The Ceremonies* is seen as a modern horror "classic." In addition to its use of intertextuality, it harbors many traditional elements of the Gothic, including possession, murder, and ultimately a monster. However, what may be most central to making the novel so utterly memorable is its haunting use of ambience. Early on, Klein has Jeremy muse on the main features of the Gothic, and he concludes that the notion of "setting *as* character" is the most "promising" of all (16). Certainly, this idea is successfully explored throughout *The Ceremonies*. Nature itself is an ominous presence from the outset, and as the novel progresses, it seems almost to become a malicious entity. The novel plays, most effectively, on our contradictory notions about the natural world: Gilead is, on the one hand, an idyllic retreat from modern urbanity, but on the other hand, it embodies the unknown and is a monstrous wilderness. Though Jeremy initially views the farm as a blissful retreat, he soon has the overwhelming sense that "*it isn't right to build so close to the woods*" (26). He begins to think in terms of "man vs. nature" and to fear this unknown environment around him. This setting conceals a wealth of mysteries, secrets, and untold dangers. This is, in the one sense, wholly exciting: in the words of Jeremy, it is "exhilarating" to see evidence of "modern superstition" (265). However, when he eventually learns of the horrors that lie hidden inside nature, he is extremely disturbed.

The Ceremonies is a truly terrifying tale that warns of humankind's naïveté in thinking they have evolved beyond outmoded superstitions. In it, Klein creates a rich and detailed world, which is both seductive and terrifying. It is little wonder, therefore, that this is a text to which fans return again and again—and one that has made such an indelible mark in the history of horror literature.

Elizabeth Parker

See also: *Dark Gods*; "The Great God Pan"; Klein, T. E. D.; Machen, Arthur; "The White People."

Further Reading

Joshi, S. T. 1990. *The Weird Tale*. Holicong, PA: Wildside Press.

Klein, T. E. D. 1984. *The Ceremonies*. New York: Viking Press.

Machen, Arthur. 2006. *Tales of Horror and the Supernatural*. Leyburn: Tartarus Press.

Mariconda, Steven J. 1986. "The Hints and Portents of T. E. D. Klein." *Studies in Weird Fiction*, Vol. 1 (Summer), 19–28.

Tibbetts, John C. 2011. "Certain Things Associated with the Night: T. E. D. Klein." In *The Gothic Imagination: Conversations on Fantasy, Horror, and Science Fiction in the Media*, 51–54. New York: Palgrave Macmillan.

CHAMBERS, ROBERT W. (1865–1933)

Robert William Chambers was a best-selling American novelist and short story writer who occasionally wrote horror fiction, including the classic work *The King in Yellow* (1895). Born in Brooklyn, New York, in 1865, he studied art in Paris for seven years and initially became a magazine illustrator. He wrote a collection about Parisian life called *In the Quarter* (1894), but his second book, *The King in Yellow*, was the first to become highly successful. In addition to several more Parisian sketches, it contained five supernatural stories, and its success caused him to turn from illustration to writing. He wrote a few other early collections containing weird fiction, but he soon became more famous for his prolific output of commercial historical romances and society novels that earned him the nickname "the Shopgirl Scheherazade." He died in 1933.

Chambers was skilled at creating an eerie atmosphere in his weird fiction, and he often employed occultist themes and sometimes out-of-context folkloric elements. The imaginative visual imagery in his work reflects his artistic background. His love of the outdoors, hunting and fishing, butterflies, and Asian antiquities often surface in his fiction as well.

In *The Maker of Moons* (1896), the titular story involves a Chinese sorcerer who is creating artificial gold near the Canadian border. The story involves a repellent creature called a Xin and headless Yeth hounds from Welsh folklore. However, the other fantasy stories in the collection are either light in tone or comical. *The Mystery of Choice* (1897), his second best collection, contains two groups of thematically related fantasies, involving revenants, death, white shadows, and strange dreamlike fugue states, and has fallen into undeserved obscurity. *In Search of the Unknown* (1904) is comprised of mostly humorous science fiction stories about a zoologist hunting for strange animals. But the first story in the book, "The Harbour Master," features an amphibious humanoid creature that anticipates the gill-man from the classic 1941 Universal horror film *The Creature from the Black Lagoon* and may have been an influence on H. P. Lovecraft's story "The Shadow over Innsmouth." In *The Tree of Heaven* (1907), a mystic in the first story predicts the events of the following tales, many of which contain supernatural elements. Years later, Chambers returned to the horror genre with *The Slayer of Souls* (1920), which expands on the framework of "The Maker of Moons" and concerns a cult of sorcerers out to cause worldwide political discontent, and a psychic woman who is out to destroy them; and *The Talkers* (1923), about a hypnotist who tampers with a woman's soul for his own ends.

In his own day Chambers was a celebrity who wrote to entertain. Today he is remembered chiefly for his contributions to horror fiction, particularly *The King in Yellow*. He died in December 1933 following surgery for an intestinal ailment.

Lee Weinstein

See also: *The King in Yellow*; Lovecraft, H. P.; Lovecraftian Horror.

Further Reading

Lovett-Graff, Bennett. 1999. "Robert W. Chambers." In *Nineteenth-Century American Fiction Writers*, edited by Kent P. Ljungquist, 69–75. *Dictionary of Literary Biography*, vol. 202. Detroit: Gale.

Weinstein, Lee. 1985. "Robert W. Chambers." In *Supernatural Fiction Writers*, edited by E. F. Bleiler, 739–745. New York: Charles Scribner's Sons.

CHARNAS, SUZY MCKEE (1939–)

Suzy McKee Charnas is an acclaimed fantasy and science fiction author, best known in horror for her vampire fictions, which include the award-winning novel *The Vampire Tapestry* (1981). Apart from vampire stories, Charnas has also produced work inspired by other horror icons, several of which were collected in *The Music of the Night* (2001). Her darkly funny werewolf story, "Boobs," won the 1989 Hugo Award for Best Short Story and has appeared in many anthologies. Poe's "Masque of the Red Death" inspired Charnas's apocalyptic horror story "Lowland Sea" (2009), and *The Phantom of the Opera* inspired her "Beauty and the Opéra or The Phantom Beast" (1996), a finalist for both the Hugo (Best Novelette) and the James Tiptree Literary Awards in 1997.

Charnas is also renowned for her groundbreaking feminist science fiction series, the Holdfast Chronicles, which includes seven novels, beginning with *Walk to the End of the World* (1974) and concluding with *The Conqueror's Child* (1999). In 2003, the Holdfast series, along with Ursula K. Le Guin's *Left Hand of Darkness*, was inducted into the Gaylactic Spectrum Hall of Fame, which recognizes significant positive gay, lesbian, bisexual, or transgender content in North American work published prior to 1998. Charnas has also been a finalist and recipient of the James Tiptree Jr. Award, winning retrospectively in 1994 for *Motherlines* and *Walk to the End of the World*, and in 2000 for *The Conqueror's Child*. In 1994, Charnas also won the Mythopoeic Fantasy Award for Children's Literature for *The Kingdom of Kevin Malone*.

Born on October 22, 1939, Charnas enjoyed a privileged education among the children of wealthy Manhattanites, but as a young woman, she spent two formative years in Nigeria working for the Peace Corps, which radically altered her perspective: "Teaching in Nigeria taught me much that American Education [*sic*] had falsified, misunderstood, or denied outright about human beings, culture, economics, history, and the world in general, and in the process did what the Peace Corps is, to my mind, supp[os]ed to do: it made me permanently marginal to my home culture" (Charnas 2011).

Charnas describes her speculative fiction as operating in the "sociological and anthropological," rather than the "technological" mode, where "smart white guys doing imaginary techno speak at each other" (Gordon 1999, 451–454). The central protagonists of her fictions tend to be women of all ages, often in subjected states, and children. Her writing is imbued with a strong eco-feminist political consciousness. For example, her werewolf story "Boobs" traces the adolescent development of young Kelsey's body and its sudden vulnerability to sexual violence and objectification. The onset of Kelsey's menstruation coincides with the onset of her lycanthropy. A decade later, this was the plot of the cult horror film *Ginger Snaps* (2000, dir. John Fawcett). Learning to love her powerful werewolf body, Kelsey avenges herself upon the boy who assaults her by devouring him without remorse.

The Vampire Tapestry is a collection of five separately published novellas that, read together, weave the tale of the charismatic, alluring predator Dr. Weyland, mostly through the eyes of various humans who encounter him. For much of the novel, Charnas preserves ambiguity, causing the reader at first to doubt that Weyland is really a vampire and then to discover he is more of a science fiction creature than a traditional romantic vampire. Weyland appears first in "The Ancient Mind at Work" as a distinguished anthropology professor at a small college who uses his sleep research to batten upon students, but housekeeper Katje de Groot, a no-nonsense Boer from South Africa, realizes he is a vampire and, after he attacks her, shoots and critically wounds him. In "The Land of Lost Content," the wounded Weyland turns up as a prisoner held by the unsavory Roger and his Satanist associate Alan Reese. Roger orders his young nephew Mark to tend to the captive, while he and Reese exploit Weyland, but Mark eventually rebels and frees the vampire. Attempting to get himself reinstated at his college, Weyland next appears in "The Unicorn Tapestry," seeking psychotherapy with Dr. Floria Landauer.

Fascinated by her patient's vampire "delusion," Floria wears down Weyland's carefully constructed barriers against intimacy with the humans he regards as his prey. Weyland is then found in Charnas's home state, New Mexico, attending *Tosca* ("A Musical Interlude"), during which, affected by his recent experiences and the splendor of the music, he loses control and kills a performer. "The Last of Dr. Weyland" wraps up the novel with Weyland, transformed by his encounters and menaced by discovery, entering a lengthy period of hibernation.

The Vampire Tapestry was shortlisted for both World Fantasy and Nebula awards in 1981. "The Unicorn Tapestry" won the 1980 Nebula Award for Best Novella and has since been adapted by Charnas into the play *Vampire Dreams*. Along with "The Ancient Mind at Work," this chapter also won the Spanish Gigamesh Award upon its translated publication in 1990.

Aalya Ahmad

See also: "The Masque of the Red Death"; Monsters; Poe, Edgar Allan; Vampires; Werewolves.

Further Reading

Charnas, Suzy McKee. 1997. "Meditations in Red: On Writing *The Vampire Tapestry*." In *Blood Read: The Vampire as Metaphor in Contemporary Culture*, edited by Joan Gordon and Veronica Hollinger, 59–67. Philadelphia: University of Pennsylvania Press.

Cranny-Francis, Anne. 1990. "De-Fanging the Vampire: S. M. Charnas's *The Vampire Tapestry* as Subversive Horror Fiction." In *American Horror Fiction: From Brockden Brown to Stephen King*, edited by Brian Docherty, 155–175. New York: St. Martin's.

Davis, Kathy S. 2002. "'Beauty in the Beast: The 'Feminization' of Weyland in *The Vampire Tapestry*." *Extrapolation* 43, no. 1: 62.

Gordon, Joan, and Suzy McKee Charnas. 1999. "Closed Systems Kill: An Interview with Suzy McKee Charnas." *Science Fiction Studies* 26, no. 3: 447–468.

"THE CHIMNEY"

"The Chimney" is a story by Ramsey Campbell, written in 1975, first published in the anthology *Whispers*, edited by Stuart David Schiff (Doubleday, 1977), and reprinted in Campbell's story collections *Dark Companions* (1982), *Dark Feasts* (1987), and *Alone with the Horrors* (1993). One of the most gripping and personal of Campbell's stories, it is the first-person account of a man (who never identifies himself, not even by his first name) who reflects on some traumatic events that occurred when he was twelve years old. As a boy he was plagued with fears—fears of the dark, and especially fears of his own upstairs bedroom—that caused his parents to be ashamed of him. The boy's father is particularly harsh, chastising his wife for coddling the boy. As Christmas approaches, the boy's terror focuses on the chimney in his room, and he remembers when, years before, he watched a television show about "two children asleep in bed, an enormous crimson man emerging from the fireplace, creeping towards them" (Campbell 2004, 156). The boy is petrified, but his mother tries to reassure him that it is only Father Christmas: "He always comes out of the chimney" (157). The boy's fears have only increased since that time, and he now insists on a fire being lit in the chimney in his room. Then, on Christmas Eve, he hears and then sees some red-costumed figure coming down the chimney—it looks as if it is charred. It turns out to be the boy's father, dressed up as Father Christmas. Years later the boy's father dies in a fire in his house: when the boy sees the burned body, he realizes that he saw a vision of it on that Christmas Eve years before.

The story is a twisted version of the strange upbringing Campbell himself endured. Shortly after his birth in 1946, his Catholic parents became estranged; but because divorce was difficult, they devised a living arrangement whereby Campbell's father remained upstairs in their house in Liverpool and had no contact with Campbell or his mother, who occupied the downstairs rooms. As Campbell testifies in a searing document, "At the Back of My Mind: A Guided Tour," "For most of my childhood . . . my father was heard but not seen. . . . I used to hear his footsteps on the stairs as I lay in bed, terrified that he would come into my room. . . . Worst of all was Christmas, when my mother would send me to knock on his bedroom door and invite him down, as a mark of seasonal goodwill, for Christmas dinner. I would go upstairs in a panic, but there was never any response" (Campbell 2011). Campbell has fused this painful episode in his early life with the British tradition of "Father Christmas" to produce an imperishable tale of domestic conflict and existential terror. "The Chimney" remains among Campbell's most celebrated and widely anthologized stories.

S. T. Joshi

See also: Campbell, Ramsey; Psychological Horror.

Further Reading

Campbell, Ramsey. [1993] 2004. "The Chimney." In *Alone with the Horrors: The Great Short Fiction of Ramsey Campbell, 1961–1991*, 153–167. New York: Tor.

Campbell, Ramsey. [1983] 2011. "At the Back of My Mind: A Guided Tour." In *The Face That Must Die*. Kindle Edition. Necon E-Books.

CISCO, MICHAEL (1970–)

American writer Michael Cisco is among the most influential, erudite, and ambitiously experimental voices in twenty-first-century weird fiction and horror. Cisco's large body of work encompasses novelistic and long-form fiction, short fiction, translations (including work by Julio Cortazar and Marcel Béalu), and theoretical and critical essays, and he often intermingles these forms to unsettling effect. Cisco's first novel, *The Divinity Student* (1999), won the International Horror Guild Award for Best First Novel for that year, and his 2011 novel *The Great Lover* was named Best Weird Novel of the year by the *Weird Fiction Review* and nominated for the Shirley Jackson Award for Best Novel of the Year.

While, like most of Cisco's fiction, *The Divinity Student* plays vertiginously with language, it is probably the closest of his novels to traditional supernatural horror and parallel-world fantasy. Drawing on Judaic, Christian, and neo-Platonic philosophy, it unfolds in a crumbling urban landscape teeming with sinister beings and governed by dreamlike physical laws. Combining bleak horror and deep amazement, merging *Bildungsroman* (a story of someone's formative education) and fable, it presents the education, death, resurrection, and strange second life of an eponymous protagonist, who embodies aspects of both the scientist and the monster of Mary Shelley's *Frankenstein*. This hybridization of the doctor with his creation serves as an apt metaphor for Cisco's authorial identity and ever-mutating writing. He even describes his literary approach in mad scientist terms, as experimenting in order "to create living monsters that will go out into the world and wreak havoc on readers" (Mills 2013). His other novels and long-form fictions, including *The Tyrant* (2003), *The Narrator* (2010), *Member* (2013), and *Animal Money* (2015), continue to combine linguistic and narrative experimentation with atmospheric horror, absurdist humor, and an exploration of alienation in many fabulous forms.

This is also true of his short fiction, which can be found in numerous anthologies, including *The Thackery T. Lambshead Pocket Guide to Eccentric & Discredited Diseases*, *Leviathan III* and *IV*, *Album Zutique*, *Grimscribe's Puppets*, and *Aickman's Heirs*. A selection from his novella *The Genius of Assassins* was included in the VanderMeers' influential omnibus, *The Weird*, and many of his earlier short stories are included in the collection *Secret Hours* (2007).

While it often incorporates horrific imagery and transfigures conventions of the horror genre, Cisco's work, like Caitlín R. Kiernan's, evades easy classification. He has described it as "de-genred" fiction, stating, "I don't negate or deny genres but to me they're like a spice rack, to be thrown together entirely along the lines of taste" (Moreland 2013). Cisco's work draws on and transfigures writing by a vast array of influences, some of the more important being Edgar Allan Poe, Franz Kafka, J. R. R. Tolkien, H. P. Lovecraft, Samuel Beckett, William S. Burroughs, Thomas Bernhard, Thomas Ligotti, and Robert Aickman. While Cisco sees pastiche as central to his literary approach, the results of his incisive engagements with other writers are often startlingly original, creating powerfully affecting, philosophically rich, and deeply troubling narratives. There is therefore ample reason to take Jeff VanderMeer's characterization of Cisco as "The American Kafka" seriously, for, in VanderMeer's words, Cisco "has forged a singular path in creating visionary, phantasmagorical settings, uniquely alienated anti-heroes, and genuinely creepy happenings—while also exhibiting a healthy absurdism and dark sense of humor" (VanderMeer 2015).

Sean Moreland

See also: Aickman, Robert; Kafka, Franz; Kiernan, Caitlín R.; Ligotti, Thomas; Lovecraft, H. P.; Poe, Edgar Allan; Smith, Clark Ashton; Surrealism; VanderMeer, Jeff.

Further Reading

Mills, Adam. 2013. "Interview with Michael Cisco." *Weird Fiction Review*, October 15. http://weirdfictionreview.com/2013/10/interview-with-michael-cisco.

Moreland, Sean. 2013. "An Interview with Michael Cisco." *Postscripts to Darkness*, November 22. https://pstdarkness.com/2013/11/22/an-interview-with-michael-cisco.

VanderMeer, Jeff. 2015. "American Kafka? The Weird, Uncanny Work of Michael Cisco." *Literary Hub*, May 27. http://lithub.com/american-kafka.

VanderMeer, Ann, and Jeff VanderMeer. 2012. "The Weird: An Introduction." In *The Weird*, edited by Ann and Jeff VanderMeer, xv–xx. New York: Tor.

COLERIDGE, SAMUEL TAYLOR (1772–1834)

Samuel Taylor Coleridge, by means of his practice as a poet as well as his lectures and publications in philosophy and literary criticism, became one of the prime movers of the English Romantic movement (ca. 1798–1832), in collaboration with his more prolific but less gifted collaborator William Wordsworth. His introduction to England of the ideas of German idealism, which had helped to guide the German literature of *sturm und drang* (storm and stress) and provided an important element of Gothic fiction, provided a similar impetus to the more sophisticated practitioners of the English movement, where they blended well with the inspiration of Byronism. His earlier friendship with the poet Robert Southey—the two of them married the sisters Sarah and Edith Fricker in 1795—caused them to make plans to found a utopian community in America under the guidance of a philosophy they called Pantisocracy, but the practical organization proved too much for them. His contributions to literary theory included the popularization of the requirement to seduce the reader's "willing suspension of disbelief" in order to underpin fantastic materials.

Coleridge suffered throughout his life from poor health, complicated by mental problems difficult to diagnose retrospectively, for both of which he made extensive use of laudanum as a palliative. As with Thomas De Quincey, the hallucinations produced by the laudanum became an important source of raw material for his literary work, especially its horrific aspects. The composition of "Kubla Khan" under that influence was famously interrupted, and he also failed to finish the equally phantasmagorical "Christabel," the first account in English of a perversely eroticized female vampire, both of which were belatedly published in 1816. The longest and most spectacular of his opium-fueled visions, however, "The Rime of the Ancient Mariner," the first version of which was published in the first edition of *Lyrical Ballads* (1798), was and remains his masterpiece; its vision of the horrific experiences of a mariner in unknown Antarctic waters, having been cursed after killing an albatross, was enormously influential on the imagery of subsequent

In Coleridge's *The Rime of the Ancient Mariner*, the eponymous narrator's account of a doomed Antarctic voyage includes many frightful moments of nightmarish dread, as when the sailors, stranded and drifting because of the narrator's sinful killing of an albatross, encounter a ghostly ship carrying two terrible presences:

> Are those her ribs through which the Sun
> Did peer, as through a grate?
> And is that Woman all her crew?
> Is that a Death? and are there two?
> Is Death that woman's mate?
>
> Her lips were red, her looks were free,
> Her locks were yellow as gold:
> Her skin was as white as leprosy,
> The Night-mare Life-in-Death was she,
> Who thicks man's blood with cold. (Coleridge 1845, 62)

The two, Death and Life-in-Death, are gambling for the sailors' fates:

> The naked hulk alongside came,
> And the twain were casting dice;
> "The game is done! I've won! I've won!"
> Quoth she, and whistles thrice. (62)

The nightmarish Life-in-Death's whistle causes the sun to sink and the stars to come out, along with a "horned moon, with one bright star / within the nether tip." Then the terrible outcome of the game becomes clear as the narrator's fellow sailors turn to look at him:

> One after one, by the star-dogged Moon,
> Too quick for groan or sigh,
> Each turned his face with a ghastly pang,
> And cursed me with his eye.
>
> Four times fifty living men,
> (And I heard nor sigh nor groan)
> With heavy thump, a lifeless lump,
> They dropped down one by one. (62)

The sailors' souls fly from their bodies, headed "to bliss or woe," and the narrator himself is left to suffer the dreadful fate of remaining in living death, completely alone.

Matt Cardin

Source: Coleridge, Samuel Taylor. 1845. *The Works of Samuel Taylor Coleridge, Prose and Verse.* Philadelphia: Thomas, Cowperthwait & Co.

marine horror stories and became a frequent reference point for subsequent writers of fantastic fiction, from Mary Shelley to William S. Burroughs and Douglas Adams. Coleridge added "glosses" to later versions that add to the intrinsic doubts as to the hallucinatory narrative's reality, occasioned by the fact that it is insistently told to a bewildered "wedding-guest."

Coleridge continued writing doggedly during the 1820s, when he was living in Highgate with the family of his physician James Gillman, mostly working on a synthesis of his philosophical explorations that he called his "opus maximus." He failed to complete it, although Gillman's house became a place of pilgrimage in the meantime for his many literary disciples.

Brian Stableford

See also: Dreams and Nightmares; Romanticism and Dark Romanticism; Unreliable Narrator.

Further Reading

Gardner, Martin. 1974. *The Annotated Ancient Mariner*. New York: New American Library.
Keane, Patrick J. 1994. *Submerged Politics: The Ancient Mariner and Robinson Crusoe*. Columbia: University of Missouri Press.

COLLIER, JOHN (1901–1980)

John Henry Noyes Collier was an English writer, poet, and screenwriter. Assessing him is difficult, for he was a writer of many parts, some of them seemingly contradictory. The best of his stories reveal him as intensely literate, a superbly gifted miniaturist, a fine satirist, adept at fantasy as well as mainstream literature, and remarkably mischievous if not at times outright cruel and misanthropic about his characters. Although there are horrific situations in his novel *Tom's A-Cold* (1933), an early postcivilization novel, it was in Collier's short stories that his talents had their best showcase, for like such earlier writers as Saki, Collier could present horrific situations and outcomes lightly and even elliptically: the murderously scheming protagonist in "Another American Tragedy" (1940) thus gets to see himself unpacked "like a Gladstone bag," whereas the vainly lecherous protagonist of "The Bottle Party" (1939), imprisoned by a jinn, finds his bottle purchased by some sailors who "used him with the utmost barbarity." "Green Thoughts" (1931) not only transforms characters into sentient plants but concludes with a horrible play on words involving the idea of cutting off somebody.

In Collier's world, love is often shown to be no protection and no solution: the narrator of "Evening Primrose" (1940) conceals himself in a department store and discovers it is inhabited by malign wraith-like beings, and though he falls in love with the girl they use as their servant, happiness is not theirs. Horrible is Maria Beasley of "Incident on a Lake" (1941), for she is "prepared to endure Hell herself if she could deprive her husband of a little of his heaven" (Collier 2003, 113), but her scheming undoes her, as it does the banal and vulgar Alice and Irwin of "Over Insurance" (1951), who insure each other and have similar ideas about expediting the collection process. Assaults on stability and happiness can come from all directions, including a droopy old parrot of "Bird of Prey" (1941), whose repetitions reveal secrets and awaken psychological horrors, but whose real secret is terrifying and reveals the vulnerability of relationships. Demons and devils may be lightly presented, as in "After the Ball" (1933), "The Devil, George, and Rosie" (1934), and "Fallen Star" (1951), among others, but there is at the stories' core the threat of perpetual damnation and, in the latter two, rape, however amusing and distracting a line such as "I said *bed*. It's singular, that is, and it'd be a lot more singular if it were plural" (Collier 2003, 46) happens to be.

Still, sometimes power encounters greater power, as in "Thus I Refute Beelzy" (1940): while pretending to be a loving parent, Simon Carter is deliberately cruel to his son Simon, belittling the boy and attempting to get the boy to renounce his imaginary friend Mr. Beelzy, but young Simon remains true to his friend, and the not-imaginary Mr. Beelzy most horrifically concludes the sham. Also oddly positive is "Mary" (1939), in which an innocent young man finds himself in thrall to a jealous pig, but true love does find a solution to Fred's problem, and sausages are on the menu. More often, though, things end just before the worst is about to occur, and in cheerfully presenting this kind of story, Collier was peerless.

"Evening Primrose" remains one of Collier's best-remembered works, both because it has been widely anthologized and because it has been adapted for radio, stage, and television, including as a one-hour musical production written for the short-lived American television anthology series *ABC Stage 67* in 1966, featuring songs by Stephen Sondheim. Collier won both an International Fantasy Award and an Edgar Award for his now-classic 1952 fiction collection *Fancies and Goodnights*. He died of a stroke in 1980.

Richard Bleiler

See also: Devils and Demons; Saki.

Further Reading

Collier, John. [1931] 2003. *Fancies and Goodnights*. New York: New York Review Books.

Indick, Ben P. 1999. "Sardonic Fantasistes: John Collier." In *Discovering Modern Horror Fiction II*, edited by Darrell Schweitzer, 121–127. Berkeley Heights, NJ: Wildside Press.

Kessel, John. 1985. "John Collier." In *Supernatural Fiction Writers: Fantasy and Horror*, edited by E. F. Bleiler, 577–583. New York: Scribners.

Warren, Alan. 1996. "John Collier, Fantastic Miniaturist." In *Discovering Classic Fantasy Fiction: Essays on the Antecedents of Fantastic Literature*, edited by Darrell Schweitzer, 68–75. Gillette, NJ: Wildside Press.

COLLINS, WILKIE (1824–1889)

William Wilkie Collins (1824–1889) was a major Victorian (British) novelist and writer, whose *The Woman in White* (1859) is often considered one of the first great sensation novels. Like his friend Charles Dickens, Wilkie Collins wrote voluminously on a variety of subjects, often with a view toward showing the workings of fate on humanity, but unlike Dickens, Collins was not a sustained literary genius, and it has been reasonably claimed that he outlived his talent. He was not helped by an addiction to laudanum that almost overwhelmed him.

There are dark and horrific elements in Collins's three most notable novels, *The Woman in White*, *Armadale* (1866), and *The Moonstone* (1868). The first involves criminals attempting to use a woman, unjustly imprisoned and with a falsified identity, to maintain their position. The second involves prophetic dreams, false identities, and murder, with an attractive and unrepentant female villain. The third has as key plot elements sleepwalking, mysterious Indian performers, and a stolen idol's eye. All made Collins one of the more popular writers of the time and established his friendship with Charles Dickens, then editing *Household Words*, though Dickens was quite willing to reject Collins's writing if he did not feel it would be appropriate for his readers. *The Moonstone* has also been claimed as the first modern English detective novel and exerted a seminal influence on later writers in the genre, including, most notably, Arthur Conan Doyle.

Although not overtly fantastic, distinctly horrific work can be found in Collins's *After Dark* (1856), a collection of six linked stories. "The Traveller's Story of a Terribly Strange Bed" (originally published under the title "A Terribly Strange Bed" in 1852), in which a successful gambler gradually realizes that his hotel bed is not only strange but lethal, is as tense and horrific as anything ever written. It has been fairly widely anthologized, and it might be Collins's best-known short story. Overtly horrific and occasionally fantastic work can be found in *The Queen of Hearts* (1859), a collection of ten loosely connected stories that is Collins's most substantial collection of these. "The Siege of the Black Cottage" (1857) describes a resourceful young woman protecting herself, her money, and her cat from dangerous burglars. "Brother Morgan's Story of the Dream Woman" (first published as "The Ostler" in 1855) involves a terrifying dream and its outcome: Isaac Scatchard dreams of a woman trying to stab him, then seven years later marries Rebecca Murdoch, the image of the woman in the dream, and—of course—elements of the prophecy come to pass. "Brother Morgan's Story of the Dead Hand" (first published as "The Double-Bedded Room" in 1857) begins with an unsettling situation, in which the traveling Arthur Holliday is forced to share a room with a dead body in the other bed, then gets even more uncomfortable, for during the night, the body moves. "Brother Griffith's Story of Mad Monkton" (first published as "The Monktons of Wincot Abbey" in 1855) details the working-out of a prophetic curse connected with the ancient Monkton family: unless all are buried in the family vault, the line will perish. With this as the premise, it is but a matter of awaiting the inevitable when the uncle of young Alfred Monkton goes missing on the European continent. His body is found, then irretrievably lost when the transport ship sinks: and so end the Monktons, done in by Fate.

Although Collins was uneven as a writer, his best stories are as good as anything of their kind. In his final years he suffered a prolonged period of declining health, and he died in 1889 several months after suffering a stroke. His two most popular novels in his lifetime, *The Moonstone* and *The Woman in White*, remain in print and continue to be his best known works, and both have been adapted several times for film and television.

Richard Bleiler

See also: Ancestral Curse; Dreams and Nightmares.

Further Reading

Ackroyd, Peter. 2012. *Wilkie Collins*. London: Chatto & Windus.

Gasson, Andrew. 1998. *Wilkie Collins: An Illustrated Guide*. Oxford: Oxford University Press.

Sanders, Judith. 2009. "A Shock to the System, a System to the Shocks: The Horrors of the Happy Ending in *The Woman in White*." In *From Wollstonecraft to Stoker: Essays on Gothic and Victorian Sensation Fiction*, edited by Marilyn Brock, 62–78. Jefferson, NC: McFarland.

Taylor, Jenny B. 1988. *In the Secret Theatre of Home: Wilkie Collins, Sensation Narrative, and Nineteenth Century Psychology*. London and New York: Routledge.

"THE COLOUR OUT OF SPACE"

"The Colour out of Space" was the only story H. P. Lovecraft published in the first pulp "scientifiction" magazine *Amazing Stories*, in the September 1927 issue. The difficulty of exacting meager payment for the story apparently deterred him from further attempting to direct his work at this particular market. This in turn probably slowed down the transformation of the implied metaphysical context of his work and maintained its obliquity until he made a more decisive move in the belatedly published *At the Mountains of Madness*, written in 1931 but not published until 1936. That said, "The Colour out of Space" might well have influenced other horrific tales of creeping extraterrestrial corruption published in the Gernsback pulps, such as A. Rowley Hilliard's "Death from the Stars" and P. Schuler Miller's "The Arrhenius Horror" (both published in 1931).

The unnamed narrator of the story, a surveyor, attempts to discover the reason why an area in the vicinity of the town of Arkham, known as "blasted heath," is avoided by the local people. Ammi Pierce, who used to farm land nearby, tells him what happened when a meteorite landed on the property of his neighbor Nahum Gardner, which brought with it some kind of radiant matter, whose "colour" is only identified by analogy, the radiation being external to the visual spectrum. Although the matter disappeared, it poisoned the ground and Gardner's well, affecting crops and local animals in strange and ominous ways. Gardner's wife and

"The Colour out of Space" on the Screen

"The Colour out of Space" is widely regarded as one of Lovecraft's best stories, and he himself felt that it represented one of his more successful efforts to convey what he considered to be the essence of cosmic horror. It has remained prominent among his works not only because of its excellence but because of its various adaptations for other media. Chief among these are three film versions. *Die, Monster, Die!* (1965) stars an aging Boris Karloff and was released by American International Pictures, the same company behind the 1960s series of successful Edgar Allan Poe adaptations. *The Curse* (1987) was directed by David Keith and starred Claude Akins, John Schneider, and Wil Wheaton. The German-language production *Die Farbe* (2010) is thought by many, including Lovecraft scholar S. T. Joshi, to be the best adaptation to date.

Matt Cardin

one of his sons went mad, and his other son disappeared. Pierce witnessed the destruction of the house and its last surviving resident as the blight's gradual effect produced a horrific climax. The narrator and a company of associates undertake further investigations, but only succeeded in restimulating the mysterious radiation and occasioning the further spread of the blight.

Lovecraft was particularly fond of the story, believing that it captured the essential mood of "cosmic horror" that he was attempting to develop and refine better than stories that attributed their baleful manifestations to traditional supernatural causes, and permitting a measured description of decay and transfiguration that he thought particularly well adapted to the effect he was trying to achieve. Although his overall approach in "The Colour out of Space" was too new to make the story immediately popular, it eventually achieved classic status as readers gradually learned to appreciate it. Because it lacks the elaborate back-stories Lovecraft provided in some of his other major fusions of horror and science fiction, such as "The Shadow out of Time" and *At the Mountains of Madness*, the story develops in a more focused and measured fashion, but that has made it less tempting for extrapolation by subsequent contributors to the "Cthulhu Mythos," requiring a significant generic shift in the most elaborate sequel by another hand, Michael Shea's *The Color out of Time* (1984). "The Colour out of Space" has also been the subject of several cinematic adaptations, including *Die, Monster, Die* (1965), *The Curse* (1987), and *Die Farbe* (2010).

Brian Stableford

See also: *At the Mountains of Madness*; Cthulhu Mythos; Lovecraft, H. P.; Shea, Michael; Transformation and Metamorphosis.

Further Reading

Cannon, Peter H. 1989. "Cosmic Backwaters." In *H. P. Lovecraft*, 82–96. Twayne's United States Author Series, 549. Boston: Twayne.

Harman, Graham. 2012. *Weird Realism: Lovecraft and Philosophy*, 78–97. Winchester: Zero Books.

Joshi, S. T., and David E. Schultz. 2001. "The Colour out of Space." In *An H. P. Lovecraft Encyclopedia*, 41–43. Westport, CT: Greenwood.

COMMUNION

Communion: A True Story (1987), by the American horror writer and later paranormal celebrity Whitley Strieber (1945–), was not the first book to explore UFO sightings and abductions. Twentieth-century culture was rife with examples of this trope, going back to such things as Orson Welles's 1938 radio adaptation of H. G. Wells's *War of the Worlds*, which thousands of people heard and believed to be factual; Erich Von Däniken's *Chariots of the Gods* (1968), which posits that humanity has been visited and influenced by alien entities since before recorded history; and the enormous box-office success of Steven Spielberg's beneficent aliens in *Close Encounters of the Third Kind* (1977). But Strieber's book managed to crystallize and complicate the American public's ongoing fascination, or obsession, with UFOs and aliens.

In *Communion* Strieber tells the story of a paranormal abduction experience that occurred while he was staying at his upstate New York cabin in the winter of 1983. Whatever one may think of the veracity of this account, the narrative power of *Communion* is undeniable. An experienced writer with eight books already in print—including four horror novels, a dark fantasy, and a co-authored post–nuclear holocaust best seller—Strieber brought to *Communion* the professionalism

---

Communion bears more responsibility for originating the idea and image of the "alien gray" than any other single work of fiction or nonfiction. With its compelling (if outlandish, by conventional standards) story, presented as truth by the author, and with its iconic cover painting by artist Ted Seth Jacobs of a gray-skinned, bulbous-headed creature with large, jet-black, almond-shaped eyes, the book may justly be credited with planting the image of the alien gray in popular consciousness and catalyzing the modern fascination with the idea of alien abduction, which swept through American popular culture—and also intellectual culture (it was the subject of a 1992 conference at MIT)—in the late 1980s and throughout the 1990s. The significance of *Communion* can still be felt in the twenty-first century, as movies, books, games, and television shows about UFOs, extraterrestrials, and paranormal abductions continue to proliferate, many of them following the basic conceptual and visual template outlined by Strieber in 1987.

Matt Cardin

and rigor of a story compellingly well told. The book's greatest strength lies perhaps in the sympathy, and in some cases the empathy, it causes the reader to feel for Strieber because of the trauma he endured. His ability to stoke this flame makes for a gripping read.

The book's subtitle, *A True Story*, is telling. *Communion* is not meant as a fiction taken to be real like Welles's broadcast; nor is it a work of amateur archaeological speculation that is easily refuted like Von Däniken's book; nor is it like Spielberg's film, which is an obvious work of fiction that plays on wish fulfillment fantasies of transcendence. Strieber's book mines a deeply felt human need to be part of something larger than oneself, to experience firsthand that which is boundless, unknowable, and true.

Communion was a best seller when it was published, and it has remained in print ever since. Most readers have apparently accepted Streiber's claims as true, or at the very least they have believed that Strieber himself believes he is relating a true experience. Critical reception, however, has been far less kind. In science fiction circles Strieber is regarded as something of an embarrassment, as his books share little with the ongoing science fiction narratives in which the genre's best authors are substantively engaged.

But to judge Strieber solely on his contributions to science fiction is to misunderstand his greater project. *Communion* is, at its heart, a work of mysticism, and its author is an explorer of alternate states of being in the tradition of such looming figures in the twentieth century's esoteric and countercultural spiritual tradition as G. I. Gurdjieff, P. D. Ouspensky, Carlos Castaneda, and Timothy Leary. The great irony of *Communion* is that while it is the most famous and influential alien abduction text ever produced, it never claims to be about extraterrestrials per se. While "the visitors," as Strieber refers to them throughout the book, could be extraterrestrial, the possibility is entertained as well that they are figments that have penetrated the author's mind, working from either an internal psychic space or from some extradimensional arena. The notion of the alien—in this case the gray alien or "grays" as they are referred to in ufology culture (a figure that, not incidentally, was largely solidified by Strieber's book)—is thus complicated in *Communion*, where it functions as a symbol of something that is fundamentally Other and consequently unknowable.

The book was filmed as *Communion* and released in 1989, with Christopher Walken playing the role of Strieber. A nonfiction sequel to *Communion* is *Transformation: The Breakthrough* (1988). Later novels by Strieber are presented as fiction and develop the notion of extraterrestrial visitors in more genre-familiar terms. At the same time, Strieber's contributions in the specific role of horror author (which he has mostly, although not entirely, left behind in his post-*Communion* career) continue to have value, especially his werewolf novel *Wolfen* (1978), his vampire novel *The Hunger* (1981), and his underrated horror/dark fantasy novel *Catmagic* (1986), about the survival of ancient nature-based witchcraft in the modern world.

Javier A. Martinez

See also: Part Two, Themes, Topics, and Genres: Horror Literature and Science Fiction; Occult Fiction.

Further Reading

Fenkl, Heinz I. 2000. "Folkroots: Abduction and Ascension—Two Sides of the Same Coin?" *Realms of Fantasy* 6 (February): 26–32.

Kripal, Jeffrey J. 2014. "Better Horrors: From Terror to Communion in Whitley Strieber's *Communion* (1987)." *Social Research* 81, no. 4: 897–920.

Pharr, Mary. 1996. "Adam's Dream: The Gothic Imagination of Whitley Strieber." In *A Dark Night's Dreaming: Contemporary American Horror Fiction*, edited by Tony Magistrale and Michael A. Morrison, 97–109. Columbia: University of South Carolina Press.

Stanley, Wiater. 1988. "Beyond Communion: A Conversation with Whitley Strieber." *Twilight Zone* 8, no. 1 (April): 22–25.

"Whitley Strieber." 2015. *Contemporary Authors Online*. Detroit: Gale.

CONJURE WIFE

Fritz Leiber's 1943 novel *Conjure Wife*, originally published in the pulp magazine *Unknown* (a.k.a. *Unknown Worlds*) in 1943 and released in book form a decade later, updates classic tales of witchcraft for a modern (sub)urban milieu. The novel's premise is simple: witchcraft continues to survive amidst contemporary women, especially those with ambitious husbands whose career goals can be advanced through sorcerous means. The protagonist, Tansy Saylor, is the spouse of a sociology professor, Norman Saylor, who moves rapidly up the academic hierarchy as a result of Tansy's potions and spells. A skeptic himself, Norman compels Tansy to give up her "neurotic" belief in the supernatural, at which point his career takes a turn for the worse, subjecting him to the conjuring wiles of his competitors' spouses.

Sharply satirical of small-town life, with its vicious gossip and petty rivalries, the novel is also profoundly frightening, especially a scene in which a stone gargoyle descends from a campus building to stalk Norman remorselessly. The horrific charge of the story derives from the eerie counterpoint between the secular mindset of modern suburbanites and the atavistic worldview of a secretive coven of female necromancers. As in Bram Stoker's *Dracula* (1897), the supernatural presence derives much of its power from the fact that skeptical modern people simply refuse to believe in it. *Conjure Wife* stands alongside a number of other Leiber stories of the 1940s—such as "Smoke Ghost" (1941) and "The Girl with the Hungry Eyes" (1949)—in being a self-conscious updating of classic horror themes within a contemporary milieu. While there are some protofeminist aspects to the story, especially its vision of sorcerous female empowerment, the tale also relies on a number of gender stereotypes, such as the wife as selfless helpmate to her husband. Nonetheless, its vision of a furtive form of female agency, with durable ancient roots, suggests possibilities for gender solidarity that echo other protofeminist texts of the period, such as Jacques Tourneur's classic film *Cat People* (1942).

Conjure Wife was an immediate mainstream success, adapted as the 1944 film *Weird Woman* and, two decades later, as *Night of the Eagle* (1962; a.k.a *Burn, Witch, Burn!*). It has also been deeply influential in American popular culture, the ur-text for all manner of tales of modern witchery, such as the 1950 stage play *Bell, Book, and Candle*, the TV series *Bewitched* (1964–1972), and the best-selling 1967 novel *Rosemary's Baby* by Ira Levin.

Rob Latham

See also: Dark Fantasy; Forbidden Knowledge or Power; "The Girl with the Hungry Eyes"; Leiber, Fritz; Psychological Horror; *Rosemary's Baby*; Witches and Witchcraft.

Further Reading

Byfield, Bruce. 1991. "Sister Picture of Dorian Grey: The Image of the Female in Fritz Leiber's *Conjure Wife*." *Mythlore* 17, no. 4: 24–28.
Leiber, Fritz. 1973. "About *Gather, Darkness* and *Conjure Wife*." *Whispers* 1, no. 2: 33.
Murphy, Bernice M. 2009. *The Suburban Gothic in American Popular Culture*. New York: Palgrave Macmillan.

COPPARD, A. E. (1878–1957)

Alfred Edgar Coppard was an English poet and short story writer whose work often contains horrific elements, often along with allusions to folkloric motifs, Judeo-Christian imagery, and a sophisticated use of English and Irish vernacular; he likewise used to great advantage sudden and strange shifts in perception. His first fantastic story, "Piffingcap" (1921), concerns a haunted shaving mug: those shaved from it do not need to be shaved again. This seemingly light premise leads directly to the deaths of three men sent to retrieve it after it is thrown from a bridge.

Coppard's best-known story may be "Adam & Eve & Pinch Me," published in 1921 in his book of the same title. It is a haunting and dreamlike account of an out-of-body experience in which Jaffa Codling witnesses three children—Adam, Eve, and Gabriel—playing in an exquisite garden. He cannot interact with them, and only Gabriel can see him. There are recurrent images and motifs—golden swords, brilliant lights, fish, fire, fruit, and the idea of *good*—and in the end Codling returns to his body and discovers his name is Gilbert Cannister, and that he has two children, but that his wife is pregnant with the one who will become Gabriel.

Physical horror is never far from the surface of many of Coppard's stories. In "The Old Venerable" (1926), the impoverished Old Venerable's dreams of independence are destroyed when his dog is shot, and he must drown the unweaned puppies, for he cannot feed them. "The Green Drake" (1931) depicts a conversation between an amiable drake and a wandering poacher; it is a conversation full of the fantastic, but the fantastic lures the duck to its death. Equally horrible is "Arabesque: The Mouse" (1920; sometimes given as "Arabesque—the Mouse"): the narrator sits in his room, watching an inquisitive mouse and recalling the horrible death of his mother, whose hands were crushed in an accident, and recalling too an encounter with a beautiful woman whose eyes were "full of starry inquiry like the eyes of mice" (Coppard 1951, 75). All recollections conclude when the trap snaps and severs the feet of the poor mouse.

Nevertheless, it would be a mistake to consider Coppard solely as a writer utilizing the physical horrors of everyday existence, for a number of his tales make effective use of psychic horror. The virginal Clorinda Smith in "Clorinda Walks in Heaven" (1922) is granted a glimpse of the afterlife, learning that heaven contains ghosts of her unrealized desires, but she fails to profit from her knowledge and dies alone and forgotten. Heaven is likewise denied the title character in "Father Raven" (1946) because he falsely attested to the virtue of his charges in order that they might enter heaven.

Like such literary compatriots as M. R. James, Coppard had no belief in either the supernatural or the fantastic, stating in the introduction to his 1946 collection of supernatural fiction *Fearful Pleasures* that "I have not the slightest belief in the supernatural. If I should ever see a ghost I should know it was time for me to consult an oculist" (Coppard 1946, vii). His stories remain acute and often psychically terrifying, but though he has received occasional academic attention, Coppard is now largely out of print, and no comprehensive collection of his fantastic fiction is available.

Richard Bleiler

See also: Body Horror; Psychological Horror.

Further Reading

Coppard, A. E. 1946. *Fearful Pleasures*. Sauk City, WI: Arkham House.

Coppard, A. E. 1951. *The Collected Tales of A. E. Coppard*. New York: Alfred A. Knopf.

Smith, Frank Edmund. 1985. "A(lfred) E(dgar) Coppard." *Supernatural Fiction Writers: Fantasy and Horror*, vol. 2, edited by Everett Franklin Bleiler, 523–528. New York: Charles Scribner's Sons.

Thompson, N. S. 2003. "A. E. Coppard." In *British Writers: Supplement 8*, edited by Jay Parini. New York: Charles Scribner's Sons.

CRAWFORD, F. MARION (1854–1908)

Francis Marion Crawford was one of the most popular novelists in the English-speaking world of his day. Although he wrote more than forty novels, mostly historical romances, today he is remembered for a few novels of some fantasy genre interest and for a handful of important short stories in the fantasy and horror genres. He was born in 1854 to American parents in Bagni di Lucca, Italy. His father, Thomas Crawford, was the sculptor who created the "armed liberty" sculpture atop the Capitol building in Washington, D.C. Julia Ward Howe, the author

"The Upper Berth": Creepy Maritime Horror

First published in 1886, "The Upper Berth" is recognized as the finest of the small number of ghost stories written by the popular American novelist F. Marion Crawford throughout a long career. It is told in the typically indirect manner of the time. Men are sitting around chatting. Boredom threatens. Then Brisbane, a solid, sensible man, tells his companions that he once encountered a ghost, or something very much like one, on a steamship, while sharing a stateroom with a man who committed suicide on the first night at sea. This, he discovered, had happened several times before, in that very room. The berth above his own was haunted. A porthole kept opening itself. The place smelled dank. Eventually a revenant was flushed out of the upper berth, something more solid than a traditional ghost: the reanimated corpse of a long-drowned man.

One of the most remarkable features of "The Upper Berth" is the deftness with which the details are handled. The hero does not overlook the obvious. The upper berth is searched with a bright light and found to be empty and dry. The porthole is screwed tightly shut. But the manifestations occur anyway. The story itself is a refutation of the old canard that the ghost story became obsolete with the invention of bright lights. When the lights come on in the story narrated by Brisbane, the Thing is still there and just as frightening.

Although Crawford's mainstream writings were critical successes in their day, it is only his ghost stories that have withstood the test of time. "The Upper Berth," which has been anthologized many times, is chief among them.

Darrell Schweitzer

of "The Battle Hymn of the Republic," was his aunt. A grandson, H. Marion-Crawford, an actor, portrayed Watson in the 1954 Sherlock Holmes television series. Francis knew eighteen languages and was an avid sailor who owned three yachts, an interest that is reflected in much of his fiction. He died in 1908.

Crawford was an accomplished writer, a romanticist who created vivid characters and colorful backgrounds, but he saw himself as a paid entertainer rather than as an artist. He led a colorful life and was convinced by friends to turn his real-life experiences into stories. His first venture into fiction writing was *Mr. Isaacs* (1882), based on people he knew in India, and cast himself pseudonymously as the first-person narrator, something he was to do repeatedly. It has only minimal fantasy or occult elements, but its success convinced him to become a novelist.

Khaled (1891) is an Arabian fantasy about a genie who is made mortal as a form of punishment and has been compared favorably to William Beckford's *Vathek*. *The Witch of Prague* (1891) is Crawford's one true horror novel, in which Unorna, feared as a witch, and her dwarf cohort experiment to extend the human lifespan by means of her possibly supernatural hypnotic powers.

Crawford is chiefly remembered today for eight ghostly short stories, written throughout his career and collected posthumously as *Wandering Ghosts* (1911). "The Upper Berth" (1886) is one the most frequently reprinted of all ghost stories. "The Dead Smile" (1899) is a tale of evil and incest, and it inspired Seabury Quinn's Jules de Grandin story, "The Jest of Warburg Tartaval." "Man Overboard" (1903), a novella originally published as a separate small book, is a seagoing tale about a pair of identical twins, one of whom is murdered by the other during a storm, and who returns as a vengeful ghost. "For Blood is the Life" (1905) is an unusual story about a female vampire. "The King's Messenger" (1907), not in the original collection but in recent reprints, involves dreams, premonitions, and death. Crawford's popular "The Screaming Skull" (1908) has been adapted for film twice, once in 1958 as *The Screaming Skull* (although the screenplay's basis in Crawford's story was unacknowledged) and again in 1973 for an American made-for-television production. Crawford died of influenza in 1908 while doing relief work for refugees from an earthquake in southern Italy.

Lee Weinstein

See also: "The Screaming Skull"; Witches and Witchcraft.

Further Reading

Joshi, S. T. 2004. "F. Marion Crawford: Blood and Thunder Horror." In *The Evolution of the Weird Tale*, 26–38. New York: Hippocampus Press.

Moran, John C. 1981. *An F. Marion Crawford Companion.* Westport, CT: Greenwood Press.

Morgan, Chris. 1985. "F. Marion Crawford." In *Supernatural Fiction Writers*, edited by E. F. Bleiler, 747–752. New York: Charles Scribner's Sons.

CTHULHU MYTHOS

"Cthulhu Mythos" is a term posthumously applied to a body of stories originated by H. P. Lovecraft and expanded upon in his lifetime and afterward by his contemporaries in *Weird Tales* and other fiction venues. Consequently, it represents the earliest example of a "shared universe" in popular culture. Cthulhu Mythos stories typically share four common elements: a scholarly narrator; otherworldly entities called the Great Old Ones; occult spellbooks such as Lovecraft's mythical Necronomicon, which are employed to invoke or understand them; and often—but not exclusively—a New England setting.

The Cthulhu Mythos originated with Lovecraft's 1928 short story "The Call of Cthulhu," which focused on an extraterrestrial being imprisoned in an undersea Pacific Ocean vault, who reaches out to psychically sensitive human beings via telepathic dreams aimed at enticing potential victims into furthering his release. Cthulhu is vast, preternatural, and, like the mythological Kraken whom he resembles, prophesied to signal the end of the world when his enforced slumber

Cthulhu Mythos Close-up: Clark Ashton Smith's "The Return of the Sorcerer"

"The Return of the Sorcerer" by Clark Ashton Smith first appeared in the September 1931 issue of the pulp magazine *Strange Tales of Mystery and Terror* and was subsequently reprinted in the Arkham House collection *Out of Space and Time* (1942). It is of some note as an early example of a story written by one of H. P. Lovecraft's friends who accepted the latter's invitation to appropriate the imagery of what subsequently became known as the Cthulhu Mythos.

In the story the narrator, in need of employment, is contacted by the reclusive scholar John Carnby, who wants his help in translating an Arabic manuscript related to the original text of the fabled *Necronomicon*—but Carnby has acquired it by nefarious means, and his insistence that the strange sounds the narrator can hear are only due to an infestation of rats ring false. In fact, the relative he murdered to get it has made use of its nasty secrets to ensure a suitably gruesome revenge.

The story follows the standard formula of Lovecraftian horror fiction methodically, but with a measured elegance unusual in what was still at the time a species of pulp fiction, demonstrating the fashion in which the flexible template might be modified in both stylistic and imagistic terms. It thus became, and remains, a valuable exemplar for practitioners of the subgenre.

Brian Stableford

concludes. Many Mythos concepts are conscious perversions or inversions of classical mythology.

Lovecraft penned only three purely Mythos stories—"The Call of Cthulhu," "The Dunwich Horror," and "The Whisperer in Darkness"—before his contemporaries commenced borrowing his concepts, characters, and impedimenta in the pages of *Weird Tales*. This pantheon was expanded especially in the stories of Clark Ashton Smith, Robert E. Howard, Frank Belknap Long, and Robert Bloch. Lovecraft himself was the first to indulge in such borrowings, including formative Mythos concepts in stories he ghostwrote for Zealia Brown-Reed Bishop and Adolphe de Castro, among others. The conceit, which functioned partly on the level of a series of sly in-jokes, proliferated rapidly among the so-called Lovecraft Circle of horror writers.

Writing to August Derleth in 1931, Lovecraft observed of his self-described "Pseudomythology," "The more these synthetic daemons are mutually written up by different authors, the better they become as general background-material! I like to have others use my Azathoths and Nyarlathoteps—& in return I shall use Klarkash-Ton's Tsathhoggua, your monk Clithanus, & Howard's Bran" (Joshi 2008, 21).

After Lovecraft's 1937 death, novelist Derleth launched Arkham House Books, reprinting Lovecraft's stories as well as those by other members of the Lovecraft

Circle. In his own Mythos contributions, Derleth commenced adding elemental beings and codifying the Mythos in terms of a Christian worldview of good and evil—something to which the arch-materialistic Lovecraft did not subscribe during his life. To Derleth goes the credit for coining the term "Cthulhu Mythos," even though Cthulhu himself was a relatively minor godlet in the growing pantheon of Great Old Ones, which included Yog-Sothoth, Azathoth, and other cosmic beings.

Until his 1971 death, Derleth exerted a proprietary influence over the Mythos, sanctioning some stories and actively suppressing others. Since his death, the Mythos has been disconnected from Derleth's peculiar set of imposed and specious limitations and his own contributions relegated to a discredited subcategory dubbed the Derleth Mythos. The Cthulhu Mythos is today recognized as the property of no individual, thus liberating any author who cares to write a story set in Lovecraft's milieu to explore and expand upon it unchallenged.

Approaching one hundred years after Lovecraft's seminal story, the Cthulhu Mythos has exploded into a cottage industry, with new themed anthologies appearing every year. The list of contributors includes such luminaries as Colin Wilson, Thomas Ligotti, Ramsey Campbell, Fred Chappell, Brian Lumley, T. E. D. Klein, and Karl Edward Wagner, among others. The Mythos has also formed the basis of a long series of role-playing games, board games, and computer games, the most prominent of which is arguably the role-playing game *The Call of Cthulhu*, first released in 1981. Elements of the Mythos have also proliferated throughout heavy metal music, as in Metallica's songs "The Call of Ktulu" and "The Thing That Should Not Be." The Mythos has also become something of a staple in monster-themed apocalyptic horror movies such as *The Gate* (1987), the *Hellboy* movies (2004 and 2008), and *The Cabin in the Woods* (2012). Ever expanding, Lovecraft's dark and disturbing universe-view promises to endure as long as practitioners of the formal horror story continue to push the boundaries of the genre beyond the mundane monsters of mythology.

Will Murray

See also: Arkham House; *At the Mountains of Madness*; Barlow, R. H.; "The Call of Cthulhu"; *The Case of Charles Dexter Ward*; Derleth, August; Devils and Demons; "The Dunwich Horror"; Howard, Robert E.; *The King in Yellow*; Long, Frank Belknap; Lovecraft, H. P.; Lovecraftian Horror; *The Mind Parasites*; Schweitzer, Darrell; Smith, Clark Ashton; *Weird Tales*.

Further Reading

Joshi, S. T. 2008. *The Rise and Fall of the Cthulhu Mythos*. Poplar Bluff, MO: Mythos Books.
Joshi, S. T. 2010. *I Am Providence: The Life and Times of H. P. Lovecraft*. New York: Hippocampus Press.

D

DAGON

Dagon is a Southern Gothic novel by Fred Chappell published in 1968. Chappell is an award-winning poet and Southern regionalist writer, and his overt references in the novel to names and themes from the Cthulhu Mythos were recognized as one of the first efforts in the literary mainstream to acknowledge the literary legacy of H. P. Lovecraft.

The novel focuses on the dramatic spiritual and psychological decline of Peter Leland, a Methodist minister on sabbatical from his church in South Carolina. Peter and his wife Sheila have just moved to a farm he has inherited in an unnamed Southern town so that he can work on *Remnant Pagan Forces in American Puritanism*, a book whose theme has grown out of a sermon that he delivered regarding the persistence in modern times of the worship of Dagon (who is, not coincidentally, an aquatic entity worshipped as a god in Lovecraft's fiction, notably in his story "The Shadow over Innsmouth"). Dagon, as Peter explains it, is a pagan god named in the Bible whose association as a fertility symbol resonates with the "frenzied, incessant, unreasoning sexual activity" (Chappell 1996, 22) that he sees rampant in the American culture of the time. During a picnic with Sheila, Peter unexpectedly meets Ed Morgan, a sharecropper living on his farm, and later Ed's daughter Mina. Though Mina is slatternly and unattractive—her fishlike features are redolent of those borne by the human-amphibian hybrids in Lovecraft's tale— Peter looks on her with "the fascination he might have in watching a snake uncoil itself lazily and curl along the ground" (19). Under the spell of Mina's erotic allure, Peter kills Sheila and moves in with the Morgans.

Over the next few months Peter is cruelly dominated by the abusive Mina and fed a steady diet of moonshine until he is reduced to a near-bestial state. Emasculated by his lover, he increasingly comes to resemble a latter-day Samson—who, as Peter reminds the reader early in the story, destroyed the temple to Dagon where he was to be sacrificed. The book's final chapters resonate with snatches of Lovecraftian references Peter hears throughout the novel as he is ritually prepared by Mina and a band of cultists as a sacrifice to Dagon.

Chappell leaves ambiguous how much of what Peter experiences in his final moments is a genuine confrontation with the cosmic horrors of Lovecraft's fiction and how much is a symbolic rendering of his collapse into mania. Nevertheless, Peter's appreciation of his suffering as "the one means of carving a design upon an area of time, of charging with human meaning each separate moment of time" (82) is an astute interpretation of the plight of humanity in an indifferent and insentient universe that informs Lovecraftian horror fiction.

Stefan R. Dziemianowicz

See also: "The Call of Cthulhu"; Cthulhu Mythos; Lovecraft, H.P.; Lovecraftian Horror.

Further Reading

Chappell, Fred. [1968] 1996. *Dagon*. Raleigh, NC: Boson.

Clabough, Casey. 2003. "Appropriations of History, Gothicism, and Cthulhu: Fred Chappell's *Dagon*." *Mosaic: A Journal for the Interdisciplinary Study of Literature* 36, no. 3: 37–53.

Lang, John. 2000. *Understanding Fred Chappell*. Columbia: University of South Carolina Press.

Schweitzer, Darrell. 1994. "A Talk with Fred Chappell." *Worlds of Fantasy and Horror*, Summer 1994, 40–43.

THE DAMNATION GAME

The Damnation Game is the first novel by the British writer Clive Barker. Published in 1985 by Sphere and met with critical praise upon publication, the novel quickly followed from Barker's celebrated debut with the *Books of Blood* (1984–1985). *The Damnation Game* is a Gothic-horror Faustian pact tale concerning an infernal arrangement between the mysterious, near-immortal European gambler Mamoulian and the reclusive wealthy businessman Whitehead. Beginning in war-torn Warsaw, the mysterious wager between Mamoulian and Whitehead, a talented gambler, is agreed over a game of cards, later resulting in Whitehead's ascent into wealth, power, and near immortality. Decades later, having profited from their dark arrangement, Whitehead now wishes to renege on his pact with Mamoulian, which has expectedly come due, and hires convict-turned-bodyguard Marty Strauss to protect him.

Barker's antiheroes like Marty Strauss are typically loners who withdraw from the everyday world, enabling them to experience something profound or magical that is hidden from everyday view. Aided by his undead zombie acolyte Breer, Mamoulian's plan to collect his infernal wager from Whitehead by any means necessary is revealed to be driven by abject loneliness; weary from immortality, Mamoulian craves a worthy companion to join him in the release of death. Strauss, a redeemed man caught between supernatural forces and his personal demons and addictions, falls in love with Whitehead's daughter Carys, a young psychic seer troubled by drug addiction. Together, Marty and Carys attempt to save Whitehead from these supernatural threats that threaten to engulf them all.

The Damnation Game established Barker as a serious author working beyond his debut in the short story medium, emphasizing his interest in combining traditional

Gothic tropes such as the Faustian pact with his uncompromising celebration of graphic body horror. This novel affirms his unique style of tight yet lyrical prose, with his material disciplined from his years of short story composition and his close editorial relationship with his publisher, Sphere. The theme of Faustian exchange and forbidden experiences would become a repeated feature in much of Barker's later fiction, as many of his novels and film adaptations explicitly revisit this motif. *The Damnation Game* is best understood, then, as a foundational text to understand Barker's core preoccupations; it reveals his authorial thematic touchstones of transcendence and metamorphosis, infernal arrangements, and the enduring hope and redemptive nature of love in the face of horror.

Drawing upon contemporary cultural and economic divisions within 1980s Britain, the novel's depiction of social inequality and insatiable avarice lends itself neatly to the contemporary invocation of the Faustian tale amidst the pronounced misery of Thatcher's economically riven era. In Barker's novel, no one is immune to the temptations of money, power, or a game of chance. It is not the most well known of Barker's horror novels (compared to, for example, *The Hellbound Heart* [1986] or *Cabal* [1988], which enjoyed film adaptations directed by Barker), but it is certainly the most devoted to the horror genre. It offers insight into Barker's rise as an influential author of visceral horror fiction, literate in the Gothic tropes and artfully splicing them into tales that feel new and speak to contemporary concerns.

Sorcha Ní Fhlainn

See also: Barker, Clive; Body Horror; *Books of Blood*.

Further Reading

Badley, Linda. 1996. "Clive Barker Writing (from) the Body." In *Writing Horror and the Body: The Fiction of Stephen King, Clive Barker and Anne Rice*, 73–104. Westport, CT: Greenwood Press.

Hoppenstand, Gary. 1994. *Clive Barker's Short Stories: Imagination as Metaphor in the Books of Blood and Other Works*. Jefferson, NC: McFarland.

Ní Fhlainn, Sorcha, ed. 2017. *Clive Barker: Dark Imaginer*. Manchester: Manchester University Press.

Winter, Douglas E. 2001. "Nowhere Land: *The Damnation Game* (1985)." In *Clive Barker: The Dark Fantastic*, 172–187. New York: HarperCollins.

THE DAMNED

Là-Bas (translated as *Down There* or *The Damned*) is a novel by French writer J. K. (Joris-Karl) Huysmans, first published in 1891, and not published in English—and then only in a private edition—until 1928. It is the story of the author Durtal, whose research on Gilles de Rais—marshal of fourteenth-century France, whose career ended in a notorious trial for Satanism, pedophilia, torture, and child murder—leads him to a firsthand encounter with the occult. Its attempt to blend naturalism with the mystical into a kind of "supernatural realism" proved influential on subsequent horror writers, most importantly H. P. Lovecraft.

The narrative (like most of Huysmans's work) is not linear, but rather a series of tableaux. It is punctuated by discussions between Durtal and fellow novelist des Hermies as they enjoy the hospitality of the local bell ringer and his wife. When Durtal says he wants to strengthen his understanding of de Rais's satanic practices, des Hermies tells him that such activities still exist. Meanwhile, Durtal is contacted by a female reader, Hyacinthe Chantelouve, who leads him further into the occult underworld.

Much of the horror in the novel comes during the interstitial episodes, as when Durtal recounts the crimes of Gilles de Rais. In Chapter XI Durtal describes how, after a particularly shocking episode, de Rais stumbled through a Brittany forest. The vegetation seems to mutate in the most horrible manner: "It seemed that nature perverted itself before him [de Rais], that his very presence depraved it" (Huysmans 1972, 106). This hallucinatory experience is among the most terrifying in the book. Another disturbing subnarrative is in Chapter IX, when the astrologer Gévingey conveys chilling details regarding incubi and succubi.

Durtal's seduction by the "femme fatale" Chantelouve becomes a metaphor for his spiritual corruption: "'For this, basically, is what Satanism is,' said Durtal to himself. 'The external semblance of the Demon is a minor matter. He has no need of exhibiting himself in human or bestial form to attest his presence. For him to prove himself, it is enough that he chooses a domicile in souls which he ulcerates and incites to inexplicable crimes'" (106).

Durtal becomes convinced he has been cursed by the leader of a local satanic cult, the defrocked abbot Canon Docre. He turns to the mysterious Dr. Johannès, a "Doctor of Theology," for supernatural protection. The novel climaxes in Chapter XIX with a horrific description of a Black Mass, "a madhouse, a monstrous pandemonium of prostitutes and maniacs" (249).

The novel is autobiographical: its three sequels document Huysmans's conversion to Catholicism. This is foreshadowed at the end of *Là-Bas* when the bell ringer says: "On earth all is dead and decomposed. But in heaven! . . . The future is certain. There will be light" (287).

Steven J. Mariconda

See also: Devils and Demons; Incubi and Succubi; Lovecraft, H. P.

Further Reading

Baldick, Robert. 1955. *The Life of J.-K. Huysmans.* Oxford: Clarendon Press.
Cevasco, George A. 1980. *J.-K. Huysmans: A Reference Guide.* Boston: G. K. Hall.
Huysmans, J. K. [1928] 1972. *Là-bas (Down There).* New York: Dover.
Ridge, George Ross. 1968. *Joris-Karl Huysmans.* New York: Twayne.

THE DARK DOMAIN

In 1986, Miroslaw Lipinski, a Polish American translator based in New York City, published a home-printed journal, *The Grabiński Reader*. It contained translations of two stories by the early twentieth-century Polish writer of the fantastic, Stefan Grabiński: "The Area" and "Strabismus." These were the first translations of Grabiński's work into English. Over the next few years, Lipinski published more Grabiński translations in further issues of *The Grabiński Reader* and in small press anthologies. Then, in 1993, Lipinski's Grabiński translations were collected in *The Dark Domain*, published by UK-based independent press Dedalus.

The Dark Domain contains stories from a number of Grabiński's collections, all from his period of peak productivity and acclaim between 1918 and 1922, including some from his themed collections: three from *The Motion Demon* (1919), which collected his railway stories, and one from *The Book of Fire* (1922).

"In the Compartment," which is from *The Motion Demon*, shows Grabiński's fusing of Henri Bergson's theory of *élan vital*—the idea that there is an internal vital impetus behind life's processes—with scientific theories of motion. It is a story of Godziemba, ordinarily timid, a day-dreamer and a sluggard, who, when riding on locomotives, is transformed by "train neurosis" into a man of dynamism, pugnacity, sexual prowess, and murderous impulse.

Another story, "Saturnin Sektor," deals with Bergson's notion of time as continuous and indivisible. A mad watchmaker seems to split his personality to argue with himself about the nature of time—in his new persona, for perpetual duration; in his old, as Saturnin Sektor, for the division of time into hours, minutes, and seconds. The tale ends with the watchmaker dead, possibly a suicide, and all the clocks in town stopped at the moment of his passing.

In the tale "The Area," Grabiński formulates a fictional counterpart, an obscure visionary writer, Wrzesmian, whose work, unlike that of other authors, which is always tied to the real world, is totally fantastic, disunited from reality, and free of influences, allusions, and allegories. But even this leaves him unsatisfied, and, led by a theory that any thought or fiction, no matter how audacious or insane, can one day be materialized, he abandons words as a creative medium and turns to projecting his psyche onto an abandoned mansion across the street from his rooms. He calls forth from the eerie house frail figures, who, when he crosses over to investigate, demand his blood and tear him apart. This story can be read as an allegory of Grabiński's own approach to composition, and perhaps also of his fear that his writings would somehow cause him harm.

Lipinski's original journal and small press translations of Grabiński were favorably noticed by writers such as Robert Bloch, Colin Wilson, and Thomas Ligotti. *The Dark Domain* received extremely positive reviews, especially in the weird fiction scene. Prominent admirers of the collection include China Miéville and Mark Samuels. Grabiński's influence continues to grow, and more translations, from Lipinski and others, have resulted.

Timothy J. Jarvis

See also: Bloch, Robert; Grabiński, Stefan; Ligotti, Thomas.

Further Reading

Lipinski, Miroslaw. 2005. Introduction to *The Dark Domain* by Stefan Grabiński, 7–12. London: Dedalus Books.

Lipinski, Miroslaw. 2012. *The Stefan Grabiński Website*. January 9. http://www.stefangra binski.org.

DARK FANTASY

Dark fantasy is a loose designation for fiction that mixes elements of the fantasy and horror genres. While this much is clear, any attempt at a stricter definition will run into difficulties. The proportions may vary, with the "dark fantasy" label encompassing both fantasy stories with horrific aspects and horror stories with fantastic aspects, but overall the tendency in the genre is toward a blending of wonder and horror, beauty and ugliness. It might be said that writers of dark fantasy are indifferent to the question of whether their work should be considered horror or fantasy.

There are a number of avenues critics can follow in a search for a more exact definition. For example, they may think about the importance of story outcomes in both genres. As most fantasies seem to possess uplifting endings, it may be that dark fantasy could be defined as fantasy of a more tragic variety, tending toward depressing or bittersweet endings. Some horror stories have more or less happy endings, in which evil is vanquished, yet this does not induce critics generally to regard them as belonging to any special or separate category like dark fantasy. Such stories are simply "lighter" horror stories.

The importance of dreams in both genres is also marked, so critics in search of a definition may look to dreams for a clue. Dreamlike horror fiction is, however, not typically considered dark fantasy either, as delirium and hallucination are common elements of horror fiction properly speaking; however, if the dream has some concrete or consistent aspect, such as locations, place names, and objects, and if that dream is not a vision of any preexisting other world, such as the conventional hell or a familiar, clichéd version of the afterlife, but something original to the tale, then it would be more appropriate to consider it dark fantasy. The otherworld of the Cenobites in Clive Barker's *The Hellbound Heart* (which inspired the *Hellraiser* films) might be close enough to a realization of the religiously canonical hell to push the story out of the genre of dark fantasy. George MacDonald's 1858 novel *Phantastes*, on the other hand, is a haunting vision of a psychedelic pastoral England. While it resembles some earlier works, the dreamlike, pagan landscape MacDonald creates is more an aesthetic idea than a religious convention, and, since horror is secondary to wonder in *Phantastes*, it is probably more appropriate to label it dark fantasy rather than horror.

Setting, another important aspect for both genres, is also sometimes used to help define dark fantasy. Dark fantasy may be defined as fantasy fiction with a

Gothic setting, or with a setting with at least a few Gothic features that play a significant role in the story. Since Gothic horror is already its own genre, dark fantasy might be defined as more modern horror fiction that nevertheless reaches back to Gothic settings.

While dark fantasy is often associated with antiheroes, the mere presence of an antihero is not enough in itself to make a story dark fantasy. It is not clear, for example, that John Gardner's 1971 novel *Grendel*, a retelling of the story of Beowulf from the point of view of the monster, would be called dark fantasy. It might be more correct to think of dark fantasy as fantasy in which the storytellers themselves have taken up an antiheroic point of view. The attitude of the writers of dark fantasy may be the most distinctive feature of the genre, as most dark fantasy stories reflect a skepticism or pessimism about fantasy that is not typical of the nondark style.

Michael Cisco

See also: *The Dark Tower*; Dreams and Nightmares; *The Drowning Girl*; Gaiman, Neil; Grant, Charles L.; Kiernan, Caitlín R.; New Weird; *The Night Land*; Smith, Clark Ashton; *Vathek*; Wagner, Karl Edward.

Further Reading

Hoppenstand, Gary. 2004. "Francis Stevens: The Woman Who Invented Dark Fantasy." Introduction to *The Nightmare and Other Tales of Dark Fantasy* by Francis Stevens, edited by Gary Hoppenstand, ix–xxv. Lincoln and London: University of Nebraska Press.

Kaveney, Roz. 2012. "Dark Fantasy and Paranormal Romance." In *The Cambridge Companion to Fantasy Literature*, edited by Edward James and Farah Mendlesohn, 214–224. Cambridge: Cambridge University Press.

Roberts, Caryn G. 2000. "Dark Fantasy." In *The Prentice Hall Anthology of Science Fiction and Fantasy*, 31–32. Upper Saddle River, NJ: Prentice Hall.

DARK GODS

In addition to his singular novel, *The Ceremonies* (1984), T. E. D. Klein has garnered fame as a horror writer from the reputation of *Dark Gods*, his 1985 collection of sinister short stories. Though these tales, on the surface of it, are wholly unconnected, some of their pervading themes are interestingly drawn together by the volume's title, which hints at the existence of monstrous deities. In each of these stories, their is the ominous sense that the Christian God (or indeed a benevolent god of *any* kind) is nowhere to be found; instead, it is gradually suggested—or revealed—that humans are at the mercy of darker, more malevolent, and ancient forces.

The stories in this collection vividly illustrate why Klein is considered a "master of the horror genre" (Mariconda 1986, 28). Moreover, they serve to highlight some of his favorite and most recurrent themes. In each, he masterfully interweaves primordial horrors with the mundaneness of modernity—hinting, darkly, that people are naïve to assume that their more ancient superstitions are today outmoded. Klein has stated that he believes horror literature is, or should be, "a tradition-conscious genre" (Tibbetts 2011, 51), and his love and knowledge of the field ensures a consistent intertextual quality to his work. Just as *The Ceremonies* is an homage to Gothic literature, and most especially to Arthur Machen, *Dark Gods* pays tribute to many of the literary masters of horror and is most consciously indebted to the works of H. P. Lovecraft. Klein's own style is distinguished by the deliberate *vagueness* of his horror; there is very little overt violence or monstrosity, as instead he delivers his own brand of the macabre through a series of ominous hints and portents. For the most part, he consciously withholds his monsters, giving only vague and horrible outlines, which readers must then color in themselves with their most personal anxieties. His specialty lies in what Mariconda has called "atmospheric tension" (20); he masterfully creates, in each of these tales, a haunting and tangible *ambience* of dread.

The collection is comprised of four stories in total. The first of these, "Children of the Kingdom," centers on the filthy—and supernatural—underbelly of modern-day New York. The narrator, who is interestingly named Mr. Klein, has just placed his grandfather in a rest home. Through his grandfather, he comes to know Father Pistachio, an elderly priest who harbors strange and sinister notions about the origins of humanity. This priest believes, vehemently, that we all originated in Central America, where we lived happily until the sudden arrival of the "Xo Tl'mi-go," or "*usurpadores*": a monstrous race that is part human, part tapeworm. He claims that humans only left America and spread out across the earth as a result of trying to flee these creatures and their lust-driven violence. Slowly, the reader is presented with evidence to suggest these monsters' continued existence. It transpires that they dwell just beneath us, in the sewers below the cities, and emerge only in the darkness to commit their atrocities. In the climax of the story, there is a citywide blackout during which the *usurpadores* horrifyingly emerge en masse. When the light returns, no one can describe exactly what has occurred in the darkness, though several of the women in the city have been impregnated in the night. These monsters are merely glimpsed—the reader knows only that they are cold, white, wet, and webbed—and consequently, they are all the more terrifying.

The second tale, "Petey," follows the story of George and Phyllis, a young couple who have just purchased a huge, isolated, and mysterious home. The story unfolds on the evening of their housewarming party. It transpires that the property was purchased, at great reduction, through underhand means: its previous occupant, an unstable recluse, was forcibly evicted to enable its sale. When he was dragged from his home, this recluse, who had no family at all, screamed repeatedly for his "son," as he was certain that "Petey" would come to his aid. Who or what "Petey" is, is only gradually revealed by fragmented and unnerving details: the reader discovers the nature of this monstrous entity primarily through a fairy tale and a tarot deck. The fairy tale tells of a lonely farmer who grows a companion—the "Petit Diablo," or "Little Devil"—who is born with the harvest. Meanwhile, one tarot card, which is out of place in its deck, shows a strange, shapeless entity from behind. This card is repeatedly shown, and the reader discovers, to his or her horror, that its subject gradually turns toward its percipient. The tale ends with George seeing that the monster on the card has now turned to face him fully . . . at the exact same moment that there is a sudden and thunderous knocking at his door. It is implied that the insidious monster, "Petey," is now born and has now arrived to exact his "father's" revenge. This is the monster from the fairy tale, and the screams of "Petey" were in fact of "Petit" as the wronged recluse summoned his creation.

The third tale, "Black Man with a Horn," centers on an old man and the interest he takes in the evil ways of an ancient Malaysian tribe, the Chauchas. His interest is sparked by a meeting with a stranger, the Reverend Mortimer. Mortimer, who is returning from Malaysia, believes he has been targeted by this ancient tribe, who have set a demon on him—the titular Black Man with a Horn, or "shugaron" in the native tongue. Soon enough, the reverend mysteriously disappears—leaving only a few fragments of lung tissue behind him—and the protagonist sets out to discover the reverend's fate. He studies the history of the "shugaron" and discovers that it is not, in fact, a "black man with a horn," but a monster with a horn-like mouth, designed to violently suck its victims and turn their lungs inside out. Once again, the reader does not see this monster directly, but increasingly fears its proximity. The protagonist realizes, by the end of the tale, that he is the demon's next intended victim.

"Nadelman's God," the final tale in the collection, won the World Fantasy Award for Best Novella in 1986 and is heralded by many as Klein's greatest piece of horror fiction. The story follows the protagonist, Nadelman, and his interactions with a young man named Arlen Huntoon, who reads one of Nadelman's poems and becomes obsessed with its content. Huntoon believes that the poem, which is about an alternative and wholly malignant god, is no work of fiction; to his mind, it is a "cookbook" for creating hideous disciples to serve this monstrous divinity. Consequently, he follows the poem's "instructions" and builds his very own terrifying effigy. Huntoon is soon killed and then Nadelman is haunted by this hideous statue. It is uncertain, even at the end, if Huntoon is simply mad, or if his twisted religion is in some way real: in other words, the reader has no idea if Nadelman's god—a truly monstrous deity we never actually see—is in any way real. This eerie little tale preys, hauntingly, on the dreamer's paranoia: what if, asks Klein, in imagining monsters, we are truly creating them?

Dark Gods illustrates the terrifying vagueness of horror for which Klein is renowned. In each of these tales, he posits truly frightening entities, each of which is merely glimpsed peripherally—and consequently embeds itself all the more deeply in the reader's subconscious. With each story, it becomes increasingly apparent that humans are now devoid of an omniscient and benevolent deity: they are all at the mercy of dark gods indeed.

Elizabeth Parker

See also: The Ceremonies; Klein, T. E. D.; Machen, Arthur; Monsters.

Further Reading

Mariconda, Steven J. 1986. "The Hints and Portents of T. E. D. Klein." *Studies in Weird Fiction*, Vol. 1 (Summer), 19–28.

Tibbetts, John C. 2011. "Certain Things Associated with the Night: T. E. D. Klein." In *The Gothic Imagination: Conversations on Fantasy, Horror, and Science Fiction in the Media*, 51–54. New York: Palgrave Macmillan.

THE DARK TOWER

The Dark Tower is a series of books by Stephen King comprising eight volumes published between 1982 and 2012. The main narrative comprises *The Gunslinger* (1982), *The Drawing of the Three* (1987), *The Waste Lands* (1991), *Wizard and Glass* (1997), *The Wolves of the Calla* (2003), *The Song of Susanna* (2004), and *The Dark Tower* (2004). In addition, there is the novel *The Wind Through the Keyhole* (2012).

Drawing on Robert Browning's epic poem "Childe Roland to the Dark Tower Came" (1855), King's story tells of Roland Deschain, a gunslinger in a dying land called Mid-World, who is on a quest to find the Dark Tower, the nexus of all creation. Around the tower coalesce a series of beams that bind an infinite number of parallel universes. Those beams are dying, which will make the Tower fall and mean the end of everything. Roland is aided by a group of fellow travelers, known as ka-tet, drawn via mystic doors from New York City as it exists in various worlds and times. They are Eddie from the 1980s, Susanna from the 1960s, and Jake from the 1970s. With them is Oy, a raccoon-like creature from Mid-World.

The Dark Tower is King's cult work, read by relatively few of his millions of Constant Readers. In part this is due to its history. Written in the late 1960s, the first volume in the series, *The Gunslinger*, was first published serially in *The Magazine of Fantasy and Science Fiction* between 1978 and 1981. In 1982 it was released as a limited edition of 10,000 copies by Donald M. Grant Publishers, making *The Gunslinger* a novel few of his fans knew. Grant published the second part in 1987, which was then released to the mass market by Sphere along with *The Gunslinger*, but sales of all the novels remained comparatively small.

The other reason why the series has not matched King's usual success is that it is a fantasy rather than a horror text, and thus has not fit the King brand. However, during the 1980s and 1990s *The Dark Tower* exerted an increasing influence on King, whose novels began to connect to Roland's adventures. Randall Flagg from *The Stand* (1978) appears in *Wizard and Glass*, while *The Waste Lands* features the enormous turtle from *It* (1986). Such links to his wider works increased in the final books, written after King was almost killed in an accident in 1999. Father Callaghan from *'Salem's Lot* appears, as does Ted Brautigan from *Hearts in Atlantis* (1999) and also King himself.

Because it is not considered part of the horror genre, *The Dark Tower* is rarely discussed as a canonical King text such as *The Shining* or *The Stand*. Yet because of this interconnectedness it is arguably the most significant of his works, and one that may come to define King's legacy, not as a bestselling author, but as a writer and creator of worlds. In 2017, after a decade in development hell, a film adaptation titled *The Dark Tower* was released, starring Idris Elba as Roland and Matthew McConaughey as the sinister Man in Black.

Simon Brown

See also: Dark Fantasy; *It*; King, Stephen.

Further Reading

Furth, Robin. 2012. *Stephen King's The Dark Tower: The Complete Concordance*. London: Hodder and Stoughton.

McAleer, Patrick. 2009. *Inside the Dark Tower Series: Art, Evil and Intertextuality in the Stephen King Novels*. Jefferson, NC: McFarland.

Vincent, Bev. 2013. *The Dark Tower Companion: A Guide to Stephen King's Epic Fantasy*. New York: Penguin.

DATLOW, ELLEN (1949–)

Ellen Datlow is an influential editor and publishing professional whose work as an anthologist of both reprint and original fiction has had a significant impact on the consideration of anthologies as important showcases for fantastic fiction. A number of stories first published in her anthologies have won the most prestigious awards in the horror and fantasy fields.

Datlow was hired as associate fiction editor at *Omni* magazine in 1979 and became fiction editor in 1981, a position she held until 1998 before moving on to online magazines *Event Horizon* and *Sci Fiction*. Between 1984 and 1989, she edited seven volumes of science fiction stories culled from the pages of *Omni*.

In 1988 Datlow and Terri Windling began editing *The Year's Best Fantasy* (a.k.a. *The Year's Best Fantasy and Horror* as of 1991), a series that would run twenty-one volumes with Datlow picking the horror and (until 2004, when Kelly Link and Gavin Grant assumed duties) Windling the fantasy fiction. The series showcased the best short horror and fantasy fiction published in the decades when those genres established themselves as major categories in trade publishing. In 2009, after the discontinuation of *The Year's Best Fantasy and Horror*, Datlow began editing *The Best Horror of the Year*.

In 1990, drawing on horror submissions that would not have been appropriate for *Omni*'s science fiction readership, Datlow edited *Blood Is Not Enough*, an anthology of new and reprint vampire fiction that expanded the definition of the vampire's predatory proclivities. She followed this with an anthology of erotic horror and science fiction stories, *Alien Sex* (1990), and a second anthology of nontraditional vampire fiction, *A Whisper of Blood* (1991). In 1993, Datlow and Windling edited *Snow White, Blood Red*, the first in a series of anthologies in which contemporary writers of fantasy and horror retell classic fairy and folk tales for modern readers.

The themes of Datlow's anthologies show considerable range and variety: sexual horror in *Little Deaths* (1994); supernatural cats in *Twists of the Tale* (1996); tributes to H. P. Lovecraft in *Lovecraft Unbound* (2009), *Lovecraft's Monsters* (2014), and *Children of Lovecraft* (2016); movies and filmmaking in *The Cutting Room* (2014); carnivals and circuses in *Nightmare Carnival* (2014); and dolls and other simulacra in *The Doll Collection* (2015).

As of 2016 Datlow has been nominated for the World Fantasy Award forty-three times and won ten times, the most for any one person. She was awarded the Horror Writer Association's Bram Stoker Award and the World Fantasy Award for lifetime achievement in 2011 and 2014, respectively.

Stefan R. Dziemianowicz

See also: Bram Stoker Award; Link, Kelly; World Fantasy Award.

Further Reading

"Ellen Datlow and Terri Windling: Depth and Heart." 2016. *Locus* 76, no. 6: (June): 12–13, 56–58.

"Ellen Datlow: Horror's Queen." 2001. *Locus* 46, no. 3 (March): 6, 83–84.

Gee, Robin. 1990. "Close-up: Ellen Datlow." In *1990 Novel & Short Story Writer's Market*, edited by Robin Gee, 368. Cincinnati: Writer's Digest Books.

Hoagland, Ericka. 2009. "Datlow, Ellen." In *Women in Science Fiction and Fantasy*, edited by Robin A. Reid, 81–82. Westport, CT: Greenwood.

Interview with Ellen Datlow

October 2016

Datlow here draws on her long career as an editor of horror, science fiction, and fantasy to talk about what defines horror literature as such, and to clarify its relationship with science fiction and several other well-defined genres such as Westerns and crime fiction. She also discusses her editorial process for identifying high-quality horror fiction, and she describes what she views as the negative impact of the late twentieth-century boom in horror publishing on horror literature itself. She concludes by offering some recommendations for classic and contemporary horror reading. In the latter capacity, she identifies what she regards as the most important trend in contemporary horror publishing.

Matt Cardin: Early in your career you distinguished yourself as a science fiction editor. Then you became prominently associated with horror. These two have a long history together, with the blending of horror and science fiction having yielded interesting—and in some cases, *classic*—results in both areas. What do you see as the relationship between

SF and horror? Where does the one start and the other leave off? And why do they work so well together?

Ellen Datlow: There *is* a long tradition of SF/horror in literature: *Frankenstein*, *The Fly*, *Who Goes There?*, "Leiningen vs. the Ants," *Invasion of the Body Snatchers*, *The Midwich Cuckoos*, and much of Harlan Ellison's short fiction, such as "I Have No Mouth and I Must Scream."

It's easy to see how dystopian and postapocalyptic fiction (Ellison's novella *A Boy and His Dog*, and Margaret Atwood's *The Handmaid's Tale*) blur over into horror, as dystopias by their nature *are* horrific. So it's quite a natural relationship.

Horror, which is more defined by tone than anything else, combines well with several genres—as it's not in itself a genre. Romance mixed with horror becomes the classic Gothic; Westerns as written by Joe R. Lansdale and James Lee Burke often contain elements of horror. Crime fiction such as the novels of Thomas Harris featuring Hannibal Lector are most definitely horror.

MC: What are your guiding principles as an editor and anthologist of horror fiction? Obviously, themed anthologies, such as your various projects centered on vampirism and Lovecraft, have their own specific sets of needs and rules. But when it comes to your "best of" anthologies, how do you go about deciding what to include? What, in your view, marks a given work of short-form horror fiction as being truly good, or even great?

ED: While reading year round for my next *Best Horror* anthology, I make a note when I find an especially good story that is horrific. Then, when the time comes for me to begin making decisions, I count up the wordage of the stories I've marked and reread them. I know how many words I have in my annual, and I always end up with as much as twice the number of words I can fit. So the rest of the process is eliminating stories to bring the book down to a reasonable size. Sometimes I'll read a story three or four times. If I still love a story after rereading it: still find it startling, still find that it provides a deep abiding feel of unease, that it continues to unnerve me—that story will likely end up in the book.

During my career I've reprinted some stories multiple times. Those are the stories that stick with me, that continue to impress me. They're the ones that I consider the best over the years. New stories are added to that "best" over time.

But essentially for any anthology, it must be the editor's personal reaction to each story that counts.

MC: In addition to vampirism and Lovecraftian fiction, your themed horror anthologies have focused on sexual horror, carnivals and circuses, dolls, and movies. Why do you think horror is so portable, as it were? Why is it so applicable to virtually any type of plot, setting, theme, or motif? And what exactly characterizes it? What makes a given story a *horror* story instead of (or in addition to) something else?

ED: I think I started to answer that in my response to the first question. Horror is not a genre. It's a tone, a way of approaching character, plot, and place. In a horror story the protagonist loses something—things are not what they seem. There is evil lurking—underground, around the corner, in an abandoned house. Even when characters survive, they usually lose something: their innocence, their sanity, their certainty in the way things should work. In addition to SF/horror, there's supernatural horror consisting of ghosts, vampires, werewolves, zombies, witches, ghouls, and so on. And there's the conte-cruel, nicely defined by H. P. Lovecraft as fiction "in which the wrenching of the emotions is accomplished through dramatic tantalizations, frustrations, and gruesome physical horrors."

MC: You worked right through the great horror publishing boom of the 1980s and 1990s, so you had a "boots on the ground" perspective on the whole thing. What do you see as the lasting results of that phenomenon? How is the field different today because of what happened then?

ED: It hurt the field immensely. Because almost every book publisher found it expedient to create a horror line and thus fill a specific number of "slots" per month, a lot of mediocre horror was published. And most of those books did not sell. This created the perception that no horror but the big names such as Stephen King, Dean Koontz, Clive Barker, and Anne Rice sold, and also that most horror was bad. It also encouraged a spate of awful, generic book covers that didn't help. It's taken decades for horror as a "market" to recover. It demonstrated quite clearly that it's better for publishers and editors to be passionate about what they publish, than just randomly publish anything that's submitted. If they care nothing about what they're publishing, why should potential readers care?

Some writers who were regularly selling novels and receiving high advances discovered that once the bubble burst, they couldn't sell their books at all, or else couldn't make as much money with them as they had. Some writers stopped writing.

The best writers continued to create ambitious horror and to sell it. Some writers switched gears to concentrate on crime/thriller writing. Serial killer novels became quite popular for a period of time; they were often horrific but were not designated horror.

Today a lot of horror novels are published by mainstream publishers, and the reader must guess (or read reviews) to discover which are horror and which are not. It all depends on your definition of horror. I'm more open than some others in the field to what I consider horror.

I don't think anyone in the 1980s or 1990s could have foreseen the range of short horror fiction being published today, especially by young writers from different cultures. This is a thrilling time for anyone who loves short stories. Horror stories are being published in venues ranging from small and large literary magazines, to science fiction and fantasy magazines, to webzines of all kinds. The challenge is finding them. There were never many horror magazines; even in the pulp era, most of those magazines published a mix of horror, dark fantasy, and fantasy.

MC: What classic works and authors of horror fiction would you recommend to the interested reader who might be looking to further his or her knowledge of the field? Can you name a few that are absolutely indispensable?

ED: As a short story reader, I advise readers to pick up anthologies and single author collections. Anthologies such as *Great Tales of Terror and the Supernatural*, the huge reprint anthology edited by Phyllis Cerf Wagner and Herbert Wise that included mainstream writers along with the Gothic writers. *A Second Century of Creepy Stories*, edited by Hugh Walpole. *The Playboy Book of Horror and the Supernatural*. Karl Edward Wagner's old *Bests of the Year*. My old *Year's Best Fantasy and Horror* series. Stephen Jones's *Best New Horror*. Checking out current *Bests* of the year is the quickest, easiest means to find out what's going on in the field from year to year. Those are all reprint anthologies.

Kirby McCauley's *Dark Forces*, published in 1980, featured all new stories by a variety of writers. Isaac Bashevis Singer, Edward Gorey, and Joyce Carol Oates rubbed shoulders with Gene Wolfe, Lisa Tuttle, Ray Bradbury, Ramsey Campbell, Theodore Sturgeon, and Joe Haldeman, among others.

MC: What about contemporary horror? Who and what should readers be watching? What are the most important trends? Where is the cutting edge located?

ED: Short horror fiction is in a golden age. That's something I and my fellow horror editors all agree upon. There are fabulous short story writers not only from the United States, Australia, Canada, and the United Kingdom, but from Japan, India, and the Philippines. Some names to watch: Priya Sharma, Alyssa Wong, Usman T. Malik, Carmen Maria Machado, Ray Cluley, Tom Johnstone, Tamsyn Muir, Livia Llewellyn, Alison Littlewood, and Carole Johnstone. That's just a tiny example of relatively new writers.

Then there are more established writers working in SF/F/H who are less noticed by horror readers because they *do* play the field: Elizabeth Hand, Brian Evenson, Jeffrey Ford, Caitlín R. Kiernan, Dale Bailey, Garth Nix, Kelly Link, Kaaron Warren, Angela Slatter, Pat Cadigan, Margo Lanagan, Paul McAuley, Stephen Graham Jones.

I could name a few dozen more easily.

In my opinion, the most important trend is the influx of new voices from non-Western cultures and an increase of females and people of color into the field (at least in short fiction). Small presses are filling the gap in single-author collections left by large, mainstream publishers who only publish them rarely.

MC: With the field being so broad and bristling right now, do you have any parting advice for readers who want to make the most of this new golden age of horror fiction?

ED: Horror stories can be found in many more places than you might think. Because horror is as much about tone as anything else, it can reside in all kinds of fiction. Literary journals, crime magazines and anthologies, science fiction and fantasy magazines all publish horror. So be open-minded.

DE LA MARE, WALTER (1873–1956)

Walter John de la Mare was born in Kent, England, on April 25, 1873, into a wealthy family (his father, James, worked at the Bank of England) and grew up to become one of twentieth-century Britain's most prolific writers. A short story writer and novelist, de la Mare is probably best known for his poetry for children, among which "The Listeners" (1912) is most remembered by legions of schoolchildren and students. He also made significant contributions to the horror genre.

"Seaton's Aunt": A Tale of (Possible) Psychic Vampirism

Published originally in *The London Mercury* in 1922, and collected in 1923 in *The Riddle, and Other Stories,* "Seaton's Aunt" is one of de la Mare's finest and most chilling psychological horror stories, and one of the foremost examples of the inconclusive ghost story for which he was known. The eponymous "Aunt" is the relative of Arthur Seaton, one of the narrator's schoolmates, with whom he agrees to stay during the holidays. Seaton's aunt is obsessed with death, and Seaton believes she is in communion with demonic spirits. While the narrator, Withers, refuses to believe that Seaton's aunt wishes her nephew dead, he too becomes disturbed by her increasingly erratic behavior, and the story concludes with the death of Seaton in mysterious circumstances.

The strength of the story as a work of psychological horror lies precisely in the reader's confusion as to whether Seaton's aunt truly is a psychic vampire who wishes him harm, or whether the reader believes, with Withers, that Seaton is embellishing details. While de la Mare provides evidence to substantiate both viewpoints, the underlying issue is not whether something horrifying is happening, but what form exactly the horror takes. If one sides with the more rational Withers, then one must acknowledge that the aunt's neglect of her charge is a consequence of disturbing psychological abuse that it is hinted she experiences at Seaton's hand. De la Mare successfully heightens the ambiguity of the narrative by couching the real human horrors of ageism and emotional abuse in ambiguous supernaturalism, and succeeds in crafting a horror narrative that disturbs on a number of levels. The story was masterfully brought to life on screen as part of the British supernatural anthology television series *Shades of Darkness* in 1983.

Ian Kinane

After an education at St. Paul's Cathedral Choir School in London, de la Mare worked as a statistician for Standard Oil Company from 1890 to 1908, during which time he began to write. His first published work, a short story entitled "Kismet," was published in *The Sketch* magazine in 1895, after which de la Mare applied himself to compiling a collection of poetry for children—which later became his first published book, *Songs of Childhood,* published in 1902 under the pen name "Walter Ramal." This was followed by his first novel, *Henry Brocken* (1904), an intriguing romance in which the wanderer-protagonist journeys through literature, encountering all manner of characters from Jane Eyre and Rochester to Shakespeare's Titania and Bottom. It was not until 1912, though, that de la Mare achieved literary renown for his children's collection *The Listeners and Other Poems* (1912).

Though comprising a relatively fractional amount of his literary output, de la Mare's horror and supernatural writings are among the best of his work. Most of this writing can be characterized by the inconclusive nature of its horror and/or supernatural elements, as de la Mare deliberately hints at but never explicitly reveals to the reader the source of apparent supernatural happenings within his stories. For example, in one of his most disturbing psychological horror stories, "Seaton's Aunt" (1922), de la Mare intimates that the title character, the elderly aunt of the narrator's school friend, Seaton, with whom he visits, may be a psychic vampire in communion with the devil, and that she is out to hurt her nephew. While nothing explicit is ever shown, de la Mare carefully manipulates the reader's perceptions of Seaton's aunt and Seaton himself, so as to heighten the story's ambiguity. At the end, when Seaton dies under mysterious circumstances, both the narrator and the reader remain unsure as to the cause, and the potentially supernatural elements of the story are left unexplained.

In addition to the supernatural, much of de la Mare's work is concerned with the power of the human imagination and with the psychological connections between the human world and the paranormal realm. Spirit possession is a common trope in de la Mare's work, particularly in *The Return* (1910), the author's second novel, in which the protagonist falls asleep on a grave on unconsecrated ground and awakes bearing the physical appearance of the grave's occupant. Spirits and ghosts also feature heavily, or are certainly strongly hinted at. The haunting central image of "The Listeners" (1912), for example, is of the crowd of silent, phantom listeners who throng the seemingly empty house to which the protagonist has journeyed. In many of his short stories, de la Mare's spirits and ghosts are intricately tied to literature or to literary figures: in "The Green Room" (1925), a young man is haunted by the ghost of a poet when he publishes her poetry posthumously; and in the novelette "A Revenant" (1936), a literature academic is haunted by the ghost of Edgar Allan Poe after he insults the writer's work.

Haunted houses also feature greatly in de la Mare's writing. In "Out of the Deep" (1923), the hero-protagonist returns to his dead uncle's house, in which memories of his childhood proceed to haunt him before he dies. In "A Recluse" (1930), the owner of a house, with whom the protagonist visits, discovers his host's dead body and realizes he has been conversing with the dead man's ghost all along. In "The House" (1936), the protagonist is so haunted by his own childhood memories that he becomes absorbed within the walls of his old home.

The great stylistic strength of de la Mare's atmospheric supernatural writing is matched by the keen insight he possesses into humankind, and by his reflections on the very real-world, human tragedies that befall us all. In his work, de la Mare ruminates on isolation, human existence, and the limits of love, and it is perhaps for his consideration of these deeper emotions that we might recognize the painful human element underlining all of his supernatural work.

While his 1921 novel, *Memoirs of a Midget*, won the James Tait Black Memorial Prize for fiction, and his *Collected Stories for Children* won the Carnegie Medal for children's fiction in 1947, de la Mare was also a great literary critic who published some very insightful nonfiction works on contemporary literature, including *Some*

Women Novelists of the Seventies (1929) and *Desert Islands and Robinson Crusoe* (1930). His writing proved a great influence on later authors of supernatural fiction, particularly H. P. Lovecraft, Robert Aickman, and Ramsey Campbell. Declining the offer of a knighthood in both 1924 and 1931, de la Mare continued to write until his death on June 22, 1956, following which he was buried in the crypt in St. Paul's Cathedral.

Ian Kinane

See also: "The Listeners"; "Out of the Deep"; *The Return.*

Further Reading

Adrian, Jack. 1998. "De la Mare, Walter." In *The St. James Guide to Horror, Ghost, and Gothic Writers*, edited by David Pringle, 174–177. London: St. James Press.

Crawford, Gary William. 1992. "On the Edge: The Ghost Stories of Walter de la Mare." In *Discovering Classic Horror Fiction I*, edited by Darrell Schweitzer, 53–56. Gillette, NJ: Wildside Press.

Whistler, Theresa. 1993. *Imagination of the Heart: The Life of Walter de la Mare.* London: Gerald Duckworth.

"THE DEATH OF HALPIN FRAYSER"

Widely considered one of Ambrose Bierce's finest tales of horror, "The Death of Halpin Frayser" was first published in *The Wave* on December 19, 1891. Two years later, it appeared in his short fiction collection *Can Such Things Be?* It is significant both as one of Bierce's finest horror tales and as a kind of forerunner of the figure of the zombie that later became so central to horror fiction and film.

The tale begins with the eponymous protagonist waking in an eerie forest from a "dreamless sleep" and uttering the name "Catherine Larue." He journeys through the forest and encounters the corpse of his mother. The second section of the story moves to Frayser's early life in Nashville, Tennessee, where it is revealed that he is a bad poet and that he and his mother possess an inordinately close bond. Despite her objections, she allows her son to travel to San Francisco, where he is kidnapped and spends a number of years at sea. The tale then moves back to the present, where bounty hunters—a deputy named Holker and a detective named Jaralson—are seeking a criminal named Branscom, who is wanted for murder. As they enter a graveyard, they find Frayser's strangled corpse lying atop a grave that, as they soon discover, is that of Catherine Larue. Putting together the facts, Holker recalls that Larue is Branscom's real name and that the woman he murdered was named Frayser. The story ends with Holker and Jaralson hearing "the sound of a laugh, a low, deliberate, soulless laugh which had no more of joy than that of a hyena night-prowling in the desert. . . . a laugh so unnatural, so unhuman, so devilish, that it filled those hardy man-hunters with a sense of dread unspeakable!" (Bierce 1984, 71).

"That Most Dreadful of All Existences": "The Death of Halpin Frayser" as an Early Zombie

"The Death of Halpin Frayser" is often described as one of the forerunners of modern zombie fiction, and it is easy to see why when reading passages like the following. Notably, it not only features what inevitably appears to the modern reader as a zombie or zombie-like creature (right down to the familiar motif of the reanimated loved one who is horribly like and yet unlike the former self), but it does so in the context of the exquisite tone of dreadful nightmare that Bierce generates throughout the story.

> The apparition confronting the dreamer in the haunted wood—the thing so like, yet so unlike, his mother—was horrible! It stirred no love nor longings in his heart; it came unattended with pleasant memories of a golden past—inspired no sentiment of any kind; all the finer emotions were swallowed up in fear. He tried to turn and run from before it, but his legs were as lead; he was unable to lift his feet from the ground. His arms hung helpless at his sides; of his eyes only he retained control, and these he dared not remove from the lustreless orbs of the apparition, which he knew was not a soul without a body, but that most dreadful of all existences infesting that haunted wood—a body without a soul! In its blank stare was neither love, nor pity, nor intelligence—nothing to which to address an appeal for mercy. (Bierce 1914, 141)

Matt Cardin

Source: Bierce, Ambrose. 1914. "The Death of Halpin Frayser." In *Neale's Monthly Magazine*. Volume 3. New York: Neale's Publishing.

Dark and unsettling in tone, oblique in upshot and meaning, "The Death of Halpin Frayser" contains two notable features that have particularly interested readers and critics alike: the Oedipus complex and a nascent form of what would later emerge as the major horror archetype of the zombie. Regarding the former, the tale does, in fact, suggest an unnatural and too-close relationship between mother and son, resulting in tragedy. Regarding the latter, the story is widely regarded as one of the progenitors of zombie fiction, as attested by, among many other things, the fact that both it and Bierce merited inclusion in 2014's *Encyclopedia of the Zombie* (2014), where the story is described as "bleak and elliptical," and as one of several stories illustrating the fact that "In Bierce's world, the dead rarely lie still, and at times may not even be dead" (Bleiler 16). One reading of "Halpin Frayser" has it that Frayser was killed by his mother's corpse, but the matter is inconclusive since the story's events can be interpreted both supernaturally and naturally. In any event, the judgment of H. P. Lovecraft, who counted Bierce as a major influence, is generally shared by those who are familiar with the story; in his groundbreaking essay *Supernatural Horror in Literature*, Lovecraft grouped "The Death of Halpin Frayser" among several others in Bierce's body of work that have a "grim malevolence stalking through all of them," and that "stand out as permanent mountain-peaks of American weird writing" (Lovecraft 2012, 66).

E. Kate Stewart

See also: Bierce, Ambrose; Zombies.

Further Reading

Bierce, Ambrose. 1984. *The Complete Short Stories of Ambrose Bierce*, compiled with commentary by Ernest Jerome Hopkins. Lincoln and London: University of Nebraska Press.

Bleiler, Richard. 2014. "Ambrose Bierce." In *Encyclopedia of the Zombie: The Walking Dead in Popular Culture and Myth*, edited by June Michele Pulliam and Anthony J. Fonseca, 15–17. Santa Barbara, CA: Greenwood.

Lovecraft, H. P. [1927] 2012. *The Annotated Supernatural Horror in Literature*. Edited by S. T. Joshi. New York: Hippocampus Press.

Talley, Sharon. 2009. "The Failed Journey to Self-Understanding in 'The Death of Halpin Frayser.'" In *Ambrose Bierce and the Dance of Death*, 17–28. Knoxville: University of Tennessee Press.

"THE DEMON LOVER"

Elizabeth Bowen's "The Demon Lover" (1944) is a compelling and ambiguous ghost story in the mold of Henry James's *The Turn of the Screw* (1898). Bowen, in fact, was one of the most important Jamesian writers of the twentieth century, a savvy chronicler of middle-class life who was deeply attentive to the subtlest shifts of psychological mood in her characters. This sensibility served her well in the modest handful of truly eerie ghost stories she wrote during her lifetime, vivid evocations of the eruption of the uncanny into mundane contemporary settings.

Set during World War II, "The Demon Lover" centers on Mrs. Drover, a prosaic middle-aged housewife who has come to check on her shuttered London home, her family having decamped to the country to escape the blitz. There she finds a letter, apparently from a former lover who died during the First World War, promising to return to claim her. Mrs. Drover at first refuses to believe the evidence of her senses: that some strange supernatural agency has intervened into her stolid middle-class life, disrupting its orderly norms forever. Bowen sustains an atmosphere of mounting dread, bordering on hysteria, as Mrs. Drover struggles to come to grips with her experience, and it culminates in an explosion of shrieking terror that lingers long in the reader's mind.

The story's title cites the folkloric tradition of demon-lover ballads, in which deceased suitors haunt and possess their former flames, but Bowen gives the genre a Freudian twist, as Mrs. Drover's passionate past wells up, like the return of the repressed (the Freudian psychoanalytic term for the tendency of unconscious thoughts and emotions to reappear spontaneously in altered form in consciousness and behavior), and overwhelms her mundane present. As in James's pitch-perfect novella, the reader is kept in suspense with regard to the reality of the demonic threat: it could be authentic, or it could be the product of a disordered mind. The tale also captures the wartime climate vividly, conveying a sense of everyday life disrupted and besieged by malign forces. It is significant that Mrs. Drover lost her lover during an earlier spasm of military violence; indeed, the story strongly suggests that the cataclysm of war is so powerful, it can shake loose potent demons of memory and regret.

Bowen, who died in 1973, was one of the finest British short story writers of the twentieth century. "The Demon Lover" is a classic.

Rob Latham

See also: James, Henry; Psychological Horror; *The Turn of the Screw*.

Further Reading

Fraustino, Daniel V. 1980. "Elizabeth Bowen's 'The Demon Lover': Psychosis or Seduction?" *Studies in Short Fiction* 17 (4): 483–487.

Hughes, Douglas A. 1972. "Cracks in the Psyche: Elizabeth Bowen's 'The Demon Lover.'" *Studies in Short Fiction* 10, no. 4: 411–413.

Thompson, Terry W. 2010. "'A Face You Do Not Expect': The Female Other in Elizabeth Bowen's 'The Demon Lover.'" *Journal of the Short Story in English* 54 (Spring). http://jsse .revues.org/1036.

DERLETH, AUGUST (1909–1971)

August Derleth was an American writer and editor of fantasy, horror, and science fiction whose reputation is inextricably bound up with that of H. P. Lovecraft, the writer for whom he was a leading exponent and advocate. As a publisher, Derleth was instrumental in establishing the specialty press as a driving force in genre publishing.

Derleth's first professional sale, "Bat's Belfry," appeared in the May 1926 issue of *Weird Tales* when he was just seventeen years old. Over the next twenty-eight years, he published several hundred more stories in virtually every magazine that catered to readers of horror and fantasy fiction, and became the second most published author in *Weird Tales*. Among Derleth's influences, as he noted in the introduction to his first short fiction collection, *Someone in the Dark* (1941), were M. R. James and Mary E. Wilkins Freeman, and although he wrote on a wide variety of horror themes, many of his stories were in the genteel ghost story tradition associated with those writers. Derleth acknowledged that most of his short weird fiction was written as filler, and he seems to have thought more highly of his mainstream fiction concerned with the people and history of Wisconsin's Sac Prairie, which was earning him a reputation as a distinguished writer of regional fiction in the1930s and 1940s. In the introduction to his third weird fiction collection, *Not Long for This World* (1948), Derleth dismissed as mediocre most of his weird fiction for his first two decades as a writer, but he did produce several outstanding weird tales, among them the humorous ghost story "Pacific 421" (1944), the amusing vampire story "Who Shall I Say Is Calling?" (1952), the "invisible friend" story "Mr. George" (1947, as by "Stephen Grendon"), and the "evil place" story "The Lonesome Place" (1948). The simplicity of Derleth's weird tales made them ideal for adaptation to other media, and thus "The Return of Andrew Bentley" (1933) and "Colonel Markesan" (1934), both written in collaboration with Mark Schorer, as well as "A Wig for Miss Devore" (1943), were all televised for Boris Karloff's *Thriller*. "Logoda's Heads" (1939) was adapted for Rod Serling's *Night Gallery*.

Derleth began corresponding with H. P. Lovecraft in the 1920s, and he was one of the first writers to attempt a pastiche of Lovecraft's fiction when "The Lair of the Star Spawn" (written in collaboration with Mark Schorer) was published in the August 1932 issue of *Weird Tales*. In the 1940s and 1950s, in a cycle of Lovecraft pastiches published mostly in *Weird Tales* and later collected in *The Mask of Cthulhu* (1958), and in the episodic novel *The Trail of Cthulhu* (1962), Derleth began to codify as the Cthulhu Mythos the myth pattern behind much of Lovecraft's weird fiction and the tales that Lovecraft's *Weird Tales* colleagues had written in the spirit of his fiction. This entailed recasting Lovecraft's extradimensional monsters as earth elementals and rethinking Lovecraft's horror of cosmic indifference in terms of battles between good and evil entities. Derleth pursued the same strategy in his so-called posthumous collaborations with Lovecraft, in which he expanded on incomplete fragments left among Lovecraft's papers, as in *The Lurker at the Threshold* (1945), or elaborated on ideas in Lovecraft's commonplace book for stories that appeared in *The Survivor and Others* (1957), *The Shuttered Room and Other Pieces* (1959), and *The Dark Brotherhood and Other Pieces* (1966). This culminated in the anthology *Tales of the Cthulhu Mythos* (1969), for which Derleth collected stories from Lovecraft and his weird fiction colleagues as well as new works by writers whom Derleth had authorized to contribute to the Cthulhu Mythos, having discouraged other writers over the preceding decades. Derleth's regulation of the Cthulhu Mythos and his protection of it as a brand associated with Arkham House, the publishing company that he founded, is regarded as controversial by many of his critics.

Derleth founded Arkham House with fellow Lovecraft acolyte Donald Wandrei in 1939 when the two were unable to interest trade publishers in a collection of Lovecraft's fiction. Initially, Derleth planned only to publish Lovecraft's fiction and letters under the Arkham House imprint, but he expanded his program and eventually published first hardcover collections of short fiction by many of the best writers from *Weird Tales*, including (among others) himself, Lovecraft, Clark Ashton Smith, Robert E. Howard, Henry S. Whitehead, Robert Bloch, Fritz Leiber, Ray

Bradbury, Frank Belknap Long, Seabury Quinn, and Mary Elizabeth Counselman. While running Arkham House, Derleth edited anthologies of weird fiction for other publishers—among them *Sleep No More* (1944), *Who Knocks?* (1946), *The Night Side* (1947), and *The Sleeping and the Dead* (1947)—that were top-heavy with contributions from Arkham House authors. Arkham House was the first of many specialty fantasy, horror, and science fiction publishers to come into existence in the twentieth century, and its success made a considerable impact on modern genre publishing.

Stefan R. Dziemianowicz

See also: Arkham House; Cthulhu Mythos; Lovecraft, H. P.; Lovecraftian Horror; Pulp Horror; *The Lurker at the Threshold*; Wandrei, Donald; *Weird Tales*.

Further Reading

Copper, Basil. 2008. "August Derleth: A Giant Remembered." In *Basil Copper: A Life in Books*, edited by Stephen Jones, 56–63. Hornsea, UK: PS Publishing.

Dziemianowicz, Stefan. 1998. "August Derleth." In *The St. James Guide to Horror, Ghost & Gothic Writers*, edited by David Pringle, 177–180. Detroit, MI: St. James Press.

Long, Frank Belknap. 2009. "The Contributions of August Derleth to the Supernatural Horror Story." In *Conversations with the Weird Tales Circle*, edited by John Pelan and Jerard Walters, 466–473. Lake Wood, CO: Centipede Press. Originally published in *Return to Derleth: Selected Essays*, vol. 2, edited by James P. Roberts (White Hawk Press, 1995).

Price, E. Hoffmann. 2001. "August W. Derleth." In *Book of the Dead: Friends of Yesteryear: Fictioneers & Others*, 267–295. Memories of the Pulp Fiction Era. Sauk City, WI: Arkham House.

Spencer, Paul. 1992. "The Shadow over Derleth." In *Discovering Classic Horror Fiction*, edited by Darrell Schweitzer, 114–119. Mercer Island, WA: Starmont.

Tweet, Roald D. 1982. "August Derleth." *Supernatural Fiction Writers, Volume II,* edited by Everett F. Bleiler. New York: Scribners.

THE DEVIL RIDES OUT

The Devil Rides Out, first published in 1934, is a novel by the British author Dennis Wheatley, who was known for his novels of occult horror infused with conservative values. It is the first and most famous of his eight black magic novels.

Wheatley had an encyclopedic knowledge of and fascination with the occult, which underpins the idea of summoning interdimensional creatures from the otherworld and makes logical both the likelihood that, as in this novel, the devil could appear at an inn when a group of friends deliberately make a magic circle, and that faith, community, trust (all good, wartime values), occult knowledge, and muscle could control and defeat its monstrous powers. Like Wheatley himself, his recurring character, the Duke de Richleau, an occult investigator, has a fine library containing occult masterpieces, and he takes his impeccable research to far-fetched but logical extremes. The duke and his tough, strongly built friend Rex van Ryn pit their wits against a satanic cult in the British countryside in *The Devil Rides Out,* which presents a blend of imperial adventure and the occult. While staying at a country inn, the duke and his friends are endangered by the advent of the devil, a terrifying hoofed beast. They "could see the cabbalistic characters between the circles that ringed the pentacle, and the revolving bookcase, like a dark shadow beyond it, through the luminous mist. An awful stench of decay" (Wheatley 1934, 99). However, they fling a powerful jewel into the center of the circle, causing searing pain, destroying it and its power. As with Bram Stoker's crucifix- and gun-wielding masculine vampire hunters in *Dracula* (1897), forceful men, harnessing occult and religious lore and objects, keep the violent, intrusive forces of evil at bay though they howl, beat their wings, or stamp their hooves.

Wheatley's horror is clean cut. Good and evil are distinct, and conservative morality regarding sexual behavior predominates. In *The Devil Rides Out* evil takes over bodies and souls of local people, who are nightly found dancing in circles in hollows in the darkened countryside lit with garish fires, clad in robes or semi-naked, their souls in thrall to the devil. However, law, order, decency, fast cars, decisive action, and religious symbols beat back the forces of darkness, preventing the devil from riding out freely into the shires. The legacy of the investment by Wheatley and others in occult knowledge fused with adventure fiction emerges in much modern horror and fantasy, as in the character of librarian Giles in Joss Whedon's *Buffy the Vampire Slayer*. Heroism, occult knowledge, and foreign evil reappear in the *Indiana Jones* films.

The Devil Rides Out was adapted to film in 1968 by Britain's Hammer Films, directed by Terence Fisher and with a screenplay by Richard Matheson. Released in the United States as *The Devil's Bride*, the film version is widely regarded as an excellent example of occult horror cinema.

Gina Wisker

See also: Blackwood, Algernon; Haggard, H. Rider; Occult Detectives; *She*; Wheatley, Dennis.

Further Reading

Baker, Phil. 2011. *The Devil Is a Gentleman: The Life and Times of Dennis Wheatley*. Sawtry, UK: Dedalus.

Caines, Michael. 2013. "Feasting with Dennis Wheatley." *The TLS Blog at The Times Literary Supplement*. December 31. http://timescolumns.typepad.com/stothard/2013/12/feasting -with-dennis-wheatley.html.

Wheatley, Dennis. 1934. *The Devil Rides Out*. London: Hutchinson.

Wisker, Gina. 1993. "Horrors and Menaces to Everything Decent in Life: The Horror Fiction of Dennis Wheatley." In *Creepers: British Horror & Fantasy in the Twentieth Century*, edited by Clive Bloom, 99–110. London: Pluto.

DEVILS AND DEMONS

Devils and demons refer to specific monsters and minor deities from the occult and religious imagination and are often connected to other magical creatures such as witches and necromancers. Historically, demons can be good, bad, or neutral. Despite this, demon narratives frequently represent them as malicious personifications of evil. Demons have no single origin, although researchers in the area of demonology and ancient religions agree that they are one of the oldest forms of supernatural belief found in various occult and religious writings dating as far back as the fourth and fifth centuries BCE. Representations of devils and demons are diverse and manifold and have been located in Egyptian, Babylonian, African, Persian, and ancient Iranian literatures. In pharaonic Egypt, demons were categorized by the illnesses that they created. In the ancient Persian culture of modern-day Iran, they were reputed to live in caves and enchant young women into marrying them. In European pagan folklore, they appear as benign nature spirits. In Christian theology, demons are malignant former angels that accompanied Satan in the fall from heaven. They are also frequently referred to in grimoires, a modern and European term to describe books of ancient knowledge and magical spells written during the medieval period. Grimoires had many purposes both practical and philosophical. The name demon is derived from the Greek word *daimon*, meaning god-like power and knowledge. Thus, one of the main purposes of grimoires was to obtain knowledge and power over nature and other worlds by summoning demons, angels, and other supernatural spirits. The sixteenth-century German legend of Faust is one of the most famous stories of the dangers of meddling with magic and demons. In the story, Faust uses a grimoire to conjure the demon Mephistopheles and bargain his soul for twenty-four years of power and pleasure. Needless to say, things don't end well for Faust.

During the eighteenth century, there was a revival of interest in demonology and grimoires among writers and intellectuals. The interest increased throughout the nineteenth century, led by the publication of Francis Barrett's *The Magus* (1804), James Frazer's *The Golden Bough* (1890), Jacques Collin de Plancy's *Dictionnaire Infernal* (1818), and the renaissance of interest in Dante's *Divine Comedy* (1308–1321). A serious intellectual interest in the supernatural occult was maintained into the twentieth century by British occultist Aleister Crowley. In *The Book of the Law* (1904), Crowley claimed that a new religion called Thelema was dictated to him by a demon entity called Aiwass. Demon summoning, however, was not a frequent activity for a lot of occultists, and, throughout its long revival, the occult came to be associated with things secret and recondite, rather than with a direct knowledge of demons. Nonetheless, imaginative depictions of demons in art, philosophy, and literature remained throughout the fin de siècle (late nineteenth-century) period and well into the twentieth century.

This was nowhere more true than in the burgeoning genre of horror fiction, which frequently features demons as nightmarish visions of metaphysical fallenness, moral temptation, and affliction. The use of demons in horror literature was concretized by the publication of Matthew Lewis's *The Monk* (1796), in which the fall of the character Ambrose is partly attributable to a licentious female demon called Mathilda. The demon lover as sexual predator, figure of conflict, and metaphor for unhealthy passions prevailed in European and American horror fiction. In those stories that center on a female protagonist, the demon often acts as misogynistic punishment for women who have stepped outside the perimeters of socially acceptable behavior. In those that focus on men, the demon lover motif tends to be a figure of decadence and moral ambiguity, signifying the sensualism, unhealthy obsessions, and queer sexuality connected to artistic genius. At the turn of the nineteenth into the twentieth century, the demon contributed to the iconic representation of urban horror in stories such as Stevenson's *The Strange Case of Dr. Jekyll and Mr. Hyde* (1886) and Machen's "The Great God Pan" (1890). Representations of demonic queerness are also present but subverted in the works of late twentieth-century horror author Clive Barker—for example, in the sadomasochistic Cenobites of *The Hellbound Heart* (1986) and Baphomet the demon king of Meridian in *Cabal* (1988).

The linking of demons to children is also prevalent in the horror literature of the nineteenth and twentieth centuries. The diabolical sexual assaults and deformed children in Machen's other stories are drawn from descriptions of incubi and succubi in the medieval occult. Similar devils and demons, distinguished by grotesque breeding, moral decay, and ancient religious practices, make up H. P. Lovecraft's fictional universe, the Cthulhu Mythos. Walter de la Mare describes a child's death at the hands of a demon in "The Guardian" (1955). A nice young girl is possessed by the devil in William P. Blatty's *The Exorcist* (1971). A satanic impregnation occurs in Ira Levin's *Rosemary's Baby* (1967), and a diabolic child features in Doris Lessing's *The Fifth Child* (1988). In Stephen King's novels it is adults such as Randall Flagg in *The Stand* (1978) that are demons and children such as Franny's unborn baby that are the antidote to their diabolical activities. Similarly in *Desperation* (1996) the boy, David, is led by visions and religious experiences into a battle with the demon, Tak.

The presentation of demons in these and many other contemporary works of horror fiction is influenced by a Christian theology, but the handling of it is quite varied. Like demons and minor devils, the representation of the supreme demon, Satan, is often unstable and variable. In fact, Satan appears only a handful of times in the Hebrew and Christian scriptures, but certain patterns and behaviors—for instance, Satan's mysteriousness, his love of trickery and game playing, and his divided nature—can be traced back not only to the Bible but to later theological writings such as Dante's *Divine Comedy* and John Milton's *Paradise Lost* (1667). Other satanic ambiguous traits such as rebelliousness, fallenness, nihilism, and human advocacy are evidenced in diverse horror works such as Mark Twain's *The Mysterious Stranger* (1916), Robert Bloch's *That Hellbound Train* (1958), Mikhail Bulgakov's *The Master and Margarita* (1966), Jeremy Leven's *Satan* (1982), Harlan

Ellison's *The Deathbird Stories* (1974), King's *Needful Things* (1991) and Barker's *The Damnation Game* (1985).

Eleanor Beal

See also: Barker, Clive; Cthulhu Mythos; *The Damnation Game*; *The Exorcist*; Incubi and Succubi; *Melmoth the Wanderer*; *Rosemary's Baby*; "Young Goodman Brown."

Further Reading

Cardin, Matt. 2007. "The Angel and the Demon." In *Icons of Horror and the Supernatural*, edited by S. T. Joshi, 31–64. Westport, CT and London: Greenwood Press.
Carus, Paul. 2008. *The History of the Devil*. New York: Dover.
Guiley, Rosemary. 1998. *The Encyclopedia of Demons and Demonology*. New York: Checkmark Books.
Owen, Alex. 2007. *The Place of Enchantment: British Occultism and the Culture of the Modern*. Chicago, IL and London: University of Chicago Press.

DICK, PHILIP K. (1928–1982)

The American writer Philip K. Dick was the author of 44 novels and 121 short stories that have exerted a profound effect on the science fiction field. His particular approach to science fiction also imbues his work with significance for the horror genre. The question of what it means to be human, the fear of losing identity, the threat of totalitarian government, and the disorienting impact of drug use and mental illness are central themes in Dick's fiction. Many of his protagonists experience dread and disorientation as they are trapped in societies in which they have no control or understanding, and Dick employs different worlds, alternate universes, and imagined futures as settings for his protagonists facing psychological isolation and horror.

Dick grew up in the San Francisco area and attended the University of California, Berkeley, where he studied history, psychology, and philosophy. He left the university without a degree in 1949 and sold his first story in 1950. Throughout most of his career Dick struggled financially. He also became addicted to amphetamines, and after several mental health episodes, which included prolonged hallucinations, he attempted suicide in 1972. Despite his lack of financial success, Dick was popular with science readers and appreciated by critics for his genre-bending use of horror and science fiction. During his life he received the Hugo Award, the John W. Campbell Memorial Award, the British Science Fiction Award, and the French Graquilly d'Or. He was also nominated for five Nebula awards.

Despite his immense productivity and praise from critics and readers of science fiction, Dick never achieved either the sales or the popularity he wanted during his lifetime. It was only later, when his work began to be adapted for film and television, that his dark work became known to a wide and appreciative audience.

The first major film adapted from one of his stories was Ridley Scott's *Blade Runner* (1982), based on Dick's novel *Do Androids Dream of Electric Sheep?* (1969). Released in 1982, *Blade Runner*—and especially the more cinematically successful director's cut of the same film—is an excellent example of Dick's combination of horror and science fiction. It is the story of a private bounty hunter working with police on a dying, dystopic earth, who finds to his growing horror that he might not be human. Dick suggests that empathy may be the way to face the fear of identity loss, but both the novel and the film posit growing despair.

Total Recall (1990), directed by Paul Verhoeven, is based on Dick's short story "We Can Remember It for You Wholesale" (1966). Again Dick examines the boundaries of science fiction and horror as he explores the confusion and disorientation of a man who has been given a memory implant and cannot tell whether his memories are real or hallucinations.

Dick employs the convention of alternate history rather than a futuristic setting in *The Man in the High Castle* (1963), which was adapted for television in 2015. He sets his story in an America that lost the Second World War to the Germans and Japanese, who now occupy the United States. In this alternate America the protagonist attempts to survive in a fascist world that has experienced one nuclear holocaust and is threatened by the real possibility of another.

In these and Dick's other works, the horror of losing one's identity to an intrusive and powerful authority in a decaying world is dramatized and explored. Dick's characters are powerless seekers caught in nightmare worlds. The continued interest in and popularity of his work, especially as it is presented in extraliterary adaptations, suggest that many readers experience similar fears.

During the last decade of his life, Dick's work as an author of fiction became increasingly intertwined with his existential reality as he experienced a series of spiritual and paranormal events that, he thought, indicated the everyday world of mundane reality is a kind of virtual construct presided over by a demiurgic higher power. He eventually termed this power VALIS (an acronym for Vast Active Living Intelligence System) and spent his final years writing novels and keeping a journal—published in 2011 as *The Exegesis of Philip K. Dick*—in which he laid out the details and ramifications of this vision. He died on March 2, 1982, after suffering two strokes.

Jim Holte

See also: Moore, Alan; Psychological Horror.

Further Reading

Arnold, Kyle. 2016. *The Divine Madness of Philip K. Dick*. New York: Oxford University Press.

Rose, Frank. 2003. "The Second Coming of Philip K. Dick." *Wired*, December 1. http://www
    .wired.com/2003/12/philip/?pg=6.
Sutin, Lawrence. 2005. *Divine Invasions: A Life of Philip K. Dick*. New York: Carroll & Graf.

DOUBLES, DOPPELGÄNGERS, AND SPLIT SELVES

The uncanny shadow, reflection, twin, or double is a key device in Gothic and horror fiction. The dread these doubles often invoke is underpinned by ancient myth.
From the earliest theologies, chaos and order or good and evil have used twins
or doubles to figure primordial warring forces, such as Gilgamesh and Enkidu
(Mesopotamia), Osiris and Set (Egypt), or Cain and Abel (Old Testament). Greek
and Roman mythology abounds in twins, as do many storytelling cycles of Native
American and African cultures. The double is a portent, one that can signify great
fortune, but more often taken as a harbinger of misfortune. Celtic and other northern folklores regard seeing one's double or "fetch" as foretelling death. Some cultures venerate twins, but many more have killed them at birth as unlucky signs.

Since the eighteenth century, post-Enlightenment thinkers have understood the
double less in metaphysical or theological terms and more as another part of the self.
This has been integral to the development of modern psychology. Indeed, the demonic, persecutory "other" typical of Gothic fiction is inextricably related to the
development of these psychological models of selfhood. Late nineteenth-century
psychologists coined the term "double personality" and were fascinated that consciousness could apparently split spontaneously or be artificially induced to divide
through hypnotism. Modern trauma theory continues this fascination through the
terminology of dissociation or multiple personality.

German romanticism explored doubles as people with strange spiritual affinities, almost occult in their connection. Jean Paul Richter, who coined the term
Doppelgänger in 1796, had a huge influence on Goethe's and Kleist's pursuit of the
theme. It was rendered Gothic by E. T. A. Hoffmann's use of the double in *The
Devil's Elixirs* (1814) and most famously in "The Sand-man" (1816). The latter's
delirious proliferation of doubles was the subject of Sigmund Freud's study of the
unheimlich or "the uncanny," where the double is theorized as a species of familiar
thing rendered unnerving or strange, such as a lifelike doll, waxwork, automaton,
corpse, or identical other. Freud, following Otto Rank's psychoanalytic essay "The
Double" (1914), reads the figure as a projection from the inside that returns as an
implacable persecutor from the outside.

Fevered horror at the double's awful proximity entered English literature most
memorably with Mary Shelley's *Frankenstein* (1818), where Victor Frankenstein's
monstrous creation becomes an intimate shadow and relentless destroyer. This
logic echoed her father William Godwin's study of paranoid persecution, *Caleb Williams* (1794), and went on to influence a whole chain of fictions about persecutory
doubles, such as James Hogg's *The Private Memoirs and Confessions of a Justified Sinner* (1824), Edgar Allan Poe's "William Wilson" (1839), and Fyodor Dostoevsky's

The Double (1846). One of the most sustained explorations of the theme was in the work of Robert Louis Stevenson, who spoke of his own double life in Edinburgh, between pious family and student debauchery, and who was fascinated by the real-life case of Deacon Brodie, the outwardly respectable Edinburgh citizen who concealed a criminal double life. His interest culminated in *The Strange Case of Dr. Jekyll and Mr. Hyde* (1886), the story of an artificial splitting of personality by a doctor in which the second self, initially more virile and energetic than the cramped and timid professional medic, spirals down into degeneracy, crime, and eventual self-destruction. The book was instantly taken up as a defining metaphor of modern man both in conventional moral terms and in modern psychological theory. Frederick Myers, who coined the term "multiplex personality" in 1885, warmly praised Stevenson for providing a new language for a psyche where consciousness was a narrow part of the spectrum, hiding the powers of the "subliminal" mind. Stevenson's double was a decidedly physical creature; Guy de Maupassant's masterpiece, "The Horla" (1887), renders the double more ambiguously a subjective, psychological split.

Frankenstein's monster warns his maker, "I shall be with you on your wedding night," and fulfills the promise, arriving to kill the bride and leave the two locked in a perpetual warring dyad. The overtones of sexual panic in the theme of the double have been constant since the myth of Narcissus falling in love with his own reflection. In the modern era, it becomes a means of exploring same-sex desire without quite naming it. This is implicit in, say, Stevenson's *Jekyll and Hyde* (although some of his first readers saw it plainly enough), or in Henry James's "The Jolly Corner" (1908), or even more obliquely in Joseph Conrad's "The Secret Sharer" (1912). Oscar Wilde, however, rendered this subtext dangerously explicit in *The Picture of Dorian Gray* (1890), and the text was used as damning evidence at Wilde's prosecution for "acts of gross indecency" in 1895. Even at this critical moment in the formation of modern sexual identities, however, the theme of the double was flexible and not always reducible to sexual meanings. In Conrad's *Heart of Darkness* (1899), the mirroring and constant inversion of the values of light and dark, West and East, Europe and Africa, Marlow and Kurtz, use doubling to very different effect to explore the complicities of geopolitical interdependence.

Since 1980 and the emergence of the diagnosis of post-traumatic stress, dissociative disorders have often been investigated in the wider culture through the Gothic trope of the double. Stephen King, for instance, has explored traumatically dissociated selves from *The Shining* (1977) to *Dolores Claiborne* (1992) and explored psychic splitting as the core of his own creative process, as in *The Dark Half* (1989). The terror of doubling haunts the films of David Lynch, as the demonic double continues to be an abiding theme of modern horror film, with perennial remakes and adaptations of *Frankenstein, Jekyll and Hyde,* and explorations of psychic splitting from *Black Swan* (2011) to the update of Dostoevsky's *The Double* (2014).

Roger Luckhurst

See also: Frankenstein; Hoffmann, E. T. A.; "The Horla"; *The Picture of Dorian Gray*; *The Private Memoirs and Confessions of a Justified Sinner*; "The Sand-man"; *The Shining*; Stevenson, Robert Louis; *The Strange Case of Dr. Jekyll and Mr. Hyde*; The Uncanny; "The Yellow Wall-Paper."

Further Reading

Binet, Alfred. 1977. *On Double Consciousness: Experimental Psychological Studies.* Washington: University Publications of America.

Freud, S. [1919] 2003. "The Uncanny." Translated by David McLintock. In *The Uncanny*, edited by A. Phillips, 121–162. New York: Penguin Books.

Rank, Otto. 2009. *The Double: A Psychoanalytic Study.* Translated by Harry Tucker. Lincoln: University of Nebraska Press.

Tymms, Ralph. 1949. *Doubles in Literary Psychology.* Cambridge: Bowes and Bowes.

DRACULA

Bram Stoker's *Dracula* (1897) was not the first vampire story published, but it was the most important, establishing the popularity and conventions of the vampire narrative. Vampires, creatures who return from the dead to feed upon the living by drinking their blood, have been popular figures in European and Middle Eastern folklore, and classical literature mentions several vampires. The history of the vampire in English is also older than *Dracula*; John Polidori's *The Vampyre* (1819) was popular, as was James Malcolm Rymer and Thomas Peckett Prest's *Varney the Vampire; or, the Feast of Blood* (1845–1847) and Sheridan Le Fanu's *Carmilla* (1872). Stoker's *Dracula*, however, fixed in the popular imagination the image of the night-stalking, garlic-fearing vampire as a dark, mysterious, cloaked European aristocrat who can transform himself into a bat and who searches out and destroys his victims, usually beautiful young women.

Dracula is an epistolary novel; it is told through the letters, journal entries, telegrams, and diaries of Dracula's victims and hunters. The novel begins with solicitor Jonathan Harker leaving London for Transylvania to assist Count Dracula, who is planning to move to England to purchase several properties. Once there he discovers that Dracula is a vampire, is attacked and bitten by him, and is left a prisoner in Dracula's castle. Dracula journeys to England by ship, and when he arrives he attacks the beautiful young Lucy Westenra and then Mina Murray, Jonathan's fiancé. Lucy dies and becomes a vampire and Mina sickens. Jonathan, who has escaped from the castle, marries Mina and together, with the help of Lucy's three suitors and a learned German doctor and vampire hunter, Professor Abraham Van Helsing, they hunt Dracula, who flees to his castle in Transylvania only to be killed by the fearless vampire hunters.

The novel is far more complex than suggested by its plot summary, which has become a stereotype after its use in the many *Dracula* film and television adaptations. Stoker's vampire narrative works because he was successful in using the plot

The Beetle by Richard Marsh: The Book That Outsold Dracula

The Beetle (1897) by Richard Marsh is a Gothic novel involving an ancient Egyptian creature that has traveled to London to take revenge upon a member of Parliament. Published at the end of the nineteenth century, The Beetle was a massive commercial success that for years outsold Bram Stoker's Dracula, which was published only two months earlier.

Situated in a period marked by increasing unease concerning Britain's growing empire as well as other issues such as the New Woman and modernity, The Beetle explores this anxiety with an unsettling finesse. Divided into four sections that are each narrated by a different character, The Beetle focuses on Paul Lessingham, a lawmaker who harbors a great secret regarding time spent in Egypt. Lessingham, a rising political star in Parliament, is pursued by the Beetle, a horrific Egyptian creature that has infiltrated London and is able to take control of the bodies of those unfortunate enough to cross its path. As a member of the political body responsible for the growth of the British Empire, Lessingham is the standard nineteenth-century colonialist whose exploits across the globe have made entire cultures and people beholden to the British crown. Yet the Beetle's pursuit of Lessingham through London raises the issue of when the colonialist becomes the colonialized; the central fear that Britain itself could be colonialized due to its central role as a colonizer are explored in haunting detail by Marsh's text. The Beetle thus voices late nineteenth-century concerns related to the fears of radical change in the social order without any strong resolution, suggesting that there is little the British people can do to reverse the change to their society that they have unwittingly brought about.

Joel T. Terranova

to develop complex characters and address significant social issues while writing an effective horror story. Dracula himself is no one-dimensional monster. Although a ruthless killer and sexual predator, Dracula is also capable of human fear and love, aware of his long history, and interested in modern life and science. Abraham Van Helsing is a professor of medicine, psychology, literature, and law who combines modern (nineteenth-century) science (he uses blood transfusions and the telegraph) with traditional religion (he carries a crucifix and a blessed communion host) to save Mina and destroy the vampire. Mina Murray Harker is probably the most complicated character. She is a "modern woman," which at the turn of the twentieth century meant that she questioned the secondary role women held in Western society. She works. She knows how to use the latest technology, including the typewriter and recording cylinder. And although in Dracula she plays the role of the traditional vampire victim, she is also the one who pulls together all of the various observations and insights about Dracula that enable the novel's male heroes to track down and finally destroy the vampire.

One of the reasons for the popularity of *Dracula* is its dramatization of the cultural conflicts facing Western readers both at the time of its original publication and afterward, right up to the present day. At the end of the nineteenth century, many European and American readers saw white, patriarchal, Christian, European society under attack from within and without. The values of colonialism and the superiority of European culture were questioned. Traditional roles of workers and employers were being challenged, and feminism raised questions about the nature of the family and sexuality. Dracula was presented as an aristocrat with "the blood of Attila" in his veins who was planning to invade England, seduce and mesmerize women (the pure heart of the family according to Victorian ideology), and infect the population with his vampirism. He represented a physical and moral threat to the English homeland. Dracula's weapons of violence, sexuality, and supernatural power could only be confronted by the best of Western culture, and Stoker's team of vampire hunters include a learned professor, a doctor, a lawyer, an American businessman, an English nobleman, and a woman pure of heart—the best of the West against the foreign threat.

Stoker secured the dramatic rights to *Dracula* when it was published, and upon his death his wife gave permission for the development of a theatrical version of the novel by British actor, director, and playwright Hamilton Deane. The production opened in London on February 14, 1927. After a successful British run the play was brought to New York, where, with Hungarian actor Bela Lugosi in the title role, it was successful again. Carl Laemmle of Universal Studios bought the film rights to the play and the novel, and in 1931 director Tod Browning's movie *Dracula* was released, with Lugosi starring in the title role. Dracula has returned to large and small screens in a variety of adaptations ever since. Among the most famous and most successful of these later versions are director Terence Fisher's *Dracula*, a.k.a. *Horror of Dracula* (1958), for Hammer Films, starring Christopher Lee as a powerful, dominating Dracula (Hammer Films went on to make six additional *Dracula* adaptations, all but one starring Christopher Lee); John Badham's *Dracula* (1979) starring Frank Langella as a romantic Dracula; and Francis Ford Coppola's *Bram Stoker's Dracula* (1992), one of the only major adaptations that attempts to remain largely faithful to the novel. A number of film critics argue that the best adaptation of *Dracula* is F. W. Murnau's *Nosferatu* (1922), which was made in Germany without the permission of the Stoker estate, and which remains one of the finest examples of silent film. Another candidate for the "best" accolade, and another example of an adaptation that remains faithful to the source novel, is Philip Saville's 1977 BBC miniseries *Count Dracula*.

In 1972 a renewed fascination with *Dracula* began with the publication of *In Search of Dracula: A True History of Dracula and Vampire Legends*, written by Raymond McNally and Radu Florescu, who asserted that Stoker based his character on Vlad Tepes, a fifteenth-century Wallachian prince who ruled Transylvania, a province in Romania, and was known as "Dracula" or "the Son of the Dragon." Vlad was popularly known as Vlad the Impaler because of his penchant for impaling his enemies on wooden stakes. Stoker's *Dracula* and the historical Dracula have thus become linked in the popular imagination, although most scholars agree that Stoker borrowed only the name "Dracula" and did not draw on the actual history of Vlad when he was imagining his immortal vampire count.

Jim Holte

See also: *Carmilla*; *The Historian*; Stoker, Bram; Vampires; "The Vampyre"; *Varney the Vampire; or, The Feast of Blood*.

Further Reading

Holte, James. 1997. *Dracula in the Dark: The Dracula Film Adaptations*. Westport, CT: Greenwood Press.

Klinger, Leslie S. 2008. *The New Annotated Dracula*. New York: W. W. Norton.

McNally, Raymond, and Radu Florescu. 1972. *In Search of Dracula: A True History of Dracula and Vampire Legends*. Greenwich, CT: New York Graphic Society.

Miller, Elizabeth, ed. 2005. *Bram Stoker's Dracula: A Documentary Volume. Dictionary of Literary Biography*, Vol. 304. Detroit: Thomson Gale.

DREAMS AND NIGHTMARES

Dreams—the sensations and images in the mind during sleep—have existed since the dawn of consciousness. When a dream causes psychological or physical terror, it is called a nightmare. The horror story is related to dreams and nightmares on many dimensions. Horror fiction attempts to emulate the *feelings* of the nightmare—panic, fear, terror, disorientation. In terms of plotting, horror stories run the gamut in their use of dreams: the entire "real" narrative is revealed to have been a dream; the story is a mix of dream and waking; the "dream" is revealed to have been real.

In *On the Nightmare* (1931), Ernest Jones—one of the pioneers of psychoanalysis—remarks that "there is in English no term that indicates the precise combination of fearful apprehension, of panic-stricken terror, of awful anxiety, dread and anguish that goes to make up the emotion of which we are treating. The striking characteristic of . . . [the] Nightmare is its *appalling intensity*" (Jones 1931, 24). He examines several motifs characteristic of the nightmare (and also of horror fiction): incubi, witches, demons, vampires, and werewolves.

Jones also focuses on a particularly intense type of nightmare that may be experienced while falling asleep or awakening. During these "hypnagogic" dreams (a term Jones does not use himself), which occur in the liminal space between waking and sleeping, the sufferer believes that he or she is conscious, and may actually rise to a state of semiconscious awareness, but it is a state characterized by physical paralysis; a crushing sense of suffocation, often felt as a literal weight on the chest;

"Lukundoo": Inspired by a Nightmare

"Lukundoo" is Baltimore schoolteacher Edward Lucas White's best known and most reprinted horror story. He wrote it in 1907, but its grotesque nature made it unsalable until 1925, when it was finally published in *Weird Tales*. White suffered from vivid nightmares, which he often turned into short stories. He said he wrote "Lukundoo" exactly as he had dreamed it, and that he had the nightmare after reading "Pollock and the Porroh Man" by H. G. Wells.

Both stories involve white men on expedition in Africa who are driven to suicide by witch doctors' curses, and both involve decapitated heads and the unreliability of human senses. In Wells's story, Pollock has a witch doctor murdered and is haunted by his decapitated head throughout his journey back to England. It is ambiguous whether it is a hallucination; he sees it, later he hears it, and then he feels it. Finally, totally unable to trust his senses, he slits his throat. In "Lukundoo," the narrator, Singleton, is taken to Ralph Stone, an explorer cursed for humiliating a Mangbetu witch doctor. Stone is afflicted with boil-like swellings on his body and has been overheard conversing with a shrill voice while alone. Singleton witnesses miniature living heads bursting through Stone's skin, and Stone slicing them off. Stone finally succumbs and dies. Singleton relates that he is still unable to believe what he saw and heard.

Generally, in White's nightmare-inspired stories, suggestive clues build up to a horrifying denouement. Here, tension builds slowly as the reader is told first of the tiny dried heads resembling the witch doctor. This is followed by Stone's unusual boils, his self-treatment by razor, the mysterious shrill voice, and finally the revelation of the curse. There are also hints that the curse is somehow connected with his past in America and his ex-wife.

Lee Weinstein

and emotions of unbearable terror. Perhaps most distressingly, the hypnagogic visions in this type of dream generally take the form of a malevolent supernatural presence, including such "classic" forms as the "night hag" (a witchlike old crone) and the demonic incubus and succubus of medieval lore. Such experiences have been reported throughout history in cultures all over the globe, and their impact on horror literature and related art has been incalculable.

One of the most prominent instances of this influence may be seen in the iconic "Nightmare" series of paintings by the eighteenth- and nineteenth-century Swiss painter Henry Fuseli, which depict a woman lying unconscious on a bed or couch with an ugly demon squatting on her chest and a supernatural horse peering out from behind a curtain in the background. This basic image, which is believed to have been inspired by Fuseli's own personal experiences with the nightmare state in question, has sometimes been called the master image of the Gothic horror genre, and it has exerted a powerful influence on literature, as in, to name just one notable case, Mary Shelley's *Frankenstein*, wherein Shelley's description of the scene when Victor Frankenstein bursts into the bedroom on his wedding night to find that his monster has murdered Elizabeth is probably modeled on Fuseli's paintings. Other instances of the classic nightmare being used to powerful effect by horror authors include E. T. A. Hoffmann's "The Sand-man" (German: *Der Sandmann*, 1816) and Guy de Maupassant's "The Horla" (1887), which stands as the paradigmatic example of the use of the hypnogogic dream in horror fiction.

In antiquity and the Middle Ages, the dream was used as a framing device for the allegorical tale. In the eighteenth and early nineteenth centuries, nightmares became prominent in the fiction of the Romantics, who saw emotion as the authentic source of aesthetic experience. Dreams featured in many Gothic novels, notably Matthew Lewis's *The Monk: A Romance* (1796) and Charlotte Dacre's *Zofloya; or, The Moor: A Romance of the Fifteenth Century* (1806). By the mid-nineteenth century, writers including Samuel Taylor Coleridge and Thomas De Quincey showed intense interest in altered states of consciousness, including nightmares. As early as 1866, when Ambrose Bierce's "An Inhabitant of Carcosa" was published, dreams were being used as a central narrative component of horror fiction; subsequent far-reaching "dream worlds" were created by authors as diverse as H. P. Lovecraft (*The Dream Quest of Unknown Kadath*) and Philip K. Dick (*The Three Stigmata of Palmer Eldritch*).

In the short story, many writers used dreams as key elements of their tales. Edward Lucas White (1886–1934) claimed that his plots came from actual nightmares. Mary E. Wilkins Freeman's "The Hall Bedroom" (1903) relates how the sounds, odors, and other sensations "leak" from the narrator's dreams into reality. F. Marion Crawford's "For the Blood Is the Life" (1911) draws parallels between the effects of chronic nightmares and vampirism. William Hope Hodgson's *The Night Land* (1912), set in the far future, is told in the form of the dreams of a man in the seventeenth century. During this period, nightmares are conspicuous in the work of Algernon Blackwood, Nikolai Gogol, Stefan Grabiński, Arthur Machen, J. Sheridan Le Fanu, and others.

The Symbolists pushed past literal narrative to accentuate dreams and the associative powers of the imagination. Lautréamont (pseudonym of Isidore-Lucien Ducasse, 1846–1870), Georges Rodenbach, Stefan Grabiński, and Daniil Kharms (1905–1942) created stories in which images and metaphors become the actual—rather than merely the literary—representations of perception. By the mid-1920s, the Surrealists declared dreaming to be no less vital than waking. Subsequent writers including Bruno Schulz, Jean Ray, Michel de Ghelderode (1898–1962), and others used a sense of intense estrangement from the generally accepted sense of reality as a source of horror. This stream reaches its apex in the "weird" work of Thomas Ligotti, whose tales often employ incongruous images to produce an effect of terror.

Steven J. Mariconda

See also: Bierce, Ambrose; Blackwood, Algernon; Coleridge, Samuel Taylor; Dick, Phillip K.; Gogol, Nikolai; Grabiński, Stefan; "The Horla"; Incubi and Succubi; Le Fanu, J. Sheridan; Lewis, Matthew Gregory; Ligotti, Thomas; Lovecraft, H. P.; Machen, Arthur; *The Night Land*; Ray, Jean; "The Sand-man"; Schulz, Bruno; *The Songs of Maldoror (Les Chants de Maldoror)*; Surrealism.

Further Reading

Brook, Stephen, ed. 2003. *The Oxford Book of Dreams*. Oxford: Oxford University Press.

Jones, Ernest. 1931. *On the Nightmare*. London: Hogarth Press.

Khapaeva, Dina. 2012. *Nightmare: From Literary Experiments to Cultural Project*. Boston: Brill.

Pepper, Dennis. 2001. *The Young Oxford Book of Nightmares*. Oxford: Oxford University Press.

THE DROWNING GIRL

Irish American writer Caitlín R. Kiernan's novel *The Drowning Girl: A Memoir* (2012) has received widespread critical acclaim, winning both a Bram Stoker and a James Tiptree Jr. award. Combining complex psychological realism with elements of dark fantasy, its fragmentary first-person narration and meta-fictional focus, like those of Kiernan's 2008 novel *The Red Tree*, are a stylistic departure from her earlier series of dark fantasy novels, from *Silk* (1999) through *Low Red Moon* (2005). *The Drowning Girl* is nonetheless connected to them both thematically and through shared settings.

Haunted by memories of her mother's suicide, *The Drowning Girl*'s narrator, a young woman named India Morgan Phelps who refers to herself as Imp, has been diagnosed with paranoid schizophrenia. Imp struggles to comprehend a series of uncanny events linked to her childhood fascination with a painting titled "The Drowning Girl" by (fictional) American painter Philip George Saltonstall, and her encounter with an enigmatic woman named Eva Canning, whom Imp at various points in the novel imagines as a mermaid, a werewolf, or a ghost. Imp gradually uncovers connections between Eva Canning and Jacova Angevine, the leader of a cult called the Open Door of Night, whose worship of the Lovecraftian marine deity Mother Hydra and eventual mass suicide are recounted in a number of Kiernan's earlier fictions, most notably the story "Houses Under the Sea" (2007). Imp's growing obsession with Eva alienates her from her lover Abalyn Armitage, leading her ever further into a mysterious world that she, and the reader, can never be entirely sure is not the product of her own schismatic psyche.

With its dedication to Peter Straub, whose classic *Ghost Story* (1979) Kiernan has often cited as an influence, and with Imp's opening statement that she is "going to write a ghost story now" (Kiernan 2012, 1), *The Drowning Girl* situates itself within the long tradition of ghost stories, but in an untraditional way. With its stream of consciousness technique, it draws inspiration from Modernist writers, including Virginia Woolf, and from postmodern novels including Mark Danielewski's *House of Leaves* (2000). Like most of Kiernan's fictions, *The Drowning Girl* engages in what she calls a "feminization of the weird"; incorporating concepts and quotations from Poe, Lovecraft, and other writers associated with the history of weird fiction into her narrative, Imp (whose name itself echoes Poe's "Imp of the Perverse") interrogates them from a queer and feminist perspective, even as she attempts to understand how they shape her own self-perception and identity. In this respect, *The Drowning Girl* also works within the female Gothic tradition. Originating with eighteenth-century Gothic novelist Ann Radcliffe and continuing through the work of writers including Charlotte Perkins Gilman in the nineteenth century and Shirley Jackson in the twentieth, the female Gothic focuses on women's struggles to define their identity against patriarchal, and often predatory, authorities.

Sean Moreland

See also: Dark Fantasy; *House of Leaves*; Jackson, Shirley; Kiernan, Caitlín R.; Lovecraft, H. P.; Radcliffe, Ann; Straub, Peter; "The Yellow Wall-Paper."

Further Reading

Brusso, Charlene. 2012. "Pernicious Thought Contagions: PW Talks with Caitlín R. Kiernan." *Publishers Weekly* (January 30): 39. http://www.publishersweekly.com/pw/by-topic/authors/interviews/article/50378-pernicious-thought-contagions-pw-talks-with-caitlin-r-kiernan.html.

Kiernan, Caitlín R. 2012. *The Drowning Girl*. New York: ROC.

Moreland, Sean. 2016. "'Not Like Any Thing of Ours': Waking (to) Poe and Lovecraft in Caitlin R. Kiernan's *The Drowning Girl*." In *The Lovecraftian Poe: Essays on Influence, Reception, Interpretation and Transformation*. Lanham, MD: Lehigh University Press.

DU MAURIER, DAPHNE (1907–1989)

Daphne du Maurier, born in London in 1907, was one of the greatest British female writers of Gothic horror in the twentieth century. She upset romantic fictions with her novel *Rebecca* (1938), exposing the damage of flawed romantic narratives that imprison and constrain women's opportunities and worldviews. Her father was the famous actor-manager Sir Gerald du Maurier, her grandfather was writer George du Maurier (who wrote *Trilby*, 1894), and her sister Angela was also a writer.

Du Maurier's first published fiction, *The Loving Spirit* (1931), is a ghost story, informed by the supernatural. Early reception of her work, including Cornwall-based *Jamaica Inn* (1936, turned into a BBC1 TV series in 2014) and *Frenchman's Creek* (1941), misunderstood it as middlebrow genre writing. Among du Maurier's short stories and novelettes are "The Birds" (1952; filmed by Alfred Hitchcock in 1963), *The Apple Tree: A Short Novel and Some Stories* (1952), *Kiss Me Again,*

"The Birds": Social Commentary and Avian Eco-Horror

First published in Daphne du Maurier's 1952 fiction collection *The Apple Tree*, "The Birds" is an influential story in the subgenre that has come to be known as eco-horror, and its status in cultural memory has been greatly enhanced by the fact of its film adaptation by director Alfred Hitchcock.

Set in coastal Cornwall, where du Maurier lived (in Fowey), "The Birds" focuses on a community that is shockingly attacked by flocks of everyday garden birds and seabirds, threatening civic order and causing unease. The story's historical setting is just after the Second World War, and the coastal attack recalls Britain's fear of invasion from the sea and the sky. Invasion and body horror are intermixed with creature horror, since the birds go for eyes, overwhelming children and adults. The main character, a farmhand, tries to protect his family by boarding up windows and hiding inside, but the birds break in. Their insistent, incessant attack is a reminder of the futility and helplessness of people when nature or war take over. The protective power of family men is also undermined, and this is a theme that du Maurier explored elsewhere, as in her story "Don't Look Now" (1952).

In 1963 *The Apple Tree* was reprinted as *The Birds and Other Stories*, and simultaneously Alfred Hitchcock filmed *The Birds*, starring Tippi Hedren, which moves the events to the United States. The film holds an iconic place in Hollywood history. In 2009 Irish playwright Conor McPherson adapted "The Birds" for the stage at Dublin's Gate Theatre.

Gina Wisker

Stranger (1953), *The Birds and Other Stories* (1963), and "Don't Look Now" (1971), which was memorably filmed by Nicholas Roeg in 1973. The time-slip novel *The House on the Strand* (1969), also set in Cornwall, presents a tale in which mind-altering drugs transport the protagonist Dick back to medieval times, where life is meaningful, if violent.

In *Rebecca*, a dark, Gothic anti-romance that was du Maurier's most popular novel, the young second wife of the dashing Maximilian de Winter moves in with him at his country house, Manderley, and is there dominated by his sinister and imperious housekeeper, Mrs. Danvers. The novel eventually reveals Maxim as the murderer of his beautiful, sexually independent first wife, Rebecca, who haunts (without actually being a ghost) both the nameless second wife—who narrates the novel—and Manderley, which serves as an index of the decadence of a partying generation that failed to see approaching war. The novel is recognized as exploring confinement, conformity, and containment of sexual rebellion and social rebellion in women. *Rebecca* was written and published in 1938, and Prime Minister Neville

Chamberlain reportedly carried a copy in his briefcase when trying to ensure peace prior to World War II.

Rebecca revitalized women's Gothic horror writing, introducing studies of domestic tensions and crimes, doppelgängers, and hauntings without a ghost, and influencing countless writers, including Ruth Rendell, Stephen King, and Angela Carter. Du Maurier's short stories, for their part, such as "The Birds" and "Don't Look Now," undercut the myth of the strong father figure's ability to cope with human and natural forces. In "The Birds," a father cannot protect his family from the invasion of the family home by garden and sea birds. In "Don't Look Now," another father, seeking his dead daughter, is murdered by a masquerading dwarf—he, too, has failed in his role as solver of mysteries and bringer of order.

Avril Horner and Sue Zlosnik revived critical interest in du Maurier in the 1990s, and a number of Cornwall-based conferences followed. Du Maurier's life and work have often been explored, and Margaret Forster focused on her work in various papers discussing and debating her lesbianism. Daphne du Maurier was made a Dame of the British Empire in 1969.

Gina Wisker

See also: Forbidden Knowledge or Power; *Trilby*.

Further Reading

Du Maurier, Daphne. 1938. *Rebecca*. London: Victor Gollancz.

Du Maurier, Daphne. 1971. "Don't Look Now." In *Not After Midnight*. London: Victor Gollancz.

Flanagan, Padraic. 2014. "Daphne du Maurier: Literary Genius Hated by the Critics?" *The Telegraph*, April 14. http://www.telegraph.co.uk/culture/books/10765991/Daphne-du -Maurier-literary-genius-hated-by-the-critics.html.

Horner, Avril, and Sue Zlosnik. 1998. *Daphne du Maurier: Writing, Identity and the Gothic Imagination*. Basingstoke: Macmillan.

Wisker, Gina. 2003. "Dangerous Borders: Daphne du Maurier's *Rebecca*: Shaking the Foundations of the Romance of Privilege, Partying and Place." *Journal of Gender Studies* 12, no. 2: 83–97.

DUE, TANANARIVE (1966–)

Tananarive Due is an American journalist and author best known for her supernatural thriller series about a secret colony of Ethiopian immortals, the Life Brothers, whose blood has the ability to heal: *My Soul to Keep* (1997), *The Living Blood* (2001), *Blood Colony* (2008), and *My Soul to Take* (2011). In addition to her "African Immortals" books and many other horror fictions, Due has also written mystery, historical, and nonfiction works. She worked as a journalist for the *Miami Herald* before turning to a full-time writing career.

Due's short fiction is frequently anthologized and she has won several literary awards, including a 2002 American Book Award for *The Living Blood*. Her first novel, *The Between* (1995), was nominated by the Horror Writers Association for a Bram Stoker award for Superior Achievement in a First Novel, and *My Soul to Keep* was also nominated for a Stoker award. Her novella "Ghost Summer" (2008) received the 2008 Kindred Award from the Carl Brandon Society, and her collection of short stories *Ghost Summer* won a 2016 British Fantasy Award. Her novels *The Good House* (2004) and *Joplin's Ghost* (2005) are also supernatural narratives. Writing with her husband Steven Barnes, Due has also published the apocalyptic zombie novels *Devil's Wake* (2012) and *Domino Falls* (2013), continuing a history of fruitful collaborations with other authors. The husband and wife writing team have also created a short film, *Danger Word*, based on a short story set in the same universe as *Devil's Wake* and *Domino Falls*. *My Soul to Keep* is also being adapted to film.

Born January 5, 1966, in Tallahassee, Florida, Due is the daughter of renowned civil rights activists. Her mother, Patricia Stephens Due, was jailed for forty-nine days in 1960 for refusing to pay a fine for sitting in at a Woolworth's counter, and, with Tananarive, co-wrote the civil rights memoir *Freedom in the Family* (2003). Due's fiction is characterized by a strong antiracist sensibility, standing out in the speculative fiction genres for placing the struggles and perspectives of black protagonists at the center of her stories. Often her protagonists grapple, not only with supernatural issues, but with the racism and multiple injustices of their societies. Her mystery novel *In the Night of the Heat: A Tennyson Hardwick Story* (2008; written with Blair Underwood and Steven Barnes) received the National Association for the Advancement of Colored People (NAACP) Image Award.

As a black author working in genres overwhelmingly dominated by whites, Due is often compared to other black speculative fiction writers, including Steven Barnes, Octavia E. Butler, and Samuel Delany. In an interview with prominent horror editor Paula Guran, Due noted the slipperiness of applying such categories as horror to nonwhite communities: "the black community draws on so many belief systems that they take the supernatural for granted. I also find that a lot of black readers are willing to share their stories of prophetic dreams or ghost sightings, and to them, that isn't horror or dark fantasy, it's true life" (Guran 1997). In a separate interview with *Publishers Weekly*, Due observed that she wanted to find her own voice as a black writer rather than attempting to be another Alice Walker or Toni Morrison, and that writing horror fiction gave her a "prism" through which to confront her fears (Dziemianowicz 2001, 81).

Critics have remarked upon the preoccupation with the ethics of using power underlying the plot conflicts in Due's works (Mohanraj 2002). For example, in *The Living Blood*, Jessica Wolde, who receives the titular blood gift from her Immortal husband, Dawit, must struggle with the ethics of dispensing her healing blood to diseased and suffering patients from her clinic in Botswana. Her daughter Fana, who received the blood *in utero*, gains even greater power than the men in the colony but must resist the temptation of the "Bee Lady" to give in to her anger and pain, and use her power to hurt those around her.

Aalya Ahmad

See also: Ancestral Curse; Bram Stoker Award; Butler, Octavia E.; Dark Fantasy; Forbidden Knowledge or Power; *Part One, Horror through History*: Horror from 1950 to 2000; Horror in the Twenty-First Century; *Part Two, Themes, Topics, and Genres*: Apocalyptic Horror; Ghost Stories; Horror Literature as Social Criticism and Commentary; Occult Fiction.

Further Reading

Due, Tananarive. 2001. *The Living Blood*. New York: Pocket Books.

Due, Tananarive, and Dianne Glave. 2004. "'My Characters Are Teaching Me to Be Strong': An Interview with Tananarive Due." *African American Review* 38, no. 4: 695–705.

Dziemianowicz, Stefan. 2001. "PW Talks to Tananarive Due." *Publishers Weekly*, March 19: 81.

Guran, Paula. 1997. "Tananarive Due: Unique Name for a New Dark Star." *Dark Echo*. http://www.darkecho.com/darkecho/archives/due.html. Originally published in *Omni Online*.

Mohanraj, Mary Anne. 2002. "Power Dynamics in the Novels of Tananarive Due." *Strange Horizons* 20. http://www.strangehorizons.com/non-fiction/articles/power-dynamics-in-the-novels-of-tananarive-due.

Morris, S. M. 2012. "Black Girls Are from the Future: Afrofuturist Feminism in Octavia E. Butler's 'Fledgling'." *Women's Studies Quarterly* 40, no. 3: 148–168.

Pough, Gwendolyn D., and Yolanda Hood. 2005. "Speculative Black Women: Magic, Fantasy, and the Supernatural." *Femspec* 6, no. 1: ix–xvi.

Thomas, Sheree, ed. 2000. *Dark Matter: A Century of Speculative Fiction from the African Diaspora*. New York: Warner Books.

"THE DUNWICH HORROR"

First published in *Weird Tales* for April 1929, "The Dunwich Horror" has long been one of the most popular and influential of H. P. Lovecraft's works. It was influenced in turn by a number of writers and stories that Lovecraft admired, including Ambrose Bierce's "The Damned Thing" and Arthur Machen's "The Novel of the Black Seal" and "The Great God Pan," the latter of which is directly mentioned by a character in "The Dunwich Horror."

The story is set in the farm country near the imaginary town of Dunwich, Massachusetts, where a child named Wilbur Whateley is born to an albino woman, Lavinia Whateley, and no known father. Lavinia's sinister father, "Wizard Whateley," makes the prophetic utterance to the startled townspeople that "some day yew folks'll her a child o' Lavinny's a-callin' its father's name on the top o' Sentinel Hill!" (Lovecraft 2001, 211). By age thirteen young Wilbur is hideous and nearly seven feet tall. Lavinia Whateley disappears, never to be seen again. Some time later, Wizard Whateley likewise disappears, but not before people note that the walls and floors of the Whateley barn have been torn out, as if to contain something immense. Intellectually precocious, Wilbur begins corresponding with scholars on esoteric matters. He tries to borrow the dreaded *Necronomicon* from the Miskatonic University library, then attempts to steal it, but is killed by the watchdog. Meanwhile,

The description of Wilbur Whateley's corpse after he is killed by the watchdog at Miskatonic University is among the high points in Lovecraft's career of envisioning hideously malformed (by human standards) monsters in the category of "things that should not be." Wilbur's top half is deformed, but "below the waist" anatomy turns to sheer nightmare:

> The skin was thickly covered with coarse black fur, and from the abdomen a score of long greenish-grey tentacles with red sucking mouths protruded limply. Their arrangement was odd, and seemed to follow the symmetries of some cosmic geometry unknown to earth or the solar system. On each of the hips, deep set in a kind of pinkish, ciliated orbit, was what seemed to be a rudimentary eye; whilst in lieu of a tail there depended a kind of trunk or feeler with purple annular markings, and with many evidences of being an undeveloped mouth or throat. The limbs, save for their black fur, roughly resembled the hind legs of prehistoric earth's giant saurians; and terminated in ridgy-veined pads that were neither hooves nor claws. When the thing breathed, its tail and tentacles rhythmically changed colour, as if from some circulatory cause normal to the non-human side of its ancestry. In the tentacles this was observable as a deepening of the greenish tinge, whilst in the tail it was manifest as a yellowish appearance which alternated with a sickly greyish-white in the spaces between the purple rings. Of genuine blood there was none; only the foetid greenish-yellow ichor which trickled along the painted floor beyond the radius of the stickiness, and left a curious discolouration behind it. (Lovecraft 2001, 223–224)

Matt Cardin

Source: Lovecraft, H. P. 2001. "The Dunwich Horror." In *The Thing on the Doorstep and Other Weird Stories*, 206–245. New York: Penguin.

whatever has been kept in the barn breaks out and terrorizes the countryside. Professor Armitage, the head librarian at Miskatonic, has figured out what is going on: the Whateleys have effected a mating between the horrific other-dimensional being Yog-Sothoth and Lavinia, so that "outside" creatures might gain a foothold in our dimension, destroying all humanity as they transform the world into a realm of unimaginable strangeness, in which Wilbur hoped to find a place. Armitage and two colleagues master enough of the spells from the *Necronomicon* to put an end to the monster, which, sure enough, calls out to Yog-Sothoth in extremis. It was Wilbur's nonidentical twin brother, which took after its father more than Wilbur did.

Here, in this story, is the basis for most of what followed from other writers as the "Cthulhu Mythos." August Derleth in particular latched onto the idea that Lovecraft's monsters could be defeated by sufficiently brave and knowledgeable humans. This led Derleth into the very un-Lovecraftian notion of "good gods" vs.

"evil gods" and an implied moral order in a dualistic universe, something Lovecraft himself completely rejected. In Lovecraft's view, if humans survive such encounters, it is entirely a coincidence and likely only for a short time. A close reading of "The Dunwich Horror" suggests that the only reason Armitage succeeded was that, with Wilbur dead, proper rites had not been performed, and the opportunity to open the way to Yog-Sothoth had already passed, so the monster was already "useless" for the grand design.

In mythic terms, if Wilbur and his brother are taken as the "hero," then this story becomes a blasphemous caricature of Joseph Campbell's Monomyth, or even of the story of Jesus: virgin birth, mysterious childhood, and finally a "savior" crying out to its father at the moment of its "crucifixion" atop a hill. Regardless, as a rip-roaring occult melodrama, "The Dunwich Horror" has never lacked readers. It was included in the landmark anthology *Great Tales of Terror and the Supernatural* in 1944 and has been anthologized many times since. In 1970 it was adapted as a campy low-budget horror movie starring Sandra Dee and Dean Stockwell, produced by Roger Corman for his American International Pictures.

Darrell Schweitzer

See also: Cthulhu Mythos; Derleth, August; "The Great God Pan"; Lovecraft, H. P.; Lovecraftian Horror; "The Novel of the Black Seal."

Further Reading

Burleson, Donald. 1981. "The Mythic Hero Archetype in 'The Dunwich Horror.'" *Lovecraft Studies* 4: 3–9.

Joshi, S. T. 2010. *I Am Providence, The Life and Times of H. P. Lovecraft*, 716–721. New York: Hippocampus Press.

Joshi, S. T., and David E. Schultz. 2001. *An H. P. Lovecraft Encyclopedia*, 79–81. Westport, CT: Greenwood.

Lovecraft, H. P. 2001. "The Dunwich Horror." In *The Thing on the Doorstep and Other Weird Stories*, 206–245. New York: Penguin.

ELLISON, HARLAN (1934–)

Extremely prolific, frequently controversial, and consistently brilliant, the acerbic American speculative fiction author and editor Harlan Ellison is known as much for his confrontational personality as for his hundreds of short, sharp stories. His first publication in 1956, and the early work that followed, established Ellison's distinctly angry narrative voice, even if it was expressed in derivative stories that were otherwise indistinguishable from other magazine fodder. By the early 1960s, however, Ellison began to hit his imaginative stride with important contributions to genre fiction in various outlets not limited to genre publications and including television (he wrote the screenplay for the 1967 *Star Trek* episode "The City on the Edge of Forever") and comics (with short but memorable 1–2 issue stints on *Detective Comics*, *The Avengers*, *Daredevil,* and *The Hulk*). He is considered to be one of the giants in the field of science fiction, fantasy, and horror. His influence has been widespread and his impact, if problematic, no less profound.

Now in his sixth decade as a published writer, Ellison has never stopped writing. As recently as 2011 he was awarded a Nebula Award by the Science Fiction Writers of America for his story "How Interesting: A Tiny Man" (2010). But the stories he is best known for were produced during an especially fertile period that ran from the mid-1960s to the late-1970s. Such stories as "Repent, Harlequin! Said the Ticktockman" (1965); "I Have No Mouth and I Must Scream" (1967); "The Beast That Shouted Love at the Heart of the World" (1968); "A Boy and His Dog" (1969); "The Deathbird" (1973); "The Whimper of Whipped Dogs" (1973); "Adrift Just Off the Islets of Langerhans: Latitude 38° 54' N, Longitude 77° 00' 13" W" (1974); and "Jeffty Is Five" (1977) showcase Ellison's remarkable strengths as a writer during this time: his efficient and creative use of language, his inventiveness, his sheer readability—remarkable given his often brutal subject matter and often grisly approach. He moves effortlessly between fictional and nonfictional genres, and while much of his output is categorized as science fiction, his work can be read just as easily as horror or dark fantasy—all the more so, perhaps, given that science fiction's concern with understanding the world is secondary to Ellison, who is more invested in highlighting the world's continued failings and the psychic fallout that results.

Many of the stories collected in *Deathbird Stories* (1975) and *Strange Wine* (1978) are significant for readers interested in horror fiction. In *Deathbird Stories* these include "The Whimper of Whipped Dogs," "Pretty Maggie Moneyeyes," "Adrift Just Off the Islets of Langerhans: Latitude 38° 54' N, Longitude 77° 00' 13" W,"

"Paingod," and "The Deathbird." In *Strange Wine* these include "Croatoan," "Hitler Painted Roses," "From A to Z, in the Chocolate Alphabet," "Lonely Women are the Vessels of Time," "Emissary from Hamelin," "The Boulevard of Broken Dreams," and "Strange Wine." (Stephen King, in his nonfiction study of the horror genre, *Danse Macabre* [1981], refers to "Strange Wine" as one of the finest horror fiction collections since 1950.) A sampling of other stories of interest include "Jeffty Is Five" and "All the Lies That Are My Life" in *Shatterday* (1980); "Djinn, No Chaser" in *Stalking the Nightmare* (1982); "Paladin of the Lost Hour" in *Angry Candy* (1988); and "Chatting with Anubis" and "Mefisto in Onyx" in *Slippage* (1997).

Ellison's best stories are often fueled by anger at what he perceives to be, and very often is, injustice and ignorance. When this anger subsumes the narrative it may come across as didactic or judgmental. But that same anger, channeled effectively, lends great weight and power to Ellison's stories. Even when his work presents problematic characterizations of women and nonwhite characters, there remains nonetheless an abiding authorial concern for the individual. Despite this empathy on his part, Ellison might also be accused of introducing into the world the very same pain to which, as the speculative literature critic John Clute has observed, he also serves as an eloquent witness. Ellison has been notoriously difficult to work with, as evidenced by the many lawsuits he has brought against companies and individuals, especially those associated with the film and television industries. He has also infuriated female writers and critics in and outside genre fiction with stories like "A Boy and His Dog," where the male protagonist chooses to cook and eat his love interest rather than sacrifice the dog he shares a psychic connection with. Though not necessarily negative, there is a quality to Ellison's oeuvre and to the author himself that seeks controversy, or at the very least attention. Some of the stories in *Strange Wine*, for example, were written in a bookshop window, allowing crowds a view of the artist at work, and the vignettes that were written in response to Jacek Yerka's art and collected in *Mind Fields: The Art of Jacek Yerka/The Fiction of Harlan Ellison* (1994) can also be considered performances of a sort. Ultimately, Ellison's polarizing personality and the contradictions found in both him and his stories point to the complexity and importance of the artist and his work.

Ellison has also been active as an editor, with his best and most important work being *Dangerous Visions* (1967) and, to a lesser degree, its companion *Again, Dangerous Visions* (1972). Compiled as in dialogue with the (mostly British) New Wave movement in science fiction, these anthologies focused perhaps too much on some aspects of the New Wave (its emphasis on sexuality and breaking of taboos) and not enough on others (its genuine concerns for injecting into science fiction literary elements modeled in part after literary Modernism). Still, there are some stories of interest to horror genre readers, especially Ellison's "The Prowler in the City at the Edge of the World" which appears in the first volume. *Medea: Harlan's World* (1985) is more formally an experiment, and a successful one, in science fiction world building (and self-mythologizing). Ellison's nonfiction includes autobiographical essays, reflection pieces on his work, and commentary, usually scathing, on the media industry, *The Glass Teat* (1970) being perhaps the best known of these.

Ellison has received numerous accolades for his work over the years, including eight Hugo Awards, four Nebula Awards, five Bram Stoker Awards, two Edgar Awards, two World Fantasy Awards (including one for lifetime achievement), the Eaton Award, and an unprecedented three Writers' Guild of America Awards. In 2011 he was inducted into the Science Fiction Hall of Fame.

Javier A. Martinez

See also: Bram Stoker Award; "I Have No Mouth and I Must Scream"; "The Whimper of Whipped Dogs"; World Fantasy Award.

Further Reading

Francavilla, Joseph, ed. 2012. *Critical Insights: Harlan Ellison*. Pasadena, CA: Salem Press.
Weil, Ellen R., and Gary K. Wolfe. 2002. *Harlan Ellison: The Edge of Forever*. Columbus: Ohio State University Press.

ETCHISON, DENNIS (1945–)

Dennis William Etchison is arguably the best American author of horror short fiction since Ray Bradbury. Starting in the 1960s, Etchison began publishing brilliant stories that won him a devoted following among horror connoisseurs—especially in Great Britain, where his savagely bleak "The Dark Country" won the 1981 British Fantasy Award—and led eventually to a series of beautifully wrought collections published by Scream Press: *The Dark Country* (1982), *Red Dreams* (1984), and *The Blood Kiss* (1987). These collections, along with *The Death Artist* (2000) and *Talking in the Dark* (2001), contain what are considered some of the finest works of horror literature published in English during the last four decades.

Etchison's short fiction explores the ambiguous landscapes of Southern California with a corrosive precision that recalls Raymond Chandler and Nathanael West. The characteristic scenes of his stories—half-empty multiplex cinemas, all-night laundromats and convenience stores, bleak highway rest-stops, neon-lit beachside motels—evoke the aimlessness and weary boredom of contemporary suburban experience, a spiritual wasteland in which sinister forces incubate. Stylistically, the tales are models of concision, stark montages of hallucinatory details pregnant with psychological nuance. "It Only Comes Out at Night" (1976) captures the accumulating dread of a driver who realizes he is being tracked by a killer, while "The Nighthawk" (1978) offers a subtle study of a young girl who suspects that her brother is a shape-shifting monster. Only a few of the tales—such as "The Late Shift" (1980), in which dead-end service jobs are staffed by reanimated corpses—are overtly supernatural, most conveying mere glimpses of the numinous that remain inscrutable, hauntingly elusive. Filled with grim hints and nervous portents, his stories amount to a collection of cryptic snapshots of contemporary suburbia and the lost souls who inhabit it.

Etchison's novels have failed to capitalize on the brilliance of his short fiction, upon which his considerable reputation rests—although he has shown skills as an editor, with award-winning anthologies such as *Meta-Horror* (1992) to his credit. His novels—*Darkside* (1986), *Shadowman* (1993), *California Gothic* (1995), and *Double Edge* (1997)—feature the author's shrewd eye for telling social detail, especially regarding California lifestyles, but they are all flawed in significant ways, informed by a retrograde nostalgia altogether lacking in his more hard-edged short stories. While his portraits of middle-class characters struggling in the ruins of their shattered ideals have at times a genuine poignancy, they also tend to degenerate into polemical disquisitions on cultural malaise. Ultimately, Etchison will be remembered for his muted, haunting, and ferociously downbeat short stories, which are among the best that modern horror has produced.

Rob Latham

See also: Bradbury, Ray; Novels versus Short Fiction; Psychological Horror.

Further Reading

Joshi, S. T. 1994. "Dennis Etchison: Spanning the Genres." *Studies in Weird Fiction* 15 (Summer): 30–36.

Mathews, David. 1998. "Arterial Motives: Dennis Etchison Interviewed." *Interzone* 133 (July): 23–26.

Schweitzer, Darrell. 1985. "The Dark Side of the American Dream: Dennis Etchison." In *Discovering Modern Horror Fiction I*, 48–55. Mercer Island, WA: Starmont House.

EWERS, HANNS HEINZ (1871–1943)

Few literary figures blurred the boundary between their fiction and their biography as thoroughly as Hanns Heinz Ewers. The fascination with blood, eroticism, and the occult exhibited by many of his characters was apparently shared by the author himself. His horror stories and novels have been admired by everyone from H. P. Lovecraft to Dashiell Hammett to Adolf Hitler. During his lifetime Ewers was among the most popular authors in his native Germany.

Born Hans Heinrich Ewers in Dusseldorf in 1871, he came by his artistic inclinations honestly; his mother Maria was a raconteur and his father Heinz was court painter for the Grand Duke of Mecklenburg-Schwerin. As a boy Ewers would often serve as the model for the grand duke's court children. Forced to stand still for hours while wearing regal finery, young Hans learned the power of storytelling from his mother's telling of fairy tales and German folklore, which she did to keep Hans entertained while he modeled for his father's canvases. Along with literary leanings, Ewers also shared with his mother a hunger for diablerie (demonic sorcery); in girlhood Maria Ewers spoke of her earnest desire to meet the Devil in the flesh. Her son would eventually tour Europe giving a lecture entitled *Die Religion des Satan* (*The Religion of Satan*).

Ewers began his publishing career in 1898 with the poem "Mutter" ("Mother"). His debut short story collection, *Das Grauen* (*The Grey*) was published in 1907, and its contents reflected many of his personal experiences from both travel and his deepening interest in Spiritualism (he was reportedly a gifted medium). In 1908, *Die Besessenen* (*The Possessed*) featured Ewers's most reprinted story, "The Spider," in which a medical student falls under the sinister spell of a hotel room where a chain of suicides have occurred. "The Spider" featured a morbidly erotic femme fatale–type character, which Ewers considered a manifestation of "the Eternal Feminine." This was to become a recurrent theme in his fiction.

He penned a trilogy of novels featuring the character of Frank Braun, a scholar, occultist, traveler, and Nietzschean soul (one aspiring to superhuman greatness of the type written about by the nineteenth-century German philosopher Friedrich Nietzsche); in other words, a thinly veiled idealization of Ewers himself. *Alraune* (1911), a gory, sexual riff on both *Frankenstein* and the mandrake myth, became the author's most successful book.

Ewers continued to write and travel until the First World War. In America, his propagation of German Nationalist literature around New York aroused the attention of the U.S. Secret Service, and in 1918 Ewers was arrested as an enemy agent. He remained imprisoned until the summer of 1920.

The Germany he returned to was embroiled in political and social turmoil. Ewers's innate nationalism seemed to flourish through the 1920s as he began to make contacts within the burgeoning Nazi Party. While these affiliations very likely saved his life, eventually Ewers's philosemitism (respect for Jews and Judaism), along with his morbidly decadent imagination and hedonistic views of sex and intoxicants (he had been using and praising hashish and alcohol since 1893), led him to being declared an unperson by the Third Reich. His books were ordered to be burned. He lived until June 12, 1943, when tuberculosis and heart failure claimed him.

In the wake of World War II, Ewers's legacy disintegrated. However, new English translations began to appear at the dawn of the twenty-first century, sparking a resurgence of interest in his grisly, passionate, and singular fiction.

Richard Gavin

See also: *Alraune*; Meyrink, Gustav; Spiritualism.

Further Reading

Ewers, Hanns Heinz. 2012. *Brevier*. Edited by Arthur Gersel and Rolf Bongs. Newcastle: Side Real Press.

"Hanns Heinz Ewers." 2003. *Contemporary Authors Online*. Detroit, MI: Gale.

Koger, Grove. 2007. "Hanns Heinz Ewers." *Guide to Literary Masters & Their Works* 1. Salem, MA: Salem Press.

THE EXORCIST

The 1971 publication of American author William Peter Blatty's novel *The Exorcist* signaled a radical change in supernatural horror fiction. Exploiting a deep-seated and practically universal human anxiety about the loss of self, autonomy, and identity to invading, invisible forces, the novel presents readers with a vividly detailed depiction of the demonic possession of a twelve-year-old girl named Regan Mac-Neil. Written in the third person, the novel reveals the progress of Regan's possession primarily through the eyes of her mother, actress Chris MacNeil, and Catholic priest and psychiatrist Damien Karras. Attempting to liberate Regan from her possessed state, Karras enlists the aid of an experienced exorcist, Jesuit priest and archaeologist Lankester Merrin, whose character is loosely based on British archaeologist Gerald Lankester Harding. The novel is among the most iconic works of twentieth-century horror fiction and remains the most influential fictional account of demonic possession ever written.

Though *The Exorcist* was Blatty's fifth novel, it was both his first foray into supernatural horror and his first major popular success. While its sales were initially slow and critical response was mixed, Blatty's appearance on *The Dick Cavett Show* helped bring the novel, and the phenomenon it treated, into the spotlight. *The Exorcist* went on to spend more than four months on the *New York Times* best-seller list, its popularity further boosted by the 1973 release of a film adaptation, scripted by Blatty and directed by William Friedkin. The film broke a number of box office records and was an unprecedented commercial success, spawning dozens of imitations in the following decades and irrevocably establishing demonic possession as among the most popular tropes of horror film. It shocked and traumatized many filmgoers, inspiring religious revivalism, moral panic, and eventually the creation of a clinical psychiatric category, "cinematic possession neurosis," to

---

The World's Scariest Christian Novel?

The fact that *The Exorcist* has generally been remembered as one of the most frightening horror novels ever published—something intimately linked to the parallel reputation of its legendary film adaptation as "the scariest movie ever made"—both fulfills and, to an extent, obscures Blatty's stated purpose in writing it. What has been lost in general public awareness of the book is that, in its aftermath, Blatty said he had intended it as a Christian novel. By his own account, he was deeply disturbed by the rising nihilism of secularized Western culture in the mid-twentieth century, and his driving ambition in writing *The Exorcist* was to convey to a jaded, despairing, and disillusioned modern public a sense of the horror of demonic evil, in the hope that this would automatically convey an accompanying emotional sense of the obverse: the existence of angels and God and eternal life, and what these would entail.

Matt Cardin

describe those who became convinced they were demonically possessed after viewing the film.

The Exorcist draws on a long history of writings about demonic possession, from those that appear in the Gospels and early Patristic writings to modern literary treatments. While not a staple of either early or Victorian Gothic fiction, demonic possession had been obliquely treated by Dark Romantic writers including E. T. A. Hoffmann and Edgar Allan Poe, who linked it most often to mesmerism as much as traditional theology. Aldous Huxley wrote about the phenomenon in *The Devils of Loudun* (1952), a lightly fictionalized treatment of a historical case that Blatty's novel makes repeated reference to. Huxley's book in turn served as the source for Ken Russell's cinematic extravaganza *The Devils*, released contemporaneously with Blatty's novel in 1971. However, where Huxley and Russell focused on the dangers of sexual repression and religious irrationalism, Blatty took an entirely different approach, producing a fast-paced thriller that fused anxieties about social change, Catholic theology, and visceral horror into an original and powerful compound.

The Exorcist was written during a period of radical social change in the United States. The civil rights movement, feminist activism, and anti–Vietnam War peace protests formed its backdrop and are implicated in the plot, as Regan's actress mother is playing the lead role in a film about student activism on the campus of Georgetown University when Regan's possession occurs. The novel also reflects conservative and Christian anxieties about the rising popularity of "New Age" and occult spiritual beliefs and practices, causally implicated as Regan is shown innocently experimenting with a Ouija board prior to her possession. Both novel and film suggestively link this experimentation to Regan's adolescent sexuality; it is her playing (Ouija) with herself that seems to trigger her possession.

Blatty, a practicing Catholic, has stated that the novel was partially inspired by his own crisis of faith, a crisis given its most acute expression through Karras, who wrestles with despair and disbelief throughout the novel. Blatty drew some of the details of the exorcism from a case he had read about while a student at Georgetown University, in which a young boy was supposedly successfully exorcised by Jesuit priest and educator William S. Bowdern. Blatty's decision to make the possessed child female both reflects the majority of reported cases of possession and plays into the conventions of Hollywood filmmaking, in which it is most often the body of a threatened woman that bears the viewer's gaze and is used to generate dramatic tension.

While Blatty's novel of satanic supernatural horror came in the wake of the popular success of Ira Levin's best-seller *Rosemary's Baby* (1967) and Roman Polanski's even more successful film of the same title (1968), the two novels are radically different creatures. Levin's is urbane, often sardonic, and satirical of, among other things, religious irrationalism and middle-class materialism. Blatty eschews liberal irony in favor of emotional immediacy, spiritual intensity, and an emphasis on visceral body horror, anticipating much of what would come during the mass market "horror boom" that followed in the late 1970s and throughout the 1980s. *The*

Exorcist's popularity influenced the creation of numerous horror novels focused on spirit possession, from "horror boom" titles including Frank di Felitta's *Audrey Rose* (1975), Stephen King's *The Shining* (1977) and *Christine* (1983), and James Herbert's *Shrine* (1983) to more contemporary reinventions including Sara Gran's *Come Closer* (2003), Andrew Pyper's *The Demonologist* (2013), and Paul Tremblay's *A Head Full of Ghosts* (2015).

Sean Moreland

See also: Devils and Demons; Possession and Exorcism; *Rosemary's Baby*.

Further Reading

Ballon, Bruce, and Molyn Leszcz. 2007. "Horror Films: Tales to Master Terror or Shapers of Trauma?" *American Journal of Psychotherapy* 61, no. 2: 211–230.

Clover, Carol J. 1992. "Opening Up." In *Men, Women, and Chain Saws: Gender in the Modern Horror Film*, 65–113. Princeton, NJ: Princeton University Press.

Mäyrä, Frans Ilkka. 1999. "The Inarticulate Body: Demonic Conflicts in *The Exorcist*." In *Demonic Texts and Textual Demons*, 143–168. Tampere, Finland: Tampere University Press.

Morgan, Chris R. 2016. "Archetypes of Exorcism." *First Things: A Monthly Journal of Religion and Public Life* 263(May): 63–64. http://www.firstthings.com/blogs/firstthoughts/2016/04/archetypes-of-exorcism.

Szumskyj, Benjamin, ed. 2008. *American Exorcist: Critical Essays on William Peter Blatty*. Jefferson, NC: McFarland.

Winter, Douglas E. 1996. "Casting Out Demons: The Horror Fiction of William P. Blatty." In *A Dark Night's Dreaming: Contemporary American Horror Fiction*, edited by Tony Magistrale, 84–96. Columbia: University of South Carolina Press.

"THE FALL OF THE HOUSE OF USHER"

Originally published in 1839, "The Fall of the House of Usher" is one of Edgar Allan Poe's most famous stories. It is a quintessential Gothic story, written at a time when the traditional Gothic novel had run its course, so that Poe's use of stock Gothic materials is turning in a new direction. Rather than merely tell of crypts and haunted castles, Poe made such elements symbolic of his characters' mental states, so that inner madness becomes physically manifest.

An unnamed narrator arrives at the crumbling mansion of his old school friend, Roderick Usher, whom he has not seen in years. He remarks at some length on how the mere sight of the place fills his soul with depressive gloom, and he observes a crack in the overall structure of the house. Roderick Usher had asked him to come, hoping that the presence of a friend would help dispel his own depression. Usher is the last of his line, suffering from a mysterious malady that has heightened all his senses. He cannot bear strong light, or any but the blandest

Edgar Allan Poe's "The Haunted Palace"

After publishing "The Haunted Palace" in a magazine in 1839, Poe incorporated it into "The Fall of the House of Usher," where it is presented as having been written by Roderick Usher himself.

In the greenest of our valleys
    By good angels tenanted,
Once a fair and stately palace—
    Radiant palace—reared its head.
In the monarch Thought's dominion—
    It stood there!
Never seraph spread a pinion
    Over fabric half so fair!

Banners yellow, glorious, golden,
    On its roof did float and flow

(This—all this—was in the olden
    Time long ago)
And every gentle air that dallied,
    In that sweet day,
Along the ramparts plumed and pallid,
    A wingéd odor went away.

Wanderers in that happy valley,
    Through two luminous windows, saw
Spirits moving musically
    To a lute's well-tunéd law,
Round about a throne where, sitting,
    Porphyrogene
In state his glory well befitting,
    The ruler of the realm was seen.

And all with pearl and ruby glowing
    Was the fair palace door,
Through which came flowing, flowing, flowing,
    And sparkling evermore,
A troop of Echoes, whose sweet duty
    Was but to sing,
In voices of surpassing beauty,
    The wit and wisdom of their king.

But evil things, in robes of sorrow,
    Assailed the monarch's high estate.
(Ah, let us mourn!—for never morrow
    Shall dawn upon him, desolate!)
And round about his home the glory
    That blushed and bloomed
Is but a dim-remembered story
    Of the old time entombed.

And travellers, now, within that valley,
    Through the encrimsoned windows see
Vast forms that move fantastically
    To a discordant melody,
While, like a ghastly rapid river,
    Through the pale door
A hideous throng rush out forever,
And laugh—but smile no more.

Matt Cardin

Source: Poe, Edgar Allan. *The Works of Edgar Allan Poe.* 1914. Vol. 10. New York: Charles Scribner's Sons. 32–33.

foods, or any but certain musical notes. Meanwhile, Roderick's sister Madeleine, with whom he has a strange, possibly incestuous relationship, is dying of a wasting illness of her own. She apparently dies, and the narrator and Roderick carry her coffin down into a crypt to leave it there for a fortnight before final burial. If this is a precaution against premature burial, it is an odd one, because they screw the coffin lid shut and close the heavy metal door to the vault. In the next few days, Roderick begins to behave strangely, and even the narrator is certain he is hearing noises from below. He tries to calm his friend by reading aloud from a chivalric romance, but even as the knight in the story strikes a gate with his mace, the two men hear a crash. As a dragon shrieks, they hear a cry. Roderick, with his heightened senses, has been aware for days that Madeleine is alive within her coffin. Now she has broken out and stands outside his chamber. When he opens it, she falls dying into his arms, and he dies too. The narrator escapes just in time, as a whirlwind crashes the entire structure into the surrounding tarn (lake).

Critics have made much of all this, citing numerous symbolic aspects, notably parallels between the disintegrating house and Roderick Usher's disintegrating mind. This is brought out even more explicitly in the poem "The Haunted Palace," which is given in the story as the composition of Roderick Usher. Poe scholar Thomas Olive Mabbott credited H. P. Lovecraft's "Supernatural Horror in Literature" for a solution to the central mystery: that Roderick, Madeleine, and the house share the same soul, and so all perish at the same instant. The story has been filmed many times, most memorably by Roger Corman in 1960.

Darrell Schweitzer

See also: "The Masque of the Red Death"; Poe, Edgar Allan; Psychological Horror; Romanticism and Dark Romanticism; Unreliable Narrator.

Further Reading

Bailey, James O. 1964. "What Happens in 'The Fall of the House of Usher'?" *American Literature* 35, no. 4 (January): 445–466.

Cook, Jonathan A. 2012. "Poe and the Apocalyptic Sublime: 'The Fall of the House of Usher.'" *Papers on Language & Literature* 48, no. 2: 3–44.

Gargano, James W. 1982. "'The Fall of the House of Usher': An Apocalyptic Vision." *University of Mississippi Studies in English* 3: 53–63.

Kendall, Lyle H., Jr. 1963. "The Vampire Motif in 'The Fall of the House of Usher.'" *College English* 24, no. 4 (March): 450–453.

Mabbott, Thomas Ollive. "The Fall of the House of Usher." 1978. In *The Collected Works of Edgar Allan Poe: Tales and Sketches 1843–1849*, 392–422. Cambridge, MA: Belknap Press of Harvard University Press.

Moss, William. 2014. "The Fall of the House, from Poe to Percy: The Evolution of an Enduring Gothic Convention." In *A Companion to American Gothic*, edited by Charles L. Crowe, 177–188. Hoboken, NJ: John Wiley.

Timmerman, John H. 2003. "House of Mirrors: Edgar Allan Poe's 'The Fall of the House of Usher.'" *Papers on Language & Literature* 39, no. 3 (Summer): 227–244.

FARRIS, JOHN (1936–)

John Lee Farris, born in Jefferson City, Missouri, is an American writer best known for his psychic horror novel *The Fury* (1976), which was made into a successful film directed by Brian De Palma in 1978. A true artistic polymath, Farris has written screenplays—most notably, the script for *The Fury*—plays, and poetry, and he even directed a film, *Dear Dead Delilah* (1973). He is, however, best known for his work in horror prose. Although substantially less popular than some of his contemporaries, especially Stephen King, alongside whom he would appear in the second volume of *Transgressions* in 2006 as one of two *New York Times* best sellers, Farris's oeuvre is vast and thematically varied.

After a first period in which he concentrated on thrillers and noirs, sometimes publishing under the pen name Steve Brackeen, Farris started to combine the successful Harrison High School series (1959–1974) with a string of horror novels. Following the television adaptation of *When Michael Calls* (1967) in 1972, Farris began working in the horror genre in earnest, which he sometimes combined with the psychological thriller and serial killer genres in novels such as *Sharp Practice* (1974), *Shatter* (1980), and *Nightfall* (1987).

The success of the telekinetic terrors of *The Fury* would lead Farris to mine more obviously occult and supernatural areas in the 1970s, 1980s, and early 1990s, and to become a full-time horror writer. His work during this, his "peak" period shows an understanding of the publishing market; the demonic *Son of the Endless Night* (1984), for instance, draws on the success of *The Exorcist* (1971) and *The Omen* (1976). But his very personal literary vision—which resorts to anything from Aztec rites in *Sacrifice* (1994) to Nordic folklore in *Fiends* (1990), voodoo cults in *All Heads Turn When the Hunt Goes By* (1977), or vanished magical civilizations in *Catacombs* (1981)—prevails.

His last horror writing period, after a brief slew of thrillers published from 1995 to 1999, began in the new millennium. Apart from the collection *Elvisland* (2004) and the novels *Phantom Nights* (2004), *You Don't Scare Me* (2007), and his first werewolf novel, *High Bloods* (2009), also his last work to date, the rest of Farris's postmillennial books have been dedicated to reviving *The Fury*.

Although Farris's books are now largely out of print, a number of his "classics" have recently become available in eBook format, a venture that has rescued some of his best novels from oblivion. In the 2010s, specialist publisher Centipede Press also paid homage to Farris by publishing five of his novels in deluxe limited editions.

Xavier Aldana Reyes

See also: *The Exorcist*; King, Stephen; Psychological Horror; Werewolves.

Further Reading

Aldana Reyes, Xavier. 2016. "John Farris." In *Lost Souls of Horror and the Gothic: Essays on Fifty-Four Neglected Authors, Actors and Others*, edited by Elizabeth McCarthy and Bernice M. Murphy, 80–82. Jefferson, NC: McFarland.

Errickson, Will. 2015. "Evil Eighties: The Paperback Horrors of John Farris." *Tor.com*, February 13. http://www.tor.com/2015/02/13/evil-eighties-the-paperback-horrors-of-john-farris.

FAULKNER, WILLIAM (1897–1962)

William Faulkner was an American writer and Nobel laureate who is best known for his novels and short stories set in the fictional Yoknapatawpha County, Mississippi, which illustrate the intricate links between race, class, and gender in the U.S. South at the turn of the twentieth century. His fiction is characterized both by distinctive writing techniques—including deconstructed timelines, shifting points of view, stream of consciousness, and unreliable narrators—and recurrent motifs such as moral and social decay in the American South, rape, lynching, incest, miscegenation, psychological distress, physical and mental disability, and pathological bonds between individuals, families, and the community.

"A Rose for Emily": Classic Southern Gothic

"A Rose for Emily" was first published in the April 1930 issue of the *Forum*, and it went on to become Faulkner's most anthologized story. Integral to the Southern Gothic tradition, it is noted for its twist ending, involving necrophilia. It is narrated in the first-person-plural point of view by the collective voice of the citizens of the fictional city of Jefferson, Mississippi, and the story unfolds in nonlinear fashion, beginning with the funeral of Emily Grierson, the last in the long line of a Southern aristocratic family. The story then examines the peculiar events of her life: a rotting smell coming from her house; the time she bought poison; and her romance with a Northern man named Homer Barron, who mysteriously disappears. It all ends with Emily's death and the townspeople's discovery of Homer's decayed corpse lying on a bed in a locked upstairs room, where Emily's silver hair is found on the pillow next to him. The clear implication is that Emily, who had long been feared and viewed as an eccentric crank by the townspeople, murdered Homer and then slept beside his corpse for years in the solitude of her reclusive abode.

"A Rose for Emily" explores the tropes of death and decay, nostalgia for a romantic past (as exemplified by the modern world's encroachment on the decaying Old South), and the iron-fisted control of Southern patriarchy. With its striking viewpoint and voice, it is an early example of a modernist take on literary horror, and it has been widely anthologized and included in high school and college literature textbooks. A PBS short film adaptation of "A Rose for Emily" was produced in 1983, starring Anjelica Huston as Emily.

Chun H. Lee

Born in 1897 in New Albany, Mississippi, Faulkner spent most of his life at his estate of Rowan Oak in Oxford, Mississippi, from which he also derived the inspiration for much of his writing. The innovative quality of his prose and his attachment to his Southern background have often led him to be categorized as an author of both the modernist movement and the Southern Renaissance. However, Faulkner's taste for disturbing, often macabre storylines, as well as uncanny atmospheres, also made him responsible, alongside authors such as Erskine Caldwell and Thomas Wolfe, for the emergence of Southern Gothic fiction in the early 1930s. Major figures of the genre have acknowledged their debt to Faulkner, such as Flannery O'Connor, who wrote that "the presence of Faulkner in our midst makes a great difference in what the writer can and cannot permit himself to do" (O'Connor 1969, 45).

Although Faulkner's reputation as a writer is currently well established, his fame came relatively late. Prior to achieving success, he spent several years in California and New Orleans publishing screenplays for Hollywood, essays and sketches, and poetry. While in New Orleans, he became acquainted with Sherwood Anderson, who recommended he should write about his native region and the idiosyncrasies of the "southern character." Following this advice, Faulkner proceeded to write the first book of the Yoknapatawpha saga, which would be published under the name *Sartoris* (1929). While waiting for it to be published, Faulkner embarked on a second novel that would be his ticket to fame: *The Sound and the Fury*.

Published in October 1929, the novel is widely regarded as a revolutionary masterpiece. It recounts the gradual decay of a Southern bourgeois family through the successive points of view of four of its members: Benjy, the youngest son, whose mental disability prevents him from having any sense of time, place, and people, to the point that he does not recognize his own image in the mirror; Quentin, the eldest son, whose incapacity to deal with his ambiguous feelings for his sister leads him to flee the South and commit suicide in the Charles River; Jason, the last son of the lineage as well as a bachelor who abuses the women of his family and drunkenly drives around the town of Jefferson chasing after his young niece; and finally, Dilsey, the black maid who has lived through the family's downfall and is the last one standing to take care of the disabled son and the estate. *The Sound and Fury* is a challenging book in both form and content. To learn the truth about the Compson family, the reader must piece together many different plot elements scattered through the broken timeline and the stream of consciousness narrations. The horror and the violence of the plot are made apparent in the process of reading, through careful innuendos, ellipsis, and understatements. This novel set the tone for the other novels and stories to come: through convoluted narrative techniques and baroque prose, Faulkner was to paint life in the South as a horror story made of violence, unruly bodies, and perverted morals and manners. Exploring the whole social, racial, and gender spectrum from the Civil War to the Great Depression, Faulkner spares his reader no gruesome details.

His next novel, *As I Lay Dying* (1930), is a macabre and ludicrous mock-epic in which a family of poor farmers embark on a disastrous journey to bury the body of the mother that has just died. The many obstacles they face see their task put to a gruesome test, especially when the corpse inside the coffin starts rotting and carrion birds start following them everywhere they go. The macabre humor of *As I Lay Dying* is also to be found in "A Rose for Emily" (1930), a short story now considered a foundational text of Southern Gothic literature. Told from the collective point of view of the townspeople of Jefferson, the story tells of Emily Grierson, an old maid from an aristocratic family of Jefferson who has probably gone mad. In a final plot twist, the town realizes on the day she dies that she murdered her lover some fifty years ago and has been sleeping next to his decaying body every night since.

With *Sanctuary* (1931), Faulkner's sulfurous detective-story, he earned the nickname "the corncob man": the story follows a young white girl named Temple Drake as she runs away from college. She falls into the hands of an impotent thug named Popeye who eventually rapes her with a corncob in an abandoned grange. Even though the rape itself is left out of the text, the suggested violence of the scene was such that the novel was almost banned, under claims that no one but a pathological reader could enjoy being sadistically aroused by it.

Light in August (1932) is a collection of intersected stories that all come together through the violent beheading of Joanna Burden by her lover Joe Christmas, who consequently gets lynched by a white supremacist bearing the ominous name of Percy Grimm. Though Joanna's murder seems to be the peak of violence in the novel, the rest of the novel is seething with racial hate and sexual abuse that is only solved through explosions of violence such as murders or lynching.

Absalom, Absalom (1936) is Faulkner's Gothic *grand oeuvre*. Very much in the tradition of Edgar Allan Poe's "The Fall of the House of Usher," it depicts the downfall of a family, brought about through generations of incestuous desires, greed, envy, and racial divides, climaxing in the literal destruction of the family home. Haunted by the presence of a member of the family whom everybody thought long gone, the Sutpen mansion goes down in flames, leaving nothing of the patriarch's dream of grandeur but a couple of ghost stories told by the elders of the community.

Faulkner's artistic vision stood in complete contradiction to the predominant discourse of the time that portrayed the South as a lost Eden. His callous prose earned him the ire of the Southern literary scene, which, as early as 1935, labeled him and other writers of the time as "the real equerries of Raw-Head-and-Bloody-Bones," "merchants of death, hell and the grave," and "horror-mongers in chief" (Bassett 1997, 352). Fellow Southern writer Ellen Glasgow called Faulkner out for letting his literature "crawl too long in the mire" (Bassett 1997, 359). She found his style too macabre, labeling it "Southern Gothic" in a pejorative way; in an attempt to disparage Faulkner, Glasgow both coined the term and tied it forever to his name. The label stuck, and distinguished authors such as O'Connor, Eudora Welty,

Carson McCullers, Truman Capote, and Toni Morrison, all of whom wrote in a Southern Gothic vein themselves (with the term eventually losing its negative connotation), held Faulkner as a major point of reference.

Elsa Charléty

See also: The Grotesque; Morrison, Toni; O'Connor, Flannery; The Uncanny; Welty, Eudora.

Further Reading

Bassett, John Earl, ed. 1997. *Defining Southern Literature: Perspectives and Assessments, 1831–1952*. Madison, NJ: Fairleigh Dickinson University Press.

Faulkner, William. 2003. *The Portable Faulkner*. New York: Penguin.

Fiedler, Leslie A. [1960] 1997. *Love and Death in the American Novel*. Normal, IL: Dalkey Archive Press.

O'Connor, Flannery. 1969. *Mystery and Manners: Occasional Prose*. Edited by Sally Fitzgerald and Robert Fitzgerald, 36–50. New York: Farrar, Straus, & Giroux.

Sundquist, Eric J. 1983. *Faulkner: The House Divided*. Baltimore: Johns Hopkins University Press.

FEAR

Fear is a novel of psychological horror by L. Ron Hubbard that was first published in the July 1940 issue of the pulp fantasy magazine *Unknown*. Editor John W. Campbell touted it as the type of horror story that he hoped other authors would contribute to his magazine of modern fantastic fiction.

The protagonist of *Fear* is James Lowry, a professor of anthropology and ethnology at Atworthy College. A scientific rationalist, Lowry has just published an article in the *Newspaper Weekly* dismissing humanity's belief in devils and demons as a type of mental illness promulgated in times past by witch doctors who hoped to control the masses through their fear of the supernatural. The head of Lowry's department interprets the article as an attack not just against superstition but against religion, and he fires Lowry for besmirching the university's reputation with what he considers an exploitative attempt at self-aggrandizement. Reeling from this unexpected twist of fate, James visits the home of his friend and colleague, Tommy Williams, who disagrees with James's rationalism and warns him that "that man is the safest who knows that all is really evil and that the air and earth and water are peopled by fantastic demons and devils who lurk to grin at and increase the sad state of man" (Hubbard 2000, 14).

At the start of the novel's second chapter, James comes to his senses, disoriented, and discovers that four hours have passed since he left Tommy's house for which he cannot account. Furthermore, he has lost the hat that he was wearing, and his hand bears a cut and a bruise whose cause he can't recall. At first James attributes his disorientation to a recent bout of malaria that he picked up during his overseas travels. But over the next few hours, he moves through landscapes of seemingly impossible topography—among them, a stairway that leads to impossible subterranean depths—and as he tries to conduct his life normally with Tommy, his wife Mary, and his students, he experiences a variety of increasingly eerie and enigmatic visions, among them the legendary hangman Jack Ketch, a young girl, an invisible thing that keeps nudging his leg at a table, and an elderly crone who warns him that "if you find your hat you'll find your four hours, and if you find your four hours then you will die!" (29). These visions culminate in a final one in which James is told that he is the only real person in the surreal universe that he is navigating, at which point he acknowledges what happened during his lost four hours—he mistakenly assumed that Tommy and his Mary were having an affair, killed them, and tried to conceal their bodies—and accepts that all of his encounters and experiences following this have been completely illusory, the product of his psychotic break with reality.

The thunderclap revelation at the end of *Fear* is that the world James has moved through for most of the novel is a completely internal landscape shaped by his denial and feelings of personal guilt over his actions. In that landscape, demons—incarnated in a pair who hover on the periphery of the narrative, speaking in editorial asides, and who present themselves as enacting Lowry's ordeal in order to teach him a lesson—do exist. As Brian Stableford observes in his critique of Hubbard's novel, "there *are* demons and they *do* torment us, but they are one with ourselves and haunt us from within" (Stableford 1979, 764). Praising the rigorous internal logic that gives the story its narrative cohesion, Stableford notes the parallels between Hubbard's novels and the tenets of Scientology, the psychoanalytic discipline he would later found: "There is surely a moral in the fact that Hubbard went on to invent a new school of psychoanalysis based on the thesis that all the ills of mankind stem from blotted out memories ('engrams'), suppressed because of their inherent unpleasantness, which plague and torment us, and that this new psychoanalysis was ultimate reincarnated as a religion whose dramatic revelation is that we are *all* potentially godlike if only we can clear away our inner demons and 'audit' ourselves back to our inherent superpowers" (764–765).

Stefan R. Dziemianowicz

See also: Devils and Demons; Hubbard, L. Ron; Psychological Horror; Pulp Horror.

Further Reading

Budrys, Algis. 1991. "Books." *Magazine of Fantasy and Science Fiction* 80, no. 4: 28–29.

Hubbard, L. Ron. [1940] 2000. *Fear*. Los Angeles, CA: Galaxy Press.

Stableford, Brian. 1979. "*Fear* and *Typewriter in the Sky*." In *Survey of Science Fiction Literature*, edited by Frank N. Magill, 761–765. Englewood Cliffs, NJ: Salem Press.

FÉVAL, PAUL (1816–1887)

Paul-Henri-Corentin Féval was born in Rennes in Brittany, France, and his interest in the history, legends, and folklore of Brittany was a strong element in his literary work, providing the basis for his early collections *Contes de Bretagne* (1844) and *Les Contes de nos pères* (1845), and a frequent stimulus to the newspaper serials he produced in great abundance, especially during the Second Empire (1851–1870), when he became famous as the chief proponent of swashbuckling *"cape-et-épée"* fiction." Such serial fiction traded very heavily in suspenseful melodrama and employed horrific motifs as a staple element of the threats prolifically addressed to their heroes and (more particularly) heroines.

Convention favored the rationalization of seemingly supernatural materials, and Féval constantly found his far-reaching imagination forced to operate within an editorially imposed straitjacket that required tokenistic explanation of supernatural manifestation in naturalistic terms, which resulted in extravagant novels like *Le Livre des mystères* (1852; also known as *La soeur de fantômes* and *Les Revenants*; tr. as *Revenants*) and *La Vampire* (1856; tr. as *The Vampire Countess*) becoming strangely awkward hybrids. More license was granted to writers when employing shorter formats, so Féval was allowed to let his love of the supernatural run riot in such exuberant novellas as *La Fille de Juif-Errant* (1864; tr. as *The Wandering Jew's Daughter*), *Le Chevalier Ténèbre* (1867; tr. as *Knightshade*), and *Le Ville-Vampire* (1875; tr. as *Vampire City*), which juxtapose their horrific elements with humor in a fashion that was not to become commonplace until the late twentieth century. *Le Chevalier Ténèbre* introduces a "double act" of two brothers who are ingenious in all kinds of evil, who also excel in telling creepy stories to divert their intended victims, while the classic *Le Ville-Vampire* features the English Gothic novelist Ann Radcliffe as a heroine, visiting the other-dimensional vampire city of Selene as an eccentric literary ancestor of Buffy the Vampire Slayer.

Féval made considerable use of naturalistic horrific motifs in his pioneering crime fiction, especially *Jean Diable* (1862; tr. as *John Devil*) and the classic series launched by *Les Habits Noirs* (1863; tr. as *The Parisian Jungle*), featuring a criminal gang with elaborate connections in all strata of society, whose nefarious exploits are masterminded by the sinister Corsican Colonel Bozzo-Corona and his brutal right-hand man Monsieur Lecoq.

After making and losing a fortune, Féval underwent an ostentatious reconversion to devout Catholicism in 1876, after which he rewrote many of his novels to reduce their horrific elements and bring them into line with pious virtue, but those he considered morally unsalvageable—including *La Vampire*, which includes some fine phantasmagorical vignettes—continued to be reprinted regardless. His son, Paul Féval fils, also became a prolific writer in various genres, similarly intruding elements of horror into much of his melodramatic fiction.

Brian Stableford

See also: The Grotesque; Hugo, Victor; Penny Dreadful; Vampires.

Further Reading

Rohan, Jean, and Jacques Dugast, eds. 1992. *Paul Féval: romancier populaire*. Presses Universitaires de Rennes.

Stableford, Brian. 2003. "Introduction" and "Afterword" in Paul Féval, *The Vampire Countess*. Encino, CA: Black Coat Press.

FORBIDDEN KNOWLEDGE OR POWER

The theme of forbidden knowledge has its roots in ancient Greek literature. Early examples revolve around a set of ideas, the comprehension of which has been prohibited by a figure of (often divine) authority. Access to this knowledge can confer superhuman or supernatural power on the individual, though this is often presented in negative terms. Contemporary fiction frequently replaces the idea of a singular authoritative figure with moral, ethical, and social proscriptions, though narratives commonly focus on the consequences of transgressing. There are two narrative traditions of forbidden knowledge, which are traditionally (though not necessarily) gendered.

One of the earliest seekers of forbidden knowledge is Prometheus in Hesiod's *Theogony* (ca. 700 BCE). In this story, Prometheus steals fire from Zeus and gives it to humanity. In *Works and Days* (ca. 700 BCE), Hesiod expands this, suggesting that the forbidden fire is related to the creation of life itself. Prometheus is punished for his crime with eternal torment. Prometheus's willful challenge of Zeus's authority is echoed in Christian narratives of Lucifer/Satan's war against God. The story of Lucifer found in Isaiah 14:12 condemns the "morning star" for his pride; however, later stories (such as John Milton's *Paradise Lost*) connect Lucifer's rebellion

---

Prometheus and Pandora

Narrative traditions of forbidden knowledge can be divided into two general streams or types:

Promethean: Named for the Greek god Prometheus, who stole fire from Zeus and gave it to mortals, this type consists of narratives in which excessive ambition leads characters to rebel against conventional limits in the search for power and/or knowledge.

Pandoran: Named for Pandora, the woman in ancient Greek mythology who inadvertently loosed evil into the world (and who was the wife of Epimetheus, Prometheus's brother), this type consists of narratives in which characters are motivated not so much by ambition as by a transgressive curiosity to know things that they, and that mortals in general, are not meant to know.

Matt Cardin

specifically with the pursuit of prohibited power and knowledge. As the devil or Satan, this figure becomes a temptation to other men, from Adam (in biblical tradition) to Faust (in German folklore and literature). Prometheus and Lucifer's desire to attain knowledge that would make them "like gods," despite the horrendous consequences, is also reflected in stories of people who attempt to transgress natural and social "laws," such as in *Frankenstein* (1818), *The Island of Doctor Moreau* (1896), and *Jurassic Park* (1990).

A parallel tradition also begins with Hesiod's *Works and Days* and the story of Pandora, the woman entrusted with a jar (or box) containing all the evils of the world. Although instructed not to open the jar, she cannot help but look inside, and thus evil enters the world. Elements of the Pandora story can be seen in various versions of Eve's temptation by Satan, where the woman is compelled to take a bite of "forbidden fruit" despite knowing exactly what will happen if she does. Transgressive curiosity is also the theme of the Bluebeard story, as told, for example, by Charles Perrault. In this folkloric tale, a young woman marries a man who prohibits her from looking in one particular room in his castle. The woman eventually looks in the room and is confronted by the bodies of her husband's former wives. Bluebeard's wife is the direct ancestor of many Gothic heroines, such as Charlotte Brontë's Jane Eyre (1847) and the unnamed narrator of Daphne du Maurier's *Rebecca* (1938), but she is also echoed in the many contemporary horror characters who are unable to resist trying something, despite receiving multiple warnings and prohibitions.

The "Prometheus" and "Pandora" traditions of seeking forbidden knowledge frequently intersect in horror fiction and, while the traditions remain gendered to some degree, it is possible to find a male Pandora or a female Prometheus. In some fiction, seekers of knowledge are depicted as rebellious and heroic; nevertheless, much contemporary horror relies on the older trope of knowledge that has been forbidden for the good of humanity.

Hannah Priest

See also: *Conjure Wife*; *Frankenstein*; *The Historian*; *The House of the Seven Gables*; Mad Scientist; "The Monkey's Paw"; "The Music of Erich Zann"; *Our Lady of Darkness*.

Further Reading

Athanassakis, Apostolos N. (trans.) 2004. *Hesiod: Theogony, Works and Days, Shield*. 2nd ed. Baltimore and London: Johns Hopkins University Press.

Colavito, Jason, ed. 2008. *"A Hideous Bit of Morbidity": An Anthology of Horror Criticism from the Enlightenment to World War I*. Jefferson, NC, and London: McFarland.

Shattuck, Roger. 1997. *Forbidden Knowledge: From Prometheus to Pornography*. San Diego, CA: Harcourt Brace.

Tatar, Maria. 2004. *Secrets Beyond the Door: The Story of Bluebeard and His Wives*. Princeton, NJ, and Oxford: Princeton University Press.

FRAME STORY

The "frame story" is a narrative device that, although now associated with horror and other genre writing, has been used by some of the foundational texts of world literature, including Chaucer's *The Canterbury Tales* (ca. 1380–1400), Giovanni Boccaccio's *Decameron* (ca. 1349–1353), and *One Thousand and One Nights* or *Arabian Nights* (ca. ninth century). The frame story usually establishes a situation in which a represented narrator (a character in the frame story) is brought together with a represented audience (other characters in the frame story) to whom he or she then imparts a story or stories.

Typically, several of these "tales within a tale" will be linked together within the frame story. The origins of the form are perhaps to be found in its expediency in corralling oral folk traditions for the printed page, imposing a structure that allows the reader to more easily navigate otherwise disparate contents. Another facet, identified by genre critic John Clute, is that its use creates a critical distance between the reader and the composite tale, facilitating a suspension of disbelief in the face of accounts of often wondrous or supernatural events. In other words, Clute has argued, we are led to understand that "a tale is being told" rather than reality being directly represented. Before the story is related, an atmosphere of contemplative expectation is usually established, and the everyday concerns of the audience are suspended for the duration of the narrative. Through this setup, actual readers feel vicariously reassured that they are free to question the veracity of the story, rather than required to accept an often incredible anecdote at face value.

In the late eighteenth and early nineteenth centuries, several Gothic novels used the device, notably Mary Shelley's *Frankenstein* (1818), but also Charles Maturin's *Melmoth the Wanderer* (1820) and *The Manuscript Found in Saragossa* (ca. 1815) by Jan Potocki, both of which significantly complicate the conceit. The increase in print culture and the associated rise of the short story form in the nineteenth century created conditions for the proliferation of the use of the frame story, since the device was a convenient and commercially expedient way whereby short stories previously published in journals could be "fixed up" into a book-length text for republication. Examples include J. Sheridan Le Fanu's *In a Glass Darkly* (1872), Robert Louis Stevenson's *New Arabian Nights* (1882), and Robert Louis and Fanny Vandergrift Stevensons' *More New Arabian Nights: The Dynamiter* (1882). Arthur Machen similarly recycled existing material within the frame story of his weird horror classic *The Three Impostors* (1895).

Clute (2011) has also identified the fin de siècle (late nineteenth century) and Edwardian periods as ones that saw the rise of what he calls the "club story." The narrowest definition of the club story involves the represented narrator relating an allegedly autobiographical experience to his fellow club members (usually male). The telling of the tale can be precipitated by something raised in preceding general discussion, which triggers a specific memory; fulfilling an expectation of the auditors (who may regularly gather for that specific purpose); or offered by way of simple entertainment to ameliorate an otherwise dull evening. Numerous ghost stories use the technique of a represented narrator recounting an "unusual" experience. Notable examples in horror fiction of the period include William Hope Hodgson's Carnacki stories and F. Marion Crawford's "The Upper Berth" (1894). However, the basic iteration of the club story motif had become so ubiquitous by 1924 that H. P. Lovecraft was critical of its overuse in *Weird Tales* magazine, describing "the club-room with well-groomed men around the fire" as "hackneyed stuff" (Lovecraft 1924, 3). Lovecraft's own "The Call of Cthulhu" (1928) represents, by contrast, a far more sophisticated deployment of the device.

Versions of the frame story persisted in horror fiction throughout the twentieth century, including, for example, Anne Rice's *Interview with the Vampire* (1976) and *The Vampire Lestat* (1985), and Clive Barker's *Books of Blood* (1984–1985). In the latter, much like his nineteenth-century antecedents, Barker uses the device to yoke together otherwise unrelated narratives. However, perhaps the most notable twentieth-century examples have been in horror cinema. During the 1960s and 1970s, the Anglo-American studio Amicus in particular produced a string of "portmanteau" horror films heavily influenced by the use of the conceit in the horror comics of the 1950s (specifically EC Comics' *Tales from the Crypt*), for example *Dr. Terror's House of Horrors* (1965), *Torture Garden* (1967), and *Asylum* (1972). The early twenty-first century has seen the frame story continue to be effectively applied in horror fiction, and interesting new formulations of the device are to be found in Mark Z. Danielewski's *House of Leaves* (2000) and Timothy J. Jarvis's *The Wanderer* (2014).

James Machin

See also: *Books of Blood*; "The Call of Cthulhu"; *House of Leaves*; *In a Glass Darkly*; *Interview with the Vampire*; Machen, Arthur; *Melmoth the Wanderer*; Stevenson, Robert Louis; Unreliable Narrator.

Further Reading

Baldick, Chris. 2008. *The Oxford Dictionary of Literary Terms*. Oxford: Oxford University Press.

Clute, John. 2011. *Pardon This Intrusion: Fantastika in the World Storm*. Essex: Beccon.

Lovecraft, H. P. [1924] 2015. Letter to J. C. Henneberger, February 2. In James Machin, "Fellows Find: H. P. Lovecraft Letter Sheds Light on Pivotal Moment in His Career." Harry Ransom Center, January 27. http://blog.hrc.utexas.edu/2015/01/27/fellows-find -h-p-lovecraft-letter/.

FRANKENSTEIN

Frankenstein, or the Modern Prometheus is a Gothic novel by Mary Wollstonecraft Shelley. It ranks among the most famous stories in modern human history and has had an immeasurable impact on the development of both horror and science fiction literature (and other media). Indeed, horror and science fiction most commonly

The Monster Wakes

Frankenstein's monster as originally portrayed in Mary Shelley's novel differs dramatically from the mute, shambling version of it that was burned into public consciousness by Universal Studios' 1931 film adaptation. So does the scene of its animation: in the novel when Victor brings his creation to life, the violent thunderstorm and Gothic laboratory full of sparking electrical equipment are distinctly absent, as are the elatedly histrionic shouts of "It's alive! It's alive!"

It was on a dreary night of November, that I beheld the accomplishment of my toils. With an anxiety that almost amounted to agony, I collected the instruments of life around me, that I might infuse a spark of being into the lifeless thing that lay at my feet. It was already one in the morning; the rain pattered dismally against the panes, and my candle was nearly burnt out, when, by the glimmer of the half-extinguished light, I saw the dull yellow eye of the creature open; it breathed hard, and a convulsive motion agitated its limbs.

How can I describe my emotions at this catastrophe, or how delineate the wretch whom with such infinite pains and care I had endeavored to form? His limbs were in proportion, and I had selected his features as beautiful. Beautiful!—Great God! His yellow skin scarcely covered the work of muscles and arteries beneath; his hair was of a lustrous black, and flowing; his teeth of a pearly whiteness; but these luxuriances only formed a more horrid contrast with his watery eyes, that seemed almost of the same colour as the dun white sockets in which they were set, his shriveled complexion, and straight black lips. (Shelley 1823, 77)

Matt Cardin

Source: Shelley, Mary. [1818] 1823. *Frankenstein. A New Edition.* London: Printed for G. and W. B. Whittaker, Ave Maria Lane.

meet in representations of scientific endeavor gone horribly awry. The origins of this cultural myth can be most clearly found in Shelley's novel.

It was first published in 1818 by the London publishing house Lackington, Hughes, Harding, Mayor and Jones. This first edition was published anonymously, though it included both a dedication to William Godwin, Mary's father, and a preface written by Mary's husband, Percy Bysshe Shelley. G. & W. B. Whittaker published a second edition of the novel in 1823. This edition contains few noteworthy changes from the 1818 text and is relatively ignored in critical histories of the novel. The major significance of the 1823 edition is in marking the first time that Mary Shelley attributed her name as author of the novel. Henry Colburn and Richard Bentley published a third "revised" edition of the novel as a single volume in 1831. Both the 1818 and 1831 versions of the text remain in print, though the latter edition is more commonly available.

Though there are substantive differences between the editions, they are subtle and thematic rather than narrative. Whereas the 1818 edition presents Victor Frankenstein as a man driven by pride and personal ambition, the 1831 version gives more scope for sympathy, presenting Victor as a victim of cruel fate. For scholars, the most significant addition to the 1831 text is Mary Shelley's preface, in which she outlines the origins of the novel (an event that has itself become a famous story in literary history). The 1831 preface has also become famous for Shelley's statement: "I bid my hideous progeny go forth and prosper" (Shelley 2012, 169). Such phrasing suggests an intended link between Shelley's creation of the novel and Victor's construction of the monster, and it has in turn had a major impact on critical and autobiographical interpretations of the novel over the last two centuries.

Shelley's implied comparison is important, as *Frankenstein* is indeed a novel about the processes and perils of creativity. Constructed as a frame narrative with multiple levels, it relates the story of Victor Frankenstein, a young nobleman who, early in life, develops a keen scientific interest. After he enrolls in the University of Ingolstadt, this interest mutates into a fixation on the origins and properties of life. In pursuit of answers he constructs a human figure from the disparate remains of corpses and successfully imbues it with life. Appalled at the monstrosity he has constructed, Victor rejects his creation. The nameless creature wanders the rural wilderness, where he discovers the nature of humanity, both in the reading of classical literature and through his own human encounters.

After a further rejection by the poor De Lacy family, the creature becomes embittered and vengeful. He returns to Victor to demand that his creator at least end his isolation by creating a mate. Victor initially agrees but, at the last moment, reflects that if these creatures were to breed, "a race of devils would be propagated upon the earth, who might make the very existence of the species of man a condition precarious and full of terror" (Shelley 2012, 119). He rends the constructed body into pieces, enraging the creature, who vows eternal vengeance. The creature systematically destroys Victor's life and family, climaxing in his promise to Victor that "I will be with you on your wedding night" (136). The threat is borne out when the creature murders Victor's beloved Elizabeth in their honeymoon bed. The promise has also served as a tool in numerous queer readings of *Frankenstein* and in those critical responses that focus on the doubling present throughout the novel. Eve Kosofsky Sedgwick, for instance, reads *Frankenstein* as part of a subgenre of "paranoid" Gothic novel in which a man finds himself "persecuted," "transparent to," and "under the compulsion" of another male (Sedgwick 1985, 91).

The novel ends with Victor pursuing the creature to the Arctic aboard a ship captained by Robert Walton, one of the novel's many narrators. Victor eventually dies before he is able to destroy his nemesis, but not before he is able to warn Walton of the dangers inherent in ambition, hubris, and the unchecked pursuit of knowledge. Walton, who was previously willing to risk his crew's life in pursuit of his own exploratory ideals, heeds the advice. The novel closes when the creature invades the cabin and bears his creator away into the freezing wastes.

Frankenstein is open to multiple, almost innumerable interpretations, further expanded by the changes between the 1818 and 1831 versions. It has been read as a biographical account, most notably revealing Mary Shelley's guilt over the death of her mother and the loss of her infant daughter. Ellen Moers describes the novel as a birth myth that is particularly female in its "emphasis not upon what precedes birth, not upon birth itself, but upon what follows birth: the trauma of the after-birth" (Moers 1979, 93).

Frankenstein has also been interpreted as both pro- and anti-revolutionary. Readers' stances on this depend largely on whether they consider the creature or the scientist to be the "real" monster of the novel. Originally the creature may have been seen to represent the threat of violent, uncivilized revolution that seemed poised to sweep across Europe in the years preceding the novel's publication. To the modern reader, however, the creature seems a sympathetic figure: a victim of authority and inhumanity that is extremely relevant in the contemporary capitalist world. The contemporary trend for redeeming monsters—making them sympathetic, understandable, even attractive—owes a huge debt to *Frankenstein*. This may be the novel's most important ongoing purpose: to force readers to rethink what is acceptable, what is moral, and what is human.

The novel has been the subject of a multitude of adaptations for stage, cinema, television, comic books, video games, and other media. The most famous adaptation is Universal Studios' 1931 film *Frankenstein*, starring Boris Karloff, which gave the world the iconic image of the rectangular-headed, bolt-necked monster.

Neil McRobert

See also: Doubles, Doppelgängers, and Split Selves; Forbidden Knowledge or Power; Frame Story; Gothic Hero/Villain; Mad Scientist; Monsters; Romanticism and Dark Romanticism; Shelley, Mary.

Further Reading

Botting, Fred. 1991. *Making Monstrous: Frankenstein, Criticism, Theory*. Manchester: University of Manchester Press.

Moers, Ellen. 1979. "Female Gothic." In *The Endurance of* Frankenstein: *Essays on Mary Shelley's Novel*, edited by George Levine and U. C. Knoepflmacher, 90–98. Berkeley: University of California Press.

Sedgwick, Eve Kosofsky. 1985. *Between Men: English Literature and Male Homosocial Desire*. New York: Columbia University Press.

Shelley, Mary. 2012. *Frankenstein*. Second Norton Critical Edition. New York: W. W. Norton.

Tropp, Martin. 1976. *Mary Shelley's Monster: The Story of Frankenstein*. Boston: Houghton Mifflin.

G

GAIMAN, NEIL (1955–)

Born in Hampshire, United Kingdom, and currently living in the United States, Neil Gaiman is a celebrated writer of dark fantasy. His works cross over from many genres and mediums. He is known for writing comics, short stories, novels, children's picture books, essays, and more. Although Gaiman does not consider himself to be a horror writer, he loves the genre and regards it to be a "condiment rather than a meal" (Gaiman and Olson 2002) in his works.

Gaiman started his writing career as a journalist, but moved on to comic books in the late 1980s. After meeting with some success in titles like *Marvel Man* and *Black Orchid*, he was offered an opportunity to take on a long-forgotten detective character from the golden age of comics named the Sandman and reinvent the comic as he wished. Gaiman's *The Sandman* was a huge departure from the detective character. It was instead an adult take on dark fantasy, centered on the god-like living personification of dreaming, one of the Endless, named Dream or Morpheus. It often featured stories of mythic gods and figures, complications of magic set upon the human world to horrific effect, and explorations into the power of dreams and nightmares. Some of the impactful characters that have come from this title include the Corinthian, a living nightmare; Death, another aspect of the Endless; and Lucifer Morningstar, Gaiman's take on the biblical figure of the Devil. Many scholars consider Gaiman's seventy-five-issue run on *The Sandman* to be a seminal work in the graphic novel field, and it is thought of as "highly allusive, psychologically astute, and brilliantly conceived" (Wolfe 2003). *The Sandman* won numerous Eisner Awards, and even the World Fantasy Award in literature. It is credited for being a major influence in putting comics into the hands of adult readers.

Gaiman firmly established himself in the literary world with the 2001 release of his dark fantasy novel *American Gods*. The book's premise, gods from the Old World surviving and fighting to exist in America, allowed Gaiman to write a travel narrative featuring fantastic American places and eccentric personalities. Charles De Lint describes Gaiman's ability to balance the light and dark aspects of the storyline to have moments that are "utterly whimsical" or "filled with doom and dread" (2001). *American Gods* won several speculative fiction awards, including the Hugo, the Nebula, and the Stoker.

Coraline (2002), the follow-up to *American Gods*, maintained the common Gaiman theme of finding magic or the unworldly in unexpectedly everyday locales, but focused it through a child's eye and her new home. *Coraline* took Gaiman ten years of sporadic writing to complete. It features a monster made to channel the fear of the familiar turned distorted and terrible. The "Other Mother" is a wonderful combination of the temptations a child Coraline's age would want from a parent and the hauntingly dreadful and unexplainable: she wants Coraline to live with her forever at the cost of having her eyes replaced by buttons. *Coraline* won several accolades and awards including the Hugo, the Nebula, and the Stoker. Gaiman went on to garner even more success with his next children's novel, *The Graveyard Book*. Featuring Nobody Owens, a young boy who escapes his own death on the night of his family members' grisly murders, *The Graveyard Book* was heavily influenced by Rudyard Kipling's *The Jungle Book*. Both texts feature a young boy raised by unconventional guardians. In the case of *The Graveyard Book*, ghosts teach important life lessons to the young boy as he develops. *The Graveyard Book* won the Newbery Medal and other prestigious speculative fiction awards. When asked why he would choose to write a children's horror novel, Gaiman replied by arguing for "inoculation" to the frightful and terrorizing.

Laurie Penny noted that while other writers may "have a political agenda, however covert," with a few exceptions in his early years, "Gaiman's work is pure escapism" (Penny 2013). His form of fantasy draws from the urge to discover and find wonders or horrors, whether they are behind a mysterious door or beyond the world of dreaming. Gaiman remains active in the dark fantasy genre, having returned in 2013 to write *The Sandman: Overture* and promising a sequel to *American Gods*. He is well known for his readings and speeches, which are often crowded media events. In 2012 his commencement address "Make Good Art" at the University of the Arts in Philadelphia garnered viral attention and eventually became a publication of its own.

Chun H. Lee

See also: Bram Stoker Award; Dark Fantasy; Kiernan, Caitlín R.; Kipling, Rudyard; World Fantasy Award.

Further Reading

De Lint, Charles. 2001. "Review of *American Gods*." *Fantasy & Science Fiction* 101 (3): 97–98.

Gaiman, Neil, and Ray Olson. 2002. "The Booklist Interview: Neil Gaiman." *Booklist* 98 (22): 1949.

"Neil Gaiman: Keynote Address 2012." 2012. The University of the Arts. May 17. http://www.uarts.edu/neil-gaiman-keynote-address-2012.

Neil Gaiman. 2016. Neilgaiman.com. June 8. http://www.neilgaiman.com.

Penny, Laurie. 2013. "An Interview with Neil Gaiman, the Internet's Favorite Fantasy Writer." *New Republic.* November 21. https://newrepublic.com/article/115682/neil-gaiman-interview.

Wolfe, Gary K. 2003. "Gaiman, Neil 1960–." In *Supernatural Fiction Writers: Contemporary Fantasy and Horror*, edited by Richard Bleiler, 369–375. 2nd ed. Vol. 1. New York: Charles Scribner's Sons.

Yuen, Wayne, Rachel Luria, and Tracy Lyn Bealer. 2012. *Neil Gaiman and Philosophy: Gods Gone Wild!* Chicago, IL: Open Court, 2012. *eBook Collection (EBSCOhost).*

GAUTIER, THÉOPHILE (1811–1872)

Théophile Gautier was a leading figure in the French Romantic movement whose principal works—most notably *Mademoiselle de Maupin* (1835), whose introduction is a manifesto of sorts—champion the doctrine of "*l'art pour l'art*" (art for art's sake). In his introduction to the third edition of Charles Baudelaire's *Les Fleurs du Mal*, published after that poet's death, he provided a similar championship of "Decadent style," taking up an adjective first hurled at romanticism as a term of abuse by the critic Desiré Nisard, but reconstrued as praise by Baudelaire. Gautier's own works, especially his stories employing horrific motifs, are archetypal models of Decadent prose style, and perfect illustrations of the manner in which focus on style, employing the artistry of representation for its own sake, transfigures horrific imagery into something beautiful as well as sublime, producing a distinctive aesthetic effect.

Gautier pioneered a rich French tradition of lush historical fantasies in "*Une nuit de Cléopâtre*" (1838), translated by Lafcadio Hearn as the leading items in the classic collection *One of Cleopatra's Nights and Other Fantastic Romances* (1882), which

---

In Gautier's "*La Morte amoureuse*" (English: "The Dead in Love," but most commonly translated as "Clarimonde"), a young Catholic priest named Romuald is seduced by a woman named Clarimonde, who turns out to be a vampire. His elderly spiritual guide, Sérapion, stands against Clarimonde and helps to rescue him from her. The story is one of the most famous nineteenth-century vampire fictions, and it contains a number of scenes that are recognizable as "classic" motifs in the world of vampire literature as a whole. Among these is the scene when Sérapion opens Clarimonde's coffin and destroys her in front of Romuald:

> He wrenched apart and tore up the lid, and I beheld Clarimonde, pallid as a figure of marble, with hands joined; her white winding-sheet made but one fold from her head to her feet. A little crimson drop sparkled like a speck of dew at one corner of her colourless mouth.
>
> Sérapion, at this spectacle, burst into fury: "Ah, thou art here, demon! Impure courtesan! Drinker of blood and gold!" And he flung holy water upon the corpse and the coffin, over which he traced the sign of the cross with his sprinkler. Poor Clarimonde had no sooner been touched by the blessed spray than her beautiful body crumbled into dust, and became only a shapeless and frightful mass of cinders and half-calcined bones. (Gautier 1908, 50).

"Clarimonde" was adapted as a 1998 episode of the vampire-themed horror television series *The Hunger*.

Matt Cardin

Source: Gautier, Théophile. [1836] 1908. "Clarimonde." In *Stories*. Translated by Lafcadio Hearn. New York: E. P. Dutton.

also contains the classic erotic vampire story "*La Morte amoureuse*" (1836; tr. under various titles, usually "Clarimonde") and another femme fatale story, "Arria Marcella" (1852). Gautier's other supernatural fantasies include *Avatar* (1856), about an identity exchange undertaken for erotic purposes, and *Jettatura* (1857; tr. as "The Evil Eye"), a more straightforwardly horrific account of a man who falls prey to the eponymous curse. *Spirite* (1866) is an account of a love affair between a young man and a female ghost written for the dancer Carlotta Grisi, although it was Carlotta's sister Ernesta who bore him two daughters, including the writer Judith Gautier (1845–1917), whose own work included several Decadent horror stories, and who was married for a while to another important Decadent fantasist, Catulle Mendès.

Gautier's short stories sometimes contained transfigured elements of horror, most notably the doppelgänger story "*Le Chevalier Double*" (1840; tr. as "The Duplicated Knight") and "*Deux acteurs pour un rôle*" (1841: tr. as "Two Actors for One Role"). The great majority of his works were collected in twenty-two volumes as *Oeuvres* (1855–1874; tr. in twenty-four volumes edited by F. C. Sumichrast). Gautier's key works represented the ultimate in Romantic fantasy; his feverish idealizations of erotic sensibility crystallized the imagery of the *femme fatale*, arguing flamboyantly that death might be a price worth paying for the rewards such magically attractive sexual partners might have to offer. He pointed the way for many subsequent writers to reinterpret the imagery of horror as a form of fabulously perverse eroticism, "*La Morte amoureuse*" being the most pivotal work in the process of the symbolic reconfiguration of vampiric lust, which eventually extended far beyond Decadent fantasy to become a staple of modern popular fiction.

Brian Stableford

See also: Doubles, Doppelgängers, and Split Selves; Dark Fantasy; Romanticism and Dark Romanticism; The Sublime; Vampires.

Further Reading

Richardson, Joanna. 1958. *Théophile Gautier: His Life and Times*. London: Max Reinhardt.
Smith, Albert Brewster. 1977. *Théophile Gautier and the Fantastic*. University, MS: Romance Monographs.

"THE GHOST SHIP"

A perennial entry in ghost-fiction anthologies, "The Ghost Ship" is not actually a horror story, but more a gentle whimsy. It contains much that is echoed in later fantasies ranging from Hope Mirrlees's *Lud-in-the-Mist* to Neil Gaiman's *Stardust*. In a rural English town, people treat their ghosts like ordinary citizens, making it the "ghostiest" place in the land. One night a storm blows a ghost ship inland, into the middle of a turnip patch. The captain proves a genial fellow, whose tasty rum is having a scandalous effect on the local ghosts. The narrator and a local parson confront the captain, who assures them that he will be leaving soon. Another storm blows the ship away with most of the local ghost population aboard and the village idiot aboard too. The captain, we learn, is the infamous pirate Bartholomew Roberts (early eighteenth century) who continues his piratical career in the hereafter. The idiot returns after two years, but, yearning for that ghostly rum, soon runs away again.

Arthur Machen wrote, "I would not exchange this sort, crazy, enchanting fantasy for a whole wilderness of seemly novels" (Machen 1913, xiv). The story is actually quite unusual for its author, most of whose output is melancholy and frequently grim. Richard Middleton (1882–1911) was of a romantic disposition and wildly impractical in day-to-day life. He tried to make his living as a poet, but the result was poverty and depression. Even though he enjoyed some success in magazines, he could not get any publisher to bring out a book of his poems or stories. He would have appreciated (and probably anticipated) the irony that as soon as he was dead (by suicide) he was proclaimed a lost genius and virtually his entire literary output, five volumes, appeared in book form within another year. A final collection followed in 1933, but in the long run he is mostly remembered for this one story, often cited as the most successful humorous ghost story in English.

Darrell Schweitzer

See also: Gaiman, Neil; Machen, Arthur.

Further Reading

Machen, Arthur. 1913. Preface to *The Ghost Ship and Other Stories* by Richard Middleton, vii–xiv. New York: Mitchell Kennerly.

Schweitzer, Darrell. 1998. "Richard Middleton: Beauty, Sadness, and Terror" in *Windows of the Imagination*, 115–120. San Bernardino, CA: Borgo Press.

GHOST STORY

Ghost Story is a 1979 novel by Peter Straub. Its significance for modern horror literature is almost incalculable, both because of its intrinsic brilliance and because of its timing. The novel appeared right at the beginning of the late twentieth-century "horror boom," and was in fact one of the central texts that helped to launch it. *Ghost Story* acknowledged its deep debt to the long tradition of ghost stories and Gothic literature that had come before it, while simultaneously presenting an original, striking, and frightening treatment of the tradition's core themes. Straub's fourth published novel, it represented a watershed both for his career and for the horror genre.

Reduced to its bare essentials, *Ghost Story* can be described as a superior tale of supernatural revenge. Five young men—Ricky Hawthorne, Sears James, Edward Wanderley, Lewis Benedikt, and John Jaffrey—accidentally kill a woman named Eva Galli. They panic and decide to cover up her death by putting her body in a car and driving it into a lake. But as the car is sinking, they glimpse Eva's face through the rear window, and for a moment it appears that she is still alive. Deeply shaken, they take a vow to keep her death a secret. The incident will, however, haunt them for the rest of their lives.

Fifty years later, the five men, now prosperous and content, still live in their (fictional) hometown of Milburn, New York, and call themselves "The Chowder Society." Although they meet regularly to swap ghost stories, they never speak of Eva. This all changes when Edward dies of fright during a party given in honor of a mysterious young woman, an actress who goes by the name Anne-Veronica Moore. The remaining members experience a series of disquieting dreams in which several of them die, leading them to conclude that Eva Galli has somehow reentered their lives and is seeking revenge.

Unable to admit fully to themselves that their past deeds have come back to haunt them, they reach out to Ed's nephew, Don Wanderley, for help. Don is a writer who has produced a horror novel titled *The Nightwatcher*, which is based on his own experiences with Eva, whom he knew by the name of Alma Mobley; the old men sense that he may have insights into their situation that may be key to their very survival. Don's arrival in town appears to serve as a signal to the evil threatening the group, resulting in the deaths of Lewis and John. The surviving members, Sears and Ricky, band together with Don and Peter Barnes, a young man who has also suffered at the hands of Eva—who has become a supernatural shape-shifter—and the supernatural minions that she now commands. Together they struggle to locate and eliminate their nemesis as Eva slowly goes about destroying all that is dear to them.

From the novel's very first sentences, Straub sets a tone that defines the whole book. Those sentences take the form of a question and response: "'What's the worst thing you've ever done?' 'I won't tell you that, but I'll tell you the worst thing that ever happened to me . . . the most dreadful thing'" (Straub 1980, 3). Straub then proceeds, through the novel as a whole, to explore the terrifying notion that ghosts may be unique to those they haunt, that victims may somehow summon their torturers from some dark place within their own psyches. Stephen King has described this as "a very Henry Jamesian theme. . . . the idea that ghosts, in the end, adopt the motivations and perhaps the very souls of those who behold them" (King 2010, 271). Straub leaves it unclear whether Eva/Alma/Anne-Veronica could thrive if she were not sustained by the belief of her victims. It is never made clear whether her existence is objective and independent, symbiotic, or dependent on those she seeks to destroy, and Straub's clues muddy the waters—apparently deliberately—as when Eva and another shape-shifter are asked, "Who are you?" and they answer with maddening ambiguity, "I am you" (Straub 1980, 26).

Straub has openly acknowledged the debt *Ghost Story* owes to Stephen King's second novel, *'Salem's Lot*, which was published four years earlier, in 1975, and which likewise had a seismic impact on the shape of modern horror fiction. Although both books do share similar themes, plot points, and even settings—a small American town besieged by a supernatural horror—'*Salem's Lot* seems to have provided a template of sorts, a kind of guide or catalyst that enabled Straub to intuit larger possibilities in the literary form of the horror novel. In the final analysis, *Ghost Story* may be seen as the marriage of two sensibilities: King's, from which it derives its more operatic moments, and Straub's, who used it to fulfill his ambition to enlarge the boundaries of the traditional ghost story. Notably, it also stands as the first example of Straub's trademark exploration of the dormant power of secrets, and of the power of storytelling to uncover core truths. Much as King's book pays homage to writers such as Bram Stoker and Richard Matheson, who had produced canonical vampire novels before him, Straub's stands as a tribute to previous writers in the long tradition of ghost stories, including some who are specifically referenced in the book (such as Nathaniel Hawthorne and Henry James) and some who are not (such as Edgar Allan Poe, Washington Irving, H. P. Lovecraft, Ambrose Bierce, and M. R. James).

Hank Wagner

See also: James, Henry; King, Stephen; Psychological Horror; Straub, Peter.

Further Reading

Andriano, Joseph. 1993. "From Fiend to Friend: The Daemonic Feminine in Modern Gothic." In *Our Ladies of Darkness: Feminine Daemonology in Male Gothic Fiction*, 135–144. University Park, PA: Pennsylvania State University Press.

Bosky, Bernadette. 1999. "Peter Straub: From Academe to Shadowland." In *Discovering Modern Horror Fiction II*, edited by Darrell Schweitzer, 3–17. Berkeley Heights, NJ: Wildside Press.

King, Stephen. [1981] 2010. *Danse Macabre*. New York: Gallery Books.

Neilson, Keith. 1980. "Ghost Story." *Magill's Literary Annual 1980*, 1–4.

Straub, Peter. 1980. *Ghost Story*. New York: Pocket Books.

THE GIRL NEXT DOOR

The Girl Next Door is an extreme horror novel written by Jack Ketchum. It was first published by Warner Books in 1989; Leisure Books published the mass market paperback in 2005. Though it has elements of horror, particularly in the stark depictions of violence, Ketchum's book is best categorized as crime fiction, as it is loosely based on the true-life events of the torture and eventual murder of Sylvia Likens in Indianapolis, Indiana, in 1965. It has been called "Suburban Gothic," given its setting and how Ketchum is able to describe such horrendous violence in what is otherwise considered a safe place.

The novel is narrated by David, an adult who is remembering his youth in what appears to be a typical 1950s suburban neighborhood, not unlike many that can be found almost anywhere across the United States. The innocuous setting only serves to intensify the horrific events that happen. Teenager Meg, along with her younger sister, Susan, are sent to live with Ruth, a single mother who is raising three boys of her own. Ruth, struggling with poverty, stress, depression, and substance abuse, allows her sons—and eventually other boys from the neighborhood—to imprison Meg in the basement and perform increasingly vile acts of torture, including rape, on the captive girl.

In 1996, a limited edition of the book was published, featuring an introduction from fellow horror writer Stephen King. In describing Ketchum, he wrote, "Jack Ketchum is a brilliantly visceral novelist whose bleak perception of human nature is perhaps only rivaled by that of Frank Norris and Malcolm Lowry" (quoted in Beahm 1998, 113). The extreme violence in Ketchum's novel divides critics and readers. While some are turned off by the gore, some, like King, understand that Ketchum has a unique ability to look into the dark soul of humanity and to plumb the depths of human depravity in order to ask why evil exists in the world.

In 2007 the novel was adapted into a film, *Jack Ketchum's The Girl Next Door*. Reviews were mixed, as most critics and audiences considered the violence too graphic to be shown on screen. The same year saw the release of another film inspired by the story of Sylvia Likens. Titled *An American Crime*, this one did not use Jack Ketchum as a source, instead choosing to go to the original murder case as inspiration.

Lisa Kröger

See also: Ketchum, Jack.

Further Reading

Beahm, George. 1998. *Stephen King from A to Z: An Encyclopedia of His Life and Work*. Kansas City: Andrews McMeel.

Hipson, Richard. 2007. "Jack Ketchum Talks About the Horrors That Live 'Next Door.'" *Dark Scribe Magazine*, November 15. http://www.darkscribemagazine.com/feature -interviews/jack-ketchum-talks-about-the-horrors-that-live-next-door.html.

"Retold: Torture Death of Sylvia Likens." 2015. *Indianapolis Star*, October 22. http://www .indystar.com/story/news/history/retroindy/2013/10/24/sylvia-likens/3178393.

Rhyne, Leah. 2014. "Prose and Conversation: 'The Girl Next Door' by Jack Ketchum." *Lit-Reactor*, February 21. https://litreactor.com/columns/prose-conversation-the-girl-next -door-by-jack-ketchum.

"THE GIRL WITH THE HUNGRY EYES"

Fritz Leiber's "The Girl with the Hungry Eyes" (1949) is a classic vampire story that updates the genre's conventions for the world of modern consumerism. Its protagonist—a lean young advertising model known simply as "The Girl"—is essentially the undead embodiment of consumer desire itself, of half-formed cravings that can never be fully satisfied. The narrator, a down-on-his-luck photographer who snaps the Girl's first promotional glossies, almost succumbs to her eerie

"The Signal-man": Urban Horror ahead of Its Time

One of the first instances of urban horror, "The Signal-Man," predates Fritz Leiber's use of the form in "The Girl with the Hungry Eyes" by nearly a century. If this 1866 ghost story by Charles Dickens, sometimes called "No. 1 Branch Line: The Signal-man," had involved nautical signals or stagecoaches, it would have been effective, but unremarkable. A man is plagued by an apparition that warns of upcoming disaster. The third time, it presages his own death. What makes this more interesting is that it is about a railway signal operator and takes place among the soot and grime of early industrial England. Dickens builds up the atmosphere deftly, the setting being the signalman's cabin in a low, dank, walled trench near the opening to a railway tunnel. The train, roaring out of the dark tunnel mouth, becomes an effective emblem of menace. The story may have been inspired by a real place, the Clayton Tunnel in England, where a notable collision occurred in 1861.

The first time the "ghost" appears, there is a train wreck. The second time, a woman dies mysteriously aboard a train, and the third time the signalman himself is hit by one. On this final encounter it is unclear whether he actually saw a ghost or the operator of the third train, who is described as waving and shouting in exactly the same manner as the apparition. This could be read as a case of precognition, not haunting in the usual sense.

Fictional ghosts had long haunted gloomy castles, remote crossroads, and lonely sea strands, but Dickens was one of the first to realize the potential of a modern, urban landscape for horror fiction. This was so far ahead of its time that it still seemed revolutionary when Fritz Leiber did something similar with "Smoke Ghost" and "The Girl with the Hungry Eyes" eight decades later.

Darrell Schweitzer

blandishments, yet manages at the last minute to shake free. Meanwhile, the Girl goes on to infest the urban marketplace, her face gazing down from billboards, her appetite as unquenchable as the inchoate longings of the hapless consumers upon whom she preys.

Like a number of Leiber's other works of the 1940s, such as "Smoke Ghost" (1941) and *Conjure Wife* (1943), "The Girl with the Hungry Eyes" takes a perennial horror icon and situates it within a contemporary milieu. In essence, Leiber asks: what would a vampire look like in a world dominated not by the Gothic trappings of the past but by the most up-to-date technologies and ideologies? A major innovation of the story is to see the vampire not as a physical predator, sucking blood, but as a psychological parasite, battening on and draining emotional energy. A possible influence was Mary Wilkins-Freeman's "Luella Miller" (1902), with its eponymous psychic leech; yet "The Girl" in Leiber's story is no shrinking violet but rather a boldly libidinous huntress stalking the modern world. Like Dracula in Bram Stoker's novel (1897), who advances his undead campaign by means of real estate agents and railway timetables, Leiber's "Girl" draws victims to her via photography agencies and fashion magazines.

"The Girl with the Hungry Eyes" is the forerunner of an entire subgenre of contemporary vampire stories that link feral appetite with modern communications media and high-tech consumption. S. P. Somtow's *Vampire Junction* (1984) and Anne Billson's *Suckers* (1992), for example, both connect vampiric thirst with consumer desire, its undead creatures animated by marketing strategies. David J. Schow's World Fantasy Award–winning story "Red Light" (1986) is virtually an homage to Leiber in its tale of a beautiful photographer's model who is both a victim of male lust and a subtle predator upon it. Leiber's tale has been filmed twice: in 1972 as an episode of Rod Serling's anthology series *Night Gallery*, and then in 1995 as a low-budget horror movie directed by Jon Jacobs.

Rob Latham

See also: Conjure Wife; Dark Fantasy; Incubi and Succubi; Leiber, Fritz; Psychological Horror; Vampires.

Further Reading

Auerbach, Nina. 1995. "Vampires and Vampires." In *Our Vampires, Ourselves*, 101–111. Chicago: University of Chicago Press.

Langan, John. 2008. "Feed Me, Baby, Feed Me: Beyond the Pleasure Principle in Fritz Leiber's 'The Girl with the Hungry Eyes.'" In *Fritz Leiber: Critical Essays*, edited by Benjamin Szumskyj, 101–115. Jefferson, NC: McFarland.

GOGOL, NIKOLAI (1809–1852)

Nikolai Gogol was a Ukrainian Russian writer and dramatist. Best known for his tales set in St. Petersburg, Russia, and for his macabre, absurdist, and grotesque style, Gogol also achieved literary prominence in his lifetime for stories inspired by Ukrainian folklore. His work demonstrates a profound attention to psychological complexity, everyday life, and the common person, prompting nineteenth-century critic Vissarion Belinsky to name him the father of the "natural school" of Russian literary realism. However, Romantic writers such as Aleksandr Pushkin and E. T. A. Hoffmann also influenced Gogol's writing, resulting in an idiosyncratic fantastic realism in which the supernatural, grotesque, and surreal violently intrude upon the banal realities of everyday life.

A tendency toward chaos, a preoccupation with the vulgarity of life, an overriding belief in evil as a ubiquitous presence, and a characteristic dark humor permeate Gogol's work from his earliest collection, *Evenings on a Farm Near Dikanka* (1831–1832). Heavily influenced by Gogol's Ukrainian childhood and by traditional Ukrainian culture and folklore, *Evenings* contains eight stories that present the Ukrainian countryside as a place of myth, magic, and the supernatural. Cossacks, maidens, witches, devils, sorcerers, ghosts, and deadly acts of vengeance haunt its pages, combining folkloric figures with Gothic literary tropes, a highly developed dark wit, and a Romantic sense of the sublime. "A Terrible Vengeance"—an unsettling tale of sorcery, dark magic, and obsession—offers an early example of Gogol's talent for depicting the grotesque, while "Christmas Eve," with its humorous portrayals of vanquished devils and comely maidens, exhibit Gogol's absurdist, cynical dark humor.

Evenings was followed by the short story collections *Mirgorod* (1835) and *Arabesques* (1835). Ranging from satire to the Gothic to the absurd, these tales demonstrate both Gogol's expansive talent and his tendency to defy classification. With *Mirgorod*, Gogol presented a cycle of tales that returned to rural Ukrainian settings and folklore. "*Viy*," a tale of witchcraft, demons, vengeance, and a less-than-pious clergyman, has left a particularly pronounced impression on both the Soviet and Russian Gothic-horror traditions and has been adapted for film numerous times both within and outside Russia. With *Arabesques*, Gogol moved his tales from rural Ukraine to his adopted city of St. Petersburg. "The Portrait," "Nevsky Prospect," and "Diary of a Madman" are perhaps the most Gothic tales in this collection, presenting a labyrinthine city dominated by rigid social hierarchies, pettiness, and vice. Gogol's characters in these tales are often young and relatively powerless artists and petty bureaucrats, easily overwhelmed by the temptations of—and social barriers to—a luxurious urban lifestyle. Here, it is both the urban environment and a pervasive bureaucracy that destroys the common person: "Diary of a Madman" and "Nevsky Prospect," for instance, depict St. Petersburg as a disorienting force overlaid by a mechanical, pointless bureaucracy that crushes the individual, while "The Portrait" is a tale of demonic ambition that recalls earlier themes from *Evenings*.

Gogol's later work prominently featured St. Petersburg as an indifferent, imposing city largely controlled by the administrative class. "The Nose" (1836) and "The Overcoat" (1842) are perhaps Gogol's most well-known short works and are both exemplars of Gogol's late absurdist, grotesque style. "The Nose," a masterful tale of pure absurdity and dark humor, depicts a civil servant of average rank who awakens to discover that his nose has not only gone missing but has also begun to pose as a human and, to his horror, has even surpassed him in rank. In "The Overcoat," obsessions with rank, social status, and the meanness of urban life drive a lowly civil servant to increase his social standing by saving for a new overcoat. When the coat is finally purchased and immediately stolen, the civil servant falls into a fever and dies, returning as a ghost to haunt—and steal overcoats from—passersby on the city streets. The tale is considered a masterwork of Russian literature and exerted a profound influence on later writers, such as Fyodor Dostoevsky, who is famously said to have proclaimed, "We all come out from Gogol's 'Overcoat.'"

Though Gogol's oeuvre was composed over the relatively short period of 1830–1842, ending with his satirical and widely praised novel-poem *Dead Souls* (1842), Gogol's influence on writers, directors, and composers has been monumental and long-lasting, resulting in numerous cinematic and operatic adaptations of his work, including the famous Soviet horror film *Viy* (1967). Gogol died in 1852 after falling into a deep depression, during which time he burned his final manuscript.

Brittany Roberts

See also: The Grotesque; Surrealism.

Further Reading

Fanger, Donald. 1979. *The Creation of Nikolai Gogol*. Cambridge, MA: Harvard University Press.

Gippius, Vasilii. 1981. *Gogol*. Translated by Robert A. Maguire. Ann Arbor, MI: Ardis.

Nabokov, Vladimir. 1944. *Nikolai Gogol*. Norfolk, CT: New Directions.

THE GOLEM

The Golem is a novel by Austrian writer Gustav Meyrink (1868–1932). Written in German under the title *Der Golem*, it was published first as a serial between 1913 and 1914, and then as a book in 1915. The first English translation appeared in 1928.

The setting is Prague, a city with a large Jewish population and a reputation for alchemy and sorcery. Meyrink draws on a Jewish legend about a wonder-working rabbi who is able to bring to life the massive clay statue of a man, the Golem, who protects the Jews of Prague from persecution. (This same legend inspired several silent films by the German Expressionist director Paul Wegener, but despite the identical titles, his films are not adaptations of Meyrink's novel.)

While Prague is the setting of the novel, it is also almost a character as well, actually manifesting itself as the Golem. The novel is alive with Meyrink's own preoccupations, involving the blending of psychology and mysticism in a way that aligns him with other contemporary writers such as Carl Jung and William Butler Yeats. The plot does not follow conventional lines of cause and effect, preferring instead to connect events using a subtle inner logic of correspondences that hints at the unfolding of an ineffable cosmic plan. This plan is impossible to understand for those who lack some form of spiritual enlightenment.

The first section of the book tells the story of a young man named Athanasius Pernath, who is framed for murder and loses everything. In the second section, however, the reader learns that Pernath's story is all a dream; the dreamer, who is also the narrator, has taken Pernath's hat away with him from a restaurant by mistake, and evidently for this reason has dreamed about him. Haunted by the dream, the narrator begins searching for Pernath. In his search, he seems to become lost in a phantasmagorical delirium of Prague. He meets the Golem, who is like the spirit of the city, a man-made thing animated by human activity but somehow lacking human consciousness. Eventually, the narrator finds Pernath, and, through him, a higher spiritual plane of existence.

The Golem is an example of the artistic movement known as expressionism. Expressionist art tries to capture the ways in which a single person's point of view alters, or distorts, experience. In painting, film, poetry, and fiction, the result is typically a work that tries to make the audience aware of the way an individual's desires shape his or her perspective. In effect, expressionism sacrifices conventional realism, the attempt to record events objectively, in order to be more realistic about the experience of an event for an individual. For this reason, much expressionist fiction is structured by affinities, rather than modeled on everyday events. Instead of depicting the way one event leads to another, expressionist novels like *The Golem* will often set events side by side because they share the same mood, or seem to point to the same mysterious idea beyond experience.

It may be noted that *The Golem* is also an important novel for its Jewish characters, some of whom correspond to the viciously anti-Semitic stereotypes of the time. Others, as if in compensation, have an equally exaggerated saintliness.

Michael Cisco

See also: Meyrink, Gustav.

Further Reading

Barnett, David. 2014. "Meyrink's *Golem*: Where Fact and Fiction Collide." *The Guardian*, January 30. https://www.theguardian.com/books/booksblog/2014/jan/30/the-golem-gustav-meyrink-books.

Irwin, Robert. 1985. "Gustav Meyrink and His Golem." In *The Golem* by Gustav Meyrink, 1995, translated by Mike Mitchell, 15–20. Monroe, OR: Dedalus.

"GOOD COUNTRY PEOPLE"

Flannery O'Connor's short story "Good Country People" was first published in *Harper's Bazaar* in 1955 and then in O'Connor's collection of short stories *A Good Man Is Hard to Find* (1955). It stands among the most anthologized tales that she ever wrote, alongside "A Good Man Is Hard to Find," "Everything That Rises Must Converge," and "The Life You Save May Be Your Own." The story is highly representative of O'Connor's dark humor as well as the Southern Gothic style: it features grotesque characters from the rural South with physical deformities and moral failings who bring about their downfall through their own stubbornness.

Mrs. Hopewell is a well-off widow who runs a farm in rural Georgia with the help of her tenants, Mrs. Freeman and her two daughters, whom she believes are "good country people." They contrast heavily with Mrs. Hopewell's own daughter, a thirty-two-year-old spinster called Joy who lost a leg in a gunshot accident. Joy came back to live on the farm after earning a PhD in philosophy but failing to make it in academia because of her physical deformity. As a consequence, she is bitter and condescending to the country people's lack of philosophical insight.

One day, a Bible salesman named Manley Pointer shows up at the farm. He shows interest in Joy and invites her on a date. Overnight, Joy pictures herself seducing the young man to mock his country ways and his faith. During the picnic, Pointer convinces Joy to go in a barn loft and to take off her prosthetic leg. He confesses that he pretends to be an innocent Bible seller in order to steal prosthetic limbs. He then runs away with the leg, leaving Joy to go back to her mother, humbled and limbless.

The story, labeled by O'Connor as a "low joke" (O'Connor 1969, 98), follows the narrative pattern of the trickster being tricked. Priding herself on her philosophical knowledge and atheism, Joy devises a scheme to expose the bigotry of country folks, but her intellectual arrogance and contempt for the material world are exposed when Pointer seduces her and steals her prosthetic leg. Joy turns out to be greatly attached to her fake limb, and the loss of it shatters her image of a detached and independent intellectual. She has to admit that her physical impairment makes her reliant on her mother and the Freeman women, whether she likes it or not.

Joy is one of O'Connor's most grotesque creations. Her moral failings and physical handicap make her amusing and horrifying to the reader. There is humor in her condescending attitude, as it becomes clear to the reader that she is a caricature of an intellectual, but there is something deeply unsettling in the sexual farce Pointer plays on her. His fetish for the leg as well as the pleasure he takes in humiliating Joy contradicts the idea that country people are inherently "good" and gives the story a dark turn. "Good country people" can be as cruel as anyone, and the fault lies both in Joy's cynical attitude toward them as well as in her mother's blindness to their potential evil, as the latter insists, until the end of the story, that they are indeed good.

Elsa Charléty

See also: Body Horror; The Grotesque; O'Connor, Flannery.

Further Reading

Di Renzo, Anthony. 1995. *American Gargoyles: Flannery O'Connor and the Medieval Grotesque*. Carbondale: Southern Illinois University Press.
Kirk, Connie Ann. 2008. *Critical Companion to Flannery O'Connor*. New York: Infobase.
O'Connor, Flannery. 1969. *Mystery and Manners: Occasional Prose*. New York: Macmillan.

GOTHIC HERO/VILLAIN

The Gothic hero/villain is a type of male character, especially found in Gothic fiction of the nineteenth century, who appears to have the qualities of both good and evil. Contrary to a traditional romance hero, represented as a dutiful, sensitive, and pious gentleman, the Gothic hero/villain is dark, brooding, and sometimes cruel or abusive, but also capable of displaying strong, passionate feelings. The aura of

---

Examples of Gothic Hero/Villains

- Manfred in Horace Walpole's *The Castle of Otranto* (1764)
- Vathek in William Beckford's *Vathek* (1786)
- Montoni in Ann Radcliffe's *The Mysteries of Udolpho* (1794)
- Ambrosio in Matthew Lewis's *The Monk* (1796)
- Victor Frankenstein in Mary Shelley's *Frankenstein* (1818)
- Lord Ruthven in John Polidori's "The Vampyre" (1819)
- Melmoth in Charles Robert Maturin's *Melmoth the Wanderer* (1820)
- Heathcliff in Emily Brontë's *Wuthering Heights* (1847)
- Dracula in Bram Stoker's *Dracula* (1897)
- Lestat in Anne Rice's *The Vampire Chronicles* (1976–)

Matt Cardin

---

mystery that surrounds him makes him both attractive and repulsive to the Gothic heroine who usually falls under his influence, and his moral ambiguity makes it difficult for the reader to place a definite judgment on him.

Heroes with moral ambiguities can be found all through the history of literature, from the protagonist Odysseus in Homer's *Odyssey* to Elizabethan theater (Hamlet, Macbeth, Faust), but the hero/villain of nineteenth-century Gothic literature finds his origin in the real-life figure of the English poet Lord Byron. As the author of narrative poems such as *Don Juan* (1823) and *Childe Harold's Pilgrimage* (1816), Lord Byron is both the creator and the inspiration for this character whom Lord Macauley described as a "proud, moody, cynical man, with defiance on his brow and misery in his heart" (Christiansen 1989, 201). Byron's tumultuous life, made of scandalous affairs and excess, bore so many echoes of the male characters found in his poetry that this type of hero would be called "Byronic."

The Gothic hero/villain is a flawed but passionate figure who challenges the ideas of his time. He conforms to neither morals nor religion, and is a believer in the ideologies of the Enlightenment, mainly those of freedom and knowledge. However, the relentless pursuit of his ideals often leads him to extremes as he indulges in abuse, excess, or self-destruction. The Gothic hero/villain embodies the darker side of romanticism, as he constantly questions and defies authority by destructive means.

Even though this male character is defined by his ambiguity, three main types of Gothic hero/villain can be identified: the satanic, the Promethean, and the Caliban hero/villain. The satanic hero/villain, much like the Satan of Milton's *Paradise Lost,* possesses a brilliant mind and a power of persuasion over weaker individuals. He manipulates people around him with subtle words and action, and seduces them, regardless of their gender. The magnetic aura that surrounds him makes him a dangerously attractive character, often to the detriment of the good hero. Examples include John Polidori's Ruthven (in "The Vampyre"), the original vampire of English literature, who was modeled directly on Byron; Ann Radcliffe's Montoni in *The Mysteries of Udolpho* (1794); and Bram Stoker's titular vampire in *Dracula* (1897).

Recalling Prometheus, the ancient Greek deity who defied the gods by giving fire to humankind, the Promethean hero/villain transgresses the essential laws of nature in pursuit of a greater good. He acts not out of love, but out of passion for science and knowledge. He is ready to cross all boundaries for the advancement of humanity, even the sacred one between life and death. Victor Frankenstein, the eponymous tragic protagonist and "mad scientist" from Mary Shelley's *Frankenstein* (1818), is a telling example, since the book's full title is *Frankenstein; or The Modern Prometheus*.

The Caliban hero/villain is a raw force of nature. Like Shakespeare's creature in *The Tempest*, the Caliban hero/villain has failed to be fully subjugated to modern civilization. He is brutal, impulsive, and cruel to humans and animals alike. His feelings are strong and unconditional, and his love is as intense as it is destructive. The best example of this type is Heathcliff, the dark and haunted lover of Catherine Earnshaw in Emily Brontë's *Wuthering Heights* (1847).

Twentieth-century incarnations of the Gothic hero/villain tend to be stripped of their Gothic component while keeping the complex moral ambiguity of the character. Crime fiction and psychological thrillers often resort to this type of character. Both genres owe much to the figure of the Gothic hero/villain for achieving some of their most characteristic effects, as he is useful for heightening tension and allowing for major plot twists. The figure of the private detective, such as Arthur Conan Doyle's Sherlock Holmes (an obsessive-compulsive maniac addicted to morphine) and Sam Spade and Philip Marlowe (grumpy alcoholic loners emblematic of noir fiction), embody this hero/villain of a new genre. Other modern examples may include the mysterious phantom from *The Phantom of the Opera* (1910), the sociopathic antihero Alex in Anthony Burgess's *A Clockwork Orange* (1962), the masked anarchist freedom fighter V. in Allan Moore's graphic novel *V for Vendetta* (1988); and Dexter, the vigilante serial killer from the HBO series of the same name.

Elsa Charléty

See also: The Brontë Sisters; Byronic Hero; *The Castle of Otranto*; *Dracula*; *Frankenstein*; Mad Scientist; *The Mysteries of Udolpho*; *The Phantom of the Opera*; Romanticism and Dark Romanticism; Vampires; "The Vampyre."

Further Reading

Behr, Kate E. 2002. *The Representation of Men in the English Gothic Novel, 1762–1820*. Vol. 69. Lewiston, NY: Edwin Mellen Press.

Christiansen, Rupert. 1989. *Romantic Affinities: Portraits from an Age, 1780–1830*. London: Random House UK.

Hogle, Jerrold E., ed. 2002. *The Cambridge Companion to Gothic Literature*. Cambridge: Cambridge University Press.

Marshall, Bridget M. 2000. "The Face of Evil: Phrenology, Physiognomy, and the Gothic Villain." *Hungarian Journal of English and American Studies (HJEAS)* 6, no. 2: 161–172.

Morrison, Robert, and Chris Baldick. 1997. Introduction to *The Vampyre and Other Tales of the Macabre*. New York: Oxford University Press.

Punter, David, and Glennis Byron. 2004. *The Gothic*. Malden, MA, and Oxford: Blackwell.

GRABIŃSKI, STEFAN (1887–1936)

Stefan Grabiński was a Polish writer of what he termed "psychofantasy" or "meta-fantasy," tales of the dark fantastic that explore the inner realm of psychological, philosophical, and metaphysical concerns. He enjoyed a brief period of critical and popular acclaim early in his career, but his renown waned and he died impoverished and forgotten. However, after World War II interest in his work was rekindled, and his reputation has grown.

Grabiński was born on February 26, 1887, in Kamionka Strumiłowa, a small town in the eastern provinces of Poland, now part of the Ukraine. He had a quiet and comfortable childhood, though marred by ill health; he inherited a genetic form of tuberculosis from his father, which, starting in his bones and later spreading to his lungs, was to cause him suffering his whole life. After Grabiński's father's death, the family moved to Lwów, capital of Polish Galicia, where Grabiński studied Polish and classical literature. After graduating, he began working as a teacher of Polish, mostly in local schools. He would remain a provincial teacher the rest of his life, a job he found frustrating, as he felt it sapped his creative energy. He was, though, by all accounts, a good teacher.

As a child, encouraged by his mother, who was a great lover of books, Grabiński would read while laid up on his sickbed. It is likely Grabiński's sickness, a constant reminder of his mortality, and his introspective personality led him to dark fantasy and to an interest in the esoteric. In his own writing he took influences from Edgar Allan Poe and writers of the Polish Decadent and avant-garde movements. He was also inspired by classical thinkers, such as Heraclitus and Plato, and contemporary philosophers, particularly Henri Bergson and Maurice Maeterlinck. And he was intensely spiritual throughout his life, a pantheist who read the Christian mystics, Eastern religious texts such as the Indian Vedas, and works of theosophy and demonology.

In 1906, supported by his mother, Grabiński began writing. In 1909, he self-published a collection of stories under a pseudonym. This book did not find an audience, but his second volume of tales, *On the Hill of Roses* (1918), published some time later, after the upheaval of World War I, had a more encouraging critical reception. In 1919 *The Motion Demon* followed, a compilation of fantastical railway stories written for magazines and newspapers. It was a very popular collection, partly due to the interest in rail travel of the time, and was well regarded by critics. Karol Irzykowski, a leading writer of the Polish avant-garde, called it a perfect example of its genre and hailed Grabiński as the "Polish Poe." Grabiński's take on the railways is mystical, based on an esoteric theory of motion. He merged Bergson's theory of *élan vital*—the idea that evolution can be explained by an internal vital impetus that drives organisms to develop—with scientific theories of motion from Sir Isaac Newton and Albert Einstein.

The Motion Demon sold well enough that it was expanded and reprinted in 1922. It was followed by further collections: *Pilgrim's Madness* (1920), *A Mystery Tale* (1922), and *Book of Fire* (1922). The latter, like *The Motion Demon*, had a unified theme.

In his stories, Grabiński is modern and does not turn to the past, to the rich folklore of Poland. But he was also an opponent of mechanization; he had a sense that the modern world was a place where humankind's original sense of self and of harmony with nature was being erased by machines, materialism, and bureaucracy. In his work, and in particular his railway tales, demonic forces are fused with modern machines.

Grabiński had a close relationship with his mother and lived with her for most of his life. Though he was married in 1917, the relationship did not last, ending in 1921 when his wife left him, taking their two daughters with her. These things may have affected his attitudes toward women: in his fiction they are often sweet, pliant, and voluptuously monstrous at the same time. Many of his stories, such as "In Sarah's House," "The Black Hamlet," and "Passion," deal with the destructive power of lust. Grabiński's focus on the erotic can also be explained by his interest in in the human mind, psychoanalysis, and madness—he relished writing the lunatics in his fiction, for they shared his maverick perspective.

In the essay "*Wyznania*" ("Confessions," 1926), Grabiński writes, "Wonder and fear—these are my guiding motives" (Lipinski 2014, 7). And he was as much a writer of ecstasy as he was of horror, balancing and mixing the two emotions in his stories.

The heights of Grabiński's early tales were never regained, and the fame and material comfort they bought faded quickly. He tried his hand at novels and dramas, but they lacked the tautness and economy that made his short fiction catch fire and were too dependent on obscure occult iconography and terminology.

During this time, Grabiński's deteriorating health increasingly kept him housebound. He became bitter. In 1929, his tuberculosis spread to his lungs, with hemorrhaging. His financial situation also grew increasingly precarious. Still he continued to work, and in 1936 he published a novel, *Itongo Island*. It received bad reviews, and it was to be his last book.

Grabiński died on November 12, 1936. On his deathbed, he complained bitterly about having been misunderstood and forgotten in his native land. But interest in his work was revitalized in Poland in the late 1940s, and he was later championed by Stanisław Lem, the great Polish science fiction writer, who edited a collection of Grabiński's work and his influence has grown since. Several Polish films have been based on his work, and in the English-speaking world, thanks largely to the pioneering translations of Miroslaw Lipinski, begun in the 1980s, Grabiński's work has found favor among writers and readers of weird fiction. In Poland, the Year of Grabiński was held in 2012, with scholarly works and symposia dedicated to the writer.

Timothy J. Jarvis

See also: The Dark Domain.

Further Reading

Lipinski, Miroslaw. 2012. *The Stefan Grabiński Website*. January 9. http://www.stefangrabinski.org.

Lipinski, Miroslaw. 2014. Introduction to *The Motion Demon* by Stefan Grabińksi, 7–11. New York: NoHo Press.

Mills, Adam. 2012. "Interview: Translator Miroslaw Lipinski on Stefan Grabiński." *Weird Fiction Review*, July 10. http://weirdfictionreview.com/2012/07/interview-translator-miroslaw-lipinski-on-stefan-grabinski.

GRANT, CHARLES L. (1942–2006)

Charles Lewis Grant was an American novelist, short story writer, and editor/anthologist who specialized in dark fantasy and what he called "quiet horror," a term that became associated with his name and eventually came to define his work in the minds of his many admiring readers. He was born in 1942 in New Jersey, and he spent most of his life as a resident of the northwestern part of the state.

Grant's first novel, *The Shadow of Alpha* (1976), was a work of science fiction. He published a number of books in that genre before the end of the 1970s, switching to horror when the market for science fiction weakened. His first work of horror was a werewolf novel titled *The Curse* (1977). Grant would subsequently publish a total of eighty-five novels in myriad genres under his own name and numerous pseudonyms, many of which had their origins in bodies of water; thus, the pen names Geoffrey Marsh, Lionel Fenn, Timothy Boggs, and Simon Lake. He penned dozens of short stories that were later collected in six books. He also edited twenty-five anthologies, among them twelve volumes of one of the enormously influential horror anthology series *Shadows* (1978–1991). As an editor, he worked with some of the biggest names in the genre, and he also gave many fledgling writers their start.

He was known as a master and champion of quiet, subtle horror, as opposed to the more visceral and gaudy horror pioneered by Clive Barker in his *Books of Blood* and by the other so-called "splatterpunks" who rose to prominence in the late 1980s. While appreciating the effects those authors created, Grant preferred to suggest the horrific rather than render it explicitly. His great influence on the field is indicated by an insightful comment from author David Morrell in Douglas Winter's book of interviews, *Faces of Fear: Encounters with the Creators of Modern Horror* (1985): "Stephen King and Peter Straub are like the luxury liners of the horror field. They're always visible on the horizon when you look over these deep, dark waters. But Charlie Grant—he's the unseen power, like the great white shark, just below the surface" (Winter 1985, 109). Besides creating a vivid mental image, the quote is notable for the accurate portrayal of Grant acting as a secret master of the genre, subtly exerting profound influence on all those in his orbit. Grant led by example, publishing the best prose he could craft, and by educating the rest of his colleagues through the numerous anthologies he edited, announcing by their inclusion in these volumes that certain writers had "arrived" and that these stories were worthy of readers' attention.

Of particular importance in Grant's own body of work is his fictional Connecticut town of Oxrun Station. Although many writers have explored the subject of small town horror—including, notably, Shirley Jackson in "The Lottery" (1948), Thomas Tryon in *Harvest Home* (1973), and Stephen King in *'Salem's Lot* (1975)—few have done it as well, or as long, or in as many and varied ways, as Grant. Starting with *The Hour of the Oxrun Dead* in 1979, he went on to write a total of eight novels and a series of four collections of novellas set in the secluded Connecticut hamlet, concluding in 1995 with the collection *The Black Carousel*. As a set, the Oxrun books represent a grand, wildly successful experiment in horror, as Grant effectively explores dread and disquiet in many forms, whether it be the threat of harm from satanic cults; classic monsters like vampires, werewolves, or mummies; the pain of loneliness; or the confusion and despair caused by mental illness. Individually, many of these stories are classics of the genre, expertly evoking fear, terror, and horror, and providing readers with fleeting, disturbing, and memorable glimpses of what lurks in the shadows.

Grant won many awards over the course of his career, including two Nebulas plus multiple World Fantasy, Bram Stoker, and International Horror Guild awards. Late in his career he was honored with awards for lifetime achievement from the Horror Writers Association, the World Horror Convention, the British Fantasy Society, and the International Horror Guild. His profound influence on the horror genre is also evidenced by two tribute collections. The first, *Quietly Now* (2004), edited by Kealan Patrick Burke, presents tributes to Grant by various writers and critics in the field. The second, *Scream Quietly* (2011), edited by Stephen Jones, presents the best of Grant's short fiction.

Grant suffered from declining health in his later years. He was residing in Newton, New Jersey, with his second wife, the speculative fiction writer and editor Kathryn Ptacek, when he died of a heart attack on September 15, 2006.

Hank Wagner

See also: Bram Stoker Award; Dark Fantasy; International Horror Guild Award; Vampires; Werewolves; World Fantasy Award.

Further Reading

Mcdonald, T. Liam. 2003. "Grant, Charles L. 1942–." In *Supernatural Fiction Writers: Contemporary Fantasy and Horror*, edited by Richard Bleiler, 2nd ed., Vol. 1, 391–402. New York: Charles Scribner's Sons.

Neilson, Keith. 1983. "The Subtle Terrors of Charles L. Grant." In *Survey of Modern Fantasy Literature*, Volume 3, edited by Frank N. Magill, 1191–1195. Englewood Cliffs, NJ: Salem Press.

Schweitzer, Darrell. 1994. "Charles L. Grant." In *Speaking of Horror: Interviews with Writers of Supernatural Horror*, 47–57. San Bernardino, CA: Borgo Press.

Winter, Douglas E. 1985. *Faces of Fear: Encounters with the Creators of Modern Horror*. New York: Berkley Books.

"THE GREAT GOD PAN"

"The Great God Pan" is a classic horror novella by the Welsh author Arthur Machen. It caused something of a sensation when it was published, and it has become one of the central texts in the history of weird fiction in the English language.

The novella's first section, "The Experiment," was originally published as "The Great God Pan" in the short-lived *Whirlwind* in 1890, which styled itself a "lively and eccentric newspaper" and whose contributors included Stéphane Mallarmé, James Abbott McNeill Whistler, and Walter Sickert. Machen expanded this original iteration into its final form for publication in *The Great God Pan and The Inmost Light* (1894), one of John Lane's "Keynotes," a book series associated with the literary Decadent movement of the 1890s.

Inspired by Robert Louis Stevenson's conceit in *Dr. Jekyll and Mr. Hyde* (1886), Machen was convinced that a similarly "scientific" plot device was necessary for

---

In Machen's "The Great God Pan," Dr. Raymond's explanation of what it means to "see the god Pan" lays out a philosophical viewpoint that resonates with weird horror fiction's central concern, and that stands as a quintessential articulation of it:

> Look about you, Clarke. You see the mountain, and hill following after hill, as wave on wave, you see the woods and orchard, the fields of ripe corn, and the meadows reaching to the reed-beds by the river. You see me standing here beside you, and hear my voice; but I tell you that all these things—yes, from that star that has just shone out in the sky to the solid ground beneath our feet—I say that all these are but dreams and shadows; the shadows that hide the real world from our eyes. There is a real world, but it is beyond this glamour and this vision, beyond these "chases in Arras, dreams in a career," beyond them all as beyond a veil. I do not know whether any human being has ever lifted that veil; but I do know, Clarke, that you and I shall see it lifted this very night from before another's eyes. You may think this all strange nonsense; it may be strange, but it is true, and the ancients knew what lifting the veil means. They called it seeing the god Pan. (Machen 1894, 3)

Matt Cardin

Source: Machen, Arthur. 1894. *The Great God Pan*. London: John Lane, Vigo St.

the modern reader to accept an unusual narrative, where traditional supernatural horror tropes would no longer be convincing. Thus the opening section of "The Great God Pan" relates a scientific (or rather, pseudoscientific) experiment on the brain of a young girl by Dr. Raymond, intended to give her access to other realms of perception.

The ensuing narrative is fragmented, offering different perspectives on the events precipitated by the experiment, provoking the reader into active construction and interpretation of the central plotline. During her ordeal, the girl encounters what is (perhaps only euphemistically) described as the Greek deity Pan, rendering her both insane and mysteriously pregnant. The resulting child, Helen Vaughan, is shunned by the rural Welsh community in which she grows up and where she is the subject of disturbing rumors. As an adult, Vaughan moves through London society leaving in her wake insanity and a series of suicides. She is eventually tracked down by two men, Villiers and Clarke, who have learned something of her history and become convinced of how dangerous she is. They confront Vaughan and coerce her into killing herself. The final paragraphs describe Vaughan's preternatural "dissolution," through a reverse evolutionary process, into protoplasmic material.

"The Great God Pan" received largely negative reviews upon publication for its gruesome subject matter as well as its association with controversial new literary freedoms. Its theme of pagan resurgence destabilizing bourgeois metropolitan society resonated with fin-de-siècle (literally "end of the century," a phrase used at the close of the nineteenth century to define what was perceived as a significant cultural and historical moment) anxieties provoked by the erosion of old religious certainties. Although the climactic physical dissolution of Vaughan has been regularly discussed in the context of the fin de siècle preoccupation with degeneration (biological, cultural, and racial), it is likely Machen was as much influenced by his formidable knowledge of medieval alchemy as he was by specific contemporary discourse.

The story has occasionally been criticized as misogynistic and cited as evidence that Machen had a morbid fear of human sexuality. Recent critics who have advanced this view include S. T. Joshi in his *Unutterable Horror: A History of Supernatural Fiction* (2012/2014), China Miéville in his essay "Weird Fiction" in *The Routledge Companion to Science Fiction* (2009), and Andrew Smith in *The Victorian Gothic: An Edinburgh Companion* (2012) (although Smith also notes that "the silence of the central female character"—which has been the focus of claims of the story's misogyny—also contributes to the story's overall narrative effect, since it increases "the mystery and terror at the heart of the story, linked to a predatory female sexuality" by maintaining the mysterious ineffability of what it means to glimpse "the Great God Pan"; see Smith 2012, 225). However, when considered within the wider context of Machen's life and work, the notion that he had a particular animus against women, or that he was squeamish about sex, seems unconvincing. Indeed, the renowned literary critic Tzvetan Todorov has used Machen as an example to demonstrate his concern that "too direct application" of psychoanalysis to litera-ture can result in both misrepresentation of the author and simple reiteration of "initial presuppositions" regarding the text (Todorov 1975, 152–153).

Indicative of the impact of "The Great God Pan" is the fact that it was almost immediately parodied, in Arthur Sykes's "The Great Pan-Demon" and Arthur Compton-Rickett's "A Yellow Creeper." However, it was also a commercial success and established Machen's reputation as a writer of weird horror in the Stevenson mold. Vernon Lee's "Dionea" (from *Hauntings*, 1890) is an interesting comparison, although Lee uses an epistolary form to relate her similar tale of a destabilizing pagan influence channeled through an amoral female character never directly rep-resented. Machen's presentation of his story as a puzzle of different testimonies from a variety of sources anticipates the similar structure used by Bram Stoker in *Dracula*, and its influence in this respect can be clearly seen in H. P. Lovecraft's "The Call of Cthulhu." Lovecraft's "The Dunwich Horror" also uses a near-identical cen-tral conceit of a child born of congress between a human and a supernatural entity. Stephen King has stated that Machen's novella is "one of the best horror stories ever written. . . . Maybe the best in the English language," and M. John Harrison's 1988 story "The Great God Pan" is so titled in explicit homage.

James Machin

See also: "The Call of Cthulhu"; *The Ceremonies*; "The Dunwich Horror"; Machen, Arthur; "The Novel of the Black Seal."

Further Reading

Joshi, S. T. 1990. *The Weird Tale*. Holicong, PA: Wildside.

Joshi, S. T. 2014. *Unutterable Horror: A History of Supernatural Fiction, Volume 1: From Gilgamesh to the End of the Nineteenth Century*. New York: Hippocampus Press.

Lovecraft, H. P. [1927] 2012. *The Annotated Supernatural Horror in Literature*. Edited by S. T. Joshi. New York: Hippocampus Press.

Luckhurst, Roger, ed. 2005. *Late Victorian Gothic Tales*. Oxford: Oxford University Press.

Miéville, China. 2009. "Weird Fiction." In *The Routledge Companion to Science Fiction*, edited by Mark Bould, Andrew M. Butler, Adam Roberts, and Sherryl Vint, 510–515. London: Routledge.

Smith, Andrew. 2012. *The Victorian Gothic: An Edinburgh Companion*. Edinburgh: Edinburgh University Press.

Todorov, Tzvetan. 1975. *The Fantastic: A Structural Approach to a Literary Genre*. Translated by Richard Howard and Robert Scholes. Ithaca: Cornell University Press.

"GREEN TEA"

One of the most frequently anthologized of supernatural stories, "Green Tea," by the Irish author J. Sheridan Le Fanu (1814–1873), first appeared in the journal *All the Year Round*, edited by Charles Dickens (1812–1870), in 1869. It was subse-quently incorporated in Le Fanu's collection *In a Glass Darkly* in 1872. The

"Green Tea" shows the influence of the eighteenth-century Swedish mystic and vision-ary Emanuel Swedenborg on Le Fanu's thought and work. The story takes one of Swedenborg's basic ideas—that of the opening of the "inner eye," the faculty of spir-itual sight—and gives it a supernatural horrific slant. The text itself essentially explains this, as it presents, at one point, several excerpts from one of Swedenborg's books, as read by the character of Hesselius:

> I lighted upon a complete set of Swedenborg's "Arcana Celestia," in the original Latin, a very fine folio set, bound in the natty livery which theology affects, pure vellum, namely, gold letters, and carmine edges. There were paper markers in several of these volumes, I raised and placed them, one after the other, upon the table, and opening where these papers were placed, I read in the solemn Latin phraseology, a series of sentences indicated by a penciled line at the margin. Of these I copy here a few, translating them into English.
>
> "When man's interior sight is opened, which is that of his spirit, then there appear the things of another life, which cannot possibly be made visible to the bodily sight."
>
> . . . "If evil spirits could perceive that they were associated with man, and yet that they were spirits separate from him, and if they could flow into the things of his body, they would attempt by a thousand means to destroy him; for they hate man with a deadly hatred." (Le Fanu 1994, 14–15)

Matt Cardin

Source: Le Fanu, J. Sheridan. [1872] 1886. "Green Tea." *In a Glass Darkly*. London: Richard Bentley & Son.

"Prologue" and "Conclusion" to "Green Tea" are integral to the narrative and should be read in conjunction with the main body of the tale.

The "Prologue" is written by an anonymous English editor responsible for dis-seminating the clinical and philosophical work of the deceased German physician Martin Hesselius. The narrative of "Green Tea"—and, by implication, the four sto-ries that follow it in *In a Glass Darkly*—have been selected by the editor not for their clinical insight but rather for the amusement they might bring to a general reader. That amusement is implicitly somewhat sardonic, for the story that follows is one of medical mismanagement and purblind dogmatism. The date of the narra-tive is not given, but the events of "Green Tea" appear to take place in London and southern England during the earlier years of the nineteenth century. Dr. Hesselius encounters the Reverend Mr. Jennings, an Episcopalian clergyman, at a London gathering. Realizing that there is something amiss with the cleric, he visits him at his London residence and learns that the scholarly gentleman is subject to a recur-rent and distressing hallucination. Jennings has, for some time, been subject to periodic visitations by a malevolent monkey, visible only to him, which at first merely stalked him silently but which latterly has begun to speak, to utter blasphemies that interrupt the sermons he delivers in his rural parish, and to encourage him to take his own life.

Hesselius counsels Jennings that the monkey is a delusion brought about by the clergyman's excessive consumption of green tea as a stimulant to support his nocturnal researches into paganism, and promises to return to him should the monkey again manifest itself to the cleric's sight. He neglects, however, to leave an address at which he might be contacted, and when the monkey returns, angry at Jennings having consulted a physician, the apparition goads his victim into suicide. Hesselius's "Conclusion," subtitled "A Word for Those Who Suffer," is a consummate exercise in deflecting the blame from the irresponsibility of the physician onto the hereditary disposition of the unfortunate patient.

"Green Tea" is a significant narrative for a number of reasons. First, it is very much implicated in the popular medicine of its day, and the notion that Jennings's vision might be affected by the innocuous beverage he has consumed parallels Ebenezer Scrooge's interpretation of why he sees the ghost of his deceased partner, Jacob Marley, in Dickens's *A Christmas Carol* (1843). Second, it is a narrative that, like Le Fanu's *Uncle Silas* (1864), is heavily influenced by the writings of the visionary philosopher Emanuel Swedenborg (1688–1772). Third, as a self-contained and disturbing short work it typifies, despite the absence of a conventional human specter, the genre of the ghost story, a tradition that is associated with, but distinct from, the Gothic novel.

William Hughes

See also: In a Glass Darkly; Le Fanu, J. Sheridan; Occult Detectives.

Further Reading

Crawford, Gary William, Jim Rockhill, and Brian J. Showers, eds. 2011. *Reflections in a Glass Darkly: Essays on J. Sheridan Le Fanu*. New York: Hippocampus Press.

Hughes, William. 2005. "The Origins and Implications of J. S. Le Fanu's 'Green Tea.'" *Irish Studies Review* 13, no. 1: 45–54.

Sullivan, Jack. 1981. "'Green Tea': The Archetypal Ghost Story." In *Literature of the Occult*, edited by Peter B. Messent, 117–138. Oxford: Oxford University Press.

Wegley, Mark. 2001. "Unknown Fear: Joseph Sheridan Le Fanu and the Literary Fantastic." *Philological Review* 27.2 (Fall): 59–77. Reprinted in *Short Story Criticism*, vol. 84, edited by Thomas J. Schoenberg and Lawrence J. Trudeau, 2006, Literature Resource Center. Detroit: Gale.

THE GROTESQUE

The grotesque in horror literature is conventionally defined by representations of human excess, the abnormal, the repulsive, the ugly, and the nightmarishly or ludicrously fantastic. Rather than being the shock that horror elicits, or the dread and imminent sense of fear that terror connotes, the grotesque is rooted in physicality and the visual. It is a physical manifestation of horror and terror that is created by deviation, dichotomy, and excess. The grotesque and horror are inextricably connected. How "the elusive nature of the grotesque" (Barasch 1968, v) is defined in relation to horror has been debated by scholars and critics from the seventeenth century into the present.

The term "grotesque" has undergone redefinition since it was first used during the Italian Renaissance to describe unearthed Roman frescos at Domus Aurea as "grottesca" from grottos or caves. As an aesthetic mode applied to visual mediums, the "grottesche" implied the fantastic imaginings of Roman artists (in the era of Vitruvius). The frescos were seen to depict chimeric images of decadence and absurdity made more sepulchral and ethereal by their discovery in grottos. Early literary usage of the term appears in the sixteenth century with Montaigne, who linked the grotesque to monstrosity and experimentation.

Flannery O'Connor's "A Good Man Is Hard to Find"

"A Good Man Is Hard to Find" is a short story written by American author Flannery O'Connor. First published in 1953, it is now the most read and recognized of O'Connor's work due to its inclusion in numerous anthologies.

It begins with the portrayal of a "comically vapid, ill-tempered, and self-centered" (Harris 1990) family from Georgia on a cross-country trip to Florida. The story shifts dramatically after a car accident, which results in the family meeting the Misfit and his homicidal gang. The Grandmother unintentionally identifies these escaped convicts, and this leads to the murder of the family.

Critics often find the character of the Misfit to be a curiosity of contradictions. For example, he is full of Southern courtesy and politeness while also killing innocent people; he agonizes over faith while also admitting he is "doing all right" without prayer; and he feels he never deserves any punishment, but admits to several instances of wrong-doing. All of this contributes to his aptly named moniker.

The story's climax, a conversation between the Grandmother and the Misfit, circles around the subject of religion. It features the grandmother undergoing a spiritual epiphany while under intense duress, a common theme in O'Connor's works.

"A Good Man Is Hard to Find" is often noted for its Southern Gothic themes, including its use of grotesque, realistic horror, outcasts, and nostalgia for an idealized South. In fact, O'Connor's work is noted for helping to establish the genre of Southern Gothic itself.

Chun H. Lee

Source: Harris, Laurie Lanzen. 1990. "Overview: 'A Good Man Is Hard to Find.'" In *Characters in 20th-Century Literature*. Literature Resource Center. Detroit: Gale.

The grotesque as an element of horror literature became enmeshed with the Gothic mode through Horace Walpole's *The Castle of Otranto*. Walpole imbued grotesque horror with buffoonery and the sublime in the preface to his second edition. In the nineteenth century, Mary Shelley stitched the grotesque body to horror fiction in *Frankenstein*.

Victor Hugo's *Preface de Cromwell* (1827) popularized the use of the term. With Edgar Allan Poe's *Tales of the Grotesque and Arabesque* (1840), and a century later H. P. Lovecraft's *Supernatural Horror in Literature* (1927), the concept of the grotesque moved toward the current idiom.

Important recent scholars of the grotesque include Geoffrey Galt Harpham, Frances K. Barasch, Justin Edwards and Rune Graulund, and Wolfgang Kayser. The latter's *The Grotesque in Art and Literature* (1963) emphasizes the horror, estrangement, and demonic as central to its definition. Theories of the grotesque that rely on power structures, aberration, and horror are visible in Michel Foucault, Julia Kristeva, and John Ruskin. Tzvetan Todorov examines the grotesque in relation to the fantastic, and Freud through the uncanny. In the nineteenth century, Ruskin's study of the symbolic grotesque merges horror with the ludicrous, where the grotesque's playful comic tendency threatens to descend into terror. He separates the noble from the barbarous grotesque, which is associated with terror and the horror genre. Mikhail Bakhtin's text *Rabelais and His World* (1965) emphasizes the carnivalesque, realism, and structures within the grotesque. Significant contributions to the literature of the term include Edgar Allan Poe's tales, Lovecraftian horror, the religious visions of Flannery O'Connor, the realistic aesthetics of Sherwood Anderson and Cormac McCarthy, the self-reflexive grotesque of Patrick McGrath, and others.

Today the grotesque is still a complex and diffuse theme with little clear consensus. Often critics describe it as a structure in which estrangement and deviation are expressed. It is tied to paradoxical combinations of the ludicrous and the terrifying. Grotesque, as a literary term, has been connected variously with the uncanny, the sublime, and the absurd as it has transformed over time. Recent scholars such as Edwards and Graulund connect a global definition of the grotesque to these associated literary themes through reliance on multiple grotesques and sociocultural contexts, thus further obscuring a concise definition. Conversely, Shun-Liang Chao and Frances S. Connelly root the grotesque back within the physical or visual, where some combination of the ridiculous and horrific is always at play.

Naomi Simone Borwein

See also: Body Horror; Hugo, Victor; Koja, Kathe; McGrath, Patrick; O'Connor, Flannery; The Sublime; Terror versus Horror; The Uncanny; Welty, Eudora.

Further Reading

Barasch, Frances K. 1968. "Introduction." In *A History of Caricature and Grotesque in Literature and Art*, by Thomas Wright (1865), vii–ix. New York: Frederick Ungar.

Edwards, Justin, and Rune Graulund. 2013. *The Grotesque*. London: Routledge.

Kayser, Wolfgang. 1963. *The Grotesque in Art and Literature*. Bloomington: Indiana University Press.

Nelson, Victoria. 2001. "Grotto, an Opening." In *The Secret Life of Puppets*, 1–24. Cambridge, MA: Harvard University Press.

H

HAGGARD, H. RIDER (1856–1925)

Like his close friend Rudyard Kipling, Sir Henry Rider Haggard was a quintessential literary spokesman for the British Empire, a devotee of the imperial ideology bringing order to the world and uplifting "uncivilized" peoples. He was of enormous cultural significance in his own day, inspiring a generation of young Englishmen to seek careers in the service of the empire. His main subjects were Africa, ancient Egypt, and the occult. His depictions of Africa in particular captured the imagination of the public. In this, he can be seen as a predecessor of Edgar Rice Burroughs, the creator of Tarzan, although unlike Burroughs he had actually been to Africa in the imperial service and was describing peoples and landscapes he knew firsthand. His racial attitudes are of his time. He never sees black Africans as equals, but desires benevolent rule for them. He thought himself a friend of the Africans, and by Victorian standards, he was. He first achieved prominence with the African adventure novel *King Solomon's Mines* (1885), written on a bet from his brother that he could not write a better book than Robert Louis Stevenson's *Treasure Island*.

Haggard was something of a believer in the occult, or at least in supernatural destiny, and it is largely for this that his work is relevant to weird fiction. His most famous novel, *She: A History of Adventure* (1886), spawned an entire subgenre of imitations: the Lost Race novel, which invariably deals with the discovery of some isolated remnant of an ancient civilization, found in a remote place, replete with some wondrous phenomenon unknown to the rest of the world. In *She* the heroes reach a lost city in Africa where Ayesha, a 2,000-year-old white queen, rules over a tribe of "savages." She is under a romantic curse, having killed her lover, Kallikrates, in ancient times, and is doomed to wait, undying, for his return. One of the explorers is the reincarnation of Kallikrates. When she tries to make him immortal and renew her own immortality, she steps into the flaming Pillar of Life, its effects are disastrously reversed, and she withers away.

The novel was a smash bestseller, and there were sequels. Ayesha herself was reincarnated as the awesome femme-fatale/sorceress in countless subsequent fantasy novels. Indeed, part of the Lost Race formula all but requires that one of the European heroes becomes romantically entangled with a fabulously beautiful princess or temptress. The influence of *She* extended ever further when Edgar Rice Burroughs transported the entire scenario to another planet in *A Princess of Mars* in 1911.

Haggard made a similar mistake in killing off the main character in his bestselling *Allan Quatermain* (1887), but then "discovered" several memoirs of earlier adventures, including the reincarnation story *The Ancient Allan* (1920), set in prehistoric times. Quatermain met Ayesha in *She and Allan* (1921).

Supernaturalism in Haggard's work otherwise varies widely. One of his rare short stories, "Only a Dream . . ." (1905), is horror. The ghost of a man's dead wife haunts him on the eve of his second marriage. She leaves her skull behind. In the novella "Smith and the Pharaohs" (1913), a man lingers in a museum after closing time and witnesses a gathering of ancient Egyptian spirits returning to their mummies. *Eric Brighteyes* (1890) is a surprisingly effective pastiche of a medieval Norse saga, with a vivid mix of heroism, dooms, and sorceries. A later novel of particular interest is *Red Eve* (1911), which begins as a costume romance set in fourteenth-century Europe, but becomes genuine weird fiction with the introduction of the character Murgh, a personification of the Black Death, who arrives in Venice on a corpse-laden ship. The hero develops a strange acquaintance with Death, and for a time he is spared. The 1903 novel *Stella Fregellius* involves a disastrous attempt to contact the dead by scientific means. There are many fantastic elements in most of Haggard's African novels. *Nada the Lily* (1892) is an epic set among the Zulus, featuring omens, fate, a sky goddess, and a supernatural wolf pack. *The Ghost Kings* (1908), which Kipling helped plot, introduces the sorcerous Ghost People, who are linked to trees and die if their trees are destroyed. However dated Haggard's ideas may sometimes seem, he remains an extremely entertaining writer, strong on both authentic detail and eerie atmosphere when the story requires it.

Darrell Schweitzer

See also: Kipling, Rudyard; *She*.

Further Reading

Cohen, Morton, 1960. *H. Rider Haggard, His Life and Work*. London: Macmillan.

Katz, Wendy, 1987. *H. Rider Haggard and the Fiction of Empire*. Cambridge, UK: Cambridge University Press.

Luckhurst, Roger. 2012. "Rider Haggard among the Mummies." In *The Mummy's Curse: The True History of a Dark Fantasy*, 185–208. Oxford: Oxford University Press.

HAINING, PETER (1940–2007)

Peter Alexander Haining was a British journalist and publishing professional who wrote and compiled numerous nonfiction books on horror, fantasy, and mystery themes, including *An Illustrated History of Witchcraft* (1975), *The Legend and Bizarre Crimes of Spring-Heeled Jack* (1977), *The Mystery and Horrible Murders of Sweeney Todd, the Demon Barber of Fleet Street* (1979), and the illustrated *The Art of Horror Stories* (1976). He also compiled "scrapbooks" and miscellanies concerned with the fiction of Edgar Allan Poe, M. R. James, and H. G. Wells, and collections of macabre fiction by John Buchan, Wilkie Collins, Charles Dickens, Edith Wharton, and Bram Stoker.

Haining is best known as a compiler of both general reprint anthologies, among them *Beyond the Curtain of Dark* (1966) and *The Unspeakable People* (1969), and thematically specific anthologies: *The Ghouls* (1971) featured horror stories that had been adapted as movies, and *The Hollywood Nightmare* (1970) stories were concerned with show business; *The Fantastic Pulps* (1976) and *Weird Tales* (1976) both drew from the rich legacy of twentieth-century pulp fiction magazines; and *The Midnight People* (1968) collected vampire stories. The themes of *The Mummy: Stories of the Living Corpse* (1988), *Supernatural Sleuths* (1986), *Zombie: Stories of the Walking Dead* (1985), and *Werewolf: Horror Stories of the Man-Beast* (1987) are self-evident. A number of Haining's best anthologies combined scholarship with their fiction reprints, including *The Penny Dreadful; or, Strange, Horrid and Sensational Tales* (1976) and *The Shilling Shockers: Stories of Terror from the Gothic Bluebooks* (1978).

Haining compiled a number of anthologies under the pseudonyms Ric Alexander, William Pattrick, and Richard Peyton, and he authored three novels. Although the reliability of his research and sources has been questioned by some scholars, his work as an anthologist helped to shape perceptions of the anthology as a vital medium for genre fiction. He was awarded the British Fantasy Society's Karl Edward Wagner Award in 2001.

Stefan R. Dziemianowicz

See also: James, M. R.; Poe, Edgar Allan; Pulp Horror; Stoker, Bram; *Weird Tales*; Wells, H. G.; Wharton, Edith.

Further Reading

Haining, Peter, ed. 1972. *Gothic Tales of Terror: Classic Horror Stories from Great Britain, Europe, and the United States 1765–1840*. New York: Taplinger.

Haining, Peter, ed. 1976. *The Penny Dreadful; Or, Strange, Horrid & Sensational Tales!* London: Victor Gollancz.

Haining, Peter. 1976. *Terror! A History of Horror Illustrations from the Pulp Magazines*. New York: A & W Visual Library.

"Peter Haining." 2007. *Contemporary Authors Online*. Detroit: Gale.

HAND, ELIZABETH (1957–)

Elizabeth Hand is an American writer of dark fantasy, horror, and neo-noir. She is perhaps best known for her thrillers featuring Cass Neary, a hard-boiled photographer and reluctant crime fighter who has been compared to Liz Salander, the lead character in Stieg Larsson's *Millennium* series. Hand has lived in rural Maine in the United States since 1988, but she also spends a significant amount of time in London, England. She has won the James Tiptree Jr. Award and the Mythopoeic Fantasy

Award for *Waking the Moon* (1994); the World Fantasy Award for her collection *Bibliomancy* (2002), her novel *Illyria* (2008), and "The Maiden Flight of McCauley's Bellerophon" (2010); and the Shirley Jackson Award for the first Cass Neary novel, *Generation Loss* (2007), which is set in Maine.

Her characters are generally troubled individuals living on the very rough edges of society, but they are also often highly creative: artists, musicians, photographers, and writers, whose interests give them access to the darker realms of modern life and culture. Hand began her career as a fantasy and science fiction writer not unlike the American feminist science fiction writer Sheri S. Tepper in style; her first novel, *Winterlong* (1990), and its sequels, *Aestival Tide* (1992) and *Icarus Descending* (1993), are set in an alternate, dystopian universe. However, it was with *Waking the Moon*, centering on a fictional university in a broadly realist Washington, D.C., that Hand gained critical recognition and began to engage with horror motifs such as ritual murder and Lovecraftian monstrosity. *Waking the Moon*, which revolves around gory sacrifices to a newly awakened Mother Goddess, is also particularly noteworthy for its subtle critique of 1990s neo-paganism and Wicca, a critique successfully balanced with a more pragmatic feminist message. This complex mix of feminism and images of genuinely frightening feminine evil is continued through the postapocalyptic *Glimmering* (1997, reissued in a new, updated edition in 2012), the historical fantasy *Mortal Love* (2004), and the haunted house novella *Wylding Hall* (2015).

Hand's work overall is heavily allusive, integrating song lyrics; references to real artists, writers, and photographers; and quotations from and echoes of the work of T. S. Eliot, Shirley Jackson, Ray Bradbury, and Peter Straub, among many others.

She published *Hard Light* in 2016, the third Cass Neary novel, even as she was working on the fourth thriller in the series, *The Book of Lamps and Banners*. In many respects, this marks a move away from horror as such, though as with much crime writing, Hand's work repeatedly integrates gothic tropes. She also indicated that she was working on another novella and some short fiction, which may extend the ongoing centrality in her *oeuvre* of violence, personal demons, and the darker aspects of myth and fantasy.

Dara Downey

See also: Bradbury, Ray; Dark Fantasy; Jackson, Shirley; Shirley Jackson Awards; Straub, Peter; World Fantasy Award.

Further Reading

Attebery, Brian. 2014. *Stories about Stories: Fantasy and the Remaking of Myth*. Oxford: Oxford University Press.

"Elizabeth Hand." 2011. *Contemporary Authors Online*. Detroit: Gale.

Mendlesohn, Farah. 2008. *Rhetorics of Fantasy*. Middletown, CT: Wesleyan University Press.

Mendlesohn, Farah, and Edward James. 2009. *A Short History of Fantasy*. Faringdon: Middlesex University Press.

Thirsty. 2016. "A Conversation with Novelist Elizabeth Hand." *Stay Thirsty Magazine*, Spring. www.staythirstymedia.com/201604-092/html/201604-hand.html.

Wein, Cherie. 2003. "Hand, Elizabeth 1957–." In *Supernatural Fiction Writers: Contemporary Fantasy and Horror*, 2nd ed., vol. 1, edited by Richard Bleiler, 413–417. New York: Charles Scribner's Sons.

THE HANDS OF ORLAC

The Hands of Orlac is an influential French 1920 horror novel written by Maurice Renard (1875–1938). Renard, who is today better known by French critics and readers than English or American ones, was a literary theorist as well as a writer who called his work "*le roman merveilleux-scientifique*" (the scientific-marvelous novel), which he considered a new literary genre. Renard's most successful novel, *Les Mains d'Orlac* (*The Hands of Orlac*), was published in 1920 and translated into English in 1929.

Orlac is the story of a famous pianist, Stephen Orlac, who loses both his hands in a train accident and receives the hands of an executed murderer in a transplant operation. He begins to believe that he is being controlled by his newly transplanted hands, and he starts to experience violent urges. When he discovers that his father has been killed by the same knife that was used by the murderer, he begins to fear he may be the culprit. Struggling for the truth and his own sanity, he eventually discovers that he has been set up by a con man.

The Hands of Orlac reflects Renard's interest in the scientific developments of his time, including in the fields of psychology, biology, and surgery. It also reflects his interest in adapting science to tales of horror and the marvelous. In practicing this approach, Renard followed the lead of H. G. Wells, who employed the same structure in his novel *The Island of Dr. Moreau* (1896), which Renard acknowledged as an influence.

Today *The Hands of Orlac* is best known as the source for director Robert Wiene's silent 1924 German Expressionist film adaptation, starring Conrad Veidt as Orlac. German Expressionism was an extreme anti-realistic cinema style in which the external images of the film, such as unusual camera angles and lighting, as well as exaggerated acting and makeup, represent the internal states of the characters. Wiene's film, now considered a classic, was a critical and financial success and has been remade several times, most successfully by director Karl Freund in 1934 as *Mad Love*, starring Peter Lorre. The film was also remade in 1960 in a version that starred Mel Ferrer and Christopher Lee.

Both the original novel and the film adaptations of *The Hands of Orlac* are significant for a number of reasons. First, Renard's novel is an excellent early example of speculative fiction, a genre that combines diverse interests and forms. Renard took contemporary developments in biology, psychology, and medical practice in the early twentieth century and placed them in the world of horror, using rational means to explore the irrational. Second, the original 1924 film adaptation is one of the earliest and best examples of body horror cinema, in which horror is caused by the disfiguration, decay, or mutilation of the body. Other well-known body horror narratives include the films *Freaks* (1932), *The Fly* (1958; remade in 1986), *The Blob* (1958; remade in 1988), *Alien* (1979), and *American Mary* (2012), all of which owe some debt to *Orlac* because of its seminal position in the subgenre. This influence can be seen even more directly in a number of horror films that offer new takes on the idea of individual body parts possessing an evil will of their own, such as *Body Parts* (1991) and *Idle Hands* (1999).

Jim Holte

See also: Body Horror; *The Island of Doctor Moreau*; Psychological Horror.

Further Reading

Goldberg, Ruth. 2002. "Of Mad Love, Alien Hands and the Film under Your Skin." *Kinoeye* 2, no. 4 (February 18). http://www.kinoeye.org/02/04/goldberg04.php.

Olney, Jan. 2006. "The Problem Body Politic, or 'These Hands Have a Mind All Their Own!': Figuring Disability in the Horror Film Adaptations of Renard's *Les mains d'Orlac*." *Literature/Film Quarterly* 34, no. 4: 294–302.

Reyes, Xavier Aldana. 2014. *Body Gothic: Corporeal Transgression in Contemporary Literature and Horror Film*. Cardiff: University of Wales Press.

HARDY, THOMAS (1840–1928)

A poet, novelist, and short story writer whose most significant work spans the final three decades of the nineteenth century and the first two decades of the twentieth, Thomas Hardy is a major figure in English literary history, renowned for his realistic treatment of rural settings and his pessimistic view of human existence as tragedy. Influenced by the evolutionary theories of Charles Darwin and Thomas Henry Huxley, Hardy's poetry and "Novels of Character and Environment" (also known as the "Wessex Novels") dramatize "the plight of mankind trapped in a universe oblivious to human feelings and ethical aspirations" (Schweik 1999, 63), usually by presenting passionately aspiring characters who become victims of indifferent forces that exceed their control and ultimately master or destroy them.

Born in the southwestern county of Dorset into a working-class family steeped in local folk traditions, Hardy also became an avid antiquarian and folklorist, committed to preserving in his fiction and poetry "a fairly true record of a vanishing life" (Hardy 1967, 22) during a period when industrialization, modernization, and urbanization were dismantling the traditional communities and folkways of the English countryside. Among the numerous traditional customs, stories, and superstitions that Hardy incorporated into his depictions of rural life in "Wessex" (a fictionalized version of his native Dorset), several figure with particular prominence throughout his career: the belief in ghosts (*Tess of the d'Urbervilles*; "The

Superstitious Man's Story"; "A January Night"; "The Harvest Supper"; "A Sound in the Night"; "At Shag's Heath"), fairies (*The Return of the Native*; *The Mayor of Casterbridge*; *Tess of the d'Urbervilles*), witchcraft ("The Withered Arm"; *Under the Greenwood Tree*; *The Return of the Native*; *The Woodlanders*), and assorted predictive superstitions such as omens, premonitions, and divination (*The Return of the Native*; *Far From the Madding Crowd*; *Jude the Obscure*; *The Woodlanders*).

In addition to providing Hardy's fiction and poetry with authentic touches of local color that are ornamental and atmospheric, the evocation of occult folk belief serves narrative and thematic purposes as Hardy routinely adapted folk traditions to the needs of plotting, tone, and symbolism. In *Tess of the d'Urbervilles* (1891), for instance, the tale of the phantom coach presaging death and perceptible only to those of true d'Urberville ancestry has a basis in the Dorset tradition of a haunted carriage that could only be seen by members of a family named Turberville. Narrative accounts by the heroine's two lovers of this spectral coach of ill-omen, in which a beautiful woman was once abducted and possibly murdered by a d'Urberville, heighten suspense around the fates of Tess and her lovers, which it obliquely fore-shadows. More profoundly, the fatal coach is also a microcosm symbolizing the prison-like universe ruled by Fate against which Hardy's archetypal heroine struggles. The ghost-coach in *Tess*, which functions both as a symbol of death and as an omen, epitomizes the role of supernatural belief in Hardy's fiction, which is to create the uncanny atmosphere of fatality and predetermination that characterizes Hardy's conception of a universe that is grotesquely indifferent to human striving.

As a narrative realist, Hardy did not generally grant the ghosts of his novels objective phenomenal existence; for the most part, they exist only as stories told by rustics and believers. Yet Hardy, in spite of his religious skepticism, was himself profoundly drawn to a belief in ghosts, and following his turn away from fiction toward poetry, Hardy became less coy about depicting ghostly phenomena, which acquire objective existence in his many ghost poems.

Hardy died in 1928, and his ashes are buried in Westminster Abbey. His heart is buried in the grave of his first wife, Emma Gifford, in Stinsford Churchyard.

Brian Johnson

See also: The Uncanny.

Further Reading

Firor, Ruth A. 1968. *Folkways in Thomas Hardy*. New York: Russell & Russell.

Gatrell, Simon. 2000. "Ghosts." In *Oxford Reader's Companion to Hardy*, edited by Norman Page, 138–139. New York: Oxford University Press.

Hardy, Thomas. [1911] 1967. "General Preface to the Novels and Poems." In *Thomas Hardy's Personal Writings*, edited by Harold Orel, 44–50. London: Macmillan.

Robson, Peter. 2011. "Thomas Hardy's Ghosts." *Tradition Today: The Journal for the Centre of English Traditional Heritage* 1: 26–34. http://centre-for-english-traditional-heritage.org/traditiontoday1a.html.

Schweik, Robert. 1999. "The Influence of Religion, Science, and Philosophy on Hardy's Writings." In *The Cambridge Companion to Thomas Hardy*, edited by Dale Kramer, 54–72. Cambridge: Cambridge University Press.

HARRIS, THOMAS (1940–)

Thomas Harris is a writer of Gothic thrillers. He was born in Jackson, Tennessee, and is most well known for creating the character of Hannibal Lecter. He has published five novels and currently resides in South Florida.

Harris started his writing career after graduating from Baylor University and working as a local newspaper reporter in Waco, Texas (something he had done while earning his English degree at Baylor). Jason Cowley notes that Harris spent time working for the Associated Press in New York "where he excelled as a crime reporter, showing an unusual curiosity in the finer details and nuances of the crimes he wrote about, no matter how bleak" (2006). In 1975 Harris published his first novel, *Black Sunday*, while also working as a reporter. It is a thriller about a terrorist attack on the Super Bowl using a blimp loaded with explosives. It met with only moderate success, but its rights were purchased by Hollywood. This gave Harris the freedom to write fiction for a living.

Harris's second book, *Red Dragon* (1981), features FBI profiler Will Graham assisting in the hunt for serial killer Francis Dolarhyde or "the Tooth Fairy." It also introduces the character of Hannibal Lecter as a psychopath that Graham must speak with in order to capture Dolarhyde. The novel is notable for its carefully detailed look into the world of FBI profiling. The research that Harris undertook for this was extensive; he even attended some behavioral science classes at the FBI Academy in Quantico. This detail-oriented focus became a signature element in Harris's writing, enhancing his horror with procedural realism and journalistic integrity.

In 1988 Harris made Lecter a major character in his next book, *The Silence of the Lambs*. This part of the Lecter series switched protagonists with the introduction of Clarice Starling as an FBI trainee who is asked to speak with the psychopath in order to find the serial killer, Buffalo Bill. The book was well received, winning the Bram Stoker and the Anthony awards for best novel. In 1991 it was adapted to film

---

Harris based the serial killer Buffalo Bill in *The Silence of the Lambs* on the real-life Ed Gein, who in 1950s Wisconsin murdered two women and robbed multiple graves to create a collection of costumes and memorabilia out of human female skin and body parts. Gein was likewise the inspiration for Norman Bates in Robert Bloch's *Psycho* (1959), Leatherface in the *Texas Chainsaw Massacre* movies, and several additional literary and cinematic serial killers and mass murderers.

Matt Cardin

by director Jonathan Demme, with Sir Anthony Hopkins taking on the role of Lecter. The film won several Oscars, including Best Picture and Best Director, and cemented Hannibal Lecter into American culture.

The third book in the Lecter series, *Hannibal* (1999), features Lecter returning to Clarice while also escaping the clutches of the deformed magnate Mason Verger. The novel's controversial ending, which involves Lecter brainwashing Clarice and taking her as a lover, divided critics and readers.

Harris's final venture into the Lecter world was a prequel titled *Hannibal Rising* (2006). It tells the story of a young Lecter extracting revenge on his sister's killers. This book met with mixed reviews, and it was suggested that the book was only written because movie producer Dino De Laurentiis intended to move forward on a cinematic version of the project with or without Harris's help.

Harris's work and his signature character of Hannibal Lecter were reconceptualized for television with the three-season run of NBC's *Hannibal* (2013–2015). Harris, known as a reclusive author, has not signaled an intent to publish another novel.

Chun H. Lee

See also: Bram Stoker Award; Psychological Horror.

Further Reading

Cowley, Jason. 2006. "Creator of a Monstrous Hit." *The Guardian*. https://www.theguardian.com/books/2006/nov/19/fiction.thomasharris.

Fierman, Daniel. 2007. "Hannibal Lecter Meets His End: One of the Best Horror Franchises in History Falls Apart." *Entertainment Weekly*. http://www.ew.com/article/2007/02/16/hannibal-lecter-meets-his-end.

Grixti, Joseph. 1995. "Consuming Cannibals: Psychopathic Killers as Archetypes and Cultural Icons." *Journal of American Culture* 18: 87–96.

Magistrale, Tony. 1996. "Transmogrified Gothic: The Novels of Thomas Harris." In *A Dark Night's Dreaming: Contemporary American Horror Fiction*, edited by Tony Magistrale and Michael A. Morrison, 27–41. Columbia: University of South Carolina Press.

HARTLEY, L. P. (1895–1972)

Leslie Poles Hartley was an English writer and reviewer who achieved considerable fame in the mid-twentieth century, especially for his 1953 novel *The Go-Between*, a best seller that was adapted multiple times for stage and screen. In addition to publishing popular novels, he wrote many short stories, thirty-seven of which are fantastic, often horrifically so.

Hartley's most horrific stories tend to work by indirection, a deliberate vagueness that adds emphasis to the horrors. The titular story of *Night Fears* (1924), his first collection, thus describes a secure and set night watchman whose snowy vigil is interrupted by a nameless stranger who, with but a few questions and sneers, destroys everything the watchman holds dear; the watchman commits suicide, and the stranger's departing footprints lead to a blind alley. "A Visitor from Down Under" (1926) uses clues and indirection to show a newly returned colonial being pursued, haunted, and ultimately removed by James Hagberd, the revenant of the man he murdered in Australia. In "Podolo" (1948) the peripherally seen horror may resemble an ape, but as the visitors to its island learn, it is devastatingly hungry and vicious.

Indirection likewise plays a role in "Someone in the Lift" (1955), which is told largely through a child's eyes: little Peter Maldon glimpses a shape in the elevator that no one else can see; he discovers its horrible identity on Christmas, when his father does not return. The admirably brief "The Waits" (1961) shows an apparently happy family visited by a pair of carolers on Christmas Eve: the ghosts of the people the father drove to murder and suicide. Several stories seem to pile on the horrors, then conclude just before anything is seen, letting the reader determine whether or not they are supernatural. For example, the nameless narrator of "A Summons" (1954) has agreed to assist his sister if she dreams of being murdered in her bed and knocks on the adjoining wall; he elects not to assist, and the knocking grows fainter and fainter. The question of what he will find remains unresolved, as it does in the marvelous "The Shadow on the Wall" (1969), in which houseguest Mildred Fanshawe learns that the room adjacent to hers is being held for the mysterious Count Olmütz. Fanshawe glimpses in the shadows a corpse with its throat cut, and from its head she recognizes it as a man she knows, but whether there is really a body is left unanswered; the story concludes with the opening of the count's door.

In his introduction to Lady Cynthia Asquith's *Third Ghost Book* (1955), Hartley provided a rationale of the ghost story: "even ghosts must have rules and obey them. In the past, they had certain traditional activities; they could squeak and gibber, for instance; they could clank chains. They were generally local, confined to one spot. Now their liberties have been greatly extended; they can go anywhere, they can manifest themselves in scores of ways" (Hartley 2001, xiii). For all that Hartley chose to show these manifestations, he recognized that too much horrific material can lose its effectiveness, and a black humor thus enlivens many stories: "The Travelling Grave" (1929), for example, contains a conversation in which baby carriages are confused with coffins. Death assumes physical reality in "Mrs. Carteret Receives" (1971), but he is very ordinary and prosaic, "ugly, dirty, and wet through" (Hartley 1986, 648).

In the past several decades, Hartley's stories have been made conveniently available to current readers in collected editions. Significantly for those who are interested in his fantastic and horrific writings, *The Collected Macabre Stories*, published by Tartarus Press in 2001, contains several stories that do not appear in *The Complete Short Stories of L. P. Hartley*, published by Beaufort (1973).

Richard Bleiler

See also: Arkham House; Machen, Arthur.

Further Reading

Athos, John. 2009. "L. P. Hartley and the Gothic Infatuation." In *Short Story Criticism*, vol. 125, edited by Jelena O. Krstovic. Detroit: Gale. Originally published in *Twentieth Century Literature* 7.4 (Jan. 1962): 172–179.

Hartley, L. P. 1986. *The Complete Short Stories of L. P. Hartley*. New York: Beaufort Books.

Hartley, L. P. 2001. *The Collected Macabre Stories*. Leyburn, UK: Tartarus Press.

Wright, Adrian. 2001. *Foreign Country: The Life of L. P. Hartley*. London and New York: Tauris Park.

HARVEST HOME

Harvest Home (1973) was the second novel by former Hollywood actor Thomas Tryon. It received both critical and popular acclaim, and is generally regarded as one of the most significant novels in the subgenre of rural horror. In the novel, myths that rural life is superior to urban life because it is more innocent and natural are inverted, along with gender roles. S. T. Joshi has described *Harvest Home* as "one of the great weird novels of our time, and a virtual textbook on how to update the form while simultaneously drawing upon history to lend texture and substance" (Joshi 2001, 200).

The plot is centered on Ned and Beth Constantine and their daughter, Kate, who move from New York City to Cornwall Coombe, Connecticut, a farming community whose inhabitants resist any changes to their longstanding way of life. These ways are derived from ancestry in Cornwall, England, where fertility rites were significant in growing corn as a staple crop. Ned, who narrates the novel, proves to be something of an unreliable narrator specifically in this area, because the information given to him about the longstanding traditions and practices of Harvest Home is oblique, and this contributes, with progressively increasing suspense, to the horror of the novel's final revelation.

The Constantines are initially welcomed into this usually closed community because the Widow Fortune—who has been mother, nurse, midwife, and overall guiding spirit to the community for many years—thinks that permitting them to move into Cornwall Coombe will provide new bloodlines to promote high-quality physical and mental health among the citizenry. Ned, however, is sterile, and this contributes to disharmony in his and Beth's marriage. Beth, for her part, proves receptive to the Widow Fortune's influence, which Ned finds increasingly oppressive and sinister. He does not readily comprehend or participate in Cornwall Coombe beliefs and customs, and thus he is ultimately ostracized and accorded drastic physical punishment for his scoffing at and interfering with "the old ways." Ironically, he does not realize that his efforts to befriend various persons, notably young Worthy Pettinger, who becomes the designated Harvest Lord for the community's climactic Harvest Festival that year—but who refuses to act as such—are deemed outrageous and dangerous by the locals. Several betrayals by community members, especially by several females (ultimately including Kate, who has adopted the area's traditions), lead to his downfall.

In the rural Gothic, pastoral settings are used for Gothic or horrific effects, often by placing city dwellers in a geographically and socially isolated pastoral environment where the local inhabitants and the landscape itself become the locus of a claustrophobic, "backwoods" type of horror as dark secrets and dreadful cultural practices are revealed. *Harvest Home* illustrates this pattern as Ned's probing of the mysteries of local life in Cornwall Coombe ultimately exposes physical and emotional violence and horrors, most appallingly in the novel's climactic scene, where Ned spies on a forest ceremony and discovers that the community's seasonal agricultural cycle is climaxed by a pagan ritual of human sacrifice. As the novel closes, Kate is teamed with local boy Jim Minerva, upcoming Harvest Lord, whose union with her will presumably produce offspring who will in turn contribute new life to the community. Kate is fully and joyfully enfolded within the community's life and traditions. And Ned inhabits his own home as a prisoner, having had his eyes put out for his transgression.

The idea of protagonists from late twentieth-century urban-technological societies stumbling upon evidence of pagan nature-based sacrificial rituals surviving in isolated rural locales was popular in early 1970s horror, with Robert Marasco's *Burnt Offerings* (1973) and writer Anthony Shaffer and director Robin Hardy's film *The Wicker Man* (1973) both being released the same year as *Harvest Home*, and both dealing with this very thing. A decade later, T. E. D. Klein's novel *The Ceremonies* (1984) mined the same territory. It has since become a recognized and established trope in the genre—a development that can be traced in no small part to the influence of *Harvest Home*.

Benjamin F. Fisher

See also: *Burnt Offerings*; *The Ceremonies*; *The Other*; Unreliable Narrator.

Further Reading

Joshi, S. T. 2001. *The Modern Weird Tale*, Jefferson, NC and London: McFarland.
"Thomas Tryon." 2003. *Contemporary Authors Online*. Detroit: Gale.

THE HAUNTED HOUSE OR CASTLE

A haunted house may be defined simply as a dwelling that is inhabited by or visited regularly by a ghost. But the variants of this—the building, the circumstances, the type of supernatural intrusion, and the potential physical and emotional repercussions—are limitless. As a classic trope and setting in horror literature, the haunted house or castle has thus been subjected to a multitude of variations.

As Sigmund Freud points out in his famous essay (1919), the very notion of "The Uncanny" could not exist without the concept of "home." The haunted house story has to have, needless to say, a house—or, as it may be, a castle, chateau, of other place of assumed safety. In terms of plot line, the haunted house has to be the nexus of a series of supernatural events, and the best tales have a backstory (the history behind the situation that exists at the start of the main story) of the provenance and discovery of these events.

Horace Walpole (1717–1797) first elevated the haunted castle from a mere setting to part of the narrative fabric in *The Castle of Otranto* (1764). Clara Reeve's *The Old English Baron* (1778) contributed skeletal remains under the floor, weird portraits turned toward the wall, and a suit of bloodstained armor. Ann Radcliffe developed these motifs to the fullest in her signature work *The Mysteries of Udolpho* (1794).

The House of the Seven Gables (1851) is the father of the modern haunted house novel. Nathaniel Hawthorne weaves the theme so finely into the fabric of the story that it dominates the novel without overpowering the plot and characterizations. J. Sheridan Le Fanu has several masterly instances of the haunted house. In "Ghost Stories of the Tiled House" (1861), a woman is literally scared to death in what may be the worst possible encounter of its kind. Even infants—as in "An Account of Some Strange Disturbances in Aungier Street" (1853) and "The Narrative of the Ghost of a Hand" (1863)—are not spared Le Fanu's terrors. "Who Knows?" (French: "Qui sait?"; 1890) is a haunted house tale that is both horrifying and amusing in manner unique to Guy de Maupassant. Returning at night from the theater, the solitary narrator feels uneasy as he approaches his house and hears a commotion. Then he realizes what the noise is: all his possessions are animate and fleeing his domicile. His efforts to recover them are correspondingly eerie.

The twentieth century saw new variants of the traditional theme. In Walter de la Mare's "A Recluse" (1926), the narrator is out for an automobile ride, but is compelled to pull over to look at what appears to be an unoccupied house. Ray Bradbury created a poignant new variant in "There Will Come Soft Rains" (1950): a mechanized house that can speak and maintain itself expires after its human occupants are vaporized by a nuclear explosion.

Shirley Jackson's *The Haunting of Hill House* (1959), widely recognized as the greatest haunted house novel, is emphatically supernatural in its premise: four individuals sensitive to psychic phenomena come to Hill House to analyze its odd manifestations, and one seems to become so psychically fused with the house that she is unable to leave it. The novel was adapted to film in *The Haunting* (1963). Robert Marasco's *Burnt Offerings* (1973) is a haunted house novel perhaps second only to Jackson's. In it, a family rents a strange old house for an unusually cheap rate. There is an elderly woman upstairs who is never seen. The wife becomes attached to the woman and to the house, which seems to regenerate in threatening ways. The novel was adapted by Hollywood in 1973. Richard Matheson's *Hell House* (1971) has a plot roughly similar to Jackson's *Hill House*—four people gather in a purportedly haunted house to investigate—and was adapted for film in the 1973 British production *The Legend of Hell House*.

The haunted house story has proved amazingly flexible in accommodating a wide variety of themes: good versus evil, science versus the supernatural, economic conflict, class, gender, and so on. Over three centuries, the theme has been a compelling vehicle for the horror narrative, and it will doubtless continue to be so.

Steven J. Mariconda

See also: Bulwer-Lytton, Edward; *Burnt Offerings*; *The Castle of Otranto*; de la Mare, Walter; *The Haunting of Hill House*; *Hell House*; *The House of the Seven Gables*; Le Fanu, J. Sheridan; Maupassant, Guy de; *The Mysteries of Udolpho*; The Uncanny; *Part Two, Themes, Topics, and Genres*: Ghost Stories.

Further Reading

Bailey, Dale. 2011. *American Nightmares: The Haunted House Formula in American Popular Fiction*. Madison: University of Wisconsin Press.

Janicker, Rebecca. 2015. *The Literary Haunted House: Lovecraft, Matheson, King and the Horror in Between*. Jefferson NC: McFarland.

Mariconda, Steven J. 2007. "The Haunted House." In *Icons of Horror and the Supernatural: An Encyclopedia of Our Worst Nightmares*, edited by S. T. Joshi, 267–306. Westport and London: Greenwood Press.

Railo, Eino. 1927. *The Haunted Castle: A Study of the Elements of English Romanticism*. London: G. Routledge & Son.

THE HAUNTING OF HILL HOUSE

The Haunting of Hill House is a Gothic novel written by Shirley Jackson, first published in 1959 by Viking/Penguin. In the novel, Jackson created Hill House, which has come to be the prototype for the haunted house. The book not only helped secure Jackson's legacy as a horror writer, earning her a nomination for the 1960 National Book Award for Fiction, but it also inspired decades of writers to pen their own ghost stories.

Jackson's novel is the quintessential haunted house story. A group of people is invited to Hill House, an old mansion, by Dr. Montague, a specialist in the occult hoping to prove the existence of a true haunting. Among his guests are Eleanor, a young woman seeking a place in the world; Theodora, a free spirit; and Luke, the heir to Hill House. The story is largely told from Eleanor's perspective, and Jackson spends a great deal of time examining Eleanor's relationship with Theodora. Both women are unique in that they explode the traditional gender roles of the day (neither woman is the typical wife and mother that would be considered the norm). These psychic detectives encounter what has now become commonplace in haunted house tales: unexpected cold spots, mysterious and ominous messages scribbled on the wall, a child's cry when no children are around. Jackson deviates from the traditional haunted house tropes by introducing Eleanor as an unstable and unreliable witness, leaving readers to speculate whether the haunting is indeed real or only a manifestation of a troubled mind. In this way, *The Haunting of Hill House* could be considered the literary heir to Henry James's ghost story *The Turn of the Screw*, in

---

Ghost Hunters

The Haunting of Hill House has been adapted twice by Hollywood, first in 1963 by director Robert Wise and again in 1999 by director Jan de Bont, both times under the title *The Haunting*. But its cinematic influence extends much further, as its central motif of paranormal investigators taking up residence in a supposedly haunted house to investigate purportedly supernatural events has been seized upon by countless additional movies and television shows. From the 1973 horror film *The Legend of Hell House* (based on Richard Matheson's 1971 novel, which took direct inspiration from Jackson) to the twenty-first century's bumper crop of "ghost hunting" paranormal shows on cable television, Shirley Jackson's most famous novel casts a long shadow across the landscape of subsequent paranormal media. This is despite the fact that she did not originate the theme in question, whose earliest clear incarnation may be Edward Bulwer-Lytton's 1859 story "The Haunted and the Haunters," which likewise has an investigator stay in a haunted house. There is also a long tradition of occult detectives and paranormal investigators in horror fiction hailing from the century between the publication of Bulwer's story and the publication of Jackson's 1959 novel. But *The Haunting of Hill House* remains the most prominent and influential such work.

Matt Cardin

---

which readers are never told whether the ghosts that plagued the governess and her two charges are real or not. Jackson was intrigued with psychic phenomenon and those who studied it; it was a scholarly interest for much of her adult life. She had the idea of writing a ghost story after learning about the Society for Psychic Research, a nineteenth-century group formed to study the possibility of ghosts. One such group rented a house that was rumored to be haunted for exactly such a purpose; once Jackson read the account, Hill House was born.

Hill House and the people who come to study the mansion have become the prototype for nearly every haunted house story that has followed the first printing of Jackson's book. Richard Matheson's *Hell House*, published in 1971, and the film adaptation that followed (*The Legend of Hell House*, 1973) are both greatly influenced by Jackson's story. Matheson's Belasco House, like Hill House, is haunted, and like Hill House, it draws a team of psychic researchers. Unlike Jackson, however, Matheson favored shock over subtlety, making the ghosts in the house undeniably real. The idea of the house that was "born bad" (as opposed to human monsters or some other outside evil) became prevalent in the horror novels of the following decades. Anne Rivers Siddons's *The House Next Door* (1978) deviates in that the house in question is not an old Gothic manor—it's a sleek modern design—but the premise is still the same: the house is a living, breathing organism that has evil intent toward any occupants who dare to step across the threshold. Stephen King has mentioned his admiration for Shirley Jackson in his nonfiction book on the horror genre, *Danse Macabre* (1981), and readers can see the influence of *The Haunting of Hill House* throughout his works. Both the novel (and the later film) *The Shining* (1977) and the television miniseries *Rose Red* (2002) feature remote places that attract the paranormal. King's novel *Carrie* (1974) even includes a brief nod to *Hill House*'s Eleanor: both Carrie and Eleanor have experienced psychic phenomena at a young age, specifically in the form of rocks raining down on the roofs of their childhood homes.

In 1963, director Robert Wise brought Jackson's novel to the silver screen with his adaptation, *The Haunting*. Wise cast Julie Harris as Eleanor and Claire Bloom as Theodora. The film was a critical success and earned Wise a Golden Globe nomination for best director. In 2014, Wise's film was nominated for a Saturn Award by the Academy of Science Fiction, Fantasy, and Horror Films. In 1999, director Jan de Bont made another adaptation of *The Haunting of Hill House*, likewise titled *The Haunting*. Though the film was cast with popular stars (Liam Neeson, Catherine Zeta Jones, Owen Wilson), de Bont's film was not met with the same critical acclaim.

Lisa Kröger

See also: The Haunted House or Castle; *Hell House*; *The House Next Door*; Jackson, Shirley; *The Shining*; *The Turn of the Screw*; Unreliable Narrator.

Further Reading

Anderson, Melanie R. 2016. "Perception, Supernatural Detection, and Gender in *The Haunting of Hill House*." In *Shirley Jackson, Influences and Confluences*, edited by Melanie R. Anderson and Lisa Kröger, 35–53. London: Routledge.

Haggerty, George E. 2006. "'Queer Company': *The Turn of the Screw* and *The Haunting of Hill House*." In *Queer Gothic*, 131–150. Urbana: University of Illinois Press.

Hattenhauer, Darryl. 2003. *Shirley Jackson's American Gothic*. Albany: State University of New York Press.

Hodges Holt, Shari. 2016. "The Tower or the Nursery? Paternal and Maternal Re-visions of Hill House on Film." In *Shirley Jackson, Influences and Confluences*, edited by Melanie R. Anderson and Lisa Kröger, 160–182. London: Routledge.

King, Stephen. [1981] 2010. *Danse Macabre*. New York: Gallery Books.

Lootens, Tricia. 2005. "'Whose Hand Was I Holding?': Familial and Sexual Politics in Shirley Jackson's *The Haunting of Hill House*." In *Shirley Jackson: Essays on the Literary Legacy*, edited by Bernice M. Murphy, 150–168. Jefferson, NC: McFarland.

Wilson, Michael T. 2015. "'Absolute Reality' and the Role of the Ineffable in Shirley Jackson's *The Haunting of Hill House*." *Journal of Popular Culture* 48.1: 114–123.

HAWTHORNE, NATHANIEL (1804–1864)

Born Nathaniel Hathorne in Salem, Massachusetts, Hawthorne, like Jane Austen, E. T. A. Hoffmann, Honoré de Balzac, and Alexander Pushkin, is a major nineteenth-century writer from European traditions whose work is speckled with but

"Rappaccini's Daughter": A Poisonous Beauty

Nathaniel Hawthorne's "Rappaccini's Daughter: From the Writings of Aubépine" (1844) was initially published alongside Edgar Allan Poe marginalia. The tale's fore-matter presents it as the work of a Gallicized persona of Hawthorne. This sixth-to-final piece of Hawthorne's short fiction culminates prior themes of scientists and inventors tampering with dangerous forces in other tales that were likewise collected in his *Mosses from an Old Manse* (1846), such as "The Birth-Mark" (1843) and "The Artist of the Beautiful" (1844). Beatrice Rappaccini, as a dying and deadly beautiful woman, literalizes a literary commonplace from contemporaries such as Louisa May Alcott and Poe.

The tale offers deep ambiguities. Student Giovanni Guascontis falls in love with Beatrice, daughter of Dr. Giacomo Rappaccini, after spying on her in her father's garden. Having grown up in the presence of the poisonous plants cultivated by her father, Beatrice is herself poisonous, so flowers and insects die upon her touch. Giovanni's feelings for Beatrice alternate between desire, loathing, and confusion, even as he himself becomes poisonous in Beatrice's father's secret experiment. A rival of Rappaccini gives Giovanni an antidote to save Beatrice, but the attempted cure kills her. The tale occurs in Padua, Italy, of unclear date, and alludes to Genesis, *Mudrarakshasa*, *The Divine Comedy*, *Macbeth*, *The Anatomy of Melancholy*, *Paradise Lost*, *St. Leon*, and *Frankenstein*.

The tale informs Oliver Holmes's romance of serpentine original sin, *Elsie Venner* (1861). Adaptations of it occur in poetry, operas, plays, radio, television, and popular music, and the Rappaccinis inspired several comic book antiheroines and villainesses. A cinematic adaptation, *Twice-Told Tales* (1963), is part of the U.S. and U.K. 1960s–1970s trend of horror anthology films. The tale's segment, unlike the others, somewhat follows Hawthorne's plot and characterizations but dampens the scientists' rivalry, irradiates Beatrice's blood, has Vincent Price play Giacomo in a mode more Freudian and Puritan, and climaxes with a triple suicide.

Bob Hodges

not exhausted by Gothic effects and supernatural overtones. In his twenties, Hawthorne added a letter to his surname (much as fellow Gothic regionalist William Faulkner would do about a century later). He almost suppressed his anonymous first Gothic romance, *Fanshawe* (1828), after its commercial failure. *Romance* is a term Hawthorne used for novel-length fictions in marvelous or imaginative modes beyond the strict, mannered realism he saw novels demand.

Hawthorne toiled on tales and literary sketches in the 1830s and 1840s for initially obscure publications, until collected reprints began to attract critical and commercial notice. *Twice-Told Tales* (2 vols., 1837, 1842), *Mosses from an Old Manse* (1846, expanded 1854), and *The Snow-Image, and Other Twice-Told Tales* (1852) collect the bulk of his short fiction. Hawthorne follows Washington Irving in using detailed U.S. locales and histories for his tales, something New England predecessors John Neal, Catharine Maria Sedgwick, and Lydia Maria Child also explored in their longer romances.

Some of the best commentary on Hawthorne comes from his successors: Herman Melville, Henry James, H. P. Lovecraft, and Jorge Luis Borges. Lovecraft in *Supernatural Horror in Literature* (1927) draws an extended contrast between the short fiction of Hawthorne and his contemporary Edgar Allan Poe. Poe represents a more calculated and impersonal supernatural fiction aimed at producing specific horrific effects on the reader often via violence, sensation, a general sense of cosmic indifference, and/or more indefinite, hence universal, settings and situations. In contrast, Hawthorne's supernatural fiction poses indefinite but persistent allegory, melancholy, specific regional and historical detail, and concern with possibly irredeemable human sin and worldly evil. Lovecraft sees Poe as the paramount artist of modern horror, but his extensive treatment of Hawthorne evidences the latter's influence on the weird. The seminal pulp magazine *Weird Tales* often reprinted nineteenth-century U.S. supernatural fiction and poetry before 1940, and they ran eight of Hawthorne's tales, more than any writer except Poe.

Several Gothic Hawthorne tales stage ambivalent encounters for the reader with revolutionary violence. In "My Kinsman, Major Molineux" (1832) Robin undertakes a confused, surreal, nocturnal journey within eighteenth-century Boston to find the titular kinsman and the advancement he offers. Robin finds his corrupt kinsman tarred, feathered, and led by a mob with a satanic Janus-faced figure at its head, which presages philosopher Walter Benjamin's Janus-like angel in "Theses on the Philosophy of History" (1940). The ghostly title figure of "The Gray Champion" (1835) manifests to spur on Puritans at key moments of political violence. The internal splits between Congress-men and King's men and the latter's doomed cause in the U.S. revolution are symbolized via a revel (which was influential on Poe's "The Masque of the Red Death" [1842]), a satanic portrait, a pestilent piece of aristocratic dress, and a timely death in Hawthorne's four-part "Legends of the Province House" (collected together 1842): "Howe's Masquerade" (1838), "Edward Randolph's Portrait" (1838), "Lady Eleanore's Mantle" (1838), and "Old Esther Dudley" (1839). "Earth's Holocaust" (1844) speculates on humanity's either past or future immolation of all tokens of political, sexual, militarist, penal, economic, literary, and religious authority.

Hawthorne's short fictions' major theme offers various haunting yet obscure epiphanies that vex characters' relations with their intimates as well as their society and its values. "Young Goodman Brown" (1835) recounts the shattering effect on the seventeenth-century Puritan title character's religious, social, and marital faiths (his wife is even named Faith) after a nocturnal forest experience or dream of a satanic encounter and a witches' sabbath. The eighteenth-century Rev. Hooper veils himself in "The Minister's Black Veil" (1836) for life and even burial against a never specified sin with seeming sexual overtones. His veil feminizes him, breaks his engagement, and makes him a social pariah. Originally intended for a longer romance, the title character of "Ethan Brand" (1850) returns home after a long, successful search for an unpardonable sin that he found within his own intellect.

One of Hawthorne's most overt ventures into the didactic is "Dr. Heidegger's Experiment" (1837), for the titular scientist's sociological experiment hinges on the short-term Fountain of Youth. Perhaps Hawthorne's most interesting film adaptation, *Twice-Told Tales* (1963), ironically adapts only that tale from the collection along with "Rappaccini's Daughter" (1844) and Hawthorne's second major romance *The House of the Seven Gables* (1851). The *Twice-Told Tales* film participates in the 1960s–1970s U.S. and U.K. trend of horror anthology films and stars Vincent Price in the midst of his ten-film cycle of (loose) Poe adaptations (1960–1969). Consequently, the segment for "Dr. Heidegger's Experiment" alters the tale into a romantic, Poe-esque rivalry between old friends over corpse preservation and resurrection occasioned by mysterious water.

Despite his central concern with sin, Hawthorne explored many variants of the Gothic. The frontier Gothic "Roger Malvin's Burial" (1832) offers the failure of funerary rites for its title character in the Fourth Anglo-Abenaki War in what is now Maine. The riddle story "Mr. Higginbotham's Catastrophe" (1834) centers upon a murder mystery. It and London's simultaneous moral confusion and intimate surveillance in "Wakefield" (1835) anticipate Poe's proto-detective tale "The Man of the Crowd" (1840) and subsequent detective fiction. "The White Old Maid" (1835) is near to a traditional ghost story, and its emphasis on unsettling feminine mourning anticipates Faulkner's "A Rose for Emily" (1930). "Feathertop" (1852) follows the Gothic tradition of asexual reproduction and synthetic life from Hoffmann's "The Sand-man" (1817) and Mary Shelley's *Frankenstein* (1818). A witch animates the title character, a scarecrow that thinks it is a man, to court a judge's daughter for an unspecified revenge. "Feathertop" is one of the most adapted Hawthorne tales, both in its original form and as extended into Percy MacKaye's stage melodrama *The Scarecrow* (1908), which adds sentiment and Satan. Hawthorne was an early U.S. speculative fiction writer with tales such as "The Birth-Mark" (1843), "The Artist of the Beautiful" (1844), and "Rappaccini's Daughter," but Feathertop's smoking iconography influences the titular automaton of the first science fiction dime novel, Edward Ellis's *The Steam Man of the Prairies* (1868).

Hawthorne's first three years of the 1850s mark one of the most impressive productive periods of any U.S. writer; in addition to his final achievements in short fiction like "Ethan Brand" and "Feathertop," he released his first three major romances: *The Scarlet Letter* (1850), *The House of the Seven Gables*, and *The Blithedale Romance* (1852). *The Scarlet Letter* presents itself, in the Gothic tradition of James Macpherson and Horace Walpole, as a found manuscript, incorporating historical figures of seventeenth-century Boston and the sinister forest surrounding it. The colony's Puritan authorities impose the eponymous scarlet "A" upon Hester Prynne for her adultery and refusal to name the father of her infant daughter Pearl. But the ambivalent symbol also has enchanted and artistic overtones, and a few years later it provides a strange communion for Pearl, an impish and religiously irreverent child. *The Scarlet Letter* is one of the most striking treatments of crime and punishment in U.S. literature, with scenes of Hester's social exclusion and her and later her secret lover's suffering on the scaffold. Hester's lover, Rev. Arthur Dimmesdale, is mercilessly shadowed by her cuckold, the sinister scholar and physician Roger Chillingworth. The reverend's and the doctor's scenario follows the combination of demonic malignancy and homoerotic intimacy within Gothic romances like *Frankenstein* and Charles Maturin's *Melmoth the Wanderer* (1820).

The Blithedale Romance (1852), a *roman à clef*, fictionalizes Hawthorne's time at the 1840s Brook Farm commune, based upon Charles Fourier's utopian socialism. The romance is Hawthorne's brightest and least Gothic, but its narrator remains dissatisfied with rural idiocy and toil in its commune as well as alienated, modern Boston. Of the two major female characters during the romance's climax, one is unveiled as the mysterious mesmerist referenced throughout, and the other, driven by a striking but unclear provocation, drowns herself. The recovery of the rigid, drowned corpse provides the most haunting scene. Hawthorne's romance likely influenced George Eliot's novella *The Lifted Veil* (1859) given their shared enervated, acute male protagonists; independent women seen as inscrutable and fatal; ingratiating, transgressive scientists; and twining of clairvoyance with modern media technology.

The House of the Seven Gables exerted a profound influence on New World Gothic and New England horror writers. But perhaps Hawthorne's most underappreciated achievement is his final complete long work. *The Marble Faun* (1860) combines Gothic romance, a novel of artists, and an Italian travelogue from Hawthorne's and his family's tour abroad. *The Marble Faun* culminates tendencies toward urban Gothic in his prior major romances and tales like "Molineux" and "Wakefield." Its descriptions of the Eternal City render Rome's catacombs and carnival as a sprawling web for his characters, at once inspiration and ensnarement. Hawthorne's intricate Roman cityscape anticipates Sigmund Freud's extended metaphor in *Civilization and Its Discontents* (1930), conjoining the psychoanalytic concept of the unconscious to the city's fragmentary and sometimes unexpected preservation of its long architectural history. The romance's plot concerns three young U.S. fine artists and the Italian count of Monte Beni. Following the mold of Walter Scott and James Fenimore Cooper, Hawthorne contrasts his two female painters. Miriam, the archetypal Dark Lady, is speculated to be of Jewish-, German-, or Afro-American ancestry with a sinister past. Joyful Count Donatello, thought to be part human and part faun, falls in love with Miriam, who inadvertently suborns him into murdering a mysterious figure from her past. The painter-copyist Hilda, the Fair Maiden, is an innocent but dreadfully harsh in her judgment of Donatello and Miriam for this crime. She is loved by the sculptor Kenyon. This romance of secret sin and ambiguous enthrallment informs Louisa May Alcott's late thrillers involving foreign liaisons and artists as well as Henry James's narratives of artists, U.S. expatriates, and tourists in Italy, despite his critical reservations about this particular Hawthorne work. The complex overlays of different narratives and its vivid descriptions of place and art make *The Marble Faun* a sophisticated elevation of Hawthorne's Gothic project.

Ill health in his last years limited Hawthorne's writing, but he left several variant manuscripts for two different romance narratives, one inspired by his consular service in England and a superstition about an ancestral curse of bloody footprints as well as another concerning the Elixir of Life in revolutionary Concord. Some of these variants were posthumously published in the nineteenth century. He died in his sleep in 1864 and is buried at Authors' Ridge in Sleepy Hollow Cemetery at Concord, Massachusetts, near Louisa May Alcott and many other renowned U.S. writers. He was survived by his wife Sophia, née Amelia Peabody, a fine artist and diarist. They had three children: Una, who edited one of her father's manuscripts but died young; Julian, a notable writer and editor of romances and mysteries; and Rose, a poet and later a nun.

Bob Hodges

See also: Alcott, Louisa May; Ancestral Curse; Gothic Hero/Villain; The Haunted House or Castle; *The House of the Seven Gables*; Lovecraft, H. P.; Mad Scientist; Poe, Edgar Allan; Romanticism and Dark Romanticism; *Weird Tales*; "Young Goodman Brown."

Further Reading

Bidney, Martin. 2008. "Fire, Flutter, Fall, and Scatter: A Structure in the Epiphanies of Hawthorne's Tales." *Texas Studies in Literature and Language* 50, no. 1: 58–89.

Brodhead, Richard. 1990. Introduction to *The Marble Faun*, ix–xxix. NY: Penguin, 1990.

Elbert, Monika. 2008. "Dying to Be Heard: Morality and Aesthetics in Alcott's and Hawthorne's Tableaux Morts." In *Death Becomes Her: Cultural Narratives of Femininity and Death in Nineteenth-Century America*, edited by Elizabeth Dill and Sheri Weinstein, 19–36. Newcastle: Cambridge.

Lovecraft, H. P. [1927] 2012. *The Annotated Supernatural Horror in Literature*. Edited by S. T. Joshi. New York: Hippocampus Press.

Pearson, Leland. 2007. *The Cambridge Introduction to Nathaniel Hawthorne*. Cambridge: Cambridge University Press, 2007.

Twice-Told Tales. 2005. DVD. Dir. Sidney Salkow. 1963. Beverly Hills, CA: MGM Midnite Movies.

Wineapple, Brenda. 2003. *Hawthorne: A Life*. New York: Random House.

HEARN, LAFCADIO (1850–1904)

Best remembered today for his volume of Japanese ghost stories *Kwaidan: Stories and Studies of Strange Things* (1904), Patrick Lafcadio Tessima Carlos Hearn was in his day the chief interpreter of Japanese culture and literature for Western audiences. In Japan he is still well regarded, although considered old-fashioned. Like many Westerners of the era, he took a romantic view of the Orient, celebrating its ancient and traditional culture at precisely the time (particularly in Japan) when that culture was vanishing in the face of rapid modernization. His writings hover on the borderline between folklore and literature, a mixture of translation, retelling, and his own embellishments.

Hearn was born on the Greek isle of Lefkada to an Irish father and a Greek mother. The father soon abandoned the family. Hearn was raised in Dublin for a time, then sent to school in France and England. He lost sight in one eye during a schoolyard "accident" in England, which may have been an incident of bullying. He was essentially dumped in America, penniless, and left to make his way. After enduring great poverty and sleeping on the streets, he eventually became a journalist in Cincinnati, where he specialized in accounts of lurid crimes and other salacious stories. He married a black woman, Alethea Foley, which was illegal at the time.

The Touch of Nightmare

One of Hearn's most fascinating contributions to the literature of horror is a little piece— part story, part essay, part memoir—titled "Nightmare-Touch." Collected in his book *Shadowings* (1900), it sets out to examine the question of why, exactly, people are afraid of ghosts. Hearn's answer is penetrating and highly memorable:

> Nowhere do I remember reading a plain statement of the reason why ghosts are feared. Ask any ten intelligent persons of your acquaintance, who remember having once been afraid of ghosts, to tell you exactly why they were afraid,—to define the fancy behind the fear;—and I doubt whether even one will be able to answer the question.
>
> . . . Now I venture to state boldly that the common fear of ghosts is *the fear of being touched by ghosts*,—or, in other words, that the imagined Supernatural is dreaded mainly because of its power to touch. Only to *touch*, remember!—not to wound or to kill.
>
> But this dread of the touch would itself be the result of experience,—chiefly, I think, of prenatal experience stored up in the individual by inheritance, like the child's fear of darkness. And who can ever have had the sensation of being touched by ghosts? The answer is simple:—*Everybody who has been seized by phantoms in a dream.*
>
> Elements of primeval fears—fears older than humanity—doubtless enter into the child-terror of darkness. But the more definite fear of ghosts may very possibly be composed with inherited results of dream-pain,—ancestral experience of nightmare. And the intuitive terror of supernatural touch can thus be evolutionally explained. (Hearn 2010, 224–225)

Matt Cardin

Source: Hearn, Lafcadio. [1900] 2010. "Nightmare-Touch." In *The Penguin Book of Ghost Stories: From Elizabeth Gaskell to Ambrose Bierce,* edited by Michael Newton, 224–230. New York: Penguin Classics.

This "scandal" cost him his job and brought more poverty. The marriage was not a success. He continued as a journalist and moved to New Orleans, and also spent some time on the island of Martinique, where his extensive writings about these places brought him some measure of fame.

Hearn always had a taste for the bizarre and colorful, and he gathered much supernatural lore. A collection of writings from this period, *Fantastics* (1914), contains stories and prose sketches, some of them developed into full stories, all in a florid, poetic style. He published several highly regarded translations, including translations of Théophile Gautier's *One of Cleopatra's Nights* (1838) and Gustave Flaubert's *The Temptation of St. Anthony* (1874).

By this time he had already showed an interest in the Orient, retelling Chinese legends as *Some Chinese Ghosts* (1887), but when Harper & Brothers sent him to Japan in 1890 to write books and magazine articles, he fell in love with the country and stayed there, eventually becoming a Japanese citizen. His Japanese tales, found in such books as *Kwaidan, Shadowings* (1900), *In Ghostly Japan* (1899), *Kotto* (1902), *The Romance of the Milky Way* (1905), and others are of great interest to connoisseurs of the fantastic and horrifying. His wandering samurai, Buddhist priests, and ordinary peasants are constantly encountering malevolent ghosts, faceless demons, a lethal female snow demon, vampire-like creatures whose heads detach and fly around at night, a corpse-eating ghost that is the spirit of a greedy priest punished for his sins, and many more spooks and situations unfamiliar to Western readers, all told in beautiful prose, which becomes more spare and restrained in Hearn's later period. Also of interest is his 1898 lecture "The Value of the Supernatural in Fiction," in which he argues that both tales of the supernatural and real-world beliefs in supernatural phenomena have their origin in dreams and nightmares.

Darrell Schweitzer

See also: Devils and Demons; Gautier, Théophile; *Kwaidan: Stories and Studies of Strange Things*; Vampires.

Further Reading

Hakutani, Yoshinobu. 1898. "(Patricio) Lafcadio (Tessima Carlos) Hearn." In *American Short-Story Writers, 1880–1910*, edited by Bobby Ellen Kimbel and William E. Grant. *Dictionary of Literary Biography* Vol. 78. Detroit: Gale.

Hearn, Lafcadio. [1898] 2008. "The Value of the Supernatural in Fiction." In *"A Hideous Bit of Morbidity": An Anthology of Horror Criticism from the Enlightenment to World War I*, edited by Jason Colavito, 267–278. Jefferson, NC, and London: McFarland.

McWilliams, Vera, 1946. *Lafcadio Hearn*. Boston: Houghton Mifflin.

HELL HOUSE

Richard Matheson's *Hell House* is a 1971 horror novel about four individuals—physicist/parapsychologist Professor Lionel Barrett, his wife, Edith; and two spirit mediums, Benjamin Fischer and Florence Tanner—employed by a wealthy, dying man named Rolf Rudolph Deutsch to investigate whether there really is life after death. As part of this enterprise, they must enter Maine's notorious Belasco House, possibly the most haunted house on Earth, and live there for a week in order to divine whatever secrets of immortality it may contain, to be rewarded later with a sum of $100,000 as compensation for enduring its reputed horrors. As is related in the book, the place earned its reputation as "Hell House" due to the diabolical activities of the previous owner, Emeric Belasco.

As the inquiry proceeds—contrasting the scientific observations of the disturbing phenomena (via Barrett) with the otherworldly aspects of what might be happening (by way of the medium Tanner)—the characters are attacked by the evil dwelling in the house, as the malevolent forces attempt to prey on each individual's personal fears and weaknesses. The author later adapted the novel into a film, *The Legend of Hell House* (1973).

Though arguably one of Matheson's better known works—a fact that is at least partly due to the popularity of the film adaptation—it is also one of his weakest offerings (something Matheson acknowledged in later interviews). The characters seem dated in retrospect, and the story drags in the second half of the book. But the main weakness is the way Matheson chose to express the notion of evil via sex and gratuitous violence. There is a distracting preoccupation with "corrupt" sexual acts (mainly in the guise of lesbianism and orgies), along with scenes of overt (and grisly) violence, both of which are uncharacteristic of the author's normal output, and which are unconvincingly rendered in places, probably due to his discomfort with such blatant demonstrations in his work. The end result is a mixed affair, and more than one reader has come away from the book disappointed and comparing the final reading experience unfavorably to author Shirley Jackson's seminal work, *The Haunting of Hill House* (1959), which Matheson himself noted later as an influence, though he was not conscious of it at the time he wrote the novel. In the end, Jackson was better able to instill a feeling of dread and fear than Matheson achieves, effectively bridging the divide between a classic Gothic tradition (especially Poe) and the modern sensibilities of jaded audiences who, by the time of *Hill House* (the late 1950s), had been exposed to the brutal horrors of two World Wars and the blossoming of the mass media with its increasingly bold radio, cinematic, and television fare. Possibly only Peter Straub, author of 1979's *Ghost Story*, would consistently approach Jackson's work in this area, but not until the mid-1970s/1980s.

Hell House undoubtedly has its adherents. Dean Koontz praised it and predicted its endurance as a major novel of supernatural horror in an introduction written for one edition of the book and later reprinted in editors Stanley Wiater, Matthew R. Bradley, and Paul Stuve's *The Twilight Zone and Other Zones: The Dark Worlds of Richard Matheson*. Laudatory blurbs from the likes of Straub and Stephen King were printed on some of the book's various published editions, with the latter declaring that it "may be the scariest haunted house novel ever written." Nevertheless, *Hell*

House could be judged a rare miss for Matheson, if success is measured in terms of content and relevance.

Jason V Brock

See also: The Haunted House or Castle; *The Haunting of Hill House*; Matheson, Richard.

Further Reading

Bradley, Matthew R. 2010. "Richard Matheson—Storyteller: Fresh Hell." Tor.com, November 9. http://www.tor.com/2010/11/09/richard-matheson-storyteller-fresh-hell.

Koontz, Dean. 2009. "Introduction to Hell House." In *The Twilight and Other Zones: The Dark Worlds of Richard Matheson*, edited by Stanley Wiater, Matthew R. Bradley, and Paul Stuve, 100–107. New York: Citadel Press Books.

Pulliam, June M., and Fonseca, Anthony J. 2016. *Richard Matheson's Monsters: Gender in the Stories, Scripts, Novels, and Twilight Zone Episodes.* Lanham, MD: Rowman & Littlefield Publishing Group.

HERBERT, JAMES (1943–2013)

James John Herbert was an English writer of horror fiction who achieved fame with his first novel, *The Rats*, in 1974. Over a 40-year career he became Britain's best-selling author of popular fiction, and his novels played a significant role in the horror publishing boom of the 1970s through the 1990s.

Herbert was born in London in 1943, the son of market stall traders, and grew up in the postwar bomb-damaged East End area of Whitechapel. Having studied graphic design and printing, he worked for an advertising agency in London, and it was there that he wrote *The Rats*, which was an instant best seller upon its publication. He went on to publish twenty-three more novels during his career, plus two nonfiction books and a graphic novel.

In his landmark survey of the horror genre, *Danse Macabre*, Stephen King describes Herbert as "probably the best writer of pulp horror fiction to come along since the death of Robert E. Howard" (King 1981, 336). King suggests that the way Herbert approaches horror is uncompromising: Herbert "seizes us by the lapels and begins to scream in our faces" (339), and this became evident early in his career. In books such as *The Rats*, *The Fog* (1975), and *The Dark* (1980), Herbert reveled in graphic depictions of violence, including a gym teacher stripped and beaten to death by his aroused students, a child eaten by rats, and an entire football stadium crowd descending into frenzied murder. King felt the need to defend Herbert, who he said was held in "remarkably low esteem by writers in the genre" (336). Arguably it was this tendency toward the explicit that branded Herbert the lesser, more "pulpy" writer, yet a lack of critical appreciation was compensated for by popularity. At the time of his death, Herbert had sold more than 50 million books.

Herbert shattered the British tradition of historically set, Gothic-inflected horror featuring middle-class intellectual heroes and aristocratic monsters. Instead, his stories are contemporary, urban, and working class. His main characters are mostly ordinary, professional men who are ill-equipped to deal with the forces against them, from bodyguard Liam Halloran facing ancient Sumerian evil in *Sepulchre* (1987) to the sleazy paparazzo Joe Creed beset by disenfranchised demons in *Creed* (1990).

Often these characters' investigations lead them from their London flats to large country estates, blue-collar men drawn into the murky world of the wealthy country elite, and Herbert never shied away from political or social commentary. He earned the wrath of the British neo-Nazi movement with *The Spear* (1978), in which Nazi sympathizers worship a zombiefied Heinrich Himmler. In *The Secret of Crickly Hall* (2006) he wrote about child abuse in orphanages, while *Others* (1999) addressed the mistreatment of disabled children. In later years he critiqued big business, such as the Magma Corporation in *Sepulchre* and the powerful yet mysterious Illuminati-like The Inner Court in *Ash* (2013).

Such commentary stemmed from Herbert's roots. Growing up in the East End, he saw successive governments fail to improve the living conditions of the poor, and his distrust of authority became the backdrop to his stories, with his heroes lifting the veil on the rich, powerful, and corrupt. Another key theme drew on his Catholicism, explored in detail in *Shrine* (1983), which tells the story of Alice, a deaf-mute girl who, after apparently seeing a vision of the Virgin Mary, can hear, speak, and perform miracles. Herbert's story involves a Catholic church that exploits the miraculous Alice and the blind followers who idolize her, only to find that she is possessed by Elnor, a seventeenth-century nun who was a witch and a spirit of evil. Herbert's critique here is aimed at all forms of blind faith and fanaticism. Alice is ultimately murdered by a lonely young man who is obsessed with Mark Chapman (John Lennon's killer) and John Hinkley (would-be assassin of Ronald Reagan).

While graphic scenes of death and sex in his first novels gave Herbert a reputation as an *enfant terrible* of pulp horror, other early works demonstrated a softer side to his writing that would eventually come to the fore. *The Survivor* (1976) downplayed horror in favor of the supernatural in its tale of pilot David Keller, the single survivor of a plane crash that kills 300 people. The book is part mystery thriller, as Keller investigates the crash and a series of other bizarre deaths that occur around the crash site, but it also increasingly becomes a Catholic-inflected musing on the afterlife. Herbert expanded on this in his next book, *Fluke* (1977), a fable about a man who dies and is reborn as a dog, and who tries in his canine form to discover the circumstances of his death. Both *Fluke* and *The Survivor* were filmed, the former in Hollywood in 1995 and the latter in Australia in 1981. *Fluke* was sold as a children's film, while *The Survivor* was a little seen and even less loved horror movie, as was *Deadly Eyes* (1982), a Canadian adaptation of *The Rats*. It was arguably the lack of success in transforming Herbert's work into movies in the early 1980s that contributed to his becoming less of a cultural icon than King.

Although he returned to gore in novels such as *The Spear, The Dark,* and *Sepulchre*, increasingly Herbert focused on the supernatural, with later novels such as *The Magic Cottage* (1986) and *Haunted* (1988) becoming progressively elegiac in tone. Herbert's softer side and huge achievement led to his eventual acceptance by the establishment. He was awarded the Officer of the Most Excellent Order of the British Empire (OBE) in 2010, and the same year he received the World Horror Convention Grand Master Award from Stephen King. In the year before his death, after a checkered relationship with screen adaptations, Herbert saw his *The Secret of Crickley Hall* adapted by the BBC into a well-received three-part miniseries.

Herbert died at his home in West Sussex in March 2013. No cause of death was given. While the gentle *Fluke* was his personal favorite, his true legacy is found in the savage early works that revolutionized British horror writing and inspired a generation of young British readers to embrace the genre.

Simon Brown

See also: Psychological Horror; *The Rats.*

Further Reading

Cabell, James. 2013. *James Herbert—The Authorised True Story 1943–2013.* London. John Blake.

Jones. Stephen. 1992. *James Herbert: By Horror Haunted.* London: Hodder and Stoughton.

King, Stephen. 1981. *Danse Macabre.* New York. Everest House.

Spark, Alasdair. 1993. "Horrible Writing: The Early Fiction of James Herbert." In *Creepers: British Horror & Fantasy in the Twentieth Century*, edited by Clive Bloom, 147–160. London and Boulder: Pluto Press.

HICHENS, ROBERT (1864–1950)

Robert Smythe Hichens was a prolific English novelist and short-story writer. He did not originally claim credit for a successful *roman à clef* (a fictional story about real people) about Oscar Wilde, *The Green Carnation* (1894), but was deeply affected by a tour of the Nile made in the company of Lord Alfred Douglas, transfigured in his phantasmagoric novel *An Imaginative Man* (1895), and seems to have retained traumatic guilt feelings from it that also fueled his work.

Lord Frederick Hamilton, editor of the *Pall Mall Magazine*, was sufficiently impressed by Hichens's account of a transmigration of souls in "A Reincarnation" (1895) to commission him to develop a plot of his own in "A Tribute of Souls," featuring a diabolical bargain. But Hamilton subsequently found Hichens's "The Cry of the Child" too nasty-minded to print. That harrowing tale of a man haunted by the ghostly cries of a child whom he allowed to die of neglect appeared in Hichens's finest collection, *Tongues of Conscience* (1900), a book of five horror stories that also featured his masterpiece, "How Love Came to Professor Guildea." The more sedate *Bye-Ways* (1897) had previously reprinted "A Tribute of Souls"

"How Love Came to Professor Guildea": A Neglected Masterpiece of Ghostly Horror

Hichens's novella "How Love Came to Professor Guildea" was first published in the collection *Tongues of Conscience* (1900) but is based on a shorter story, "The Man Who Was Beloved," published in the October 1897 issue of *Pearson's Magazine*. The central character, a scientist, is fond of explaining to his only friend, a priest, that there is no scope in his well-ordered life for emotion or affection, but he then becomes the object of the slavish infatuation of a ghostly stalker that suffers from a severe mental deficiency. The ghost is invisible to him but not to his pet parrot, whose mimicry of the moronic phantom reveals her fawning all too clearly. In the first version of the story, the idea of the parrot's mimicry is simply used as a twist in the tale, but the fuller version brings out the desperate unease of a man who has eliminated love from his existence but finds himself persecuted by it in an insidious fashion that seems uniquely horrible to him.

Although many ghost stories are, in effect, tales of stalking, those prior to the publication of Hichens's story that credited amorous motives to the specters tended to render the eroticism more rewarding, unless or until spoiled by jealousy. Hichens provides a far more distinctive and intense psychological study, which makes the novella one of the great English ghost stories. It has been widely anthologized, although it has somehow escaped the attention of most scholars of horror and supernatural fiction. It has also been adapted several times for radio and television, including an episode of the popular 1940s CBS radio show *Escape* and an episode of the pioneering 1950s horror-suspense television series *Lights Out*.

Brian Stableford

alongside "The Charmer of Snakes," in which a man loses his wife to the seductive music of a snake-charmer.

Flames (1897) is a remarkable novel in which an effortlessly moral socialite wants to feel the temptations that torment his imperfect friend, and so he proposes a magical exchange of souls that goes awry. The friend's body is possessed by the soul of an evil occultist, whose influence threatens to corrupt him irredeemably. *The Dweller on the Threshold* (1911) revisits the theme of *Flames*, and Hichens wrote a third, more enigmatic version of the plot in "The Sin of Envy," published in his *The Gardenia and Other Stories* (1934). In the title story of *The Man in the Mirror* (1950) a portraitist attempts to paint his doppelgänger, with disastrous consequences.

Hichens never quite made up his mind where he stood on the matter of the fashionable occultism that pervaded British and American culture in the late nineteenth and early twentieth centuries. This uncertainty in the face of supernatural phenomena weakened many of his horror stories, but the strange psychology of his work remains a fascinating case study.

Brian Stableford

See also: Doubles, Doppelgängers, and Split Selves; Psychological Horror.

Further Reading

Cooper, Frederic T. [1912] 2008. "Robert Hichens." In *A Hideous Bit of Morbidity: An Anthology of Horror Criticism from the Enlightenment to World War I*, edited by Jason Colavito, 307–324. Jefferson, NC: McFarland.
Stableford, Brian. 1998. "Robert Smythe Hichens." In *The St. James Guide to Horror, Ghost and Gothic Writers*, edited by David Pringle, 268–270. Detroit: St. James Press.

HILL, JOE (1972–)

Joe Hill is the pen name for Joseph Hillstrom King, an American author. Born in 1972 to horror writer Stephen King and his wife Tabitha, also a writer, Hill chose a pseudonym to achieve success on his own, apart from his famous family name. He was able to write for nearly a decade, publishing a collection of short stories, while keeping his identity secret. He is best known for horror and science fiction novels and comic books.

His first book, a critically acclaimed short story collection titled *20th Century Ghosts* (2005), garnered numerous awards, including a Bram Stoker Award for Best Fiction Collection and two British Fantasy Awards. Hill has said that his fiction, particularly his short fiction, is greatly influenced by Bernard Malamud, especially the idea that short stories can contain elements of fantasy and magic next to stark reality. Critics have described his writing style as "slipstream," which crosses and combines genre elements of horror, science fiction, fantasy, mystery, and literary fiction.

With the publication of his first novel, *Heart-Shaped Box* (2007), Hill won literary success, but he also found that he could no longer hide the connection to his famous father. Eventually, he gave in to the family connection and published several Kindle Singles with his father, including *In the Tall Grass* (2012) and *Throttle* (2012). Like Stephen King, Hill is probably best known for his horror novels: *Heart-Shaped Box*, *Horns* (2010), *NOS4A2* (2013), and *The Fireman* (2016). In 2014, *Horns* was adapted into a feature film starring Daniel Radcliffe and Juno Temple, directed by Alexandre Aja. *NOS4A2* inspired a comic series called *Wraith: Welcome to Christmasland* (2013–2014). *Wraith* followed on the heels of *Locke and Key* (the first in the series debuted in 2008), another comic book series penned by Hill and illustrated by Gabriel Rodriguez. In 2011, a television series adapted from *Locke and Key* was highly anticipated by fans, and a pilot was filmed, though the Fox network ultimately passed on the project. Hill has continued to work with various artists and IDW Publishing on several horror comic projects, including *The Cape* (2012) and *Thumbprint* (2013).

In 2016, a landmark year in Hill's writing career, *The Fireman* hit #1 on the *New York Times* hardcover best-seller list, the first work of his to reach the top spot. In interviews, Hill has said that he identifies more as a comic writer than anything else, though he continues to write across mediums. At the time of this writing, a new television adaptation of *Locke and Key* was rumored to be still in the works, with Hill saying that he did not want to give up on the project.

Lisa Kröger

See also: King, Stephen.

Further Reading

Dionne, Zach. 2013. "Owen King and Joe Hill on Their New Novels, Sibling Rivalry, and Stephen King's Shadow." *Vulture*, May 2. http://www.vulture.com/2013/04/joe-hill-owen-king-interview.html.

"Joe Hill." 2016. *Contemporary Authors Online*. Detroit: Gale.

Joe Hill Fiction. 2016. Accessed June 15. http://www.joehillfiction.com.

Niehart, Ben. 2007. "Prince of Darkness." *New York Times Magazine*, March 18. http://www.nytimes.com/2007/03/18/magazine/18hill.t.html?_r=0.

HILL, SUSAN (1942–)

British author Susan Hill, winner of the Whitbread, Somerset Maugham, and John Llewellyn Rhys awards and shortlisted for the Booker Prize, is well known as an accomplished author of contemporary ghost stories: *The Woman in Black* (1983), *The Mist in the Mirror* (1992), *The Man in the Picture* (2007), several short stories, and also crime and other contemporary fictions. Both her tales of the strange living and of the dead impinging on the living depict individual feelings and the confusion of relationships and hidden family secrets. She creates social microcosms with delicacy, vulnerability, and a sense of threat.

Hill's revival of the British ghost story in *The Woman in Black* (1983) engages readers with the power of Gothic horror to reveal horrible secrets of the past and their deadly legacy in the present, putting spectral flesh on hidden, repressed stories, versions, perspectives, and lives, and inviting readers to look again at social mores and understand them differently. The titular woman in black is the marginalized and maddened ghost of Jennet Humfrye, who wreaks fatal revenge on local children for the loss of her illegitimate child Nathaniel, who, after being adopted by Jennet's wealthy sister, Mrs. Drablow, drowned in an accident crossing the marshy spit to her remote mansion. The novel is interpretable in light of Julia Briggs's feminist exploration of women's ghost stories, which recuperated and emphasized their importance for reading the hidden lives of women in periods when they had no property and little education, and were expected to be silent. Ghosts, says Briggs, lure readers into a space of tension "between certainty and doubt, between the familiar and the feared, between rational occurrence and the inexplicable" (Briggs 2012, 176).

In Hill's *The Mist in the Mirror*, on a dark and rainy night Sir James Monmouth returns to England after a lifetime of traveling, intent on discovering more about himself and his obsession, explorer Conrad Vane. Sir James, warned against following Vane's trail, experiences disturbing events leading to questions concerning a sad little boy, an old woman hidden behind the curtain, chilling screams, and desperate sobbing. Travel and entrapment reappear in *The Man in the Picture*, set in Cambridge, London, a remote country house, and Venice at Carnival time, a popular city for tales of ghosts, death, confusion, and loss (as in Thomas Mann's *Death in Venice*, 1912; Daphne du Maurier's "Don't Look Now," 1971; and Ian McEwan's *The Comfort of Strangers*, 1981). Here people wear masks concealing secrets, which are revealed in a terrifying painting in which the man in the picture comes to life. Hill's dark short stories also dramatize ghostly revenge. For example, in "The Small Hand" (2010) a murdered child leads a researcher close to death, reenacting his own drowning at the hand of the man's brother, who, faced with his own guilt, commits suicide. Retribution, malice, and uncanny returns dominate Hill's socially engaging horror.

Gina Wisker

See also: The Woman in Black.

Further Reading

Briggs, Julia. 2012. "The Ghost Story." In *A New Companion to the Gothic*, edited by David Punter, 176–185. Oxford: Blackwell.

Hill, Susan. 1983. *The Woman in Black*. London: Vintage.

Hill, Susan. 1992. *The Mist in the Mirror*. London: Sinclair Stevenson.

Hofer, Ernest H. 1993. "Enclosed Structures, Disclosed Lives: The Fictions of Susan Hill." In *Contemporary British Women Writers, Narrative Strategies*, edited by Robert E. Hosmer Jr., 128–150. New York: St. Martin's Press.

Jackson, Rosemary. 1982. "Cold Enclosures: The Fiction of Susan Hill." In *Twentieth-Century Women Novelists*, edited by Thomas F. Staley, 81–103. Totowa, NJ: Barnes & Noble Books.

Quema, Anne. 2006. "Family and Symbolic Violence in *The Mist in the Mirror*." *Gothic Studies* 8, no. 2: 114–135.

THE HISTORIAN

The Historian is the 2005 debut novel by Elizabeth Johnson Kostova (1964–). It involves characters in three different decades attempting to discover the truth behind the legends surrounding the ruthless fifteenth-century Romanian leader Vlad Tepes (Vlad the Impaler), the historical figure who may have served at least in part as an inspiration for Bram Stoker when he created the character of Dracula.

In the earliest of three interwoven threads, historian Professor Bartholomew Rossi searches for Dracula in Eastern Europe in the 1930s. In 1952, one of Rossi's doctoral students, known only as Paul, tries to discover what happened to Rossi after he disappeared under mysterious circumstances. Finally, in 1972, the student's unnamed daughter searches for her father. As they travel the European continent, each scours libraries for hidden clues about where Tepes was buried. The three historians come to believe that Tepes really was a vampire and that he survives to this day. Except for the 1972 storyline, the novel is told through discovered letters, some many pages long, mirroring the epistolic style (i.e., told in the form of letters) of *Dracula*.

The unnamed narrator learns that she is a direct descendant of Dracula. When the vampire finally enters the story, he is unable to live up to the legend. He admires modern developments—the atomic bomb and the Cold War, for example—but he seems interested in little more than cataloging his vast library. He waxes poetic about the purity of evil, but is not very threatening and is apparently dispatched by a silver bullet to the heart.

Kostova was inspired by stories her father told her as a child while they lived in Slovenia and traveled throughout Europe. She researched and wrote the novel over a ten-year period, in part while teaching at various universities. In search of creative mentoring, she entered the MFA program at the University of Michigan, where the as-yet-incomplete manuscript won the Hopwood Award in 2004.

The book drew immediate interest from publishers and made headlines because of the $2 million advance paid for it at auction, as well as a similar payment from Sony for the film rights. Due to its reliance on solving puzzles and uncovering ancient conspiracies, Little, Brown and Company marketed the novel by comparing it to Dan Brown's *The Da Vinci Code*, despite the fact that *The Historian* is much slower paced than the Brown thriller.

The Historian was the first debut novel to land at number one on the *New York Times* best-seller list during its first week and is still the fastest-selling debut novel in U.S. history. Reviews, however, were decidedly mixed, in part due to the lack of variation in voice among the various narrators. The movie adaptation has never been produced.

The Historian ends in a manner that invites a sequel—either Dracula is still alive or one of his minions has taken his place—but Kostova has stated that she has no intentions of continuing the story, preferring to leave it for her readers to speculate about what happens next.

Bev Vincent

See also: Dracula; Forbidden Knowledge or Power; Gothic Hero/Villain; Psychological Horror; Vampires.

Further Reading

"Elizabeth Kostova." 2010. *Contemporary Authors Online*. Detroit: Gale.

"Interview: Elizabeth Kostova Discusses Her First Novel, 'The Historian.'" 2005. *Weekend Edition Sunday*. NPR, June 26.

Sanow, Anne. 2005. "Vivifying the Undead." *Publishers Weekly* 11 (April): 32.

HODGSON, WILLIAM HOPE (1877–1918)

William Hope Hodgson was a British author known for his science fiction-based horror fiction. He was born in Essex in 1877, the second of twelve children of an Anglican priest. At fourteen he left school and joined the Merchant Marines, first as a cabin boy and later as a first mate, a deeply traumatic experience that was to inform his writing. While at sea he took up photography and also body-building. He died in 1918.

After quitting the sea, Hodgson wrote and sold articles about physical culture and life at sea. Self-taught, he soon began writing fiction. His short horror stories and novels do not feature standard supernatural elements such as ghosts or vampires, but monstrous life forms, sometimes evolved here on earth, and sometimes invading from other planes of existence.

Hodgson's recurrent themes include horror at sea, most often the Sargasso Sea, and people besieged by monsters. His earliest published horror story, "A Tropical Horror" (1907), is typical, involving sailors barricading themselves against a huge, dangerous, but unknown sea creature. His two best short stories are "The Voice in the Night" (1907; adapted for the television series *Suspicion* in 1958) and "The Derelict" (1912). The former concerns a couple marooned on an island covered with a strange gray fungus, and the latter is about an abandoned ship that hosts a horrifying new form of life.

His first published novel, *The Boats of the Glen Carrig* (1907), is about shipwreck survivors who encounter trees that absorb people and a ship besieged by tentacled humanoid creatures. In *The House on the Borderland* (1908) a man experiences involuntary visionary trips beyond the solar system and into the remote future. *The Ghost Pirates* (1909) is set aboard a ship that is attacked and eventually overtaken by other-dimensional beings. *The Night Land* (1912) is a visionary tale of the remote future that is at once horror, science fiction, and romance. *Carnacki the Ghost-Finder* (1910) is a collection about an occult detective who investigates hauntings caused by quasi-scientific phenomena.

Hodgson's fiction anticipates that of H. P. Lovecraft, who independently created a similar approach to horror. But the Lovecraftian universe is harsh and apathetic, whereas Hodgson's balances good and malign forces. Hodgson's stories also often include overly sentimental romantic elements. He was notable for being able to create and sustain a mood of horror, even at novel length. He is primarily remembered for *The House on the Borderland*, *The Night Land*, "The Voice in the Night," "The Derelict," and the Carnacki stories, which are still being written today by other authors who expand on Hodgson's original concept.

His writings were critically well received at the time but nearly forgotten until their rediscovery in the 1940s. He died in Ypres, Belgium, in 1918, a casualty of World War I.

Lee Weinstein

See also: The House on the Borderland; Lovecraft, H. P.; *The Night Land*; Occult Detectives.

Further Reading

Berruti, Massimo, S. T. Joshi, and Sam Gafford, eds. 2014. *William Hope Hodgson: Voices from the Borderland: Seven Decades of Criticism on the Master of Cosmic Horror*. New York: Hippocampus Press.

Bloom, Harold. 1995. "William Hope Hodgson." In *Modern Horror Writers*, 93–107. New York: Chelsea House.

Bruce, Samuel W. 1997. "William Hope Hodgson." In *British Fantasy and Science-Fiction Writers Before World War I*, edited by Darren Harris-Fain, 121–131. *Dictionary of Literary Biography*, vol. 178. Detroit: Gale.

Gafford, Sam. 1992. "Writing Backward: The Novels of William Hope Hodgson." *Studies in Weird Fiction* 11 (Spring): 12–15.

Joshi, S. T. 2012. "William Hope Hodgson: Things in the Weeds." In *Unutterable Horror: A History of Supernatural Fiction, Vol. 2: The Twentieth and Twenty-First Century*, 445–451. Hornsea, England: PS Publishing.

The Night Land: The Weird Fiction of William Hope Hodgson. Accessed August 15, 2016. http://nightland.website.

Warren, Alan. 1992. "Full Fathom Five: The Supernatural Fiction of William Hope Hodgson." In *Discovering Classic Horror Fiction I*, edited by Darrell Schweitzer, 41–52. Mercer Island, WA: Starmont.

Weinstein, Lee. 1980. "The First Literary Copernicus." *Nyctalops* 15 (January). https://leestein 2003.wordpress.com/the-first-literary-copernicus.

HOFFMANN, E. T. A. (1776–1822)

Ernest Theodore Wilhelm (Amadeus) Hoffmann was a German writer, artist, composer, lawyer, and theater manager. He was one of the most important figures in the cultural movement known as romanticism, and a highly influential writer in both European and American literature.

Hoffmann was born in the city of Königsberg, which at that time was in Germany; Königsberg is now part of Russia and has been renamed Kaliningrad. He trained initially for a career in the law and practiced as a lawyer. However, his interest in art was both deep and wide; he wrote novels, short stories, and poetry; he painted and created illustrations; and he also both performed and composed music. His passion for Mozart's music was so great that he began replacing one of his middle names, "Wilhelm," with "Amadeus," which was also Mozart's middle name. Hoffmann even composed an opera, "Undine," which was based on a fantastic 1811 novella by his friend Friedrich de la Motte Fouqué, who assisted him with the lyrics.

His first short story was published in 1809, and his first collection, *Fantasiestücke in Callots Manier* (*Fantasy Stories in the Style of Callot*), appeared in 1814. Much of this collection was devoted to writings about music; however, it also included an important early tale, "The Golden Pot: A Fairytale of Modern Times." In this story, the somewhat awkward hero, Anselmus, falls in love with Serpentina, the daughter of a salamander escaped from Atlantis. The story presents a more light-hearted and bizarre side of Gothicism than many of his later tales, and resorts to the unusual tactic of bringing the narrator directly into the story in order to finish it. Crossing the boundaries between the real and the unreal would prove to be a constant theme running through Hoffmann's work.

His first novel, *Die Elixiere des Teufels* (*The Devil's Elixir*) appeared in 1815 and proved to be a far darker story than "The Golden Pot." The influence of *The Monk*, by Matthew Lewis, on *The Devil's Elixir* is obvious. In this novel, the figure of the double, or "doppelgänger," plays an important role, and Hoffmann's subsequent writing was full of secondary characters who seemed to reflect the main characters.

In 1817, what is today arguably Hoffmann's most famous work, "The Sand-man," was published in his collection *Nachtstücke* (*Night Pieces*). It is the story of a young man named Nathanael who, as a boy, may have witnessed the death of his father during an alchemical experiment. His father was not alone at the time, but in the company of the mysterious and terrifying Coppelius, a man the young Nathanael suspects might be the actual Sand-man. In German folklore, the Sand-man is an evil spirit who steals the eyes of children. As a young man, Nathanael encounters an Italian eyeglass-maker named Coppola, who seems to be Coppelius in disguise, and falls in love with his beautiful, shy daughter Olimpia. When Nathanael realizes that Olimpia is actually an "automaton," a machine built by Coppola, he goes mad. The theme of reality and unreality runs through "The Sand-man," which is a sustained meditation on the reliability of vision, of experience, as a way of understanding reality. Sigmund Freud, the most important figure in modern psychotherapy, wrote extensively on "The Sand-man" in his 1919 psychological treatise, *The Uncanny*.

Hoffmann's next collection, *Die Serapionsbrüder* (*The Serapion Brethren*), published in 1819, included the now-classic tale "Nutcracker and Mouse-King," which inspired Tchaikovsky's ballet "The Nutcracker." Other well-known stories from this collection include "The Mines of Falun," "Councillor Krespel," and "Mademoiselle de Scuderi," which is considered by many to be the first story of the detective genre. While much of Hoffmann's fiction would not appear in English until the 1850s, it is generally believed that Edgar Allan Poe was inspired by "Mademoiselle de Scuderi" to write his own important early detective story, "The Murders in the Rue Morgue."

In general, Hoffmann's style is important for the way he combines the psychological and the supernatural. While he recycles certain Gothic images, settings, and situations, drawing from Gothic sources such as Matthew Lewis and, particularly, the short fiction of Horace Walpole, Hoffmann is original in the way he handles Gothic material. By reexamining the Gothic from a fresh point of view, which was formed by the developments in German philosophical thinking about the nature of the mind and its relationship to experience, Hoffmann was able to bring a new dimension into Gothic fiction. His delirium and grotesqueness are not just exciting Gothic effects; they give him a way to question humanity's grasp on reality itself. Time and again, Hoffmann's characters are swept up in the tumult of their own desires and become unable to tell what is dream and what is not; but they are not fools—their problem is only a more acute form of a problem faced by all human beings. Hoffmann deliberately withholds whatever information would be necessary to establish beyond a shadow of a doubt that the experiences of his narrators are not supernatural. Understanding this tendency helps to explain the importance of delusional personas, figures like Coppelius, who act as a focus for the delusion of the main character. These personas are often depicted as malevolent beings who are aware of the role they play and seek to carry it out as if it were a mission.

Hoffmann's influence is extensive. Major authors both in and out of the horror genre reflect the results of reading Hoffmann, including not only Edgar Allan Poe and Nathaniel Hawthorne in the United States, but Russian authors such Fyodor Dostoyevsky and Nikolai Gogol, Charles Dickens and George MacDonald in England, and Charles Baudelaire in France. H. P. Lovecraft's story "The Music of Erich Zann" has a decidedly Hoffmann-like quality, and J. Sheridan Le Fanu's character, Dr. Hesselius—a scholar of supernatural events and a forerunner of Bram Stoker's Dr. Van Helsing—bears a resemblance to some of Hoffmann's characters as well. The composer Jacques Offenbach wrote an opera entitled *Tales of Hoffmann*, which was adapted for film in 1951. In later days, animators such as the Brothers Quay and Jan Svankmajer seem to have derived some inspiration from Hoffmann, who was fond of depicting inanimate objects coming to life and moving of their own accord.

Michael Cisco

See also: Baudelaire, Charles; Doubles, Doppelgängers, and Split Selves; Gogol, Nikolai; Hawthorne, Nathaniel; Le Fanu, J. Sheridan; Lewis, Matthew Gregory; *The Monk*; "The Music of Erich Zann"; Poe, Edgar Allan; Romanticism and Dark Romanticism; "The Sand-man"; The Uncanny; Walpole, Horace.

Further Reading

Duroche, Leonard L. 1988. "Hoffmann, E. T. A. 1776–1822." In *Writers for Children: Critical Studies of Major Authors Since the Seventeenth Century*, edited by Jane M. Bingham, 283–288. New York: Charles Scribner's Sons.

Freud, Sigmund. [1919] 2003. "The Uncanny." In *The Uncanny*, translated by David McLintock, 121–162. New York: Penguin.

Willis, Martin T. 1994. "Scientific Portraits in Magical Frames: The Construction of Preternatural Narrative in the Work of E. T. A. Hoffmann and Arthur Machen." *Extrapolation* 35, no. 3: 186–200.

"THE HORLA"

The influential short story "Le Horla" (The Horla) by the French writer Guy de Maupassant is a salient example of French weird fiction, praised by H. P. Lovecraft in *Supernatural Horror in Literature* (1927). A stark tale about the metaphysics of invisibility that takes the form of a confession to a physician, it was published under the title "Lettre d'un fou" (Letter from a Madman) in *Gil Blas*, a popular Parisian magazine, in February 1885 under the pen name of "Maufrigneuse." Maupassant then published (also in *Gil Blas*) the first version of "Le Horla" in October 1886, with the tale now featuring a framing device legitimating the narrator's sanity—and thereby inviting the reader into a macabre world that casts light on the limitations of the natural sciences when confronting the impossible. The final version of the story was published as "Le Horla" (1887) in *Le Horla*, a collection of Maupassant's short stories edited by Paul Ollendorff.

In the final version, Maupassant cuts out the frame narrative, instead organizing the story as a chronological series of journal entries told entirely from a first-person perspective and expressed in a lucid prose style. The narrator's protracted reflections on nonhumans and the strange occurrences to which he bears witness, however, veer uncontrollably into metaphysical abstraction and Schopenhauerian (in the style of the nineteenth-century German philosopher Arthur Schopenhauer) pessimism, thereby engendering affective dread and despair. The story describes the arrival on earth of an invisible entity from beyond the veil of human knowledge, an arrival that implies for its narrator the obliteration of the human species by extradimensional beings. The narrator's commitments to reason and faith collapse when confronting the titular "Horla," thus opening onto a vision of an incomprehensible cosmos. The tale illustrates weird fiction's penchant for speculating on realities that horrify readers before returning them to mundane reality with a more complex understanding of their embeddedness in cosmic immensities.

The narrator's inability to rationalize the manifestations of the invisible creature leads him to concoct a plan to trap it in his house with iron shutters in order to burn it alive. Yet, in his frantic efforts to rid himself of Le Horla, he forgets to inform his servants of his plan, and they are killed in the process. The story concludes grimly with the narrator, who is trapped in an existential nightmare in which he believes the horrid being is still alive, choosing to commit suicide.

In 1892, only five years after the publication of "Le Horla," Maupassant would himself attempt suicide, thereby paving the way for critics to speculate on the relationship between the story and the author's life. Regardless of biographical relevance, "Le Horla" remains a striking monument to the weird's capacity to unsettle and horrify both philosophically and psychologically, and it has had a profound influence on subsequent horror literature, including Lovecraft's classic story "The Call of Cthulhu" (1928) and Ambrose Bierce's "The Damned Thing" (1893). It has been adapted as, and/or has exerted an influence on, multiple movies and radio and television program, including a loose adaptation as the 1963 American horror film *Diary of a Madman*, starring Vincent Price.

Sean Matharoo

See also: "The Call of Cthulhu"; Doubles, Doppelgängers, and Split Selves; Dreams and Nightmares; Frame Story; Maupassant, Guy de; Psychological Horror; Unreliable Narrator.

Further Reading

Fitz, Brewster E. 1972. "The Use of Mirrors and Mirror Analogues in Maupassant's *Le Horla*." *The French Review* 45 (5): 954–963.

Goulet, Andrea. 2013. "Neurosyphilitcs and Madmen: The French *Fin-de-siècle* Fictions of Huysmans, Lermina, and Maupassant." In *Literature, Neurology, and Neuroscience: Neurological and Psychiatric Disorders*, edited by Stanley Finger, François Boller, and Anne Stiles, 73–91. Amsterdam and Oxford: Elsevier.

Showers, Brian J. 2010. "The Horla." In *Encyclopedia of the Vampire: The Living Dead in Myth, Legend, and Popular Culture*, edited by S. T. Joshi, 146–148. Santa Barbara, CA: Greenwood.

THE HOUND OF THE BASKERVILLES

The Hound of the Baskervilles is one of four novels by Arthur Conan Doyle that feature fictional detective Sherlock Holmes and his loyal friend Dr. John Watson. Serialized in *The Strand* magazine from 1901 to 1902, it was the first Sherlock Holmes story to be published since 1893, when Doyle memorably killed off his hero in *The Final Problem*. However, due to immense public pressure to write more Sherlock Holmes stories, Doyle produced *The Hound of the Baskervilles,* set sometime before Holmes's fateful battle with Professor Moriarty at the Reichenbach Falls.

Like the majority of Sherlock Holmes stories, the story is told by Dr. Watson's narrative, but also in the epistolary format using letters and old manuscripts. Regarded as a little old-fashioned by the advent of the twentieth century, when modernism was on the rise, this format is nevertheless used to great effect by Doyle in *The Hound of the Baskervilles* as the mystery is gradually explained. Though typically classed as a detective story, the novel features many tropes common to Gothic literature, for example, the Gothic mansion of Baskerville Hall and the windswept moors. But unlike many Gothic and horror stories, there is a rational explanation for all of the strange events that occur.

The mystery in *The Hound of the Baskervilles* is a complex one, with a multitude of characters, multiple plot strands, and many false clues. Due to its length, Doyle was able to develop a much more intricate story than in the short fiction he had

The scene late in *The Hound of the Baskervilles* when the title creature is finally revealed remains as thrilling today as it was to Arthur Conan Doyle's readers in 1901–1902. Holmes, Watson, and Lestrade (a detective from Scotland Yard, and an old acquaintance of Holmes's) are out on a fog-shrouded moor at night when they first hear the hound, followed by its appearance:

> There was a thin, crisp, continuous patter from somewhere in the heart of that crawling bank. The cloud was within fifty yards of where we lay, and we glared at it, all three, uncertain what horror was about to break from the heart of it. I was at Holmes's elbow, and I glanced for an instant at his face. It was pale and exultant, his eyes shining brightly in the moonlight. But suddenly they started forward in a rigid, fixed stare, and his lips parted in amazement. At the same instant Lestrade gave a yell of terror and threw himself face downward upon the ground. I sprang to my feet, my inert hand grasping my pistol, my mind paralyzed by the dreadful shape which had sprung out upon us from the shadows of the fog. A hound it was, an enormous coal-black hound, but not such a hound as mortal eyes have ever seen. Fire burst from its open mouth, its eyes glowed with a smouldering glare, its muzzle and hackles and dewlap were outlined in flickering flame. Never in the delirious dream of a disordered brain could anything more savage, more appalling, more hellish be conceived than that dark form and savage face which broke upon us out of the wall of fog. (Doyle 1902, 251–252)

Matt Cardin

Source: Doyle, Sir Arthur Conan. February 1902. "The Hound of the Baskervilles." *The Strand Magazine.* Volume XXIII.

published previously. The mystery focuses on the ill-fated Baskerville family, who are apparently haunted by a demonic hellhound. Holmes does not believe in hellhounds, of course, and he and Watson set out to solve a puzzle with a very human (and canine) evil at its center.

Like the contradictory character of Holmes himself, *The Hound of the Baskervilles* combines the outrageous with the reassuringly rational. Doyle uses many sensational elements in his novel, such as diabolical criminals, ghostly seeming hounds, and manhunts across the moors, but always reduces the apparently uncanny to something explicable.

The Hound of the Baskervilles was a huge success, and it led to Doyle's reviving Sherlock Holmes in *The Adventure of the Empty House*, with the detective dramatically revealing he had faked his own death. The novel has been adapted for both the cinema and the television screen on numerous occasions. It has even lent its name to a statistical observation known as "the Baskerville effect," the effect being that mortality due to heart attacks is increased by psychological stress. It continues to be one of the best-known and most popular Sherlock Holmes stories. It has also earned a place in the horror canon, a fact demonstrated by Christopher Frayling's choice to include it along with three other iconic works of horror literature—Mary Shelley's *Frankenstein*, Bram Stoker's *Dracula*, and Robert Louis Stevenson's *The Strange Case of Dr. Jekyll and Mr. Hyde*—in his 1996 BBC series *Nightmare: The Birth of Horror* and its accompanying book, in which he details the background, origin, and impact of each work.

Carys Crossen

See also: Ancestral Curse.

Further Reading

Frank, Lawrence. 2003. *Victorian Detective Fiction and the Nature of Evidence: The Scientific Investigations of Poe, Dickens and Doyle.* Basingstoke: Palgrave Macmillan.

Frayling, Christopher. 1996. "The Hound of the Baskervilles." In *Nightmare: The Birth of Horror*, 162–214. London: BBC Books.

Kestner, Joseph A. 2010. *Masculinities in British Adventure Fiction, 1880–1915.* Farnham: Ashgate.

Priestman, Martin, ed. 2003. *The Cambridge Companion to Crime Fiction.* Cambridge: Cambridge University Press.

THE HOUSE NEXT DOOR

The House Next Door is a 1978 novel by Anne Rivers Siddons. While at its core *The House Next Door* is a haunted house story, it could also be considered the anti–haunted house story. After all, the haunted house in question is not even built when the novel opens, and no ghosts actually come into the storyline, even though horrific things happen to anyone who moves into the home.

The novel is told from the perspective of Colquitt Kennedy, a Caucasian housewife living an ideal life in suburban Atlanta with her husband, Walter. Their domestic bliss is interrupted, however, when architect Kim Dougherty (whose orphan status and red hair makes him a prime candidate to be the source of the novel's evil) builds his masterpiece next door. The novel is told in three parts, each detailing the three families who move in. Drawing heavily on haunted houses such as Shirley Jackson's Hill House, the titular house next door to the Kennedys appears to have been created with horror inside its bones; the structure itself houses some kind of evil that brings about the downfall of its inhabitants. Unlike her predecessors, Siddons forgoes the traditional Gothic mansion in favor of a contemporary home, with a sleek and modern design. The home itself isn't menacing; rather, the true horror comes from witnessing the effects of the new structure on the families who live there—and, by proximity, the Kennedys, who stand as witness. By removing the traditional elements of a horror story, Siddons is able to highlight the real horror that plagues humanity: war, loss, broken relationships, damaged trust.

In his book on the nature of horror, *Danse Macabre*, Stephen King devotes an extended section to *The House Next Door*, comparing it both to the haunted house tradition of Shirley Jackson and to the Southern Gothic tradition of William Faulkner. Even though Siddons strips away the traditional architecture of the haunted house, King claims that she still holds on to the heart of the horrific, in that carefully constructed social norms have been broken down to the point that they are irreparable. The Kennedys are forever changed; in the end, they cannot return to their former suburban lives.

In 2006, Siddons's novel was adapted into a made-for-television movie for Lifetime, with Lara Flynn Boyle playing the character of Col Kennedy, Colin Ferguson as her husband (named Walker for the film), and Mark-Paul Gosselaar as the architect Kim. The film did not receive good reviews.

Lisa Kröger

See also: Burnt Offerings; Faulkner, William; The Haunted House or Castle; *The Haunting of Hill House, Part Two, Themes, Topics, and Genres:* Horror Literature as Social Criticism and Commentary.

Further Reading

Bailey, Dale. 1999. "Middle-Class Nightmares: Robert Marasco's *Burnt Offerings* and Anne Rivers Siddons's *The House Next Door*." In *American Nightmares: The Haunted House Formula in American Popular Fiction*. Bowling Green, OH: Bowling Green State University Popular Press.

Eggener, Keith. 2013. "When Buildings Kill: Sentient Houses in Fiction and Film." *Places Journal*, October. https://placesjournal.org/article/when-buildings-kill.

King, Stephen. [1981] 2010. *Danse Macabre*. New York: Gallery Books.

HOUSE OF LEAVES

House of Leaves is an experimental horror novel by American author Mark Z. Danielewski. It was originally published on Danielewski's website and circulated in the early years of Internet "viral" culture. Since its publication in print form in 2000, it has become a touchstone of postmodern writing and a referent for almost all subsequent experimental horror fiction.

House of Leaves is a difficult text to synopsize. It is comprised of a series of concentric but interlinked narratives. At the center of the novel, both structurally and thematically, is the house on Ash Tree Lane belonging to photographer Will Navidson and his young family. Navidson discovers a profound spatial paradox when a hallway appears in his home, leading down into a labyrinth that vastly exceeds the dimensions of the house. He puts his visual skills to good use in a recorded exploration of the impossible space and its malign influence on his family. The novel's textual appearance mirrors the physical labyrinth at the heart of the story. Danielewski uses color, typography, layout, and elaborate citation to present a textual composition that is dizzying and difficult to navigate.

Navidson's video is the subject of *House of Leaves'* bifurcated, competing narratives. The majority of the text is devoted to a pseudo-academic analysis of Navidson's film, written by the reclusive, blind Zampanò. His analysis, "The Navidson Report," is an in-depth deconstruction that parodies academic discourse while illustrating the uncanny, frightening properties of Navidson's home. It is full of footnotes and citations, some of which reference authentic sources, while others are entirely fictitious.

Just as Zampanò reflects upon Navidson's film, his analysis is in turn the subject of the next layer of the text: a stream-of-consciousness account by Los Angeles drop-out Johnny Truant. Johnny is the involuntary recipient of Zampanò's study after he finds it in the dead man's apartment. He appoints himself an unofficial editor of "The Navidson Report" and relates his own experience in the marginalia and footnotes to that text. As well as a commentary on the report, however, his narrative reveals the sinister consequence of reading Zampanò's work. He becomes increasingly paranoid, convinced that he is being pursued by an entity that may or may not reside in Navidson's labyrinth. The implication, of course, is that the same fate may befall the reader in turn. As Johnny explains: "focus on these words and whatever you do don't let your eyes wander past the perimeter of this page. Now imagine just beyond your peripheral vision, maybe behind you, maybe to the side of you, maybe even in front of you, but right where you can't see it, something is quietly closing in on you" (26).

The horrors in *House of Leaves* are many and varied and exist at every level of the text: Johnny's paranoia, Zampanò's lonely death, the destruction of the Navidsons' domestic space, and the death of their friends in the labyrinth. At the heart of the novel, however, is the notion of fallible truth: the idea that reality itself is unstable. This is foregrounded in various ways. The most shocking occurs late in the novel when Navidson finds himself alone and lost in the labyrinth reading a book by the light of a burning page. The book, of course, is revealed to be *House of Leaves*. Thus the text becomes as impossible a space as the labyrinth itself, and any perspective on what is "real" (within the context of the fiction) is entirely lost.

Danielewski's novel has been influential in the development of a critically aware, self-reflexive, media-savvy breed of horror fiction. Marisha Pessl's *Night Film* (2013) and Paul Tremblay's *A Head Full of Ghosts* (2015) both follow in *House of Leaves'* wake as horror fictions focused on the uncanny properties of media and mediation, and both have been termed successors to Danielewski's novel. Its influence may also be discerned in Caitlín R. Kiernan's Bram Stoker Award–winning novel *The Drowning Girl* (2012). Danielewski has himself returned to the elaborate experimental form in the first two volumes of an intended twenty-seven-volume novel, *The Familiar.* It remains to be seen, however, whether any novel will equal the marriage of self-conscious commentary, innovative technique, and existential horror presented in *House of Leaves*.

Neil McRobert

See also: *The Drowning Girl*; Frame Story; The Haunted House or Castle; New Weird; The Uncanny; Unreliable Narrator; *Part One, Horror through History*: Horror in the Twenty-First Century; *Part Two, Themes, Topics, and Genres*: Ghost Stories; Horror Criticism; Horror Literature in the Internet Age; Small Press, Specialty, and Online Horror.

Further Reading

Belletto, Steven. 2009. "Rescuing Interpretation with Mark Danielewski: The Genre of Scholarship in House of Leaves." *Genre Forms of Discourse and Culture* 42, nos. 3–4 (Fall/Winter): 99–117.

Danielewski, Mark Z. 2015. *The Familiar, Volume 1: One Rainy Day in May.* New York: Pantheon.

McCaffery, Larry, and Sinda Gregory. 2003. "Haunted House: An Interview with Mark Z. Danielewski." *Critique* 44/2: 99–135.

Pessl, Marisha. 2013. *Night Film.* New York: Random House.

Pressman, Jessica. 2006. "*House of Leaves*: Reading the Networked Novel." *Studies in American Fiction* 34, no. 1: 107–28.

Tremblay, Paul. 2015. *A Head Full of Ghosts.* New York: William Morrow.

Watkiss, Joanne. 2012. *Gothic Contemporaries: The Haunted Text.* Cardiff: University of Wales Press.

THE HOUSE OF THE SEVEN GABLES

Published in 1851, Nathaniel Hawthorne's second major romance, *The House of the Seven Gables,* competes with his first, *The Scarlet Letter* (1850), for pride of place amidst his oeuvre. Its influence as both a Gothic romance and a work of literature in general has been immense.

The titular gabled *House*, modeled after one in Salem, is set in a nameless New England town and built on land seized by one Col. Pyncheon via a false accusation of warlockery against Matthew Maule, who, as he was being hanged for witchcraft, laid a bloody curse on the Pyncheons. The primary action occurs in the mid-nineteenth century as Hepzibah Pyncheon, a destitute aristocrat, opens a shop and takes a boarder in the gabled house. The boarder, Holgrave, is a daguerreotypist (early photographer) and mesmerist (hypnotist), smitten with Hepzibah's newly arrived cousin, Phoebe. Hepzibah's paroled brother Clifford returns unhinged by prison after another cousin, Judge Jaffrey Pyncheon, probably framed Clifford for Jaffrey's uncle's death from Maule's curse or a hereditary Pyncheon condition. The "curse" kills Jaffrey, which allows the Pyncheon siblings to inherit his estate and escape the house, and permits Holgrave, a Maule descendant, to become engaged to Phoebe.

The romance has had four cinematic adaptations. The two most interesting star Vincent Price. *Twice-Told Tales* (1963) adapts "Dr. Heidegger's Experiment" (1837), "Rappaccini's Daughter" (1844), and *House* in three segments. Made while Price was in the midst of his ten-film cycle of (loose) Poe adaptations (1960–1969), the

Built over an Unquiet Grave

In this paragraph from the opening pages of *The House of the Seven Gables*, Hawthorne lays the groundwork for the curse and the haunting that serve as the novel's main focus. He also establishes the brooding and gloomy tone that will dominate throughout, as well as the narrator's habit of referring to local gossip in framing perceptions of people and events:

> After the reputed wizard's death, his humble homestead had fallen an easy spoil into Colonel Pyncheon's grasp. When it was understood, however, that the colonel intended to erect a family mansion—spacious, ponderously framed of oaken timber, and calculated to endure for many generations of his posterity—over the spot first covered by the log-built hut of Matthew Maule, there was much shaking of the head among the village gossips. Without absolutely expressing a doubt whether the stalwart Puritan had acted as a man of conscience and integrity, throughout the proceedings which have been sketched, they nevertheless hinted that he was about to build his house over an unquiet grave. His home would include the home of the dead and buried wizard, and would thus afford the ghost of the latter a kind of privilege to haunt its new apartments, and the chambers into which future bridegrooms were to lead their brides, and where children of the Pyncheon blood were to be born. The terror and ugliness of Maule's crime, and the wretchedness of his punishment, would darken the freshly-plastered walls, and infect them early with the scent of an old and melancholy house. (Hawthorne 1851, 13)

Matt Cardin

Source: Hawthorne, Nathaniel. 1851. *The House of the Seven Gables*. Boston: Ticknor, Reed, and Fields.

segment highlights the influence of Edgar Allan Poe's less subtle "The Fall of the House of Usher" (1839) on *House* as well as other sensational elements of Poe's and Hawthorne's supernatural fiction as walls and Col. Pyncheon's portrait bleed, Phoebe cum Alice is buried alive, Hannah cum Hepzibah is a witch, Price as Gerald cum Jaffrey is a maniacal killer, and the house collapses. Universal's *The House of the Seven Gables* (1940) hews closer to the romance but rearranges Pyncheon family structure and assigns a lengthy murder trial to Price as Clifford. Ironically, given Hawthorne's racism and lack of support for abolition, Holgrave becomes an abolitionist jailed alongside Clifford, and Jaffrey swindles a gullible deacon into embezzling abolitionist funds into the slave trade.

H. P. Lovecraft admired *House* the most among Hawthorne's works but frankly assessed that Hawthorne's singular style, unlike Poe's, had inspired few inheritors. That assessment has its truth, but subsequent history allows nuance. A vicious, variegated New England horror tradition succeeded without imitating Hawthorne, including occasional works by Edith Wharton, Lovecraft himself, and Shirley Jackson. Moreover, the cursed aristocratic inheritance exerts tremendous influence on high achievements of twentieth-century New World Gothic: William Faulkner's *Absalom, Absalom!* (1936), Isabel Allende's *The House of the Spirits* (1982), and Toni Morrison's *Beloved* (1987).

Bob Hodges

See also: Ancestral Curse; *Beloved*; Forbidden Knowledge or Power; The Haunted House or Castle; Hawthorne, Nathaniel; Jackson, Shirley; Lovecraft, H. P.; Poe, Edgar Allan; Romanticism and Dark Romanticism; Wharton, Edith; Witches and Witchcraft; *Part One, Horror through History*: Horror in the Nineteenth Century; *Part Two, Themes, Topics, and Genres*: Gender, Sexuality, and the Monsters of Literary Horror; The Gothic Literary Tradition.

Further Reading

Bailey, Dale. 1999. "The Sentient House and the Ghostly Tradition: The Legacy of Poe and Hawthorne." In *American Nightmares: The Haunted House Formula in American Popular Fiction*, 15–24. Bowling Green, OH: Bowling Green State University Popular Press.
The House of the Seven Gables. 2010. DVD. Dir. Joe May. 1940. Universal City: Universal.
Lovecraft, H. P. [1927] 2012. *The Annotated Supernatural Horror in Literature.* Edited by S. T. Joshi. New York: Hippocampus Press.
Martin, Terence. 1983. "The House of the Seven Gables." In *Nathaniel Hawthorne*, revised edition. Twayne's United Authors Series 75. Boston: Twayne Publishers.
Siebers, Tobin. 1983. "Hawthorne's Appeal and Romanticism." In *The American Renaissance: New Dimensions*, edited by Harry R. Garvin and Peter C. Carafiol, 100–117. London and Toronto: Associated University Presses.
Twice-Told Tales. 2005. DVD. Dir. Sidney Salkow. 1963. Beverly Hills: MGM Midnite Movies.

THE HOUSE ON THE BORDERLAND

The House on the Borderland by William Hope Hodgson, first published in 1908, is a portmanteau novel (one consisting of multiple different parts) in which four narrative episodes and two brief connecting passages, allegedly contained in a manuscript, are presented within a frame narrative, prefaced by an introduction and a poem. Two of the episodes describe the haunting of a house in Ireland by creatures from a nearby pit; one of the others is a vision in which a replica of the house is surrounded by a fabulous landscape inhabited by loathsome monsters, and the last a cosmic vision in which the dreaming narrator witnesses the end of the world and visits the binary star at the center of the universe, which is also an allegory of human life and death.

Although it represented a decisive break from the sea stories that were Hodgson's principal stock in trade as he tried to make a living as a professional writer, the novel transports the metaphysical schema outlined in several of those stories, with its attendant psychological fascinations, into a broader visionary area in order to display them more elaborately. The enigmatic house is symbolic of the troubled mind of its inhabitant; the pit on whose brink it is precariously situated is the well of his unconscious. The main visionary sequence is both an attempt to place human existence in the frame of space and time established as true by contemporary science and an attempt to develop a metaphysical framework that might make that placement meaningful, subjectively if not objectively.

The idea of a marginal region incompletely separating our world from another plays a significant role in almost all of Hodgson's fiction, where breaches in the barrier and irruptions from the world beyond are invariably seen as baleful; significantly, they are usually characterized as animalistic even when frankly supernatural; his "phantoms" always have a carnal repulsiveness about them, often porcine, as in this instance. That aspect of Hodgson's work is distinctive, at least in the intensity of his preoccupation with it.

The fact that the novel is a patchwork of pieces that were presumably written separately makes its narrative flow awkward and detracts from its overall coherency, but the resulting disorder is by no means inappropriate to the nature of the exercise, and is amply compensated in terms of its imaginative ambition and graphic imagery. As in Hodgson's *The Night Land*, to which it is closely related in terms of its underlying endeavor, its clumsiness is part and parcel of its ambition, a consequence of its reach exceeding its grasp. For that reason, *The House of the Borderland* has exerted a long-lasting fascination over many devoted admirers and remains a key work in the history of imaginative fiction that defies easy classification. Its influence on subsequent writers of horror and fantasy fiction, including major figures such as H. P. Lovecraft and Clark Ashton Smith, has been profound. In 2001 a graphic novel adaptation of the novel was published by the Vertigo imprint of DC Comics.

Brian Stableford

See also: Dreams and Nightmares; The Haunted House or Castle; Hodgson, William Hope; *The Night Land*; *Part One, Horror through History*: Horror from 1900 to 1950; *Part Two, Themes, Topics, and Genres*: Horror Literature and Science Fiction; Weird and Cosmic Horror Fiction.

Further Reading

Berruti, Massimo, S. T. Joshi, and Sam Gafford, eds. 2014. *William Hope Hodgson: Voices from the Borderland: Seven Decades of Criticism on the Master of Cosmic Horror*. New York: Hippocampus Press.

Bloom, Harold. 1995. "William Hope Hodgson." In *Modern Horror Writers*, 93–107. New York: Chelsea House.

Gafford, Sam. 1992. "Writing Backward: The Novels of William Hope Hodgson." *Studies in Weird Fiction* 11 (Spring): 12–15.

Joshi, S. T. 2012. "William Hope Hodgson: Things in the Weeds." In *Unutterable Horror: A History of Supernatural Fiction, Vol. 2: The Twentieth and Twenty-First Century*, 445–451. Hornsea, England: PS Publishing.

Warren, Alan. 1992. "Full Fathom Five: The Supernatural Fiction of William Hope Hodgson." In *Discovering Classic Horror Fiction I*, edited by Darrell Schweitzer, 41–52. Mercer Island, WA: Starmont.

HOWARD, ROBERT E. (1906–1936)

Robert E. Howard, who was born and lived most of his life in rural Texas, was a prolific American writer for pulp fiction magazines. Although he wrote for a wide variety of fiction markets, including adventure and sports publications, he is best known as the creator of Conan the Barbarian and the fantasy subgenre of sword-and-sorcery. He was a titan of the pulp era in American popular fiction, and his work crossed over in many significant ways with dark fantasy and horror.

"Pigeons from Hell": Atmospheric Southern Gothic Horror

"Pigeons from Hell" was first published in the May 1938 issue of *Weird Tales*. One of Howard's best-known tales of horror, it is set in an unspecified rural locale in the American South where two young men, Griswell and John Branner, stop overnight at an abandoned mansion. During the night Griswell awakens from sleep to see Branner ascend the stairs as though in a trance and then return as a walking corpse, his head split with a hatchet which he is bearing to kill Branner. Griswell flees the house in terror and runs into Buckner, the local sheriff, who accompanies him back to the house. From Buckner and Jacob, a black voodoo man living nearby, Griswell learns that the house is the ruins of the Blassenville plantation, which fell into decline after the American Civil War. Local legend has it that the pigeons that flock to the house are the souls of the Blassenvilles, let out of hell at sunset. Celia Blassenville, the last of the family, was notorious for abusing her slave, Joan, and it is believed that Joan went through an occult ritual to become a *zuvembie* (a type of immortal monster) to avenge herself on Celia. When Branner and Buckner decide to stay the night, they discover the truth about the *zuvembie* who murdered John Branner.

"Pigeons from Hell" is an atmospheric Southern Gothic story, one of several that Howard based on the regional folklore of his native Texas. Perhaps its most impressive aspect is its successful use of its rich setting to generate an atmosphere of almost unbearable dread from what amounts to a kind of mixed kettle of horror tropes. It was memorably adapted as an episode of Boris Karloff's *Thriller* television series in 1961 and has been adapted several times in comic book form.

Stefan R. Dziemianowicz

Howard made his first professional fiction sale in 1925 to *Weird Tales*, the magazine that would become his best market. The April, 1926 issue carried his "Wolfshead," a werewolf tale whose muscular style and historical setting anticipated his approach in much of his heroic fantasy fiction. Other sales to *Weird Tales* included the witchcraft tale "Sea Curse" (1928), the ghost story "Man on the Ground" (1933), and the Native American–themed "Old Garfield's Heart" (1933). Several of Howard's most highly regarded works of horror were published posthumously, among them "Black Canaan" (1936) and "Pigeons from Hell" (May, 1938). Both of these stories are Southern Gothic tales steeped in the folklore of Howard's native American South: they bristle dramatically with racial tensions between blacks and whites, and they are memorable for horrors rendered in Howard's trademark visceral style. "The Dead Remember," a tale of vengeance from beyond the grave published in the August 15, 1936 issue of *Argosy*, is another notable regional horror tale.

Howard began corresponding with fellow *Weird Tales* contributor H. P. Lovecraft in 1930, and he contributed to the Cthulhu Mythos, the shared world of cosmic horror fiction inspired by Lovecraft's stories. As Marc Cerasini and Charles Hoffman have noted, most of Howard's mythos tales—including "The Children of the Night" (1931), "The Thing on the Roof" (1932), "The Fire of Asshurbanipal" (1936), and "Dig Me No Grave" (1937)—do not represent his best work, since his attempts to evoke the futility of human endeavor that distinguishes Lovecraft's fiction forced him to suppress the heroics characteristic of his best fiction. An exception is "The Black Stone" (1931), an effective Lovecraftian horror story about a contemporary traveler in Hungary who is privy to a vivid dream vision of an ancient rite of sacrifice to a monstrous entity. This story introduced the mad poet Justin Geoffrey and the book of occult lore, the *Unaussprechlichen Kulten* (*Nameless Cults*), both referenced afterward in stories by Lovecraft and other contributors to the mythos.

Many tales featuring Howard's serial heroes are punctuated with incidents of horror and the supernatural. "Worms of the Earth" (1932), featuring Pict warrior Bran Mak Morn, is one of several stories in which Howard developed the theme of a bestial prehistoric race, driven underground, that later gave rise to folk legends of the little people. In "Red Shadows" (1928), "The Moon of Skulls" (1930), "The Walking Dead" (1930), and "Wings in the Night" (1932), Howard's puritan swordsman Solomon Kane becomes enmeshed in sorcerous intrigues in Africa. In many of Howard's tales of Conan, incidents of physical horror and the supernatural provide challenges to the masculine prowess of the hero.

Howard committed suicide in June 1936 as his dying mother lay in a coma. The 1996 film *The Whole Wide World* depicts the romantic and intellectual relationship between Howard (played by Vincent D'Onofrio) and Novalyne Price (played by Renée Zellweger), as based on Price's memoirs of her time with Howard.

Stefan R. Dziemianowicz

See also: Cthulhu Mythos; Dark Fantasy; Lovecraft, H. P.; Lovecraftian Horror; Pulp Horror; *Weird Tales; Part One, Horror through History:* Horror from 1900 to 1950.

Further Reading

Bleiler, Everett F. 1985. "Robert E. Howard: 1906–1936." In *Supernatural Fiction Writers,* edited by Everett F. Bleiler. New York: Scribner's.

Cerasini, Marc A., and Charles Hoffman. 1987. *Robert E. Howard: Starmont Reader's Guide 35.* Mercer Island, WA: Starmont House.

HUBBARD, L. RON (1911–1986)

Lafayette Ronald Hubbard is best known as the founder of Scientology, a controversial religious system advocating the acquisition of knowledge and spiritual fulfillment through a course of study and training. Hubbard is also known as a prolific author of science fiction, having produced more than 250 short stories and novels. Nineteen of his books have appeared on the *New York Times* best-seller list. He began his authorial career writing science fiction, fantasy, and adventure stories for such pulp magazines as *Thrilling Adventures* and *Astounding Science Fiction* in the 1930s, and he continued to publish in those genres through the 1950s, a period that has been called the "Golden Age" of pulp fiction, during which time he achieved a considerable reputation, especially as a science fiction writer. Some of his work also touched on themes of horror, especially of the psychological variety.

Return to the Stars (1954) and *Battlefield Earth* (1982), both traditional science fiction narratives, are Hubbard's best-known novels. Two other works, *Typewriter in the Sky* (1940) and *Fear* (1940), explore questions of identity and perception within the framework of the horror narrative.

Typewriter in the Sky, first published as a two-part serial, uses the conventions of a time-travel narrative to explore the growing fear of the loss of identity and self-awareness. The hero, Mike de Wolf, receives an electric shock and is thrown back to the sixteenth century, where he has high adventures in the Caribbean. He becomes aware that during his adventures he can hear the keys of a typewriter, and he begins to question his existence, wondering whether he is human or simply a character in someone else's novel.

Even more disquieting is *Fear.* Ethnologist James Lowrey returns from an expedition to Central America to discover that he is being fired from his college for denying the existence of a spiritual world. During the course of the novel, Lowrey, suffering from the effects of malaria, blacks out for four hours and then begins to experience visual, auditory, and tactile hallucinations. As he searches for his lost hours, demons and devils speak to him, offering godlike powers of perception and/ or horrible death. He slowly loses his connections to reality, and in the end of the novel Lowrey discovers or imagines that he has killed his wife and best friend with an axe. *Fear* is widely considered a masterful description of a descent into madness and is recognized as a significant example of psychological horror.

In much of his fiction Hubbard develops themes related to Scientology, depicting establishment systems and beliefs, such as the banking system, the law, and especially psychiatry and psychology, as oppressive structures blocking the development of self-awareness and the acquisition of the means to develop human potential. In *The Typewriter in the Sky* and especially *Fear*, he dramatizes the internal horror of psychological deterioration and the inability of rational systems to provide help. Although the prominence of Scientology in popular consciousness has mostly eclipsed the memory of Hubbard's career as a novelist, several of his novels, including these two, still stand as significant works of speculative fiction with connections to the literary horror tradition.

Jim Holte

See also: Devils and Demons; *Fear*; Psychological Horror.

Further Reading

Adrian, Jack. 1996. "L. Ron Hubbard: Overview." *St. James Guide to Fantasy Writers*, edited by David Pringle. New York: St. James Press.

Hubbard, L. Ron. 1950. *Dianetics: The Modern Science of Mental Health*. New York: Hermitage House.

Hubbard, L. Ron. 1977. *Fear & Typewriter in the Sky*. New York: Popular Library.

Miller, Russell. 1988. *Bare-Faced Messiah: The True Story of L. Ron Hubbard*. New York: Holt.

Stableford, Brian. 1979. "*Fear* and *Typewriter in the Sky*." In *Survey of Science Fiction Literature*, vol. 2, edited by Frank N. Magill, 761–65. Englewood Cliffs, NJ: Salem Press.

HUGO, VICTOR (1802–1885)

Victor-Marie Hugo was a French poet, novelist, and playwright who is regarded as one of France's greatest writers. He became the effective figurehead of the French Romantic movement (which dominated French literature in the first half of the nineteenth century) following the premiere of his play *Hernani* in February 1830. The French consider him one of their greatest poets, but internationally his fame rests more on his novels, especially *Les Misérables* (1862) and *Notre-Dame de Paris* (1831), the latter of which is better known to English-speaking readers as *The Hunchback of Notre Dame*.

Hugo's authorial career was divided into several phases by the fallout from mid-nineteenth-century French political events. His Republican sympathies led to his taking an active part in the 1848 Revolution against the monarchy of Louis-Philippe, and he accepted a post in the new government. However, when the elected president, Louis-Napoléon, staged the coup d'état in 1851 that transformed the Republic into the Second Empire, Hugo was exiled; he refused to accept the offer of amnesty made some years later, and he did not return to France until the emperor was forced to abdicate in 1870. Hugo completed the second major phase of his literary work while residing on the Isle of Jersey; the third, begun after his return to France, was ended by a disabling stroke that he suffered in 1878.

Hugo was sixteen years old when he initially wrote his novel *Bug-Jargal*, about the friendship between a French military officer and the eponymous African prince during the 1791 slave revolt in the French colony of Saint-Domingue that led to Haitian Revolution, but he revised the text before publishing it in 1826. It features a dwarfish obi (a sorcerer or witch-doctor) and includes a fanciful account of the syncretic process that created the religion later known as voodoo. Much of Hugo's subsequent prose fiction, including *Han d'Islande* (1823; translated as *Hans of Iceland*), features a similar mixture of melodrama and political polemic, embodying an odd fascination with human deformity that would now be considered politically incorrect. The supernatural plays no explicit role in Hugo's fiction, where the horrors are always naturalistic. *Le Dernier jour d'un condamé à mort* (1829; translated as *The Last Day of a Condemned Man*) obtained him a reputation as a pillar of what Charles Nodier dubbed the "frenetic school" of French horror fiction (Hughes 2013, 107), while emphasizing the seriousness of his crusading purpose.

Hugo's most famous novels, *Notre-Dame de Paris—1482* and *Les Misérables*, retain an element of the frenetic but operate on a larger scale with far greater artistry. The former, especially in its characterization of the lustful cleric Claude Frollo and his remarkable protégé Quasimodo, the deformed bell ringer, provided a significant archetype for the writers of popular newspaper serials who laid the foundations of modern popular fiction in the 1840s and 1850s; its imagery is prolifically echoed in the works of Alexandre Dumas, Eugène Sue, and Paul Féval. The novel likewise influenced popular film, with *The Hunchback of Notre Dame* receiving several memorable cinematic treatments, including, especially, the silent 1923 version starring Lon Chaney as Quasimodo and the lavish 1939 Hollywood production starring Charles Laughton.

Hugo's superbly flamboyant melodrama *L'Homme qui rit* (1869; translated as *The Man Who Laughs*) recounts the bizarre adventures of Gwynplaine, the last victim of a child-mutilating *comprachicos* (or "child-buyer," a term coined by Hugo to refer to those who, according to folkloric accounts, mutilated children in order to make them sellable as exotic specimens) before and after he comes into his legitimate inheritance as an English peer, having been saved from an early death by the vagabond philosopher Ursus and his pet wolf Homo. Gwynplaine's particular mutilation—the cutting of his mouth into a perpetual grin—has been memorably portrayed in a number of films, most notably the 1928 American silent film *The Man Who Laughs*, directed by the German Expressionist filmmaker Paul Leni and starring Conrad Veidt. Hugo's reach into the fantastic and speculative realms of international popular culture was further extended when Veidt's portrayal of Gwynplaine later contributed to the inspiration behind Batman's arch-nemesis, The Joker, "another mutilated, grinning character who defies the established order and demonstrates its weakness" (Heldenfels 2015, 98).

Brian Stableford

See also: Baudelaire, Charles; Féval, Paul; The Grotesque; Romanticism and Dark Romanticism.

Further Reading

Brombert, Victor. 1984. *Victor Hugo and the Visionary Novel.* Cambridge, MA: Harvard University Press.

Heldenfels, Richard D. 2015. "More Than the Hood Was Red." In *The Joker: A Serious Study of the Clown Prince of Crime*, edited by Robert Moses Peaslee and Robert G. Weiner, 94–108. Jackson: University Press of Mississippi.

Houston, John Porter. 1974. *Victor Hugo.* Boston: Twayne.

Hughes, William. 2013. *Historical Dictionary of Gothic Literature.* Lanham, MD; Toronto, Canada; and Plymouth, UK: Scarecrow Press.

HUYSMANS, J. K. (1848–1907)

Charles Marie Georges Huysmans was a nineteenth-century French author who wrote under the name Joris-Karl (J. K.) Huysmans, and whose Decadent and Symbolist writings were an important influence on horror fiction. His fierce blend of the antihuman, the antisocial, and the antirational, coupled with a hypnotic prose style that combines realist precision with strange flights of fancy, inspired not merely H. P. Lovecraft and his followers, but also Clark Ashton Smith, Thomas Ligotti, Poppy Z. Brite, and others. Huysmans's fiction contains little supernaturalism, but is punctuated by compelling intervals of the horrible.

Huysmans's career had three phases. In the first phase (1874–1884), he worked as a naturalist under the influence of Émile Zola. This effort enabled Huysmans to develop an astonishing mastery of description that he put to use subsequently when describing the bizarre, the repulsive, and the ineffable. In the second phase (1884–1891), which is of most relevance here, his novels embodied the concept of "supernatural realism," where narrative precision is occasionally pushed into the realm of the eccentric when something hideous is described. In the final phase (1895–1907), Huysmans recounted his religious conversion.

Huysmans influenced horror fiction, first, with his sensibility. He seems to find something of the sublime in things that would normally evoke disgust. Second, Huysmans discarded linear plot development for a series of loosely connected set-pieces or tableaux. Instead of incidents, he made language itself—that is, the mood or atmosphere of the narrative—the central feature of his work.

The influential *À Rebours* (variously translated as *Against the Grain* or *Against Nature*, 1884) is the primary example of Decadent literature, in which the artificial is seen as superior to the natural world. The jaded des Esseintes secludes himself in the countryside and attempts to amuse himself with, among other things, grotesque flowers and plants, strange literature and art, and a "mouth organ" that dispenses "inner symphonies" of liqueurs. Some of the narrator's flights of fancy, such as his wild imaginings regarding Gustave Moreau's painting *L'Apparition* (1874), shade into the realm of horror.

In *En Rade* (variously translated as *Becalmed, A Haven,* or *Stranded*, 1887), Jacques Marles takes refuge from his Parisian creditors in a remote, run-down château. He finds the countryside disturbing, the local peasants offensive, and the house potentially haunted. Interspersed with the narrative are three dream sequences that include some of the most excitingly weird prose Huysmans wrote.

In *Là-Bas* (*Down There* or *The Damned*, 1891), the novelist Durtal undertakes biographical research on fourteenth-century satanist and child-murderer Gilles de Rais, and discovers that occult rites are still being practiced in Paris. Huysmans's vivid description of a Black Mass is as hideous as anything in modern horror fiction.

Steven J. Mariconda

See also: Baudelaire, Charles; Brite, Poppy Z.; The Haunted House or Castle; Ligotti, Thomas; Lovecraft, H. P.; Romanticism and Dark Romanticism; Smith, Clark Ashton; The Sublime; *Part One, Horror through History*: Horror in the Nineteenth Century; *Part Two, Themes, Topics, and Genres*: The Gothic Literary Tradition.

Further Reading

Antosh, Ruth B. 1986. *Reality and Illusion in the Novels of J.-K. Huysmans.* Amsterdam: Rodopi.

Baldick, Robert. 1955. *The Life of J.-K. Huysmans.* Oxford: Clarendon Press.

Cevasco, George A. 1980. *J.-K. Huysmans: A Reference Guide.* Boston: G. K. Hall.

Ridge, George Ross. 1968. *Joris-Karl Huysmans.* New York: Twayne.

I AM LEGEND

A dystopic vampire novel from 1954, *I Am Legend* is one of writer Richard Matheson's best-known works. The plot concerns the fate of the last remaining human on earth, Robert Neville, who is a survivor of a war-driven plague that has turned the rest of humanity into monstrous versions of themselves with symptoms resembling vampirism. Neville, who has lost his entire family, is desperate to find a cure for the pandemic, to which he alone is immune.

Frightened and lonely, he barricades himself in his house, which becomes a symbol for the last vestiges of society as it was before the catastrophe. Groups of vampires try to overwhelm him every night, led by Ben Cortman, his neighbor. Eventually, in his daily forays to find food and supplies (the plague victims cannot go out in the daytime), he stumbles upon a woman, Ruth, who appears to be uninfected. After a time, he learns that she is a spy sent by the others to gather data, and that she was slowly able to overcome the aspect of the illness that prevented her from traveling in the daylight, thus enabling her to masquerade as a human.

After a warning to leave or he will be killed, Neville is injured mortally in another skirmish with the nocturnal army of vampires. As he is dying, Neville realizes that he is simply a memory waiting to happen, the residue of an older time. In the new society that will live after him, he will be remembered as a legend. He hastens his own end by committing suicide rather than dying from his wounds or facing execution at the hands of his adversaries.

The relationship between *I Am Legend* and its multiple cinematic adaptations is more than a little ironic. The first direct adaptation, 1964's *The Last Man on Earth*, retained the novel's identification of the reanimated dead as vampires. The second, 1971's *The Omega Man*, changed this to nocturnal albino mutants. Then 1968's *Night of the Living Dead*, which was largely inspired by Matheson's novel, recast the novel's vampires as shambling, flesh-eating ghouls and created the modern image and idea of the zombie. Four decades later, in 2007, another cinematic adaptation of *I Am Legend* appeared, this one titled directly after the book—but the word "vampire" is never mentioned in it, and the monsters are now presented as murderous mutants that are, effectively, zombies.

Matt Cardin

With this important novel—which appears to expand on similar ideas from the masterful 1951 novella *Dark Benediction* by Walter M. Miller Jr.—Matheson firmly established himself as a force in American horror literature and a major influence on subsequent writers in the genre (including Stephen King, who has cited Matheson, and particularly *I Am Legend*, as a chief influence on his own writing). Rife with symbolism and infused with a rich thematic subtext—the new consuming the old and effecting change (revolution); groupthink as an infectious and toxic technique to blunt individualism; the dangers of technology run amok; the crushing hell of existential nothingness—the book is still a benchmark in the field, and it holds up well more than six decades after its first publication. Transcending the vampire myth, it has been a chief inspiration for the postapocalyptic zombie and disease tropes so prevalent in the postmodern era, especially in film and comics—beginning with the first film adaptation of the book, *The Last Man on Earth* (1964), starring Vincent Price and penned by Matheson himself under the pseudonym of Logan Swanson (a name he reserved for works he contributed to, but which were altered beyond his comfort level as a creator). There have also been two additional versions, *The Omega Man* (1971), starring Charlton Heston, and *I Am Legend* (2007), starring Will Smith. The book's profound impact on popular culture is also visible in the precipitous rise and eventual dominance of zombies in horror entertainment; *I Am Legend* was a prime catalyst for George A. Romero's original *Night of the Living Dead* (1968), the movie that introduced the now-iconic zombie of pop culture.

In 2011 the Horror Writers Association gave the novel a special one-time Bram Stoker Award for Best Vampire Novel of the Century.

Jason V Brock

See also: Vampires; Zombies; *Part One, Horror through History*: Horror from 1950 to 2000; *Part Two, Themes, Topics, and Genres*: Apocalyptic Horror; Horror Literature as Social Criticism and Commentary; Page to Screen: The Influence of Literary Horror on Film and Television; Vampire Fiction from Dracula to Lestat and Beyond.

Further Reading

Clasen, Mathias. 2010. "Vampire Apocalypse: A Biocultural Critique of Richard Matheson's *I Am Legend*." *Philosophy and Literature* 34, no. 2: 313–328.

Ketchum, Jack. 2009. "On *I Am Legend*." In *The Twilight and Other Zones: The Dark Worlds of Richard Matheson*, edited by Stanley Wiater, Matthew R. Bradley, and Paul Stuve, 57–61. New York: Citadel Press Books.

Miller, Walter M., Jr. 1951. "Dark Benediction." *Fantastic Adventures* 13, no. 9 (September). Chicago: Ziff-Davis.

Pulliam, June M., and Anthony J. Fonseca. 2016. *Richard Matheson's Monsters: Gender in the Stories, Scripts, Novels, and Twilight Zone Episodes*. Lanham, MD: Rowman & Littlefield Publishing Group.

"I HAVE NO MOUTH AND I MUST SCREAM"

First published in 1967, Harlan Ellison's "I Have No Mouth and I Must Scream" is a bleak, postapocalyptic story that takes place more than a century after a nuclear war between the United States, Russia, and China. The nuclear holocaust is initiated when one of the three nations' supercomputers becomes sentient. The self-named AM, frustrated by its disembodiment, kills every human being in the world except for five individuals, whom it has psychologically and physically altered and kept alive to torture.

The story is told from the perspective of the youngest among them, Ted, an unreliable narrator who suffers from paranoia, but who considers himself to be the only unaffected individual in the group. The other four characters include Benny, a former scientist who has been transformed into a near-mindless, ape-like figure with grotesquely enlarged sexual organs; Gorrister, formerly a principled intellectual who is now apathetic and in a constant state of languor; Nimdok, so named by AM and the oldest of the group, who suggests that they go on a quest for a cache of canned food; and Ellen, the sole woman and African American among them, whom AM has altered to be sexually insatiable. The story follows these characters on their journey to find sustenance, all the while being tortured in various ways by AM. The supercomputer (or A.I., as it would be more commonly called today), starves them only to later provide a menu of increasingly disgusting foodstuff, which the protagonists have no choice but to consume. As well, AM creates bizarre creatures that hunt them, tortures them with sounds, blinds Benny, and continuously plays on their collective angst. After an arduous journey the group finally reaches the stash of canned foods, but realize they have no way of opening the cans. The entire expedition, it seems, has been a ruse crafted by AM, a seed of false hope planted as another means of torment. At this point Ted, realizing that killing his fellows is the only way to save them from their predicament, attacks and kills Benny and Gorrister. Ellen, reaching the same conclusion, kills Nimdok and is in turn killed by Ted. AM, furious at what has occurred, alters Ted into a blob of flesh, trapping his consciousness forever in an unresponsive and helpless physical and mental prison.

The events that motivate "I Have No Mouth and I Must Scream" read like a checklist of cultural anxieties especially prevalent at the time the story was published: cold war paranoia, fear of nuclear destruction, and distrust of technology, especially the increasingly widespread use of computers in industry. These concerns and others are displayed in full force in the story and are given additional weight by Ellison's unabashed narrative voice that revels in the extremity of the author's terrible vision.

A well-received video game based on the story and with input from Ellison was published in 1995. In 2009 the story was selected for inclusion in the Library of America's two-volume anthology *American Fantastic Tales*, representing the best in American fantastic and horror fiction that has been published from the eighteenth century to the present.

Javier A. Martinez

See also: Ellison, Harlan; Unreliable Narrator; "The Whimper of Whipped Dogs"; *Part Two, Themes, Topics, and Genres*: Apocalyptic Horror; Horror Literature and Science Fiction; Horror Literature as Social Criticism and Commentary.

Further Reading

Francavilla, Joseph, ed. 2012. *Critical Insights: Harlan Ellison*. Pasadena: Salem Press.
Weil, Ellen R., and Gary K. Wolfe. 2002. *Harlan Ellison: The Edge of Forever*. Columbus, OH: Ohio State University Press.

IN A GLASS DARKLY

One of the most lauded and studied works by J. Sheridan Le Fanu (1814–1873), the collection of short fictions *In a Glass Darkly* represents the height of its author's subtle power in penning terror and suspense alongside keen insights into the human mind and conscience. Collected in three volumes in 1872, the year before Le Fanu's death, *In a Glass Darkly* includes five previously published tales now presented together as case studies from the personal papers of Dr. Martin Hesselius, a German physician and practitioner of metaphysical medicine.

Comprising the first volume of *In a Glass Darkly*, the three tales "Green Tea," "The Familiar," and "Mr. Justice Harbottle" exhibit a specific similarity in that they each recount the story of an esteemed professional (a reverend, a naval officer, and a judge, respectively) who becomes haunted by a presence that no one else can see. Le Fanu plays skillfully with the uncanny, providing some evidence for the reality of these supernatural entities while also including more than a suggestion that these men are—more naturally—haunted by their own flaws, the entities they see being only psychological manifestations of moral failings or selfish compulsion.

The latter interpretation is further supported by the theme of the fourth tale, *The Room in the Dragon Volant*, a masterful nod to the earliest staples of the Gothic genre—an adventurous mystery of romance and evil intent. While part of the mystery involves a room known to have been the place of mysterious disappearances, the narrative is one of the "supernatural explained." The mysterious room is a setting only of mere human deceits, but deceits that nearly cost the protagonist his life as he becomes ensnared in a confidence scheme to steal his fortune and is nearly buried alive. As in the previous stories, Le Fanu suggests that this mystery is also a moral tale exposing the weaknesses of romantic, idealistic, and selfish thinking when such supersedes proper restraint.

The finale of *In a Glass Darkly* is also Le Fanu's most influential work: the homoerotically charged vampire novella *Carmilla*. In contrast to the previous stories, *Carmilla* is undeniably fantastical. The vampire is real, and the young protagonist, Laura, is saved from danger by the insights of Baron Vordenburg's occult scholarship. Several attributes of *Carmilla* were a direct influence on Bram Stoker's *Dracula* (1897), including the sexualizing of the vampire and the juxtaposition of ancient superstition with modern science. Dr. Martin Hesselius and Baron Vordenburg serve as models for Stoker's Abraham Van Helsing. Like Stoker's more famous work, *Carmilla* draws attention to the moral and physical dangers of sexual and intellectual repression in civilized society. Only in facing challenges responsibly with knowledge and temperance may people find victory over that which haunts them. Removed from danger, Laura concludes her story, explaining that "often from a reverie I have started, fancying I heard the light step of Carmilla at the drawing-room door" (Le Fanu 1993, 319). Whether real or imagined, the fears Le Fanu masterfully mirrors in *In a Glass Darkly* are clear reflections of the human psyche.

Mark Wegley

See also: Carmilla; Gothic Hero/Villain; "Green Tea"; Le Fanu, J. Sheridan; Psychological Horror; Terror versus Horror; The Uncanny; Vampires.

Further Reading

Crawford, Gary William, Jim Rockhill, and Brian J. Showers, eds. 2011. *Reflections in a Glass Darkly: Essays on J. Sheridan Le Fanu*. New York: Hippocampus Press.

Harris, Sally. 2003. "Spiritual Warnings: The Ghost Stories of Joseph Sheridan Le Fanu." *Victorians Institute Journal* 31: 9–39.

Le Fanu, Sheridan. [1871–1872] 1993. *Carmilla*. In *In a Glass Darkly*, 243–319. Oxford: Oxford University Press.

Melada, Ivan. 1987. *Sheridan Le Fanu*. Boston: Twayne.

Sullivan, Jack. 1978. *Elegant Nightmares: The English Ghost Story from Le Fanu to Blackwood*. Athens: Ohio University Press.

Tracy, Robert. 1993. Introduction. *In a Glass Darkly*. Oxford: Oxford University Press.

Wegley, Mark. 2001. "Unknown Fear: Joseph Sheridan Le Fanu and the Literary Fantastic." *Philological Review* 27, no. 2 (Fall): 59–77.

INCUBI AND SUCCUBI

Incubi and succubi are male and female demons that, according to folklore and legend, engage in sexual intercourse with human beings, draining their life force and, if allowed to continue, eventually destroying them. Beliefs about such demons have played an important role in the religious and folkloric belief of Western Christian culture for more than a thousand years. Incubi and succubi have also played a significant role in horror literature and cinema.

The idea of sexual contact between humans and the ghost world seems to be a very old one. The Chaldeans, a Semitic people in the south of Mesopotamia (ca. first millennium BCE), had their "demons of nocturnal emission," and the Israelites also knew a cult involving sexual contact with demonic goats, which was forbidden by the Bible (Leviticus 17:7). The Greeks had their fauns and sylvan spirits, and Middle Eastern peoples believed in *djinn* who lusted after women.

The first mention of incubi (the male variety of these demons) can be found in the writings of Aurelius Augustinus (354–430 CE)—better known as Saint Augustine—especially in his monumental *De Civitate Dei* or *The City of God* (written between 413 and 426). He asserts that common folk call the dreaded fauns and sylvan ghosts "incubi," but he is not sure whether these beings are capable of sexual intercourse with humans since they only have an "aerial" body (Augustinus 1841, book 15, chapter 23). It is worth remarking that Augustinus saw these pagan spirits as demons, so through him they became a part of the Christian religious system.

From the eleventh century CE, incubi and succubi were treated as scientific fact in Western culture. Authors such as Albert the Great (ca. 1200–1280), Bonaventura (1221–1274), John Duns Scotus (ca. 1266–1308), William Durandus (1230–1296), and Peter of Aquila (d. 1361) asserted that demons have a body that is apt to have intercourse with humans. The most important propagator of this opinion was the great Catholic scholastic theologian Thomas Aquinas (ca. 1225–1274). He affirmed in his highly influential *Summa Theologica* (written ca. 1265–1273) that sexual contact between demons in the form of incubi or succubi and humans cannot be denied. Aquinas thought it possible that children may be born of such a union. These children, he said, are not the children of demons but of humans, since demons are not able to produce semen. They collect it as succubi from male persons and pass it over to women after having changed their form into that of incubi (Thomas Aquinas 2012, p. I, qu. LI, art. III).

This concept of incubi and succubi became an integral part of the later witch trials that began as a mass phenomenon throughout Europe in the late 1400s and reached their peak (having spread to America as well) in the late 1500s and early 1600s. The most notorious book on witches and witchcraft, the witch-hunt manual *Malleus Maleficarum* (*The Hammer of the Witches*), first published in 1487, has a lot to say about incubi and succubi. The author of this book, the German Catholic clergyman Heinrich Kramer, was of the same opinion as Aquinas concerning procreation by demons, teaching that they can beget children by stealing semen. They feel no lust, says Kramer; their only purpose is to lead humanity into sin. The witch, on the other hand, lusts after the incubus and embraces him willingly, so she sins of her own free will.

Nicholas Rémy (ca. 1530–1612), a provost (judge) of Nancy (a city in Lorraine, a territory on the border between France and Germany, eventually annexed by France in 1766), wrote an important book on witchcraft, *Daemonolatreia* (1595), in which he treats incubi and succubi among many other subjects. He writes that the demons assume bodily form, "but I think that body will be either the corpse of a dead man, or else some concretion and condensation of vapours" (Rémy 2008, 12). Following Aquinas's theory, Rémy maintains that the incubus injects the semen he previously collected as a succubus, and he adds that "if the Demon emits any semen, it is so cold that they [the witches] recoil with horror on receiving it" (12–13). In contrast to Thomas Aquinas and the *Malleus Maleficarum*, Rémy does not believe that children can be born from the borrowed semen.

The Franciscan theologian Ludovico Maria Sinistrari (1622–1701) produced a whole book on the subject of incubi and succubi under the title *De Daemonialitate et Incubis et Succubis*, written around 1700 but not published until 1875. Sinistrari details all the theories here described, plus many stories of the workings of the demonic incubi and succubi, but he introduces a new element that might explain why his book was not printed during his lifetime. In contrast to the teachings of the church authorities, he sees the incubi and succubi not only as spiritual beings but also as corporeal beings: " those creatures would be made from the most subtile part of all elements. . . . God Himself, through the medium of Angels, made their body as He did man's body, to which an immortal spirit was to be united" (Sinistrari 1927, 35, 36). Sinistrari calls these beings animals, and he is of the opinion that they have a soul and are capable of salvation. So for him they lose a great part of their demonic nature and return to what they initially were: fauns and sylvan beings.

This deep history of theological speculation and, as it may seem to modern sensibilities, supernatural obsession lies behind the long-lived substream of horror stories about sexual demons (or sometimes, if not specifically demons, then supernatural sexual predators), even in those instances when the incubus and succubus are not explicitly named, and/or when the basic idea of them has been abstracted away from overtly theological concerns as such and placed in the service of fictional works more generally concerned with evoking a thrill of horror. A notable early example is Matthew Lewis's classic novel *The Monk* (1796), in which the succubus-like character of Mathilda, empowered by the Devil himself, seduces the saintly priest Ambrosio with her sexual wiles, leading him inexorably to his eventual doom and spiritual damnation. Additional examples could be multiplied almost indefinitely. J. K. Huysmans deals with incubi and succubi along with many other supernatural and occult matters in his 1891 novel *The Damned*. F. Marion Crawford's "For the Blood Is the Life" (1905) relates the tale of a murdered woman's vampiric spirit that drains the vitality of the young man she loved from afar in life. F. Scott Fitzgerald's "A Short Trip Home" (1927), published in *The Saturday Evening Post*, tells of a young female college student being seduced by an incubus, in this case the ghost of a dead young man. In *Rosemary's Baby* (1967) Ira Levin has the Devil himself, aided by a modern-day coven of witches, play an incubus-like role by impregnating a woman. In Ray Russell's *The Incubus* (1976), a series of rapes and murders in a California coastal town are the work of a demonic incubus that is trying to impregnate human women. In Frank De Felitta's *The Entity* (1978)—a fictionalized account of a real-life paranormal assault case in 1974—two parapsychology graduate students investigate the case of a California woman who has been repeatedly raped and assaulted in her home by an invisible presence.

Rosemary's Baby, *The Incubus*, and *The Entity* were all adapted to film (the first in 1968, the latter two in 1982), and the results represent just three entries—the first a classic horror film directed by Roman Polanski, the second something considerably lesser, the third a notorious and increasingly valorized entry in modern horror cinema—in the onscreen careers of demonic sexual spirits. As with the literary incarnations of incubi and succubi, additional examples in cinema are plentiful. But of more significance in establishing the import of incubi and succubi for horror fiction is the fact that near the end of the eighteenth century, the Swiss painter Henry Fuseli (1741–1825) produced what has sometimes been characterized as the master image of the entire Gothic horror movement, and this took the form of an explicit representation of the incubus. Fuseli's *The Nightmare*, which he painted in 1781 and then went on to reproduce in several alternate versions when it proved extremely popular, depicts a woman fallen backward across a bed in a swoon while a spectral horse peers out from behind a curtain. On the woman's stomach squats a leering, apelike gargoyle or demon. The specific meaning is unclear, but the painting's subject is plainly that of a woman being assaulted and oppressed in her sleep by an imp or demon, whether real or the product of a nightmare. London's Tate Britain museum, in notes written for a 2006 exhibition of works by Fuseli and William Blake, describes the painting as "an enduring image of sexual terror" ("Gothic Nightmares" 2006).

Fuseli apparently suffered from what would now be called sleep paralysis—an experience of coming to consciousness from sleep and finding oneself paralyzed with a sense of suffocating weight on one's chest, often accompanied by terrifying perceptions of a threatening supernatural presence—and his painting is often interpreted today as a depiction of that experience. Not insignificantly, this same experience was the original referent of the English word "nightmare," which has since devolved to mean simply a bad dream. Also not insignificantly, it has often been invoked in the modern world as an explanation for the many firsthand reports throughout history of apparent attacks by incubi and succubi. Whatever the case, Fuseli's painting caused a sensation when it was first displayed in 1782 at the annual Royal Academy exhibition in London, and it went on to exert a profound influence over Gothic and horror fiction, being used as a model, for instance, by Mary Shelley in *Frankenstein* for her description of the scene in which the monster kills Elizabeth, and then again by director James Whale for the analogous scene in the classic 1931 Universal Studios adaptation of Shelley's novel. Echoes of it, and thus of the basic incubus/succubus dynamic, have also been discerned in much vampire fiction and film, where the basic idea of the vampire, which drains people's life blood—a trope that is obviously and easily relatable to the sexual drainings of the victims of incubi and succubi—is often presented in scenes of a sleeping man or woman being assaulted by a creature that leans or hovers over them.

The upshot for the world of horror literature is that the incubus and the succubus are not just two monstrous figures existing on a level with many others (such as the zombie, the werewolf, and the mummy), but are somehow implicated in the roots of literary horror as a whole. Originally conceived in Western Christian culture as sexually predatory demons that try to destroy people's bodies and souls, and given paradigmatic treatment by such towering figures as Augustine and Aquinas, the incubus and succubus were incorporated into horror literature on a veritably genetic level right from the start.

Michael Siefener and Matt Cardin

See also: The Damned; Devils and Demons; Dreams and Nightmares; *The Monk*; *Rosemary's Baby*; Russell, Ray; "A Short Trip Home"; Vampires; Witches and Witchcraft.

Further Reading

Andriano, Joseph. 1993. *Our Ladies of Darkness: Feminine Daemonology in Male Gothic Fiction*. University Park, PA: Pennsylvania State University Press.

"Gothic Nightmares: Fuseli, Blake and the Romantic Imagination: Room 8." 2006. Tate. http://www.tate.org.uk/whats-on/tate-britain/exhibition/gothic-nightmares-fuseli-blake-and-romantic-imagination/gothic-6.

Moffitt, John F. 2002. "A Pictorial Counterpart to 'Gothick' Literature: Fuseli's *The Nightmare*." *Mosaic: A Journal for the Interdisciplinary Study of Literature* 35, no. 1: 173–196.

Rémy, Nicolas. [1595, 1930] 2008. *Demonolatry: An Account of the Historical Practice of Witchcraft*. Translated by E. Allen Ashwin. Introduction and notes by Montague Summers. Mineola, NY: Dover.

Sinistrari, Ludovico Maria. [ca. 1700, 1927] 2014. *Demoniality*. Translated by Montague Summers. Whitefish, MT: Literary Licensing.

Stephens, Walter. 2002. *Witchcraft, Sex, and the Crisis of Belief*. Chicago and London: University of Chicago Press.

Stewart, Charles. 2002. "Erotic Dreams and Nightmares from Antiquity to the Present." *Journal of the Royal Anthropological Institute* 8, no. 2 (June): 279–309.

INTERNATIONAL GOTHIC ASSOCIATION

The International Gothic Association (IGA) is the organization that brings together critics and scholars of the Gothic from around the world. It does so in various ways: through its website, through its biennial conferences, and through its journal, *Gothic Studies*. It also acts as an informal network, which has had tremendous benefits in terms of joint publication, multiauthored books, and research projects. It was founded in 1991 at the University of East Anglia, United Kingdom.

The IGA's website, www.iga.stir.ac.uk, is currently hosted by the University of Stirling and provides information about current and future events, including conferences, publications, and contact details, as well as a Postgraduate Forum and a Directory that offers links to other Gothic-related resources.

The biennial conferences have been held over the years at the universities of East Anglia, Stirling, Liverpool Hope, Lancaster, Surrey, and at St. Mary's College Twickenham in the United Kingdom; at Mount Saint Vincent, Simon Fraser, and Montréal/Wilfrid Laurier universities in Canada; at the University of Aix-en-Provence in France; and at the University of Heidelberg in Germany. The 2017 conference was held in Mexico.

Gothic Studies was first published in 1999 and is a fully refereed journal appearing twice a year. Its founding editor, William Hughes, remains in that post; at present the journal alternates between "general issues" and issues devoted to a special theme in the Gothic. A particularly impressive spin-off from the journal is the new series of books, *International Gothic*, published by Manchester University Press.

The IGA elects a president for a two-year period, although this has often been extended to four years by mutual agreement. Past presidents include the late Allan Lloyd Smith; Robert Miles; Jerrold E. Hogle; Steven Bruhm; Avril Horner and Sue Zlosnik; and, currently, Catherine Spooner and Angela Wright. It operates through an Executive Committee, consisting of the president(s), the executive officer, the chair of the IGA Advisory Committee, and the editor of *Gothic Studies*. The Advisory Committee, a larger body, has an additional number of members, between fifteen and twenty; its chair is David Punter. There is an Annual General Meeting of the IGA each year, in person during conference year and electronically in the other years.

The IGA is committed to furthering and promoting the study of the Gothic in all its forms, from traditional Gothic fiction through contemporary Goth culture, including arts ranging from literature to the visual arts and music. It seeks to capture and discuss Gothic as it has manifested itself historically, from the medieval to the modern, and to ensure that scholars of the field are able to access resources—human and technological—that will aid them in their research.

The IGA has proved resilient in its approach to changing practices in research, as well as in contemporary developments in the meaning of Gothic, which continue to evolve as Gothic finds new modes of expression in cultures worldwide. The IGA has proved itself, and continues to do so, an organization responsive to new trends, even as it endeavors to keep alive the memory of past cultural traditions.

David Punter

See also: Part Two, Themes, Topics, and Genres: The Gothic Literary Tradition; Horror Criticism.

Further Reading

International Gothic Association. Accessed June 27, 2016. http://www.iga.stir.ac.uk.

INTERNATIONAL HORROR GUILD AWARD

The International Horror Guild (IHG) (originally the International Horror Critics Guild) was created in 1995 as a means of recognizing the achievements of creators in the field of horror and dark fantasy, supplementing other similar genre awards such as the Bram Stoker Award and the World Fantasy Award. The last awards (for works from 2007) were announced in 2008.

The IHG Awards, which were spearheaded in their last years of existence by editor and critic Paula Guran, were decided by a jury of notable, knowledgeable horror/dark fantasy critics and reviewers. Over the years, Edward Bryant, Stefan Dziemianowicz, William Sheehan, Ann Kennedy Vandermeer, Fiona Webster, and Hank Wagner served as judges for the awards. Although it was a juried award, the IHG judges requested recommendations from the public to help them in their search for the most deserving candidates. Those recommendations were then considered when determining the nominees for the awards. The judges decided on winners in each category from the final ballot of nominees. The list of categories included Novel, Long Fiction, Mid-Length Fiction, Short Fiction, Collection, Anthology, Periodical, Illustrated Narrative, Nonfiction, and Art.

The IHG Awards were usually announced annually during a special presentation at a convention or other event. The awards were hosted by the World Fantasy Convention (WFC), World Horror Convention (WHC), and Dragon*Con. The IHG was in no way officially affiliated with WFC, WHC, or with Dragon*Con, nor was it considered a sponsor of any event.

Each year, the IHG presented a "Living Legend" award for outstanding contributions to the field. Harlan Ellison was the first recipient in 1995, and Peter Straub was the last in 2008. Along the way, several other notables were recognized, including Ramsey Campbell, Chelsea Quinn Yarbro, Gahan Wilson, Richard Matheson, Stephen King, Hugh B. Cave, E. F. Bleiler, William F. Nolan, Ray Bradbury, and Clive Barker.

A lasting legacy of the IHG Awards is their usefulness to readers who are interested in discovering high-quality work in the fields of horror and dark fantasy, since the works of those named as Living Legends by the IHG can provide a valuable guide to recommended reading, as provided by a knowledgeable group of judges who loved and respected genre fiction. The annual listings of the nominees in each award category are also helpful. As of this writing, a listing of all nominees and winners is still being maintained at www.horroraward.org.

Hank Wagner

See also: Barker, Clive; Bleiler, E. F.; Bradbury, Ray; Bram Stoker Award; Campbell, Ramsey; Dark Fantasy; Ellison, Harlan; King, Stephen; Matheson, Richard; Nolan, William F.; Shirley Jackson Awards; World Fantasy Award; Yarbro, Chelsea Quinn.

Further Reading

International Horror Guild. 2008. http://www.horroraward.org/index.html.

INTERVIEW WITH THE VAMPIRE

Interview with the Vampire is the first novel by Anne Rice. Published in 1976, it raises existential questions about the meaning of good, evil, life, and death in the modern world, and it contributed to a renewed cultural fascination with the vampire by abandoning the conventionally tyrannical villain in the *Dracula* mold that had become a staple of the genre.

The novel is presented as an interview with one Louis de Pointe du Lac, who, in the late twentieth century, recounts the story of how he was turned into a vampire in the eighteenth century by a vampire named Lestat; how he struggled against his

A Template for Goths

Interview with the Vampire was not commercially successful when it was first published, but its reputation steadily grew, and this was linked in part to its profound influence on the nascent Goth subculture. As Gothic scholar Catherine Spooner has observed, "Despite preceding the first wave of Goth, *Interview with the Vampire* (1976) created, in its angst-ridden hero Louis and hedonistic anti-hero Lestat, Goth fictional icons. . . . The novel provided a template for the emergent Goth scene to project itself onto" (Spooner 2012, 358).

Matt Cardin

Source: Spooner, Catherine. 2012. "Goth Culture." In *A New Companion to the Gothic*, edited by David Punter, 350–366. Malden, MA: Wiley-Blackwell.

vampire nature, regularly clashing violently with his maker, who encouraged him to embrace this dark gift; and how the two settled into an unsettling domestic unity in New Orleans, following their "creation" of Claudia, a vampire destined to remain a child in body, if not mind, for eternity. Through Claudia, Rice introduces one of the more disturbing characters in horror literature. Claudia is a taboo-breaking creation who crosses many cultural and social boundaries, embodying both innocent victim and monstrous creation; child and lover; the dead child but also the child who will never die. While Louis is the narrator, it is Claudia's story that haunts the novel, bubbling beneath the surface, generating unease and discomfort because she is fundamentally unknowable. Through this unholy union between Louis, Lestat, and Claudia, the novel offers a fascinating and perverse representation of family, bound by blood and death.

Key influences on Rice's novel were Richard Matheson, whose horror and science fiction writing reimagined familiar genres through a contemporary lens, and the Universal horror film *Dracula's Daughter* (1936), which is notable for its sympathetic and yet morally complex female vampire, who longs for release from the curse of vampirism, while remaining driven by her insatiable physical desire for blood. Rice would draw into her novel the film's exploration of the tension between desire and guilt, between self-loathing and the sensual pleasure in being a vampire. These characteristics were enhanced by the novel's first-person narration.

While Rice did not originate the figure of the sympathetic vampire, her novel emphasized the importance of the vampire having its own voice, making the novel particularly significant in a period when marginalized groups sought to articulate their perspective through the civil rights, gay rights, and women's movements. This is one reason, alongside the novel's evocation of polymorphous sensuality among its primarily male vampires, that it was perceived to operate as an elongated allegory for homosexual desire, an exploration of identity, and a celebration of alternative sexualities. Ultimately, Rice offered a new model of a soulful vampire that continues to haunt contemporary literature and media.

Interview with the Vampire was adapted to film in 1994 by director Neil Jordan, with Tom Cruise as Lestat, Brad Pitt as Louis, and Kirsten Dunst as Claudia. The film version was nominated for two Academy Awards.

Stacey Abbott

See also: Rice, Anne; Vampires; *Part One, Horror through History*: Horror from 1950 to 2000; *Part Two, Themes, Topics, and Genres*: Horror Publishing, 1975–1995: The Boom Years; Page to Screen: The Influence of Literary Horror on Film and Television; Vampire Fiction from Dracula to Lestat and Beyond.

Further Reading

Benefiel, C.R. 2004. "Blood Relations: The Gothic Perversion of the Nuclear Family in Anne Rice's *Interview with the Vampire*." *Journal of Popular Culture* 38 (2): 261–273.

Tomc, S. 1997. "Dieting and Damnation: Anne Rice's *Interview with the Vampire*." In *Blood Read: The Vampire as Metaphor in Contemporary Culture*, edited by Joan Gordon and Veronica Hollinger, 95–113. Philadelphia: University of Pennsylvania Press.

Wood, Martin J. 1999. "New Life for an Old Tradition: Anne Rice and Vampire Literature." In *The Blood Is the Life*, edited by Leonard G. Heldreth and Mary Pharr, 59–78. Bowling Green, OH: Bowling Green State University Popular Press.

THE INVISIBLE MAN

The Invisible Man, published in 1897 by H. G. Wells, is a novel that explores the moral and social consequences of scientific progress through a tale of a scientist who renders himself invisible. The story begins as a mysterious man, wrapped from head to toe, takes a room in the West Sussex village of Iping. The man's strange and solitary behavior attracts the curiosity of the villagers. In a dispute over money, the stranger throws off his clothing to reveal he is entirely invisible. After causing a panic, the Invisible Man takes shelter in the home of a university friend, Kemp, and reveals himself as Griffin, a young physics student who has discovered how to render living tissue invisible. Griffin had experimented on himself to ensure he would have full credit for his discovery. His desperate escape from London, however, has left him without money, clothing, or access to the equipment he needs to become visible again, driving him insane. Rather than assist in Griffin's declared "Reign of Terror," Kemp alerts the police. After a struggle, Griffin is overwhelmed by a mob and killed, his body again becoming visible in death.

As a moral tale, Wells's novel dramatizes the Ring of Gyges episode from Plato's *Republic*, which questions whether or not morality is really the product of the fear of being caught. In addition, Wells draws much symbolism from who can and cannot "see" Griffin; Wells uses visibility in a similarly symbolic way in the 1904 short story "The Country of the Blind."

The initial horror of the Invisible Man comes from his coverings, which mark him as a man-machine hybrid. Later, when Griffin has shed his disguise, it is not his otherness that is unsettling, but his ability to move unseen into private spaces and homes. Not only a tale of scientific overreach, *The Invisible Man* also demonstrates how society rejects the abnormal: Griffin's inability or unwillingness to find help pushes him from marginal figure to antagonist.

As with Wells's other "scientific romances," scientific pursuit holds an occult power over the scientist figure, in which the abstractions of scientific research are somehow more "real," Also typical for Wells, however, the Invisible Man's extraordinary nature must contend with everyday life. Wells pits the conflict of the Invisible Man against the villagers of Iping in terms of the antagonism of town and country, of cosmopolitan progress versus tradition and superstition.

The story has since been adapted numerous times, notably in a 1933 film by director James Whale. *The Invisible Man* is an equally engaging investigation into experimentation on the body and society's resistance to scientific pursuit.

Miles Link

See also: Gothic Hero/Villain; Mad Scientist; The Uncanny; Wells, H. G.; *Part Two, Themes, Topics, and Genres*: Horror Literature and Science Fiction.

Further Reading

Beiderwell, Bruce. 1983. "The Grotesque in Wells's *The Invisible Man.*" *Extrapolation* 24 (4): 301–310.

The Invisible Man. 2014. Directed by James Whale. Los Angeles: Universal Studios Home Entertainment, DVD.

MacLean, Steven. 2009. *The Early Fiction of H.G. Wells: Fantasies of Science*. London: Palgrave Macmillan.

IRVING, WASHINGTON (1783–1859)

Born April 3, 1783, in Manhattan, New York, to Scottish-English parents, Washington Irving was a writer of short stories as well as an essayist, historian, and biographer, who became one of the first American authors to achieve international notoriety and commercial success for his work. Named after General George Washington, the revolutionary hero (and, later, first president of the United States), who had negotiated the British ceasefire the same week in which young Irving was born, Washington Irving is most famous for his 1819–1820 publication *The Sketch Book*, written under the pseudonym Geoffrey Crayon, in which his best-known stories "Rip Van Winkle" (1819) and "The Legend of Sleepy Hollow" (1820) first appeared.

Irving's career as a writer began in the *Morning Chronicle*, in which he wrote scathing social and cultural commentaries under a pseudonym (a habit he would maintain throughout his fictional works), before he founded *Salmagundi*, a literary magazine, in 1807, which also satirized New York cultural life. After the success of his first book, *A History of New York* (1809), Irving edited *Analectic Magazine* and began writing biographies. From 1819 to 1820, Irving's *The Sketch Book of Geoffrey Crayon, Gent.* was published in installments, and with its great success Irving lobbied hard for stronger legal practices to protect his lucrative copyright on both sides of the Atlantic.

Though he was and is famed more for his fictional histories and biographies of well-known historical figures than his horror fiction, Irving's "The Legend of Sleepy Hollow," a romantically Gothic tale of the headless Hessian horseman who haunts the eponymous town of Sleepy Hollow, has long been preserved in America's cultural imagination. Noted for its Gothic imagery and for its representation of local superstitions, myths, ghost stories, and the dreamy quality of pastoral life in upstate New York, "Sleepy Hollow" is lent a haunting gravitas by Irving's earlier experiences in the real-life town of Sleepy Hollow near Tarrytown, New York, where Irving recuperated from illness as a child. The story has provided the basis for one of director Tim Burton's most beautifully realized Gothic films, *Sleepy Hollow* (1999), as well as Fox TV's supernatural drama of the same title.

Other short stories published in *The Sketch Book* included "Rip Van Winkle," a Gothic pastoral folk tale cum ghost story set in the haunting Catskill Mountains, and "The Spectre Bridegroom," a Gothic drama in which a slain bridegroom returns to fulfill a promise to his bride-to-be, set in a German castle near the Rhine. *Tales of a Traveller*, published in 1824 (which includes the supernatural horror story "The Devil and Tom Walker"), was also published under Irving's Geoffrey Crayon pseudonym. Later in his life, Irving published famed biographies on Christopher Columbus, Oliver Goldsmith, the prophet Muhammad, and George Washington, as well as other works of fiction inspired by his time in Spain, where he lived from 1842 to 1846, serving as the U.S. minister to Spain.

Irving died on November 28, 1859, at seventy-six years of age. His literary reputation and his impact on American culture is one of the greatest among his contemporaries. A little-known fact is that Irving was the first to call New York City "Gotham," the name that later became famous in the Batman comic book universe. The surname of his fictional historian persona, Diedrich Knickerbocker, has become the colloquial name for New Yorkers. Irving is also responsible for reimagining American Christmastime in his writing, and he was the first to introduce the (false) idea that Europeans previously believed the earth to be flat, prior to European voyages of discovery. As a writer of Gothic horror, Irving's output was minimal, but the influence of his most well-known works on the genre (particularly "Sleepy Hollow") cannot be overstated.

Ian Kinane

See also: "The Legend of Sleepy Hollow"; *Part One, Horror through History*: Horror in the Nineteenth Century; *Part Two, Themes, Topics, and Genres*: Ghost Stories.

Further Reading

Burstein, Andrew. 2007. *The Original Knickerbocker: The Life of Washington Irving*. New York: Basic Books.

Irving, Pierre M. 1862. *Life and Letters of Washington Irving*, edited by Richard D. Rust. New York: G. P. Putnam.

Irving, Washington. 1969–1986. *The Complete Works of Washington Irving*, edited by Richard D. Rust. Wisconsin: Twayne.

Williams, Stanley T. 1935. *The Life of Washington Irving*. Two Volumes. Oxford: Oxford University Press.

THE ISLAND OF DOCTOR MOREAU

The Island of Doctor Moreau, published in 1896 by H. G. Wells, is a novel about scientific ethics and human identity. The story is told by Edward Prendick, sole survivor of a shipwreck in the South Pacific. He is rescued by Montgomery, a former medical student fleeing scandal, now carrying a consignment of animals to an isolated island. On the island, Prendick discovers several menacing, strange-looking men. Prendick initially fears that Moreau is transforming humans into animals; Moreau explains, however, that his experiments shape animals into human form. The resulting "Beast People" are held in check by a strict set of laws meant to suppress their instincts, especially the tasting of blood.

One day, Moreau is accidentally killed by a half-finished creation. Without their supreme authority figure, the Beast People revolt, and Montgomery is killed as well. Prendick lives an uneasy existence with the Beast People, who revert slowly to animal instinct, until he escapes the island by boat.

Moreau echoes the tale of Circe from the *Odyssey*, and also John Milton's *Comus*. Both of these older works depict a malevolent magician transforming lost travelers into animals. The book also draws from Jonathan Swift's inverted critique of society in *Gulliver's Travels*, especially the ending: upon his return to England, Prendick finds it difficult to distinguish human beings from animals, and, like Gulliver preferring the company of his horse, chooses to live out his days in isolation.

The novel's primary concern is the ethics of scientific experimentation. Moreau was driven out of England following a sensationalist exposé, "The Moreau Horrors." However, Moreau himself is untroubled by any moral objections to vivisection. Prendick is impressed by Moreau's scientific resolve, yet repulsed by the carelessness with which Moreau discards his finished experiments. The novel asks what responsibility scientists hold for their creations.

Most importantly, Wells blurs the dividing line between humans and animals. Moreau's laws, which recast instinct as sinful behavior, are an early form of the Freudian view that civilization is only possible by suppressing desire, or a jaded version of Thomas Hobbes's social contract. In addition, Prendick's conjecture that the Beast People have been hypnotized into submission suggests a critique of mass culture, drawing a parallel with the newspaper-led controversy that drove Moreau from England. The Beast People's ritual cry, "Are we not Men?" is thus a poignant question, picked up by subsequent film adaptations (notably in 1996, and in 1932, as *The Island of Lost Souls*). "Moreau" has subsequently become a byword for unethical scientific practice.

Miles Link

See also: Body Horror; Mad Scientist; *The Strange Case of Dr. Jekyll and Mr. Hyde*; Wells, H. G.; *Part Two, Themes, Topics, and Genres*: Horror Literature and Science Fiction.

Further Reading

Glendening, John. 2002. "'Green Confusion': Evolution and Entanglement in H.G. Wells's *The Island of Doctor Moreau*." *Victorian Literature and Culture* 30 (2): 571–597.

The Island of Lost Souls. [1932] 2011. Directed by Erle C. Kenton. New York: Criterion Collection. DVD.

Parrinder, Patrick. 1995. *Shadows of the Future: H. G. Wells, Science Fiction, and Prophecy*. Syracuse: Syracuse University Press.

IT

It (whose title is sometimes capitalized as *IT*) is an award-winning novel by the American novelist and horror writer Stephen King. At over 1,300 pages in paperback, *It* is among the longest of his many works. Published in 1986, the novel centers on a battle between good and evil in a small Maine town. Though ostensibly fictional, Derry is heavily based upon the real-life environs of Bangor, Maine, where King relocated specifically to write the novel, and where he still resides. Today the Bangor "Stephen King Tour" focuses on many of the locations that either inspired or are directly included in the novel.

It depicts the conflict between the "Losers Club"—a band of misfit childhood friends—and an otherworldly evil that emerges every thirty years to terrorize Derry. This "IT" takes the form of its victim's innermost fear, a conceit that allows King to indulge his love of pulp horror staples. "IT" manifests most frequently as a terrifying clown figure known as Pennywise, but its real nature is stranger by far and strays into the Lovecraftian territory that forms a loose metaphysical backdrop to much of King's supernatural fiction. The children confront and defeat Pennywise, but three decades later a spate of child murders heralds the reeruption of trouble in Derry, and the adult members of the Losers Club are drawn back from each of their disparate lives to do battle once more.

The length and complexity of *It* means that this straightforward good-versus-evil plot is only one strand in the novel. Indeed, Pennywise the Clown is not actually named (except in a single authorial intrusion) until well past page 500. The central plot expands into a nostalgic meditation on childhood, friendship, and memory. In addition, King offers a detailed sketch of a small New England city in the mid-twentieth century, where the threat of Sputnik (the Russian satellite by which the

Soviet Union gained a lead on the United States in the "space race") and "the bomb" are balanced against the prosaic anxieties of adolescence.

It contains numerous references to King's wider universe. Pennywise, or another of his species, appears in the final volume of *The Dark Tower*, while other characters are referenced in various stand-alone novels. For instance, Dick Halloran, a major character in *The Shining*, appears as a younger man, and one of the "losers," Eddie Kaspbrak, is mentioned in *Misery* as a childhood neighbor of protagonist Paul Sheldon.

King fans often list *It* as a personal favorite among his works, usually second only to the equally epic apocalyptic novel *The Stand* (1978). Pennywise is perhaps King's most iconic villain, and his impact is due to both the huge success of the book—the best-selling novel of 1986—and Tim Curry's portrayal of the character in the 1990 television miniseries. Critics have also pointed to links between Pennywise and serial killer John Wayne Gacy, who performed as a party clown. The novel's greatest influence, arguably, is in elevating the figure of the monstrous clown to the pantheon of contemporary Gothic monsters. *It* remains King's grandest novel and the most comprehensive distillation of his thoughts on fear, childhood, imagination, and community, which together form the thematic spine of his writing career.

It was the winner of the 1987 British Fantasy Award for best novel and was also nominated for the Locus Award and World Fantasy Award. In 2017 the first part of a planned two-part feature film adaptation of the novel was released, directed by Andrés Muschietti and starring Bill Skarsgård as Pennywise.

Neil McRobert

See also: *The Dark Tower*; King, Stephen; Lovecraftian Horror; Monsters; *Part One, Horror through History*: Horror from 1950 to 2000; *Part Two, Themes, Topics, and Genres*: Horror Literature and Science Fiction; Horror Publishing, 1975–1995: The Boom Years; Weird and Cosmic Horror Fiction.

Further Reading

Drey, Mark. 1999. *The Pyrotechnic Insanitarium: American Culture on the Brink*. New York: Grove Press.

Magistrale, Tony. 1992. "Art versus Madness: *It* and *Misery*." In *Stephen King: The Second Decade, Danse Macabre to The Dark Half* by Tony Magistrale, 101–133. New York: Twayne.

Magistrale, Tony. 1988. *Landscape of Fear*. Bowling Green, OH: Bowling Green University Press.